The Appraisal of Real Estate

Third Canadian Edition

Appraisal Institute®

*Professionals Providing
Real Estate Solutions*

Appraisal Institute
of Canada

Institut canadien
des évaluateurs

ACKNOWLEDGMENTS

The Appraisal Institute of Canada gratefully acknowledges the contribution of the Appraisal Institute (United States) for the use of The Appraisal of Real Estate, 13th Edition, which served as the basis for this 3rd Canadian Edition.

The Appraisal Institute of Canada also wishes to acknowledge the contribution of the following persons who acted as authors, editors, and reviewers:

- Larry Dybvig, AACI, PApp, MAI
- Sharon Gulbranson, MBA
- John Bridal, BCom, MEd
- André Gravelle, BCom
- Tsur Somerville, PhD, Faculty of Commerce, UBC
- Georges Lozano, MPA
- Ian Saxon, BCom

FOR EDUCATIONAL PURPOSES ONLY

Published by:

SAUDER
School of Business

Real Estate Division

The appraisal of real estate / Larry Dybvig, editor. – 3rd Canadian ed.

Includes bibliographical references and index.
ISBN 978-0-88865-727-5

1. Real property – Valuation. I. Dybvig, Larry. II. University of British Columbia. Real Estate Division III. Title.
HD1387 .A664 2010   333.33'2

First printing 2010

TABLE OF CONTENTS

FOREWORD

Welcome to the Appraisal of Real Estate, Third Canadian Edition! For more than 60 years, *The Appraisal of Real Estate* has served generations of North American appraisers and their clients as the comprehensive repository of appraisal knowledge. The 13th edition of the US Appraisal Institute textbook that forms the basis of this third Canadian edition continued that tradition, focusing on fundamentals to provide a solid foundation on which to build a broad and substantial understanding of real property valuation.

This third Canadian edition of *The Appraisal of Real Estate* appears at a time when appraisers face challenging markets and increased expectations from stakeholders, employers, and clients. Economies and marketplaces have been particularly uncertain at the time of publication, but amid this uncertainty, appraisers can still count on *The Appraisal of Real Estate* to remain a steadfast primary resource and reference for the profession.

As technology and the market for real estate appraisal services evolve, the tools required by an appraiser change; revisions to this text are in response. For example, given the increasing availability of market data and the capabilities of modern desktop computers, users of appraisal reports look to see increased use of statistics and modeling in appraisal practice. Consequently, this edition gives more emphasis to statistics, moving the topic out of the appendixes and into a freestanding chapter that expands on the theory and concepts discussed in earlier editions. Elsewhere, insights are provided on the related topics of the emerging data standards and new information technology tools as well as the many data sources available to real property appraisers in the 21st century.

Like information technology, construction techniques and building design have changed in recent years, as economic and environmental sustainability issues have reached a broad audience. Appraisers are still gathering market data and debating the appropriate valuation techniques to apply to green buildings; this text includes a discussion of sustainable architecture and development that should spur thought and conversation on the subject in years to come.

Looking back over recent events in the appraisal profession and the broader business world, the financial repercussions of the subprime lending crisis have hit close to home, stirring up memories of the savings and loan crisis of the late 1980s. The lending practices that fuelled the recent market downturn may feel all-too-familiar to long-time appraisers, and the need for a strong commitment to professional standards and ethical conduct is increasingly apparent. In the wake of financial scandals and increased scrutiny of auditing and accounting, real property appraisers have new opportunities to diversify by leveraging their expertise in developing market-based opinions of fair value for financial reports. *The Appraisal of Real Estate* now takes a closer look at the concept of fair value and the discipline of valuation for financial reporting.

Professional standards for appraisers continue to evolve from year to year. The third edition of *The Appraisal of Real Estate* reflects current editions of the Canadian Uniform Standards of Professional Appraisal Practice, the Code of Professional Ethics of the Appraisal Institute of Canada, and the International Valuation Standards. Although no textbook can keep pace with incremental changes in successive editions of these documents, the current edition of the textbook incorporates the most significant changes in recent years, with particular emphasis on the process of developing an appropriate scope of work in real property appraisal assignments.

The generosity of the Directors and staff of the American Appraisal Institute in making their text available for editing into this Canadian edition has been essential and is greatly appreciated. Production of this text succeeds only because of the contributions of dozens of notable appraisers, educators, and consultants, as noted in the Acknowledgements provided earlier and below. The textbook reviewers and consultants who volunteered their services for this project have clearly demonstrated their confidence in and commitment to the profession and to furthering the body of knowledge, as represented by the content of this textbook. Their efforts are greatly appreciated, and their expertise in the classroom, in the courtroom, and in the field are plain to see in the many improvements, large and small, readers will discover in these pages.

In publishing the American edition of this text, the US Appraisal Institute acknowledged the active involvement of many real estate professionals, and the Appraisal Institute would like to gratefully acknowledge the following contributors, reviewers, and consultants: Mark F. Bates, MAI, Peter D. Bowes, MAI, Andrew P. Brorsen, MAI, SRA, Theddi Wright Chappell, MAI, Stephanie Coleman, MAI, SRA, Ron D. DeVries, MAI, SRA, Julian Diaz, MAI, SRA, John D. Dorchester Jr., MAI, Robert W. Dunham, MAI, SRA, Larry O. Dybvig, MAI, Don M. Emerson, MAI, SRA, Stephen F. Fanning, MAI, Jeffrey Fisher, Kenneth G. Foltz, MAI, SRA, W. West Foster, MAI, Howard C. Gelbtuch, MAI, Brian A. Glanville, MAI, Craig M. Harrington, SRA, Alan Hummel, SRA, Thomas O. Jackson, MAI, Jeffrey A. Johnson, MAI, Bruce A. Kellogg, MAI, Thomas R. Kirby, MAI, SRA, David C. Lennhoff, MAI, SRA, Mark R. Linné, MAI, Kenneth M. Lusht, MAI, SRA, Joseph C. Magdziarz, MAI, SRA, George R. Mann, MAI, SRA, Stephen A. Manning, MAI, SRA, Richard Marchitelli, MAI, Michael S. MaRous, MAI, SRA, Maureen Mastroieni, MAI, Mark R. Rattermann, MAI, SRA, Stephen D. Roach, MAI, Don (Randy) Scheidt, MAI, SRA, John A. Schwartz,

MAI, Lee B. Smith, MAI, Gary P. Taylor, MAI, SRA, Chris Thorne, Lee H. Waronker, MAI, SRA, Danny K. Wiley, SRA, Marvin L. Wolverton, MAI, and Janice F. Young, MAI, SRA.

Special recognition must be given to Richard Marchitelli, Chair of the US AI Publications Review Panel, and the members of its textbook development team who led the review teams responsible for topical sections of the text and reviewed the final manuscript: Peter Bowes, Don Dorchester, Stephanie Coleman, Stephen Fanning, Joseph Magzdiarz, Mark Rattermann, Stephen Roach and Marvin Wolverton. Their contributions were invaluable.

Larry Dybvig,
AACI, PApp, MAI
Editor
Vancouver, 2010

CHAPTER 1

REAL PROPERTY AND ITS APPRAISAL

Land provides the foundation for the social and economic activities of people. It is both a tangible physical commodity and a source of wealth. Since land is essential to life and society, it is important to many disciplines, including law, economics, finance, sociology, and geography. Each of these disciplines may employ a somewhat different concept of real property.

Within the vast domain of the law, issues such as the ownership and the use of land are considered. In economics, land is regarded as one of the four agents of production, along with labour, capital, and entrepreneurial coordination. Land provides many of the natural elements that contribute to a nation's wealth. Finance applies the principles of economics within a market economy to furnish capital for the exchange of property, and it helps market participants act knowledgeably and prudently. Sociology focuses on the dual nature of land:

- As a resource to be shared by all people
- As a commodity that can be owned, traded, and used by individuals

Geography focuses on describing the physical elements of land and the activities of the people who use it.

Lawyers, economists, sociologists, and geographers have a common understanding of the attributes of land:

- Each parcel of land is unique in its location and composition.
- Land is physically immobile.
- Land is durable.
- The supply of land is finite.
- Land is useful to people.

Real estate appraisers view these attributes as the foundation of real estate's value. Contrasted with the physical character of land, value is an economic concept. Appraisers recognize the concepts of land used in other disciplines,

> Land is investigated and analyzed in a variety of disciplines—government, the law, economics, geography, and environmental studies.

but are most concerned with how the market measures value. Markets reflect the attitudes and actions of people in response to social and economic forces and the constraints of law and legal encumbrances.

CONCEPTS OF LAND

Although one can view land and improvements in a physical sense, there are other concepts of land that are less obvious. These concepts help to characterize the importance of land and provide the foundation for land value systems.

Geographic and Environmental

The study of land includes consideration of its diverse physical characteristics and how these characteristics combine in a particular area. Each land parcel is unique, and location is a very important attribute. The utility of land and the highest and best use for land can be significantly affected by the physical and locational characteristics of the land and other related considerations (broadly referred to as geography).

Land is affected by a number of processes. Ongoing physical and chemical processes modify the land's surface, biological processes determine the distribution of life forms, and socioeconomic processes direct human habitation and activity on the land. Together, these processes influence the characteristics of land use.

Land can be used for many purposes:

- Agriculture
- Commerce
- Industry
- Habitation
- Recreation

In addition, land use decisions may be influenced by many factors:

- Climate
- Topography
- The distribution of natural resources, population centres, and industry
- Trends in economics, population, technology, and culture

The influence of each of these factors on a particular parcel of land varies. Geographic considerations are particularly significant to appraisers. The importance of physical characteristics such as topography, soils, water, and vegetation is obvious, but the distribution of population, facilities, and services and the movement of people and goods are equally important. The geographic concept of land, which emphasizes natural resources, the location of industry, and actual and potential markets, provides much of the background knowledge required in real estate appraisal.

Government and Legal

Land use derives from the mandates of organized society. In countries where the ownership and marketability of land are not free, government often dictates the use of land. Free market economies regulate land use by a framework of laws. To understand how the various forces affecting land operate, the basic role of law must be recognized.

Society reflects its cultural, political, governmental, and economic attitudes in its laws. The law does not focus on the physical characteristics of land but on the rights and obligations associated with various interests in land. Canada primarily uses British-derived common law, which provides that the holders of the land actually have land tenure (permission from the Crown to hold land) rather than absolute ownership.

In the United States, individuals maintain the right to own and use land for material gain, while the law gives people to right to use the land. In other words, the law recognizes the possible conflict between private ownership and public use. In many undeveloped parts of the world, land cannot be privately owned, with its rights retained by others. For example in Fiji, lands are considered to be held by the village, with decisions respecting its use made by a hereditary chief. Occupants of such indigenous lands lack security of tenure, and thus risk losing improvements made to land.

The choice of early Canadians to remai n closely tied to the British Empire had a major impact on the development of property rights in this country. The Canadian system of land ownership, more accurately called real property ownership, does not permit the same level of rights and freedoms over land as the US system allows.

In the United States, landowners usually hold title to the mineral resources located beneath their land; in Canada, this is never the case.

Originally, the British monarchy held the rights to the land, and now the Canadian government holds the rights to most Canadian land. All Canadian land is subject to the rights of the Crown (the federal government). Laws governing real property ownership have been under provincial control since the Confederation Act of 1867. Landowners pay royalties for mineral exploration to the provinces, which forms a major part of provincial revenue. Landowners never profit from the discovery of mineral resources underneath their property.

"Whose is the land, his it is, to the sky and the depths". This ancient maxim is the basis of the following legal definition:

> Land ... includes not only the ground, or soil, but everything that is attached to the earth, whether by course of nature, as are trees and herbage, or by the hand of man, as are houses and other buildings. It includes not only the surface of the earth but everything under it and over it. Thus in legal theory, the surface of the earth is just part of an inverted pyramid having its tip, or apex, at the centre of the earth, extending outward through the surface of the earth at the boundary lines of the tract, and continuing on upward to the heavens.[1]

This definition suggests that land ownership includes complete possession of land from the centre of the earth to the ends of the universe. In practice, however, the extent of rights available to private ownership is legally limited due to governmental controls, at the federal, provincial, first nation, and municipal level. Since land owner-

---

[1]   Werner, R.J. and Kratovil, R. 1993. *Real Estate Law*, 10th ed. Englewood Cliffs, N.J.: Prentice-Hall, Inc. p4.

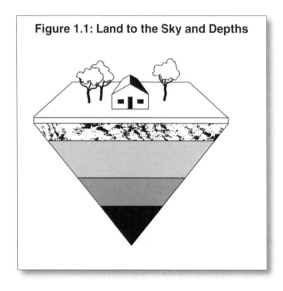

Figure 1.1: Land to the Sky and Depths

ship can be limited, ownership rights are the subject of law.[2] The value of these rights is the focus of real property appraisal.

The laws that govern the use and development of land in Canada give landowners great freedom in deciding how to use their land. However, this freedom is not without restrictions. The basic concept of private ownership calls for unrestricted use so long as such use does not unreasonably harm the rights of others. In the past, the test of harm focused on owners of adjacent properties. The concept of harm has recently been expanded to encompass broader social and geographic concerns. Many court cases have argued the definition of reasonable use.

Legal matters of particular concern to appraisers include the following:

• Easements
• Access regulations
• Use restrictions
• The recording and conveyance of titles

In addition, appraisers must be familiar with local and provincial laws, which constitutionally have primary jurisdiction over land.

Economic

Land is a physical entity with inherent ownership rights that can be legally limited for the good of society. Land is also a major source of wealth, which, in economic terms, can be measured in money or exchange value. Land and its products have economic value only when they are converted into goods or services that are useful, desirable, paid for by consumers, and limited in supply. The economic concept of land as a source of wealth and an object of value is central to appraisal theory.

The economic concept of land reflects a long history of thought on the sources and bases of value, which is referred to as value theory.[3] Value theory contributes to the value definitions used in appraisals and appraisal literature, and it is an important part of the philosophy on which professional appraisal practice is founded.

---

2   See "1991 Analysis of Property Rights and the Constitution - Government of Canada Collection" *dsp-psd.tpsgc.gc.ca/Collection-R/LoPBdP/BP/bp268-e.htm*

3   Wendt, P.F. 1974. *Real Estate Appraisal: Review and Outlook.* Athens, Ga.: University of Georgia Press. p. 17.

Social

Modern society has become increasingly concerned with how land is used and how rights are distributed. The supply of land is fixed, so increased demand for land exerts pressure for land to be used more intensively. Conflicts often arise between-groups that hold different views on proper land use. Those who believe that land is a resource to be shared by all want to preserve the land's scenic beauty and important ecological functions. Others view land primarily as a marketable commodity. They believe society is best served by private, unrestricted ownership.

For example, the developer of a proposed shopping centre or a business park may view a particular parcel of land as developable green space in a desirable and affordable location serving a definable market area. On the other hand, local residents might argue that, as the site of a significant battle in the War of 1812, the parcel deserves government protection if taxpayers could be persuaded to support such a public investment in historical preservation. These conflicting views do not alter the constitutional rights of ownership or market concepts of land. Rather, they reflect controversies that arise between the property rights of the individual and those of society. As a resource, land may be protected for the good of society. As a marketable commodity, the ownership, use, and disposal of land are regulated so that individual rights are not violated.[4]

The origin of property rights in the original British colonies of North America evolved from the British legal system, in which all land rights were granted by the "Crown". These grants were not absolute; the Crown held all retained rights. The American Revolution severed the link with the British Crown, with many of the retained rights subsequently forming part of private property rights. In Canada, the Canadian government has assumed the role of the Crown in taking responsibility for and reaping the benefits of ownership rights that were originally the privilege of the monarchy. Consequently, property rights in Canada are less than those available in the United States, and this distinction has an implication in the understanding of property rights in North American appraisal.

In 1876, the US Supreme Court established the government's right to regulate "the manner in which [a citizen] shall own his own property when such regulation becomes necessary for the public good". The court quoted the words of England's Lord Chief Justice Hale: "When private property is 'affected with a public interest', it ceases to be *juris privati* only."[5] Throughout American history, land ownership has been recognized as fundamental. John Adams wrote, "If the multitude is possessed of real estate, the multitude will take care of the liberty, virtue, and interest of the multitude in all acts of government."[6]

In the 21st century, the principle restrictions on land use in Canada arise from the planning and zoning provisions of public authority. By the imposition, removal,

---

[4]   See also Roe, C.E. 2000. "Land Use: The Second Battle of Gettysburg". *The Appraisal Journal*. October 2000. pp441-449.

[5]   94 U.S. 113 (1896). Quoted in Babcock, R.F. and Feurer, D.A. "Land as a Commodity Affected with a Public Interest" in Andrews, R.N.L. 1979. *Land in America*. Lexington, Mass.: D.C. Heath and Company. p110.

[6]   Ibid., 31.

or alteration of land use controls, a public authority may dramatically increase or decrease the value of land by changing the permitted uses that may be made of it.

All laws and operations of government are intended to serve the public. Thus, in the public interest, society may impose building restrictions, zoning and building ordinances, development and subdivision regulations, and other land use controls. These controls affect what may be developed, where development may occur, and what activities may be permitted subsequent to development. In recent decades, the Canadian government has increased its efforts to regulate the air and water emissions from manufacturing processes and to reduce pollution caused by dirt, chemicals, and noise. Protective controls over land use extend to wetlands, beaches, and navigable waters and to the preservation of the habitats of endangered species.[7]

As the nature and extent of land use controls change, so do the nature and extent of private land ownership. Such changes influence markets and ultimately real estate values. Consequently, real estate appraisers must be familiar with the regulations and restrictions that apply to land use and understand how these regulations affect a specific property.

REAL ESTATE, REAL PROPERTY, AND PERSONAL PROPERTY

Real estate appraisal makes an important distinction between the terms *real estate* and *real property*. Although these concepts are different, some provincial laws and court decisions treat them synonymously for legal purposes. The separate definitions that follow recognize the traditional distinction in appraisal theory between the two concepts.

Real estate is land, buildings, and other affixed improvements as a tangible entity. The term pertains to the physical land and appurtenances affixed to the land, e.g., structures. Real estate is immobile and tangible. The legal definition of real estate includes the following tangible components:

- Land
- All things that are a natural part of land, such as trees and minerals
- All things that are attached to land by people, such as buildings and site improvements

In addition, all permanent building attachments such as plumbing, electrical wiring, and heating systems as well as built-in items such as cabinets and elevators are usually considered part of the real estate. Real estate includes all attachments, both above and below the ground.

Real property includes the interests, benefits, and rights inherent in the ownership of physical real estate. A right or interest in real estate is also broadly referred to as an estate. Specifically, an estate in land is the degree, nature, or extent of interest

---

[7]   For more information on the government's control of land use, see Anne Warner La Forest. 2009. *Anger & Honsberger Law of Real Property,* Third Edition. Aurora, ON: Canada Law Book, and Eaton, J.D. 1995. *Real Estate Valuation in Litigation,* 2nd ed. Chicago, IL: Appraisal Institute.

that a person has in it. To qualify as an estate in land, the legal interest(s) must allow possession – now or in the future – and specify duration. Estates are distinguished by their duration and fall into two categories: freehold and leasehold estates as shown in Figure 1.2.

A bundle of rights represents the total range of private ownership interests in real property. Imagine a bundle of sticks where each "stick" represents a distinct and separate right or interest. The bundle of rights contains all the interests in real property, including the right to use the real estate, sell it, lease it, enter it, and give it away, and each "stick" can be separated from the bundle and traded in the market. These rights are subject to certain rights retained by government, subject to limitations and restrictions, which are discussed in Chapter 6.

> The distinction between real estate and real property is fundamental to appraisal.
>
> real estate
> Land, buildings, and other affixed improvements, as a tangible entity.
>
> real property
> The interests, benefits, and rights inherent in the ownership of real estate.
>
> Source: Canadian Uniform Standards of Professional Appraisal Practice, 2010.

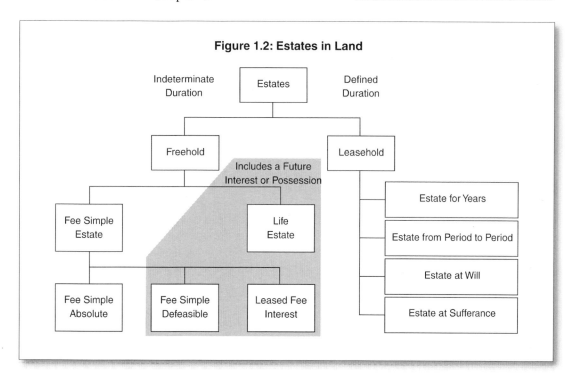

Figure 1.2: Estates in Land

Appraisers not only distinguish between real estate and real property, they also differentiate between real estate, personal property, and trade fixtures, as illustrated in Tables 1.1 and 1.2. Appraisers must know whether an item is personal property or a fixture to determine whether it will be included in the property value indication. If an item is classified as a fixture, it is part of the real estate. Since the distinction between fixtures and personal property is not always obvious, appraisers should read leases carefully and know how these items are treated in their market area and its legal precedents. Personal property that is related to real estate and is to be included in the opinion[8] of value must be identified in the appraisal process and described in the appraisal report (see Chapter 26).

Table 1.1: Distinctions Between Real Estate, Personal Property, and Trade Fixtures

Real Estate	Characteristics	Items that have been installed or attached to the land or building in a rather permanent manner. All real estate improvements were once personal property; when attached to the land, they become real estate.
	Examples	• Land • Buildings • Fixtures – e.g., plumbing, lighting, heating, and air-conditioning in a residential property
Personal Property	Characteristics	Movable items of property that are not permanently affixed to, or part of, the real estate. Personal property is not endowed with the rights of real property ownership.
	Examples	• Furniture and furnishings not built into the structure such as refrigerators and freestanding shelves • Items such as bookshelves and window treatments installed by a tenant that, under specific lease terms, may be removed at the termination of the lease
Trade Fixtures	Characteristics	Unlike fixtures, which are regarded in law as part of the real estate, trade fixtures are not real estate endowed with the rights of real property ownership. They are personal property regardless of how they are affixed. A trade fixture is to be removed by the tenant when the lease expires unless this right has been surrendered in the lease. Also known as a *chattel fixture*.
	Examples	• Restaurant booths • Gasoline station pumps • Storage tanks • Fitness equipment in a health club • Plumbing, lighting, heating, and air-conditioning in an industrial building • Industrial equipment such as air hoses, water pipelines, craneways, and bus ducts

---

[8]   Personal Property is "identifiable portable and tangible objects which are considered by the general public as being "personal", e.g. furnishings, artwork, antiques, gems and jewellery, collectibles, machinery and equipment; all property, tangible and intangible, that is not classified as real estate." (CUSPAP 2008)

Table 1.2: Criteria for Distinguishing Between Personal Property and Fixtures

Criteria	Explanation
The manner in which the item is affixed	Generally an item is considered personal property if it can be removed without serious injury to the real estate or to itself. There are exceptions to this rule.
The character of the item and its adaptation to the real estate	Items that are specifically constructed for use in a particular building or installed to carry out the purpose for which the building was erected are generally considered permanent parts of the building.
The intention of the party who attached the item	Frequently the terms of the lease reveal whether the item is permanent or is to be removed at some future time.

Source: Werner, R.J. and Kratovil, R.J. 1993. *Real Estate Law, 10th ed.* Englewood Cliffs, N.J.: Prentice-Hall, Inc. pp11-17.

APPRAISAL PRACTICE

In our complex society, the words *appraiser* and *appraisal* can take on many meanings. It is important to use these terms correctly and to distinguish among the individuals involved in the valuation process.

Buyers and sellers purchase and sell real estate and make decisions relating to prices and other real estate matters. Home buyers often have little or no background in real estate and must rely on others to make their decisions. The only "appraisal" they make is an evaluation of the conditions they observe or facts that are made known to them. At the opposite end of the spectrum, institutional investors may have personnel who are trained in appraising.

Real estate salespeople are licensed to sell real estate. They have training in their field, but may or may not have extensive appraisal training. They are generally familiar with properties in a given locale and have access to market information. They frequently use sales and other market information for property comparison purposes in pricing. Some may develop appraisal expertise. As a group, real estate salespeople evaluate specific properties, but they typically do not consider all the factors that professional appraisers do.

Real estate financial officers and executives include loan officers, closing agents, agents at title companies, relocation officers and agents, and others. This group also includes government officials who deal with land or land values in the private marketplace. These professionals vary in their ability to understand market forces in a given locale, develop opinions of value, and apply appraisal concepts. Real estate investment advisors may have extensive training in understanding appraisals even if they do not develop appraisals themselves. Members of this group work with or review appraisals developed by others. While they are knowledgeable about appraisals, they are rarely trained appraisers.

In Canada, four provinces currently regulate various aspects of appraisal: Nova Scotia, New Brunswick, Quebec, and Alberta. These provinces have established entities that become involved in such professional matters as education and standards. Other than the four regulating provinces, appraisers do not need any professional license, registration, or membership.

In Quebec, l'Ordre des évaluateurs agréés du Québec (the Order) was established by the provincial government in the 1970s as a corporation recognizing professional appraisers; it grants members qualified in appraisal with the designation "EA" (évaluateurs agréés). The Order is not a formal licensing body, although in order to be a chief assessing officer and sign an assessment roll, the EA designation is mandatory.

In Alberta, the province mandated an existing provincial regulator, the Real Estate Council of Alberta (RECA), to regulate appraisers. RECA has formal provincial authority in this mandate, so violators of its policies can be breaking the law.

In Nova Scotia and New Brunswick, registration of appraisers is required through the Nova Scotia Real Estate Appraisers Association and New Brunswick Association of Real Estate Appraisers respectively. A private members bill in the provincial legislature established these self-regulating associations; thus, they do not formally represent government policy. The registering organizations do not receive government funding, but have professional standards and ethics to which their members must adhere; a failure to do so could lead to deregistration. An appraiser lacking registration cannot practice in these provinces.

In matters such as professional qualifications and appraisal standards, government regulators can rely on professional appraisal associations: the Appraisal Institute of Canada (AIC) makes available membership on a national basis; almost all professional real estate appraisers across the country belong to it. A member of the Appraisal Institute of Canada meets educational, experience, and testing requirements set by the Institute and can perform appraisals across the country, subject to provincial requirements. They must conform to standards developed by the Institute, the foremost of which is Canadian Uniform Standards of Professional Appraisal Practise (CUSPAP).

The type of properties that individuals can appraise depends on the level of qualification they hold. For example, the Appraisal Institute of Canada grants two professional designations: AACI, which indicates general competence, and CRA, which denotes single-family residential competence. The Appraisal Institute of Canada requires its designated members to meet continuing education requirements and must adhere to the Canadian Uniform Standards of Professional Appraisal Practice or risk disciplinary action, including possible loss of designation. The legislated provincial appraisal bodies can impose standards and ethical requirements for their members. These requirements are intended to provide even higher protection of the public served by these professionals.

USPAP (the American Appraisal Standard) defines an appraiser as "one who is expected to perform valuation services competently and in a manner that is independent, impartial, and objective". By that definition, any potential client of the appraiser should be able to expect a certain level of professionalism from anyone representing himself or herself as an appraiser.

CANADIAN UNIFORM STANDARDS OF PROFESSIONAL APPRAISAL PRACTICE (CUSPAP)

Current standards of the Appraisal Institute of Canada (AIC), developed for appraisers and the users of appraisal services by the Standards Committee of the AIC. The intent of the Standards is to promote and maintain a high level of public trust in professional appraisal practice by establishing requirements for appraisal, review, and consulting assignments. These Standards begin with the Ethics Standard, which sets out the requirements for integrity, impartiality, objectivity, independent judgement, and ethical conduct. The Standards apply to all activities of any member involving an analysis, opinion or conclusion relating to the nature, quality, utility, or value of a specified interest in – or aspects of – identified real estate.

Adherents must develop and communicate his or her analysis, opinions, and advice in a manner that will be meaningful to the client, that will not be misleading in the marketplace, and that will be in compliance with these Standards.

Full-time professional real property appraisers spend the majority of their time appraising. These individuals have extensive training and experience and are committed to the profession. This group includes those who perform and review real property appraisals. Professional appraisers are bound to strict compliance with regulatory requirements; in Canada, they are members of the Appraisal Institute of Canada and the Order, organizations that foster participation in professional activities and educational development. Members agree to peer review of their ethical conduct or work performance, which reflects their strong commitment to professionalism.

Continuing education is the cornerstone of professional development. By pursuing continuing education, appraisers demonstrate their commitment to maintaining their skills at a level far above the bare minimum required to satisfy provincial licensing requirements. Individuals who complete a rigorous educational program and earn recognized professional designations enhance their employment and business prospects. A commitment to professionalism helps regulate the industry and ensures quality appraisal work.

According to CUSPAP, appraisal practice includes, but is not limited to, three types of valuation services:

- Appraisal
- Appraisal Review
- Appraisal Consulting

Appraisers engage in appraisal practice – i.e., "acting as an appraiser", as the definition states – while a variety of professionals may provide valuation services, according to the definitions in the professional standards. A wide range of activities, from measuring the size of a building to developing a detailed market study, qualify as appraisal practice but do not fit the definitions of the three types of valuation services. Table 1.3 compares the characteristics of valuation services, and Figure 1.3 illustrates the relationship of the professional standards to the various professional activities an appraiser might engage in.

The application of appraisal procedures and the level of detail in the report that communicates the appraiser's conclusions are guided by the nature of the property, the type of opinion to be developed, the intended use, and the intended users. To avoid misunderstandings, it is imperative that the client and the appraiser address these issues at the outset of the assignment.

Table 1.3: Comparison of Appraisal, Appraisal Consulting, and Appraisal Review

Appraisal

Definition	A formal opinion of value: prepared as a result of a retainer; intended for reliance by identified parties, and for which the appraiser assumes responsibility; the act or process of developing an opinion of value.
Characteristics	Appraisal involves selective research into appropriate market areas, the assemblage of pertinent data, the use of appropriate analytical techniques, and the application of knowledge, experience, and professional judgement to develop an appropriate solution to an appraisal problem. The appraiser provides the client with an opinion of real property value that reflects all pertinent market evidence.
Examples	• An opinion of market value for a fee simple estate, leasehold estate or other estate (i.e., to assist in mortgage lending decisions, to assist in purchase or sale decisions) • An opinion of investment value or some other properly defined value of an identified interest in real estate as of a given date (i.e., for insurance purposes, for relocation purposes, for property tax appeal work)

Appraisal Consulting

Definition	The act or process of developing an analysis, recommendation, or opinion to solve a problem, where an opinion of value is a component of the analysis leading to the assignment results.
Characteristics	Current market activity and evidence are studied to form a conclusion that is not in itself a value indication. An appraiser develops a value opinion in an appraisal consulting assignment as part of the process of answering some other question about real estate, such as whether a proposed use of a given property is economically feasible.

Appraisal Review

Definition	The act or process of developing and communicating an opinion about all or part of an appraisal.
Characteristics	A reviewer examines the work of another appraiser and expresses an opinion about the quality of that work.

Definitions cited from the Definitions section of the Canadian Uniform Standards of Professional Appraisal Practice (2010 edition)

Figure 1.3: Valuation Services and Appraisal Practice

	Valuation Services		
	Other Roles (e.g., brokerage, property management)	Other Services	Appraisal, Appraisal Review, and Appraisal Consulting
Pertains to aspects of value	✓	✓	✓
Performed by individual acting as an appraiser		✓	✓
Obligation to comply with USPAP		✓	✓
Performance and reporting requirements (Standards 1-10)			✓
Record keeping and workfile requirements			✓

Source: Uniform Standards of Professional Appraisal Practice, 2008-2009 ed., Advisory Opinion 21, A-69

Appraisal Reporting Options

Appraisal reports are generally of three types:

- Narrative – comprehensive and detailed
- Short Narrative – concise and briefly descriptive
- Form – a standardized format combining check-off boxes and narrative comments

The most significant differences in the reporting options are in the level of detail reported on the information analyzed, the appraisal methods and techniques employed, and the reasoning that supports the analyses, opinion, and conclusions. In a narrative appraisal report, there is full description of the data and analyses used in the assignment. In a short narrative appraisal report, a summary of the data and analyses used in the assignment is given. There is less detail provided in the summary appraisal report than in the narrative appraisal report. In a form appraisal report, the conclusions of the appraisal are stated, and the data (or analyses) used in the appraisal is presented in summary form only. It is not necessary for the appraiser to provide the data and analysis needed to fully develop those conclusions within the report where the appraiser and client have agreed that a form appraisal report is appropriate for the assignment.

Appraisal reports may also be delivered orally. Oral or verbal reports are given in court testimony and in tribunals such as appraisals, as well as in other circumstances (Chapter 26 discusses appraisal reporting formats in more detail).

The distinction between the *appraisal* and the *appraisal report* is important. The service the appraiser supplies to a client is to provide a credible opinion of value, as of a specified date, according to a specified definition of value, for a specified intended use. The service is not simply to deliver an appraisal report. The report is merely the means by which the appraiser's opinion of value is communicated.

In addition, the complexity of the appraisal problem need not affect the physical size of a written report. A value opinion developed through the application of a complex appraisal process might be communicated in a form appraisal report. The appraisal development process and the appraisal reporting process are separate, and one is not dependent on the other.

Purpose and Intended Use of an Appraisal

The purpose of an appraisal is to develop an opinion of some type of value that must be defined at the outset. The defined value may include the following:

> An appraiser produces a report that is appropriate for the intended use, and is incapable of misleading the intended user. CUSPAP does not dictate the form, format, or style of reporting. These are functions of the needs of users and appraisers. The substantive content of a report determines its compliance.

- Market value
- Use value
- Investment value
- Assessed value
- Business value
- Fair value
- Other types of value

Chapter 2 discusses distinctions among these terms.

The intended use of an appraisal is the appraiser's intent as to how the client and other intended users, if any, would use the appraisal report. In other words, what the client needs to know or the client's problem to be solved determines the intended use of an appraisal. For example, a client may need to know the market value of a residence to avoid paying too much for it or accepting too little for it in a sale. The local government may need to know the value of property taken through expropriation.

> The **purpose** and the **intended use** of an appraisal are related, but distinct, concepts.
> *Purpose of an Appraisal:* The stated reason for an appraisal assignment, i.e., to develop an opinion of the defined value of any real property interest or to conduct an evaluation study (consulting assignment) pertaining to real property decisions.
> *Intended Use of an Appraisal:* The manner in which a client will employ the information contained in an appraisal report.
> Appraisals are commonly used in situations involving the transfer of ownership, financing and credit, litigation, taxation, and investment counselling and in other business decision-making.

Since an appraisal provides a basis for a decision concerning real property, the intended use of an appraisal depends on the decision the client wishes to make. In defining the appraisal problem, the appraiser should consider the client's requirements and reach an understanding that is acceptable to the client and the appraiser and is consistent with accepted standards of professional appraisal practice.

An appraisal may be requested in a number of situations. While Table 1.4 does not reflect all possible uses for appraisals, it provides a broad sampling of professional appraisal activities.

Table 1.4: Typical Uses of Appraisals

Transfer of ownership
- To help prospective buyers set offering prices
- To help prospective sellers determine acceptable selling prices
- To establish a basis for real property exchanges
- To establish a basis for reorganizing or merging the ownership of multiple properties
- To determine the terms of a sale price for a proposed transaction
- Financing and credit
- To develop an opinion of the value of the security offered for a proposed mortgage loan
- To provide an investor with a sound basis for deciding whether to purchase real estate mortgages, bonds, or other types of securities
- To establish a basis for a decision to insure or underwrite a loan on real property

Litigation

Expropriation proceedings
- To develop an opinion of the market value of a property as a whole – i.e., before a taking
- To develop an opinion of the market value of the remainder after a taking
- To estimate the damages to a property created by a taking

Property divisions
- To develop an opinion of the market value of a property in contract disputes
- To develop an opinion of the market value of partnership interests

Environmental litigation
- To estimate damages created by violations of environmental laws
- To estimate damages created by environmental accidents

Tax matters
- To develop an opinion of assessed value
- To separate assets into depreciable (or capital recapture) items such as buildings and non-depreciable items such as land, and to estimate applicable depreciation (or capital recapture) rates
- To develop an opinion of the value of the real estate component of an estate plan that represents the foundation for future capital gains, often in the context of an inheritance
- To determine gift tax credits

Investment counselling, decision-making, and accounting
- To set rent schedules and lease provisions
- To determine the feasibility of a construction or renovation program
- To help corporations or third parties purchase homes for transferred employees
- To serve the needs of insurers, adjusters, and policyholders
- To facilitate corporate mergers, the issuance of stock or the revision of book value
- To develop an opinion of liquidation value for forced sale or auction proceedings
- To counsel clients by considering their investment goals, alternatives, resources, constraints, and the timing of their activities
- To advise planners, zoning authorities, and courts, among others, on the probable effects of proposed actions
- To assist in arbitrating valuation issues
- To analyze supply and demand trends in a market
- To ascertain the status of real estate markets
- To value fixed assets and assist in asset value allocations

Appraiser Liability

As users of appraisal services increase their reliance on the services of appraisers, the scope of appraiser responsibility and potential liability grows. Appraisers may be held liable for negligence, misrepresentation, fraud, breach of contract, or lack of compliance with the standards imposed by court rulings, government agencies, and those of professional associations such as the Appraisal Institute of Canada. Areas of potential exposure include matters involving privity of contract, disclosure, and litigation, e.g., discovery proceedings, interrogatories, and affidavits. For example, an inflated appraisal can be a component of property flipping, one form of mortgage fraud.

The vast majority of appraisers perform their assignments ethically and competently. However, appraisers are advised to take measures to safeguard themselves from unintentional or involuntary malpractice. Preparing well-documented reports and ensuring competency through continuing education, the use of checklists and backup reviews, and strict adherence to the Canadian Uniform Standards of Professional Appraisal Practice can help reduce an appraiser's exposure to civil action. Professional liability insurance is mandatory for all members of the Appraisal Institute of Canada and required by most clients. Appraisers are advised to review all exclusions and retroactive dates in their insurance policies and to take normal precautions in their business practices.

> Appraisers may be held liable for professional violations or related misconduct.
>
> **liability**
> In appraisal, a legal obligation to render services in compliance with professional standards and to refrain from malpractice, which includes negligence, misrepresentation, fraud, and breach of contract.

Contested opinions of value may result from rapid changes in market conditions, the presence of contaminated materials on appraised properties, enforcement of environmental and preservation easements, and changes in legal and regulatory guidelines. The proliferation of legal proceedings suggests that litigation will continue to increase in the appraisal field as it has in other professions.

THE NATURE OF VALUE

FACTORS OF VALUE

The economic concept of value is not inherent in the commodity, good, or service to which it is ascribed. Rather, it is created in the minds of the individuals who make up the market. The relationships that create value are complex, and values change when the factors that influence value change.

Typically, four interdependent economic factors create value:

1. Utility
2. Scarcity
3. Desire
4. Effective purchasing power

The four factors interact in the marketplace to influence the relationship of supply and demand.

Utility

Utility is the ability of a product to satisfy a human want, need, or desire. All properties must have utility to tenants, owner-investors, or owner-occupants. Residential properties satisfy the need for shelter and commercial properties generate income. Both may have design features that enhance their attractiveness. These features are

> Four interdependent factors create value: utility, scarcity, desire, and effective purchasing power. Utility and scarcity are supply factors. Desire and effective purchasing power are demand factors.

called amenities. The value of amenities is related to their desirability and utility to an owner-occupant or tenant-occupant. The value of ownership may be measured from the prices paid for residences. The value to a tenant can be converted into income in the form of rent. The benefits derived from income-producing properties can usually be measured in terms of cash flow. The influence of utility on value depends on the characteristics of the property. Size utility, design utility, location utility, and other specific forms of utility can significantly influence property value.

> **utility**
> The ability of a product to satisfy a human want, need, or desire.
>
> **scarcity**
> The present or anticipated undersupply of an item relative to the demand for it. Conditions of scarcity contribute to value.
>
> **desire**
> A purchaser's wish for an item to satisfy human needs (e.g., shelter, clothing, food, companionship) or individual wants beyond essential life-support needs.
>
> **effective purchasing power**
> The ability of an individual or group to participate in a market, i.e., to acquire goods and services with cash or its equivalent.

The benefits of real property ownership are derived from the bundle of rights that an owner possesses. Restrictions on ownership rights may inhibit the flow of benefits and, therefore, lower the property's value. Similarly, a property can only achieve its highest value if it can legally perform its most useful function. Environmental regulations, zoning regulations, title restrictions, and other limitations on the rights of ownership can enhance or detract from a property's utility and value.

Scarcity

Scarcity is the present or anticipated supply of an item relative to the demand for it. In general, if demand is constant, the scarcity of a commodity makes it more valuable. For example, land is still generally abundant, but useful, desirable land is relatively scarce and, as a result, has greater value.

No object, including real property, can have value unless scarcity is coupled with utility. Air, which has a high level of utility, has no definable economic value because it is abundant, but to a scuba diver who is 30 metres underwater with a tank that is almost empty, it is extremely valuable. The question again becomes one of supply and demand.

Desire

Desire is a purchaser's wish for an item to satisfy human needs (e.g., shelter, clothing, food, companionship) or individual wants beyond the essentials required to support life.

Effective Purchasing Power

Effective purchasing power is the ability of an individual or group to participate in a market – that is, to acquire goods and services with cash or its equivalent. A valid opinion of the value of a property includes an accurate assessment of the market's ability to pay for the property.

Supply and Demand

The complex interaction of the four factors that create value is reflected in the basic economic principle of supply and demand, which is discussed in more detail in the following chapter. The utility of a commodity, its scarcity or abundance, the intensity of the human desire to acquire it, and the effective power to purchase it all affect the supply of and demand for the commodity in any given situation.

Demand for a commodity is created by its utility and affected by its scarcity. Demand is also influenced by desire and the forces that create and stimulate desire.

Although human longing for things may be unlimited, desire is restrained by effective purchasing power. Thus, the inability to buy expensive things affects demand.

Similarly, the supply of a commodity is influenced by its utility and limited by its scarcity. The availability of a commodity is affected by its desirability. Land is a limited commodity, and the land in an area that is suitable for a specific use will be in especially short supply if the perceived need for it is great. Sluggish purchasing power keeps the pressure on supply in check. If purchasing power expands, the supply of a relatively fixed commodity will dwindle and create a market-driven demand to increase the supply for which there is latent or pent-up demand.

THE HISTORY OF VALUE THEORY

The development of modern value theory began in the 18th and 19th centuries when economic thinkers of the classical school first identified the four agents of production – labour, capital, coordination, and land, which are discussed in more detail in the following chapter – and examined the relationships between the basic factors that create value and supply and demand, e.g., utility, scarcity, desire, and effective purchasing power. Classical theory was largely based on the contributions of the physiocrats, whose ideas were put forth in reaction to the mercantilist doctrines that dominated earlier economic thought.

Mercantilism focused on wealth as a means of enhancing a nation's power. National wealth was equated with an influx of bullion into the national treasury. Mercantilists sought to maintain a favourable balance of trade by selling goods to accumulate gold, the chief medium of exchange. Between the 15th and 18th centuries, economic activity in Western Europe was associated with overseas exploration, colonization, and commerce. Mercantilist doctrine promoted strong, central economic controls to maintain monopolies in foreign trade and ensure the economic dependency of colonies.

Physiocratic thinkers of the mid-18th century objected to the commercial and national emphasis of mercantilism. They stressed other considerations in formulating a theory of value. Agricultural productivity, not gold, was identified as the source of wealth, and land was cited as the fundamental productive agent. The physiocrats also identified the importance of factors such as utility and scarcity in determining value.[1]

The Classical School

The classical school expanded and refined the tenets of physiocratic thought, formulating a value theory that attributed value to the cost of production. The Scottish economic thinker Adam Smith (1721-1790) suggested that capital, in addition to land and labour, constituted a primary agent of production. Smith acknowledged the role

---

[1] A physiocrat was a member of an 18th century group of French economists who held that agriculture, rather than manufacturing or trade, was the source of all wealth and that agricultural products should be highly priced. Francois Quesnay (1694-1774) and Anne Robert Turgot (1727-1781) put forth an individualistic, agrarian-based concept of economic behaviour without centralized state control. They stressed the necessity of free trade and popularized the phrase *laissez-faire*, "to let people do as they choose", which underscores their individualistic approach. See Roll, E. 1964. *A History of Economic Thought*, 3rd ed. Englewood Cliffs, N.J.: Prentice-Hall, Inc. p134.

of coordination in production, but did not study its function as a primary agent. He believed that when the agents of production were brought together to produce a useful item, value was created.

In *The Wealth of Nations* (1776), the first systematic treatment of economics, Smith considered value as an objective phenomenon. By virtue of its existence, an item was assumed to possess utility. Scarcity also imparted exchange value to goods. The "natural price" of an object generally reflected how much the item cost to produce. In contemporary appraisal practice, the classical theory of value has influenced the cost approach.

Later economic thinkers who are regarded as members of the classical school offered theoretical refinements on the cost of production theory of value, but none contested its basic premises. David Ricardo (1772-1823) developed a theory of rent based on the concept of marginal land and the law of diminishing returns. Land residual returns were referred to as rent. Ricardo's theory contributed significantly to the concept of highest and best use and the land residual technique used in the income approach to value.

John Stuart Mill (1806-1873) reworked Adam Smith's ideas in *The Principles of Political Economy* (1848), which became the leading economic text of its time. Mill defined the relationship between interest and value in use, which he referred to as "capital value"; the role of risk in determining interest; and the inequities of "unearned increments" accruing to land.[2] Confident in his analysis of the cost of production theory, Mill asserted, "Happily, nothing in the laws of value remains for the present or any future writer to clear up; the theory of the subject is complete."

Challenges to the Classical Theory

In the second half of the 19th century, two serious challenges to classical value theory were put forward. One was the labour theory of value, an extreme position advocated by Karl Marx (1818-1883). Marx claimed that all value is the direct result of labour and that increased wages to labour would lower capitalistic profits. Marx envisioned an inevitable struggle between the social classes that would eventually result in a violent political upheaval.

The other challenge was presented by the marginal utility, or Austrian, school, which was critical of both the classical and Marxian theories. The central concept of marginal utility links value to the utility of, and demand for, the marginal, or additional, unit of an item. Thus, if one more unit than is needed or demanded appears in a given market, the market becomes diluted and the cost of production becomes irrelevant. Value is regarded as a function of demand, with utility as its fundamental precept.[3] Marginal utility is the theoretical basis for the concept of contribution.

---

[2]   For further discussion of value theory, see Burton, J.H. 1982. *Evolution of the Income Approach*. Chicago: American Institute of Real Estate Appraisers..

[3]   Eugen von Boehm-Bawerk (1835-1882) defined value as "the significance a good acquires by contributing utility toward the well-being of an individual." William Stanley Jevons (1835-1882), a founder of modern statistics and a principal proponent of marginal utility, wrote, "Labour once spent has no influence on the future value of any article: it is gone and lost forever." Jevons, W.S. 1965. *The Theory of Political Economy,* 5th ed. New York: Augustus M. Kelley. p164; Burton, p17.

The Neoclassical Synthesis

These formidable challenges to the classical theory of value inspired economists to reconsider the issue. In the late 19th and early 20th centuries, the neoclassical school successfully merged the supply-cost considerations of the classicists with the demand-price theory of marginal utility. Alfred Marshall (1842-1924) is credited with this synthesis, which forms the basis for contemporary value theory. [4]

Marshall compared supply and demand to the blades of a pair of scissors because neither concept could ever be separated from the determination of value. He stressed the importance of time in working out an adjustment between the two principles. Marshall maintained that market forces tend toward equilibrium where prices and production costs meet. Utility-demand considerations operate in the limited span of a given market. In the short term, supply is relatively fixed and value is a function of demand. Cost-supply considerations, however, extend over a broader period, during which production flows and patterns are subject to change. Marshall believed that a perfect economic market would eventually result and that price, cost, and value would all be equal.[5]

Marshall was the first major economist to consider the techniques of valuation, specifically the valuation of real estate. In this regard, his writings and the writings of those who built upon his work are the source of the distinction between value theory and valuation theory, i.e., the method of estimating, measuring, or forecasting a defined value. Marshall anticipated and developed many of the concepts employed in contemporary appraisal practice. These concepts include the determination of site value through capitalization of income, the impact of depreciation on buildings and land, and the influence of different building types and land uses on site value.

Marshall is also credited with identifying the three traditional approaches to value: market (direct) comparison, reproduction or replacement cost, and capitalization of income. Irving Fisher (1867-1947), an influential American economist associated with the neoclassical school, fully developed the income theory of value, which is the basis for the income capitalization approach used by modern appraisers.[6]

Modern Appraisal Theory

Scholars and business professionals interested in economic thought read the writings of Marshall, Fisher, and other economists of the late 19th and early 20th centuries. At the same time, the field of real estate appraisal was emerging and a few practitioners were gaining experience estimating market value and other kinds of value for properties of various types. In the 1920s and 1930s, several events helped to establish appraisal as a young, but viable, real estate function.

---

[4]   In 1890, Marshall published *Principles of Economics*, which succeeded Mill's *Principles of Political Economy* as the authoritative text on economic thought. In this book, Marshall advocated a dynamic theory of value to explain real world events. See Marshall, A. 1920. *Principles of Economics*, 8th ed. London: MacMillan and Company; reprint 1982, Philadelphia: Porcupine Press. pp288-290, 664-669.

[5]   See Heilbroner, R.L. 1964. The Worldly Philosophers, rev. ed. New York: Simon and Schuster. pp178-179 and Wendt, P.F. 1974. Real Estate Appraisal: Review and Outlook. Athens: University of Georgia Press. pp18-19.

[6]   Wendt, P.F. 1974. Real Estate Appraisal: Review and Outlook. Athens: University of Georgia Press. pp18-19.

One motivating force was the introduction of land economics as an academic discipline. Land economics developed from the interrelationship of several disciplines and attracted scholars and students who contributed significantly to real estate and appraisal literature over the next 40 years.[7]

The publication of *Real Estate Appraising* by Arthur J. Mertzke in 1927 was a significant event in appraisal history. This publication adapted Alfred Marshall's ideas to develop a tangible link between value theory and valuation theory. Mertzke translated economic theory into a working appraisal theory, helped establish a clear emphasis on the three approaches to value, and explained the use of capitalization rates as indices of security. The pre-eminence of the three approaches to value in the appraisal process was underscored in publications by K. Lee Hyder, Harry Grant Atkinson, and George L. Schmutz.[8] Their works established systematic procedures for applying the direct comparison, cost, and income approaches. Schmutz presented a model in which appraisal activity leads to a conclusion of value, which was later incorporated into *The Appraisal of Real Estate*, first published by the American Institute of Real Estate Appraisers in 1951.

Appraisal theory and the language used to describe that theory have continued to evolve. Today's education requirements are stringent and appraisers make use of many analytical methods and techniques. Applying these methods and techniques to an expanding database presents new challenges and raises questions as to how applicable the valuation model is to actual appraisal assignments, how well it analyzes the forces that affect value, and how accurately it interprets the actions and motivations of market participants.

DISTINCTIONS AMONG PRICE, COST, AND VALUE

Contemporary appraisers make careful distinctions among the related terms *price*, *cost*, and *value*. The term price refers to the amount a particular purchaser agrees to pay and a particular seller agrees to accept under the circumstances surrounding the transaction. A price, once finalized, refers to a sale or transaction price and implies an exchange. In other words, price is an accomplished fact.

Generally the circumstances of a transaction reflect conditions within one or several markets because a property might have demand from more than one market. A market is a set of arrangements in which buyers and sellers are brought together through the price mechanism. A market may be defined in terms of geography, products or product features, the number of available buyers and sellers, or some other arrangement of circumstances.

---

[7] This influential group included Richard T. Ely (1854-1943), the founder of land economics as an academic subject, Frederick Morrison Babcock (1898-1983), Ernest McKinley Fisher (1893-1981), and Arthur J. Mertzke (1890-1970). Ely, Babcock, and Fisher contributed to the Land Economics series published by the National Association of Real Estate Board (now the National Association of Realtors), which was the first major publication effort designed to provide real estate professionals with current technical information. The first texts in this series were Fisher's *Principles of Real Estate* (1923), Ely and Moorehouse's *Elements of Land Economics* (1924), and Babcock's *The Appraisal of Real Estate* (1924).

[8] Hyder, K.L. 1936. "The Appraisal Process". The Appraisal Journal. January 1936; Atkinson, H.G. 1936. "The Process of Appraising Single-Family Homes". *The Appraisal Journal*. April 1936; and Schmutz, G.L. 1941. *The Appraisal Process*. North Hollywood, CA: the author.

A real estate market is created by the interaction of individuals who exchange real property rights for other assets such as money. Specific real estate markets are defined on the basis of various attributes:

> The terms price, cost, and value are used and defined carefully by appraisers.

- Property type
- Location
- Income-producing potential
- Typical investor characteristics
- Typical tenant characteristics
- Other attributes recognized by those participating in the exchange of real property

Examples of specific real estate markets might include new, single-unit residences selling for $250,000 in a well-defined neighbourhood or older apartment buildings located near the central business district and available for renovation.

Many people use cost and value synonymously, but appraisal practice requires more precise definitions. The term cost is used by appraisers in relation to production, not exchange. Cost may be either an accomplished fact or a current estimate.

Costs may be identified with the project phase to which they pertain, i.e., either actual construction cost or overall development cost. Construction cost of components or the entirety normally includes the direct costs of labour and materials, as well as indirect costs such as administrative fees, professional fees, and financing costs. Development cost is the cost to create a property, including the land, and bring it to an efficient operating state. Development cost includes acquisition costs, actual expenditures, and the profit required to compensate the developer or entrepreneur for the time and risk involved in creating the project.

Real estate-related expenditures are directly linked to the price of goods and services in competitive markets. For example, the costs of roofing materials, masonry, architectural plans, and rented scaffolding are determined by the interaction of supply and demand in specific areas. Thus, they are subject to the influence of social, economic, governmental, and environmental forces.

> For appraisers the term value alone can be misleading. Appraisers typically refer to a particular type of value rather than use the word value on its own.

Value can have many meanings in real estate appraisal: the applicable definition depends on the context and usage.[9] In the marketplace, value is commonly perceived as the anticipation of benefits to be obtained in the future. Since value changes over time, an appraisal reflects value at a particular point in time. Value as at a given time represents the monetary worth of property, goods, or services to buyers and sellers. To avoid confusion, appraisers do not use the word value alone. Instead they refer to more specific terms such as market value, fair value, use value, investment value, and assessed value. Market value is the focus of most real property appraisal assignments.

---

[9]   See Smith, H.C. 1977. "Value Concepts as a Source of Disparity Among Appraisals". *The Appraisal Journal*. April 1977: pp203–208 and Shlaes, J. 1993. "Value: More than Ever, In Your Eye". *The Appraisal Journal*. January 1993: pp71–78.

MARKET VALUE

The concept of market value is of paramount importance to business and real estate communities. Vast sums of debt and equity capital are committed each year to real estate investments and mortgage loans that are based on opinions of market value. Real estate taxation, litigation, and legislation also reflect an ongoing, active concern with market value issues. In virtually every aspect of the real estate industry and its regulation at local, provincial and federal levels, market value considerations are essential to economic stability.

CUSPAP requires that an appraisal report must include a relevant definition of the value found and a citation of the source of the definition. A number of different definitions of market value can be found in a variety of sources, including appraisal texts, real estate dictionaries, professional standards, federal regulations, lease and option-to-purchase agreements, and court and tribunal decisions. Despite differing opinions on individual aspects of the market value definition, it is generally agreed that market value results from the collective value judgments of market participants. An opinion of market value must be based on objective observation of the collective actions of the market. Since the standard measure of these activities is cash, the increases or diminutions in market value caused by financing and other terms of sale are measured against an all-cash value.

> Market value is the major focus of most real property appraisal assignments. Both economic and legal definitions of market value have been developed and refined. Continual refinement is essential to the appraisal profession.
> Various definitions of market value have been developed by the Appraisal Institute of Canada, the Appraisal Institute of the United States, the Appraisal Foundation, the International Valuation Standards Committee, and others.

The definition that follows incorporates the concepts that are most widely accepted, such as willing, able, and knowledgeable buyers and sellers who act prudently as of a given date, and this definition gives the appraiser a choice among three bases: all cash, terms equivalent to cash, or other precisely revealed terms. The definition also requires increments or diminutions from the all-cash market value to be quantified in terms of cash.

Market Value

The most probable price, as of a specified date, in cash, or in terms equivalent to cash, or in other precisely revealed terms, for which the specified property rights should sell after reasonable exposure in a competitive market under all conditions requisite to a fair sale, with the buyer and seller each acting prudently, knowledgeably, and for self-interest, and assuming that neither is under undue duress.

This definition represents the concept of value in exchange, a concept made explicit in the market value definition developed by the International Valuation Standards Committee (IVSC) and used in the International Valuation Standards. These standards define market value as:

[T]he estimated amount for which a property should exchange on the date of valuation between a willing buyer and a willing seller in an arm's-length transaction after proper marketing wherein the parties had each acted knowledgeably, prudently, and without compulsion.[10]

The general valuation concepts and principles guiding the International Valuation Standards reiterate the concept that market value "reflects the collective perceptions and actions of a market", not the "preconceived view or vested interest of a particular individual". The market value basis of valuation of the International Valuation Standards is consistent with other discussions of market value in professional standards.

In addition to the requirements of professional standards, to clarify the nature of value reported, an appraisal report might need to set out the following items:

- Identification of the specific property rights to be appraised.

- Statement of the effective date of the value opinion.

- Specification as to whether cash, terms equivalent to cash, or other precisely described financing terms are assumed as the basis of the appraisal.

- If the appraisal is conditional upon financing or other terms, specification as to whether the financing or terms are at, below, or above market interest rates and/or contain unusual conditions or incentives. The terms of above- or below-market interest rates and/or other special incentives must be clearly set forth; their contribution to, or negative influence on, value must be described and estimated; and the market data supporting the opinion of value must be described and explained.

Although these requirements include non-cash equivalent financing terms within the scope of the market value of appraised property rights, these rights are valued in relation to cash. Increments or diminutions in market value attributable to financing terms are measured against an all-cash standard, and the dollar amount of variance from the cash standard must be reported.

Citable definitions of market value can be found in provincial and federal regulations, laws, or publications. For example, the following definition is from the federal government's Expropriation Act (R.S. 985 c. E-21).

the value of an expropriated interest is the market value thereof, that is to say, the amount that would have been paid for the interest if, at the time of its taking, it had been sold in the open market by a willing seller to a willing buyer.

A similar definition is contained in the Expropriation Act of British Columbia [RSBC] Chapter 125:

The market value of an estate or interest in land is the amount that would have been paid for it if it had been sold at the date of expropriation in the open market by a willing seller to a willing buyer.

---

10   International Valuation Standards Committee. 2007. *International Valuation Standards*, 8th ed. London. p76.

In addition to the IVSC definition, CUSPAP provides:[11]

> One definition of market value is:
>
> The most probable price which a property should bring in a competitive and open market as of the specified date under all conditions requisite to a fair sale, the buyer and seller each acting prudently and knowledgeably, and assuming the price is not affected by undue stimulus.
>
> The definition may be expanded by adding:
>
> Implicit in this definition are the consummation of a sale as of the specified date and the passing of title from seller to buyer under conditions whereby:
>
> • buyer and seller are typically motivated;
> • both parties are well informed or well advised, and acting in what they consider their best interests;
> • a reasonable time is allowed for exposure in the open market;
> • payment is made in terms of cash in Canadian dollars or in terms of financial arrangements comparable thereto;
> • the price represents the normal consideration for the property sold unaffected by special or creative financing or sales concessions granted by anyone associated with the sale.

The intended use of an appraisal dictates which definition of market value is applicable to a specific assignment. Client wishes or instructions do not change the basic requirement that the appraiser must identify an appraisal's intended use and cite an appropriate definition of market value for that use. Appraisers must understand why a particular definition of market value should be used, apply that definition according to established standards, and communicate these requirements clearly to the clients they serve.

OTHER TYPES OF VALUE

Appraisals of the market value of real property are the most common assignments, but appraisers are also called upon by clients to develop opinions of a variety of other types of value.

Fair Value

When the accounting profession refers to the value of an asset, it uses different terms and definitions; recently, these have been undergoing change. Historically, the accounting profession in Canada and the United States has used the depreciated purchase price for reporting the value of corporate assets for tax purposes and for use in financial statements. Canadian accounting practises followed Generally Accepted Accounting Principles, or GAAP, that for practical reasons were highly standardized relative to those in the United States. In some other countries, entities report

---

[11] Canadian Uniform Standards of Professional Appraisal Practice, 2010 Edition, 12.16. Ottawa: Appraisal Institute of Canada.

asset values having a basis in the marketplace, pursuant to International Accounting Standards, or AS, (maintained by the International Accounting Standards Board, or IASB). As at 2001, IASB defined fair value as:

> The amount for which an asset could be exchanged, or a liability settled, between knowledgeable, willing parties in an arm's length transaction.

For reasons that include improved transparency and consistency, interest in asset accounting based on current value has grown in Canada, accelerated by auditing scandals from 2000 to 2004 involving asset values reported by some publicly traded companies.

In 2006, the Canadian Institute of Chartered Accountants adopted a definition of fair value as:

> The amount of the consideration that would be agreed upon in an arm's length transaction between knowledgeable, willing parties who are under no compulsion to act.

This definition effectively harmonized Canadian GAAP with International Financial Reporting Standards (IFRS) with respect to the recognition and measurement of financial assets and financial liabilities. The Canadian accounting profession continued to adopt further IAS policies, which were themselves changing to standardize guidance for financial statements. In May 2008, the IASB issued a policy proposal that defined fair value as:

> the price that would be received to sell an asset or paid to transfer a liability in an orderly transaction between market participants at the measurement date.

This definition is very similar to a market value opinion as appraisers have long defined the term. Like market value, fair value measurement assumes that the asset or liability is exchanged in an orderly transaction between market participants to sell the asset or transfer the liability at the measurement date. An orderly transaction is a transaction that assumes exposure to the market for a period prior to the measurement date to allow for marketing activities that are usual and customary for transactions involving such assets or liabilities. It is not a forced transaction, e.g., a forced liquidation or distress sale. The transaction to sell the asset or transfer the liability is a hypothetical transaction at the measurement date, considered from the perspective of a market participant who holds the asset or owes the liability. Therefore, the objective of a fair value measurement is to determine the price that would be received to sell the asset or paid to transfer the liability at the measurement date, i.e., an exit price.

Market participants are buyers and sellers in the principal (or most advantageous) market for the asset or liability that are:

1. Independent of the reporting entity, i.e., they are not related parties

2. Knowledgeable, having a reasonable understanding about the asset or liability and the transaction based on all available information, including information that might be obtained through due diligence efforts that are usual and customary

3. Able to transact for the asset or liability

4. Willing to transact for the asset or liability, i.e., they are motivated but not forced or otherwise compelled to do so

The fair value of the asset or liability should be determined based on the assumptions that market participants would use in pricing the asset or liability.

A fair value measurement assumes the highest and best use of the asset by market participants, considering the use of the asset that is physically possible, legally permissible, and financially feasible at the measurement date. The highest and best use of the asset establishes the valuation premise used to measure the fair value of the asset, specifically:

1. In use. The highest and best use of the asset in use would provide maximum value to market participants principally through its use in combination with other assets as a group.

2. In exchange. The highest and best use of the asset is in exchange if the asset would provide maximum value to market participants principally on a stand-alone basis.

The real estate appraiser may need to report both values so that the user of the report can make an informed decision.

The International Valuation Standards point out that fair value and market value are not necessarily synonymous in the International Financial Reporting Standards, where market value is used in differing contexts.

Use Value

Use value is the value a specific property has for a specific use. In estimating use value, the appraiser focuses on the value the real estate contributes to the enterprise of which it is a part, without regard to the highest and best use of the property or the monetary amount that might be realized from its sale. Real property has both a use value and a market value, which may be the same or different depending on the property and the market. For example, an older manufacturing plant that is still used by the original owner may have considerable use value to that owner but only a nominal market value for another use. Use value may vary depending on the management of the property and external conditions such as changes in business operations. For example, a factory designed around a particular assembly process may have one use value before a major change in assembly technology and another use value afterward.

Use value appraisal assignments may be performed to value assets (including real property) for mergers, acquisitions, corporate financial reporting, or security issues. This type of assignment is sometimes encountered in appraising industrial real estate when the existing business includes real property.

Court decisions and specific statutes may also create the need for use value appraisals. For example, some jurisdictions require agricultural use appraisals of farmland for property tax purposes (i.e., value based on productivity) rather than

---

USE VALUE, VALUE IN USE, AND INVESTMENT VALUE OR WORTH

The term value in use is often used by appraisers synonymously with use value, but the former term has specific meanings in other contexts, which can cause confusion. The International Financial Reporting Standards defines value in use as "(t)he present value of estimated future cash flows expected to arise from the continuing use of an asset and from its disposal at the end of its useful life." This definition is quoted in the International Valuation Standards (IVS) in relation to valuation for financial reporting.

Earlier editions of the International Valuation Standards included a different definition of value in use as part of International Valuation Standard 2: Bases Other Than Market Value, but that definition was recently deleted, eliminating the possible confusion between value in use and investment value or worth. The current definition of investment value or worth is not specifically related to financial reporting as value in use now is in IVS.

---

opinions of value based on highest and best use. Some option to purchase agreements in lease documents call for valuation of a property under a specified use (generally that of the tenant).

Use value appraisals often involve limited-market properties, i.e., properties of a type that has relatively few potential buyers at a particular time. Large manufacturing plants, railroad sidings, and research and development properties are examples of limited-market properties that typically appeal to relatively few potential purchasers. Many limited-market properties, such as houses of worship, museums, schools, public buildings, and clubhouses, include structures with unique designs, special construction materials, or layouts that restrict their functional utility to the use for which they were originally built. These properties usually have limited conversion potential and, consequently, are also called specialized, special-use, special-purpose, or special-design properties.

Limited-market properties may be appraised based on their current use or the most likely alternative use. Due to the relatively small markets and lengthy market exposure needed to sell such properties, there may be little evidence to support an opinion of market value based on the current use. If a market exists for a limited-market property, the appraiser must search diligently for whatever evidence of market value is available.

If a property's current use is so specialized that there is no demonstrable market for it but the use is viable and likely to continue, the appraiser may render an opinion of use value if the assignment reasonably permits a type of value other than market value. Such an estimate should not be confused with an opinion of market value. If no market can be demonstrated or if data is not available, the appraiser cannot develop an opinion of market value and should state so in the appraisal report. However, it is sometimes necessary to render an opinion of market value in these situations for legal purposes. In these cases, the appraiser must comply with the legal requirement, relying on personal judgement and whatever direct market evidence is available and making explanations and disclosures that are relevant and that can fully inform the intended users of the appraisal. Note that the type of value developed is not dictated by the property type, the size or viability of the market, or the ease with which that value can be developed. Rather, the intended use of the appraisal determines the type of value to be developed.

Just as use value should not be confused with market value, it should be distinguished from investment value, discussed next.

Investment Value

Investment value represents the value of a specific property to a particular investor. As used in appraisal assignments, investment value is the value of a property to a particular investor based on that person's or entity's investment requirements. In contrast to market value, investment value is value to an individual, not necessarily value in the marketplace.

Investment value reflects the subjective relationship between a particular investor and a given investment. It differs in concept from market value, although investment value and market value indications sometimes may be similar. If the investor's requirements are typical of the market, investment value will be the same as market value.

When measured in dollars, investment value is the price an investor would pay for an investment in light of its perceived capacity to satisfy that individual's desires, needs, or investment goals. To render an opinion of investment value, specific investment criteria must be known.

> **investment value**
> The specific value of a property to a particular investor or class of investors based on individual investment requirements; distinguished from market value, which is impersonal and detached.

Business Value

A going concern is an established and operating business with an indefinite future life. For certain types of properties (e.g., hotels and motels, restaurants, bowling alleys, manufacturing enterprises, athletic clubs, landfills), the physical real estate assets are integral parts of an ongoing business. The market value of such a property (including all the tangible and intangible assets of the going concern, as if sold in aggregate) is commonly referred to by laymen as *business value* or *business enterprise value*, but in reality it is market value of the going concern including real property, personal property, and the intangible assets of the business. (See Figure 2.1.)

Appraisers may be called upon to develop an opinion of the investment value, use value, or some other type of value of a going concern, but most appraisals of the value of the going concern relate to market value. Due to the nature of the different types of value included, the appraiser should be careful that he or she has the experience and competence to complete this type of valuation assignment. It may be necessary for the real estate appraiser to collaborate with a personal property appraiser or a business appraiser or both on such an assignment.

Traditionally, the term *going-concern value* has been defined as the value of a proven property operation. The current definition of the term highlights the assumption that the business enterprise is expected to continue operating well into the future (usually indefinitely).

> **going concern**
> All tangible and intangible assets of an established and operating business with an indefinite life.

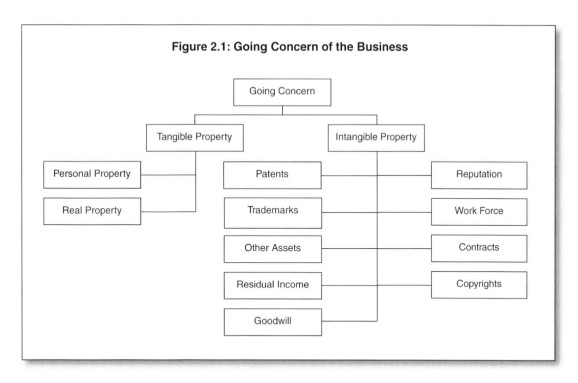

Figure 2.1: Going Concern of the Business

In contrast, liquidation value assumes that the enterprise will cease operations. Going-concern value includes the incremental value associated with the business concern, which is distinct from the value of the tangible real property and personal property. The value of the going concern includes an intangible enhancement of the value of the operating business enterprise, which is produced by the assemblage of the land, buildings, labour, equipment, and the marketing operation. This assemblage creates an economically viable business that is expected to continue. The value of the going concern refers to the total value of the property, including both the real property and the personal property attributed to business value (see Figure 2.2).

It may be difficult to separate the market value of the land and the building from the total value of the business, but such a division of realty and non-realty components of value may be required by the intended use of the appraisal. When an appraiser cannot effectively separate the market value of the real estate from its business value, it is appropriate to state that the reported opinion of value includes both market value and business value and that the appraiser has not been able to distinguish between them. Only qualified practitioners should undertake these kinds of assignments, which must be performed in compliance with appropriate CUSPAP standards.

Public Interest Value

Public interest value is a general term covering a family of value concepts that relate the highest and best use of property to non-economic uses. Public interest value is driven by social, political, and public policy goals. It is not based on economic principles. Rather, public interest value is based on a non-economic highest and best use.

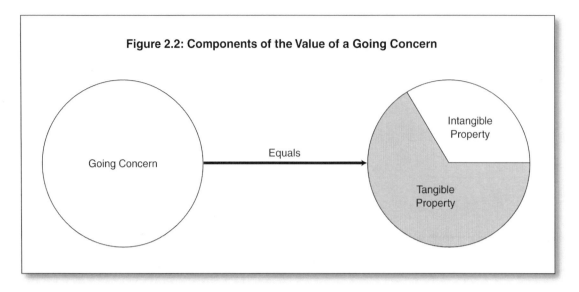

Figure 2.2: Components of the Value of a Going Concern

Public interest value has sometimes been referred to as natural value, intrinsic value, aesthetic value, scenic value, preservation value, and similar terms.

Large amounts of public funds are at stake over what has been a highly controversial issue. Proponents of the public interest value concept recommend a redefinition of highest and best use and market value (to recognize preservation or conservation as a highest and best use), extension of the market concept to include public agencies and conservation groups, and adoption of alternative valuation models. Opponents contend that because non-economic uses are not responsive to market forces, such uses cannot give rise to market value, the basis of which can only be economic highest and best use. They argue that the application of public interest value concepts invariably results in opinions of value that exceed those derived from economic highest and best use analyses. Opponents further point out that government is a different type of market participant, not constrained to follow market economic rules.

The notion of public interest value does have an important potential application when it is defined and applied in public benefit terms. For example, a highway department acquiring private land for a highway might adopt a policy of determining market value of each parcel to be acquired. Then, in the public interest, the highway department determines it appropriate to offer 25% more than market value to avoid potential transaction and litigation costs that would be required in expropriations. This formula would demonstrate that the first 100% was the department's opinion of market value and the last 25% (of the 125% paid) was paid in the public interest rather than directly for market value. Government buildings that have increased security structures that exceed normal market needs are an example of how costs that exceed the normal costs of office buildings may be justified in public interest value terms. These are only two of many examples that may illustrate how the decisions of individual market participants regarding market value differ from the construct and basis of decisions that are made by or on behalf of the public.

Assessed Value

Assessed value applies in ad valorem taxation and refers to the value of a property according to the tax rolls. Assessed value may not conform to market value, but it is usually calculated in relation to a market value base. Some assessing jurisdictions estimate both an assessed value and a market value.

Insurable Value

Insurable value is the value of an asset or asset group that is covered by an insurance policy. Insurable value may be based on the replacement or reproduction cost of physical items that are subject to loss from hazards. This value is often controlled by provincial law and varies from province to province.

assessed value
The value of a property according to the tax rolls in ad valorem taxation; may be higher or lower than market value, or based on an assessment ratio that is a percentage of market value.

Actual Cash Value

Actual cash value is an insurance concept that refers to the calculation of compensation due in an insurable loss. Strictly

insurable value
The value of an asset or asset group that is covered by an insurance policy; can be estimated by deducting costs of noninsurable items (such as land value) from market value.

defined as replacement cost minus normal depreciation, actual cash value is determined in the courts through a review of legal precedents. A building on a site where market conditions favour redevelopment to a higher and better use might have little actual cash value, even though it has a remaining physical value.[12]

---

[12]   Black's Law Dictionary, Bryan A. Garner, Editor in Chief, Thomson West, St. Paul, Eighth Edition, 2004

CHAPTER 3

FOUNDATIONS OF APPRAISAL

Real property is the focus of real estate appraisal activity. Society generally perceives real property to be a good investment, allowing individuals to achieve economic goals through the ownership and successful management of real estate. Real estate markets have always been turbulent and probably always will be. For example, in the early 1980s, the Bank of Canada (and the federal government) increased interest rates to combat inflation, and house prices fell sharply as mortgages became unaffordable. Eighteen years later, to stimulate a slowing economy, regulators dropped interest rates to near historic lows, reducing the cost of mortgage financing and stimulating housing demand and increasing house price levels. In the United States, aggressive subprime lending in the 2000s contributed to an abundance of foreclosured properties and brought on federal scrutiny and intervention. Developers often perceive public controls and municipal development levies as excessive. Nevertheless, real estate markets remain an important investment vehicle and a generator of economic activity.

In determining their level of participation in the real estate market, individuals consider their wants and needs as well as the variety of options available to them at different times. Their choices help support a free market economy. Thus, both individual and collective decisions contribute to the nation's economic success. Similarly, the production of goods, services, and income depends on the combined effects of four essential economic ingredients, commonly referred to as the four agents of production:

- Land
- Labour
- Capital
- Entrepreneurial coordination

AGENTS OF PRODUCTION

Traditional economic theory holds that four agents of production are combined to create real estate and that the sum of the costs to develop a property is one of the basic measures of real property value available to appraisers. In other words, combining land, labour, capital, and entrepreneurial coordination creates a finished real estate product. An appraiser might develop a well-supported opinion of value through systematic analysis of each of these components, their interrelationships, and their relationship to the property as a whole.

Land

The first thing an entrepreneur generally considers in developing a property is the cost of acquiring the land. The cost of a vacant site or parcel of raw land is the cost of acquisition. The appraiser anticipates that an owner will add improvements and market the property to tenants or multiple end users.

Labour

The labour component comprises all direct and indirect costs required to construct and market the product as land alone or with improvements. Direct costs include not only the wages paid to individuals, but also the cost of materials used in construction. Indirect costs consist of permit fees, marketing expenses, taxes, overhead, the cost of project coordination or supervision, and financing costs that are not included in the rate paid to the lender over the development period.

Capital

Real estate development requires physical capital such as equipment (e.g., machinery and tools), buildings, and infrastructure (that is, capital goods) that can produce other goods.

Entrepreneurial Coordination

No prudent developer will undertake to construct and market a property without anticipating receipt of a profit in addition to the return of the equity investment. The purchaser who continues an existing land use is not creating value, only maintaining value through proper management of the property. A developer, on the other hand, invests not only equity in a development, but also time and expertise. Accordingly, an entrepreneur expects a reward – known as entrepreneurial incentive (and measured in the marketplace as entrepreneurial profit) – for creating and marketing a real estate product through the coordination of land, labour, and capital. More precisely, entrepreneurial incentive is a forecast of the amount the devel-

---

entrepreneurial coordination
The ability of an entrepreneur to combine land, labor, and capital in the development of real property; a component of real estate value that represents the investment of time, expertise, and equity by an entrepreneur (or developer) in the development of a property.

oper expects to receive. This forecast is developed before construction is complete. Entrepreneurial profit is the actual amount received after the property is complete. The fourth agent of production, entrepreneurial coordination, accounts for that investment of time and expertise. Chapter 17 discusses entrepreneurial incentive and entrepreneurial profit in greater detail.

ANTICIPATION AND CHANGE

The human actions that collectively shape market operations reflect the pursuit of economic goals. To analyze the many dynamic and interactive factors that influence people's attitudes and beliefs about value, an appraiser must address the fundamental principles of anticipation and change.

> **anticipation**
> The perception that value is created by the expectation of benefits to be derived in the future.
>
> **change**
> The result of the cause and effect relationship among the forces that influence real property value.

Anticipation

The anticipation of future benefits creates value. In real estate markets, the current value of a property is usually not based on its historical prices or the cost of its creation; rather, value is based on the market participants' perceptions of the future benefits of acquisition.

> Value is created by the anticipation of future benefits.

> **opportunity cost**
> The cost of options foregone or opportunities not chosen.

The basis for value of owner-occupied residential property is primarily the expected future advantages, amenities, and the opportunity cost of ownership and occupancy. Prior to the property's sale, the primary investment return is measured in these amenities and the economic benefit of owning rather than renting property, not in the receipt of income. The basis of value for income-producing real estate is the future income it will produce. As a result, real property appraisers must be aware of local, regional, and national real estate trends that affect the perceptions of buyers and sellers and their anticipations of the future. Historical data on a property or a market is relevant only insofar as it helps interpret current market anticipations.

Change

The dynamic nature of the social, economic, governmental, and environmental forces that influence real property value accounts for change. Although change is inevitable and continuous, the process may be gradual and not easily discernible. In active markets, change may occur rapidly, with new properties put up for sale and others sold on a daily basis. Plant or government facility closures, tax law revisions, the start of new construction, or natural disasters can precipitate abrupt changes. The pervasiveness of change is evident in the real estate market, where the social, economic, governmental, and environmental forces that affect real estate are in constant transition. Changes in these forces influence

> *All values are anticipations of the future.*
> – Justice Oliver Wendell Holmes, Jr.

> The principles of anticipation, change, supply and demand, competition, and substitution are fundamental to understanding the dynamics of value.

the demand for and supply of real estate and, therefore, individual property values. Appraisers attempt to identify current and anticipated changes in the market that could affect current property values, but, because change is not always predictable, opinions of value are said to be valid only as of the specified date of valuation. An appraiser's analyses and conclusions reflect what the market anticipates, rather than what the appraiser or the owner anticipates.

Shifts in market preferences also provide evidence of change. Real estate is not readily adaptable to new consumer preferences and thus often suffers obsolescence, i.e., an impairment of desirability and usefulness. The physical, functional, and economic impairments observed in buildings as they age result in depreciation, which is defined as a loss in property value from any cause. Depreciation may be seen as the difference between the cost to reproduce or replace a property and its present value. In general, deterioration or obsolescence causes losses in property value. Since obsolescence can begin in the design phase and deterioration may start while a building or improvement is still being constructed, the different types of deterioration and obsolescence found in a property have unique implications in appraisal. Chapter 19 presents a detailed discussion of deterioration and obsolescence.

SUPPLY AND DEMAND, SUBSTITUTION, BALANCE, AND EXTERNALITIES

The appraisal principles of supply and demand, substitution, balance, and externalities can be applied to the unique physical and legal characteristics of a particular parcel of real property. When these basic economic principles are in proper accord, they indicate the highest and best use of the parcel of land, which has great significance in real property appraisal. Chapter 12 discusses highest and best use in detail.

Supply and Demand

In economic theory, the principle of supply and demand states that the price of a commodity, good, or service (or, in a real estate context, the price of real property) varies directly, but not necessarily proportionately, with demand and inversely, but not necessarily proportionately, with supply. Thus, an increase in the supply of an item or a decrease in the demand for an item tends to reduce the equilibrium price. The opposite conditions produce an opposite effect. The relationship between supply and demand may not be directly proportional, but the interaction of these forces is fundamental to economic theory. The interaction of suppliers and demanders, or sellers and buyers, constitutes a market.

Supply

Property values usually vary inversely with changes in supply. If properties for a particular use become more abundant relative to demand, their equilibrium value declines. By contrast, if properties become more scarce and supply declines relative to demand, the equilibrium price of the properties increases. The supply of and demand for commodities always tend to move toward equilibrium. At this theoretical point (which almost never occurs), market value, price, and cost are equal.

In real estate, supply is the amount of a type of real estate available for sale or lease at various prices in a given market at a given time. Typically, markets will supply more of an item at a higher price and less at a lower price. Therefore, the supply of an item at a particular price, at a particular time, and in a particular place indicates that item's relative scarcity, which is a basic factor of value.

The supply of real estate is dependent on the costs of the four agents of production, which are brought together to produce a product that is offered for sale. Increasing demand in a particular market will drive up property values and the quantity of new properties offered for sale generally increases. When the supply of the agents of production declines, property values again tend to rise. On the other hand, increases in the productivity of labour, greater technological efficiency, improvements in capital goods, or the utilization of more capital goods per worker tend to reduce development costs. A building boom set in motion by developer's rising expectations of profit may result in an oversupply of properties.

Since real property is both a physical commodity and a service, the supply of real estate refers to the amount of service, or the usability of the space as well as the quantity of physical space. Consequently, those involved in real estate are primarily concerned with the supply of land suitable for a specific use, not simply the total number of hectares or acres available.

Generally the quantity of space supplied for a given use is slow to adjust to changes in price levels. The length of time needed to build new structures, the large amount of capital required, and government regulations often hamper a supplier's ability to meet changes in the market. However, the quality of space can change more rapidly because suppliers can convert non-productive space to alternative uses, cure deferred maintenance, and partition existing space into smaller units.

Demand

Demand is the desire and ability to purchase or lease goods and services. In real estate, demand is the amount of a certain type of real estate desired for purchase or rent at various prices in a given market for a given period of time. Typically a market will demand less of an item at a higher price, and more at a lower price.

Since it is difficult to augment the supply of real property for a specific use in a short time, current demand strongly affects values. Demand, like supply, can be characterized in terms of both quantity and quality. For example, the number of households in the market area and the household incomes as well as the size and characteristics of the households and specific housing preferences may define demand in a residential market. Demand supported by purchasing power results in effective demand, which is the type of demand considered by the market. Appraisers must interpret market behaviour to ascertain the existing relationship between the supply of and the demand for the type of property being appraised.

Competition

Competition between buyers or tenants represents the interactive efforts of two or more potential buyers or tenants to make a purchase or secure a lease. Between sellers or landlords, competition represents the interactive efforts of two or more potential sellers or landlords to effect a sale or lease. Competition is fundamental to the dynamics of supply and demand in a free enterprise, profit-maximizing economic system.

Buyers and sellers of real property operate in a competitive market setting. In essence, each property competes with all other properties suitable for the same use in a particular market segment and often with properties from other market segments as illustrated in the following examples:

- A profitable hotel faces competition from newer hotels nearby.
- Existing residential subdivisions compete with new subdivisions.
- Downtown retail properties compete with suburban shopping centres.

Over time, competitive market forces tend to reduce unusually high profits. Profit encourages competition, but excess profits tend to attract ruinous competition. For example, the first retail store to open in a new and expanding area may generate more profit than is considered typical for that type of enterprise. If no barriers to entry exist, owners of similar retail enterprises will likely gravitate to the area to compete for the surplus profits. Eventually there may not be enough business to support all the retailers. A few stores may profit, but others will fail. The effects of competition and market trends on profit levels are especially evident to appraisers making income projections as part of the income approach to value.

> **competition**
> Between purchasers or tenants, the interactive efforts of two or more potential purchasers or tenants to make a sale or secure a lease; between sellers or landlords, the interactive efforts of two or more potential sellers or landlords to complete a sale or lease; among competitive properties, the level of productivity and amenities or benefits characteristic of each property considering the advantageous or disadvantageous position of the property relative to the competitors.
>
> **substitution**
> The appraisal principle states that when several similar or commensurate commodities, goods, or services are available, the one with the lowest price will attract the greatest demand and widest distribution. This is the primary principle upon which the cost and direct comparison approaches are based.

Substitution

The principle of substitution states that when several similar or commensurate commodities, goods, or services are available, the one with the lowest price attracts the greatest demand and widest distribution. This principle assumes rational, prudent market behaviour with no undue cost due to delay. According to the principle of substitution, a buyer will not pay more for one property than for another that is equally desirable.

The price of acquiring an equally desirable substitute property tends to set property value. The principle of substitution recognizes that buyers and sellers of real property have options, in that other properties are available for similar uses. The substitution of one property for another may be considered in terms of use, structural design, or earnings. The cost of acquisition may be the cost to purchase a similar site and construct a building of equivalent utility, assuming no undue cost due to delay; this is the basis of the cost approach. On the other hand, the cost of acquisition may be the price of acquiring an existing property of equal utility, again assuming no undue cost due to delay; this is the basis of the direct comparison approach.

The principle of substitution is equally applicable to properties such as houses, which are purchased for their amenity-producing attributes, and properties purchased for their income-producing capabilities. The amenity-producing attributes of residential properties may include excellence of design, quality of workmanship, or superior construction materials. For an income-producing property, an equally desirable substitute might be an alternative investment property that produces equivalent investment returns with equivalent risk. The prevailing prices, rents, and rates of equally desirable substitutes tend to set the limits of property prices, rents, and rates. The principle of substitution is fundamental to all three traditional approaches to value: direct comparison, cost, and income.

Although the principle of substitution applies in most situations, the market perceives the characteristics of a product to be unique. The demand generated for such products may result in unique pricing.[1] For example, a market may not have ready substitutes for special-purpose properties like a historic residence, medical office building, or high-tech manufacturing plant. In those situations, the appraiser may have to research substitute properties in a broader market or employ analytical techniques appropriate for limited-market properties.

Balance

The principle of balance holds that real property value is created and sustained when contrasting, opposing, or interacting elements are in a state of equilibrium. This principle applies to relationships among various property components as well as the

> The principles of balance, decreasing marginal utility, contribution, surplus productivity, and conformity explain how the integration of property components affects property value.

relationship between the costs of production and the property's productivity. Land, labour, capital, and entrepreneurial coordination are the agents of production, but for most real property the critical combination is the land and improvements. Economic balance is achieved when the combination of land and improvements is optimal, i.e., when no marginal benefit or utility is achieved by adding another unit of capital.

The principle of balance governs the related principles of diminishing returns, contribution, surplus productivity, and conformity. The law of diminishing returns holds that increments in the agents of production added to a parcel of property produce greater net income up to a certain point. At this point, the point of decreasing or diminishing returns, maximum value is achieved. Any additional expenditure will not produce a return commensurate with the additional investment. When the point of decreasing returns is reached, further increments in the agents of production will cause productivity to decline proportionally. This is also known as the principle of diminishing marginal productivity.

---

[1]   The specific issues involved in the valuation of unique properties are addressed in Frank E. Harrison, *Appraising the Tough Ones: Creative Ways to Value Complex Residential Properties* (Chicago: Appraisal Institute, 1996).

> **balance**
> The principle that real property value is created and sustained when contrasting, opposing or interacting elements are in a state of equilibrium.
>
> **law of decreasing returns**
> The premise that additional expenditures beyond a certain point (the point of decreasing returns) will not yield a return commensurate with the additional investment; also known as law of diminishing returns.
>
> **law of increasing returns**
> The premise that larger amounts of the agents of production produce greater net income up to a certain point (the point of decreasing returns).

The fertilization of farmland provides a simple example. Applying fertilizer to a land parcel increases crop yield only up to a point. Beyond that point the additional fertilizer will produce no further increase in the marginal output of the acreage. The optimum amount of fertilization is achieved when the value of the increment in yield resulting from the last unit of fertilizer equals the additional expenditure on fertilizer. This is the point of balance.

As a further illustration, consider a developer who is deciding how many bedrooms to include in a single-unit house being developed for sale on the residential market. The typical single-unit house in this residential market has three bedrooms. It may be uneconomic to include a fourth bedroom if the cost to build exceeds the value added to the property.

The principle of balance also applies to the relationship between a property and its environment. A proper mix of various types and locations of land uses in an area creates and sustains value. A residence near other residences has much more market appeal than a residence next to a landfill or an all-night gas bar.

The principle of balance and the principles of contribution, surplus productivity, and conformity are interdependent and crucial in highest and best use analyses and market value estimation. These concepts form the theoretical foundation for estimating all forms of depreciation in the cost approach, making adjustments in the direct comparison approach, and calculating expected earnings in the income approach.

Contribution

The principle of contribution states that the value of a particular component is measured in terms of its contribution to the value of the whole property or as the amount that its absence would detract from the value of the whole. The cost of an item does not necessarily equal its value. A swimming pool that costs $30,000 to install does not necessarily increase the value of a residential property by $30,000. Rather, the pool's dollar contribution to value is measured in terms of its benefit or utility in the market. The swimming pool's contribution to value may be one of the following:

- Higher than its cost if properties with swimming pools are in very high demand in the market.

- Equal to its cost.

- Lower than its cost, though still contributing positively to value. This is the most common situation, i.e., more than zero but less than its cost.

- No contribution to value if adding a swimming pool would have no effect on the value of that property in that market at that time.

- A negative contribution to value if the swimming pool may need to be removed at an additional cost for the property to reach its highest and best use.

The contribution of the existing improvements may not be in proper balance with the total property. Especially in transitional areas, a property's present use may underutilize the land. Nevertheless, an existing, less-than-optimal use, called an interim use, will continue until it is economically feasible for a developer to absorb the costs of converting the property, either by razing and replacing the existing improvements or by rehabilitating them.

> **contribution**
> The concept that the value of a particular component is measured in terms of its contribution to the value of the whole property or as the amount that its absence would detract from the value of the whole.

Surplus Productivity

Surplus productivity is the net income to the land remaining after the costs of the other agents of production have been paid. The classical economists of the 18th and 19th centuries identified the surplus with land rent, which they understood to account for land value. Traditionally, the principle of surplus productivity has provided the basis for the residual concept of land returns and residual valuation techniques (See Chapter 22). The principles of surplus productivity and residual returns to the land are useful in establishing the highest and best use of land and in analyzing which option among alternative land use options will yield the highest value. Some 20th century economists argue that surplus productivity should be ascribed to a different agent of production, i.e., the entrepreneurial coordination required to combine the land, labour, and capital into a complete real estate product.

> **surplus productivity**
> The net income that remains after the costs of various agents of production have been paid.
> **conformity**
> The appraisal principle that real property value is created and sustained when the characteristics of a property conform to the demands of its market.

Conformity

Conformity holds that real property value is created and sustained when the characteristics of a property conform to the demands of its market. The styles and uses of the properties in a given area may conform for several reasons, including economic pressures and the shared preferences of owners for certain types of structures, amenities, and services. The imposition and enforcement of zoning ordinances and plans by local governments to regulate land use may also contribute to conformity. Standards of conformity set by the market are subject to change. Local building codes and private restrictions, which tend to establish conformity in basic property characteristics such as size, style, and design, are often difficult to change and may hasten the pace of obsolescence.

Individual markets also set standards of conformity, especially in terms of price. According to the principle of progression, a lower-priced property will be worth more in a high-priced neighbourhood than it would in a neighbourhood of comparable properties. Under the principle of regression, a higher-priced property will be worth less in a low-priced neighbourhood than it would in a neighbourhood of comparable properties. Of course, there are exceptions to these principles. The seasonal cottages and luxurious vacation homes that line a popular recreational lake may exert no effect, either positive or negative, on the value of one another because the market accepts the diversity.

Externalities

The principle of externalities states that factors external to a property can have either a positive or negative effect on its value. Bridges and highways, police and fire protection, and a host of other essential structures and services are positive externalities that are provided most efficiently through common purchase by the government. Negative externalities result when the actions of others impose inconveniences on property owners.

> externalities
> Factors outside a property, or externalities, exert both positive and negative influences on the property's value.

For example, a firm that violates environmental law by dumping hazardous waste and manages to evade responsibility imposes the cleanup costs on others.

Since real estate is physically immobile, external influences affect it more strongly than most other economic goods, services, or commodities. Externalities may refer to the use or physical attributes of properties located near the subject property or to the economic conditions that affect the market in which the subject property competes. For example, an increase in the purchasing power of the households that constitute the trade area for a retail facility will likely have a positive effect on the sales (income-producing) potential of the property.

On a broad level, international economic conditions can influence real estate values through externalities such as the availability of foreign capital or the effect of increasing foreign trade on the growth of the national economy. The effects of foreign trade are particularly strong in Ontario, Montreal, and British Columbia, areas that have economies subject to shifts in trade volume with the United States, European, and Pacific Rim areas respectively .

National fiscal policy also plays a vital role in the economy and, consequently, in real estate markets. Government policy changes that influence the taxation or financial performance of real estate can affect its appeal and value.

National economic trends have had varying effects in different areas of Canada. In the 1990s, the West Coast economy strengthened as a result of expanded Pacific Rim trade, while the prairies suffered from low agricultural commodity prices. Areas with more diversified economies did not experience as severe a recession. Throughout the 1990s, the growth of the information technology industry in various pockets across the country – greater Ottawa, Vancouver, and Kitchener-Waterloo, among others – had profound impacts on real estate values in those areas. In Newfoundland, economic growth from off-shore oil development created strong economic growth

TAX POLICY AND REAL PROPERTY MARKETS

Changes to the Income Tax Act in 1972 made gains in the value of investment real estate in Canada taxable; before that, such "capital gains" were free of tax. Further reforms at the same time prevented rental investors from claiming depreciation charges (called capital cost allowances or CCA) as deductions against income from other sources. These changes had a far-reaching effect on the value of investment-grade properties. Due in part to the tax advantages available prior to 1970, some real estate markets had been overbuilt. After the tax law was changed, the oversupply was recognized and values in these markets declined significantly.

In 1974, the multiple-unit residential building (MURB) provision of the Income Tax Act restored the favourable CCA treatment for rental apartment developments. The MURB provision was extended several times – it was in effect from 1974 to 1979 and was reinstated from 1980 to 1981. The purpose of the MURB provision was to stimulate investor interest in rental housing; at this it proved successful, as many syndicated MURB tax shelter rental projects were built across Canada during this time. However, in 1978, depreciation rates for MURBS were reduced, and in 1979 and 1981, the deductibility of expenses for rental investors was limited, making this type of investment less attractive. During the recessionary period that commenced in 1981, demand for rental multi-unit developments disappeared. By the mid 1980s, low interest rates stimulated a gradual economic recovery and sales of new and existing homes picked up.

during the decade following 2000; oil and gas development in Alberta, and to a lesser extent in Saskatchewan and eastern British Columbia led to escalating real estate values, with the rapidly increasing incomes of Alberta residents leading to high demand for recreational property in British Columbia. Manitoba's economy increased steadily in the first decade of the century, with good agricultural prices augmenting growth in the manufacturing and services sector.

The Maritime provinces changed markedly throughout the 20th century, partly as a result of global and national economic trends, and partly as a result of government intervention. Each sub-region within the Maritimes has developed over time to exploit different resources and expertise. Saint John became a centre of the timber trade and shipbuilding and is currently a centre for oil refining and some manufacturing. The northern New Brunswick region is focused on the pulp and paper industry and some mining activity. Historically a railway centre, Moncton has changed its focus by becoming a multi-modal transportation centre with associated manufacturing and retail interests. The Halifax metropolitan area has come to dominate peninsular Nova Scotia as a retail and service centre, but the province's industries have traditionally extended from the coal and steel industries of industrial Cape Breton and Pictou counties, the mixed farming of the North Shore and Annapolis Valley, and the fishing industry on the South and Eastern Shores. Prince Edward Island is largely dominated by farming, fishing, and tourism, and experienced strong growth from 2004 to 2008, due to the strength of these sectors.

Quebec has three distinct economic regions: the agricultural St. Lawrence River Valley, the natural resource-rich areas north of the St. Lawrency River Valley, and Greater Montreal. The agricultural St. Lawrence River Valley experienced strong growth from 2004 to 2008, following high demand for agricultural commodities. The natural resource-rich areas north of the St. Lawrence River Valley also experienced strong growth during this decade, although pulp, paper and lumber demand fell off as the US economy slowed starting in 2006. Greater Montreal is a service, manufacturing, technology and distribution centre and particularly benefited from the strength of the aerospace sector until the global economic downturn in 2008.

In Canada's North, the service and natural resource sectors have dominated. Recent development of diamond mines in Northwest Territories and Nunavut, and pipeline projects in the Northwest Territories and Yukon have added economic activity and affected real estate markets.

At the community and neighbourhood levels, property values are affected by local laws, local government policies and administration, property taxes, economic growth, and social attitudes. Different property value trends can be found in communities in the same region and among neighbourhoods in the same community. Appraisers should be familiar with external events at all levels that can impact property values.

FORCES THAT INFLUENCE REAL PROPERTY MARKETS

The value of real property reflects and is affected by the interaction of four basic forces that influence human activity:

- Social forces
- Economic circumstances
- Governmental controls and regulations
- Environmental conditions

The forces are interactive; they exert pressure on human activities and are, in turn, affected by these activities. The interaction of these forces influences the value of every parcel of real estate in the market.

An understanding of value-influencing forces is fundamental to the appraisal of real property. To develop an opinion of value, an appraiser investigates how the market views a particular property, and the scope of this investigation is not limited to static, current conditions. Rather, the appraiser analyzes trends in the forces that influence value to determine the direction, speed, duration, strength, and limits of these trends. Chapters 4, 8, and 9 further discuss the observation and analysis of value influences.

> An appraiser must study the interaction of the social, economic, governmental, and environmental forces that affect property value.

Social Forces

The social forces studied by appraisers primarily relate to population characteristics. Appraisers need to properly analyze and interpret demographic trends because the demographic composition of the population reveals the potential demand for real estate. Real property values are affected not only by population changes and characteristics, but also by the entire spectrum of human activity. The total population, its composition by age and gender, and the rate of household formation and dissolution strongly influence real property values. Social forces are also reflected in attitudes toward education, law and order, and lifestyle options.

Economic Forces

To determine the influence of economic forces on value, appraisers analyze the fundamental relationships between current and anticipated supply and demand and the economic ability of the population to satisfy its wants, needs, and demands through its purchasing power. Many specific market characteristics are considered in the analysis of economic forces:

- Employment
- Wage levels
- Industrial expansion
- The economic base of the region and the community
- Price levels
- The cost and availability of mortgage credit
- The stock of available vacant and improved properties
- New development under construction or in the planning stage
- Occupancy rates
- The rental and price patterns of existing properties
- Construction costs

An appraiser might study other economic trends and considerations as the analysis focuses on successively smaller geographic areas.

Governmental Forces

Political and legal activities at all levels of government can have a great impact on property values. The legal climate at a particular time or in a particular place may overshadow the natural market forces of supply and demand. As mentioned previously, the government provides many necessary facilities and services that affect land use patterns. Therefore, appraisers must diligently identify and examine how the following factors could influence property values:

- Public services such as fire and police protection, utilities, garbage collection, and transportation networks

- Local zoning, building codes, and public health codes, especially those that obstruct or support land use

- National, provincial, and local fiscal policies

- Special legislation that influences general property values:

  ◦ Rent control laws

  ◦ Foreclosure and bankruptcy laws

  ◦ Restrictions on forms of ownership such as those imposed on condominiums and timeshare arrangements

  ◦ Environmental legislation regulating new developments and wetlands as well as the control of hazardous or toxic materials

- Legislation affecting the types of loans, loan terms, and investment powers of mortgage lending institutions

- Legislation protecting the right to farm, and reserving forest or agricultural lands

- Fisheries laws, which limit upland activities that directly or indirectly diminish food or habitat for fish

Environmental Forces

The natural and man-made environmental forces that may be analyzed for real estate appraisal purposes include the following:

- Climatic conditions such as snowfall, rain fall, temperature, and humidity

- Topography and soil

- Toxic contaminants such as asbestos, radon, and PCBs

- Natural barriers to future development such as rivers, mountains, lakes, and oceans

- Primary transportation systems, including federal and provincial highway systems, railroads, airports, ports and navigable waterways

- The nature and desirability of the immediate area surrounding a property

---

location
The time-distance relationships, or linkages, between a property or neighborhood and all other possible origins and destinations of people going to or coming from the property or neighborhood.

linkage
1. Time and distance relationship between a particular use and supporting facilities, e.g., between residences and schools, shopping, and employment.
2. The movement of people, goods, services, or communications to and from the subject site, measured by the time and cost involved.

All of these factors are environmental, although market participants usually associate the term with the conservation of natural resources (e.g., wildlife, timberlands, and wetlands) and the regulation of man-made pollution. Chapter 10 discusses the treatment of hazardous substances in real estate appraisal.

The environmental forces that affect the value of a specific real property may be understood in relation to the property's location. Location considers time-distance relationships, or linkages, between a property or neighbourhood and all possible origins and destinations of residents coming to or going from the property or neighbourhood. Location has both an environmental and an economic character. Time and distance are measures of relative access that an appraiser considers in terms of site ingress and egress, the characteristics of the neighbourhoods through which traffic to and from the site passes, and transportation costs to and from the site.

To analyze the value influence of location, the linkages between the property and important points or places outside the property are identified, and the distance and time required to cover those distances by the most commonly used types of transportation are measured. Depending on the area and the property type, the appraiser may investigate the property's access to the following:

- Public transportation
- Schools
- Stores
- Service establishments
- Parks
- Recreational and cultural facilities
- Places of worship
- Sources of employment
- Product markets
- Suppliers of production needs
- Processors of raw materials

The proximity of industrial properties to residential areas provides the businesses located there with access to workers, but proximity to potentially hazardous substances may penalize the market for residential properties.

CHAPTER 4

REAL ESTATE MARKETS

Buyers and sellers of different types of properties interact in different areas for different reasons. Thus, real estate markets are divided into categories based on property type and their appeal to different market participants. The markets for various categories of real estate are further divided into sub-markets, which correspond to the preferences of buyers and sellers. Differentiating real estate markets facilitates their study.

All real estate markets are influenced by the attitudes, motivations, and interactions of buyers and sellers of real property, which in turn are subject to many social, economic, governmental, and environmental influences. Real estate markets may be studied in terms of their geographic, competitive, and supply and demand characteristics, which relate to overall real estate market conditions.

The identification and interpretation of real estate markets are analytical processes. To answer questions about real estate markets and sub-markets, appraisers analyze the utility and scarcity of property as well as the desires and effective purchasing power of those who seek to acquire property rights.

CHARACTERISTICS OF REAL ESTATE MARKETS

The efficiency of a market is tied to the behaviour of buyers and sellers as well as the characteristics of the products traded. Real estate markets can differ significantly from the markets for other goods and services and have never been considered truly efficient markets (see Table 4.1). Real estate products are heterogeneous, and information about real estate is often incomplete due to the confidentiality of transactions. Also, changes in supply lag behind changes in demand for a specific real estate product because of the time needed to bring a new building to market. In a more efficient market, like a stock exchange, supply quickly reacts to changes in demand.

In recent years, real estate markets have become more efficient than they once were because of the securitization of real estate and increased access to property and transaction information, along with other changes in the larger economy. Efficiency in the real estate market has a direct bearing on rate of return requirements.

Table 4.1 Comparison of Efficient Markets and Real Estate Markets

Efficient Markets	Real Estate Markets
Goods and services are essentially homogeneous items that are readily substituted for one another.	No two parcels of real estate are physically identical.
A large number of market participants creates a competitive, free market, and none of these particular type of property at one time, in one price participants have a large enough share of the market to have a direct and measurable influence on price.	There are usually only a few buyers and sellers interested in a particular type of property at one time, in one price range, and in one location. An individual buyer or seller can influence price through exertion of control on supply or demand or both.
Supply and demand are never far out of balance. The market returns to equilibrium quickly through the effects of competition.	In stable real estate markets, supply and demand are considered causal factors and price is the result of their interaction. Price changes usually are preceded by changes in market activity. Often supply or demand may shift suddenly in a period of no activity, increased activity, or when properties are in transition.
Buyers and sellers are knowledgeable and fully informed about market conditions, the behaviour of other market participants, past market activity, product quality, and product substitutability. Any information needed on bids, offers, and sales is readily available.	Buyers and sellers of real estate may not be well informed.
Buyers and sellers are brought together by an organized market mechanism, such as the New York Stock Exchange. Sellers can easily enter and exit the market in response to demand.	Buyers and sellers are not brought together formally.
Goods are readily consumed, quickly supplied, and easily transported from place to place.	Real estate is a durable product and, as an investment, it may be relatively unmarketable and illiquid.
Market efficiencies lead to low transaction costs.	Market inefficiencies lead to high transaction costs, e.g., broker's fees and commissions, closing costs on financing.
Market participants can act on new information quickly to take advantage of opportunities to increase supply to meet demand.	Market participants are not able to act quickly on new information, e.g., an increase in market demand will be followed by a lag as developers attempt to increase supply but are hampered by the long development times for new real estate products.

Consequently, a purchaser who understands the inefficiencies of the real estate market can gain benefits in terms of rates of return, relatively stable income, inflation protection (usually), and other factors.

Real estate market analysis focuses on the motivations, attitudes, and interaction of market participants as they respond to the particular characteristics of real estate and to external influences that affect its value. This focus underscores the need for objective real estate appraisal in a free market economy and the responsibility of appraisers to the communities they serve. Chapter 9 discusses real estate market analysis in detail.

Market Segmentation and Delineation

A real estate market is a group of individuals or firms that are in contact with one another for the purpose of conducting real estate transactions. Possible market participants include the following:

- Buyers
- Sellers
- Renters
- Lessors
- Lessees
- Mortgagors
- Mortgagees
- Developers
- Builders
- Managers
- Owner-users
- Investors
- Brokers

Each market participant does not have to be in contact with every other participant. A person or firm is part of the market if that person or firm is in contact with another subset of market participants.

The actions of market participants are prompted by their expectations about the uses of a property and the benefits that property will offer its users. Therefore, *market segmentation* differentiates the most probable users of a property from the general population by their consumer characteristics. The activity of individual market participants in a real estate market focuses on a real estate product and the service it provides. Product *disaggregation*, therefore, differentiates the subject property and competitive properties from other types of properties on the basis of their attributes or characteristics.

> **sub-market**
> A division of a total market that reflects the preferences of a particular set of buyers and sellers.
>
> **market segmentation**
> The process by which sub-markets within a larger market are identified and analyzed.
>
> **disaggregation**
> Grouping properties together based on similar attributes or characteristics.

> Specific real estate markets can be identified by property type, property features, market area, substitute properties, and complementary properties.

A *market segment* is delineated by identifying the market participants likely to be interested in the subject real estate and the type of real estate product and service it provides. Product disaggregation includes both the subject property and competitive and complementary properties. Thus, market analysis combines market segmentation and product disaggregation. The characteristics of a subject property and its *market area* that are investigated by an appraiser in the process of delineating the market are illustrated in Figure 4.1.

Figure 4.1: Market Delineation Process

To identify a specific real estate market, an appraiser investigates the following factors:

1. Property type (e.g., single-unit residence, retail shopping center, office building).
2. Property features such as occupancy, customer base, quality of construction, and design and amenities.
   a. Occupancy – single-tenant or multi-tenant (residential, apartment, office, retail).
   b. Customer base – the most probable users. Data on population, employment, income, and activity patterns is analyzed. For residential markets, data is broken down according to the profile of the likely property owner or tenant. For commercial markets, data is segmented according to the likely users of the space. For retail markets, the clientele that the prospective tenants will draw represents the customer base. For office markets, the customer base reflects the space needs of prospective companies leasing office units.
   c. Quality of construction (class of building).
   d. Design and amenity features.
3. Market area – defined geographically or locationally. A market area may be local, regional, national, or international in scope. It may be urban or suburban. It may correspond to a district or neighborhood of a city. Retail and residential market areas are often delineated by specific time-distance relationships.
4. Available substitute properties – i.e., equally desirable properties competing with the subject in its market area, which may be local, regional, national, or international.
5. Complementary properties – i.e., other properties or property types that are complementary to the subject. The users of the subject property need to have access to complementary properties, which are also referred to as support facilities.

Defining Geographical Boundaries

The boundaries of *market areas*, *neighbourhoods*, and *districts* identify the areas that influence a subject property's value. The area of influence, commonly called a *neighbourhood*, can be defined as a group of complementary land uses. A residential neighbourhood, for example, may contain single-unit homes and commercial properties that provide services for local residents. A *district*, on the other hand, has one predominant land use. Districts are commonly composed of apartments, commercial, industrial, or agricultural properties. In broader terms, appraisers analyze the market area within which a subject property competes for the attentions of buyers and sellers. A market area can encompass one or more neighbourhoods or districts or both.

These boundaries may coincide with observable changes in land use or demographic and socioeconomic characteristics. Physical features such as structure types, street patterns, terrain, vegetation, and lot sizes help to identify land use districts. The following items can also be significant boundaries:[1]

- Transportation arteries such as highways, major streets, and railroads

- Bodies of water such as rivers, lakes, and streams

- Changing elevation such as hills, mountains, cliffs, and valleys

To identify the boundaries of a market area, an appraiser:

- examines the subject property. The process of defining a market area's boundaries must start with an analysis of the subject property;

- examines the area's physical characteristics. The appraiser should drive or walk around the area to develop a sense of place, noting the degree of similarity in land uses, structure types, architectural styles, and maintenance and upkeep. Using a map, the appraiser can identify points where these characteristics change and note any physical barriers – e.g., major streets, hills, rivers, railroad tracks – that coincide with these points;

- draws preliminary boundaries on a map. The appraiser draws lines on a map of the area to connect the points where physical characteristics change; and

- determines how well the preliminary boundaries correspond to the demographic data. The market area boundaries are often overlaid on a map of geographical areas, e.g., postal code local delivery areas, census divisions and census subdivisions, block groups. The appraiser's observed market area and the areas for which data is available seldom match up perfectly. The information available for municipalities, postal code forward sortation areas and census divisions/subdivisions must be segmented to delineate pertinent sub-markets.[2] Reliable data may also be available from provincial, regional and municipal governments, local chambers of commerce, universities, and research organizations, often through online sources.

---

[1] In defining a district, variations in the relevant characteristics of properties may indicate that more limited boundaries should be established. For example, consider an urban area where many high-rise apartment buildings are constructed along a natural lakeshore and separated from other land uses by major transportation arteries. In this type of district, there may be great variations in apartment prices, sizes, views, parking availability, proximity to public transportation, and building ages. These variations suggest limited district boundaries that must be identified to reveal market and sub-market characteristics.

[2] The collection of statistics in Canada is a responsibility of the federal government. Under the Statistics Act, Statistics Canada is required to "collect, compile, analyse, abstract and publish statistical information relating to the commercial, industrial, financial, social, economic and general activities and conditions of the people of Canada." In addition to conducting a census every five years, Statistics Canada (www.statscan.gc.ca) conducts about 350 active surveys on virtually all aspects of Canadian life, including the collection and analysis of data on population and housing characteristics, employment, and earnings. For information on applying census and other data to the analysis of market areas, see Stephen F. Fanning, *Market Analysis for Real Estate: Concepts and Applications in Valuation and Highest and Best Use* (Chicago: Appraisal Institute, 2005), Chapters 7 and 8.

In unusual cases, an appraiser might consider surveying area residents to identify relevant characteristics. Appraisers may also interview business people, brokers, and community representatives to establish how far they think the market area extends. Through experience, an appraiser learns to observe changes and recognize how inhabitants perceive their market areas.

Legal, political, and economic organizations collect data for standardized or statistically defined areas, such as cities, regional districts, urban and rural municipalities and counties, census areas, or postal code based analysis, such as forward sortation areas and subset data. Although this data may be relevant, it rarely conforms to the market area boundaries identified for property valuation. If such secondary data is used to help identify market area boundaries, the appraiser should verify and supplement the data with primary research.

REAL ESTATE CYCLES

In the twenty years following World War II (1946–1966), distinct patterns emerged in real estate and general business cycles. As business prospered, the demand for capital intensified, inflation accelerated, and an oversupply of goods and services was produced. Then Bank of Canada monetary policy and other economic controls was used to slow the pace of the economy and keep inflation in check. If the economy slowed too much, a recession would ensue.

When governments wanted to revive the economy, the real estate industry provided economic stimulation, particularly home building.[3] Programs and legislation were developed to provide abundant, moderately priced mortgage money. These programs initially involved mortgage insurance or guarantees to induce capital managers to participate, programs now institutionalized in their availability. In 2009 and 2010, federal tax credits stimulated housing renovation. Because there was a substantial demand for housing, the programs were well received and residential development expanded, increasing employment in all economic sectors. Business improved for the manufacturers of hardware, supplies (e.g., heating, plumbing, and electrical), paints, furniture, equipment, and other goods. The economy finally revived, then inflation started to accelerate, and the cycle was repeated. When loan insurance programs supplied inexpensive long-term capital, real estate prospered and the general economy expanded.

The larger economic cycle (see Figure 4.2) influences the real estate cycle, and so do demographic cycles and business cycles. As the economy expands, competition for capital intensifies, the costs of goods and services increase, and inflation escalates. Canada's central bank, the Bank of Canada then seeks to combat inflation by tightening money and credit until the economy slows down. The demand for funds subsides, interest rates decline, and economic conditions become stable enough for businesses to expand. When the frequency of the economic cycle accelerates and its range increases, business and money conditions change drastically and rapidly. This creates an unattractive economic environment for long-term investments.

[3]   In developing countries and countries making the transition from a state-controlled economy to a market economy, promoting home ownership has been seen as a way of stabilizing the economy and establishing a middle class.

Real estate appraisers need to know where a real estate market is in its cycle because certain types of assignments are more prevalent at different stages of the cycle:

- Foreclosures, bankruptcies, and tax appeal assignments are more common during a market contraction or recession.

- Appraisals for financing and traditional real estate transactions are more common during the upswing of a cycle, i.e., both the recovery and expansion phases.

- Many clients need appraisal consulting services when a market is expanding or contracting around its peak, the best time to sell an investment-grade property.

Similarly, real estate investors want to know when to hold or sell a property, when to write a long-term or short-term lease, when to hold down expenses, and when to invest in renovations and refurbishment. These questions and others require an opinion of the state of the real estate cycle.

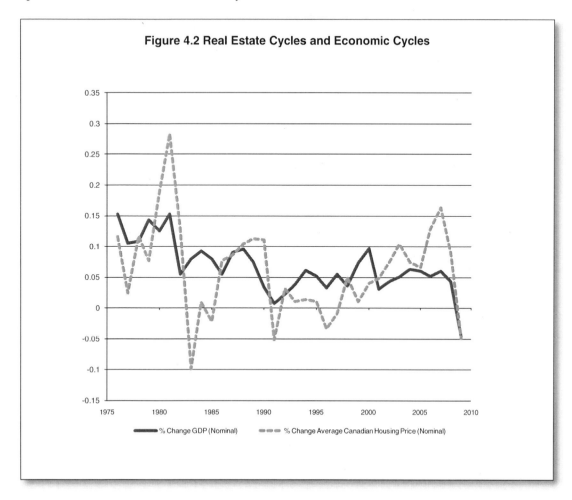

Figure 4.2 Real Estate Cycles and Economic Cycles

The position of a real estate market in its cycle (see Figure 4.3) is determined by several factors:

- Supply
- Demand
- Vacancy
- Rents
- Capitalization rates

The first four factors relate to the markets for real estate space, while the last factor is a function of the financial markets (see Chapter 5).

Trends in real estate markets can be measured by the interaction of several related market statistics:

- Vacancy rates
- Rental growth rates
- Capitalization rates
- Home price changes
- Changes in supply

If vacancy rates rise, rents will fall and capitalization rates will rise. If vacancy falls, then rents will rise and capitalization rates will fall. There is a lag in real estate markets while the market participants react to new information. If vacancy rates begin to fall, rental rates will not change until the market has noticed the change in vacancy. Similarly, capitalization rates will not change until the trend in rental rates (and the potential gross income for a property) is evident.

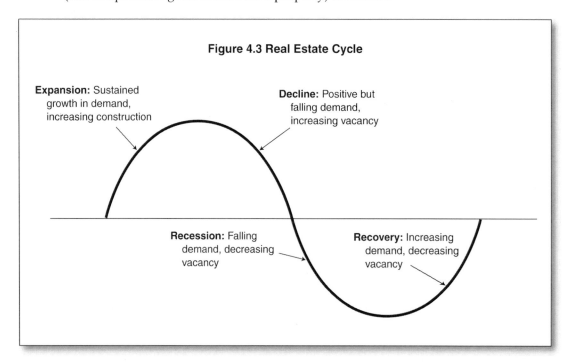

Figure 4.3 Real Estate Cycle

Expansion: Sustained growth in demand, increasing construction

Decline: Positive but falling demand, increasing vacancy

Recession: Falling demand, decreasing vacancy

Recovery: Increasing demand, decreasing vacancy

In the 1990s, what became known as the "new economy" promised to eliminate, or at least smooth, the traditional business cycle of expansion, contraction, recession, and recovery. Applying information technology to inventory control was supposed to ensure that production never got too far ahead of sales, improving the efficiency of the operations of manufacturing companies. The economic downturn in the G8 economies at the end of the 1990s proved some of these claims to be overly optimistic, but continued gains in productivity could be realized from greater use of information technology. The internet is generally acknowledged as reducing transaction costs, promoting disintermediation, and helping reduce the lag in real estate markets between the interrelated cycles of vacancy rates, rents, and capitalization rates.

MARKET AREAS, NEIGHBOURHOODS, AND DISTRICTS

Social, economic, governmental, and environmental forces influence property values in the vicinity of a subject property. As a result, they affect the value of that property. Therefore, to conduct a thorough analysis, the appraiser must delineate the boundaries of the area of influence. Although physical boundaries may be drawn, the most important boundaries are those that identify factors influencing property values, i.e., neighbourhoods, districts, and market areas.

The term market area may be more relevant to the valuation process than either neighbourhood or district for several reasons:

- Using the umbrella term market area avoids the confusing and possibly negative implications of the other terms.

- A market area can include neighbourhoods, districts, and combinations of both.

- Appraisers focus on market area when analyzing value influences. A market area is defined in terms of the market for a specific category of real estate and thus is the area in which alternative, similar properties effectively compete with the subject property in the minds of probable, potential purchasers and users.

To identify a market area's boundaries, an appraiser examines the subject property's surroundings. The investigation begins with the subject property and proceeds outward, identifying all relevant actual and potential influences on the property's value that can be attributed to the property's location. The appraiser extends the search far enough to encompass all of the influences the market indicates will affect a property's value. When no more factors that would impact the value of the subject and surrounding properties are found, the boundaries for analysis are set. The appraiser's conclusions regarding the market area's impact on a property's value are meaningful only if area boundaries have been properly drawn.

Market areas are defined by a combination of factors – e.g., physical features, the demographic and socioeconomic characteristics of the residents or tenants, the condition of the improvements (age, upkeep, ownership, and vacancy rates), and land use trends.

Analyzing the market area helps to provide a framework, or context, in which the opinion of property value is developed. The analysis identifies the area of influence and establishes potential limits within which the appraiser searches for data that can be used to apply the approaches to value. Analyzing the market area also helps the appraiser determine an area's stability and may indicate future land uses and value trends.[4]

> **market area**
> The geographic or locational delineation of the market for a specific category of real estate, i.e., the area in which alternative, similar properties effectively compete with the subject property in the minds of probable, potential purchasers and users.
>
> **neighbourhood**
> A group of complementary land uses; a congruous grouping of inhabitants, buildings, or business enterprises.
>
> **district**
> A type of market area characterized by homogeneous land use, e.g., apartment, commercial, industrial, agricultural.

Change and Transition in Market Areas

In market area analysis, an appraiser recognizes the potential for change and tries to determine how an area may be changing. Appraisers usually consider trends in area growth and composition when analyzing patterns of change. They also investigate whether a market area is in a state of transition from one type of land use to another, which, although related to the principle of change, is a separate concept. Land in transition can be perceived as land that has acquired value chiefly as a result of economic forces outside of the property itself, unlike land that acquires value in the traditional manner, e.g., through the construction of new improvements on the land or the renovation of existing improvements. In essence, transition is the result of change. For example, the arrival of a major new employer in a market area may cause a change in demand for residential property, and that change in market conditions may then lead to the transition of formerly undeveloped land within the market area to a more intensive use as the site of new homes or apartments.

Change and transition can occur at different rates and can affect different properties in the same market area. Change can be good or bad for the community, but transition is what causes positive or negative effects on value. Change can last for a short or long time, but transition from one land use to another is usually long term. Most problems in determining highest and best use do not occur in areas where change is occurring, but rather in areas in transition because land in transition often has an interim use before it is ready for development.

The Life Cycle of a Market Area

Because market areas are observed, organized, constructed, and used by people, each has a dynamic quality. Appraisers describe this quality as a market area's life cycle. The complementary land uses that make up neighbourhoods and the homogeneous land uses within districts typically evolve through four stages:

---

[4]   What has traditionally been called neighbourhood analysis is referred to in this text as market area analysis, in part to distinguish that concept from market/marketability analysis, which is covered in Chapter 9. Market area analysis focuses on the identification of a market area's boundaries and the social, economic, governmental, and environmental influences that affect the value of real property within those boundaries. In conducting market/marketability analysis, the appraiser addresses the competitive supply and demand for the subject property more directly.

1. Growth is a period during which the market area gains public favour and acceptance

2. Stability is a period of equilibrium without marked gains or losses

3. Decline is a period of diminishing demand

4. Revitalization is a period of renewal, redevelopment, modernization, and increasing demand

Transition often occurs in the revitalization stage, when a land use that is no longer financially feasible is discontinued in favour of a more productive use.

Although these stages can describe the life cycle of market areas in a general way, they should not be used as specific guides to market trends. No set number of years is assigned to any stage in the cycle. Many market areas remain stable for a long time, and decline is not necessarily imminent in all older areas. Unless decline is caused by a specific external influence – e.g., the construction of a new highway that changes traffic patterns – it may proceed at an imperceptible rate and can be interrupted by a change in use or a revival of demand. A market area has no set life expectancy and the life cycle is not an inexorable process. At any point in the cycle, a major change can interrupt the order of the stages. For example, a strong negative influence such as a major employer suddenly pulling out of a community or the closing of a military base can cause a market area that is growing to decline rather than stabilize.

After a period of decline, a market area may undergo a transition to other land uses or its life cycle may begin again due to revitalization. Revitalization often results from organized rebuilding or restoration undertaken to preserve the architecture of significant structures. It may also be caused by a natural resurgence of demand. For example, the rebirth of an older, inner-city neighbourhood may simply be due to changing preferences and lifestyles.

Evidence of Transition

Transition is often indicated by variations within the market area. New uses may indicate potential increases or decreases in property values. For example, a residential neighbourhood in which some homes are well maintained and others are not may be undergoing either decline or revitalization. The introduction of different uses, such as rooming houses or offices, into a single-unit residential neighbourhood also indicates potential transition to a more intensive use.

Changes in one market area are usually influenced by changes in other, competing areas and in the larger region of influence. Growth of one market area may lead to the downfall of a competing market area. Suburban business centres may interfere with the success of a city's central

---

Market areas often pass through a four-stage life cycle of growth, stability, decline, and revitalization. Some market areas may bypass stages in this cycle.

growth

A stage in a market area's life cycle in which the market area gains public favour and acceptance.

stability

A stage in a market area's life cycle in which the market area experiences equilibrium without marked gains or losses.

decline

A stage of diminishing demand in a market area's life cycle.

revitalization

A stage in a market area's life cycle characterized by renewal, redevelopment modernization, and increasing demand.

business district. Newer residential areas may affect older areas. The added supply of new homes may cause residents to shift from old homes to new ones and place older homes on the market. This increase in supply may affect the market values of all homes in the area. If a market area's location makes it attractive for conversion to more intensive land uses, the existing improvements in that area may be remodelled or torn down to make way for redevelopment.

ANALYZING VALUE INFLUENCES

Forces that influence value are important in the analysis of market areas. Similar characteristics point to influences that have affected value trends in the past and may affect values in the future. A market area's character may be revealed by examining why occupants live or work in the area. Occupants are attracted to a location for its status, amenities, services, affordability, and convenience.

GENTRIFICATION AND DISPLACEMENT

Gentrification is a phenomenon in which middle- and upper-income people purchase properties in a residential neighbourhood to renovate or rehabilitate them. The residents displaced by this process are often lower-income individuals who moved into these older, urban neighbourhoods when middle- and upper-income groups left because they found the neighbourhoods unappealing and unattractive. Often two or more low-income households would occupy what was formerly a single-unit residence. Such neighbourhoods often became blighted.

Gentrification, which reverses the process of decline, appears to be the result of a large number of small families and single people who choose to live in urban areas. "Urban pioneers" will tolerate higher crime rates and poorer services in exchange for lower housing prices and the potential for great appreciation in property value as the character of the once blighted neighbourhood improves. Often, as demand and property values in a gentrifying area increase, the burden of increasing property taxes and increasing rents on long-time residents with lower incomes can become too great, leading to the displacement of those residents.

Displacement is often associated with public improvement projects: when individual residential properties are bought up for public redevelopment schemes such as the urban renewal efforts in the 1950s and 1960s or for land consolidation and redevelopment of commercial or larger scale mixed use schemes. Residents must be relocated, although affordable housing is not always readily available. Displacement also occurs when home owners, businesses, or farm operations are forced to vacate the properties they occupied as a result of governmental action, such as a taking through expropriation.

Social Influences

In the analysis of a market area, an appraiser identifies relevant social characteristics and influences. To identify and describe these characteristics, the appraiser must know that the social or demographic characteristics that influence property values most in a community tend to overlap. Of course, price levels in the subject market in relation to prices in competing areas reflect the overall desirability of the subject market area.

In the analysis of a market area, relevant demographic characteristics include the following:

- Population density, which is particularly important in central business districts and high-rise residential neighbourhoods.

- Educational characteristics, skill levels, and employment categories, which are particularly important in industrial or high-technology districts.

> Market area analysis focuses on the four forces – social, economic, governmental, and environmental – that influence value. Analysis of the four forces is performed by investigating specific factors pertaining to each.

- Age levels, which are particularly important in residential neighbourhoods.

- Household size.

- Employment levels and types of unemployment, e.g., temporary, seasonal, or chronic.

- Extent of crime.

Other related information that may be useful in characterizing an area includes the extent of litter observed, the quality and availability of educational, medical, social, recreational, cultural, and commercial services, and the presence of community organizations such as improvement associations, neighbourhood block clubs, and crime watch groups.

Although an appraiser can compile demographic information, it is difficult, if not impossible, to identify the social preferences of the individuals making up a given market and to measure how these preferences affect property value. Therefore, an appraiser should not rely to a large extent on social influences when arriving at a value conclusion. From an appraiser's viewpoint, the social characteristics of a residential neighbourhood are significant only when they are considered by the buying public and can be objectively and accurately analyzed. Although race, religion, and national origin are social characteristics, they have no direct relationship to real estate values. Appraisers must perform unbiased analyses of neighbourhoods, districts, and market areas.[5]

Economic Influences

Economic considerations relate to the financial capacity of a market area's occupants and their ability to rent or own property, to maintain it in an attractive and desirable condition, and to renovate or rehabilitate it when needed.

The economic characteristics that an appraiser may consider include the following:

- Mean and median household income levels
- Per capita income
- Income distribution for households
- Extent of owner occupancy
- Property rent levels and trends

---

[5] See Canadian Uniform Standards of Professional Appraisal Practice, 2010, 7.10 and 7.28

- Property value levels and trends
- Vacancy rates for various types of property
- Amount of development and construction

The physical characteristics of the area and of individual properties may indicate the relative financial strength of area occupants and how this strength is reflected in local development and upkeep. Ownership and rental data can also provide clues to the financial capability of residents. The income levels revealed by recent census information and private studies may indicate the prices at which occupants can afford to rent or purchase property. Using vacancy statistics compiled by Canada Mortgage and Housing Corporation (CMHC), apartment owner associations and other fact-finding agencies along with information about the number of properties for rent or sale found in classified newspaper ads, an appraiser can estimate the strength of demand and the extent of supply, as shown in Chapter 9.

The presence of vacant lots or acreage suitable for development in an area may indicate future development or a lack of demand. Current construction creates trends that affect the value of existing improvements. A careful study of these market trends can help an appraiser forecast the future desirability of an area. Block-by-block information helps identify the direction of growth. A trend may be a local phenomenon or it may affect the entire metropolitan area. A change in the economic base on which a community depends (e.g., the addition or loss of a major employer) is frequently reflected in the rate of population growth or decline. Ownership demand tends to remain strong and rental occupancy levels are high when the population is growing. Demand weakens and occupancy levels decrease when the population is declining.

To analyze the economic characteristics of a market area, an appraiser expands the analysis to include economic trends over a three- to five-year period. Then the appraiser decides which economic variables contribute most to value differences among locations and compares the economic characteristics of competing market areas.

Governmental Influences

Governmental considerations relate to the laws, regulations, and property taxes that affect properties in the market area and the administration and enforcement of these constraints, such as zoning laws, building codes, and public health codes. The property tax burden associated with the benefits provided and the taxes charged for similar benefits in other areas are considered. The enforcement of applicable codes, regulations, and restrictions should be equitable and effective.

The governmental characteristics an appraiser considers in the analysis of a market area include the following:

- Property tax burden relative to services provided, compared with other areas in the community
- Special assessments
- Local government development levies, e.g., impact fees
- Zoning, building, and subdivision codes or by-laws

- Quality of public services, such as fire and police protection, schools, and other governmental services

- Environmental regulations

The appraiser gathers data on these characteristics of the market area and compares them with the characteristics of other, competing areas.

Divergent tax rates or impact fees may affect market value. Local taxes may favour or penalize certain property types. Therefore, an appraiser should examine the local structure of assessed values and tax rates to compare the tax burdens created by various forms of taxes and ascertain their apparent effect on the values of different types of real estate.

Local zoning by-laws and like policies regulate land use and the density of development. With varying degrees of success, communities maintain zoning to direct, regulate, halt, or slow growth. To encourage new development, they may expand capital improvement programs and construct sewage treatment facilities, fire stations, streets, and public recreational facilities. In the absence of zoning, the appraiser should determine if any other public policies or private restrictions are in place that would protect long-term property values.[6]

Zoning is the common tool employed to enforce a community's land use plan or comprehensive plan, which is usually based on economic growth projections though it may be modified for purely political reasons. The appraiser should be aware of the assumptions on which the land use plan is based and of the potential for revision. The appraiser must also consider the date that the plan was adopted and the plan's projection term. Land use plans are typically projected five to ten years into the future. The more recent the land use plan was adopted, the more meaningful it will be.

Environmental concerns have prompted increased regulation of land development at federal, provincial, and local levels. Zoning by-laws and building codes impose additional costs on developers. To preserve environmental quality, developers are required to consider the impact that large developments will have on an area's ecology and on the larger environmental system. Developers may be required to improve public roads, construct sewage treatment facilities, preserve natural terrain, or take other actions to conform to the recommendations of local, regional, or provincial planning agencies. These regulations can significantly increase the time required to complete a development and hence increase its final cost. The value of subdivision land is influenced by environmental regulations, which can affect costs and the amount of time required to develop and sell the sites.

The creation or modification of a transportation system is a government action. The government bases its action on an analysis of the direct and indirect impacts the system has on users and non-users. An improvement in the transportation system can affect a site's accessibility and, thus, its value. Improved transportation routes often cause new areas to be developed, which affects the value of other sites that must compete with the increased supply. To a great extent, the suburbanization of an

---

[6]   Private restrictions on land use may be established by private owners through provisions in deeds, land registries or title certificates. These restrictions may specify lot and building sizes in a subdivision, permitted architectural styles, and property uses. Condominium by-laws also restrict property use. The appraiser considers if private restrictions limit property uses inordinately.

urban population results from improvements in highways, commuter railroads, and bus routes.

In some communities, the movement of commercial and retail enterprises from downtown areas to the suburbs has changed real estate markets and placed new emphasis on zoning systems, the administration of local government, and public expenditures. The highway system has opened certain regions to development and increased their comparative advantage by decreasing the cost of transporting products to markets.

A municipality's willingness to provide public services to outlying areas can affect the direction and amount of development. Regulations such as moratoriums on expansion of sewer service, multi-unit housing, or other types of property have been used effectively to control local growth. This type of restriction can increase the value of existing developments if demand is pressing on a limited supply.

Environmental Influences

Environmental considerations consist of any natural or man-made features that are contained in or affect the market area and its location, including the following:

- Building size, type, density, and maintenance
- Topographical features, e.g., terrain and vegetation
- Environmental features important to wildlife habitat
- Navigable waterways
- Open space
- Nuisances and hazards emanating from nearby facilities such as shopping centres, factories, and schools – e.g., odours, noises, litter, vibrations, fog, smoke, and smog
- The adequacy of public utilities such as streetlights, water, sewers, and electricity
- The existence and upkeep of vacant lots
- General maintenance
- Street patterns, width, and maintenance
- The attractiveness and safety of routes into and out of the area
- Effective ages of properties
- Changes in property use and land use patterns
- Microclimate characteristics, e.g., high winds in a localized area, temperature and humidity differences between the area on the edge of a body of water and the surrounding area
- Environmental liabilities, e.g., threat of landslides or flooding

- Access to public transportation (and type of system, e.g., bus, rail, rapid transit), schools (and quality of schools), stores and service establishments, parks and recreational facilities, houses of worship, and workplaces

Topographical features can have positive or negative effects on property values in a given market area. The presence of a lake, river, bay, or hill in or near a market area may give it a scenic advantage. A hill may mean little in a mountainous area, but in a predominantly flat area, an elevated or wooded section can enhance property value. A river subject to severe flooding may cause the value of homes along its banks to decline due to the risk of such a hazard. Sometimes a river, lake, or park serves as a buffer between a residential district and commercial or industrial enterprises. Excessive traffic, odours, smoke, dust, or noise from commercial or manufacturing enterprises can make a residential neighbourhood less desirable.

Environmental features important to wildlife habitat, such as nutrient-bearing streams, raptor nests, and deer trails, can cause regulators to restrict development on or near these lands. For example, the presence of spotted owls, an endangered species, in forested areas in the Northwest led to bans on logging and development.

Gas, electricity, water, telephone service, cable television, and storm and sanitary sewers are essential to meeting the accepted standard of living in most municipal areas. A deficiency in any of these services tends to decrease property values in a market area. Access to fibre optic communications lines is becoming an increasingly important, and sometimes even essential, utility in most commercial districts. The availability of utilities also affects the direction and timing of growth or development.

A market area's environmental characteristics cannot be judged on an absolute scale. Instead, they must be compared with the characteristics of competing areas. For example, an appraiser analyzes whether the terrain, vegetation, street patterns, density, property maintenance, public utilities, and other attributes of one market area make it more or less desirable than other areas.

Location may refer to the siting of a property and the effect of siting on accessibility, e.g., the ease of access to a corner lot compared to an interior lot. It can also refer to the time-distance relationships, or linkages, between a property or market area and all other possible origins and destinations of people going to or coming from the property or market area. Time and distance are measures of relative access. Usually all the properties in a well-defined market area have the same or similar locational relationships.

To analyze the impact of a market area's location, an appraiser must identify important linkages and measure their time-distances by the most commonly used types of transportation. The type of transportation usually depends on the preferences and needs of neighbourhood occupants. It is not enough to note that transportation exists. The type of service provided and how it addresses the needs of local residents must be considered.

Linkages should be judged in terms of how well they serve the typical users of real estate in the market area. For example, in analyzing a single-unit residential neighbourhood, an appraiser considers where typical occupants need to go. If adequate facilities are not available for necessary linkages, the neighbourhood will not be regarded as favourably as competing neighbourhoods with better linkages. For single-unit residential neighbourhoods, linkages with schools, grocery stores, and employment centres are usually the most important. Linkages with recreational facilities, houses of worship, restaurants, and retail stores may be less important. For a neighbouring industrial district, linkages to the available labour supply in those residential neighbourhoods are as important as access to trade routes, both for receiving raw materials and distributing finished goods.

The distance to public transportation is considered in relation to the people who will use it. Access to public transportation is more important in a residential neighbourhood with a high percentage of residents who cannot afford a car or choose not to drive than it is in a neighbourhood where car ownership is predominant. A study of local transportation facilities must consider the territory through which users must pass. Most people would rather avoid poorly lit streets and rundown areas. Generally, the closer a property is to good public transportation, the wider its market.

CITY ORIGINS AND GROWTH PATTERNS

Appraisers of urban and suburban property recognize that growth and change in a community can affect neighbourhoods, districts, and other market areas differently. An appraiser must understand the factors that contribute to urban and suburban growth patterns to analyze the market area where the subject property is located and to determine how the area affects the quantity, quality, and duration of the subject property's future income or the amenities that create value.

The structure of land uses in an urban community usually reflects the settlement's origin; this is known as the siting factor. Some Canadian cities were established at transportation centres such as seaports, river crossings, or the intersection of trade routes. Others were founded near power sources useful to manufacturing, and still others were located for defensive, commercial, or political reasons. As the national standard of living improved, climate and other natural advantages became siting factors responsible for the development of retirement areas, recreational resorts, and other specialized communities. From its initial site, a community grows outward in a pattern dictated by the nature and availability of developable land, the evolution of technology, and the government's ability and willingness to provide essential public services.*

Where land is scarce, communities often experience an increase in land use density. Development corridors channel new construction to usable land. New technology, building materials, and construction methods make it possible to construct high-rise buildings in cities without bedrock and those subject to earth tremors.

Transportation improvements and the proliferation of automobiles have also shaped modern cities. Improved transportation allows urban settlements to expand and serve larger markets. The pattern of city growth is influenced by the local transportation network. Growth usually radiates from the central business district along major transportation routes. Major freeway systems can cause widespread migration from the city's core.

* Various conceptual models of urban growth are used to describe land use patterns. These "social ecology" models include the concentric zone theory, the sector (wedge) theory, the multiple nuclei theory, and the radial (axial) corridor theory. For a more complete discussion of urban growth patterns, see Stephen F. Fanning, *Market Analysis for Real Estate: Concepts and Applications in Valuation and Highest and Best Use* (Chicago: Appraisal Institute, 2005), Chapter 5.

When current zoning does not restrict changes from the present land use or when a change in land use is evident, the appraiser may need to examine linkages in terms of both the current land use and the anticipated land use in the market area.

The market's idea of what makes market areas desirable can be studied by analyzing comparable sales. The dollar and percentage differences among the sale prices of similar properties in different locations can provide the basis for this analysis.

CHARACTERISTICS OF REAL ESTATE DISTRICTS

The value influences that affect different types of districts – e.g., residential districts, commercial districts, industrial districts – are the same as those affecting larger, more diverse market areas, but the emphasis and relative importance of the factors change with the type of district being analyzed.

The availability of public utilities, including sanitary sewers and municipal or well water, is one important factor that affects land value in all districts. Prevailing levels of real estate and personal property taxes also influence the desirability of districts and may be reflected in real estate values. Of course, the four market forces that influence all real estate value will also affect districts.

Single-Unit Residential Districts

Home ownership has long symbolized economic prosperity, and the residents of an area dominated by owner-occupied single-unit homes often take an active role in maintaining or enhancing the value of their properties. Through formal home owners' associations, which often enforce conditions, covenants, and restrictions in a development, or voluntary associations such as crime watch groups and neighbourhood block clubs, property owners attempt to ensure conformity of land uses within a residential district and thus safeguard the character, appeal, and value of neighbouring homes.

Community spirit, which is evidenced in activities such as block parties and street fairs, and activist efforts, such as lobbying against undesirable rezoning or development, can make a residential area more stable or even reverse a trend toward declining property values.

In built-up urban areas, single-unit homes will usually be integrated into the complementary land uses that make up a residential neighbourhood. In outlying suburban areas where developable green space is relatively cheap, single-unit residential districts can cover large amounts of land. In some growing metropolitan areas, suburban sprawl has become as much of a social problem as flight from central cities was in the 1960s and 1970s. Therefore, the value of residential districts in distant suburbs is influenced by commuting time.

Just as the availability of labour and consumer purchasing power is essential to the economic health of commercial and industrial districts, proximity to employment opportunities significantly influences property values in a residential district. As employers relocate from central cities to areas closer to their employees' homes, former bedroom communities can develop thriving commercial districts. These districts can rival the central business district of the larger metropolitan area and may serve as an economic base for surrounding residential areas. Long-term migratory patterns within a metropolitan area can be analyzed to forecast possible growth trends.

Table 4.2: Characteristics of Single-Unit Residential Districts

Defining characteristic	• Predominance of owner-occupied homes
Subdistricts	• Custom-built subdivisions • Attached housing, e.g., condominiums, townhouses • Senior housing: congregate care and living • Rural housing
Value influences	• Access to workplaces • Transportation service • Access to shopping centres and cultural facilities • Quality of local schools • Reputation of area • Residential atmosphere and appearance and protection from unwanted commercial and industrial intrusion • Proximity to open space, parks, lakes, rivers, or other natural features • Supply of vacant land likely to be developed could make present accommodations more or less desirable • Private land use restrictions – e.g., conditions, covenants, and restrictions

The topographical and climatic features of land in a residential district are generally analyzed as possible amenities or potential hazards. As discussed earlier, access to a body of water can increase a home's value if the location provides a scenic view, but the same lake or stream may reduce value if flooding occurs frequently. Natural features such as a river, lake, hill, or park may provide a buffer between a residential district and commercial or industrial areas and thereby reinforce the residential area's identity.

In recent years, the growth of the telecommuting work force has made rural and exurban[7] areas far from urban and suburban employment centres into feasible residential communities by eliminating the commute. On a national level, the combination of telecommuters and the self-employed working at home makes up a small percentage of the total workforce, but the number of home workers increased significantly in the 1990s, before levelling off in the first decade of the 21st century. Various Statistics Canada surveys suggests the number and proportion of employees doing some or all of their regularly scheduled work at home rose from 6% of the work force in 1995 to 10.2% in 2000 and then dipped to 9.8% in 2005. Employees in social sciences and education had the highest incidence, at 29%, with sales and service occupations registering a low incidence (6%).[8] The impact of telecommuting on the supply of and demand for housing in a residential district can be significant, depending on the

[7]   The Canadian Oxford Dictionary defines "exurb" as "a town or community beyond the suburbs of a large city".

[8]   Ernest B. Akyeampong. 2007. "Working at Home - An Update". June 2007. *Perspectives*, Statistics Canada Catalogue no. 75-001-XIE. See also Matthew Mariani. 2000. "Telecommuters". *Occupational Outlook Quarterly* (Fall 2000): 10-17; and William C. Wheaton. 1999. "Telecommuting: The Real Story" (January 1999), available at *www.twr.com*.

demographics of the area. Table 4.2 provides a summary of information about single-unit residential districts.

Multi-Unit Residential Districts

In large cities, multi-unit residential districts usually cover an extensive area. In smaller cities such districts may be dispersed or limited in size. Units may be rented, i.e., apartments, or privately owned as condominiums. Multi-unit districts are subject to many of the same influences that single-unit residential areas are, but the importance of certain influences differs in multi-unit districts because of their higher density. Table 4.3 provides a summary of information about multi-unit residential districts.

In most urban centres, statistics on the supply of apartments, vacancy rates, and rent levels are available from government and commercial sources. When statistics are not available, the appraiser will have to gather data through primary research.

Table 4.3: Characteristics of Multi-Unit Residential Districts

Defining characteristic	• Generally a predominance of renter occupancy and higher density than single-unit residential districts
Subdistricts	• Multi-storey/high-rise buildings • Garden apartments • Row houses • Townhouses • Cooperative apartments
Value influences	• Access to workplaces • Transportation service • Access to shopping centres, cultural facilities, and entertainment • Reputation of area • Residential atmosphere and appearance, and protection against unwanted commercial and industrial intrusion (However, proximity to employment may be highly desirable for multi-unit residential districts, which often act as buffers for commercial and industrial districts.) • Proximity to open space, parks, lakes, rivers, or other natural features • Supply of vacant apartment sites that are likely to be developed and could make present accommodations more or less desirable • Parking for tenants and guests • Vacancy and tenant turnover rate

Commercial Districts

A commercial district is a group of offices or stores. Included in this category are the following:

- Highway commercial districts, i.e., enterprises along an arterial business street or freeway service road and developments adjacent to a traffic intersection

- Retail districts, e.g., regional, super-regional, and neighbourhood shopping centres

- Downtown central business districts (CBDs)

To analyze a commercial district, an appraiser identifies its trade area, i.e., the area the businesses serve. Because a commercial district's economic health depends on the vibrancy of the surrounding trade area, the type and character of nearby land uses and other factors that influence the values of surrounding properties affect the property values in a commercial district. Table 4.4 provides a summary of information about commercial districts.

Office Districts

Office districts can contain combinations of buildings ranging from small structures to large, multi-storey buildings. The buildings in an office district may be owner-occupied structures or serve a variety of tenants. The offices may serve multinational corporations, local corporations, small service companies, and professionals.

> **trade area**
> The geographic area from which a retail facility consistently draws most of its customers (also called market area).

Office districts include planned office parks and strip developments on or near major traffic arteries. Suburban office parks, which are also known as business parks, often have industrial users among their tenants because the parks offer good locations, easy access, attractive surroundings, and utility without the congestion and high rents of the CBD. Office parks increasingly provide facilities for service industries as well as retailers, restaurants, computer stores, branch banks, day care centres, and other businesses. Since office parks and industrial parks rely on surrounding areas to supply the labour force, they are often located near residential districts and their park-like appearance may be an advantage in the eyes of nearby residents.

Retail Districts

More than any other type of real estate, retail properties rely on the local trade area for their economic base. The customers for all but the largest destination shopping centres are drawn from the surrounding areas. The common types of retail property can be classified by the sizes of the trade areas they serve:

- Regional shopping centres and super regional centres can serve hundreds of thousands of people in many communities along major transportation routes.

- Community shopping centres serve a neighbourhood or group of neighbourhoods within a three- to five-mile radius.

- Neighbourhood and strip shopping centres serve their immediate neighbourhoods.

Table 4.4: Characteristics of Office Districts

Defining characteristic	• Office uses with supporting retail services and other related services
Subdistricts	• Central business districts • Suburban office parks • Concentrations of office properties of a particular class, as defined by the market
Value influences	• Significant locational considerations such as the time-distance from potential labour force, access, highway medians, and traffic signals • Physical characteristics such as the visibility, attractiveness, quality of construction, and condition of properties • Direction of observable growth • Character and location of existing or anticipated competition • Availability of land for expansion • Pedestrian or vehicular traffic count

Table 4.5: Characteristics of Retail Districts

Defining characteristic	• Concentration of competing retail locations, often along a major street
Subdistricts	• Regional and super-regional shopping centres • Community shopping centres • Neighbourhood shopping centres • Specialty centres
Value influences	• Focus on quantity and quality of the purchasing power of the population likely to patronize a shopping area and any trends affecting purchasing power • Significant locational considerations such as the time-distance from potential customers, access, highway medians, and traffic signals • Physical characteristics such as the visibility, attractiveness, quality of construction, and condition of properties • Direction of observable growth • Character and location of existing or anticipated competition • Retailers' inventory, investments, leasehold improvements, and enterprise • Availability of land for expansion and customer parking • Pedestrian or vehicular traffic count • The 100% location or anchors and core groupings

Specialty shopping centres, such as outlet malls, warehouse clubs, and power centres, serve a wide range of trade areas, depending on the tenant makeup and demographic and psychographic target markets.

Although the appraiser focuses on the sales potential of a given retail trade area, various other considerations can complicate the analysis of value influences.

Like certain central business districts, some retail districts may contain a destination shopping attraction. Multiplex movie theatre anchors in regional shopping centres in urban or suburban areas often serve as destinations for consumers from a wider trade area than a similar-sized shopping centre would normally attract. On the other hand, the growth of online shopping and continued competition from catalogue retailers may weaken the sales potential of existing shopping centres.[9]

Table 4.6: Characteristics of Shopping Centres

Neighbourhood Shopping Centre

Typical size	30,000 to 100,000 sq. ft.
Typical trade area	• Immediate neighbourhood • Population of 3,000 to 40,000 • Radius of 3 miles • Driving time of 5 to 10 minutes
Leading tenant	Supermarket

Community Shopping Centre

Typical size	100,000 to 450,000 sq. ft.
Typical trade area	• Population of 40,000 to 150,000 • Radius of 3 to 6 miles • Driving time of 10 to 20 minutes
Leading tenant	Junior department store, large variety, discount, or department store

Regional Shopping Centre

Typical size	300,000 to 900,000 sq. ft. (one or more department stores of around 200,000 sq. ft. each plus small tenant space)
Typical trade area	• May include several neighbourhood centres • Minimum population of 150,000 • Radius of 5 to 15 miles • Driving time of 20 minutes
Leading tenant	• One or two full-line department stores

Super-Regional Centre

Typical size	500,000 to 2.0 million sq. ft. or more
Typical trade area	Trade areas are also extended by major transportation arteries and linkages, so the trade areas for some super regional centres transcend provincial boundaries. • Minimum population of 300,000 • Radius of 5-25 miles • Driving time of 30 minutes or more
Leading tenant	Three or more full-line department stores

---

[9] For additional discussion of retail market research and trade area delineation, see Joseph Rabianski, "Elements of Retail Market Research", *Real Estate Review*, vol. 27, no. 4 (Winter 1998): 52-55.

When analyzing a group of local retail enterprises that are not located in a shopping centre, an appraiser also examines the zoning policies that govern the supply of competing sites, the reasons for vacancies and business failures, and the level of rents compared with rent levels in new buildings. Table 4.5 provides a summary of information about shopping centres.

Table 4.6: Characteristics of Shopping Centres *(continued)*

Specialty Centres

Outlet centre	• An aggregation of factory outlet stores • No specific anchor tenant
Off-price centre	• Typically between the size of community centres and regional centres • Specializing in name-brand merchandise sold significantly below the price at full-line department stores • Formerly known as discount centre
Power centre	• Large community shopping centre (more than 250,000 sq. ft.) with at least one super anchor store (e.g., discount department store, home improvement store) with more than 100,000 sq. ft. • Several smaller, category-specific anchor tenants (20,000 to 25,000 sq. ft.) • Floor space not owned by shopping centre management • Small shop space not more than 10% to 15% of total gross leasable area • Trade area similar in size to regional shopping centre
Off-price megamall	• Up to 2 million sq. ft. in size • Usually located on a major highway on the exurban fringe of a metropolitan area • Trade area of more than 25 miles
Urban entertainment centre	• Combination of entertainment, dining, and retail uses in a pedestrian-oriented environment
Fashion centre	• Concentration of fashion retailers • Usually no specific anchor tenant • Wide range of trade areas, i.e., similar to neighbourhood, community, or regional shopping centre depending on the target market sector as defined by quality, taste, and price • Often higher-quality finishes and materials, lower parking ratios, higher sales per customer
Festival centre	• Tourist-oriented centre in a large city; forerunner of urban entertainment centre • Large proportion of specialty restaurants and food vendors

Sources: *Shopping Center Development Handbook*, 3rd ed. (Washington, D.C.: Urban Land Institute, 1999); *Dollars and Cents of Shopping Centers/The Score 2008* (Urban Land Institute and International Council of Shopping Centers, 2008); James Vernor, Joseph Rabianski, *Shopping Center Appraisal and Analysis*, 2nd Ed. (Chicago: Appraisal Institute, 2009).

Central Business Districts

A central business district (CBD) is traditionally the core, or downtown area, of a city where the major retail, financial, governmental, professional, recreational, and service activities of the community are concentrated. Over the past 25 years, some CBDs have not experienced the same pattern of growth and development that other commercial districts have. The development of suburban commercial centres in edge cities and the corresponding decline of inner urban areas have undercut the predominance of CBDs. Even in smaller cities and exurban towns, the development of commercial districts centred on a category-killer retailer outside the town centre can have a negative impact on the economic viability of the area's traditional business core and the value of aging properties there.

Appraisers should be aware of this trend but should also recognize that some CBDs have brighter prospects than others, possibly as a result of economic development efforts or a concentration of companies in strong business sectors. The economic life cycle of CBDs is often scrutinized closely by analysts. Transportation facilities in most cities are oriented to the CBD. Through downtown development associations, many merchants have made efforts to revitalize CBDs with improved public transportation, larger parking areas, better access, and coordinated sales promotion programs.

The diverse enterprises located in CBDs usually reflect several types of land use, e.g., housing, retail stores, offices, financial institutions, and entertainment facilities. In some communities, land use decision-makers believe that housing is not an essential land use within a central business district, but it can help to revitalize or maintain an area's viability. In others, the CBD is a popular location to live, and has high residential values, e.g., Vancouver.

> central business district (CBD)
> The core, or downtown area, of a city where the major retail, financial, governmental, professional, recreational and service activities of the community are concentrated.

Retail clothing stores may primarily serve office employees, and other retail establishments tend to locate where large numbers of people work, shop, and live. Financial institutions are often found in areas with other financial institutions. In major cities, entertainment and cultural facilities usually operate in or near CBDs to serve the greatest number of residents and out-of-town visitors. Different parts of the CBD attract different users, and the enterprises within a single general use category may be diverse. For example, office buildings in different parts of a CBD may house a wide variety of business and professional firms.

Appraisers should recognize that shifting functions within CBDs can lead to changes in land use and potential increases in real estate values. For example, the addition of entertainment uses to an area dominated by office uses may attract more restaurants, art galleries, and specialty shops to a downtown area. In the 1990s, some major CBDs promoted specific uses to develop a reputation as destination locations. Many include prominent stores with well-known names and complementary entertainment or recreational facilities. Quite often, destination shopping is an outing that allows the entire family to participate in both shopping and entertainment activities.

To assess the viability of a CBD, an appraiser must consider the sales potential of various commercial products and services and determine whether establishments in the CBD can attract a share of the market. To evaluate the utility of a particular location within a CBD, the appraiser considers which use or mix of uses – e.g., office, hotel, retail, housing, entertainment – is most appropriate. Table 4.7 provides a summary of information about central business districts.

Table 4.7: Characteristics of Central Business Districts

Defining characteristic	• Located in a concentration of major retail, financial, governmental, professional, recreational, and service activities of a city
Subdistricts	• Broad range of uses – office, hotel, retail, housing, and entertainment
Value influences	• Local population (residents and workers) • Transportation linkages • Pedestrian traffic • Municipal land use policies (e.g., signage ordinances) • Density and mix of uses • Vacancy and rental rates

Industrial Districts

Industry is often the engine of economic growth in a community. Governmental and public-private economic development efforts are often targeted at manufacturing and other industrial concerns that may bring high-paying jobs to an area. Since the 1980s, major manufacturers sought to control inventory costs by implementing just-in-time production techniques, and the suppliers who serve those companies began to cluster around their headquarters.

Industrial districts range from those that contain heavy industry, such as steel plants, foundries, and chemical companies, to those that contain assembly, distribution, and other "clean" operations. In most urban areas, heavy industry and light industry districts are established by zoning by-laws, which may limit uses and place controls on air pollution, noise levels, and outdoor operations. In the oldest manufacturing or warehouse districts, obsolete, multi-storey, elevator buildings are typical and parking and expansion areas are limited. Newer manufacturing districts and industrial parks usually consist of one-storey buildings with greater ceiling heights than were typical previously. Each industrial district has a value pattern that reflects the market's reaction to its location and the characteristics of its sites and improvements. Table 4.8 provides a summary of information about industrial districts.

The environmental liabilities incurred by industrial properties are considerably more complex than those that affect other property types. Industrial properties may contain underground storage tanks for a broad range of chemicals. The presence of contaminants, such as asbestos and PCBs, may be more widespread. Long-term contamination tends to be more severe in industrial districts than in commercial and residential districts, and cleanup costs can be high. Chapter 10 discusses environmental liabilities in more detail.

Table 4.8: Characteristics of Industrial Districts

Defining characteristic	• Cluster of related industrial concerns, e.g., a manufacturer and its suppliers
Subdistricts	• Manufacturing facilities • Research & development facilities/science parks • Warehouse/distribution facilities
Value influences	• Nature of the district (distribution, manufacturing, R&D, etc.) • Availability of labour • Transportation facilities • Availability of raw materials • Distribution facilities • Political climate • Availability of utilities and energy • Effect of environmental controls

Agricultural Districts

Agricultural districts can be as small as a portion of a township or as large as several counties, regional districts, or rural municipalities. Often, important value influences relate to individual properties rather than to entire agricultural districts because farms may be far apart and soil and microclimate conditions localized. Nevertheless, an agricultural district's physical features are usually representative of the individual farms within it and contribute to their desirability.

Agricultural activities are wide ranging, including soil based agriculture and animal husbandry.[10] Greenhouses can yield substantial crops using hydroponic systems that do not involve soil cultivation at all. In some communities, people actively cultivate and manage trees, either for fruit and other crops, or for the timber or Christmas trees yielded.

The importance of different value influences in an agricultural district depends on what is produced there. Agricultural production areas are served by highways that lead to marketing centres where farm products are sold. Like an urban neighbourhood, the farm community depends on government services such as roads and schools and on the availability of services such as electricity.

Infrastructure to support the particular land use dominant in a district is important in all districts, but it is particularly important in agricultural districts. The infrastructure for agriculture includes land uses such as the following:

- Equipment sales and repair
- Outlets for seed, feed, fertilizer, herbicides, etc.
- Processors or intermediaries to buy farm products

For many years urban encroachment into agricultural districts and the erosion of the agricultural infrastructure has been a concern of property owners in rural

---

[10]   The Canadian Oxford Dictionary defines "animal husbandry" as "the science of breeding and caring for farm animals".

areas because urban land uses generally do not complement agricultural uses. Governmental attempts to preserve agricultural land have had limited effectiveness because the causes of encroachment are so complex.

Environmental liabilities on agricultural properties may include cattle vats which were used in the early 1900s to treat animals for ticks and other pests, turpentine stills, fertilizers, pesticides, and underground storage tanks. Table 4.9 provides a summary of information about agricultural districts.

Table 4.9: Characteristics of Agricultural Districts

Defining characteristic	• Undeveloped land used for production of foodstuffs, timber, and other agricultural products
Subdistricts	• Grain farms • Orchards, groves, and nurseries • Grasslands • Dairies • Timberland and sod farms
Value influences	• Climate • Topography • Soil types • Crops grown • Animals raised • Typical land use • Average size of the farming operations in the district • Whether the farming operations are run by owners or tenants • Transportation • Availability of farm labour/immigration

Specialty Districts

Individual properties are sometimes appropriate only for an existing special-purpose use. Similarly, if some specialized activity is predominant in a market area, that area may qualify as a specialty district, such as the following:

- Forestry district
- Medical district
- Research and development park
- High technology park
- Education district
- Historic district

The value influences at work in these specialty districts may be similar to those affecting areas where traditional land uses dominate (in particular, office districts), but the emphasis often changes depending on the activity that characterizes the specialty district. Table 4.10 provides a summary of information about specialty districts.

Forestry Districts

In Canada, most large scale forestry activities involve publicly owned lands, sometimes turned over to a private firm for management and harvesting. Private land holdings tend to be smaller and near urban areas. The value of the standing timber on a forested property can substantially exceed the market value of the land after logging. Often, logged land is subdivided and taken out of forestry use. Government regulations can restrict or prevent nonforestry use of lands in forestry districts.

Land use conflicts exist between the logging industry, environmentalists, the tourism industry, and First Nations people. Governments often have conflicting objectives and regulations that attempt to preserve natural values, jobs, economic activity, commercial fish stocks and yet meet international free trade standards.

Medical Districts

A medical district may be composed entirely of hospitals, health care facilities, and physicians' offices. A medical district may include one or more hospitals with related facilities such as parking lots, patient services buildings, a number of physicians' offices, laboratories and specialized testing facilities, and several pharmacies. Medical districts can be found in densely populated urban areas and in spacious, park-like settings, although the general trend of suburbanization may be causing medical uses to spread out.

The desirability and value of a property such as a doctors' office building depend on its age and proximity to hospitals and other medical offices. The quality of professional personnel and the availability of modern equipment are also important considerations.

Demographics are an additional concern. Medical buildings in or near residential neighbourhoods with many seniors, the prime consumers of health care services, may have an advantage over medical buildings in other areas and those with poor access to public transportation.

Utilities are a particular concern in medical districts because power outages can have disastrous effects on hospitals. To increase reliability, most hospitals augment the electrical service available from the power grid with backup systems. Also, the disposal of medical waste and potentially infectious materials has become highly controversial. Many hospitals incinerate their waste; others have shipped it offshore.

Research and Development Parks

Characterized by a mix of office and industrial uses, research and development parks (also known as science parks) may contain the research and development departments of large drug, chemical, or computer companies, or they may cater to firms specializing in research activities. Research firms are usually small and specialize in identifying and developing new products, which are sold to other firms. Occasionally a small research firm will create, develop, and market a new product with considerable success, but then the nature of the firm must shift from research to marketing.

Research and development parks are often sponsored and promoted by universities, which provide a convenient source of technical expertise and qualified employees. Universities may sponsor a park to sell excess land, provide employment for students and faculty, and raise an area's level of economic activity.

Table 4.10: Characteristics of Specialty Districts

Type	Characteristics/Value Influences
Medical district	• Potential for functional obsolescence of improvements • Proximity to hospitals and other medical offices • Quality of professional personnel • Availability of modern equipment • Demographics (i.e., proximity to residential districts with many seniors who are the primary consumers of medical services) • Linkages (e.g., public transportation) • Reliability of power sources/backup power systems • Waste disposal, particularly infectious materials
Research and development park	• Mix of office and industrial uses • Often sponsored and promoted by universities, which supply technical expertise and qualified employees
High technology park	• Clustered around high-tech companies • Sometimes receive favourable financing packages from local government and economic development corporations
Education district	• May contribute economically as well as socially and culturally to the surrounding community • Should be accessible to surrounding residential neighbourhoods if student housing is needed • Access to public transportation important for institutions that appeal to commuters
Historic district	• May include residential, commercial, industrial, or other types of property alone or in combination with one another • Designated to preserve an area's architectural character or informally recognized by residents • A heritage-related charge on title, or inclusion of a property on a heritage registry can complicate future use of the property and might affect value.

High Technology Parks

Firms engaged in high-tech activities often locate near one another or in parks where technical expertise may be available from a nearby university or research facility. Electronics and computer firms have dominated high technology parks, but firms involved with space equipment, drugs, cosmetics, and aviation may also have offices in these areas.

Sometimes local governments and economic development corporations will create designated technology corridors hoping to attract high technology companies. Real estate developments in technology incubator areas may benefit from favourable financing packages.

Education Districts

Local schools, colleges, and universities may constitute a district if they have several buildings or facilities and are considered an integral part of the surrounding residential neighbourhood. Education districts may contribute economically as well as socially and culturally to the surrounding community.

Colleges and universities often attract students from far away who bring income to the community and thus contribute to its economic base. In some towns and smaller cities, universities and colleges may provide most of the economic base. An education district should be accessible to the surrounding residential neighbourhood if student housing is needed. Access to public transportation is more important to educational institutions that appeal to commuters.

Historic Districts

Interest in preserving historically and architecturally significant properties has grown and given rise to a unique type of district.[11] The establishment of historic districts is one of the most widely applied and rapidly developing techniques for preserving cultural heritage. Overlay districts also can be used to preserve an area's architectural character.

Historic districts may be informally perceived by observers, or they may be formally designated by local, provincial, or federal agencies. Incentives such as density bonuses are often available to encourage retention of significant heritage features.

Historic districts may include residential, commercial, industrial, or other types of property alone or in combination with one another. Appraisers of historic property must become thoroughly familiar with each community's heritage designation policies and these criteria are, or may be, applied to properties of significant design or history, or within district boundaries. Heritage preservation agreements are often lodged on the title of a property that benefitted from public assistance or development bonuses in return for preservation efforts; these can limit the future redevelopment or use of a property and thereby impact value, either negatively or positively.

---

[11] Russell V. Keune, ed., *The Historic Preservation Yearbook* (Bethesda, Md.: Adler & Adler, 1984), 461. See also Judith Reynolds, *Historic Properties: Preservation and the Valuation Process*, 3rd ed. (Chicago: Appraisal Institute, 2006); Paul K. Asabere and Forrest E. Huffman, "Historic Designation and Residential Market Value", *The Appraisal Journal* (July 1994): 396–410; and Patrick Haughey and Victoria Basolo, "The Effect of Dual Local and National Register Historic District Designations on Single-Family Housing Prices in New Orleans", *The Appraisal Journal* (July 2000): 283-289.

CHAPTER 5

THE MONEY AND CAPITAL MARKETS

In valuing real property, the real estate appraiser must consider how real estate competes with other investment options for available investment dollars. Each good and service has its own distinct market, but each must also compete with other products that the market at large may consider as substitutes for that particular good or service. Market participants with desire and adequate purchasing power must make decisions such as whether to:

- Rent an apartment or buy a house
- Buy stocks and bonds or invest in real estate securities or investment-grade property

Thus, the appraiser must understand the characteristics, advantages, strengths, weaknesses, and mechanisms of the competing investment markets that most influence real estate.

Although it is called a "market", the money market is not formally organized like the Toronto Stock Exchange. Rather, it is an over-the-counter operation that employs sophisticated communications and computer systems to provide traders with accurate, up-to-the-minute information on national and international transactions. Since the Bank of Canada regulates the Canadian money supply, it influences daily trading activity in the money market and the cost (i.e., interest rates) of money market funds. The money market, in turn, greatly affects the real estate industry because its short-term financing vehicles are needed to fund real estate construction and development. This is one of many ways in which the availability and cost of money regulates the volume and pace of activity in the real estate industry.

> The two **sources of capital for real estate** are the money market, trading in short-term money instruments, and the capital market, trading in long-term money instruments.
>
> money market
> The interaction of buyers and sellers who trade short-term money instruments.
>
> capital market
> The interaction of buyers and sellers trading long- or intermediate-term money instruments.

A capital market reflects the interaction of buyers and sellers trading long-term or intermediate-term money instruments. Long-term and intermediate-term instruments usually mature in more than one year and include the following:

- Bonds or debentures
- Stocks
- Mortgages
- Deeds of trust

Although stocks are capital market items, they are equity investments with no fixed maturities. The distinction between money markets and capital markets is not sharply defined because both involve trading in funds for varying terms and both are sources of capital for all economic activities, including real estate.

In the money and capital markets, there are observable relationships between various instruments that stem from their differing interest rates, maturities, and invest-ment risks. Normally, an individual who invests in a long-term instrument is believed to assume greater risk than one who invests in a short-term instrument. Therefore, long-term instruments usually offer higher yields. This situation is graphically portrayed in what has come to be known as the normal yield curve (see Figure 5.1).

Sometimes the relationship is reversed. For example, if investors expect future interest rates to be lower than current interest rates (in other words, they expect the economy to slow or even decline in the long term), the yield of long-term debt instruments can be lower than that of short-term debt instruments of similar credit quality, e.g., 10-year Canadian government treasury bills vs. 1-year Canadian government treasury bills. Thus, an inverse or inverted yield curve sometimes precedes a recession. Another source of an inverse yield curve can arise when the central bank increases short-term interest rates (the only rates it can effectively influence) in order to combat high inflation. This action is intended to be temporary, lasting just long enough to dampen investors' inflationary expectations, but it may cause short-term yields to be greater than long-term yields, in which case the yield curve is said to be inverted.

For many years, appraisers and others involved in real estate investment have debated the degree to which returns on real estate may be analogous with, or even directly parallel to, yields on other forms of investment, such as real estate securi-ties. The ongoing securitization of some forms of real estate investment has been accompanied by the evolution of a four-quadrant capital market as illustrated in Figure 5.2. This development has brought about a structural change in capital market financing for real estate. The pricing of publicly traded asset shares reflects continu-ous transactions in the securities market. The pricing of asset shares in the private market quadrants is readily linked to activity in the public markets. This process is more advanced in the United States, with its more extensive secondary markets for securitized debt, mortgage backed securities, and equity in the form of real estate investment trusts (REITs). In contrast, 29% of Canadian residential mortgage loans had been securitized as of 2009.[1] While this more than doubled since 2004, the Canadian market still has less than half of the securitization activity of the United

---

[1]   Kiff, John. 2009. "Canadian Residential Mortgage Markets: Boring But Effective?" IMF Working Paper.

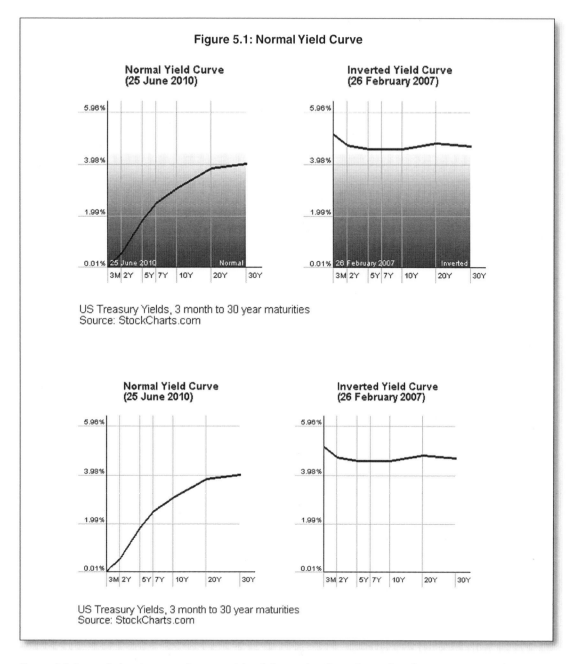

Figure 5.1: Normal Yield Curve

**Normal Yield Curve
(25 June 2010)**

**Inverted Yield Curve
(26 February 2007)**

US Treasury Yields, 3 month to 30 year maturities
Source: StockCharts.com

**Normal Yield Curve
(25 June 2010)**

**Inverted Yield Curve
(26 February 2007)**

US Treasury Yields, 3 month to 30 year maturities
Source: StockCharts.com

States.[2] Most of the interest in securitized loans in Canada is for those guaranteed by the Canada Mortgage and Housing Corporation (CMHC), indicating that investors have little interest in mortgage backed securities that are not guaranteed by the Canadian government.[3]

---

[2]   "The American Mortgage in Historical and International Context". Green, Richard and Wachter, Susan. The Journal of Economic Perspectives. Vol. 19, No. 4. 2005.

[3]   Ibid.

There are both advantages and disadvantages associated with investor-driven pricing in contrast to real estate user-driven prices. Returns on certain real estate investments are becoming even more closely related to the returns on non-real estate investment alternatives. However, real estate is an economic sector, not just another asset class. The value of real estate depends on performance, not simply investor behaviour.

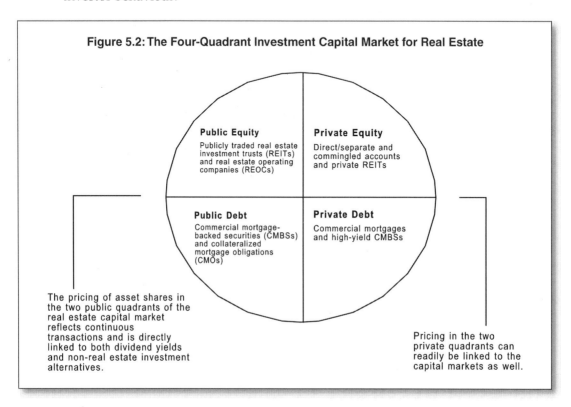

Figure 5.2: The Four-Quadrant Investment Capital Market for Real Estate

Public Equity
Publicly traded real estate investment trusts (REITs) and real estate operating companies (REOCs)

Private Equity
Direct/separate and commingled accounts and private REITs

Public Debt
Commercial mortgage-backed securities (CMBSs) and collateralized mortgage obligations (CMOs)

Private Debt
Commercial mortgages and high-yield CMBSs

The pricing of asset shares in the two public quadrants of the real estate capital market reflects continuous transactions and is directly linked to both dividend yields and non-real estate investment alternatives.

Pricing in the two private quadrants can readily be linked to the capital markets as well.

RELATIONSHIP TO VALUATION PROCESS

The various money market and capital market instruments and facilities described in this chapter should not be thought of as isolated elements. All are interrelated and exhibit sympathetic interest rate or yield movements. Certain rates such as the overnight and Canadian bond rates are foundational; they are closely followed by traders and investors and their movements set rate levels and velocity throughout money markets.

In the real estate industry, development and construction sectors employ short-term and medium-term funds, the cost of which largely influences a project's economic feasibility. Since this financing is priced on a variable-rate basis, and its cost is tied to an index such as the *commercial bank* prime lending rate, cost estimating and project budgeting require interest rate forecasts covering the development period. Thus, it is critical that a real estate appraiser be familiar with money markets and their activities.

Direct Comparison Approach

When mortgage financing is readily available at moderate cost, real estate markets function freely. They tend to slow when funds become scarce, prohibitively expensive, or otherwise unobtainable. Using high interest rates as an inflation antidote usually generates *disintermediation* in the banking and life insurance industries. Scarce, expensive mortgage money causes market slowdowns. This prompts efforts to find alternative financial arrangements, or creative financing, to maintain sales volumes.

In the residential real estate market, sellers are often compelled to take back purchase-money mortgages (also called seller-financing or vendor-financing) in amounts and at rates buyers can afford. If sales are structured around existing low-interest rate mortgages that are not due on sale, secondary mortgage financing must be sought from sellers or other financial sources. When large, high-quality commercial properties are involved, buyers capable of paying all cash can and do pre-empt the market. This action crowds out buyers who require mortgage financing, which is scarce and expensive. For intermediate commercial grade and more modest properties, the investment market dries up and dies.

In such situations, more than lower interest rates are needed to improve mortgage capital availability. There must be proper relationships between certain money rates. For example, if commercial bank certificate of deposit rates maintain a significant margin over short-run Canadian government bond rates, most savers will be persuaded to place their money in money market investment funds rather than in depository institutions. None of this money will be available for mortgage loans.

Drastic money fluctuations and unpredictable interest rates are negative factors that retard mortgage activity and slow real estate investment activity. Under these conditions, lenders are constrained to keep very liquid, investing their available funds in high-quality, short-term debt instruments rather than in long-term, fixed-rate mortgages.

> **disintermediation**
> The act of investing directly, rather than saving in a financial intermediary. It is "skipping the middleman" (the intermediary).

Income Approach

The income approach is based on anticipation. Value may be expressed as the present worth of anticipated future benefits, and valuation involves a discounting of these benefits. One key element is the selection of an appropriate discount rate. One view is that the discount rate is basically a weighted average of the costs of the mortgage capital and equity funds used to create the investment. Credit stringency causes intense capital competition and high rates. More available credit loosens the market and tends to moderate rates. Changes of this sort clearly affect capitalization rates.

Although the capitalization rate may be a key valuation element, the forecast of investment benefits is of equal importance. An investor looks for income earnings over the term of the investment and hopes to realize reversionary profits upon its disposition. These benefits are clearly influenced by monetary conditions, particularly those related to inflation. The forecast of anticipated benefits should be based on the most complete information obtainable on real estate, capital, and money markets and employ logical and appropriate procedures.

RISK

Every real estate transaction contains an element of risk. A lender accepts the risk that a borrower may default on a loan. A landlord accepts the risk that tenants will not renew at the termination of a lease. Home buyers accept risks related to the quality and condition of unseen building elements and, on a larger level, the likelihood that property values in the neighbourhood will go up or down in the future. Risk increases as the range of possible outcomes grows. The rate of return necessary to attract investment increases along with risk levels.

Various types of risk can affect an investment:

Market risk

Definition: Risk that net operating income will be affected by changes in the market, e.g., shifts in demand or supply or both

Influenced by:

- Type of property
- Location of property
- Stage in cycle

Financial risk

Definition: Risk related to the use of debt to finance an investment, e.g., default, prepayment, contractual financing terms that cannot respond to interest rate changes

Influenced by:

- Amount of debt
- Type of debt

Capital market risk

Definition: Risk that market value will be affected by changes in capital markets, e.g., mortgage yield rates, equity yield rates, overall yield rates (due to the changes in mortgage or equity yield rates), or overall and terminal capitalization rates (due to changes in overall yield rates)

Influenced by:

- Changes in levels of interest rates
- Changes in availability of capital (both mortgage and equity)
- Rate of return for alternative investment opportunities

Inflation (purchasing power) risk

Definition: Risk that unexpected inflation will cause cash flow from operations and reversion to lose purchasing power

Influenced by:

- Lease provisions that provide inflation protection

Liquidity (marketability) risk

Definition: Difficulty of converting a real estate investment into cash at market value in a reasonable amount of time

Influenced by:

- Inefficiency of real estate market

RISK, *continued*

Environmental risk

Definition: Risk that the market value of a property will be affected by its physical environment

Influenced by:

- Perceived health hazards
- Costs associated with dealing with potential environmental problems
- Acts of nature such as earthquakes and weather conditions

Legislative risk

Definition: Risk that legal factors will affect the market value of a property

Influenced by:

- Tax law changes
- Environmental regulations
- Change in land use regulations (zoning)

Ability to navigate permitting process

Management risk

Definition: Risk that the management cannot ensure that the property meets defined goals

Influenced by:

- Competency of management
- Type of property, e.g., regional malls require more intensive management than warehouses

Each of these types of risk can influence a property separately or in combinations. For example, a change in federal tax laws (legislative risk) may lead to changes in the required equity yield rate (capital market risk), or unexpected inflation (inflation risk) can cause mortgage interest rates to rise (capital market risk).

Comparable properties in the income approach should have the same degree of risk as the subject because risk is a consideration in the selection of overall capitalization and yield rates.

Cost Approach

Money market and capital market activities are important in the cost approach because they affect land values, cost estimates, and depreciation.

Land Values

An owner of land for sale usually capitalizes ownership costs such as debt service and taxes. Inflationary interest rate escalations certainly cause mortgage debt service increases. Cities and towns incur higher capital borrowing costs in providing municipal services, and this brings about substantial increases in real estate tax burdens.

Cost Estimates

Proper cost estimates require interest rate forecasts covering the contemplated building period. Many real estate projects are so large that two to three years are required to complete construction and to achieve full occupancy and stabilized operation. To finance these efforts, construction funds are acquired through building loan contracts with variable costs (interest rates) tied to an index such as the commercial bank prime lending rate.

Although certain loans include rate float ceiling and floor limitations, the more common arrangement provides for unlimited movement. Because building loan interest is the major soft, or indirect, construction cost, its proper estimation calls for a long-term interest rate forecast. Since interest rates are volatile and affected by the Bank of Canada's monetary policies, the task is difficult but necessary. Hard construction costs, such as materials and labour, are also influenced by interest rate variations. Price escalations of this nature are called *cost-push inflation*.

Depreciation

Depreciation is often described as the difference between cost and value. During inflationary periods, when money costs escalate sharply, construction costs rise rapidly. As a result, the base building cost from which depreciation is subtracted shows substantial growth.

For income-producing properties such as rental housing, income growth often lags behind operating expense increases, which erodes net earnings. At the same time, capitalization rates rise in response to interest rate escalations. This results in a reduction in property values, and with rising replacement costs, the measure of depreciation grows substantially. For other types of income-producing properties such as shopping centres and office buildings, leases may call for rent escalations and overages that match and sometimes exceed the growth of operating expenses. In these cases, depreciation does not experience inflation-related growth.

THE MONEY MARKET

Supply and demand relationships set the cost, or price, of money. When money becomes plentiful, the price declines. As it becomes scarce, the price rises. The price of money is expressed as an interest rate, i.e., the cost to borrow funds. Interest rates are particularly important in the real estate industry because most investments are created by combining debt and equity funds. When the demand for money is high and its supply is low, capital costs, or interest rates, increase. These higher interest rates, which are components of the capitalization and discount rates developed for valuation, affect real property values.

There is a difference between money and other commodities on the supply side of the pricing formula. The demand for money is a product of the operation of economic forces. The supply of money available for lending is a function of the level of savings, which reflects personal, corporate, and governmental accumulation, both domestic and foreign.

In Canada, the money supply is regulated by the credit policies of the Bank of Canada, the fiscal policies of the Department of Finance, and supply and demand relationships.

Economics determines the amount of savings, but the quantity of Canadian currency is subject to regulation by the Bank of Canada. The Bank has the power to regulate general interest rate levels, which strongly influence the discount rates and overall capitalization rates used in real estate valuation.[4] Housing affordability is greatly influenced by prevailing mortgage rates. For example, an increase of a single percentage point in the effective annual interest rate, from 6% to 7%, on a $200,000 mortgage, amortized over 20 years, would increase the monthly mortgage payment by approximately $110, which may cause a significant number of households with a certain level of purchasing power to be priced out of the market for home ownership. Canada Mortgage and Housing Corporation (CMHC), a federal crown corporation, can affect mortgage lending practises through its mortgage insurance programs; due to a concern about a "housing bubble" (house price inflation) in 2010, it increased down payment requirements, reduced amortization periods and increased debt service ratios for the insurance of new mortgages. This created downward pressure on housing demand and stabilized prices.

The bills and coins that constitute money are interchangeable (fungible) and can be used in all economic activities. Holders of capital will invest in whatever they believe will produce the optimum yield, considering the risk and maturity involved. Competition for capital involves all economic sectors.

Fiscal Policy

While the Bank of Canada determines monetary policy, the Department of Finance manages the government's financial activities by raising funds and paying bills. When income matches spending, the federal budget is balanced. When the outflow of funds exceeds collections, a federal deficit results. Spending that is not covered by tax funds produces deficits, which are financed by the sale of public debt instruments such as government bonds, bills, and notes issued by the Government of Canada and managed by the Department of Finance. When deficits are monetized by selling large amounts of debt, the Bank of Canada is tacitly expected, though not mandated, to cooperate by supplying the banking system with sufficient reserves to accommodate the debt sales program and still leave enough credit for the private sector.

Money Market Instruments

The prices of financial instruments, which are established in a free and active money market, determine their investment yields. These yields consist of the instruments' face, or stated, interest rates plus any price discounts earned or minus any price premiums paid. The price or cost of money is properly called an interest rate because when a borrowing instrument is created, it carries that day's market interest level for the risk rating and maturity involved.

Money markets, which deal in instruments with maturities of one year or less, are especially important to real estate development activities. Construction loans are short-term mortgages with variable interest rates that are tied to market indices.

[4] In foreign countries, various central banks perform the same functions as the Bank of Canada and they generally have the same powers. In the US, this role is played by the US Federal Reserve System, the "Fed". In Britain, the Bank of England is the equivalent, with the Deutsche Bundesbank being Germany's central bank.

Short-term money market instruments include loans made at the overnight and bank rates, treasury bills and notes, special purchase and resale and reverse purchase and resale agreements, certificates of deposit, commercial paper, bankers' acceptances, municipal notes, and Eurodollars.

For example, borrowing costs in the market might be two to four percentage points above the *prime rate*, which is the short-term loan rate that commercial banks offer to favoured customers. When the demand for short-term money is intense and the supply is limited, market interest rates escalate and construction funds become expensive. The high real estate carrying costs that result can destroy economic feasibility and cause project failures and even bankruptcies.

The anticipated cost and availability of short-term funds are key considerations for developers, and their perceptions cause real estate activity to expand or contract. Appraisers must factor projected construction loan costs, which constitute a large portion of soft costs, into their cost approach valuations. This is particularly important when appraising projects that will require more than one year to complete.

In money markets, various instruments and arrangements are offered and sold by the federal government, banks, corporations, and local governments. Important instruments include the following:

- Overnight market loans
- Canadian government treasury bills and bonds
- Provincial government and crown corporation bonds
- Repurchase and reverse repurchase agreements
- Certificates of deposit
- Commercial paper
- Banker's acceptances
- Municipal notes
- Eurodollars

Table 5.1 defines these instruments.

CAPITAL MARKETS

Traditional real estate investment practices involve the use of two types of capital – debt and equity – and a typical venture is structured with a substantial mortgage amount and a smaller equity contribution. The most common capital market instruments are the following:

Long-term and intermediate-term capital market instruments include bonds, stocks, mortgages (including junior liens and home equity loans), and deeds of trust.

- Bonds
- Stocks
- Mortgages
- Deeds of trust

Appraisers must keep in mind that the conditions influencing the use of long-term, fixed-rate, or variable-rate instruments may change over time. Appraisers and market analysts must keep abreast of shifts in monetary policy that invariably produce market changes and interpret how they may influence the financing arrangements discussed below.

Table 5.1: Money Market Instruments

Instrument	Characteristics
Overnight market	Funds available for maturities of one day, typically by and for deposit taking institutions. The Bank of Canada targets a band for the overnight rate. It then sets the bank rate, the rate at which the Bank of Canada will make short-term advances to members of the Canadian Payments Association (chartered banks), at the top of the band. Member banks may borrow funds at the bank rate to meet Bank of Canada requirements.
Treasury bills	Short-term securities with maturities of three months to one year.
Other government securities	Securities created and sold by provincial governments and crown corporations.
Special purchase and resale agreements and reverse repurchase and resale agreements	Short-term financing arrangements made by securities dealers, banks, and the Bank of Canada in which a person who needs funds for a short period uses a portfolio of money market investments as collateral and sells an interest in the portfolio with the obligation to repurchase it, with interest, at a specified future time. A reverse repurchase agreement refers to the obligation of the security dealer, bank, or Bank of Canada to relinquish control over the portfolio upon fulfilment of the terms by the borrower; also called repos.
Certificates of deposit (CDs)	A financial instrument that represents a time deposit with a banking organization.
Commercial paper	A corporation's promissory notes used to borrow short-term funds for current operations. Through trading, organizations with excess cash lend to those in need of money.
Bankers' acceptances	A bank's obligation or promise to pay; similar to commercial paper in that it is a marketable, short-term obligation.
Eurodollars	Monies such as US dollars deposited outside their countries of origin and used in foreign money markets, especially markets in Europe and Asia.

Bonds

A bond is a capital market instrument with a fixed interest rate issued for a term of one year or more. The bond market is closely related to real estate investment activities. Real estate is normally bought with a combination of equity capital and medium-term to long-term debt funds, called mortgage money. Most real estate deals are structured with a substantial amount of mortgage money and a smaller amount of equity, or venture, funds. Institutions with long-term capital to invest usually survey bond markets, then examine mortgage opportunities, and finally make investment decisions to secure the best earnings for the risk involved by charging interest. The interest rate will be set some number of basis points higher than the interest rate charged on a bond of the same maturity. Government, crown corporation, and corporate bond yields observed in daily trading reflect investors' earnings requirements for a wide range of risk ratings. Popular proxies for these bonds are the different Scotia Capital bond indices, which are published in the financial press. Some bonds are traded on organized exchanges such as the Toronto Stock Exchange, but many others are traded over the counter. Figures 5.3 and 5.4 later in this chapter provide examples of rate trends for key Canadian investments.

US FINANCIAL SYSTEM: THE FEDERAL RESERVE SYSTEM AND CREDIT REGULATION

In the United States, the regulation of the money supply is done by the Federal Reserve System (the Fed). It is independent of the US Congress and the president. This independence distinguishes it from the Bank of Canada, and central banks in most other countries, which are government entities. Although the Fed is independent, it functions within the general structure of the US Government, operating in accordance with national economic policies.

The Federal Reserve regulates money and credit, which are the lifeblood of the real estate industry.

The Fed uses three principal credit-regulation devices to accomplish the duties assigned to it by Congress:

- Reserve requirements
- The discount rate
- The Federal Open Market Committee

In periods of economic crisis, the Fed supplies financial markets with necessary liquidity.

Reserve Requirements

Within statutory limits, the Federal Reserve board can fix the amount of reserves that member banks must maintain. If the Fed wants to restrict the money supply, it increases deposit reserve obligations. If it wants to increase the supply, it lowers the obligations. The 1991 *Bank Act* eliminated reserve requirements as a policy instrument in Canada.

Federal Discount Rate

Banks in the Federal Reserve System can borrow from the Fed to meet reserve requirements and obtain funds for their customers even in periods of great demand. To get these loans, member banks agree to pay the Federal Reserve interest at its established discount rate. The Fed can deny loan requests when it believes that borrowing is not in the best interests of the national or regional economy. The Bank of Canada uses the bank rate, set at upper end of the overnight rate band, in the same way.

The borrowing privilege is a vehicle for expanding the monetary supply. Curtailing that privilege limits or contracts credit. The federal discount rate helps determine the prime rate, the interest rate that a commercial bank charges for short-term loans to borrowers with high credit ratings. The federal discount rate is generally about two percentage points below the prime rate.

Federal Open Market Committee

The Federal Open Market Committee (FOMC) is probably the most extensively used and most potent of the Federal Reserve's credit-regulating devices. The FOMC buys and sells US government securities in the open market, thereby exerting a powerful influence on the supply of money and the interest rate. In fact, through its daily operations, the FOMC maintains short-term money rates at selected target levels. This power in Canada is concentrated in the hand of the Governor of the Bank of Canada. However, the Governor is directly responsible to the Minister of Finance.

YIELD LEVELS

Appraisers consult daily financial market reports to study money market activity for indications of changing monetary costs and values. These reports provide information on various debt and equity instruments and their yield rates. This information represents the market's discounting of economic futures, reflecting the state of the economy and possibly affecting real estate industry operations directly or indirectly.

The yield levels of bonds are fixed by the contract between the buyer and seller of the bonds, but in real estate few of the elements needed to forecast yield and risk can be fixed in that manner. Comparing the yield spreads with some designated riskless rate that investors require for various assets in competitive markets indicates the levels of risk associated with a real estate investment. Given a range of yield rates, investors make judgments about the investment's uncertainties based on the characteristics of the property or the community in which it is located.

Yield levels are most sensitive to the following:

- Cost to construct, remodel, or acquire
- Loan ratio to cash costs
- Interest rate and rate of repayment of principal
- Real estate taxes
- Operating expenses
- Cost of land*

Several of these items are characteristics of real estate markets and others are characteristics of the financial markets.

* Stephen P. Jarchow (editor). 1992. *Graaskamp on Real Estate.* Washington, DC: Urban Land Institute, p. 253.

STOCKS/REITS

A stock is an ownership share in a company or corporation. A stock corporation is a common legal entity in which investors provide organizational capital by buying shares that represent ownership and a right to all proprietary benefits. These shares are subject to the prior claims of operating expenses and debt service on the capital raised by selling bonds, debentures, and other money market instruments. Shareholder benefits consist of any cash or stock dividends declared, augmented by share price appreciation or diminished by price depreciation.

Historically, real estate owners and developers have accessed stock markets for capital by taking real estate corporations public and issuing shares to the public. In the United States, these firms did not look to stock markets as capital sources until real estate securitization began to grow in the early 1990s. Since then, many traditional real estate development companies restructured themselves as real estate investment trusts (REITs), which can offer stock on the open market to raise capital for real estate acquisition and development and take advantage of the tax benefits REIT status allows.

This form of ownership allows revenues from real estate assets to be passed through to investors without being taxed at the REIT level. To qualify, though, there are strict limits on the type of activities in which REITs may engage and the uses of revenues from properties. In the United States, 75% of assets must be real estate assets (equity or debt), cash, or government securities, and 90% of net revenues must be passed through to unitholders[5]. In Canada, 75% of income must come from rents, mortgages, or reversion gains on properties situated within the country. To avoid taxation at the REIT level, 100% of net taxable income must be passed through to unitholders.[6]

In the United States, growth was tremendous between 1990 and 1997, with the number of REITs increasing from 119 to 211 and their market capitalization per REIT increasing by over 8 times. Since then, consolidation in the industry has reduced the number of REITs to 142, but the combined market capitalization of these organizations has increased from $89 billion to $2.71 billion.[7] While the stock market establishes the value of REITs, the income performance of these assets tracks that of real estate markets. REIT prices tend to be less volatile than the Standard and Poor's 500 or the TSE 300.

REIT growth in Canada has lagged that in the United States because of differences in laws and the ability of real estate owners and developers to access capital elsewhere. The total number of REITs in Canada was 30 at the end of 2009, combining for an overall market capitalization of $21 billion.[8] Thus, REIT capitalization in Canada in 2009 was only 7.6% of that in the United States. As a distinct entity, REITS have existed for over 40 years in the United States, as the legislation establishing their special status, the REIT Act, was passed in 1960. The tremendous growth in the early to mid 1990s came on a base of an existing and known form. There is no special REIT legislation in Canada; instead, they are organized under the Income Tax Act as "mutual fund trusts". The first Canadian REIT was established in 1993 from the assets of a real estate mutual fund.

> **bond**
> A debt instrument issued for a period of more than one year for the purpose of raising capital by borrowing. The federal government, states, cities, corporations, and many other types of institutions sell bonds. A bond is generally a promise to repay the principal along with interest on a specified date (maturity).
>
> **stock**
> The ownership shares of a company or corporation.

REITs in Canada suffer from several disadvantages relative to those in the United States. First, because they are organized as trusts, investors retain liability for REIT actions in cases involving environment concerns. This has been an especially important concern for institutional investors. Second, unlike the United States, Canada has no legislation allowing an umbrella REIT (UPREIT) structure. This has been a key catalyst for the supply of properties for REITs because it allows holders of real property to exchange for units that can be converted at a future date to REIT shares. Taxation incidence is delayed until units are actually converted to shares.

Still, starting from a small base, REITs in Canada have grown substantially. Between 1993 and 1997 the number of REITs in Canada grew from one to twelve, and the average capitalization per REIT grew by over seven times between 1994 and 2000. In the early 2000s, REITs in Canada were still relatively small, with only one, RioCan,

---

[5]   A "unitholder" is the REIT equivalent of a corporation shareholder.

[6]   "Worldwide REIT Regimes". PriceWaterhouseCoopers. 2007.

[7]   "Real Estate Investment Trusts: Performance, Recent Findings, and Future Directions". Liu, Peng. Cornell Hospitality Quarterly. 2010.

[8]   "Against all odds". Global Real Estate Investment Trust Report. Ernst & Young. 2010.

having a market capitalization above $1 billion. However, by 2010, over 20 REITs are in existence, seven of which exceed $1 billion in market capitalization.

Mortgages

A mortgage is a legal instrument for pledging a described property interest as collateral or security for the repayment of a loan under certain terms and conditions. Mortgage loans supply most of the capital employed in real estate investments. A borrower gives a lender a lien on real estate as assurance that the loan will be repaid. If the borrower fails to make the debt service payments, the lender can foreclose the lien and acquire the real estate, thereby offsetting the loss.

The parties to a mortgage are usually free to contract in any fashion they desire, subject only to limitations of usury and public policy. Mortgage loans in Canada typically have terms of 5 years or less, with amortization schedules of 25 years or less, and rates are usually fixed over the term. However, variable rate mortgage rates are floating. In contrast, in the United States mortgage loans are made for long terms of 20 to 30 years and carry fixed interest rates. A level payment mortgage, which requires the same dollar amount of payment each period for the entire loan term, is the most popular contract. The payments are calculated to pay interest at a certain rate and to amortize the loan fully over its term so that less of each successive payment is required for interest and more is available for debt reduction. Other payment arrangements and schedules are also used, the most notable examples being variable rate and balloon mortgages. Table 5.2 shows other types of mortgages categorized by their repayment characteristics.

A borrower may pledge a real property interest to more than one lender, thereby creating several liens. In such cases, the time sequence or order of the liens is important.

- The first loan contract executed and recorded is the first mortgage, which has priority over all subsequent transactions.

- Second and subsequent mortgages are sometimes referred to as junior liens. Because they involve more lending risk than first mortgages, higher rates of interest are charged for second and third mortgages, which typically have shorter terms.

- Home equity loans are another common type of junior lien, often with interest only payments and the principal repaid in a lump sum at the end of the loan term. Alternatively, they are often structured as a line of credit (HELOC: home equity line of credit), in order to lower the interest rate relative to an unsecured line of credit. Home owners often use this type of financing for renovations or for non-real estate purchases such as cars or appliances, which were formerly made by instalment contracts.

Mortgages can also be categorized based on how they are protected against the risk of default. The two major categories are the following:

- Insured: e.g., National Housing Act (NHA) mortgages, where CMHC provides the insurance

- Conventional: neither insured nor guaranteed.

Table 5.2: Repayment Characteristics of Mortgages

Type	Repayment Characteristics
Interest only mortgage	Non-amortizing loan in which the lender receives interest only during the term of the loan and recovers the principal in a lump sum at the time of maturity.
Level-payment mortgage	A mortgage repaid in periodic, usually equal, instalments that include repayment of part of the principal and the interest due on the unpaid balance. Although the payments are level, the amount of principal and interest varies with each payment. Most commonly, the interest component decreases with each payment while the principal or amortization component increases.
Adjustable variable rate mortgage	Mortgage with an interest rate that may move up or down following a specified schedule or in accordance with the movements of a standard or index to which the interest rate is tied.
Wraparound mortgage	A mortgage subordinate to, but inclusive of, any existing mortgage(s) on a property. Usually, a third-party lender refinances the property, assuming the existing mortgage and its debt service which are wrapped around a new, junior mortgage. A wraparound lender gives the borrower the difference between the outstanding balance on the existing mortgage(s) and the face amount of the new mortgage. Wraparound mortgages became widespread in periods of high mortgage rates and appreciating property values, but they have generally fallen into disuse with declining mortgage rates. This type of mortgage is not currently used in Canada, as they are legally unenforceable.
Participation mortgage	The lender receives a share of the income and sometimes the reversion from a property on which the lender has made a loan. Lenders may opt for this type of arrangement either as a hedge against inflation or as a means of increasing their total yield on the loan.
Shared appreciation mortgage	The borrower receives assistance in the form of capital when buying the real property in return for a portion of the property's future appreciation in value.
Convertible mortgage	The lender may choose to take an equity interest in the real estate in lieu of cash amortization payments by the borrower. In this way the mortgage interests of the lender may be converted into equity ownership at specified times during the life of the mortgage.
Graduated payment mortgage	Designed to aid borrowers by matching mortgage payments to projected increases in income, this type of mortgage has periodic payments that start out low and gradually increase. Because the borrower's payments in the early years of the loan are not sufficient to pay the entire interest due or to amortize the mortgage, the borrower actually borrows the difference between the payments and the current interest due.
Zero coupon mortgage	Debt secured by real estate with interest payments accruing rather than being paid by the borrower. In some circumstances, a rate of interest may be ascribed, e.g., for income taxation.
Reverse annuity mortgage (RAM)	A negative amortization mortgage that allows owners to use some or all of the equity they have accumulated in their property as retirement income while retaining ownership of the property. Typically, the loan increases as more money is borrowed and unpaid interest on the outstanding balance accumulates up to an agreed-upon amount, which is generally scheduled to coincide with the sale of the property.
Vendor takeback mortgage (VTB)	A mortgage that is given by a purchaser to a seller in lieu of cash as partial payment for the purchase of real property. If the purchaser defaults on a payment, the seller may foreclose. A VTB is an alternative to an institutional loan and often resembles a junior lien.

Loans without NHA insurance are limited to an 80% conventional loan-to-value (LTV) ratio. With NHA insurance, LTVs can be as high as 95%.

The effects of competition for capital are clearly evident in mortgage markets. In a volatile economic climate, some investors may resist long-term positions and fixed rate instruments because they provide little protection against inflation. In response to erratic conditions during the late 1970s and early 1980s, partially amortized mortgages become the norm in Canada, and more recently variable rate mortgages and adjustable rate mortgages are becoming commonplace. These mortgage instruments provide for periodic adjustment of interest rates to keep yields competitive with those available in capital markets. However, this raises the possibility of borrowers qualifying for payments at low initial rates, but unmanageable payments when interest rates rise. This was a major contributor to the "sub-prime mortgage crisis" in the US in the mid-2000s.

> **mortgage**
> A pledge of a described property interest as collateral or security for the repayment of a loan under certain terms and conditions.
>
> **deed of trust**
> A legal instrument similar to a mortgage, which, when executed and delivered, conveys or transfers property title to a trustee.
>
> **agreement for sale**
> Also called land contract or installment (sale) contract. A contract in which a purchaser of real estate agrees to pay a small portion of the purchase price when the contract is signed and additional sums, at intervals and in amounts specified in the contract, until the total purchase price is paid and the seller delivers the deed; used primarily to protect the seller's interest in the unpaid balance because foreclosure can be exercised more quickly than it could be under a mortgage. Also called contract for deed or installment (sale) contract.

Agreements-For-Sale / Deed of Sale or Escrow title delivered after full or partial

A mortgage is a contract between a borrower (the mortgagor) and a lender (the mortgagee). The lender registers a charge against title as security for a loan, such that if the borrower does not meet the repayment terms, the lender's funds can be recovered via foreclosure proceedings. However, the borrower holds title or ownership of the property.

In contrast, an agreement-for-sale, or instalment sale contract or land contract, provides for the future delivery of a property's title to a buyer only after certain conditions are met. A seller finances the sale of a property by permitting the buyer to pay for it over a period of time, but the title is delivered only after all payments are made. In the event of default, the buyer normally forfeits all payments made and the seller may also elect to hold the buyer to the contract.

RATE RELATIONSHIPS

Observing daily trading activity over a period of time may reveal relationships among the earning rates of various instruments traded in money and capital markets (see Figures 5.5 and 5.6). For example, there may historically be a relatively constant spread of 50 basis points between the yields on three-month and six-month Canadian government treasury bills. However, market volatility can cause the spread between these yields to increase or decrease at times. Similarly, the spread between three-month and six-month commercial paper may widen to 70 basis points and remain steady at that level for several months. These observations are significant because they reveal how the length of an instrument's maturity influences its yield.

A key investment yield is reflected in the weekly auction of Canadian government treasury bills. Because these instruments represent top credit quality and short maturity, their yields establish a base from which market participants measure all short-term money costs, including some real estate construction loan rates. Money market and capital market rate relationships are created by prime investment considerations, which include borrowers' credit, loan maturity, monetary supply and demand conditions, and existing and anticipated inflation rates. All of these factors are important in rating the risk of various investments.

Figure 5.3: Key Canadian Interest Rates 2006-2010 (as of July 30)

	2006	2007	2008	2009	2010
Prime rate	6.00	6.25	4.75	2.25	2.75
Overnight	4.2418	4.4994	3.0055	0.2281	0.7472
Bank rate	4.50	4.75	3.25	0.50	1.00
1-year mortgage	6.60	7.05	6.95	3.75	3.50
5-year mortgage	6.95	7.24	7.15	5.85	5.79
3-month Tbill	4.15	4.56	2.41	0.24	0.66
6-month Tbill	4.22	4.66	2.76	0.32	0.88
10-year Bond	4.38	4.58	3.81	3.53	3.22

Source: Bank of Canada: www.bankofcanada.ca/en/rates/index.html#interestl

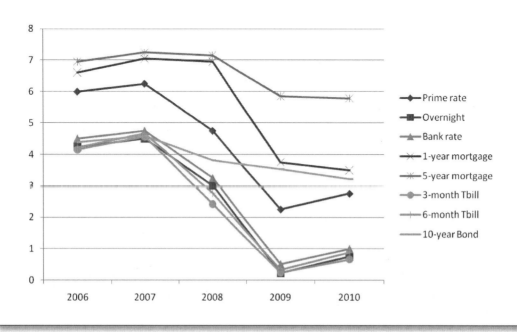

Understanding rate relationships can help appraisers correlate real estate investment risk with the risks associated with actively traded capital market instruments, providing support for market-derived discount and capitalization rates. The financial press contains a plethora of pricing and yield information to facilitate this process.

SOURCES OF CAPITAL FOR REAL ESTATE

Equity and debt investors reveal their different aspirations through their market actions. The debt investor participates in bonds or mortgages, usually pursuing conservative paths in search of certain income and the repayment of principal. This type of investor expects a priority claim on investment earnings and often looks for security in the form of a lien on the assets involved. While a debt investor is relatively

Figure 5.4: Key Rate Trends 1989-2009

	1989	1990	1991	1992	1993	1994	1995	1996	1997	1998	1999	2000	2001	2002	2003	2004	2005	2006	2007	2008	2009
Overnight Market Rate	11.9	12.9	9.0	6.6	4.6	5.1	6.9	4.3	3.3	4.9	4.7	5.5	4.2	2.4	2.9	2.3	2.6	4.0	4.3	3.0	0.4
Bank Rate	12.3	13.0	9.0	6.8	5.1	5.8	7.3	4.5	3.5	5.1	4.9	5.8	4.3	2.7	3.2	2.5	2.9	4.3	4.6	3.2	0.7
Corporate bonds*	10.8	11.9	10.8	9.9	8.8	9.4	9.0	8.1	7.0	6.2	6.6	7.1	7.1	7.0	6.5	6.1	5.4	5.4	5.4	-	-
5-10-year Government of Canada Bonds	9.8	10.8	9.4	8.2	7.2	8.3	7.9	6.9	5.9	5.3	5.6	6.0	5.3	5.1	4.5	4.3	3.9	4.2	4.3	3.4	2.8
Mortgage Rate 1 year - Chartered Bank	12.9	13.4	10.1	7.9	6.9	7.8	8.4	6.2	5.5	6.5	6.8	7.9	6.1	5.2	4.8	4.6	5.1	6.3	6.9	6.7	4.0
Mortgage Rate 5 year - Chartered Bank	12.1	13.4	11.1	9.5	8.8	9.5	9.2	7.9	7.1	6.9	7.6	8.4	7.4	7.0	6.4	6.2	6.0	6.7	7.1	7.1	5.6

* Scotia-McLeod Bond Yield, Corporate bonds, Long term (These series were terminated at the end of June 2007)

Sources: Bank of Canada (*www.bankofcanada.ca/en/rates.htm*)

passive, an equity investor is active. An equity investor is more willing to assume risk, and the funds used for equity investment are known as *venture capital*.

Home owners and other owner-occupants of single-unit residential property are also equity investors and are major sources of capital. The investment criteria of home owners differ from those of investors in income-producing property. An owner-occupant trades the potential of receiving rental income for the enjoyment of the amenities provided by the property during the ownership period and the future financial benefit of the equity reversion when the house is eventually sold.

Equity

Equity investors realize that their earnings are subordinate to a project's operating expenses and debt service requirements. Equity income earnings are called dividends. One-year's worth of income to an equity investment is an *equity dividend*. However, equity dividends are only one part of the total return that the investor anticipates.

INFLATION

Inflation occurs when the general level of prices rises. The inflation rate is the rate of change in the price level as reflected in the Consumer Price Index (CPI). Other useful measures of inflation include the wholesale price index and the GDP implicit price deflator.

Inflation and appreciation have similar effects on future dollars but different effects on yield rates. Inflation tends to increase yield rates (and most rates of return) because investors require a higher nominal rate of return to offset the loss in purchasing power due to inflation. Appreciation will not affect the yield rate unless the risk associated with the property has changed.

In oversupplied markets, real estate may not always keep up with inflation. In an inflationary environment, the value of real estate may tend to increase with the value of other investments such as stocks and bonds. Rents under annual leases can be adjusted upward periodically, while the interest and dividends paid on longer-term securities are more fixed. In oversupplied commercial markets, rent spikes are sometimes used to allow market rents to catch up to levels that would have otherwise been achieved by annual inflationary increases in rents. Rent spikes are generally a function of demand.

The economic importance of inflation can be seen in the concept of *real interest rates*. *Nominal interest rates*, which are reported daily in the financial press, are said to be composites of the real cost of funds, or the real interest rate, and the premiums that investors demand to protect their currency value from being eroded by inflation. Thus, the nominal rate equals the real interest rate plus a premium for expected inflation. Economists suggest that the real interest rate has historically remained steady at 3% to 4%. Therefore, if the capital market were to show a nominal rate of 6%, the real interest rate concept would indicate an inflation premium of 2%.

6% (nominal rate) ᴄ 4% (real interest rate) ᵅ 2% (inflation premium)*

An appraiser can account for the effects of inflation in capitalization by expressing future benefits in constant dollars, which are adjusted to reflect constant purchasing power. An appraiser can also express the yield rate as a real, uninflated rate of return on capital. In practice, however, appraisers usually project income and expenses in unadjusted, inflated dollars and express the discount rate as a nominal, or apparent, rate of return on capital that includes an allowance for inflation.

* In countries with low inflation, this formula is an adequate approximation. A more precise formula for computing the real interest rate would be:

1 + nominal rate1 + inflation rate = 1 + real interest rate
1 + 0.061 + 0.02 = 1.03921, rounded to 1.04, or a real interest rate of 4%

Investors may also expect the value of their original investment to increase, remain stable, or decrease, depending on the type of property and market conditions. The total return the investor anticipates is called the *equity yield*. An equity dividend represents the cash flow component of the equity yield.

Real Estate Investment Trusts (REITs)

Real estate investment trusts (REITs) have been successful in pooling the funds of both individual and institutional investors to acquire real estate investment positions that could not be handled by these investors individually. The liquidity of these securities is an attractive feature. Buying shares of REIT stock is not the same as direct investment in a given property. REITs offer shareholders freedom from most sources of personal liability (from all liability in the United States), the benefit of expert management, and readily transferred shares. With complicated income-measuring practices, these trusts attempt to pay out almost all their net income and, therefore, are substantially restricted in establishing reserves for possible losses.

When analyzing comparable sales, appraisers should consider whether a REIT paid a premium to add the property to its portfolio. REITs tend to purchase properties with the following characteristics:

- Superior locations in superior markets
- Limited lease expiration exposure in any given year
- Improvements with minimal incurable obsolescence
- Considerable value
- Favourable management characteristics

> The capitalization of real estate is divided into debt investment and equity investment (or venture capital).
>
> equity
> The ownership claim on property. Property value is the total of debt and equity. Equity investors assume greater risk and their earnings are subordinate to operating expenses and debt service. They are compensated with dividends (cash flows) and possible appreciation in the value of their investments. Equity includes the residual claim to the assets, which is solely possessed by the owners.
>
> debt
> One of two characteristic types of investment, the other being equity. The debt investor expects a priority claim on investment earnings and looks for security in the form of a lien on the assets involved. Debt investors participate in bonds or mortgages and receive fixed or variable interest on investments with repayment of the principal upon maturity.

> REITs, partnerships, syndications, joint ventures, insurance companies, pension funds, and international equity capital are sources of equity investment.

A partnership is a common vehicle for pooling real estate equity funds. It is a business arrangement in which two or more persons jointly own a business and share in its profits and losses.

A general partnership is an ownership arrangement in which all partners share in investment gains and losses and each is fully responsible for all liabilities. A general partner has complete liability for the acts of the other partners and is responsible for debts incurred by them. This is one major disadvantage of this type of business arrangement. The most attractive feature of a general partnership in a real estate investment is the ability to pass the tax-shelter benefits of depreciation, interest, and real estate taxes through to partners.

A limited partnership is an ownership arrangement consisting of general and limited partners. General partners manage the business and assume full liability for partnership debt, while limited partners are passive and liable only to the extent of their own capital contributions. Limited partnerships are popular because they permit an uneven distribution of tax-shelter benefits. Although limited partners' financial liability is restricted to their capital contributions, they may receive tax benefits in excess of that amount.

Syndications

A syndication is a private or public partnership that pools funds for the acquisition and development of real estate projects or other business ventures. Private syndications are limited to small groups of investors and are relatively free from government regulation. Public syndications involve large groups of investors and generally operate in more than one province.

Joint Ventures

A joint venture is a combination of two or more entities that join to undertake a specific project. Although a joint venture often takes the form of a general or limited partnership, it differs from a partnership in that it is intended to be temporary and project specific. The parties may later embark on other ventures, but each venture is the subject of a separate contractual agreement.

A joint venture arrangement is frequently used in large real estate projects. One party, usually a financial institution, supplies most of the required capital and the other party provides construction or management expertise. Life insurance companies and pension trusts have joined with entrepreneurial building organizations in joint ventures to develop large offices, shopping malls, and other major real estate projects.

Pension Funds

Private and government-operated pension funds, such as Caisse de dépôt et placement du Québec (Canada's largest private pension fund),[9] the Canada Pension Plan, the Ontario Teachers' Pension Plan, and Ontario Municipal Employees Retirement System, are a large and rapidly growing source of investment capital. Usually the pension contributions of employers and employees are placed with a trustee, who is obliged to invest and reinvest the money prudently, accumulate funds, and pay designated plan benefits to retirees. The trustee may be a government body, a trust company, an insurance company, private investment management firm, or an individual. In performing these duties, an individual trustee may employ the trust departments of commercial banks, insurance companies, and other financial institutions.

Traditionally, pension funds have been involved primarily in securities investments such as stocks and bonds. Between 1997 and 2006, the largest 100 pension

---

[9]   "Canada finance: Top ten pension funds". Industry Briefing, Economist Intelligence Unit website. June 2007. *www.eiu.com*

funds in Canada (which includes public and private pension plans) invested, as a group, about 3.5 to 5% of their total portfolios in real estate related assets, although there is some variation between pension funds. For example, as of 2010, the Canadian Pension Plan (CPP) had 5.5% of its assets invested in real estate,[10] the Ontario Teachers' Pension Plan (OTPP) had 18% of its assets invested in real estate,[11] and the Ontario Municipal Employees Retirement Scheme (OMERS) stated a policy of having approximately 12.5% of their assets in real estate. CPP, OTPP, and OMERS are three of the largest pension funds in Canada. Pension funds may hold assets themselves or, through banks and life insurance companies, acquire high-quality real estate equities, pool the investments in separate accounts, and supply the necessary portfolio management for a fee. Pension trusts commit funds to these accounts and share in all earnings, which consist of both income returns and sales profits. The real property holdings of a pension fund may be in a separate account or in a commingled fund with other investments.

Life Insurance Companies

Life insurance companies have always invested heavily in real estate. Their activities include both mortgage lending (debt) and property ownership (equity investment). Life insurance companies usually acquire real estate positions that are long term and relate well to their regular business, in which policy premiums are collected over extended periods. Their investment officers regard equities as attractive earning situations that offer growth potential and reasonable protection against the capital erosion caused by inflation.

International Equity Capital

Although foreign investors represent only a fraction of total Canadian real estate investment, they supply needed equity capital to realty ventures in this country. Legislation like the North American Free Trade Agreement (NAFTA) eliminates some of the obstacles to foreign investment. International capital comes from a variety of sources, such as foreign individuals, countries, financial institutions, and pension funds. The use of Eurodollars has a stabilizing effect on international exchange rates, which can have a negative effect on investment returns and impede foreign investment.

A foreign investor interested in buying Canadian property usually hires a Canadian appraiser to value the property. A Canadian investor considering underwriting part of a real estate project in a foreign country also needs a meaningful appraisal report, and often retains a Canadian appraiser to work on the assignment with a local appraisal firm. When analyzing sales of Canadian property involving foreign investors, it can be important for the Canadian appraiser to understand the motivations of the foreign investor and the behaviour of foreign investors in general. For example, long-term prospects for exchange rate shifts or a special tax advantage may make investment in Canadian properties especially attractive. The investment

---

[10]   CPP Investment Board: Asset Mix website. *www.cppib.ca* (accessed September 1, 2010)

[11]   Ontario Teachers' Pension Plan: Real Estate website. *www.otpp.com* (accessed September 1, 2010)

horizon of foreign clients may be considerably longer than that of Canadian investors. The appraiser should understand if foreign investment has influenced market transactions, particularly if the transactions are "outliers".[12]

An example of the considerations arise with foreign direct investment can be seen in Canada's experience with increased real estate involvement from Asian investors, particularly Japanese investors, in the 1980s. The favourable cost of capital in their native countries allowed these investors to make offers that did not make sense for Canadian investors. Despite the interest from foreign investors, not all Canadian properties qualified as potential acquisitions. Appraisers had to be cautious in not applying the investment criteria of foreign investors when the property in question was not appropriate for offshore capital. Ignoring this could dramatically over-value the property in terms of what domestic investors might be willing to pay.

Foreign direct investment in the United States rebounded in the 21st century, spurred by the globalization of financial markets. The relatively free and open US real estate market remained attractive to investors from Germany, Latin America, Australia, Japan, the United Kingdom, Canada, and the Netherlands. Japanese investment in US real estate, which has traditionally accounted for the highest share of foreign investment, dropped in 2005 with German and Latin American investors steadily increasing their shares. Competition from emerging markets globally may be balanced by the declining value of the dollar. China, in particular, has gained ground significantly on the United States as a destination for foreign investment in real estate in the 2000s.

Between 1999 and 2009, total foreign direct investment in Canada increased steadily from $253 billion to $549 billion. Between 1999 and 2003, foreign direct investment directed toward real estate rose from $8.5 billion to $10.8 billion, but has since fallen to $4.7 billion. Today, foreign investment in real estate accounts for less than 1% of total foreign direct investment in Canada.

Debt

Since mortgage money is so important in real estate, investors, appraisers, and analysts must be familiar with the sources and costs of debt capital. Increased regulation in the wake of the savings and loan crisis of the 1980s prompted many traditional providers of debt capital to restrict their lending activity in non-residential real estate. The focus of these institutions has been redirected to residential lending. Although commercial banks and life insurance companies are not precluded from originating loans for commercial real estate, increased reserve requirements make real estate a less attractive investment option.

Chartered Banks

Chartered banks are federally-regulated, privately owned institutions that offer a variety of financial services to businesses and individuals. In keeping with their role as short-term lenders, commercial banks are the primary suppliers of construction and development loans. For short-term, construction (interim) financing, developers of for-lease properties are usually required to obtain commitments from long-term,

---

[12]   For further discussion of international valuation, see Chapter 27.

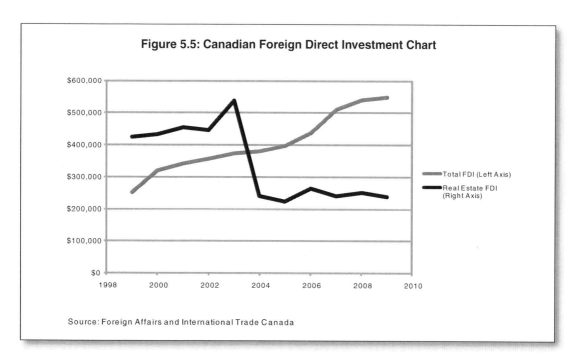

Figure 5.5: Canadian Foreign Direct Investment Chart

Source: Foreign Affairs and International Trade Canada

permanent lenders, whereby the lenders agree to "take-out" the "end loan" with the developer once the project has been completed. Large commercial banks have also become a principal source of takeout financing, i.e. long-term permanent

Chartered banks, trusts, credit unions and caisses populaires, insurance companies, junior mortgage originators, and the secondary mortgage market (MBSs, CMBSs) are sources of debt investment.

mortgage loans and end loans, usually for commercial and industrial properties. Most of the restrictions on bank residential mortgage lending were lifted in 1967. As a result, between 1970 and 1990, chartered banks increased the share of their assets in residential mortgages from 3.6% to 20.1%. The Bank Act of 1991 allowed chartered banks to acquire trust companies that had, up to then, been the dominant providers of mortgage loans in Canada along with life insurance companies. In 2007, chartered banks held 56% of outstanding residential mortgage debt, while all deposit taking institutions together held 69%.[13] In contrast, in the United States, deposit taking institutions were responsible for 75% of residential mortgage loans in 1970, but only 30% in 2007.

Life Insurance Companies

Up until 1967, life insurance companies were the largest source of mortgage funds in Canada. Their share has dropped dramatically with the increased role of chartered banks, from 59.4% of residential mortgage debt in 1960 to 3.9% in 2001. However, they still retain an important role in commercial mortgages. The mortgage investments of life insurance companies cover the full range of realty types, e.g., residences, apartments, offices, shopping malls, hotels, and industrial properties. Since many life insurance companies manage large portfolios, they have been important in

---

[13] "Canadian Residential Mortgage Markets: Boring But Effective?" Kiff, John. IMF Working Paper. 2009.

providing mortgage loans for large, income-producing properties like office buildings and shopping malls.

Trust Companies

Trust companies are usually depository institutions that also act to provide a
fiduciary function by administering assets that they do not own (as part of estate
planning, for example), although some trusts do not take deposits. Both federal and
provincial governments regulate them. Mortgages have historically been the principal
lending activity of trusts. The Bank Act of 1991 permitted trust companies to make
commercial loans, making their functions very similar to chartered banks. As of 2010,
most of the major trust companies were subsidiaries of the large chartered banks.

Credit Unions and Caisses Populaires

These are cooperative non-profit financial institutions that take deposits and are
regulated by the provinces. Depositors and borrowers are the shareholders. They
emerged, in part, because chartered banks tended to focus on commercial lending,
leaving small borrowers without an institutional source of capital. Alphonse
Desjardins founded the first cooperative financial institution in Quebec in 1900 and by
the 1930s they had spread across Canada. Credit unions in English-speaking Canada
were primarily rural, while the caisses populaires in Quebec were more urban. Prior
to 1980, credit unions were not part of the national cheque-clearing system, relying
instead on provincial-level regional unions or centrals to clear cheques and act as a
lender of last resort to member institutions. Currently, the Credit Union Central of
Canada allows for the transfer of funds between provincial centrals.

Credit unions and caisses populaires are most important in British Columbia,
Quebec, and Saskatchewan. Nationally, the assets of the 485 credit union and caisses
populaires in the 4th quarter of 2009 were reported to be $133 billion,[14] just less than
6% of the total assets of deposit taking institutions in Canada.[15] Credit unions and
caisses populaires play a significant role in residential real estate finance. They make
both mortgage loans to home buyers and construction loans to builders and developers and, in 2010, they held 19% of residential mortgage holdings in the industry.[16]
Going forward, credit unions may gain further traction in mortgage markets due
tonewly implemented rules that allow them to incorporate federally.[17]

Junior Mortgage Originators

Junior mortgages can be used to raise substantial amounts of mortgage funds and to
achieve various investment goals, such as creating additional leverage and facilitating
sales of properties with first mortgages that cannot be refinanced. Junior mortgages

---

[14] System Results Largest 100 Credit Unions. Credit Union Central of Canada. 2010.

[15] StatsCan. Banking - Balance sheet and income statement. *www.statcan.ca* (accessed Sept 1, 2009)

[16] "Canada credit unions may challenge big banks-report". April 27, 2010. Reuters UK website: *uk.reuters.com*

[17] Ibid.

involve greater risk than senior liens do and therefore command higher interest rates and shorter loan terms and amortization periods.

Canada's regulatory environment usually precludes banks, trust companies, credit unions, and life insurance companies from making large junior mortgage loans. Other private lenders such as REITs, Mortgage Investment Companies (an investment vehicle created by Canadian tax law), and private investors provide secondary financing as a regular line of business. They offer expensive secondary financing in the form of junior mortgages or subordinated land sale-leasebacks, but they are supervised by different regulators and to a lesser extent than institutional lenders.[18]

Secondary Mortgage Market

Canada Mortgage and Housing Corporation (CMHC) acts to stimulate home building through the secondary mortgage market. In this market, mortgagees sell packages of NHA insured mortgages at prices consistent with existing money market rates. Selling mortgages frees up capital, creates liquidity, and permits mortgagees to lend when they might otherwise lack funds.

In Canada, all residential secondary mortgage market activity is generated by CMHC. Banks, credit unions and caisses populaires, trusts, mortgage loan companies, and insurance companies with mortgage-originating capability will sell loan portfolios of NHA insured loans to CMHC. These loans are pooled and used to back securities such as bonds or pass through certificates. At the peak in 2008, 16% of residential mortgage credit was securitized as NHA mortgage backed securities.[19] NHA mortgage backed securitization grew steadily since 1987, when the total value of securitized mortgages was $460 million. The outstanding value of NHA mortgage backed securities exploded between 2002 and 2008, and as of 2009 they have a total outstanding value of around $130 million (illustrated in Figure 5.6). Enthusiasm for securitized products was diminished by the sub-prime mortgage crisis, but the total value of mortgage backed securities in Canada will likely continue to grow, at a slightly slower pace.

> **secondary mortgage market**
> A market created by government and private agencies for the purchase and sale of existing mortgages, which provides greater liquidity for mortgages.

In the United States, mortgages typically carry a 30-year term, fixed interest rates, and no restrictions on pre-payment of principal. In combination with certain tax and regulatory changes, lenders have a strong incentive to remove mortgages from their balance sheets by selling them to federal government and government sponsored agencies such as the Federal National Mortgage Association (Fannie Mae), Federal

[18]   A Mortgage Investment Corporation or MIC is an investment and lending company designed specifically for mortgage lending (primarily residential mortgage lending) in Canada. Owning shares in a Mortgage Investment Corporation (MIC) allows investment in a diversified and secured pool of mortgages. Shares of a MIC are qualified investments under Section 130.1of the Income Tax Act (Canada) for RRSPs, RRIFs, DPSPs, or RESPs. A MIC mortgage portfolio can include everything from small second mortgages on residential property to commercial and development mortgages on new projects. MICs are organized for investing in pools of mortgages. Profits generated by MICs are distributed to its shareholders according to their proportional interest. The mortgages are secured on real property, often in conjunction with other forms of security, such as personal and corporate guarantees, general security agreements, and assignments of material contracts, such as insurance policies, prepared by lawyers for the MIC.

[19]   Calculations based on data from CMHC (*www.cmhc-schl.gc.ca*) and Kiff, John. 2009. "Canadian Residential Mortgage Markets: Boring But Effective?" IMF Working Paper

Home Loan Mortgage Corporation (Freddie Mac), and the Government National Mortgage Association (Ginnie Mae), who in turn issue a variety of securities backed by these mortgage pools. In 2008, 46% of the $10.6 trillion (USD) of outstanding residential mortgage debt in the US was held by these and similar agencies.[20]

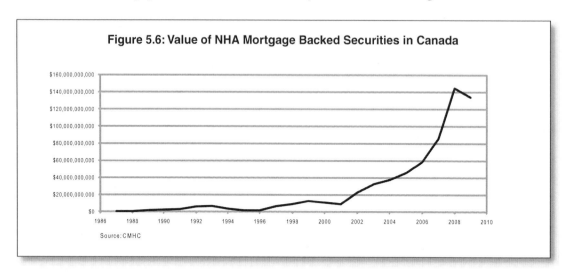

Figure 5.6: Value of NHA Mortgage Backed Securities in Canada

Source: CMHC

Securitization of Real Estate Investment Markets

Just as questions have arisen about realty and non-realty components of property value, new attention has focused on the basic nature of real estate. As new investment vehicles proliferate, appraisers will want to know when to value the individual real estate and when to reflect any differences attributable to the ownership vehicle, within which the property is grouped with other properties.

Security vs. Real Estate

Although public market pricing has some advantages, investor-driven pricing does not necessarily reflect the value of the underlying real estate asset. There is wide variation among real estate securities, depending on the structure of the particular investment vehicle. For example, REITs are subject to stringent requirements as to the dividends paid to investors (expectations of higher or lower dividends can influence pricing) or to legal restrictions limiting the amount of property that can be sold in any given year. REITs can also employ investment leverage, which increases the potential return on the investment but can create difficulties for the investment in market downturns.

One of the newer real estate investment securities vehicles divides real estate interests into a series of layers called tranches. Property investments have long been divided into equity and mortgage layers, sometimes even into a series of mortgage layers. In the 1960s, L. W. Ellwood and others showed that the typical leased fee or fee simple estate was purchased with a combination of equity and mortgage funds and that analysis of the income and return requirements of each of these layers represented a valid approach to appraisal. The modern tranche goes well beyond this concept, but the mathematical processes used in investment analyses still apply. In 1998 and again in 2007, the CMBS market came to a near halt as almost no one was willing to buy securities in the higher-risk tranches, which was explained by most analysts as a "flight to quality" sparked by concerns about financial institution stability.

DEBT AND EQUITY RELATIONSHIPS

In money markets and capital markets, when the risks associated with different investments are comparable, funds flow to the investment that offers the best prospective yield. Risks are related to rewards. If capital is to be attracted, competitive yields must be offered. The most persuasive indicators of competitive yield levels are found in money markets where billions of dollars of capital are traded daily, traders are sophisticated and well informed, and investments are often professionally rated for risk.

In an unstable economic climate, appraisers are well advised to search money markets and capital markets for data to support the conclusions they have developed from real estate market data. There are hundreds of thousands of transactions each day in financial markets and billions of dollars are involved. These transactions reflect the discounting of economic futures by well-informed investors and provide useful insights for investment analysts.

> The securitization of real estate interests through the trading of secondary mortgage market issues, MBSs, REITs, and CMBSs links real estate capitalization and discount rates to financial market activity.
>
> securities
> A class of investments represented by engraved, printed, or written documents that show ownership or creditorship in a corporation or other form of business organization; includes creditorship in public bodies, e.g., bonds, stocks, mortgages, notes, coupons, scrips, warrants, rights, options.

The largest equity market is the trading of common stocks. Transactions are reported daily, and share prices and current dividend rates are revealed. Most major newspapers carry full details on stock market operations, and financial publications and online sources offer abundant information about corporate earnings and general conditions in commercial and industrial enterprises. This data provides the basis for risk rating the securities issued by businesses. In the field of debt investments (bonds and debentures), the rating task is often performed by professionals such as Toronto-based DBRS, Standard & Poor's, owned by McGraw-Hill Cos, and Moody's Investors Service, owned by Moody's Corp. Their opinions are widely published and respected by the financial community.[21] Other information is furnished by the securities analysts of major banking institutions, brokerage companies, and the investment banking industry. Their opinions are readily available to investors.

---

[21] For publications and research from the ratings agencies on the performance of stocks and bonds, see *www.standard-poors.com*, *www.moodys.com*, *www.dbrs.com*, and *www.fitchratings.com*.

Analysts' reports and financial publications do not reveal prospective stock yields, but they do provide information from which investment indices can be drawn. Since value is the present worth of future income and reversion combined, a key element of value is anticipated appreciation or depreciation. In the stock market, securities analysts are the best sources of the type of in-depth information on which the investment community bases its growth or depreciation forecasts. In this regard, a securities analyst functions like a real estate appraiser, who arrives at an opinion of value by discounting market-supported income and reversion forecasts.

The second, larger component in real estate investment is the debt capital segment, or mortgage funds. Again, capital markets offer abundant information on investor yield requirements for a great variety of debt instruments with different maturities and risk ratings. In the bond and debenture markets, there are hundreds of thousands of daily transactions involving billions of dollars. Each transaction represents one investor's discounting of perceived future economic conditions. The entire volume of transactions presents an excellent picture of well-informed expectations of debt capital performance.

Investment Yields

There are differences in the investment yields produced by debt and equity instruments. With a debt instrument, the original lender is entitled to interest at a specified rate, either fixed or variable, and full payment of the loan amount at maturity. The arrangement may call for periodic payments of interest only and full repayment of the principal at maturity, as in the case of bonds, or it may require periodic payments that combine interest and debt reduction, as in most mortgage loans.

If the original lender sells the investment during its contractual term, a different yield may be realized. If financial market conditions are tight and interest rates are higher than when the loan was originated, the lender must sell the position at a discount. If money is freer and rates are lower, the lender may be able to sell at a premium. The purchaser collects the amount of interest specified in the original contract, but the instrument's yield rate relates to a new investment basis. When the loan is repaid at maturity, the purchaser receives the full face amount. The instrument's investment yield comprises the interest collected, plus any gain or minus any loss realized at loan maturity, and repayment.

It can be seen that the investment yield on a debt instrument is largely a contractual matter. Income earnings are defined in the instrument as a fixed or variable percentage of the debt's face amount and are paid at specified times over the term of the loan. The reversion is limited to the original face amount of debt, which may be more or less than the amount paid by the final holder of the instrument.

An equity investment has none of the contractual certainty or specificity of a debt position. The income or dividend earnings are simply the amount of a venture's income, if any, after operating expenses and debt service are paid. This cash flow can be positive or negative, depending on whether there is an excess or deficiency of income after all expenses. The reversion is simply the venture's market value at the end of the investment holding period, i.e., a future value. When entering into an investment, an investor considers the forecast dividend earnings and reversion in relation to the acquisition price. This relationship reflects the prospective equity yield.

Upon termination of the investment, the dividends and reversion realized are related to the original amount of the investment to reflect the historic equity yield.

Leverage

The term leverage refers to how borrowed funds increase or decrease the equity return. The leverage an investor obtains by using borrowed funds to finance an investment is accompanied by risk. The investor seeks compensation for this risk by requiring a higher equity yield rate. In analyzing cash flows, positive leverage is indicated when the overall

> **leverage**
> The effect of borrowed funds, which may increase or decrease the yield that would be realized on equity free and clear.

capitalization rate is greater than the mortgage capitalization rate. The difference between the two rates directly benefits the equity owner, so the equity capitalization rate is higher than it would be if the investment did not have a mortgage. The same relationships hold for overall, equity, and mortgage yield rates. (See Table 5.3).

Table 5.3: Types of Leverage

Using equity capitalization rates	Using equity yield rates
If $R_o > R_M$ then $R_E > R_o$ leverage is positive	*If* $Y_o > Y_M$ then $Y_E > Y_o$ leverage is positive
If $R_o = R_M$ then $R_E = R_o$ leverage is neutral	*If* $Y_o = Y_M$ then $Y_E = Y_o$ leverage is neutral
If $R_o < R_M$ then $R_E < R_o$ leverage is negative	*If* $Y_o < Y_M$ then $Y_E < Y_o$ leverage is negative

The analysis of leverage is important because positive or negative leverage can affect the level of risk associated with a real property investment and the yield required to satisfy an investor willing to assume the risk. The use of leverage tends to magnify fluctuations in cash flow and enhanced variability translates into risk. If property performance falls below expectations and periods of insufficient cash flow are protracted, the investor may become strapped for cash to service the debt on the property. If market conditions become illiquid, the investor may be unable to command a price for the property that allows for repayment of the debt.

CHAPTER 6

REAL PROPERTY OWNERSHIP AND INTERESTS

Real property ownership involves not only the identification and valuation of a variety of different rights, but also the analysis of the many limitations on those rights and the effect that the limitations have on value. Some limitations on ownership, such as expropriation, are public while others such as title or deed restrictions are private. Holding a form of ownership in real property means having an interest in that real property. This chapter examines the bundle of rights theory, the types of real estate ownership interests, and the various forms of property ownership. Chapter 29 discusses the valuation of partial interests.

THE BUNDLE OF RIGHTS

The most complete form of ownership is the *fee simple interest* – i.e., absolute ownership unencumbered by any other interest or estate, subject only to the limitations imposed by the four powers of government: taxation, expropriation, police power, and escheat. These powers are discussed in detail in a later section of the chapter. Although fee simple interest represents the most complete form of ownership, often an appraiser will be asked to appraise something less than the fee simple interest, i.e., a partial interest or a fractional interest.

> **FEE SIMPLE IN THEORY AND IN PRACTICE**
>
> The complexity of real property ownership in Canada today suggests that a true fee simple interest seldom exists because nearly all properties are encumbered to some degree by easements, reservations, or private restrictions. Although most appraisers define the interest being appraised as a fee simple interest, once a lease or a mortgage creates a partial interest, the fee simple interest becomes largely theoretical. Even so, many assignments call for the valuation of the fee simple interest.

The bundle of rights concept compares real property ownership to a bundle of sticks. Each stick in the bundle represents a separate right or interest inherent in the ownership. These individual rights can be separated from the bundle by sale, lease, mortgage, donation, or another means of transfer. The complete bundle of rights includes the following:

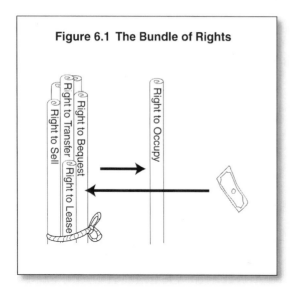

Figure 6.1 The Bundle of Rights

- The right to sell an interest
- The right to lease an interest
- The right to occupy the property
- The right to mortgage an interest
- The right to give an interest away

Ownership of the fee simple interest is equivalent to ownership of the complete bundle of sticks, while one or more of the sticks (or a portion of individual sticks) can represent a partial interest in a specific property (see Figure 6.1). Each individual right in the bundle has some potential value; if any or all are removed from the fee simple interest, one or more partial interests are created and will have to be valued.

A fee simple interest is subject only to the limitations imposed by the four powers of government. Although many appraisers state in their appraisals that the interest being valued is the fee simple interest, a true fee simple interest seldom exists. Often the valuation of a fee simple interest is hypothetical and is performed as the first step in the valuation of a partial interest. For example, in the valuation of a leased fee interest, the fee simple interest must also be valued to allow comparison between the

partial interest
Divided or undivided rights in real estate that represent less than the whole.

divided interest
An interest in part of a whole property, e.g., a lessee's interest.

undivided interest
Fractional ownership without physical division into shares, e.g., a joint tenant or tenant in common.

two interests, which in turn will allow the appraiser to determine whether a leasehold interest is positive or negative. Since all partial and fractional interests are "cut out" of the fee simple interest, the appraiser must have an understanding of the fee simple interest in a property prior to appraising a fractional or partial interest.

PARTIAL INTERESTS IN REAL PROPERTY

Partial interests can be created in several ways:

- Economically
- Legally
- Physically
- Financially

Figure 6.2 illustrates alternatives an appraiser must consider when identifying the real property interest being appraised.

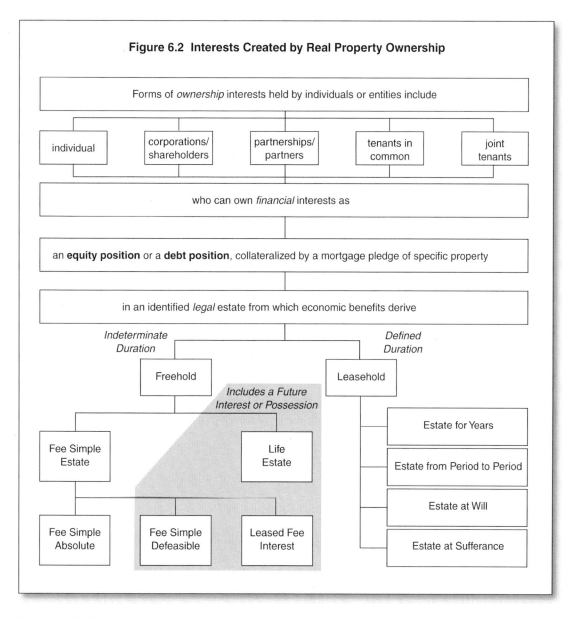

Figure 6.2 Interests Created by Real Property Ownership

Economic Interests

The most common type of economic interest is created when the fee simple interest is divided by a lease. In such a circumstance, the lessor and the lessee each obtain partial interests, which are stipulated in contract form and are subject to contract law. The divided interests resulting from a lease represent two distinct but related interests: the leased fee interest and the leasehold interest. Additional economic interests, including subleasehold (or sandwich) interests, can be created under special circumstances.

Leased Fee Interests

A leased fee interest is the lessor's, or landlord's, interest. A landlord holds specified rights that include the right of use and occupancy conveyed by lease to others. The rights of the lessor (the leased fee owner) and the lessee (leaseholder) are specified by contract terms contained within the lease. Although the specific details of leases vary, a leased fee generally provides the lessor with the following rights:

- Rent to be paid by the lessee under stipulated terms

- The right of repossession at the termination of the lease

- Default provisions

- The right of disposition, including the rights to sell, mortgage, or bequeath the property, subject to the lessee's rights, during the lease period

When a lease is legally delivered, the lessor must surrender possession of the property to the tenant for the lease period and abide by the lease provisions.

The lessor's interest in a property is considered a leased fee interest regardless of the duration of the lease, the specified rent, the parties to the lease, or any of the terms in the lease contract. A leased property, even one with rent that is consistent with market rent, is appraised as a leased fee interest, not as a fee simple interest. Even if the rent or the lease terms are not consistent with market norms, the leased fee interest must be given special consideration and is appraised as a leased fee interest.

> Leases specify the rights of the lessor (e.g., to collect rent, to repossess the property upon lease expiration, to dispose of the property through sale or transfer) and the rights of the lessee (e.g., to use, occupy, improve, and sublease the property).

Leasehold Interests

The leasehold estate is the lessee's, or tenant's, estate. When a lease is created, the tenant usually acquires the rights to possess the property for the lease period, to sublease the property (if this is allowed by the lease and desired by the tenant), and perhaps to improve the property under the restrictions specified in the lease. In return, the tenant is obligated to pay rent, surrender possession of the property at the termination of the lease, remove any improvements the lessee has modified or constructed (if specified), and abide by the lease provisions. The most important obligation of a tenant is to pay rent.

The relationship between contract and market rent greatly affects the value of a leasehold interest. A leasehold interest may have value if contract rent is less than market rent, creating a rental advantage for the tenant. This relationship, in turn, is

> **fee simple interest**
> Absolute ownership unencumbered by any other interest or estate, subject only to the limitations imposed by the governmental powers of taxation, expropriation, police power, and escheat.
>
> **leased fee interest**
> The ownership interest held by the lessor, which includes the right to the contract rent specified in the lease plus the reversionary right when the lease expires.
>
> **leasehold interest**
> The right held by the lessee to use and occupy real estate for a stated term and under the conditions specified in the lease.

likely to affect the value of the leased fee interest. The value of a leased fee interest encumbered with a fixed rent that is below market rates may be worth less than the unencumbered fee simple interest or the leased fee interest with rent at market levels. When contract rent exceeds market rent, the leasehold is deemed to have negative value. However, the contract advantage of the leased fee may not be marketable. Even in such circumstances, the tenant still has the right to occupy the premises and, despite the contractual disadvantage, may have other benefits that warrant continued occupancy. It is also possible that the contract disadvantage imperils the tenant's business and increases the risk of continued occupancy.

Subleasehold or Sandwich Interests

Normally a tenant is free to sublease all or part of a property, but many leases require that the landlord's consent be obtained. A *sublease* is an agreement in which the tenant in an existing lease conveys to a third party the interest that the lessee enjoys (the right of use and occupancy of the property) for part or all of the remaining term of the lease. In a sublease, the original lessee is "sandwiched" between a lessor and a sublessee (see Figure 6.3). The original lessee's interest has value if the contract rent is less than the rent collected from the sublessee. Subleasing does not release the lessee from the obligations to the lessor defined in the lease agreement. A sublease may affect all the parties, including the owner of the leased fee interest, and such arrangements are common and increasingly upheld by the courts.

A lease contract may contain a provision that explicitly forbids subletting. Without either the right to sublet or a term that is long enough to be marketable, a leasehold position cannot be transferred and, therefore, has no market value. Furthermore, the value of the leased fee interest would likely be diminished in this case because a lessee who no longer has need of the leased premises and is not allowed to sublease the space is likely to default on the lease.

A tenant under a sublease may not have any of the rights of the leasehold interest under the original lease contract. It is also possible that the holder of the sandwich interest may offer various economic benefits that include allowing the new tenant to sublease the property. Thus, the contract between the original tenant and the subtenant may contain provisions that go beyond, but do not violate, the provisions of the original lease.

> **sublease**
> An agreement in which the lessee in a prior lease conveys the right of use and occupancy of a property to another, the sublessee, for a specific period of time, which may or may not be coterminous (expire at the same time) with the underlying lease term.
>
> **sandwich lease**
> A lease in which an intermediate, or sandwich, leaseholder is the lessee of one party and the lessor of another. The owner of the sandwich lease is neither the fee owner nor the user of the property; he or she may be a leaseholder in a chain of leases, excluding the ultimate sublessee.

Legal Interests

Virtually every property is subject to some kind of easement or other legal restriction on use that creates a partial interest. Some are permanent easements, while others

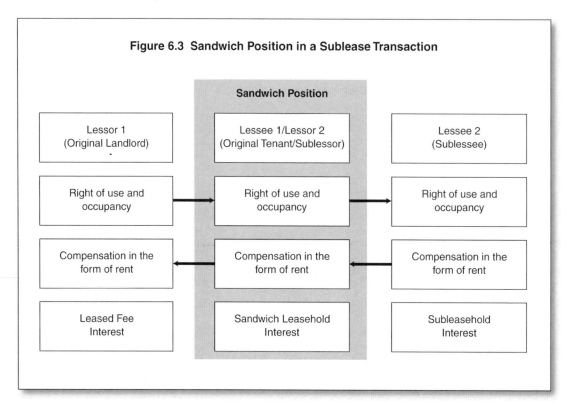

Figure 6.3 Sandwich Position in a Sublease Transaction

may only exist for a short time. Often appraisers have to either estimate the value of property subject to an easement or estimate the value of the easement itself. In certain ownership situations, a life estate may be created, which in turn creates several partial interests. Transferable development rights (TDRs) are another type of special partial interest that can be created by legal circumstances, where some or all of a property's development capability is sold to another (e.g., increase allowable density of a neighbouring property).

Life Estates

A life estate is defined as the total rights of use, occupancy, and control of a specified property limited to the lifetime of a designated party. The designated party is generally known as the life tenant and is obligated to maintain the property in good condition and pay all applicable taxes during the term of the life estate. Two interests are created when a life estate is created, and both may need to be valued by an appraiser: the interest of the *life tenant* and the *remainder interest*, which acquires the possessory interest in the property upon the death of the life tenant. Life estates can be created in several ways:

- By operations of law
- By wills
- By deeds of conveyance

For example, a fee owner may leave a will that gives land to his widow for her remaining lifetime and, at her death, the land is passed on to their children. Thus, the widow acquires a life estate and functions as a life tenant with the children becoming the remaindermen. A living fee owner may deed his property to a family member as remainderman and, by the terms of the conveyance, retain a life estate

> **life tenant**
> One who owns an estate in real property for his or her own lifetime, the lifetime of another person, or an indefinite period limited by a lifetime.
>
> **remainder interest**
> A person who is entitled to an estate after a prior estate or interest has expired; also called remainderman or remainder.

for himself. This practice might eliminate the expense of probating the will after the owner dies, but it may also call for the assessment of a gift tax.

If the life estate generates income, the appraiser may estimate its probable duration from life expectancy statistics compiled in actuarial studies. Once the appraiser established the net operating income from the estate and its duration, an appropriate discount rate can be applied. If the life estate does not generate income, the appraiser may project its future value and then discount this value back to the current date. Because death is certain but its timing is indeterminable, discounting is generally accomplished by applying a safe rate or risk-free rate (the uncertainty of the timing may require the use of a range of years, which would call for a higher discount rate than the safe rate). The discount rate selected also depends on the age and life expectancy of the person who holds the life estate.

Variations exist in life estates. Someone might leave a residential property to a relative to live in for the remainder of his or her life, with the property to transfer to the individual with the remainder interest when the life estate holder dies or ceases to live in the home. In this circumstance, an appraiser might decide to increase the discount rate to reflect the uncertainty that the life estate holder might move from the property years before he or she dies.

Easements

An easement is an interest in real property that transfers use, but not ownership, of a portion of an owner's property. Easements usually permit a specific portion of a property to be used for identified purposes, such as access to an adjoining property or as the location of a certain underground utility. Although surface easements are the most common, subterranean and overhead easements are used for public utilities, subways, and bridges. Other easements may prohibit the owner of the underlying fee simple interest from certain uses of the property without giving the owner of the easement any possessory interest in the real estate, e.g., scenic easements and facade easements.

Clearly, a property that enjoys the benefit of an easement gains additional rights, while a property that is subject to an easement is burdened. The easement attaches to the property benefitted and is referred to as an *easement appurtenant*. The property whose owner acquires an easement is known as the *dominant tenement*; the property that is subject to the easement is called the *servient tenement*. Easement rights can be

easement

An interest in real property that transfers use, but not ownership, of a portion of an owner's property. Access or right-of-way easements may be acquired by private parties or public utilities. Governments accept conservation, open space, and preservation easements on private property.

easement appurtenant

An easement that is attached to, benefits, and passes with the transfer of the dominant estate; runs with the land for the benefit of the dominant estate and continues to burden the servient estate, although such an estate may be transferred to new owners.

conservation easement

A restriction that limits the future use of a property to preservation, conservation, or wildlife habitat.

preservation easement

A restriction that prohibits certain physical changes in a historic property; usually based on the property's condition at the time the easement was acquired or immediately after proposed restoration of the property.

transferred in perpetuity (indefinitely) or for a limited time. An easement can be created in several ways:

- By a contract between private parties
- By adverse possession in accordance with provincial law
- By governmental entities or public utilities through the exercise of expropriation

Transferable Development Rights

Transferable development rights (TDRs), sometimes referred to as severable use rights, emerged in the real estate industry of the United States during the 1970s. A transferable development right is a development right that is separated from a land owner's bundle of rights and transferred, generally by sale, to another land owner in another location. Some TDRs preserve property uses for agricultural production, open space, or historic buildings. In this arrangement, a preservation district and a development district are identified. Land owners in the preservation district are assigned development rights, which they cannot use to develop their own land but can sell to land owners in the development district. These land owners can use the transferred rights to build at higher densities than zoning laws in the development district would normally permit.

In Canada, some municipalities allow for the transfer of development rights from a particular site in the form of density. This might arise as part of a heritage preservation arrangement, where a developer rejuvenating a heritage facility would receive bonus density to offset the cost of the heritage preservation effort. The municipality might require the bonus density to be used only on the heritage site,

transferable development right (TDR)

A development right that cannot be used by the land owner, or that the owner chooses not to use, but can be sold to land owners in another location; generally used to preserve agricultural land; may also be used to preserve historic sites or buildings and open space or to protect scenic features. TDRs are said to be transferred from a land owner in a sending district to the use of a land owner in a receiving district.

or on other specified sites. Sometimes, the bonus density becomes available for sale and transfer to a particular area, with no specific development site identified at the time of the density grant.

Density transfers have also been allowed where the density is sold to an adjacent development site, thus allowing consolidation of development onto a particular site. In Vancouver, a large high-rise office development, e.g., Park Place, was constructed in part using density purchased and transferred from an adjacent house of worship, which remains as a low-rise development.

Another situation in which development rights are transferred results from the constrained capacity of an existing utility. For example, consider a community that decides to impose a construction moratorium pending the expansion of its present sewage plant or the building of a new plant. Before the moratorium, a land owner was granted the right to hook up 100 projected single-family residences to the existing plant. A second land owner, however, did not obtain the right to link up his 50 proposed single-family residences to the sewage treatment plant and will have to wait for expansion of the plant's capacity. The second land owner risks financial loss if he cannot develop the land immediately, so he eagerly purchases the right to link up his 50 residential units to the plant from the first land owner.

Although such rights may vary from province to province, TDRs are generally an interest in real property only as long as they are attached to the land. When they are sold, they become personal property, becoming real property again when they are attached to another tract of land.

Physical Interests

Physical interests in real property can be achieved either horizontally or vertically. The most common methods of creating horizontal divisions of real property are through *subdivision* and *assemblage*. In subdivision, a large tract of land is broken down into smaller units, which are then marketed individually. In assemblage (or plottage), two or more parcels of real estate are combined into one parcel and a higher value is created for the assembled parcel than exists for the individual parcels. Consider two adjacent, half-acre industrial sites in an area where one-acre sites are most desirable. The value of the half-acre sites is $200,000 each, but when assembled the one-acre site has a value of $500,000. Conversely, when the market seeks smaller sites, the unit values of larger sites will likely be lower. Most appraisers are familiar with the valuation of horizontal interests, and traditional valuation techniques are usually applicable.

Vertical interests in real property may have to be considered separately by the appraiser in sales, leases, mortgages, and other realty transactions. The most common vertical interests in real property are *sub-surface rights* and *air rights*. A sub-surface right is the right to the use of and profits from the underground portion of a designated property. The term usually refers to the right to extract minerals from below the earth's surface and to construct tunnels for railroads, motor vehicles, and public utilities. Air rights are the property rights associated with the use, control, and regulation of air space over a parcel of real estate. Both of these fractional interests represent portions of a fee simple estate, and each embodies the idea of land as a three-dimensional entity.

The vertical division of real property is significant because engineering advances have dramatically affected land use and, therefore, highest and best use considerations. The development of steel-framed building construction, the passenger elevator, deep tunnel excavation techniques, and communications technology have sub-surface rights

The rights to the use and profits of the underground portion of a designated property; usually refers to the right to extract coal, minerals, oil, gas, or other hydrocarbon substances as designated in the grant; may include a right of way over designated portions of the surface.

air rights

The right to undisturbed use and control of designated air space above a specific land area within stated elevations. Such rights may be acquired to construct a building above the land or building of another or to protect the light and air of an existing or proposed structure on an adjoining lot.

all helped to shape the modern urban landscape. As the density of building in urban areas increases, fewer sites are available for new construction and land values escalate. This trend has produced a growing interest in developing air rights.

Air rights can be sold in fee, with the seller retaining one or more easements for a specialized use such as the operation of a railroad. They may also be subdivided, as when the owner of the fee simple interest sells or leases only the land and air that are to be occupied by a particular improvement. Air rights can be transferred in various ways as well. Often the air rights to one property are shifted to another within the same building zone under legal planning regulations. The transfer of air rights allows developers to adjust the density of land use without putting adverse pressure on owners, neighbourhoods, or districts. This practice underscores the importance of local zoning authorities, which regulate building heights, building functions, setbacks, and other variables involved in the development of air rights.

Financial Interests

The financial aspects of property interests have a major impact on real estate investment practices. The analysis of mortgage and equity components is of particular importance. Mortgage funds are secured debt positions, while equity investments are venture capital. Fee simple, leased fee, and leasehold interests can all be mortgaged, thereby subdividing these interests into mortgage and equity components. Other possible financial arrangements include senior and subordinated debt, sale-leaseback financing, and equity syndications.

Equity Interests

The equity in real property is the owner's interest after all claims and liens have been satisfied. An equity interest, like a mortgage loan, represents a financial interest in real property. Equity ownership in real property can be legally accomplished in several ways, e.g., as an individual owner, joint owner, partner, or shareholder in a corporation. The legal form of equity ownership does not affect property value in most appraisal assignments. However, an appraiser is sometimes called upon to render an opinion of the value of a specific legal form of equity interest.

For example, an appraiser may be asked to value a limited partner's equity interest in a partnership that was created solely to make the individual the legal owner of certain limited rights in the real property. Partial interests can have value less than their pro rata share of ownership, especially if the holder of the partial interest does not have any voice in the management or control of the asset. An assignment to value a limited partnership interest may be undertaken to appraise assets for estate tax purposes or for sale or purchase decisions.

Mortgage Interests

The purchase and ownership of real property often involves debt capital secured with the real estate as collateral. Mortgage investments have a great impact on real property value and equity yield rates.

REAL PROPERTY OWNERSHIP

Public and Private Ownership

One major distinction in real property ownership is the difference between private ownership and public ownership. Public ownership of real property takes many forms. Streets and roads, municipal utility systems, and other public facilities such as city halls, prisons, and public works facilities are usually owned by governmental bodies for the benefit of all citizens in a jurisdiction. School districts own land on which school buildings, athletic fields, and other facilities are maintained. Library districts create public libraries. Park, recreation, and conservation entities acquire land for recreation, conservation, and preservation.

Response to public necessity or public demand creates most public ownership. For example, in one community it might be necessary to acquire land for a school using the power of expropriation. In another community, there might be sufficient demand by residents to acquire land for the development of soccer fields using money generated by real estate taxation. Rather than being concerned with the economic issues that are of importance to private owners of real property, a governmental entity often is more concerned with how publicly owned real property, which is usually not subject to real estate taxation, can be used in the best interests of the public.

Police power also regulates land use, and its application can reflect the difference in a property viewed from the perspective of public versus private ownership. For example, a large municipal park might be an ideal location for industrial development, but the zoning imposed through the application of police power will ensure that the park continues to be used for recreational purposes. Also, government regulations will dictate how property acquired by a governmental entity through the process of escheat (i.e., when someone dies intestate) will best benefit the general public.

Although many appraisal assignments involve the valuation of publicly owned real property, most involve the valuation of private ownership interests. As discussed in this chapter, ownership of property can take many forms. The form of ownership is usually selected based on the needs of the owner or owners. For example, a husband and wife might own a single-unit residence in joint tenancy with the right of survivorship. However, a more appropriate type of ownership for a chain of food stores might be as a beneficial interest in a bare land trust or a limited

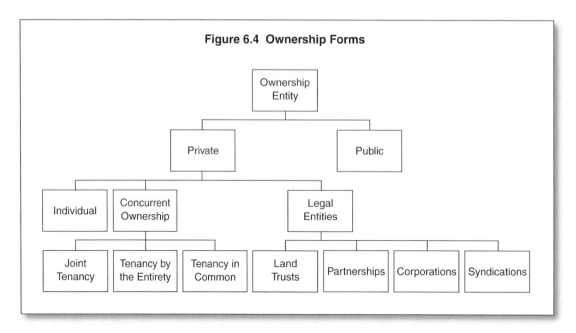

Figure 6.4 Ownership Forms

taxation
The right of government to raise revenue through assessments on valuable goods, products, and rights.

expropriation
The right of government to take or modify an individual's property right, especially through eminent domain, the inherent power of a government to take privately owned property, especially land, and convert it to public use, subject to reasonable compensation for the taking.

liability corporation. Figure 6.4 illustrates the relationship of various types of real property ownership.

Canadian Uniform Standards of Professional Appraisal Practice (CUSPAP) require the appraiser to identify which interest is to be valued in an assignment, but the interest valued need not reflect "what exists." For example, an appraiser can value a fee simple interest even though the property is leased. The interest appraised depends on the intended use of the appraisal and what interest the client needs to know the value of.

Public Restrictions on Ownership

In Canada, private ownership of real property rights is subject to certain restrictions, known as the four powers of government:

1. Taxation
2. Expropriation
3. Police power
4. Escheat

Taxation is the right of government to raise revenue through assessments on goods, products, and rights. The Canadian constitution effectively precludes the federal government from taxing real property directly. The right to tax property is reserved for provincial and local governments.

Eminent domain is the right of government to take private property for public use upon the payment of just compensation. This right can be exercised by a government agency or by an entity acting under governmental authority such as a housing authority, school district, park district, or right of way agency. Expropriation is the act or process of enforcing the right of eminent domain.

Police power is the right of government through which property is regulated to protect public safety, health, morals, and general welfare. Examples of police power include zoning ordinances, use restrictions, building codes, air and land traffic regulations, public health codes, and environmental regulations.

Escheat is the right of government that gives the government titular ownership of a property when its owner dies without a will or any statutory heirs.

> **police power**
> The right of government through which property is regulated to protect public safety, health, morals and general welfare.
>
> **escheat**
> The right of government that gives the state titular ownership of a property when its owner dies without a will or any ascertainable heirs.

> **right of way**
> A privilege to pass over the land of another in some particular path; usually an easement over the land of another; a strip of land used in this way for railroad and highway purposes, for pipelines or pole lines, and for private or public passage.
>
> **party wall**
> A common wall erected along the boundary between adjoining properties; the respective owners have a common right of use.

Private Restrictions on Ownership

Private restrictions on property ownership can limit the use or development of a property and might limit the manner in which ownership can be conveyed. The purchaser of a property may be obligated to use the property subject to a private restriction such as *right of way* or a *party wall* agreement. The systems used to register interests in land vary across Canada, and appraisers must have competence in researching the system that applies to individual properties under appraisal.

Under the land registry system of some provincial jurisdictions, usually an appraiser must look into past actions of a property owner or developer to determine if private restrictions currently affect the property. Deed restrictions and subdivision covenants and restrictions are relatively easy to discover: they can be found in deeds recorded at the registry or in information provided by a property owner. Restrictions such as easements and rights of way may be more difficult to uncover. They may only be found in title reports or through a diligent search of public records. Other restrictions such as an unrecorded agreement relative to water rights may be nearly impossible to discover. Under the land titles system of some provinces, a single title status report can be obtained that shows all the claims registered against the title of a property, and that lists some public agency notifications and interests such as easements that benefit the property.

FORMS OF OWNERSHIP

Concurrent Ownership of Real Property

Real estate can be owned by one or more entities. Individual ownership is legally known as *ownership in severalty*. However, individuals can hold ownership under certain legal entities, such as 100% ownership of the beneficial interest in a land trust or 100% ownership of the stock of a corporation that owns real estate. *Tenancy* is defined as the holding of property by any form of title.

Concurrent ownership includes joint tenancy, tenancy by the entirety, and tenancy in common. Joint tenancy is joint ownership by two or more persons with the right of survivorship. Under this arrangement, each party has an identical interest and right of possession. Upon the death of one joint tenant, ownership is automatically vested in the remaining joint tenant or tenants. Tenancy by the entirety is an estate held by a husband and wife in which neither has a disposable interest in the property during the lifetime of the other, except through joint action. It has the same survivorship provision as a joint tenancy, but tenancy by the entirety applies only to spouses. Tenancy in common is an estate held by two or more persons, each of whom has an undivided interest. In this estate, the undivided interests might or might not be equally shared by the holders and there is no right of survivorship. One tenant in common may sell off an undivided interest without the approval or knowledge of the other tenant or tenants in common.

> Various tenancy arrangements apply to property ownership by two or more persons.
>
> tenancy
> The holding of property by any form of title.
>
> joint tenancy
> Joint ownership by two or more persons with the right of survivorship.

> land trust
> A legal vehicle for partial ownership interests in real property in which independently owned properties are conveyed to a trustee; may be used to assemble land for development or, in some cases, to facilitate the assigning of property as collateral for a loan.

Legal Entity Ownership of Real Property

In addition to individual ownership, real property can be owned by a variety of different legal entities:

- Land trusts
- Partnerships
- Corporations and companies
- Syndications

Like individuals, these entities can own a fee simple interest or partial interests in real property.

Land Trusts

Trusts are sometimes used as legal vehicles to create partial ownership interests in real property. In a land trust, one or more properties are conveyed by special deed to a trustee, which then owns the real property. Either the original owners or some other designated individual or persons become the owners of the beneficial interest in the trust. A trust agreement is established outlining the duties and functions of the trustee. A trustee is usually a separate, specialized company or an independent department of a bank.

A trustee can take no actions other than those specified and allowed in the trust agreement without written permission of the owner or owners of the beneficial interest. For example, in one trust agreement a trustee may be required to manage a property actively and collect rents. However, in another trust agreement regarding a different property, the same trustee will be prohibited from managing the property and collecting rents. One important legal aspect of a trust arrangement is that a judgment against a beneficiary is not a lien against the real estate.

Partnerships

A partnership is a business arrangement in which two or more persons jointly own a business and share in its profits and losses. Partnerships are used extensively in real estate acquisition because they pool individual funds for property ownership and operation. Two types of partnerships are prevalent in the ownership of real property: general partnerships and limited partnerships.

In a general partnership, all partners share in business gains and each is personally responsible for all liabilities of the partnership.

One important aspect of a general partnership is that the agreement automatically terminates when a general partner dies.

Limited partnerships have both general partners and limited partners. All partners participate by pooling funds. However, unlike general partnerships in which all partners actively participate in the business of the partnership, in a limited partnership the partners can be either active or passive. General partners are active members of the partnership who manage the business and assume full liability for partnership obligations. Limited partners, on the other hand, are passive members of the partnership. They are not actively involved in the business of the partnership, and their liability is restricted to the amount of their capital contribution. Through a limited partnership, a group of investors can jointly acquire real property that they might be unable to acquire as individuals.

> **partnership**
> A business arrangement in which two or more persons jointly own a business and share in its profits and losses.
>
> **general partnership**
> An ownership arrangement in which all partners share in investment gains and losses and each has personal and unlimited responsibility for all liabilities.
>
> **limited partnership**
> An ownership arrangement consisting of general and limited partners. General partners manage the business and assume full liability for partnership debt, while limited partners are passive and liable only to the extent of their own capital contributions.

Stock Corporations

Like partnerships, stock corporations allow many investors to pool funds to purchase and own real property. However, unlike partnerships, the individual investors in a stock corporation do not hold an interest in the real property; rather, they own shares of stock, usually recognized as personal property. The owner of the real property is the legal entity, the corporation.

A stock corporation may be organized to hold title to a single asset, such as a parcel of real estate, or multiple assets, such as a portfolio of property investments. Ownership of the corporate entity is divided into partial interests by selling shares to an investment group. Any specific stock holding represents a percentage of total corporate ownership. For example, if a particular investor owns 250 shares out of 10,000 total shares issued by the corporation, that investor owns 2.5% of the corporation. This percentage is an ownership share in the corporation, not a percentage of any real property in the corporation.

> **stock corporation**
> A common legal entity in which investors provide organizational capital by subscribing to shares that represent ownership and a right to all proprietary benefits but are subject to the prior claims of operating expenses and debt service on capital raised by selling bonds, debentures, and other money market instruments.

Limited Liability Companies

A limited liability company incorporates features of both a corporation and a partnership. The owners of a limited liability company are members, rather than shareholders or partners. Unless otherwise specified, management is generally vested in the members in proportion to their contributions of capital. Members may separate their right to a share of the company profits from the right to participate in management or to vote on matters affecting the company. These separated rights can then be assigned to a transferee.

Syndications

Syndications are another means for selling interests or rights in real property. A syndication creates a private or public partnership to pool funds for the acquisition, development, holding, management, and/or disposition of real estate. Syndications are established when an individual or group purchases interests in real property for the purpose of transferring them to a limited partnership, which in turn sells the interests to investors.

At one time, syndications were popular because the investment value of syndicate shares usually included income tax shelter benefits. Such investments offered small income returns during the early years, when the value of the investment was perceived to lie largely in its income tax benefits, i.e., tax deductions and tax deferrals. However, tax reforms have significantly reduced the use of real estate investments as income shelters.[1]

> **syndication**
> A private or public partnership that pools funds for the acquisition and development of real estate projects or other business ventures.

Although syndications usually involve some sort of partnership, they differ from partnerships insofar as the rights of investors in a syndication are different from the rights of general or limited partners in a partnership. In theory, syndication arrange-

---

[1]   Rules 6.2.9 and 7.10 of Appraisal Standards Rule of CUSPAP require an appraiser identify and analyze timesharing interests arising from real property.

ments may be simple, but in practice they are often complex because syndications frequently purchase more than real estate, e.g., management services.

Special Forms of Ownership

In addition to concurrent ownership and ownership by legal entities, there are several special forms of ownership, including the following items:

- Condominium ownership
- Cooperative ownership
- Timesharing

Condominium Ownership

A condominium is a form of ownership of separate units or portions of multi-unit buildings. While residential and retail properties were once the main types of property held in condominium ownership, most property types now exist in condominium ownership, including offices, industrial buildings, retail structures, and even garden plots, marina slips, and undeveloped land where the access roads and utilities are the common property. A condominium unit is a separate ownership, and an individual owner holds title. The unit may be separately leased, sold, or mortgaged. In a traditional condominium, the owner holds title to an individual unit and an undivided partial interest in the common areas of the total condominium project, e.g., the land, the public portions of the building, the foundation, the outer walls, and the spaces provided for parking and recreation. Thus, the owner possesses a three-dimensional space within the outer walls, roof or ceiling, and floors and, along with other owners, has an undivided interest in common areas. In certain condominium projects, limited common elements also exist. In this arrangement, certain common elements – e.g., parking stalls, storage units, plots of surrounding land – are reserved for the use of some, but not all, of the condominium owners. The owners of units in a condominium project usually form an association to manage the project in accordance with adopted by-laws. The expenses of management and maintenance are divided proportionately among the owners, who pay a monthly fee.

> condominium ownership
> A form of fee ownership of separate units or portions of multi-unit buildings that provides for formal filing and recording of a divided interest in real property.

Cooperative Ownership

In certain areas, cooperative (co-op) ownership of apartments is popular. In a co-op, a stock corporation is organized, acquires title to an apartment building, prices the various apartments, and issues an authorized number of shares at a specified par value. Individual owners purchase shares of stock, with the price per unit determining the number of shares that an occupant must purchase. In cooperative ownership, each owner of stock receives a proprietary lease on a specific apartment and is obligated to make a monthly payment that represents the proportionate share of

cooperative ownership
A form of ownership in which each owner of stock in a cooperative apartment building or housing corporation receives a proprietary lease on a specific apartment and is obligated to pay a monthly maintenance charge that represents the proportionate share of operating expenses and debt service on the underlying mortgage, which is paid by the corporation. This proportionate share is based on the proportion of the total stock owned.

operating expenses and debt service on the underlying mortgage, which is paid by the corporation. The lease obligates the occupant to pay a monthly maintenance fee, which may be adjusted at times by the corporation's board of directors. The fee covers the expenses of management, operations, and maintenance of public areas. Since the shareholders can vote their shares in electing directors, they have some control over property conditions.

Cooperatives are less attractive forms of ownership than fee simple ownership for a variety of reasons. It can be difficult to obtain financing based on a cooperative interest, and control over individual units can be less.

In Canada, cooperative ownership is often associated with government subsidy programs aimed at low and moderate-income households. Shares in these projects often have nominal value, due to restrictions arising from the cooperative and subsidy agreements. Provincial and local government restrictions aimed at the preservation of rental housing stock can make creation of a private housing cooperative difficult.

Timesharing

Timesharing involves the sale of either limited ownership interests in or rights to use and occupy residential apartments or hotel rooms. There are two forms of timesharing: fee timeshares and nonfee timeshares. It is imperative that appraisers distinguish between the forms when appraising timeshare projects or analyzing timeshare comparables. In the first form, fee timesharing, the purchaser of a fee timeshare receives a deed that conveys title to a unit for a specific part of a year, thereby limiting the ownership. The purchaser has the right to sell, lease, or bequeath the timeshare. The interest can be mortgaged and title can be recorded. The second form of timesharing, non-fee timesharing, does not convey a legal title in the property. Typically, a purchaser receives only the right to use a timeshare unit and related premises.

There are subcategories for both types of timesharing. The two types of fee timesharing are timeshare ownership and interval ownership. In timeshare ownership, a purchaser receives a deed to a particular unit as a tenant in common. Each purchaser agrees to use the unit only during the time stipulated in the deed. In interval ownership, the ownership period may only last for the duration of the project. At the end of the specified time, the ownership reverts to the interval owners as tenants in common. They then have the option of selling the property and dividing the proceeds, or continuing as tenants in common and renewing the interval estate. Timeshare owners and interval owners pay operating expenses, including a proportionate share of taxes, insurance, and other costs and a fee for common area maintenance (CAM) and management. In many projects, 50 one-week intervals are created; the remaining two weeks of each year are reserved for maintenance and major repairs.

The three types of non-fee timesharing are leasehold interest, vacation license, and club membership.[2] The leasehold interest type of timesharing is essentially a prepaid lease arrangement. A vacation license involves the transfer of a license from the developer to the purchaser, giving the latter the right to use a given type of unit for specified times over the life of the vacation license contract. In the club membership form of ownership, timeshare patrons purchase membership for a specified number of years in a club that owns, leases, or operates the timeshare property. The purchaser receives the right to use a particular type of unit for a specified period during each year of membership.

> **timesharing**
> Limited ownership interests in, or the rights of use and occupancy of, residential apartments or hotel rooms. There are two forms of timesharing: fee timeshares and nonfee timeshares. Fee timeshares may be based on timeshare ownership or interval ownership. There are three types of nonfee timeshares: a prepaid lease arrangement, a vacation license and a club membership.

---

[2]   Under the laws of some provinces, vacation licenses and club memberships are not considered interests in real estate, but personal property.

CHAPTER 7

THE VALUATION PROCESS

The valuation process is a systematic procedure an appraiser follows to provide answers to a client's questions about real property value. It is a model that can be adapted to a wide variety of questions that relate to value. It can also be used, perhaps with some modification, to answer questions not directly related to value, as in the case of appraisal review and real property consulting assignments.

The valuation process begins when the appraiser enters into an agreement with a client to provide a valuation service. Generally, the terms of the agreement are fulfilled when the appraiser delivers the assignment results (opinions and conclusions) to the client. The objective of most appraisal assignments is to render an opinion of market value. The valuation process contains all the steps appropriate to this type of assignment. The model also provides the framework for developing an opinion of other defined values.

The valuation process is accomplished through specific steps. The number of steps followed depends on the intended use of the assignment results, the nature of the property, the scope of work deemed appropriate for the assignment, and the availability of data. The model provides a pattern that can be used in any appraisal assignment to perform market research and data analysis, to apply appraisal techniques, and to integrate the results of these activities into an opinion of defined value. In addition to assisting appraisers in their work, models that apply the valuation process are recognized by the market of appraisal users and facilitate their understanding of appraisal conclusions.

> The valuation process is a systematic set of procedures an appraiser follows to provide answers to a client's questions about real property value.

Research begins after the appraisal problem has been identified and the scope of work required to solve the problem has been determined. The analysis of data relevant to the problem starts with an investigation of trends observed at the market level: international, national, regional, or neighbourhood. The market analysis helps the appraiser understand the interrelationships among the principles, forces, and factors that affect real property value in the specific market area. Research also provides raw data from which the appraiser can extract quantitative information and other evidence of market trends. Such trends may include positive or negative percentage changes in property value over a number of years, the population movement into an area, and the number of employment opportunities available and their effect on the purchasing power of potential property users.

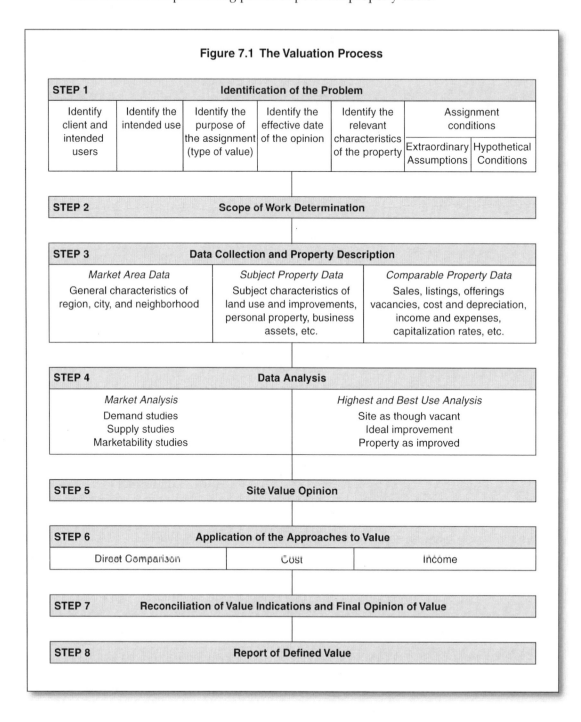

Figure 7.1 The Valuation Process

STEP 1	Identification of the Problem					
Identify client and intended users	Identify the intended use	Identify the purpose of the assignment (type of value)	Identify the effective date of the opinion	Identify the relevant characteristics of the property	Assignment conditions	
					Extraordinary Assumptions	Hypothetical Conditions

STEP 2	Scope of Work Determination

STEP 3	Data Collection and Property Description		
	Market Area Data	*Subject Property Data*	*Comparable Property Data*
	General characteristics of region, city, and neighborhood	Subject characteristics of land use and improvements, personal property, business assets, etc.	Sales, listings, offerings vacancies, cost and depreciation, income and expenses, capitalization rates, etc.

STEP 4	Data Analysis	
	Market Analysis	*Highest and Best Use Analysis*
	Demand studies Supply studies Marketability studies	Site as though vacant Ideal improvement Property as improved

STEP 5	Site Value Opinion

STEP 6	Application of the Approaches to Value		
	Direct Comparison	Cost	Income

STEP 7	Reconciliation of Value Indications and Final Opinion of Value

STEP 8	Report of Defined Value

In assignments to develop an opinion of market value, the ultimate goal of the valuation process is a well-supported value conclusion that reflects all of the pertinent factors that influence the market value of the property being appraised. To achieve this goal, an appraiser studies a property from three different viewpoints, which are referred to as the approaches to value. The three approaches are described below:

- In the *cost approach*, value is estimated as the current cost of reproducing or replacing the improvements (including an appropriate entrepreneurial incentive or profit) minus the loss in value from depreciation plus land or site value.

- In the *direct comparison approach*, value is indicated by recent sales of comparable properties in the market.

- In the *income approach*, value is indicated by a property's earning power, based on the capitalization of income.

Traditionally, specific appraisal techniques are applied within the three approaches to derive indications of real property value. One or more approaches to value may be used depending on which approaches are necessary to produce credible assignment results, given the intended use.

The three approaches are interrelated.[1] Each requires the gathering and analysis of data that pertains to the property being appraised. This chapter outlines each approach briefly and subsequent sections of the textbook discuss each approach in detail. From the approaches applied, the appraiser derives separate indications of value for the property being appraised. To complete the valuation process, the appraiser integrates the information drawn from market research, data analysis, and the application of the approaches to form a value conclusion. This conclusion may be presented as a single point estimate of value or, if the assignment permits, as a range within which the value may fall (or as a point referenced from a benchmark). An effective integration of all the elements in the process depends on the appraiser's skill, experience, and judgment.

The steps in the valuation process are depicted in Figure 7.1.

IDENTIFICATION OF THE APPRAISAL PROBLEM

The first step in the valuation process is the development of a clear understanding of the problem to be solved. This step sets the parameters for the assignment. To solve any problem, appraisers must first identify the problem and only then can the problem be solved with an appropriate solution. In appraisal practice, problem identification logically precedes scope of work determination.

Identification of the appraisal problem involves identifying each of the following:

- Client
- Intended users in addition to the client
- Intended use of the appraisal
- Type of value and its definition

---

[1]   The direct comparison approach was once known as the "market approach". However, this is a misnomer because all three approaches to value are "market" approaches in that they rely on market data.

- Effective date of the analysis, opinions, and conclusions
- Identification of the characteristics of the property that are relevant to the type and definition of value and intended use of the appraisal (including its location, the property rights to be valued, and other features)
- Assignment conditions, including extraordinary assumptions, hypothetical conditions, and additional requirements to be followed

Before identifying the characteristics of the property and any extraordinary assumptions and hypothetical conditions that are relevant to the purpose of the assignment, the appraiser must clearly identify the client, intended users, intended use of the appraisal, purpose of the assignment, and effective date of the opinion of value. Once the appraisal problem has been identified, the appraiser can determine the appropriate scope of work for the assignment.

Client

The client is the person who engages the appraiser. The client can be one person (such as an individual investor), one entity (such as a bank), or a number of people or entities acting together. The client may or may not be the intended user of the appraisal service, e.g., when the client is acting as an agent of the intended user.

Intended Users

The intended user is the person or entity who will use the results of the appraisal for some purpose. The client may provide the appraiser with information about other potential users of the appraisal, but the appraiser ultimately determines who the appropriate users are given the appraisal problem to be solved. It is necessary for the appraiser to identify the intended users so that the appraiser can report the opinions and conclusions developed in the appraisal in a manner that is clear and understandable to the intended users.

Parties who receive or might receive a copy of the appraisal report are not necessarily intended users. The appraiser's responsibility is to the intended user identified in the report, not to all readers of the appraisal report. The client may request that the intended user not be identified in the report, but the appraiser must still retain that information in the workfile and provide a notice in the report that the identity of the intended user is being withheld upon request.

Intended Use

It is essential that an appraiser identifies the intended user and intended use of an assignment for the determination of the scope of work. That is, the appraiser must identify who needs the services and for what purpose that person or entity will use the information the appraiser provides.

Some intended uses of an appraisal relate to the following:

- Financing
- Litigation

- Condemnation
- Divorce proceedings
- Buy/sell decisions
- Tax reporting
- Portfolio evaluation
- Arbitration
- Partnership value
- Estate value
- Charitable donation
- Valuation for financial reporting

In addition to its critical role in determining the scope of work, the intended use of the appraisal helps the appraiser identify the appropriate level of detail to provide to the intended user. For example, the intended user of an appraisal of the market value of a one-unit house requested for lending purposes is not likely to need the same level of detail that would likely be required by an investor ordering an appraisal of the market value of a suburban office complex to facilitate a buy/sell decision.

> **intended use of the appraisal**
> The appraiser's understanding of how the intended users will employ the information contained in an appraisal report.

Type of Value and its Definition

The type of value (e.g., market value, investment value, use value, and others) appropriate for a specific assignment depends on the nature of the appraisal problem. Likewise, the definition of the type of value used in the assignment may depend on the intended use and user. Market value may be defined differently by government agencies, lenders, and individuals, so a clear statement of the definition of the type of value being appraised helps the intended user of the appraisal better understand the appraiser's conclusions.

In appraisal review and appraisal consulting assignments, where developing an opinion of value is not the purpose of the appraisal, an appraiser still must identify the type of opinion being developed. An appraisal review may lead to an opinion of the quality of another appraiser's work. A consulting assignment may produce one of a broad variety of analyses, recommendations, or conclusions that may involve value.

> **definition of value**
> A statement specifying the type of value to be estimated; must be included in every appraisal report.

Effective Date of the Opinion of Value

Market forces are dynamic, and the appraiser's opinions and conclusions refer to a specific point in time. Given the client's needs and the nature of the assignment, the appraiser must identify the exact date the value opinion would be valid. The effective date of the opinion of value can be a current date, a retrospective (historical) date, or a prospective (future) date.

The date of the opinion of value should not be confused with the date the appraisal report or letter of transmittal is signed. The effective date of the appraisal

date of the opinion of value
The date for which an opinion of value is valid. The sale of a property might be negotiated months or even years before the closing or final disposition of the property. In this case, an adjustment for changes in market conditions between the date the contract is signed and the effective date of value may be appropriate.

effective date
The date at which the analyses, opinions, and advice in an appraisal, review, or consulting service apply..

refers to the point in time as of which the analyses and conclusions are developed for the intended use of the appraisal, not the date on which the report is prepared or delivered to the client.

Relevant Property Characteristics

The subject property is the focus of the appraisal assignment, and a clear understanding of the nature of the real property is a prerequisite for the analyses that follow. The analysis of the subject property must account for characteristics that affect value, i.e., the characteristics affecting the utility that the land and improvements provide.

Some of the most important characteristics relating to value include the following:

- The real property rights being appraised, e.g., the complete fee simple or a partial interest
- Location
- Other physical characteristics, e.g., size, layout, quality of construction
- Economic characteristics, e.g., rent, financing terms

Legal Characteristics

Legal Characteristics for the subject property include land use and zoning regulations. Some of the relevant information will be provided by the client, and some will be researched by the appraiser through interviews with property owners and market participants, firsthand observation of the subject property, and other activities. A complete legal description is commonly used to identify the subject property.

Assignment Conditions

Assignment conditions include extraordinary assumptions, hypothetical conditions, supplemental standards, and jurisdictional exceptions. The nature of the appraisal problem determines whether any of the assumptions or limiting conditions applies to the specific assignment. It is of upmost importance that appraisers disclose information about assumptions and limiting conditions so that the client is not misled by the omission of essential information about the scope of work of the assignment.

An example of an extraordinary assumption refers to an appraisal based on the premise that proposed construction will be completed on the effective date of value, i.e., a prospective date of value. The appraiser assumes that the construction will be completed as planned, but at the time the appraisal is performed, it is not known if that will indeed come to pass.

Hypothetical conditions deal with factors that are known to be false but are presumed to be true for the purposes of the appraisal. For example, if the client wanted to know the value of a proposed development as if it were complete at the current time, the appraisal assignment could be performed under the hypothetical condition that the nonexistent improvements were already in place and ready for use as proposed.

An appraiser may not be able to identify extraordinary assumptions and hypothetical conditions that affect an appraisal until the analysis has actually begun. An effort should still be made to identify possible (or probable) extraordinary assumptions and hypothetical conditions affecting the assignment during the preliminary conversations with the client.

A supplemental standard is a requirement that might apply in assignments for some entities; for example, a government agency could have additional requirements beyond the professional standards to which appraisers must adhere. Jurisdictional exceptions are even rarer, but can affect an appraisal assignment when a relevant law or public policy contradicts professional standards. Where they exist, appraisers must identify supplemental standards and jurisdictional exceptions at the beginning of an appraisal assignment, not after the fact.

SCOPE OF WORK DETERMINATION

Scope of work refers to the type and extent of research and analysis in an assignment. The scope of work applied must be sufficient to result in opinions and conclusions that are credible in the context of the intended use of the appraisal. The appraiser has the burden of proof to support the scope of work decision and the level of information included in a report. The appraiser is responsible for determining the appropriate scope of work in the appraisal assignment.[2] Scope of work for an assignment is acceptable if it leads to credible assignment results, is consistent with the expectations of parties who are regularly intended users for similar assignments, and is consistent with what the actions of the appraiser's peers would be in the same or a similar assignment.

The scope section of the report should reflect the circumstances of each particular assignment. An appraiser must have sound reasons to support the scope of work decisions and must be prepared to support the decision to exclude any information or procedure that would appear to be relevant to the client, an intended user, or the knowledgeable and experienced appraisers.

In the appraisal report, appraisers must clearly disclose the scope of work applied to develop the opinions and conclusions. The scope of work disclosure must be sufficient so that the intended users understand the scope of work performed. The scope of work discussion should address the following topic areas:

> **scope of work**
> The type and extent of research and analyses in an assignment. The undertakings set out under scope of work refer to the due diligence undertaken by the appraiser, including the terms of reference from the client.

> Scope of work for an assignment is acceptable if it leads to credible assignment results, is consistent with the expectations of parties who are regularly intended users for similar assignments, and is consistent with what the actions of the appraiser's peers would be in the same or a similar assignment.

[2] See also CUSPAP Appraisal Standard Comments 7.5, 7.17, and 7.30 and Practise Notes 12.17; also see and Stephanie Coleman, Scope of Work (Chicago: Appraisal Institute, 2006).

- The extent to which the property was identified
- The extent to which the property was inspected
- The type and extent of data researched
- The type and extent of analyses applied

For example, the appraiser may identify easements, covenants, restrictions, and other encumbrances on the subject property based solely on examination of the title report, or the appraiser might investigate each possible encumbrance independently, depending on the extent to which those encumbrances affect the assignment conclusions. The extent of the inspection of the subject and comparable properties can vary as well, from a personal inspection of all properties involved to a "drive-by" inspection (i.e., viewing the exterior of the subject property from the street), again as dictated by the needs of the assignment.

The scope of work discussion must address what was done and what was not done if an intended user might expect that a certain component of the valuation process had been performed. If any of the three approaches to value were excluded, their exclusion must be explained. In addition, if one or more persons provided significant real property appraisal assistance but did not sign the report, their contributions must be explained.

While it is possible to describe the scope of work in various sections of the appraisal report, it is generally best to include a separate section for this topic.

Planning the Appraisal

To complete an assignment quickly and efficiently, an appraiser should plan and schedule each step in the valuation process. Time and personnel requirements will vary with the amount and complexity of the work. While some assignments may be completed in a few days, more complex appraisal problems may take weeks or months gathering, analyzing, and applying all pertinent data.

Some assignments can be performed by a single appraiser, while others require the assistance of other staff members or appraisal specialists. Sometimes an appraiser may require the assistance of specialists in other fields. For example, in valuing a hotel property, the appraiser's findings may be augmented by the professional opinion of a personal property appraiser. Recognizing when work can or must be delegated improves efficiency and enhances accuracy, but appraisers should also be aware of the responsibilities inherent in the use of reports prepared by others (Such concerns are addressed in the Appraisal Institute of Canada's Claim Bulletin CP-05). The appraiser or appraisers signing the certification bear the ultimate responsibility for the assignment; where the work delegated entails significant professional assistance, it must be disclosed in the certification of the report.[3] With a comprehensive view of the assignment, the appraiser can recognize the type and volume of work to be done so that the appraiser can schedule and delegate that work properly.

---

[3]   CUSPAP Appraisal Standard Comments 7.28 and 7.29 requires that at least one appraiser must sign a report; all appraisers signing a report assume responsibility for the entire report, including technical assistance in the form of factual information that an assistant collected. Technical assistance is not significant professional assistance unless it involves analysis, opinions, and conclusions. Professional assistance involves support to the appraiser that has a direct and significant bearing on the outcome of his or her report.

The appraiser's work plan usually includes an outline of the proposed appraisal report. The appraiser delineates the major parts of the report and notes the data and procedures involved in each section. Using this outline, data can be assembled intelligently and the appropriate amount of time can be allocated to each step in the valuation process.

DATA COLLECTION AND PROPERTY DESCRIPTION

Following the preliminary analysis (i.e., the identification of the appraisal problem and determination of the scope of work), the appraiser gathers data on the market area, the subject property, and comparable properties in the market. The data needed by appraisers can be divided into *general data* and *specific data.*

General data includes information about trends[4] in the social, economic, governmental, and environmental forces that affect property value in the defined market area, e.g., trends such as population shifts, declining office building occupancy rates, and increased housing starts in a market area. General data can contribute significantly to an appraiser's understanding of the marketplace.

Specific data relates to the property being appraised and to comparable properties. This data includes legal, physical, locational, cost, and income and expense information about the properties and the details of comparable sales. Financial arrangements that could affect selling prices are also considered.

Data on comparable properties can be either general data that an appraiser has on file or specific data that must be gathered for a particular assignment. More often, comparable property data is specific supply and demand data that relates to the competitive position of properties similar to the subject in its future market. Supply data includes inventories of existing and proposed competitive properties, vacancy rates, and absorption rates. Demand data may consist of population, income, employment, and survey data pertaining to potential property users. This data develops an estimate of future demand for the present or prospective use or uses of the subject property.

The amount and type of data collected for an appraisal depend on the approaches used to develop an opinion of value and on the defined scope of work. In a given valuation assignment, more than one approach to value is usually appropriate and necessary to arrive at a value indication. Depending on the problem or problems to be addressed, one approach may be given greater emphasis in deriving the final opinion of value. In conducting a particular assignment, the appraiser's judgment and experience and the quantity and quality of data available for analysis may determine which approach or approaches are used.

The data collected should be meaningful and relevant. All pertinent value influences, facts, and conclusions about trends should be clearly indicated in the report and related specifically to the property being appraised. Since the data selected forms the basis for the appraiser's judgments, a thorough explanation of the significance of the data reported ensures that the reader will understand these judgments.

---

4   A trend is defined as a momentum or tendency in a general direction brought about by a series of interrelated changes.

DATA ANALYSIS

Once the appropriate data on the market area, subject property, and site has been collected and reviewed for accuracy, the appraiser begins the process of data analysis, which has two components: *market analysis* and *highest and best use analysis*. Even the simplest valuation assignments must be based on a solid understanding of prevalent market conditions and the highest and best use of the real estate. The two forms of analysis are related. In fact, an appraiser's investigation into trends affecting the economic base of the market area leads directly into the determination of highest and best use.

Market Analysis

Market analysis refers to a study of market conditions for a specific type of property. A description of prevalent market conditions helps the reader of an appraisal report understand the motivations of participants in the market for the subject property. Broad market conditions provide the background for local and neighbourhood market influences that have direct bearing on the value of the subject property.

Market analysis, which Chapter 9 discusses in detail, serves two important functions:

- Provides a background against which local developments are considered

- Provides knowledge of the broad changes that affect supply and demand, which gives an appraiser an indication of how values change over time

The data and conclusions generated through market analysis are essential components in other portions of the valuation process. Market analysis yields information needed for each of the three traditional approaches to value. In the cost approach, market analysis provides the basis for adjusting the cost of the subject property for depreciation, i.e., physical deterioration and functional and external obsolescence. In the income approach, all the necessary income, expense, and rate data is evaluated in light of the market forces of supply and demand. In the direct comparison approach, the conclusions of market analysis are used to delineate the market and thereby identify comparable properties.

The extent of market analysis and the level of detail appropriate for a particular assignment depend on the appraisal problem under examination. When appraisers are doing business in a generally stable market on a daily basis, they should have all the necessary demographic and economic information to document market conditions on file. When the appraisal assignment is complex, a more detailed market analysis will be required, e.g., an analysis of the feasibility of a subdivision development. Regardless of the assignment's complexity, the logic of the market analysis should be communicated clearly to the reader in the appraisal report. The level of detail may depend on the report option used.

> Analyses of market conditions and highest and best use are crucial to the valuation process when a market value opinion is the objective of the assignment.

Highest and Best Use Analysis

When a market value opinion is developed, some degree of highest and best use analysis is necessary. If a market value opinion is developed of the land as though vacant, analysis of the highest and best use of the land as though vacant is essential. If a market value opinion is developed for the improved property, analysis of the highest and best use as improved is essential. Through highest and best use analysis, the appraiser interprets the market forces that affect the subject property and identifies the use or uses on which the final opinion of value is based. Chapter 12 discusses highest and best use analysis in detail.

> Analysis of highest and best use may include consideration of both the land as though vacant and the property as improved. The conclusion is specified in terms of use, timing, and market participants.

Analyzing the highest and best use of the land as though vacant helps the appraiser identify comparable properties. Whenever possible, the property being appraised should be compared with similar properties that have been sold recently in the same market. Potentially comparable properties that do not have the same highest and best use are usually eliminated from further analysis. Estimating the land's highest and best use as though vacant is a necessary part of deriving an opinion of land value.

There are two reasons to analyze the highest and best use of the property as improved. The first is to help identify potentially comparable properties. Each improved property should have the same or a similar highest and best use as the improved subject property, as though vacant and as improved. The second reason to analyze the highest and best use of the property as improved is to decide which of the following options should be pursued:

- Maintain the improvements as is
- cure items of deferred maintenance and retain the improvements
- Modify the improvements, e.g., renovate, modernize, or convert
- Demolish the improvements

In some situations, a property may be subject to restrictions that prevent the improvements from being demolished and the property from being developed to its highest and best use, e.g., a heritage covenant that is registered on title.

The highest and best use conclusion should specify the optimal use or uses, when the property will be put to this use or achieve stabilized occupancy, and who would be the most likely purchaser or user of the property, e.g., an owner-operator of the property or an equity or debt investor.

Land Value Opinion

Land value can be a major component of total property value. Appraisers often develop an opinion of land value separately, even when valuing properties with extensive building improvements. Land value and building value may change at different rates because improvements are almost always subject to depreciation. For many appraisals, a separate opinion of land value is required.

Although a total property value estimate may be derived in the direct comparison or income approach without separating land and improvement values, it may be necessary to estimate land value separately to isolate the value the land contributes to the total property. In the cost approach, the value of the land must be estimated and stated separately.

Developing an opinion of land value can be considered a separate step in the valuation model or an essential technique for applying certain approaches to value, depending on the defined appraisal problem as well as highest and best use analysis. The relationship between highest and best use and land value[5] may indicate whether an existing use is the highest and best use of the land.

An appraiser can use several techniques to obtain an indication of land value:

- Direct comparison
- Extraction
- Allocation
- Subdivision development
- Land residual
- Ground rent capitalization

The most common way to estimate land value is by direct comparison. However, when few sales are available or when the value indications produced through direct comparison need additional support, procedures like extraction or allocation may be applied.

The other methods of land valuation, which all involve income capitalization techniques, are subject to more limitations and are used less often in everyday appraisal practice. The subdivision development technique is a specialized valuation method useful in specific land use situations.[6] The land residual technique is used most often in highest and best use analysis to test the feasibility of various uses than to estimate land value as part of one of the traditional approaches to value, and it is a method commonly applied by a developer when evaluating the acquisition of land for a specific development scheme. Ground rent capitalization can be used when land rents and land capitalization rates are readily available, e.g., for appraisals in well-developed areas. Chapter 16 discusses land valuation techniques in detail.

> Of the various techniques that can be applied to estimate land value, direct comparison is usually the most reliable for many assignments.

APPLICATION OF THE APPROACHES TO VALUE

The valuation process is applied to develop a well-supported opinion of a defined value based on an analysis of pertinent general and specific data. Appraisers develop an opinion of property value with specific appraisal procedures that reflect three distinct methods of data analysis:

---

[5]   Appraisers distinguish between land (the earth's surface, both land and water, and anything that is attached to it, whether by the course of nature or by human hands) and a site (land that is improved so that it is ready to be used for a specific purpose). The distinctions between the two terms are discussed more fully in Chapter 10.

[6]   The valuation of subdivisions is discussed more fully in Don Emerson, *Subdivision Valuation* (Chicago: Appraisal Institute, 2008).

- Direct comparison
- Cost
- Income

One or more of these approaches are used in all esti-
mations of value. The approaches employed depend
on the type of property, the intended use of the
appraisal, the applicable scope of work, and the quality and quantity of data available
for analysis.

> One of the three approaches – cost,
> direct comparison, and income –
> may be especially effective in a
> given situation. An appraiser often
> employs more than one approach.

All three approaches are applicable to many appraisal problems, but one or more
of the approaches may have greater significance in a given assignment. For example,
the cost approach might not be applicable in valuing properties with older improvements that suffer substantial depreciation, which might be difficult to estimate. The
direct comparison approach might not be applicable to specialized properties such as
garbage disposal plants because comparable data may not be available. The income
approach is not often used in the valuation of single-unit homes. In addition, the
income approach can be particularly unreliable in the market for commercial or
industrial property where owner-occupants outbid investors. Appraisers should
apply all the approaches that are applicable and for which there is data. The alternative value indications derived can either support or refute one another.

Direct Comparison Approach

The direct comparison approach is most useful when a number of similar properties
have recently been sold or are currently for sale in the subject property's market.
Using this approach, an appraiser produces a value indication by comparing the
subject property with similar properties, called comparable sales. The sale prices of
the properties that are judged most comparable tend to indicate a range in which the
value indication for the subject property will fall.

The appraiser estimates the degree of similarity or difference between the subject
property and the comparable sales by considering various elements of comparison:

- Real property rights conveyed
- Financing terms
- Conditions of sale
- Expenditures made immediately after purchase
- Market conditions
- Location
- Physical characteristics
- Economic characteristics
- Use, zoning, and land use controls
- Non-realty components of value

Appraisers derive an indicated value for the subject property by applying dollar
or percentage adjustments to the known sale price of each comparable property.
Appraisers may also apply qualitative analysis techniques for elements of comparison
for which quantitative adjustments cannot be developed. Through this comparative
procedure, the appraiser renders an opinion of the value that was defined in the
problem identification as of a specific date.

The direct comparison approach can provide an indication of value for either fee simple or leased fee and leasehold interests, depending on what real property rights are represented in the sales of comparable properties.

Income multipliers and capitalization rates may also be extracted through analysis of comparable sales, though these factors are not regarded as elements of comparison in the direct comparison approach. Instead, they are usually applied in the income approach.

Cost Approach

The cost approach is based on the understanding that market participants relate value to cost. In the cost approach, appraisers derive the value of a property by adding the estimated value of the site to the current cost of constructing a reproduction or replacement for the improvements and then subtracting the amount of depreciation (i.e., deterioration and obsolescence) in the structures from all causes. Entrepreneurial profit or incentive may be included in the value indication. This approach is particularly useful in valuing new or nearly new improvements and properties that are not frequently exchanged in the market. Cost approach techniques can also be employed to derive information needed in the direct comparison and income approaches to value, such as the costs to cure items of deferred maintenance.

The current costs to construct the improvements can be obtained from cost estimators, cost manuals, builders, and contractors. Depreciation is measured through market research and the application of specific procedures. Land value is estimated separately in the cost approach.

Typically, the cost approach provides an indication of the value of the fee simple interest. The value indication may need to be adjusted accordingly if a leased fee or other partial interest is being valued.

Income Approach

In the income approach, appraisers measure the present value of the future benefits of property ownership.. A property's income and resale value upon reversion may be capitalized into a current, lump-sum value. There are two methods of income capitalization: direct capitalization and yield capitalization. In direct capitalization, the relationship between one year's income and value is reflected in either a capitalization rate or an income multiplier. In yield capitalization, the relationship between several years' stabilized income and a reversionary value at the end of a designated period is reflected in a yield rate. The most common application of yield capitalization is discounted cash flow analysis. Given the significant differences in how and when properties generate income, there are many variations in both direct and yield capitalization procedures, which are addressed in Chapter 20.

Like the direct comparison and cost approaches, the income approach requires extensive market research. Data collection and analysis for this approach are conducted against a background of supply and demand relationships, which provide information about trends and market anticipation.

The specific data that an appraiser investigates in the income approach might include the property's gross income expectancy, the expected reduction in gross income caused by vacancy and collection loss, the anticipated annual operating expenses, the pattern and duration of the property's income stream, and the anticipated reversionary value. After income and expenses are estimated, the income streams are capitalized by applying an appropriate rate or factor or converted into present value through discounting. In discounted cash flow analysis, the quantity, variability, timing, and duration of a set of periodic incomes and the quantity and timing of the reversion are specified and discounted to a present value at a specified yield rate. The rates used for capitalization or discounting are derived from acceptable rates of return for similar properties.

Like the other approaches to value, the income approach is applicable in the valuation of various property interests. Real property that produces income in the form of rent is usually leased, which creates legal estates of the ownership interests of the lessor and lessee, i.e., the leasehold and leased fee interests. The valuation of the fee simple interest of property that entails one or more leases, which is a common appraisal assignment, may or may not require the valuation of the individual interests.

FINAL RECONCILIATION OF VALUE INDICATIONS

The final analytical step in the valuation process is the *reconciliation* of the value indications derived into a value conclusion. Reconciliation occurs within each approach to value, but the final reconciliation occurs at the end of the valuation process. The nature of reconciliation depends on the appraisal problem, the approaches that have been used, and the reliability and adequacy of the data used.

When an appraisal contains all three approaches, the appraiser examines the three separate indications and considers the relative dependability and applicability of each approach. In the reconciliation section of the report, the appraiser can explain variations among the indications produced by the different approaches and account for differences between the value conclusions and methods applied.

> **reconciliation**
> The last phase of any valuation assignment in which two or more value indications derived from market data are resolved into a final value opinion, which may be either a final range of value or a single point estimate.

The final opinion of defined value, which is the goal of the valuation process, is usually expressed as a single figure. However, it may be expressed as a range of value or as a value in relation to some stated benchmark amount, i.e., more than or less than a given dollar amount.

REPORT OF DEFINED VALUE

An appraisal report is the tangible expression of the appraiser's work. The preparation and delivery of the appraisal report is generally the last step in the valuation process. The report may be communicated to the client in writing or orally. Most reports are written and most clients mandate written reports. To the extent it is both possible and appropriate, each oral real property appraisal report, including expert testimony that addresses value, must comply with professional appraisal standards. Chapter 26 describes the requirements for appraisal reports and the circumstances under which they are prepared and submitted.

The report of the value opinion, which is the last step in the valuation process, addresses the data analyzed, the methods applied, and the reasoning that leads to the value conclusion.

---

final opinion of value

The opinion of value derived from the reconciliation of value indications and stated in the appraisal report; may be expressed as a single point, as a range, or in relation to a benchmark.

report

Any communication, written or oral, of an appraisal, appraisal review, or appraisal consulting service that is transmitted to the client upon completion of an assignment.

CHAPTER 8

DATA COLLECTION

In real estate appraisal, the quality and quantity of information available for analysis are as important as the methods and techniques used to process the data and complete the assignment. Therefore, the ability to distinguish between different kinds of data, to research reliable data sources, and to manage information is essential to appraisal practice.

Dealing with the requisite market, property, and transaction data in the valuation process involves three related processes:

- Data collection
- Data organization
- Data analysis

Appraisers need patience, judgment, and research skills to direct the preliminary steps of data collection and analysis and to gather and manage information efficiently.

Identifying comparable properties and collecting other market data for use in the valuation process was once a time-consuming and expensive process. The growth of data vendors and the increasing accessibility of market data through electronic sources have shifted the historical emphasis of appraisal practice from data collection to analysis. However, collecting accurate, reliable data remains an essential task because the conclusions of appraisers' analyses are only as good as the data that supports them.

> Data collection, organization, and analysis are essential tasks in appraisal.

Uncovering all the necessary data remains a challenge for appraisers, even with technological innovations that facilitate the process. Data collection can be the same or very different from province to province. Many provinces have open property records available to appraisers, but some are non-disclosure provinces where sales data can only be collected from the actual parties to the sale. Also, professional appraisal standards and government programs can require different levels of data collection and documentation. For example, the data required to complete a "desktop" appraisal – where an appraiser does not visit the subject property and completes only preliminary valuation analyses – would be inadequate for a comprehensive appraisal that meets the requirements of Canadian Uniform Standards of Professional Practice (CUSPAP). In order for the appraisal to qualify as a self-contained appraisal under these guidelines, appraisers must obtain and include additional information in the various sections of the report.

Before beginning the process of data collection, the appraiser determines which types of data – general, specific, or competitive supply and demand data – will be useful in the different portions of the valuation process. However, the nature of the data collected is greatly dependent on the property type being appraised and the market conditions within the market area identified by the appraiser. The appraiser communicates the type of data chosen for analysis to the client in the scope of work section of the appraisal report. In many cases, an appraiser collects general data on the demographics of the market area and competitive supply and demand data on competitive properties to perform market analysis. Additional data will be needed for highest and best use analysis, which requires specific data such as information on the physical characteristics of the subject property, zoning restrictions, and the income anticipated from alternative uses. The analysis undertaken in the application of the three approaches to value generally requires both specific data on the subject property, such as cost data for the subject property improvements in the cost approach, and competitive supply and demand data, such as information on comparable sales transactions in the direct comparison approach.

Understanding the content and sources of general and specific appraisal data facilitates data analysis in valuation and appraisal consulting assignments. However, before analyzing the data an appraiser must organize all the specific data accumulated in the investigation. Market data grids, like the cost survey worksheet used in the cost approach, the adjustment grid used in the direct comparison approach, and the reconstructed operating statement used in the income approach, are carefully prepared spreadsheets that provide a tabular representation of market data organized into useful, measurable categories. If the information to be analyzed is complex, the appraiser may need to design several different types of market data grids to isolate and study specific data.

Once the appraiser collects and organizes the data, it can be analyzed to solve the problem posed by the appraisal assignment. Market analysis and highest and best use analysis are the most obvious forms of data analysis, but each of the three approaches to value is also a form of analysis that relies on market data gathered through an inferred or fundamental market analysis as support for the value conclusions derived. The validity of each approach's conclusions and, ultimately, the final opinion of market value depend largely on how well market data can support those conclusions.

In the appraisal report, the analysis must answer the reader's question, "Why is this information relevant?" The analysis should tie the economic and financial data to the real estate market in general and to the particular market in which the real estate being appraised is located. For example, if the appraiser's economic data shows that the rate of employment growth is decreasing, then the appraisal report should illustrate how this will impact the market in general, the type of property specifically, and the particular property being appraised.

TYPES OF DATA

In most appraisal analyses, appraisers will need to gather and examine more than one type of data, including:

- General data
- Specific data
- Competitive supply and demand data

Appraisers obtain this data from either primary or secondary sources. General data, which does not relate directly to the subject property, is usually acquired through secondary sources such as Statistics Canada publications, provincial and local government agencies, and private demographic data services. In other words, secondary data is information that has not been personally confirmed by the appraiser. Specific data and competitive supply and demand data, which deal with the subject property and comparable properties in the subject market, are most often obtained by appraisers themselves and therefore qualify as primary data.

General Data

An appraiser working in a specific market on a daily basis will often have general data on file. General data consists of information about the social, economic, governmental, and environmental forces that affect property value. This information is part of the background knowledge that appraisers bring to their assignments. All general data is ultimately understood in terms of how it affects the economic climate in which real property transactions occur. General data is most frequently used in the analysis of a region or city and to a lesser degree in the analysis of a smaller market area. In analyzing general data, appraisers observe the operation of appraisal principles by studying the interaction of the four forces that affect an area's property values. Although the four forces provide convenient categories for examining general data, it is the interaction of those forces that creates trends and ultimately influences property value.

> **general data**
> Items of information on value influences that derive from social, economic, governmental, and environmental forces and originate outside the property being appraised.
>
> **specific data**
> Details about the property being appraised, comparable sale and rental properties, and relevant local market characteristics.

Economic Trends

Appraisers must recognize and understand the economic trends that affect the value of real property. It is not enough to know that economic changes have occurred; the probable direction, extent, impact, and cause of these changes must also be studied to identify and forecast trends.

The particular trends considered by an appraiser vary with the appraisal problem and the type of real estate being appraised. For example, to develop an opinion of the market value of a shopping centre with the income approach to value, the appraiser

Table 8.1: Economic Trends and Useful Economic Indicators

Trends	Useful Economic Indicators
International economic trends	Changes in: • Balance of foreign trade • Rates of foreign exchange • Commodity price levels • Wage levels • Interest rates • Industrial production levels • Volume of retail sales
National and regional economic trends	Changes in: • Gross national product • Gross domestic product • National income • The balance of payments to other nations • Price level indexes • Interest rates • Aggregate employment and unemployment statistics • The number of housing starts and building permits issued • The dollar volume of construction • Other general data Note: A time series of economic indicators, which describes and measures changes or movements over a period of time, may reveal fluctuations in long-term trends and help put current statistics in perspective, i.e., help determine the current position of the economic cycle.
Local economic trends	Changes in: • Population • Net household formation • The diversity of the economic base of the community • The level and stability of employment • Wage rates • Household or family income
Economic trends affecting rural land	Changes in: • Size and complexity of business operations in farming, ranching, timber-harvesting, rilling, or mining • Level of mechanization or labour-intensiveness • Degree of dependence on government subsidies or government-leased lands • Prospective competition from imports

must forecast the base rent and overage rent under a percentage lease.[1] The shopping centre's total potential gross income depends on trends in the number of households in the trade area, the income of these households, and their typical expenditures on the goods and services supplied by the centre's tenants. The availability of alternative shopping facilities also must be considered. Table 8.1 lists useful economic indicators appraisers often track to analyze trends in the marketplace.

International Economic Trends

In the global economy, the economic well-being of one nation may directly and indirectly affect other nations. There is much foreign investment in Canadian real estate, partly because the stability of the Canadian government gives foreign investors some measure of protection. As a result, political instability in other countries can influence the demand for, and value of, real estate in Canada.

International economic trends can have significant effects on local economies and specific real estate markets. For example, the status of the Asian economy can affect the level of international trade, which in turn has a major impact on the economy of Pacific Rim port cities (and perhaps the demand for warehouse space). Increasingly, trends in international financing can influence local real estate markets as well. In the 1980s, using financing techniques unavailable to American investors, Japanese investors could pay inflated prices for prestigious properties in Hawaii and California, including most of the luxury hotel rooms in Hawaii. At the time, real estate appraisers in Hawaii had to provide two different values reflecting the influence of Japanese investment practices (often without the benefit of a pro forma statement, lease analysis, or market study) and traditional US lending practices. The collapse of the Japanese economy, due in part to bad loans made by Japanese banks, eventually caused prices in the Hawaiian real estate market to plunge, with Japanese investors losing billions of dollars on their investments.

National and Regional Economic Trends

The state of the national economy is basic to any real estate appraisal. Financial institutions must compete for funds to lend, not only with one another, but also with money market mutual funds. Lending rates reflect this ongoing competition, and demand in the market adjusts itself accordingly.

Federal programs and tax policies can affect the value of real estate. Reforms made in 1972 to the Income Tax Act made gains in the value of investment real estate in Canada taxable; before that, such capital gains were free of tax. Further reforms at the same time prevented rental investors from claiming depreciation charges (called capital cost allowances, or CCA) as deductions against income from other sources. These changes had a far-reaching effect on the value of investment-grade properties. Due in part to the tax advantages available prior to 1970, some real estate markets had been overbuilt. After the tax law was changed, the oversupply was recognized and values in these markets declined significantly.

The national economy also reflects the economic condition of the various geographic regions of Canada. The economic health of a region depends on the

---

[1]   See Chapter 21 for the definitions of percentage lease, base rent, and overage rent.

status of its economic activity, which in turn encompasses the economic activities in individual areas and communities within the region's geographic boundaries. Minor disruptions in the economic growth of one community may not appreciably affect the entire region if the regional and national economies are strong.

The extent to which an appraiser is concerned with the national or regional economy and the economy of the city or market area depends on the size and type of property being appraised. For example, a large regional shopping centre that serves a trade area of 500,000 people and an automobile assembly plant that employs 5,000 workers are more sensitive to the general state of the economy than are medical-dental office buildings or retail service operations in suburban residential areas.

Local Market Considerations

To understand how national and even international economic trends influence property value, an appraiser studies how the region and community where the subject property is located may respond to these trends. The appraiser should examine the economic structure of the region and the community, the comparative advantages that each possesses, and the attitudes of local government and residents toward growth and change. For example, the increasing number of elderly house-holds in the nation is less significant to property values in Ottawa than to values in Victoria or Kelowna, BC, which attract more retirees. A community with a no-growth policy may have substantially different local demographics and economic potential than one that does not discourage growth.

Regional economies influence local market conditions, but local markets do not necessarily parallel regional markets. Macroeconomic studies, which are concerned with broad areas such as cities and regions, are important to understanding real estate and real estate trends. These studies should not be confused with microeconomic studies, which appraisers perform to evaluate the factors influencing the market value of a particular real estate parcel. For example, regional trends may suggest an expected increase in population, but the local data available to the appraiser may indicate that the particular area will not benefit from this trend. While both studies are important, local trends are more likely to influence property values directly.

Trends Affecting Rural Land

Appraisers of rural land should understand the links between the local rural economy, the regional economic base (agricultural, extractive, or recreational), and the national economy as well as the encroachment of suburban and urban land uses on rural land. The subject property should be analyzed in relation to comparable properties in the immediate agricultural, mining/drilling/extraction, or recreational district.

Climatic data can be important in analyzing many rural land uses. A drought in a grain-producing area or icy conditions in a fruit-growing region can have economic repercussions beyond disrupting local agricultural production. Tourism and recreational uses of rural land may be affected by the severe weather, and restaurants and hotels in the region may be forced to raise prices to keep up with the rising cost of food.[2]

Demographics

The population of a market and its geographic distribution are basic determinants of the need for real estate. Real estate improvements are provided in response to the demand generated by a population with effective purchasing power. A *household* – i.e., persons who occupy a group of rooms or a single room that constitutes one housing unit – imposes a basic demand for housing units. In analyzing a local housing market, it is crucial that appraisers have knowledge of trends in the formation of households and household characteristics. The age, size, income, and other characteristics of households must be considered to determine the demand for housing.

Two demographic categories generate demand for two different types of space:

- Households generate demand for space designed to fulfill basic human needs such as housing, retail, and medical services.

- Employment generates demand for space used in producing goods and services such as warehouse, industrial, office, and retail space.

Often households and employees generate demand for the same type of space, such as medical research and development space.

The demand for commercial and industrial real estate is created by a population's demand for the goods and services to be produced or distributed at these sites. Appraisers must be aware of changes in the characteristics and distribution of the population that consumes goods and services as well as changes in the work force that produces them. A changing population, coupled with technological advances, can rapidly alter the demand for the services provided by property, which can affect property value. Chapter 9 discusses economic base analysis and how appraisers use employment data to estimate supply and demand.

> **household**
> A number of related or unrelated persons who live in one housing unit; all the persons occupying a group of rooms or a single room that constitutes one housing unit. A single person, a couple, or more than one family living in a single housing unit may make up a household.

Government Regulations

To properly develop an opinion of value, the appraiser should understand the government regulations and actions that affect the subject property. The comparable properties selected for analysis should be similar to the subject property in terms of zoning and other characteristics.

In response to social attitudes, the government establishes land use regulations and provides public services such as transportation systems and municipal utilities. Information on zoning, master plans, environmental impacts, transportation systems,

---

[2] For further discussion of trends affecting rural property, see *The Appraisal of Rural Property*, 2nd ed. (Denver and Chicago: American Society of Farm Managers and Rural Appraisers and Appraisal Institute, 2000).

local annexation policies, and other regulations reveals governmental and social attitudes toward real estate.

Canadian governments have passed a variety of laws that affect rural and other land. Private property rights are not entrenched, and governments can take away private property rights, through enactment of zoning and other laws, without consultation or compensation. For example, many provinces discourage conversion of farmland to alternative uses, preferring to encourage soil-based agriculture. These policies can affect the utility, investment appeal, and thus the value of agricultural lands. A variety of laws also constrain forested lands and in Prince Edward Island, laws limit ownership of real estate by non-residents.

Trends in Building Activity

A property's value as of a specific date may rise or fall due to fluctuations in building activity. Housing starts and the construction of commercial and industrial properties fluctuate in response to business cycles, political events, and the cost and availability of financing. These fluctuations follow the long-term trend of new construction. Short-term fluctuations result in temporary misallocations of supply, which can depress rents and prices.

The standing stock of housing units at any point in time consists of all units, occupied and vacant. The stock is continually altered by the construction or conversion of units in response to developers' perceptions of the demand for new housing and by the need to replace existing units.

Six months to two years may pass between the time a developer decides to supply units and the time those units enter the market. During this period, changing conditions may reduce demand, and the units coming on the market may remain unrented and unsold, thus increasing vacancy rates. Developers may continue to produce additional units for some time, even in the face of rising vacancies. Once these excess units are produced, they remain on the market and can depress rents or prices until demand increases to remove the surplus. When the market tightens, the supply of units lags behind the increase in demand, resulting in abnormally low vacancy rates and upward pressure on rents and prices. Ultimately, supply materializes as developers respond to increased demand.

Fluctuations in the local supply of and demand for real estate (i.e., the life cycle of the market area) are influenced by regional and national conditions. Therefore, an appraiser looks for regional and national trends that may indicate a positive or negative change in property values at the local level. Although not all regions may experience the same slump in construction, tight monetary policy affects the cost and availability of mortgage credit and exerts a moderating influence on supply, even in a rapidly growing region.

Commercial real estate is affected by business conditions and the cost and availability of financing. Since business firms pass their high financing costs on to consumers, residential construction may be restricted. If the demand for the goods and services produced or supplied by a business remains strong, the firm can raise prices and continue to expand even when credit is tight and interest rates are high.

Building Costs

The cost of replacing a building tends to follow the general price levels established over a long period, but these price levels vary from time to time and from place to place. Building costs generally decline or stabilize in periods of deflation and increase in periods of inflation. These costs are affected by material and labour costs, construction technology, architect and legal fees, financing costs, government development levies and extractions, building codes, and public regulations such as zoning ordinances, environmental requirements, and subdivision regulations.

Construction costs can alter the quantity and character of demand and, therefore, the relative prices of property in real estate submarkets. The high cost of new buildings increases the demand for, and prices of, existing structures. When the cost of new structures increases, rehabilitation of existing buildings may become economically feasible. High building costs increase prices in single-unit residential submarkets, which can increase the demand for rental units and their prices. The size and quality of the dwelling units demanded decrease when building costs increase more rapidly than purchasing power.

Cost services, such as Marshall & Swift, R.S. Means, and others, are the primary sources of information on building costs. Appraisers can also collect information on building costs from properties that have been developed in a market area. Chapter 18 discusses building cost estimates in more detail.

Taxes

Local governments (cities, townships, municipalities, and counties) and taxing authorities, (i.e., school, fire, water, library, local improvement district) can levy property taxes. The taxing body reviews the annual budget to determine the amount of money that needs to be raised. After revenues from other sources (such as development taxes, licensing and user fees, provincial or federal revenue sharing, and interest on investments) are deducted, the remaining funds must come from property taxes. Assessing officers estimate the value of each parcel of real estate in the jurisdiction periodically. Real estate taxes are based on the assessed value of real property, hence the term *ad valorem* ("according to value") taxes. The assessed value of property is normally based on, but not necessarily equivalent to, its market value.

The ratio of assessed value to market value is called the *common level ratio* or *assessment ratio*. If, for example, the tax rate is $60 per $1,000 of assessed value and the assessment ratio is 50%, then the annual real estate tax (or effective tax rate) equals 3% of market value:

$$\$60 \div \$1,000 \times 50\% = 3\%$$

If assessed value is not based on market value, the formula is modified to reflect the difference. An effective tax rate can also be calculated by dividing the total amount of taxes by the market value of the property. Effective tax rates can be used to compare the tax burden on properties.

In jurisdictions where ad valorem real estate tawx assessments have an established or implied relationship to market value, appraisal services may be required to resolve property assessment appeals. In some communities, the trend in real estate taxes is an important consideration. In cities where public expenditures for schools and municipal services have increased, a heavy tax burden can cause real estate values to decline. Under these circumstances, new construction may be discouraged. There may be several tax districts in a metropolitan area, each with a different policy. Understanding the system of ad valorem taxation in an area facilitates the appraiser's analysis of how taxes affect value.

Different levels of sales taxes, personal property taxes, and taxes on earnings can also affect the relative desirability of properties. Although these taxes may be uniform within a province, properties in different provinces often compete with one another. To attract new residents and industries, a province may impose taxes that are lower than those of surrounding provinces; this may increase demand and enhance property values in the province relative to values in bordering provinces. For example, consider two adjacent provinces competing for the location of a commercial printing operation. The printing company owns machinery and equipment worth millions of dollars that may be taxed as personal property rather than real property, which is more often the case for industrial operations than for commercial operations. The province that does not have a personal property tax would be a more attractive location than the province that levies a personal property tax.

Financing

The cost of financing includes the interest rate and any points, discounts, equity participations, or other charges that the lender requires to increase the effective yield on the loan. Financing depends on the borrower's ability to qualify for a loan, which may be determined by the loan-to-value ratio, the housing expense-to-income ratio allowed for loans on single-unit homes, the amortization period, and the debt coverage and break-even ratios required for loans on income-producing properties (Chapter 22 discusses these ratios). The cost and availability of financing typically have an inverse relationship. High interest rates and other costs are usually accompanied by a decrease in the demand for credit and the number of borrowers able to qualify.

The cost and availability of credit for real estate financing influence both the quantity and quality of the real estate demanded and supplied. When interest rates are high or mortgage funds are limited, households that would have been in the home ownership market find that their incomes cannot support the required expenses. Individuals delay purchases and buy smaller homes with fewer amenities. The cost of land development financing and construction financing is reflected in the higher prices asked for new single-unit homes, and higher prices reduce the quantity of homes demanded.

The rental market is affected by the demand pressure of households that continue to rent and by the high cost of supplying new units, which results in part from financing costs. Occupancy rates and rents rise. Businesses try to pass on their higher occupancy costs to customers by increasing the prices of their products or services.

If businesses cannot fully recover the increased occupancy cost, the value of these properties will decline or the quantity of commercial and individual space supplied is reduced.

Specific Data

Specific data includes details about the property being appraised, comparable sales and rental properties, and relevant local market characteristics. In appraisals, this data is used to determine highest and best use and to make the specific comparisons and analyses required to develop an opinion of market value. The specific data about a subject property provided in land and building descriptions helps the appraiser select specific data pertaining to comparable sales, rentals, construction costs, and local market characteristics.

In analyzing general data, an appraiser emphasizes national, regional, and local trends in value. In an analysis of specific data, an appraiser studies the characteristics of the subject property and comparable properties. At the conclusion of the general data analysis, the appraiser needs to spell out clearly what this data and analysis means or implies for the specific market and property being valued. It is the same process used in gathering comparable sales data, analyzing it, and indicating what it means in relation to an opinion of value for the subject property. From relevant comparable sales, an appraiser extracts

> Specific data comprises information on the subject property, comparable properties, and market transactions.

specific sale prices, rental terms, income and expense figures, rates of return on investment, construction costs, estimates of the economic life of improvements, and rates of depreciation. These figures are used in calculations that lead to an indication of value for the subject property.

An appraiser needs specific data to apply each of the three approaches to value. The appraiser uses the data to derive adjustments for value-influencing property characteristics, to isolate meaningful units of comparison, to develop capitalization rates, and to measure depreciation. By extracting relevant data from the largest quantity of data available, an appraiser develops a sense of the market. This perception is an essential component of appraisal judgment, which is applied in the valuation process and in the final reconciliation of value indications.

The appraiser analyzes specific data through comparison. In each approach to value, certain items of information must be extracted from market data to make comparisons. Specific data is studied to determine if these items are present or absent and if they can be used to make reliable comparisons with the subject property. Such specific data can include information about properties that have sold as well as properties that have not sold. If, for example, the subject property is an apartment building, the appraiser could use sales of other apartment buildings to support adjustments for changes in market conditions, locational differences, or the contribution of various physical characteristics. An appraiser can also use apartment buildings that have not sold in order to obtain information on rental rates and expenses.

The appraiser's analysis of the highest and best use of the land as though vacant and the property as improved determines what comparable specific data is collected and analyzed. The comparable properties must have the same highest and best use as the subject property. The nature and amount of research needed for a specific assignment depend on the property type, the purpose of the appraisal, and the complexity of the required analysis.

Competitive Supply and Demand Data

The valuation process requires that a property be appraised within the context of its market. Of particular significance to the analysis are the supply of competitive properties, the future demand for the property being appraised, and its highest and best use. After inspecting the subject property and gathering property-specific data, the appraiser inventories the supply of properties that constitute the major competition for the property in its defined market.

Competitive Supply Inventory

The supply inventory includes all competitive properties:

- Rental units
- Properties that have been sold
- Properties being offered for sale
- Properties under construction
- Proposed properties

The subject property will have to be able to compete in a future market. Therefore, the appraiser's investigation must cover not only existing competition, but also prospective projects that will compete with the subject.

Demand Study

Along with the supply inventory of major competitive properties, the appraiser analyzes the prospective demand for the subject property. The appraiser cannot assume the current use is necessarily the use for which the most demand will exist in the future. Even in the most stable markets, subtle shifts in the market appeal or utility of a category of properties can put some properties at a competitive disadvantage and benefit others. Even in volatile markets characterized by rapid changes due to factors such as accelerating growth, precipitous decline, or an upturn in proposed construction, appraisers need to quantify demand in some manner.

The specific techniques applied to study market demand can be highly sophisticated and may fall outside the scope of normal appraisal practice. In some cases, the appraiser might use data compiled by special market research firms (proprietary data) to supplement the appraisal. However, all appraisers should develop an understanding of market research techniques and acquire the skills needed to conduct basic demand studies. Chapter 9 discusses market research and analysis techniques in more detail.

DATA COLLECTION

The scope of work of an appraisal assignment includes consideration of the extent of the data collection process. If the assignment is simple, the appraiser may rely on general data on file and specific data about the subject and comparable properties. For a complex assignment, the data collection process may be much more difficult.

Sources of General Data

The general data needed to appraise real property is available from a wide variety of sources. A substantial amount of information is compiled and disseminated by federal, provincial, and local agencies. Trade associations and private business enterprises may also provide data. Table 8.2 lists some common sources of general data.

General data is an integral part of an appraiser's office files. Data obtained from various sources can be catalogued and cross-indexed. General data such as multiple listing information and census data can be accessed by computer. In addition to Statistics Canada and the provincial and territorial government's statistical offices, many local and regional planning and development agencies computerize the following information by geographic area:

> Sources of general data include federal government publications, provincial and local government offices, trade associations, and private research firms.

- Housing inventory and vacancies
- Demolitions and conversions
- Commercial construction
- Household incomes
- New land use by zoning classification
- Population and demographics
- Housing forecasts

In recent years, many databases have been developed for online access to information. Such databases cover a broad range of topics and offer many options to appraisers performing general or specialized research. The information available is virtually unlimited and includes topics such as the following:

- Current and historical news
- Industry analyses and reports
- Corporate earnings and analyses
- Local, regional, and national internet listings
- Publication indexes and articles

Developments in computer software and hardware have resulted in low-cost, high-performance database combinations for appraisers. Hundreds of individual programs are now used with desktop systems in appraisal offices. Some databases are contained in a single computer, while others are shared by several computers or terminals through local or telecommunication networks. Improvements

Table 8.2: Commonly Used Sources of General Data

Statistics Canada

Publications	*The Daily* *Canadian Social Trends* *Households and the Environment* *Insights on the Canadian Economy*
Information Available	• Current and historical population and distribution • Population estimates • Income • Labour statistics • Total output, income, and spending • Employment, unemployment, and wages • Production and business activity • Labour force, employment, and industrial production • Housing and construction • Prices • Tourism • Income trends • Environmental matters
Where To Find It	*www.statcan.gc.ca*

Bank of Canada

Publications	The Bank in Brief Annual Report Bank of Canada Review Monetary Policy Report Weekly Financial Statistics
Information Available	Gross national product Gross domestic product National income Mortgage markets Interest rates Instalment credit Sources of funds Business activity Money, credit, and security markets Federal finance International statistics International finance
Where To Find It	*www.bank-banque-canada.ca*

Provincial and local departments of development, local and regional planning agencies, provincial statistics agencies, and regional or metropolitan transportation authorities

Information Available	• Population • Households • Employment • Master plans • Present and future utility • Transportation systems

Table 8.2: Commonly Used Sources of General Data (continued)

Chambers of Commerce and Boards of Trade

Information Available	Information, often obtained from secondary sources such as the census, on

- Local population
- Local business
- Local issues, particularly of a business nature
- Employment
- Industry

Where to Find It	www.chamber.ca

National Brokerages. National commercial brokerages publish national, regional, and select city data on office, retail, and industrial markets

Information Available	Information on national, regional, and select data on office, retail and industrial markets

- Inventory and Supply
- Absorption
- Rents
- Rates of Return
- Vacancy Rates
- Key transactions and developments

Associations of Real Estate Professionals

Where to find it   *www.colliers.com*
www.cushwake.com
www.cbre.ca
www.dtzbarnicke.com
www.avisonyoung.com

Publications   Many publications with data useful to appraisers

- *Canadian Property Valuation*
- *REM - Real Estate Magazine*
- *Journal of Real Estate Research*
- *Valuation Insights & Perspectives*
- *Real Estate Value Cycles*
- *BOMA International/Cushman & Wakefield Market Intelligence Report*
- *BOMA Experience Exchange Report*
- *Real Estate Issues*
- *Assessment Journal*
- *Ratio Study Practices*
- *The National Association of Realtors Commercial Real Estate Quarterly*
- *National Real Estate Review: Market Conditions Report*

Where to Find It

Appraisal Institute of Canada	*www.aicanada.ca*
Canadian Real Estate Association	*www.crea.ca*
American Real Estate Society (ARES)	*www.aresnet.org*
American Society of Appraisers (ASA)	*www.appraisers.org*
American Society of Farm Managers and Rural Appraisers (ASFMRA)	*www.asfmra.com*
Appraisal Institute	*www.appraisalinstitute.org*

Table 8.2: Commonly Used Sources of General Data (continued)

Building Owners and Managers Association (BOMA)	www.boma.org
Counsellors of Real Estate	www.cre.org
International Association of Assessing Officers (IAAO)	www.iaao.org
Risk Manager's Association	www.rmahq.org
Mortgage Bankers Association of America (MBA)	www.mbaa.org
Urban Land Institute (ULI)	www.uli.org
National Association of Realtors® and its affiliates	

Homebuilders Associations

Publications	Canadian Homebuilders Association:	The National (www.chba.ca)
	National Association of Homebuilders:	Sales and Marketing Management Magazine
		Survey of Buying Power

Chambers of Commerce and Boards of Trade

Information Available	Information, often obtained from secondary sources such as the census, on
	• Local population
	• Local business
	• Local issues, particularly of a business nature
	• Employment
	• Industry
Where to Find It	www.chamber.ca

Private sources such as banks, utility companies, university research centres, private advisory firms, multiple listing services, cost data services

Publications	White papers and research reports
Information Available	• Bank debt
	• Department store sales
	• Employment indicators
	• Land prices
	• Corporate business indicators
	• Mortgage money costs
	• Wage rates
	• Construction costs
	• Deeds and Titles
	• Mortgage recordings
	• The installation of utility meters
Where To Find It	Internet search on key words and market names

in telecommunication programs and facilities, word processing, and electronic spreadsheets have facilitated appraisal analysis and report writing as has the use of database information.[3]

---

[3] For further information on databases and electronic commerce, see Bennie D. Waller, "Electronic Data Interchange and Electronic Commerce: The Future of Appraising", *The Appraisal Journal* (October 1999): 370-374; Phill Britt, "E-Commerce and the Rise of Big Box", *Valuation Insights & Perspectives* (2003 Q4), Appraisal Institute; Gordon Jenkins and Ray Lancashire, *The Electronic Commerce Handbook: A Quick Read on How Electronic Commerce Can Keep You Competitive* (Etobicoke, Ontario, Canada: EDI Council of Canada, 1994); and Richard D. Wincott, "Addressing Electronic Commerce, Impact of Capital Markets in the Real Estate Industry, and Changes in Appraisal Licensing Regulations", *The Appraisal Journal* (July 1999): 313-314.

Sources of Specific Data

Like sources of general data, sources of specific data are diverse. In addition to the data obtained from public records and published sources, personal contact with developers, builders, brokers, financial and legal specialists, property managers, local planners, and other real estate professionals can provide useful information. Thus, practicing appraisers need communication skills as well as analytical techniques to research sales, improvement costs, and income and expense data thoroughly in the process of performing appraisal assignments.

> Sources of specific data include public records (e.g., deeds, title transfers, recorded leases), newspapers and internet sales facilities (e.g., advertised sale prices and rentals), multiple listing services, cost-estimating manuals, and market participants such as brokers, lenders, contractors, owners, and tenants.

Public Records

The appraiser searches public records for a copy of the property deed or title transfer documents for the subject or comparable properties as needed. In some jurisdictions, public property records can be searched electronically. The deed or title transfer provides important information about the property and the sales transaction, including the full names of the parties involved and the transaction date, a legal description of the property, the property rights included in the transaction, and any encumbrances, notices, and outstanding liens on the title.

Occasionally the names of the parties may raise a concern that unusual motivations were involved in the sale. For example, a sale from John Smith to Mary Smith Jones may be a transfer from a father to a daughter. A sale from John Smith, William Jones, and Harold Long to the SJL Corporation may be a change of ownership in name only, not an arm's-length transaction arrived at by unrelated parties under no undue pressure or duress.

In some provinces, the law requires that the consideration paid (money or other) upon transfer of title be shown on the transfer document. However, this consideration does not always reflect the actual sale price. To reduce transfer taxes, some purchasers, such as buyers of motels or apartments, deduct the estimated value of personal property from the true consideration paid. Because these personal property values are sometimes inflated, the recorded consideration for the real property may be less than the actual consideration. In one situation, the consideration indicated on the transfer may be overstated to obtain a higher loan than is warranted; in another, the consideration may be understated to justify a low property tax assessment. Although some provinces require that the actual consideration be listed on the transfer, other provinces – i.e., non-disclosure provinces – allow the consideration to be reported as "$10 and other valuable consideration."

The local tax assessor's records may include property cards for the subject property and comparables properties, with land and building sketches, area measurements, sale prices, and other information. This information is often available subject to administrative and privacy restraints. In some locations, legal or private data services issue information about current property transfers.

Listings and Offerings

Whenever possible, an appraiser should gather information about properties offered for sale. An appraiser can request to be added to the distribution lists of brokers and others who offer properties for sale. Classified ads and internet listings of listed properties suggest the strength or weakness of the local market for a particular type of property and the sales activity in a particular area. Information on purchase offers may also be obtained from brokers or managers. *Listings*, which represent the owner's perception of the property's value, usually reflect the upper limit of value. *Offers*, which represent the buyer's perspective, commonly set the lower limit of value.

Listings and offerings can be useful indicators of the values anticipated by sellers and buyers and reflect the likely turnover of competitive properties. Listings are usually set at a level that will excite market interest and therefore may be employed to test market activity; they are relevant market phenomena that the appraiser considers in analyzing competitive supply and demand. The appraiser may find that tabulating information about competitive properties in a market data grid facilitates comparing the market position of the subject property to that of the competition.

> **listing**
> A written contract in which an owner employs a broker to sell his or her real estate.
>
> **offering**
> A set of terms presented by the bidder, a prospective buyer or tenant, that are subject to negotiation. If the other party, a seller or landlord, accepts these terms, the offer will result in a contract.

In many communities, the local real estate board maintains electronic databases of listings, which are known as multiple listing services (MLS). These sources primarily contain data on residential properties listed for sale during the calendar year or fiscal quarter and cite their listing prices. They contain fairly complete information about these properties, including descriptions and brokers' names. However, details about a property's square footage, basement area, or exact age may be inaccurate or excluded. Many appraisers become members of the local real estate board as a way to obtain the more comprehensive MLS information available to board members and salespersons. Only a small percentage of commercial, industrial, or special-purpose properties are included in traditional MLS books, so appraisers must investigate other databases, often those of a commercial Board of Realtors.

The national MLS landscape is in a state of flux, as new business models challenge the historical domination of property data by local MLS organizations, which have previously controlled the dissemination of information relating to sales, listings, pending sales, and withdrawn sales. There have been some mergers and consolidation of MLS organizations to address overlapping territories and to make operations more efficient.

In recent years, large national brokerage companies have aggregated a variety of disparate data in a national footprint and made this information available to consumers. However, competition among aggregators to amass the largest number of listings may lead to poor quality data, i.e., institutional emphasis on quality control increases the likelihood of duplicates, dated information, and incorrect information in the databases. Commercial enterprises have partnered with some provincial assessment agencies to make data on property and transactions available, at a cost. These entities make it possible to obtain inventory data on properties that have sold and on general property characteristics in an identifiable subset, even if no trades have occurred.

The potential for misuse of pooled data is a concern. Ensuring the confidentiality of certain information in real property transactions is a continuously evolving issue. Both the Canadian Uniform Standards of Professional Appraisal Practice and federal legislation such as the *Personal Information Protection and Electronic Documents Act* (PIPEDA), federal legislation made in 2000, set forth privacy regulations regarding confidential information. Certain shared databases allow for restricted access to certain fields within data records deemed confidential by the contributor of the data; other databases only pool data that is not considered confidential.

THE NATIONAL DATA STANDARD (NDS) AND REAL ESTATE TRANSACTION STANDARD (RETS) OF CANADIAN REAL ESTATE BOARDS

The development and implementation of data standards is well underway in North America. The National Data Standard (NDS) is the internal standard of the Canadian Real Estate Association, and is used by almost all boards across the country to provide it data. NDS data is usually not made available to non-members. The Real Estate Transaction Standard (RETS) for real estate data providers is another standard that is in common use in Canada; it too is used internally by the Boards, and available only to members. These standards are expected to supersede the electronic data interchange (EDI) efforts of the 1980s and 1990s and facilitate data transfer between partners in the real estate industry. Creating and improving RETS is a collaborative effort of real estate brokers, franchises, associations, and their technology partners [e.g., MLS vendors, Internet Data Exchange (IDX) vendors, transaction management and electronic forms vendors], and others to simplify moving real estate information from system to system and simplify solution development efforts. For example, as NDS and RETS usage matures and expands, multiple listing services with geographic overlaps will be able to create data-sharing policies that provide their members with a single point of entry to search multiple MLS data sets. The goal of RETS is to create standards that provide brokers efficient control over their listing data. With the adoption of a single standard across the industry, brokers will be able to enter listings once and deliver them when and where they want, including national property databases. A standardized data format will also increase the accuracy and timeliness of data by eliminating duplication and avoiding the cost and time involved in converting data into different formats.

It is national policy across North America that all MLS providers adopt either NDS or RETS; however the vast majority of MLS providers already support RETS and this new MLS policy.

The significance of these standards for appraisers is that NDS and RETS provide a common basis for extracting data from MLS sources without the need for data input.

A broad based organization of real estate information, Open Standards Consortium for Real Estate (OSCRE), have developed data standards that allow different systems to communicate directly. The standards are a contextualized set of definitions and rules that facilitate the automatic transfer of data between different software packages.

For further information, see www.reso.org and *www.oscre.org*

Published News

Most city newspapers feature real estate news, and many business trade publications cover real estate activity on a local, regional, or national basis. Although some of the news may be incomplete or inaccurate, an appraiser can use this secondary source to confirm details because the names of the negotiating brokers and the parties to transactions are usually published.

Market Participants

Other real estate professionals such as brokers, appraisers, managers, and bankers can often provide information about transactions and suggest valuable leads. Individual sources may be definitive, but if the information obtained from real estate professionals is third-party data, the appraiser should look for separate verification.

Sources of Competitive Supply and Demand Data

A competitive supply inventory is compiled in several steps:

1. The appraiser first conducts a field inspection to inventory competitive properties in the subject market area and competitive market areas.

2. The appraiser then can interview owners, managers, and brokers of competitive properties in the area as well as developers and city planners. Field inspection and interviews are especially important because investors rely heavily on local competitive supply and demand analyses.

3. An examination of building permits (both issued and acted upon), plat (subdivision) maps, and surveys of competitive sites provides insight into prospective supply.

4. Data on available space, as well as vacancy, absorption, and turnover rates in specific property markets, can be obtained from electronic databases and reports prepared by real estate research firms.

Demand can be estimated using demographic data (population and vital statistics) and economic data (employment and income statistics) for the market area. Statistics Canada and a variety of provincial and local agencies compile and publish statistical data, which is often also available in electronic form. Other private and public sources provide historical data and projections based on small area populations. Appraisers who rely on projections prepared by market research firms should have a clear understanding of the methodology used to make the projection. Otherwise, the data may represent little more than a blind data set. To test the reasonableness of small area projections, comparisons should be made between the demographic data and the supply data collected in the specified market. Supply data may include building permits and market sales or absorption rates kept by public agencies such as building inspection, city planning, and public works departments.

> Sources of competitive supply and demand data include field inspections, interviews with market participants, building permits and plat maps, proprietary data, and demographic and economic data compiled by Statistics Canada, Canada Mortgage and Housing Corporation, and other public agencies.

Personal observation is also useful in estimating local demand. For example, the planned closing of a military base should be considered in analyzing the future demand for adjacent commercial properties such as dry cleaners, motels, bars, and restaurants. An appraiser who has observed development near highway interchanges will be able to anticipate that a proposed freeway interchange will generate future demand for shops, service stations, and motels catering to the needs of motorists and tourists.

DATA SAMPLING

Appraisers rarely have access to all available information for use in their analyses. Even when an appraiser has conducted extensive research, sample information frequently must be used. Therefore, the principles and implications of sampling should be understood.

Appraisers must frequently deal with incomplete information. Research involves the collection of both specific data and sample data for analytical purposes. The data used by appraisers is seldom a random sample. To establish a framework for selecting and drawing a random sampling, strict requirements must be met. More often, appraisers deal with judgment samples, i.e., sample data that is selected based on personal judgment and is thought to constitute a representative group. While certain statistical tests used with random samples cannot be applied to judgment samples, in many circumstances judgment samples can produce superior results. For example, data selected from five shopping centres by an experienced analyst may be more comparable to the subject shopping centre than a random sampling of data from a broader array of shopping centres.

The use of sample data has both strengths and weaknesses:

Strengths

- Samples are generally less expensive and more readily obtained than complete data. Selected samples are sometimes more indicative than a broader survey.
- Samples are easily tabulated, lend themselves to cross-referencing, and provide a foundation for statistical inference, including probability studies.
- Often samples may be the only source of data available.

Weaknesses

- Sampling must be conducted carefully and the data must be properly interpreted. If not, the results can be inaccurate and misleading, cost more than they are worth, and be less reliable than they appear.
- Sampling requires special training and understanding. Many people misunderstand or mistrust samples for a variety of reasons.

Whether or not the appraiser conducts formal sampling, the extent to which sample data has been used should be considered in the analytical process. The risks associated with identified sample data and the uncertainties associated with other potential data must be considered.

Data samples may be particularly important when other data is scarce or when the available data is less applicable due to market changes. Sampling may be the only way to obtain some types of data. Samples are particularly important in the following areas:

- Quantifying market demand
- Defining market characteristics
- Identifying market attitudes, perceptions, and motivations
- Analyzing market behaviour
- Interpreting market activities and intentions

Geographic Information Systems

A geographic information system (GIS) is any system that captures, stores, analyzes, manages, and presents data that are linked to location. Technically, a GIS is a system that includes mapping software and its application to remote sensing, land surveying, aerial photography, mathematics, photogrammetry, geography, and tools that can be implemented with GIS software. GIS data is available from a variety of government and private sources, for example see GeoGratis, a utility provided by Natural Resources Canada (*www.nrcan.gc.ca*). Most provinces today have GIS utilities that can be accessed via the internet and many municipalities have quite sophisticated systems that show property particulars, utility services, time series aerial photographs, zoning, land use controls, and other features. Internet utilities such as Google have developed extensive services related to satellite, aerial, and street level views of neighbourhoods and often of individual properties.

Geographic information system technology facilitates the addition of geographic reference data to individual items in real estate databases. Personal computers and larger, networked computer workstations can draw on this information to map or model the spatial referents and show the spatial relationships among the data points. Equally important, spreadsheets or tabular grids can be produced in written formats, which can help the user better understand these relationships.

Data from public sources at local, provincial, and national levels is available and, in most cases, less expensive than the cost of undertaking primary research. A combination of public data and other data available from proprietary sources allows an appraiser to assemble and map information and then analyze that information in ways previously regarded as technically infeasible or too costly. Initially, real estate professionals were most interested in the mapping capabilities of GIS, but new technology is helping expand opportunities for data analysis and promoting greater understanding of the results of such analysis.

> **geographic information systems (GIS)**
> An organized collection of computer hardware, software, geographic data, and personnel designed to efficiently capture, store, update, manipulate, analyze, and display all forms of geographically referenced information.
>
> Many local, regional, provincial, territorial, and federal government agencies and private service providers maintain GIS systems available for public use.

> Geographic information systems facilitate the graphic presentation of geocoded data and the analysis of physical characteristics and geographic relationships in a market area.

GIS can integrate digital maps with point-specific or area-specific data to answer basic questions such as the following:

- What is found in a specific location?
- Where within a given area is a specific feature, activity, or event located?
- What changes have occurred in an area over a given period of time?
- What type of spatial patterns characterize a given area?
- What impact will a specific change have on the area?

The data used to generate such maps is typically found in computer databases that include referents to a specific point on the earth's surface (i.e., latitude and longitude) or a specific area (e.g., city, postal code area, census tract).

Given sufficient information, the system can quickly pinpoint properties with specific characteristics. For example, the system can identify the locations of all parcels of vacant land in a given community that have the following characteristics:

- Contain 40 or more acres

- Meet specific soil suitability standards

- Equipped with municipal water and sewer lines

- Zoned for residential use

- Have an elementary school within a one-half mile radius and are adjacent to residential neighbourhoods where median home value exceeds $250,000

The dramatic increase in the use of GIS equipment is the result of three factors:

1. The decline in the price of high-powered personal computers
2. Improvements in GIS software
3. Expansion of commercially available geocoded data

In addition to commercially available GIS data, accurate digital base maps for most areas of the Canada are available at reasonable prices from various federal government agencies. Many local governments sell geocoded digital data on individual parcels that are compiled from assessment data and public record information. In the future, data vendors will continue to expand the amount of commercially available data compatible with GIS. Chapter 10 discusses topography and land or site analysis in more detail.

Selecting Comparable Data and Establishing Comparability

Descriptions and classifications of the characteristics and components of comparable properties are assembled in land and improvement analyses. The appraiser selects data from these analyses and analyzes it in the direct comparison, cost, and income approaches. The data used for comparison in the three approaches should come from properties that are similar to the property being appraised. The selection of comparables is directed to some extent by the availability of data. Investigation of an active market usually reveals an adequate and representative number of transactions within a restricted area and time period.

An appraiser gathers broad information about a market from its pattern of sales. Important market characteristics can be revealed by significant factors such as the following:

- Number of sales
- Period of time covered by the sales
- Availability of property for sale
- Rate of absorption
- Rate of turnover, i.e., volume of sales and level of activity

- Characteristics and motivations of buyers and sellers
- Terms and conditions of sale
- Use of property before and after its sale

While analyzing data to establish comparability and select sales, an appraiser begins to form certain conclusions about the general market, the subject property, and the possible relationships between the data and the subject property. The appraiser ascertains the following:

- Market strengths and weaknesses

- The probable supply of, demand for, and marketability of properties similar to the property being appraised

- The variations and characteristics likely to have the greatest impact on the value of properties in the market

Thus, an appraiser analyzes data against a background of information about the particular area and the specific type of property.

The information needed to apply the cost and income approaches must often be obtained from market sources other than sales. This information may also be used to refine adjustments made in the direct comparison approach. In the investigation of general and market area data, an appraiser learns about trends on the following items:

- Construction costs
- Lease terms
- Typical expenses
- Vacancy rates

Examining trends in the market where the subject property is located provides additional specific data that can be used to derive value indications and successfully complete valuation assignments.

The geographic area from which comparable sales can be selected depends on the property type. In valuing certain types of retail property, only properties with main street frontage may be pertinent. For many large industrial properties and most investment properties, the entire community should be studied; for larger properties, regional or national markets may be relevant. For a residential appraisal, adequate data can sometimes be found within a block of the subject property. However, even in these cases, the appraiser should consider the broader market to place the subject property and the comparables in a general market context.

When comparable sales data is scarce in the subject property's immediate area, the appraiser may need to extend the data search to adjacent market areas and similar communities. The appraiser must establish the comparability of the alternative market before using data from that market. When the selection of data is limited to an unacceptably narrow sample of current market activity, the appraiser may decide to use sales that are less current or to interview brokers, buyers, sellers, owners, and tenants of similar properties in the area to obtain evidence of potential market activity such as listing prices or offers to purchase.

In general, comparable properties fall into two categories:

- The first and preferred category includes properties that are comparable to and competitive with the property being appraised or have a demonstrable effect on prices or other relevant components of the market in question.

- The second category includes properties that are comparable to, but not competitive with, the subject.

With computer analysis, a large number of properties can be studied in the course of a single assignment, which may generate a deeper understanding of each property's contribution to, and influence on, a given market.

The appraiser should pay attention to several factors to judge if data is useful:

- The degree of comparability
- The quantity of information available
- The authenticity and reliability of the data

The appraiser must not assume that all data pertinent to an assignment is completely reliable. Sales figures, costs, and other information subject to misrepresentation should be scrutinized for authenticity.

Appraisers seek data that will facilitate accurate comparisons, but every real estate parcel is unique. The comparability of properties varies, and the appraiser may find it necessary to place less confidence on a given comparable. Nevertheless, the appraiser may want to consider this comparable for its evidence of, and effect on, the marketplace.

Appraisers have a special responsibility to scrutinize the comparability of all data used in a valuation assignment. They must fully understand the concept of comparability and should avoid comparing properties with different highest and best uses, limiting their search for comparables, or selecting inappropriate factors for comparison.

DATA ORGANIZATION

Market data grids are the most common tool used to organize data; they can be as detailed as the analysis dictates. In a basic data array grid, the appraiser lists significant characteristics of the subject and comparable properties that have been isolated. This type of grid summarizes the data presented and allows the appraiser to identify those factors that may account for differences in value and those that probably do not. The data array grid only presents data; it is not used for comparing the properties. In an adjustment grid, the sale properties are compared to the subject and specific adjustments are made to their prices.

A market data grid should include the total sale price of each comparable property and the date of each sale, which can be expressed in relation to the subject property's date of valuation, e.g., one month ago or sixteen months ago. The grid also includes information about the property rights conveyed, the financial arrangements of the sale, and any unusual motivations of the buyer or seller that may have resulted in a negotiating advantage, such as a desire to liquidate a property for inheritance tax or to acquire a particular property for expansion.

The market data grid can include characteristics of the subject and comparable properties, information on sales transactions, and pertinent market data from other sources. The appraiser may choose to use two or more market data grids, i.e., one grid for comparable sales data and other grids for information derived from other sources. Isolating specific data may indicate the type of information the appraiser will be able to derive from the collected data and identify variations among properties that may be significant to their value.

In examining the market data grid, the appraiser may find that certain data is not pertinent and will not be useful in applying the approaches to value. For example,

---

DATA STANDARDS

The clients of appraisers have been creating the impetus toward data standards, demanding more consistency, efficiency, and transparency within the appraisal process. Those clients have been moving in this direction because of the demands of their own customers, i.e., consumers.

Mediocre data makes good analysis more difficult. The availability of standardized and even enhanced data will facilitate analysis that is more robust and enhance research opportunities. These types of research efforts are needed to determine the appropriate analytic techniques and metrics for a data-rich real estate environment. Furthermore, mundane tasks relating to the standardization of data sets are easily taken care of using the XML format that has become a de facto Internet standard.

Three major standards groups involved in the development and dissemination of appraisal data standards are:

- The Commercial Appraisal Report Standards (CARS) project team of the Appraisal Institute
- The Mortgage Industry Standards Maintenance Organization (MISMO)
- The Open Standards Consortium for Real Estate (OSCRE)

The CARS effort recognizes that the appraisal industry must integrate data and adhere to international professional standards, which will allow information to flow to the end user through the appraisal report, providing added value as the profession moves into a global market. Initiatives include the completion of the Appraisal Institute data glossary (with sorting capabilities), affiliation with OSCRE and MISMO, and the development of an educational seminar for appraisers, who will adopt these standards for everyday use and for their clients.

The mortgage industry, an important driver in the broader real estate industry, has been working toward data standardization through the Mortgage Industry Standards Maintenance Organization (MISMO), formed in 1999 as a nonprofit subsidiary of the Mortgage Bankers Association. MISMO first worked on developing standards for the residential real estate mortgage industry and more recently began work on standards for the commercial real estate industry. Industry adoption and buy-in has been growing within the financial marketplace with the involvement of Freddie Mac, Fannie Mae, life insurance companies, and the Commercial Mortgage Securities Association.

The Open Standards Consortium for Real Estate is a rapidly growing global organization that brings together data standards from every sector of real estate. Appraisal is just one segment of its dictionary; other areas include construction, brokerage, government, and management. OSCRE is different from MISMO in that MISMO's core focus is data standards specific to mortgage-related and real property reporting information, whereas OSCRE goes beyond data standards into business process standards. MISMO and OSCRE are working to establish common data terms so that, throughout the life cycle of a building, all parties are able to use terms consistently.

if an appraiser who is valuing an industrial property finds that the subject and the comparables all occupy one-acre sites, site size will probably not account for differences in the properties' sale or unit prices. However, if the percentages of office space in the properties vary, the difference may have an effect on value.

Analysis of the data array grid may indicate that additional data is required and that the appraiser needs to create other grids to include more information or to isolate the data required for specific approaches. Appraisers should see data analysis as a process and the market data grid as a tool that facilitates this process and the derivation of valid indications of property value. Although many market data grids may be prepared in the development of an appraisal, not all grids are necessary for the appraisal report; only those that will help to explain the significance of the data to the client need to be included in the appraisal report. Chapter 14 provides further discussion and examples of the use of adjustment grids for data analysis.

CHAPTER 9

MARKET AND
MARKETABILITY ANALYSIS

The term market analysis is used broadly in economics but has more specific meaning within the appraisal discipline. For appraisers, market analysis is a process for the identification and study of the market for a particular economic good or service. Appraisers generally consider market analysis at two levels:

- From the perspective of a broad market, when a specific property is not the focus of the study the term market study is normally employed

- From the perspective of the market in which a given property competes

Although there is a logical continuum from the general to the specific, market analysis applied to a specific property is of particular importance in the valuation process and should not be confused with general market analysis or related studies. For a specific property, the term applied is *marketability study*. This market analysis may be either an inferred or fundamental analysis depending on the property type and market conditions. Although the process is commonly referred to as market analysis, all appraisals must include a *marketability analysis* as well. Marketability analysis includes market analysis as well as an estimate of capture; a market analysis seeks a *capture rate*.

Market/marketability analysis in real estate valuation is unique because it requires the appraiser to analyze the buyer/seller market as well as the user market (see Figure 9.1). The market area for the buyer/seller market is usually different from the market area for the user market. The market area for the buyer/seller market could be international, say, for a hotel, while the user market for the hotel could be within the local community. Thus, market delineation for valuation has two main parts:

- Analysis of the user market (owners, occupants, and the competition)

- Analysis of the buyer/seller market

> **market analysis**
> A process for examining the demand for and supply of a property type and the geographic market area for that property type. This process is sometimes referred to as *a use in search of a site.*
>
> **marketability study**
> A process that investigates how a particular piece of property will be absorbed, sold, or leased under current or anticipated market conditions; includes a market study or analysis of the general class of property being studied. This process is sometimes referred to as *a site in search of a use.*

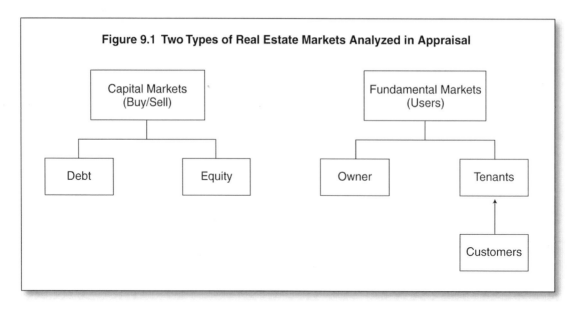

Figure 9.1 Two Types of Real Estate Markets Analyzed in Appraisal

In the appraisal of a specific property, market/marketability analysis must show how the interaction of supply and demand affects the property's value. If current market conditions do not indicate adequate demand for a proposed development, market/marketability analysis may identify the point in time when adequate demand for the project will likely emerge. Thus, market/marketability analysis helps an appraiser forecast the timing of a proposed improvement and the amount of demand anticipated in a particular period of time. The marketability study helps the appraiser forecast how much the subject property will capture, e.g., future absorption and operations outlook for future occupancy and rents

Market/marketability analysis also provides a basis for determining the highest and best use of a property. An existing or proposed improvement under a specified use may be put to the test of maximum productivity only after it has been demonstrated that an appropriate level of market support exists for that use. In-depth market/marketability analyses go much further in specifying the character of that support. Such studies may determine key marketing strategies for an existing or proposed property, address the design characteristics of a proposed development, or provide estimates of the share of the market the property is likely to capture and its probable absorption rate.

To measure the market support for a specified property use, the analyst must identify the relationship between demand and competitive supply in the subject real

> **capture rate**
> The estimated percentage of the total potential market for a specific type of property (e.g., office space, retail space, single-family homes) that is currently absorbed by existing facilities or is forecast to be absorbed by proposed facilities. For example, the capture rate of a retail center depends on the size of its trade area, the anchor tenants in the facility, competition within the trade area, and the relative position of the subject facility compared to the competition. Short-term capture is referred to as *absorption*; long-term capture is referred to as *share of the market*.

estate market, both now and in the future. This relationship indicates the degree of equilibrium or disequilibrium that characterizes the present market and the conditions likely to characterize the market over the forecast period. Markets are typically in a state of disequilibrium created by

> Market/marketability analysis investigates the relationship between the demand for and competitive supply of real estate in a defined market.

market actions, e.g., there is natural lag in meeting demand and reaching a point of equilibrium because of the time that elapses between identifying a need and developing new buildings.

The market value of a property is largely determined by its competitive position in its market. Familiarity with the characteristics and attributes of the subject property (generally called property productivity analysis) enhances the appraiser's ability to identify competitive properties (supply) and to understand the comparative advantages and disadvantages that the subject offers potential buyers or renters (demand). An understanding of economic conditions, their effect on real estate markets, and the momentum of these markets helps an appraiser appreciate the externalities affecting a property. Therefore, in its broadest sense market/marketability analysis provides vital information needed to apply the three approaches to value, as shown in Table 9.1.

Table 9.1   Market/Marketability Analysis in the Approaches to Value

Approach to Value	Uses of Market/Marketability Analysis
Cost	Market/marketability analysis provides an appraiser with information about current building costs and market conditions. This information helps the appraiser estimate the profit an entrepreneur will expect (or, for an owner-built property, the intangibles associated with owner occupancy) and any economic advantage or obsolescence the property may have suffered since its construction.
Direct comparison	Market/marketability analysis helps the appraiser identify competitive properties and determine their exact degree of comparability with the subject. With a thorough understanding of current market conditions gained through market/marketability analysis, the appraiser can adjust the sale prices of comparable properties for changes in market conditions that may have occurred since the sales occurred as well as support an adjustment for the economic characteristics of comparable properties.
Income	In the market/marketability analysis process, an appraiser collects data on vacancy and absorption rates, market rents, current and anticipated rates of return, and the competitive position of the subject property in its specific market. In the income approach, this information is used to determine the anticipated lease-up or sell-out rate for the subject, the share of the market that the subject is likely to capture, the future income stream it is likely to enjoy, and an appropriate discount rate or capitalization rate to apply to the income stream projection or annualized income expectancy. Market/marketability analysis also helps appraisers forecast supply and demand and stabilized revenue, i.e., develop a revenue forecast for the subject.

FUNDAMENTAL CONCEPTS

Market Definition and Delineation

At the outset of the market/marketability analysis process, the appraiser must clearly identify the real estate product and the real estate market in which the subject competes. These two tasks may be considered complementary. The identification and analysis of the real estate product provides a portion of the information needed in the next step – identifying the market area in which the property competes. In the property productivity analysis, the appraiser identifies the characteristics of the appraised property and further analyzes the physical, legal, and locational characteristics that affect the property's ability to compete for demand in the defined market area. Analyzing the characteristics and attributes of the real estate product helps the appraiser identify competitive properties that constitute the applicable market. Defining the real estate market for the subject property clearly enhances the appraiser's understanding of how externalities affect the subject. Through market/ marketability analysis, the appraiser breaks down a specific real estate market into market segments (i.e., the market participants), and the appraiser disaggregates the properties by characteristics, e.g., class of property, location.

Demand

Demand reflects the needs, material desires, purchasing power, and preferences of consumers. Demand analysis focuses on identifying the potential users of a subject property. i.e., the buyers, renters, clientele, or customers it will attract. For each particular type of property, demand analysis focuses on the end product or service that the real estate provides. Thus, a demand analysis for retail space would attempt to determine the demand for retail services generated by potential customers in the market area. A demand analysis for office space would attempt to identify businesses in the area that occupy office space and their space or staffing needs.

Demand analyses for residential and retail markets specifically investigate the households in the subject's market area. In addition to the number of households in the market area, these analyses focus on the disposable income or effective purchasing power of the households and the ages, gender, preferences, and behavioural patterns of household members.

The demand for housing and most retail space is projected based on growth rates in population, income, and employment levels.[1] The four key points discussed below can be especially useful in understanding demand projections for a particular land use.

First, the rate of household formation varies significantly with income and age groups in the existing population. This rate is even more sensitive to migration. Estimating the number of households in an area by dividing the total population by the average household size may result in considerable error. The rate of household formation is much higher for people between the ages of 25 and 34 and those between

---

[1]   See Chapter 8 for a discussion of the sources of the data used to estimate the demand for and competitive supply of a specific property type or use.

IMPORTANT FACTORS IN DEMAND ANALYSIS FOR A RESIDENTIAL MARKET

- Population of the market area, size and number of households, rate of increase or decrease in household formation, composition, and age distribution
- Per capita and household income, mean and median
- Major employers, types of jobs, and unemployment rate
- Percentage of owners and renters
- Financial considerations such as savings levels and lending requirements, e.g., interest rates on mortgages, points charged, and loan-to-value ratios
- Land use patterns and directions of city and area growth and development
- Factors affecting the physical appeal of the neighbourhood, e.g., geography and geology (climate, topography, drainage, bedrock, and natural or man-made barriers)
- Local tax structure and administration, assessed values, taxes, and special assessments
- Availability of support facilities and community services, i.e., cultural institutions, educational facilities, health and medical facilities, fire and police protection

---

IMPORTANT FACTORS IN DEMAND ANALYSIS FOR A RETAIL MARKET

- Population of trade area(s), size and number of households, rate of increase or decrease in household formation, composition and age distribution of households
- Per capita and household income, mean and median
- Percentage of household income spent on all retail purchases and percentage of disposable income (effective purchasing power) spent on various specific retail categories
- Rate of sales retention in the trade area
- Required volume of sales for a retail facility to operate profitably and existing sales volume per square foot
- Retail vacancy rate and trends in the market
- Percentage of retail purchases captured from outside the trade area
- Land use patterns and directions of city growth and development
- Accessibility (transportation facilities and highway systems) and cost of transportation
- Factors that affect the appeal of the retail centre, e.g., image, quality of goods, and tenant reputation

---

35 and 54 than for people between the ages of 15 and 24. However, precise data may be difficult to obtain.

Second, household size is not a constant. Over the past several decades, average household size has declined significantly. Between 1970 and 2006, census household size in Canada fell from 3.7 to 3.0.[2]

Third, while average or median income is generally projected in current dollars, the average real income per capita in Canada that is calculated in constant dollars did not grow between 1976 and 1984, increased very modestly between 1985 and 1989, declined between 1989 and 1993, and then increased steadily until 2007. Income

---

[2]   Source: Statistics Canada, Catalogue no. 91-213-X. Note that the rate of decline occurred mostly during the 1970s; average census household size in 1986 was 3.1, and has since held fairly constant.

projections based on current dollars will thus reflect future, inflated dollars; if real incomes are diminishing, effective demand might be decreasing in spite of the apparent increase in affordability.[3]

Finally, population projections for small areas are published by public agencies and market research firms, but such projections can be misleading. Therefore, the appraiser should also consult projections for the overall metropolitan area. The availability of land and the adequacy of the infrastructure in the subject area will help determine how much of the overall projected growth will go to that area.

IMPORTANT FACTORS IN DEMAND ANALYSIS FOR AN OFFICE MARKET

- Area employers who use office space; current and estimated future staffing needs
- Average square foot area of office space required by an office worker. Requirements vary according to the category of work, the rank of the office worker, and the location of the office, e.g., in the suburbs or the central business district
- Vacancy rate for the specific class of office building
- Move-up demand for space in higher quality buildings (Class A and Class B) or fall-out demand for space in lower quality buildings (Class B and Class C)
- Land use patterns and directions of city growth and development
- Accessibility (transportation facilities and highway systems) and cost of transportation
- Factors that affect the appeal of the office building (quality of construction, management, and tenancy) and the availability of support facilities (shops, restaurants, recreational centres)

IMPORTANT FACTORS IN DEMAND ANALYSIS FOR AN INDUSTRIAL MARKET

- Presence of raw materials
- Exchange capability, e.g., currency values and trade barriers
- Area employers who use industrial space; current and estimated availability of skilled and unskilled labor
- Land use patterns and directions of city growth and development
- Accessibility (transportation facilities and highway systems) and cost of transportation
- Employment in manufacturing, wholesale, retail, transportation, communications, or public utilities
- International, national,. and regional economic growth that affects local demand
- Overall employment growth
- Retail sales (applicable in market analysis for retail storage and wholesale distribution properties)
- Cargo flows by transport type (e.g., truck, rail, water, air) and product type (e.g., high or low bulk)

Demand in industrial property markets is generally more limited than demand in residential or commercial markets.

---

[3]   Statistics Canada, Income Trends in Canada 1976 to 2007, table 2020402. See http://www.statcan.gc.ca/pub/13f0022x/2007000/s4-eng.htm for more information.

Competitive Supply

Supply refers to the production and availability of the real estate product. To analyze supply, the appraiser must compile an inventory of properties that compete directly with the subject. Competitive properties include the stock of existing units, units under construction that will enter the market, and projects in planning. The appraiser must be careful in developing and analyzing data on proposed or announced projects because ultimately some may not be constructed. The appraiser must also determine the number of units lost to demolition and the number added or removed through conversion. Appraisers gather data in various ways:

- Field inspection
- Review of building permits (issued and acted upon), research into sales of development sites, and surveys of competitive sites
- Commercial data providers
- Interviews with developers, marketers, and city planners

FACTORS STUDIED IN ANALYZING THE SUPPLY OF COMPETING PROPERTIES

- Quantity and quality of available competition (standing stock)
- Volume of new construction (competitive and complementary) – projects in planning and under construction
- Availability and price of vacant land
- Costs of construction and development
- Currently offered properties (existing and newly built)
- Owner occupancy versus tenant occupancy
- Causes and number of vacancies
- Conversions to alternative uses
- Special economic conditions and circumstances
- Availability of construction loans and financing
- Impact of building codes, zoning ordinances, and other regulations on construction volume and cost

---

Market Equilibrium

Over the short term, the supply of real estate is relatively fixed and prices are responsive to demand. If demand is unusually high, prices and rents will start to rise before new construction can begin. The completion of a building may lag considerably behind the shift in demand. Thus, disequilibrium generally characterizes markets over the short term.

Theoretically, the supply of and demand for real estate move toward equilibrium over the long term. However, this point of equilibrium is seldom achieved or maintained. In some markets, such as those characterized by a very specialized economy, supply responds slowly to changes in demand. Even when an excess in the quantity of

market equilibrium
- The theoretical balance toward which the supply of and demand for real estate move over the long run – a balance that is seldom achieved.
- The balance created at any given point by the interaction of market participants, i.e., sellers representing the supply of properties and buyers representing the demand for properties.

market disequilibrium
A general characteristic of real estate markets over the short term in which the supply and demand for real estate are out of balance.

active market
A market characterized by growing demand, a corresponding lag in supply, and an increase in prices.

depressed market
A market in which a drop in demand is accompanied by a relative oversupply and a decline in prices.

buyer's market
A depressed market in which buyers have the advantage; exists when market prices are relatively low due to an oversupply of property or a reduced number of potential buyers.

seller's market
An active market in which the sellers of available properties can obtain higher prices than those obtainable in the immediately preceding period; a market in which a few available properties are demanded at prevailing prices by many users and potential users.

strong market
A market that reflects either high demand and increasing price levels or a large volume of transactions.

weak market
A market characterized by low demand and declining price levels; also called a soft market

goods offered for sale becomes apparent, projects currently under construction generally have to be completed. More stock will continue to be added to the existing surplus, causing greater disequilibrium. A decline in demand may also occur while new real estate units are being constructed, further exacerbating the oversupply.

Trends in Market Activity

Analysts and market participants describe the activity of real estate markets in a variety of ways. An *active market* is a market characterized by growing demand, a corresponding lag in supply, and an increase in prices. An active market is also referred to as a *seller's market* because the sellers of available properties can obtain higher prices. A *depressed market* is a market in which a drop in demand is accompanied by a relative oversupply and a decline in prices. A depressed market is also referred to as a *buyer's market* because buyers have the advantage.

Descriptive terms applied to markets are subject to interpretation. For example, markets are sometimes characterized as strong or weak. *Strong markets* may reflect either high demand and increasing price levels or a large volume of transactions. *Weak,* or *soft markets* may be identified by low demand and declining price levels. Other loosely defined terms include broad and narrow markets, loose and tight markets, and balanced and unbalanced markets.[4]

Not all markets can be described with simple characterizations. Sometimes supply and demand do not act as expected. Supply may fail to respond to increasing demand because the rate of demolition exceeds the rate of new construction. In this case, prices will continue to rise. Alternatively, supply may outpace rising demand because of a glut of existing properties on the market, and prices will decline.

As shown in Chapter 4, the activity of the real estate market is cyclical. Like the business

4   For further discussion of categorizing real estate markets, see Neil Carn, Joseph Rabianski, Ronald Racster, and Maury Seldin, *Real Estate Market Analysis* (Englewood Cliffs, N.J.: Prentice-Hall, 1988), 76-77 and 81-82.

cycle, the real estate cycle is characterized by successive periods of expansion, decline, recession, and recovery. However, the real estate cycle is not synchronized with the business cycle. Real estate activity responds to both long-term and short-term stimuli. The long-term cycle is a function of changes in the characteristics of existing employment, population, income, and shifts in consumer preferences. The short-term cycle is largely a function of the availability of credit.

LEVELS OF MARKET/MARKETABILITY ANALYSIS

The principles of market/marketability analysis seem simple, but the techniques and procedures applied by market analysts can be extremely sophisticated. Market/marketability studies can be developed into elaborate analyses. The levels of market/marketability analysis that can be performed reflect a spectrum of increasingly complicated methodologies.[5]

Estimates of demand are formulated differently depending on the level of analysis. In some cases, demand may simply be inferred from current market conditions, or rates of change may be used to develop projections. Because of shortcomings in this simple approach, caution is advised. To perform an in-depth analysis of forecast (fundamental) demand, the analyst must gather and segment extensive data and apply sound judgment to make projections. The analyst refines the forecast demand estimate by considering the perceptions of market participants and assessing the likelihood that current trends will continue.

Inferred Analysis and Fundamental Analysis

An appraiser can use current and historical market conditions to infer future supply and demand conditions. In addition, to forecast subject-specific supply, demand, absorption, and capture over a property's projection period, the appraiser can augment the analysis of current and historical market conditions with fundamental analysis. Table 9.2 summarizes the distinctions between inferred and fundamental demand analysis and indicates the levels of analysis associated with each.

Inferred analysis, which is sometimes called *trend analysis*, is descriptive and emphasizes historical data rather than future projections. The focus can be general, with selected comparable properties representing the larger market, or more specific and include area-wide market data and subject-specific conclusions.

Fundamental analysis is a more detailed study of market conditions, focusing on the specific submarket of the subject property and providing strong reasoning and quantifiable evidence for projections of future development. This level of analysis is based on the premise that real estate value is tied to the services the property provides and that a study of the market for those services will reveal influences on the value of the real estate.

> **fundamental analysis**
> Investment analysis that investigates both basic and economic factors and conditions affecting specific sectors and industries.
>
> **inferred demand**
> Demand projected on the basis of current market conditions, rates of change, and absorption patterns.

[5] For a comprehensive discussion of the various levels of market/marketability analysis, see Stephen F. Fanning, *Market Analysis for Real Estate: Concepts and Applications in Valuation and Highest and Best Use* (Chicago: Appraisal Institute, 2005).

Table 9.2: Types and Levels of Analysis

Levels of Analysis*			
Inferred Demand Studies		**Fundamental (Derived) Demand Studies**	
Level of Study A	B	C	D
Inferred subject attributes		Quantified subject attributes	
Inferred locational determinants of use and marketability by macroanalysis		Quantified and graphic analysis of locational determinants of use and marketability by macro-and microanalysis	
Inferred demand from general economic base analysis conducted by others		Inferred demand derived by original economic base analysis	
Inferred demand by selected comparables		Forecast demand by subject-specific market segment and demographic data	
Inferred supply by selected comparables		Quantified supply derived by inventorying existing and forecasting planned competition	
Inferred equilibrium/highest and best use and capture conclusions		Quantified equilibrium • Highest and best use – graphic – map • Timing – quantified capture forecast	
Emphasis is on: • Instinctive knowledge • Historical data • Judgment		Emphasis is on: • Quantifiable data • Forecast • Judgment	

Note: An appraisal without a fundamental demand study – e.g., Level C or D market/marketability analysis – is designed to estimate value only in a certain and stable market.

* As defined in Stephen F. Fanning, *Market Analysis for Real Estate: Concepts and Applications in Valuation and Highest and Best Use* (Chicago: Appraisal Institute, 2005), 18–30.

TYPES OF ANALYSIS

In addition to different levels of analysis, the discipline of market/marketability analysis comprises several related types of analysis. For a given appraisal assignment, the appraiser must determine which of the following variations of market/marketability analysis is most appropriate for the appraisal problem:

- Economic base analysis
- Market studies and marketability studies
- Feasibility analysis

The types of market/marketability analysis differ more in scope than in procedure. All forms of market/marketability analysis investigate local economic activity and factors influencing the supply and demand of a particular type of property or in a specific market area, not always focusing on a specific property. In addition, the conclusions of these analyses all lead the appraiser into the highest and best use analysis required in the valuation process.

Economic Base Analysis

As defined in Chapter 4, the economic base of a community is the economic activity that allows local businesses to generate income from markets outside the community's borders. Thus, economic base analysis is a survey of the industries and businesses that generate employment and income in a community as well as of functions of employment such as the rate of population growth and levels of income.

Employment figures serve as a proxy for income in economic base analysis. Basic employment industries provide the economic foundation for a community by producing goods and services that can be exported to bring money into the local economy. Although some segments of the service sector can be considered basic economic activities, most service industries are nonbasic because the service provided and the income generated remain within the community's borders. Growth in basic employment can reflect changes in population, household income, or other economic factors influencing land use and real estate value.

Often the structure of a community's business sector can be discussed using the North American Industry Classification System (NAICS) developed in a cooperative effort between the statistical agencies of Canada, the United States, and Mexico and used by Statistics Canada.[6] NAICS is used throughout Statistics Canada reporting for the variety of statistics and surveys requiring industrial activity classification, e.g., census, employment surveys, enterprise and establishment surveys, household surveys, and the System of National Accounts.

Surveys and other data-gathering techniques employed in economic base analysis generate primary data that can be used in other types of market/marketability analysis.

Market Studies and Marketability Studies

A macroeconomic market study provides a broad picture of supply and demand conditions for a specific property type (e.g., residential units, retail space, office space, industrial plant, agricultural operation) or for a specific area. In a market study, the appraiser does not focus on a specific property; for most valuation assignments, a more detailed marketability study is necessary.

In a marketability study, the appraiser investigates how a particular property will be absorbed, sold, or leased under current or anticipated market conditions; a market study or analysis of the general class of property should be included. In contrast to market studies, a marketability study is property-specific. It should identify the characteristics of the subject's market and quantify their effect on the value of the property. A marketability study includes a market study.

A marketability study is founded on analysis of four factors that create value, i.e., utility, scarcity, desire, and effective purchasing power. The interaction of these four factors will determine the marketability of a property. Utility and scarcity are supply-side factors, while desire and effective purchasing power are demand-side factors.

The development of a property usually entails a construction, conversion, or renovation phase and a marketing phase. The marketability study must describe the

---

[6] In 1997, the Standard Industrial Classification system (SIC) was replaced by the North American Industry Classification System (NAICS). NAICS is revised on a five-year cycle in order to ensure that the classification continues to reflect the rapidly changing structure of the economy. NAICS 2007 groups economic activity into 20 sectors and 928 Canadian industries. See *www.statcan.gc.ca* for more information.

market study

A macroeconomic analysis that examines the general market conditions of supply, demand, and pricing or the demographics of demand for a specific area or property type. A market study may also include analyses of construction and absorption trends.

marketability study

- A microeconomic study that examines the marketability of a given property or class of properties, usually focusing on the market segments in which the property is likely to generate demand. Marketability studies are useful in determining a specific highest and best use, testing development proposals, and projecting an appropriate tenant mix.

- Analysis of how a particular property is expected to be sold, absorbed, or leased under current and anticipated market conditions; includes a market study or analysis of the general class of property being studied.

demand and supply situation under current market conditions (for the estimate of "as is" value) as well as the demand and supply situation over the planned construction period (for the value upon completion) and the marketing period (for the estimate of value upon stabilization). In other words, a marketability study for a property must focus on each point on the development timeline for which a value is to be estimated.

Appraisers also use a marketability study for an existing property. Appraisers forecast income and occupancy, e.g., whether the market expects the subject property to maintain or lose tenants and how much rent the owners can expect in the future. Likewise for vacant land, appraisers must forecast the timing for use in order to select and adjust comparables. This too is treated as a marketability study. The demand and supply analysis must investigate market conditions, both current and future, to determine the absorption rate and other factors that will affect value during the marketing period.

An appraiser must be careful not to misinterpret data or use historical data as an absolute prediction of the future. For example, an appraiser can incorrectly assume the absorption rate experienced by competitive projects will indicate the absorption rate for the subject when it is actually an indication of demand. Consider an appraiser who is analyzing a proposed residential subdivision and finds three competitive subdivisions in the subject's market area. Over the past year, these subdivisions have had average sales rates of three lots per month, five lots per month, and seven lots per month. Simply using the average sales rate for the three competitive subdivisions, five lots per month, as the estimated absorption rate for the subject would most likely be incorrect. However, the appraiser can use the total lot sales for the three competitive subdivisions as an indication of the total historical demand for similarly developed residential lots in the subject's market area – i.e., 15 lots per month is the implied demand for this type of real estate product. The appraiser should study additional market factors, including growth patterns and the development of new competitive subdivisions, to support the estimate of total demand over the subject's marketing period.

The subject's marketing period can be determined by analyzing the supply of competitive residential subdivision lots in the market area, including the subject and all other proposed and existing subdivisions.

Consider the following situation:

- The appraiser expects the three existing subdivisions mentioned above to continue to sell off lots during the subject's marketing period.

- Another proposed subdivision will be added to the competition in the subject's market during this period.

- Total demand is 15 lots per month.

Thus, the average absorption rate for the five subdivisions will be three lots per month. The appraiser can then determine whether the subject's absorption rate will be the same as, higher than, or lower than the average rate. The appraiser should explain the reasoning for the rate chosen in the appraiser's conclusion.

If the appraiser uses a marketability study prepared by another party in the valuation, the appraiser must recognize that this study represents secondary data. The appraiser should carefully review the study to determine its validity and whether it can be used.

A MARKETABILITY STUDY MUST ANSWER THE FOLLOWING QUESTIONS:

- Who will the end users be, i.e., buyers or tenants?
- What are the characteristics of the expected end users? (e.g., age, family size, space needs, and preferences as to facilities and amenities)
- Does the utility of the improvements, whether proposed or existing, satisfy the requirements of the intended market?
- What is the demand for the proposed or existing property that is to be marketed?
- How many end users would want the property? (desire)
- How many potential users can afford it? (effective purchasing power)
- What share of demand is the property likely to capture? (capture rate)
- What is the supply of competitive properties that will be marketed?
- How many competitive units currently exist?
- How many competitive units are under construction?
- How many competitive units are planned?
- What is the estimated absorption rate for the proposed property to be marketed?
- If already developed, what future rent and occupancy are expected?
- Are there alternative uses for the property that would provide a higher return on the investment?
- What are the relative risks associated with the alternative uses?

Feasibility Analysis

Economic feasibility analysis is defined as an analysis undertaken to investigate whether a project will fulfill the objectives of an investor. Thus, the profitability of a specific real estate project is analyzed in terms of the criteria of a specific market or investor. Alternatively, the term may be defined as an investment's ability to produce sufficient revenue to pay all expenses and charges and to provide a reasonable return on and recapture of the money invested.[7] Economic feasibility is indicated when the market value or gross sellout of a project upon achievement of a stabilized condition equals or exceeds all costs of production. Market value applies to a planned rental property, while gross sellout applies to a project that will be developed as multiple units to be sold to multiple users.

---

[7]   *The Dictionary of Real Estate Appraisal*, 5th ed. (Chicago: Appraisal Institute, 2009). The terms feasibility analysis, economic feasibility analysis, and financial feasibility analysis are often used interchangeably. See also Stephen Fanning, *Market Analysis for Real Estate: Concepts and Applications in Valuation and Highest and Best Use* (Chicago: Appraisal Institute, 2005), 185, fn. 1.

Analyzing the feasibility of proposed uses requires appraisers to forecast future market conditions and the timing of events such as the sellout of new homes in a subdivision. Inadequate analysis of development projects, large or small, can contribute to a project's failure.

Highest and best use and feasibility analysis are interrelated, but feasibility analyses may involve data and considerations that are not directly related to highest and best use determinations. Such analyses may be more detailed than highest and best use analyses, have a different focus or require additional research. Generally, the feasibility of developing real estate under a variety of alternative uses is studied. The use that maximizes value represents the highest and best use. Table 9.3 provides a comparison of general market analysis, feasibility analysis, and highest and best use analysis.

Table 9.3: Comparison of Real Estate Analyses

Goal/Purpose

General market analysis	Identify demand for appropriate potential uses
Marketability analysis	Identify demand for a particular property
Feasibility analysis	Compare cost and value and analyze if specific market or investor criteria are fulfilled
Highest and best use analysis	Of the appropriate potential uses, determine the use that yields the maximum value

Processes/Steps

General market analysis	Perform supply and demand analysis for appropriate potential uses
Marketability analysis	Follow the six-step process described below
Feasibility analysis	Calculate NOI/cash flows of appropriate potential uses and select appropriate cap rate/discount rate (based on data collected during market/marketability analysis – e.g., residual land value, rate of return, capitalized value of overall property)
Highest and best use analysis	Specify terms of use, timing, and market participants (e.g., user of the property, most probable buyer) and compare values of appropriate potential uses

Results (Data Generated)

General market analysis	Forecasts over- or undersupply and the effect on absorption rates and probable rents or prices for appropriate potential uses
Marketability analysis	Forecasts how a specific property will perform under current or anticipated market conditions
Feasibility analysis	States whether potential uses are feasible based on respective data
Highest and best use analysis	Determines which alternative use (or alternative uses) creates the highest value

SIX-STEP MARKET ANALYSIS PROCESS

Most market/marketability analysis assignments can be performed using a six-step process, which is illustrated in Table 9.4. For proposed properties, a seventh step can be added to perform financial feasibility analysis of alternative uses and threshold testing, often using the break-even point of the investment as the threshold.

In Step 1, the property productivity analysis step, the appraiser or analyst identifies which features of the subject property shape productive capabilities and potential uses of the property. Those attributes can be physical, legal, or locational; they will be the basis for the selection of comparable properties as well as shaping conclusions about the capture of forecasted marginal demand.

In Step 2, given the potential uses of the subject property, the appraiser identifies a market for the defined use or more than one market if the property has alternative uses. Economic base analysis is the foundation of this analysis of existing and anticipated market demand.

In Step 3, the appraiser studies population and employment data to analyze and forecast demand. The scope of work required by the assignment (as well as time and budgetary constraints) will dictate to what extent the appraiser must investigate demand-side variables.

In Step 4, the appraiser analyzes the existing and anticipated supply of the property type under investigation.

In Step 5, the analyst investigates the interaction of supply and demand to determine if marginal demand exists and then makes predictions as to when the market will move out of equilibrium.

In Step 6, by comparing the productive attributes of the subject property to those of competitive properties, the analyst can judge the market share the subject is likely to capture given market conditions, demand, and competitive supply.

Market/marketability analysis assignments can be elaborate undertakings, particularly if a large amount of primary research is required. The following examples outline the procedures and thought processes an appraiser will apply in using the six-step process to analyze the markets for various types of property.

Analyzing Housing Demand

For a Proposed Single-Family Residential Subdivision

Real estate developers often want to know how many homes they can build in a subdivision, what prices they could expect to receive for those properties, and the timing of sales over an anticipated holding period. A typical market analysis for a new single-family residential subdivision involves the following considerations in the six-step process:

Step 1. *Property productivity analysis.* As in any market/marketability analysis, the first step is a preliminary analysis of the legal, physical, and locational attributes of the subject units and units in competitive subdivisions. Important characteristics of a new subdivision include the following:

Table 9.4: Six-Step Process

Step 1.   **Define the Product (Property Productivity Analysis)**

A.   Physical attributes
B.   Legal and regulatory attributes
   1.   Private
   2.   Public
C.   Location attributes
   1.   Identification of economic attributes – the association between land uses and their linkages
   2.   Identification of the movement of demand in relation to the direction of urban growth

Step 2.   **Market Delineation**

A.   Market area delineation concepts
   1.   Time-distance concepts and standards
   2.   Area over which equally desirable substitute properties tend to compete with the subject.
B.   Market delineation techniques
   1.   Gravity models
   2.   Customer spotting

Step 3.   **Demand Analysis**

A.   Demand segmentation
     Identification of characteristics of most probable user (consumer profile)
B.   Tastes and preferences: behavioral, motivational, and psychological factor
C.   Inferred demand analysis
     Analysis of historical growth and absorption data
D.   Fundamental demand forecast
     Submarket specific demand forecast
     Major demand drivers
   1.   Population (creates households)
   2.   Income (creates retail buying power)
   3.   Employment (creates offices/industrial users)

Step 4.   **Supply Analysis (Survey and Forecast of Competition)**

A.   Existing stock of competitive properties
B.   Properties under construction of competitive properties
C.   Potential competition.
   1.   Proposed construction
   2.   Probable additional construction
D.   Attributes and characteristics of competitive properties
   1.   Economic and financial
   2.   Locational
   3.   Site
   4.   Structure

Table 9.4: Six-Step Process (*continued*)

Step 5.	**Analyze the Interaction of Supply and Demand**

    A.   Competitive environment
    B.   Residual demand concepts

Step 6.	**Forecast Subject Capture (Market Penetration Concepts)**

    A.   Inferred methods
        Comparison of subject to general market indicators
- Comparable property data
- Secondary data surveys and forecasts
- Subject historical performance
- Local economic analysis
- Other

    B.   Fundamental capture methods
        Estimate subject capture potential of fundamental demand forecast by such methods as:
- Share of market
- Adjust by quantifiable rating techniques
- Subject historical capture rate
- Other

    C.   Reconcile subject capture indications derived by analysis of inferred and fundamental methods

Use of Study Process (Six Step) Conclusions

- Economic demand data for financial testing of highest and best use alternatives
- Economic demand data for the valuation models

- Infrastructure
- Zoning
- Title restrictions
- Linkages to major employers and amenities
- Public planning for growth
- Population trends

Step 2. *Market delineation.* To analyze the characteristics of likely buyers of the specified housing units, the analyst develops a consumer profile describing income levels, household size, age, and preferences. The market area of potential buyers may be defined in terms of the following:

- Time-distance relationships, e.g., the commuting time to employment centres and support facilities
- Social or political boundaries, e.g., school districts, voting precincts
- Man-made or natural boundaries, e.g., major thoroughfares, physical barriers
- The location of competitive housing

Step 3. *Forecast demand.* Demand for single-family homes is generally analyzed using demographic data. Once the market area is defined, the analyst can compile various figures for that area:

- The current and projected population within the defined market area.
- The current and projected number of households, keeping in mind that household size varies with the age of the head of the household.
- The number of current and projected households headed by owners and those headed by renters. (There may be an overlapping category of renters who can afford to buy.)

With that population information, the analyst can break down the number of owner-occupied households according to their income levels to determine the percentage of households that are or will be able to meet the mortgage payments required by local lending practices and interest rates and other housing costs such as expenses for maintenance, insurance, and taxes. Adjusting the number of owner-headed households that can or will be able to afford the housing by the vacancy rate in the market yields measures of the existing and anticipated demand for the subject property.

Step 4. *Competitive supply analysis.* An inventory of competitive supply includes identifying the number of the following:

- Existing competitive properties within the subject's identified market area
- Properties under construction in that area
- Planned properties in the area for which building permits have been obtained
- Proposed properties in the area

The total number of competitive properties in the defined market area for the projection period can be refined by checking the total number of building permits issued against those actually put to use in recent years. In addition to quantitative measures of current and anticipated supply, this step in the analysis process includes comparison of the subject and its competition for specific amenities and attributes that give housing units a competitive advantage or disadvantage.

Step 5. *Equilibrium or residual analysis.* Analysts can compare existing and potential demand with current and anticipated competitive supply to determine whether demand for additional units or square footage of housing (marginal demand) exists or when it may develop.

Step 6. *Forecast subject capture.* The final step in the market/marketability analysis process for a proposed subdivision is to analyze the competitive rating to forecast the likely capture rate for the subject, i.e., the market share the subject property is likely to capture. The analyst makes qualitative judgments regarding the relative appeal of the subject property in the marketplace that must be reconciled with the quantitative evidence of marginal demand.

The goal of the market/marketability analysis for a proposed subdivision is often more than just a forecast of subject capture. Many clients also want to know if the project is economically feasible and what prices the market will accept for the product. In the optional seventh step of the market/marketability analysis process, the analyst tests the feasibility of various market scenarios. The break-even point, where expected construction costs and the client's desired profit margin match the anticipated sale price, often serves as a starting point for testing pricing alternatives. The analyst can also test exceptionally optimistic or pessimistic market forecasts, providing best- and worst-case scenarios.

For an Existing Apartment Complex

To retain its value over time, an existing apartment complex needs to be able to compete effectively in the marketplace. The subject property's vacancy rate is one indicator of the relative health of a property, but market/marketability analysis for such a property involves additional considerations.

Step 1. *Property productivity analysis.* As for most property types, the first step in market/marketability analysis for an apartment building involves a preliminary analysis of the legal, physical, and locational attributes of the subject property and similar buildings in competitive apartment districts. Important characteristics of an existing apartment complex include the following:

- Design and appearance of the property
- Number, size, and mix of units
- Site improvements and amenities (in units and for complex as a whole)
- Parking
- Zoning (particularly the possibility of a zoning change for potential condominium conversion)
- Infrastructure
- Public planning for growth
- Natural features and land use trends
- Linkages to major employers and amenities

Step 2. *Market delineation.* The market area of potential renters is similar to that of potential home buyers. The boundaries of the market area for an existing apartment are based on the following:

- Time-distance relationships, e.g., the commuting time to employment centres and support facilities
- Social or political boundaries, e.g., school districts, voting precincts
- Man-made or natural boundaries; e.g., major thoroughfares, physical barriers
- The location of competitive housing

In addition, the analyst investigates the tenant profile (e.g., occupational profile, income level, and other demographic information) for the subject property and the market area in this step of the market/marketability analysis process.

Step 3. *Forecast demand.* Analysts forecast the demand for an existing apartment complex using both inferred and fundamental methods. The inferred (trend) analysis of the subject's market area includes investigation of the following:

- General growth trends
- Residential construction trends
- Historical absorption figures
- Real rental rates

Relevant information gathered in the fundamental analysis of apartment demand includes the following:

- The current and projected population within the defined market area
- The current and projected number of households (dividing population figures by average household size)
- The number of current and projected households occupied by owners and those occupied by renters
- The number of households that are or will be able to meet the monthly rent on units in the subject property

An adjustment for *frictional vacancy* in the market may need to be made for proposed construction, but for existing projects, the analysis usually focuses on the ability of the subject property to capture actual occupancy so an adjustment is not necessary. Additional adjustments may be needed for move-up demand, which is generated by the upward mobility of lower-income households, and latent (or pent-up) demand, which is often a result of underbuilding or high financing costs that restrict new construction.

Step 4. *Competitive supply analysis.* The competitive supply of apartments in a market area takes into account the following:

- Existing competitive properties
- Properties under construction
- Planned properties for which building permits have been obtained
- Proposed properties

To complete this step, the analyst compares the location, age, and amenities of the subject to those of the competitive properties.

Step 5. *Equilibrium or residual analysis.* A net excess or shortage of apartment units in the market can be determined by comparing the results of the analyses in Steps 3 and 4.

Step 6. *Forecast subject capture.* The inferred analysis of the market area is revisited along with additional fundamental analysis to generate a subject capture rate. The subject's current occupancy can be compared to the estimated number of occupied units in the market, or a pro rata share can be calculated by dividing the total number of units in the subject with the total number in the market. In addition, the analyst compares competitive ratings for the subject property and competitive properties. If the analyst uses more than one form of fundamental analysis to calculate a capture rate, the separate conclusions should be reconciled.

> **frictional vacancy**
> The amount of vacant space needed in a market for its orderly operation. In a stabilized market, where supply and demand are in balance, frictional vacancy allows for move-ins and move-outs. In markets for income-producing property, frictional vacancy measures the lost rental income as leases roll over and expire.

Analyzing Retail Space Demand

To forecast the demand for an existing or proposed community shopping centre at a specific site over a given period (e.g., 5 or 10 years), an appraiser follows these steps:

Step 1. *Property productivity analysis.* Analysis of the legal, physical, and locational attributes of the subject retail centre and competitive centres in or near its trade area focuses on current industry standards. Retail properties can become outdated quickly as industry norms change. Analysts pay particular attention to the following attributes of the subject site and improvements:

- Land-to-building area ratio
- Building area
- Parking
- Frontage, visibility, and signage
- Topography
- Utilities
- Landscaping
- Design and building layout
- Amenity features
- Store size
- Store depth
- Tenant mix and marketing

Locational factors are also important for retail properties. The locational attributes that analysts should investigate include the following:

- Land uses and linkages with the surrounding community
- Site location in relation to patterns of urban growth
- Proximity to competitive supply

Step 2. *Market delineation.* Effective analytical tools for defining the primary and secondary trade areas of a shopping centre have been objects of study for many years. The most commonly used techniques include the following:

- Trade area circles, in which preliminary trade area boundaries are adjusted for the specific geographic, demographic, and economic characteristics of the community

- Gravitational models, a variation of trade area circles that takes into account the effects of competition[8]

- Customer spotting, a more detailed form of trade area circles in which actual customer addresses are surveyed to determine distances and linkages

Step 3. *Forecast demand.* Inferred analysis of retail demand may include study of the following:

- Economic base and city growth trends
- Citywide retail centre occupancy
- Competitive centre occupancy

---

[8] See William Reilly, *Methods for the Study of Retail Relationships* (Austin: University of Texas, 1959).

Fundamental demand for retail space requires further scrutiny of market data, including the following:

- Overall population of the trade area
- Number of households
- Average household income
- Percentage of average household income spent on retail purchases
- Percentage of retail purchases typically made at shopping centres similar to the subject
- Percentage of purchases made at the subject shopping centre allocated to primary and secondary trade areas
- Volume of sales per square foot of retail area required to support the subject
- Normal vacancy rate in the market

The estimates of inferred and fundamental demand can be reconciled with a ratio analysis of the trade area in which the analyst compares the current amount of occupied retail square footage per capita to the future population forecast. The conclusions of these analyses may be further adjusted to account for retail income from outside the trade area and leakage of retail income to other areas.

Step 4. *Competitive supply analysis.* As for other property types, an inventory of competitive retail space covers the following:

- Existing competitive properties
- Properties under construction
- Planned properties for which building permits have been obtained
- Proposed properties

To complete the analysis, the supply of competitive space is rated according to the following:

- Size
- Access and location
- Quality of merchandise
- Reputation
- Rental rates
- Vacancy
- Tenant mix

The analysis of competitive supply should yield estimates of the square footage of specific competition, the market rent the subject can expect to generate in the current market, and a comparative ranking of the subject.

Step 5. *Equilibrium or residual analysis.* The difference between supportable leasable space and the amount of existing and anticipated retail space will be the estimate of additional space needed. Sales per square foot in individual retail stores may also indicate the performance level of an existing shopping centre, the centre's share of the market, and whether there is opportunity for expansion. Analysts may use this data to check the reasonableness of the estimate of additional space demanded. If there is a current surplus of retail space, the forecast of market conditions may identify when in the future the available retail space will be absorbed and demand for additional retail space will begin to come on line.

Step 6. *Forecast subject capture.* Since retail concepts can change so quickly, subject capture is especially difficult to forecast for retail properties. In addition to inferred analysis of historical capture rates of the subject and competitive properties, analysts can use several fundamental methods to support an estimate of subject capture:

- Quantitative ratings of the subject and its competition

- The size-of-the-centre technique, in which the drawing power of a shopping centre is related to its size relative to competing properties

- Ratio analysis, which is applied like the size-of-the-centre technique but segments demand to the subject property only

Analyzing Office Space Demand

To forecast the demand for existing or proposed office space in a particular *node* or district over a given period, an appraiser analyzes the relationship between supply and demand in the overall market area and the district's actual and potential share of the existing and projected demand. The time when a proposed building will reach stabilized occupancy can be forecast in this way. An appraiser can estimate demand for office space in the overall market area with the following steps:

Step 1. *Property productivity analysis.* Tenancy and class are primary identifiers of an office building's competitive status. Physical items of comparison include the following items:

- Building design and construction materials
- Signage
- Exterior lighting
- Street layout
- Utilities
- Parking
- Lot and building lines
- Landscaping and grading
- Office space layout
- Quality and style of finish in tenancies
- Floor sizes
- Stairways, corridors, and elevators
- Electrical system
- Heating, ventilation, and air-conditioning
- Amenities
- Security
- Building management and tenant mix

Locational considerations for office buildings are often analyzed both in terms of the subject's location within a cluster of office buildings and that node's location relative to other nodes in the competitive market area.

Step 2. *Market delineation.* Unlike residential and retail trade areas, which are defined by the consumers they serve, an office market is tied more to the reputation of the businesses housed in the office than by the convenience of the location. The market area for an office building is generally diffused over a broad metropolitan area, with law firms and financial institutions often seeking space in prestigious, centrally located buildings, while businesses providing other types of services may prefer suburban offices with ample parking facilities and reasonable rents.

Step 3. *Forecast demand.* To estimate office demand, the analyst must investigate various types of information:

- Size of the workforce occupying office space, segmented by occupational category[9]
- Size of the workforce occupying office space in the subject's class
- Requisite space per worker[10]
- Normal vacancy rate

Analysts may make projections in annual, biannual, or multi-year increments. If an appraiser develops a 10-year forecast and steady growth is anticipated, the demand for the first period is subtracted from the demand for the last period and the difference is divided by the number of periods in the forecast to yield an annual demand estimate.

Step 4. *Competitive supply analysis.* In addition to competitive space under construction or in planning, the competitive supply of office space in a market may be affected by demolitions, renovations, and the adaptation of space now put to other uses. Information on proposed office properties may be difficult to obtain, especially reliable information on the timing of new construction and its completion. Important characteristics of competing properties include the following:

- Size (gross building area or rental area)
- Age
- Vacancy level
- Access
- Parking
- Tenant quality
- Building management
- Building quality and condition
- Amenities
- Support facilities

Step 5. *Equilibrium or residual analysis.* In comparing the existing and projected demand for office space with the total supply of current and anticipated competitive office space, the appraiser should consider potential move-up or fall-out demand for Class A and Class B buildings. Some tenants move up from Class B to Class A space in a down market with declining rents, while others fallout from Class A to Class B space in an active market where rents are increasing. In an in depth analysis, an appraiser also

---

[9]   One way to calculate the number of office space occupants in economic and occupational sectors involves establishing the ratio between the number of office workers and the number of total workers in each sector. In a sector such as finance, insurance, and real estate (FIRE), a high percentage (more than two-thirds) of all office workers occupy space in freestanding office buildings, i.e., buildings entirely occupied by office workers. The number of FIRE office workers in freestanding buildings may be estimated by multiplying the total number of workers by this percentage. In sectors such as manufacturing, however, a very low percentage of office workers occupy space in freestanding office buildings. Using these ratios, the number of office workers in each sector can be determined and the aggregate of office workers in all sectors can be calculated. See Ian Alexander, Office Location and Public Policy (New York: Chancer Press, 1979).

[10]   The average space required for an office worker ranges from 125 to 150 square feet. Very general estimates of average area requirements are published by the Building Owners and Managers Association (BOMA). Because the square foot area required per employee varies widely with community size and the type of employment in the community, market analysts should compare BOMA estimates with area-per-worker data developed as part of the competitive supply analysis. Estimates obtained from other national and local sources may also vary.

considers space subject to pre-leasing and space that will become vacant when current tenant leases expire. If an appraiser anticipates that demand for space will grow at a steady rate, the total supply that is available for occupancy may be divided by projected annual demand to determine the absorption period. At the end of the absorption period, additional space will be required. This point in time represents a "window" for development.

Step 6. *Forecast subject capture.* An appraiser must analyze development patterns in the district in order to determine a particular node or district's share of the overall market projection. Central business districts are characterized by the greatest density of development, while suburban office complexes attract tenants with lower rents and easier access, for both employees and customers. Not all suburbs share equally in the market for office space. Analysts should compare development patterns in areas that closely resemble the subject district. Key demographic features such as total population and educational and income levels are believed to be closely correlated with the ability of a suburban area to support an office building.

> **node**
> A cluster of properties with the same or complementary uses, Generally a nucleus of office buildings and retail stores. Downtown central business districts (CBDs), the primary sites of office building nodes, usually house financial institutions, corporate headquarters, and government offices. Other office building nodes include uptown areas, which develop along the axis between the CBD and the suburbs; office parks, which accommodate the needs of research and development and manufacturing industries; and shopping centres, which provide office space for tenants serving residents of the trade area.

The appraiser can develop a ratio by dividing the amount of existing office space in the district by the amount of office space in the overall market area. Such a ratio only reflects the district's *fair share* of the market, however, and may not provide an accurate forecast. The appraiser must also consider market preferences in determining the ratio.

To forecast when a proposed building will reach stabilized occupancy, the appraiser can estimate the construction period and an absorption rate based on pre-leasing and the historic performance of competitive buildings. Analysts interpret historic performance and use it to forecast expectations, but this information must be considered in its proper context. Performance may have been especially high during periods of rapid growth and unusually low during periods of stagnation. Detailed data on occupancy may describe not only nodal and district patterns, but also absorption rates for different building types (e.g., low-, mid-, and high-rise) or different building classes (e.g., Class A, Class B, Class C) and different occupants, e.g., anchor tenants or non-anchor tenants, corporate management, research and development departments, professional services.

> **fall-out demand**
> In markets characterized by increasing rents, office building tenants who "fall out" of the market for Class A space to Class B space or from Class B to Class C space.
>
> **move-up demand**
> In markets characterized by declining rents, office building tenants who "move up" from Class B to Class A space or from Class C to Class B space.

Analyzing Hotel Demand

The source of demand for hotel rooms depends largely on the nature of the subject property, i.e., whether it is a commercial establishment, a convention hotel, or a leisure or resort property. A proposed hotel near an established suburban office park would probably target business travelers, and the future absorption of office space in that submarket may be a good indicator of demand growth in the commercial sector. A large resort hotel in an undeveloped coastal area would draw from a much different demographic, and the market/ marketability analysis process would differ as well, if only in the sources of data used by the analyst.

Step 1. *Property productivity analysis.* In general, the following attributes of a hotel's site and improvements are important factors in determining the property's competitiveness:

- Size
- Room rate structure
- Overall decor and physical appearance
- Quality of management
- Chain affiliation
- Quality and character of the market area
- Facilities and amenities offered
- Revenue per available room (RevPAR), which is a common unit of comparison used in the lodging industry to compare the income of competing facilities

The importance of these factors may depend on the type of lodging being analyzed. Access and visibility will be more important factors in the competitive ability of a highway-oriented property, but amenities will be more important for a resort hotel.

The location of a hotel often indicates the likely clientele:

- Airport hotels and highway-oriented hotels cater to transient guests.
- Centre city hotels draw both tourists and business travelers.
- Hotels in suburban locations often rely on adjacent commercial or industrial businesses.
- Convention centre hotels or resort properties are themselves the destination rather than any nearby land use.

Step 2. *Market delineation.* Defining the market area for a hotel can be difficult because this type of property does not necessarily rely on households in nearby communities to generate demand. Instead, linkages to sources of visitations in the area can be more significant than the characteristics of the surrounding neighbourhood. Hotel development often occurs in clusters, and the emergence of a new cluster nearby can have an impact on the competitiveness of existing properties.

Step 3. *Forecast demand.* The inferred analysis of demand for hotel rooms may include study of the following:

- Travel and tourism data
- Hotel employment data and convention centre activity
- Office space absorption and employment statistics – particularly regarding wholesale and retail trade; financial, insurance, and real estate (FIRE); and services
- Occupancy rates at competitive lodging facilities in the subject's class and market area

Fundamental analysis of the demand for hotel rooms is based on historical occupancy and room rate data. Interviews with demand generators such as major employers or officials at chambers of commerce or visitor information centres may yield information that supports an estimate of hotel demand calculated from occupancy figures. Data useful in quantifying hotel demand includes the following:

- Number of nights per stay
- Number of people per room
- Periods of use during the year
- Prices paid for rooms
- Food, beverage, entertainment, and telephone usage
- Methods of travel

Analysts must consider seasonal fluctuations in demand for leisure-oriented properties.

Step 4. *Competitive supply analysis.* Information on existing hotel properties and developments under construction is generally available, but the difficulty of obtaining hotel financing and the influence of foreign investors complicate the analysis of proposed hotels. Even if market evidence supports demand for a proposed property, new development may be hindered by external factors such as fluctuations in the economies of foreign countries whose citizens invest in Canadian hotel properties. The analysis of all the hotels in the market area concludes with a comparison of the relative competitiveness of all existing and planned properties.

Step 5. *Equilibrium or residual analysis.* Analysts can compare current and anticipated demand for hotel rooms, measured in total room nights per year with the existing and planned supply of available rooms. There may be a lag between when demand is evident and when supply can be added to the marketplace to accommodate that demand.

Step 6. *Forecast subject capture.* The ratio of room nights that any hotel in a market area can be expected to capture can be derived from the fair share allotted to the property adjusted for competitive penetration factors. Analysts can refine the allocation of the total number of room nights demanded between competitive properties by considering customer preferences such as the following:

- Room price
- Travel distance
- Quality of facilities
- Amenities
- Management
- Image

Hotels with particularly high market penetration in one segment will generally have lower penetration rates in other segments.

Analyzing Industrial Properties

Market/marketability analysis for industrial properties is complicated by three factors:

- The market areas for these properties are more widely scattered.
- Demand is more limited.
- Supply is highly differentiated according to the operation of the enterprise.

The market for industrial real estate reflects the unique characteristics of the property type. High-priced industrial machinery is generally custom-built, and, except for the flex space in multi-tenant research and development (R&D) facilities, industrial plants are typically custom-designed to the needs of the particular production line. The owners and users of industrial real estate have necessarily made a long-term commitment. Many older industrial firms are precluded from ever moving due to the difficulty and expense of relocation. Newer industrial facilities are less specialized, providing for more flexibility in the marketplace when growing tenants move to larger facilities or tenants leave for other reasons.

Plants are often built with custom financing, which is the result of lengthy negotiation. Transactions may vary considerably even for highly similar properties, particularly when a business is sold along with the real estate. In the latter situation, transactional information may be confidential, so market data will not be readily available.

Market/marketability analysis is generally much easier for multi-tenant warehouses and distribution centres than for facilities housing more specialized industrial operations.

Step 1. *Property productivity analysis.* Location and access to transportation are primary determinants of a distribution facility's competitive ability. All industrial properties need access to an adequate supply of skilled labour, to meet both the current demand and any anticipated growth in the industrial sector. If warehouse tenants provide parts or raw materials for manufacturing operations in the immediate area, proximity to those businesses is essential. However, access to major trade routes is more important to large distribution centres that serve a wider market area, such as a regional distribution hub for a major retailer. Manufacturing plants that produce potentially hazardous waste materials need to be located near or have affordable access to disposal sites.

Physical elements of comparison include the following:

- Size (and land-to-building ratio or floor area ratio)
- Ceiling height
- Loading capacity
- Climate control
- Percentage of office space
- Automated operations (including the use of robotics and other evolving technologies)
- Utilities
- Security
- Building management and tenant mix
- Environmental regulations

Step 2. *Market delineation.* Established trade routes can define the boundaries of the competitive market for multi-tenant industrial space. Since warehouses and distribution centres must be close to major highways or railroad lines, industrial development will tend to cluster around those features, especially major freeway interchanges in centrally located provinces where a large percentage of the region's or even the country's population can be within a day's drive.

Step 3. *Forecast demand*. Demand analysis for industrial space is similar to the procedure for analyzing office space, but the analysis of industrial demand must take into account the functional limits on the use of industrial property and the different physical characteristics of warehouses and distribution centres. Analysts place less emphasis on general population change. Export activity may be a better indicator of industrial demand in a market area than population growth because the businesses that occupy warehouse space generally serve a wider clientele than the local community. The analyst investigates the following:

- Employment in manufacturing, wholesale, retail, transportation, communications, or public utilities
- Cost of available labour force in relation to alternative locations
- Patterns and directions of industrial growth and development, which often cluster along major highways and around intersections
- Presence of raw materials
- Exchange capability

For retail storage and wholesale distribution properties, the level of retail sales in a market may serve as an indicator of demand for that type of industrial space.

Step 4. *Competitive supply analysis*. Because industrial operations are such a fundamental part of a community's economic base, information on the competitive supply of warehouse space and vacancy levels is often compiled in research reports. Analysts can compare competing properties in terms of the following items:

- Size, particularly in relation to other industrial buildings
- Age
- Vacancy level
- Access
- Building management and tenant quality
- Building quality and condition
- Building size and tenant quality are particularly important factors. Large, single-tenant distribution facilities do not compete with smaller, multi-tenant warehouses and a building housing several closely related industrial tenants may not be competitive with buildings with more diverse tenant mixes.

Step 5. *Equilibrium or residual analysis*. Industrial real estate markets can react to increasing demand with more agility than the markets for other types of properties can because raw storage space is easier to construct than most other sorts of buildings with more intensive finishes. When comparing the existing and projected demand for industrial space with the total supply of current and anticipated industrial space and historical absorption trends, an analyst should keep in mind an industrial real estate market's potential for sudden change.

Step 6. *Forecast subject capture*. As long as the forecast period is not extended too far into the future, the share of marginal demand that a warehouse or distribution centre can expect to capture can be estimated with about as much certainty as the capture rate for office space. Historical absorption rates may help support an estimate of the general length of cyclical shifts in demand and supply for industrial space of the subject's type.

Analyzing Agricultural Properties

Like industrial properties, agricultural properties often have large market areas, with limited demand and highly segmented supply based on the agricultural product at a given operation. However, forecasting demand for agricultural land is even more difficult. To conduct market/marketability analysis for agricultural properties, appraisers must examine factors as diverse as national and regional economic trends, ecological and environmental considerations, and the character of the subject agricultural district. Land prices are affected by both short-term commodity prices and long-term federal policy involving farm subsidies and the leasing of adjacent public lands for grazing range or timber stands. The condition of the regional economy generally exerts an influence on land prices also. For example, a boom or slump in an energy or extractive industry that represents a region's economic base (e.g., oil in Alberta, lumber in British Columbia, or minerals in Quebec and Ontario) may generally enhance or depress property values.

Rural appraisers must consult statistical data on soil productivity and crop yields as well as analyses of the effects of erosion on future soil productivity and forecasts of artesian (aquifer) reserves and water available for irrigation. The appraiser should be aware of current and future environmental legislation and any momentum toward land or wildlife conservation.

Finally, the appraiser must be familiar with the characteristics of the immediate agricultural district and the specific types of agriculture and complementary land uses found in the area (e.g., fodder production for a livestock ranch or dairy farm). Other essential information includes local assessment rates, the principal type of ownership (e.g., family farm or agribusiness), and the level of recent sales activity or foreclosures.s

CHAPTER 10

LAND AND SITE ANALYSIS

An appraiser may undertake appraisal assignments to develop an opinion of the value of land only or to value both land and improvements. In either case, the appraiser must provide a detailed description and analysis of the land. Land can be raw or improved; raw land can be undeveloped or put to an agricultural use. Land may be located in rural, suburban, or urban areas and may have the potential to be developed for residential, commercial, industrial, agricultural, or special-purpose use.

This chapter focuses on the description and analysis of the land component of real property. Since appraisers typically deal with land that has been improved to some degree, the term site is often more precise than land; therefore, the term site is used predominantly in this chapter. The information needed to complete a full site description and analysis is noted and explained and sources for obtaining this information are presented. Although this discussion relates primarily to the property being appraised, the same type of data is collected and examined in analyzing the comparable properties used in the appraisal.

A parcel of land can have various site improvements that enable the vacant parcel to support a specific purpose. A site can have both on-site and off-site improvements that make it suitable for its intended use or development. Off-site improvements may include utility lines, access to roads, and water, drainage, and sewer systems. On-site improvements may include landscaping, site grading, access driveways, drainage improvements, accessory buildings, and support facilities.

> **site description**
> A comprehensive listing of site data, including a legal description, other title and record data, and information on the site's physical characteristics.

In valuing any type of property, the appraiser must describe and analyze the site. Site description consists of comprehensive factual data, information on land use restrictions, a legal description, other title and record data, and information on pertinent physical characteristics. Site analysis goes further. It is a careful study of factual data in relation to the market area characteristics that create, enhance, or detract from the utility and marketability of specific land or a given site as compared with other sites with which it competes.

> **raw land**
> Land on which no improvements have been made; land in its natural state before grading, construction, subdivision, or the installation of utilities.
>
> **site**
> Land that is improved so that it is ready to be used for a specific purpose.

One primary objective of site analysis requires the appraiser to gather data that will indicate the highest and best use of the site as though vacant so that the appraiser can estimate the land value for a specific use. Whether a site or raw land is being valued, the appraiser must determine and evaluate its highest and best use. When the highest and best use of land is for agriculture, the appraiser usually analyzes and values the land by applying the direct comparison approach. If the land is to be developed for urban use, the appraiser may use a more sophisticated technique such as subdivision development analysis. Chapter 12 discusses highest and best use in detail.

LEGAL DESCRIPTIONS OF LAND

Land boundaries differentiate separate ownerships, and the land within one set of boundaries may be referred to as a *parcel*, *lot*, *plot*, or *tract*. An appraiser may apply these terms to all types of improved and unimproved land and market participants often use them interchangeably. However, the appraiser should use the terms consistently in the appraisal report to avoid confusing the client.

A parcel of land generally refers to a piece of land that can be identified by a common description and is held in one ownership. Every parcel of real estate is unique. To identify individual parcels, appraisers rely on legal descriptions, surveys, or other descriptive information typically provided by the client or found in public records. A legal description identifies a property in such a way that it cannot be confused with any other property. An appraiser usually includes or references a legal description in an appraisal report, although it is not required.

In Canada, three methods are commonly used in legal descriptions of real property:

> **legal description**
> A description of land that identifies the real estate according to a system established or approved by law; an exact description that enables the real estate to be located and identified.

- Metes and bounds system
- Rectangular survey system
- Lot and block system

An appraiser should be familiar with these forms of legal description and know which form or forms are common in the area where the appraisal is being conducted.

Metes and Bounds

The oldest known method of surveying land is the metes and bounds system, in which land is measured and identified by describing its boundaries. A metes and bounds description of a parcel of real property describes the property's boundaries in terms of precise reference points. To follow a metes and bounds description, one starts at the point of beginning (POB), a primary survey reference point that is tied to a benchmark or adjoining surveys, and moves along past several intermediate reference points before finally returning to the POB. The return to the POB is called closing and is necessary to ensure the survey's accuracy.

Surveyors in the field increasingly rely on modern "total stations" to collect data in digital form. The familiar surveyor's measuring instrument mounted on a tripod uses infrared technology and today is augmented by portable computer technology. The data is downloaded into the surveyor's office computer for plotting the property boundaries and computing the land area. Coordinate geometry software and global positioning system (GPS) technology allow for more accurate determinations of directions, distances, and areas. GPS technology is only limited by physical obstructions that prohibit receiving satellite transmissions, and its use in surveying will probably increase.

> In Canada, the three principal methods used to describe real property are the metes and bounds, rectangular survey, and lot and block systems.

> **metes and bounds system**
> A system for the legal description of land that refers to the parcel's boundaries, which are formed by the point of beginning (POB) and all intermediate points (bounds) and the courses or angular direction of each point (metes).

The metes and bounds system is an older method of describing real property, and is found most often in provinces with the oldest land registry systems, e.g., the Maritime provinces. It is used across the country as a corollary to the rectangular survey system, especially in describing unusual or odd-shaped parcels of land.

Rectangular Survey System

The rectangular survey system is also known as the Dominion Land Survey (DLS) and the section and township system. It is commonly used in western Canada, and to a lesser extent in Ontario.

The initial reference points for government surveys were established in 1871, shortly after Manitoba and the Northwest Territories became part of Canada. From each point specified, true east-west and north-south lines were drawn. The north-south reference points for government surveys were established firstly as being west of specified meridians. (The prime meridian of 98 degrees lies approximately 12 miles west of Winnipeg). East-west reference points commence at the 49th parallel of latitude. From each point specified, true east-west and north-south lines were drawn. The east-west lines are called base lines and the north-south lines are called principal meridians. Each

> **rectangular survey system**
> A land survey system. called the Dominion Land Survey (DLS), used in western Canada and to a lesser extent, Ontario; it divides land into townships approximately six miles square, each normally containing 36 one-square-mile sections of 640 acres, except when adjusted for the curvature of the earth.
>
> **base line**
> In the government survey system of land description, a line running due east and west through the initial point of a principal meridian from which township lines are established.
>
> **principal meridian**
> In land surveying, major north-south lines established as general reference points. They converge towards the North Pole. Therefore, the north edge of every township is slightly shorter than the south.

principal meridian has a unique number and is crossed by its own base line. Using these base lines and principal meridians, land can be located accurately.

The land surveyed under the rectangular survey system is divided by north-south lines six miles apart called range lines, and by east-west lines six miles apart called township lines. The system has its basis in the imperial system of measurement: as no province has undertaken a comprehensive program of metric conversion, dimensions remain in imperial until resurveying occurs. The rectangles created where these lines intersect are called townships. The standard township is six miles square and contains 36 square miles. When applied to surveying, the term township has two meanings: a location on a line north or south of a base line and a square of land that measures six miles by six miles. In Ontario, townships were oriented to geographic features including Lake Ontario, the St. Lawrence River, and early military roads. Concession lines defined townships and subdivisions involved lot surveys. The Ontario system is referred to as the township lot and concession system. Township can also refer to a political subdivision similar to a county, regional district, or rural municipality.

The intersection of a base line and a principal meridian is the starting point from which the range lines and township lines are counted to locate a specific township in a legal description. Ranges are numbered east and west from the principal meridian; townships are numbered north and south from the base line.

Townships are divided into 36 sections, each of which is one mile square and contain 640 acres. For a more specific description of a parcel, a section may be divided into quarter sections and fractions of quarter sections. To accommodate the spherical shape of the earth, additional lines called guide meridians are drawn every 24 miles east and west of the principal meridian. Other lines, called standard parallels, are drawn every 24 miles north and south of the base line. These correction lines are used to adjust the rectangular townships to fit the curvature of the earth.

Lot and Block System

The *lot and block system* was developed as an outgrowth of the rectangular survey system and can be used to simplify the locational descriptions of small parcels, particularly for lots in densely populated metropolitan areas, suburban areas, and exurbs. This system is sometimes referred to as the *recorded plat survey system* or the recorded map survey system. The system was established when developers subdivided land in the rectangular survey system and assigned lot numbers to individual sites within blocks. The maps of these subdivisions were then filed with the local government to establish a public record of their locations. Each block was identified precisely using a ground survey or established monuments.

Applying the lot and block system to old, unsurveyed communities helped to identify each owner's site or parcel of land. Typically, a surveyor located the boundaries of streets on the ground and drew maps outlining the blocks. Then lot lines were established by agreement among property owners. A precise, measured description was established for each lot and each was given a number or letter that could be referred to in routine transactions. For example, a lot in a rectangular survey area might be described as follows: Lot 5 of Block 18, registered plan 5396, southwest quarter of Section 10, Township 3 North, Range 3 East. This information was recorded in public records and was known as a recorded plat of the defined area or subdivision.

TITLE AND RECORD DATA

Before making an on-site inspection, an appraiser should obtain an appropriate description and other property data from the client or from published sources and public documents. Most jurisdictions have a government office (which increasingly is accessible via the internet) where transactions are documented and made public. Under the registry system, the accessibility of public records, which is legally known as constructive notice, ensures that interested individuals are able to research and, if necessary, contest deed transfers. Most registry offices keep index books for land deeds and mortgages, from which the book and page number of a recorded deed may be found. An appraiser might also find pertinent information in the property's abstract of title, which includes a summary of conveyances, transfers, and other facts used as evidence of title as well as any other public documents that may impair title. Under the Torrens system, this information is shown on the certificate of title. In addition, official municipal consolidated legal plans may exist and be available for examination at local or regional government offices.

Sometimes public records do not contain all relevant information about a particular property. Although official documents are the most dependable sources of information, they may be incomplete or not suited to the appraiser's purposes. Useful support data can be found in land registration systems, land data banks, and asses-

THE TORRENS SYSTEM

A system of land registration used in some Canadian provinces in which the land title authority issues title certificates covering the ownership of land, which often serve as title insurance. The system was first introduced in Australia in 1858, to combat the problems of uncertainty, complexity, and cost associated with prior title systems, which depended on profit of an unbroken chain of title back to a good "root" of title. Under the common-law form of prior title systems, land owners needed to provide their ownership of a piece of land back to the original grant of land by the Crown to its first owner. (This is the deeds registration system associated with the Registry system found in eastern Canada.) The documents relating to transactions involving the land were collectively known as the "title deeds" or the "chain of title". The original land grant could have occurred many years prior, and be influenced by many changes in the land's ownership, or of interests affecting it. A person's ownership over land could be challenged, possibly causing great expense to land owners and hindering its development. Even an exhaustive search into the chain of title would not give an owner complete security because of the possibility of undetected outstanding interests; claims by others might not be obvious.

sors' maps. The availability of internet access to government land titles or registry records simplifies reference to title and deed information.

WHERE TO FIND – TITLE DATA AND OWNERSHIP INFORMATION

Most provinces now make available title and registry information through the internet. Some commercial data providers maintain reporting services available on a subscription basis, and title search companies will conduct customized research for a fee. Provincial agencies such as the assessor's office make land titles data such as sales reports available.

A property's legal owner and type of ownership can be ascertained from the public records maintained at the provincial or territorial land titles or land registry office. This information is often available online for a fee, and local title search or abstract companies may also provide useful information.

Ownership Information

If an appraiser values a partial interest in a property rather than the fee simple interest, the appraiser should indicate and carefully analyze the excluded elements of title. An appraiser who is asked to develop an opinion of the value of a fractional ownership interest must understand the exact type of legal ownership to define the property rights to be appraised.

After defining the property rights being appraised, the appraiser must identify any excluded rights that may affect value. In addition, Canadian Uniform Standards requires appraisers to analyze and report any prior sales occurring within a specified number of years. In most assignments, the appraiser will also investigate the presence and nature of surface and subsurface rights through a title report, an abstract of title, or other documentary evidence of the property rights to be appraised. Title data indicates easements, rights of way and other restrictions that might limit the use of the property, as well as special rights such as air rights, rights-to-purchase, reversionary rights, mineral rights, obligations for lateral support, and easements for common walls. Typically, the appraiser is not an expert in title information but must rely on legal opinions, title research reports, and title data provided by other professionals. Easements, rights of way, and private and public restrictions affect property value.

Easements may provide for overhead and underground electrical transmission lines, underground sewers or tunnels, flowage, aviation routes, roads, walkways, and open space. Some easements or rights of way acquired by utility companies or public agencies may not have been used for many years, and the appraiser's physical inspection of the property may not disclose any evidence of such use. In certain jurisdictions, easements that are not used for a finite period of time may be automatically terminated. Use of a property for access without the owner's written permission may give the user a prescriptive easement across the property. This type of easement usually must be used for several years without being contested or challenged by the property owner. Restrictions cited in the deed or title may limit the type of building or business that may be conducted on the property. A typical example is a restrictive covenant that prohibits the sale of liquor or gasoline in a certain place. Often a title report will not specify the details of private restrictions. The appraiser must read a copy of the deed or other conveyance to identify the limitations imposed on the property; interpretation can require legal training or the advice of a lawyer. Appraisers often include a limiting condition in their appraisal reports regarding easements or private restrictions that have not been recorded in public records.

Zoning and Land Use Information

Local governments such as cities, towns, and regional districts usually regulate land use and development, but they are often subject to regional, provincial, and federal controls as well. In analyzing land use controls, an appraiser considers all current regulations and the likelihood of a change in the law. Usually a zone calls for a general use such as residential, commercial, or industrial and then specifies a type or density of use. Zoning and other land use regulations often control use and building standards, with the latter including the following:

- Height and size of buildings
- Lot coverage or floor space ratio (FSR) density[1]
- Required landscaping or open space
- Number of units allowed
- Parking requirements
- Sign requirements
- Building setbacks
- Plan lines for future street widenings
- Other factors of importance to the highest and best use of the site

Most zoning ordinances identify and define the uses to which a property may be put without reservation or recourse to legal intervention. This is referred to as a *use by right*. They also describe the process for obtaining nonconforming use permits, variances, and zoning changes, if permitted. In areas subject to floods, earthquakes, and other natural hazards, special zoning and building regulations may impose restrictions on construction. In coastal and historic districts, zoning restrictions may govern building location and design.

The appraiser must also consider potential changes in government regulations. If, for example, a building moratorium or cessation of land use applications is in effect for a stated period, a property's prospective highest and best use may have to be delayed. The appraiser must consider the appropriateness of the current zoning and the reasonable probability of a zoning change. Highest and best use recommendations may rely on the probability of a zoning change. One of the criteria for the highest and best use conclusion is that the use must be legally permissible. If the highest and best use of a site is predicated on a zoning change, the appraiser must investigate the probability that such a change will occur. The appraiser may interview planning and zoning staff and study patterns of zoning change to assess the likelihood of a change. The appraiser can generally eliminate those uses that are clearly not compat-

---

[1] SR (floor space ratio) is synonymous with the term FAR (floor area ratio) and is defined as the ratio or percentage of the site area that can be built upon, e.g., if a property has 100,000 square feet and a 0.5 or 50% FSR, then the buildable area is 50,000 square feet (100,000 x 0.5)

ible with existing uses in the area as well as uses that have previously been denied. After reviewing available public and private land use information, the appraiser may also prepare a forecast of land development for the area. If the zoning of the subject site is not compatible with the probable forecast uses, the probability of a change in the zoning is especially high or speculative. However, the appraiser should recognize that a zoning change is never 100% certain and should alert the client to that fact if it is relevant to the purpose of the appraisal.

WHERE TO FIND – ZONING AND LAND USE INFORMATION

Although zoning by-laws and maps are public records that are available at zoning offices or on the internet, an appraiser may need help from planning and zoning staff to understand the impact of zoning regulations. Often an appraiser must contact several agencies. Zoning and land use restrictions are not usually listed in the recorded title to a property, so confirmation from controlling agencies is necessary.

Assessment and Tax Information

Real property taxes in all jurisdictions are based on ad valorem assessments. Taxation levels are significant in considering a property's potential uses. From the present assessment, the current tax rate and a review of previous tax rates, the appraiser can form a conclusion about future trends in property taxation. Assessed values might not be good indicators of the market value of individual properties because mass appraisals based on statistical methodology tend to equalize the application of taxes to achieve parity among assessment levels in a given district. Nevertheless, in some areas and for some property types, assessed value may approximate market value if the enabling legislation requires market value assessments. The reliability of local assessments as indicators of market value varies from district to district.

WHERE TO FIND – ASSESSMENT AND TAX INFORMATION

The records of the assessor or tax collector can provide details concerning a property's assessed value and annual tax burden. Often, an appraiser obtains property information from the local assessment authority in the early stages of an appraisal to confirm legal description, address, and other property particulars.

PHYSICAL CHARACTERISTICS OF LAND

In site description and analysis, an appraiser describes and interprets how the physical characteristics of the site influence value and how the physical improvements relate to the site and to neighbouring properties. Important physical characteristics include the following:

- Site size and shape
- Corner influence
- Plottage

- Excess land and surplus land
- Topography
- Utilities
- Site improvements
- Accessibility
- Environment
- Size and Shape

A size and shape description states a site's dimensions such as street frontage, width, and depth and lists any advantages or disadvantages caused by these physical characteristics. The appraiser describes the site and analyzes how its size and shape affect property value. The appraiser should pay special attention to any characteristics that are unusual for the neigh-

> The physical characteristics of a site relate to size, shape, plottage potential, corner influence, the presence of excess or surplus land, topography, available utilities, on-site and off-site improvements, location, and environment.

bourhood. The effects of the size and shape of a property vary with its probable use. For example, an odd-shaped parcel may be appropriate for a dwelling but unacceptable for certain types of commercial or industrial use. A triangular lot may not have the same utility as a rectangular lot due to its size and shape.

The size of a parcel of land is measured and expressed in different units, depending on local custom and land use. In Canada, professional land surveyors' work is normally completed using the metric system; however, the real estate industry continues to work with the imperial system. Large tracts of land are usually measured in acres or hectares. Smaller parcels are usually measured in square feet or square metres. Imperial dimensions are expressed in feet and tenths of feet, not inches, for easy calculation.

Frontage is the measured footage of a site that abuts a street, lake or river, railroad, or other feature recognized by the market. The frontage may or may not be the same as the width of the property because a property may be irregularly shaped or have frontage on more than one side.

Size differences can affect value and are considered in site analysis. Reducing sale prices to consistent units of comparison facilitates the analysis of comparable sites and can identify trends in market behaviour. Generally, as size increases, unit prices decrease. Conversely, as size decreases, unit prices increase. The functional utility or desirability of a site often varies depending on the types of uses to be placed on the parcel. Different prospective uses have ideal size and depth characteristics that influence value and highest and best use. An appraiser should recognize this fact when appraising sites of unusual size or shape. An appraiser can observe value tendencies by studying market sales of lots of various sizes and their ability to support specific uses or intensities of development. In residential appraisal, a large triangular lot may not have any greater value because only one dwelling unit can be built on it according to zoning and subdivision regulations. The large undeveloped remainder would be surplus land, which is discussed below.

Metric	Imperial
Distance – Metre(m)	Distance – Feet (Ft)
1m = +/-3.028084 feet	1 ft = 0.3048006 metre
Distance – Kilometre (km)	Distance – Mile (mi)
1km = +/-0.621371 mile (3,280.84 feet)	1 mi = +/- 1.609.35 kilometres (1,609.35 metres)
Area – Hectare (ha)	Area – Acre (ac)
1 ha = 2.471054 acres (107,639.1 square feet)	1 ac = 0.404687 hectare (4,046.87 square metres)

Corner Influence

In the layout of building improvements and the subdivision of large plots, corner lots have more flexibility and higher visibility than interior properties. A store on a corner may have the advantage of direct access from both streets and prominent corner visibility and exposure. Corner exposure may provide advantageous ingress and egress for a drive-in business. For residential properties, corner locations may have negative implications; quiet, cul-de-sac sites in the interior of a subdivision may be more desirable and command higher prices. Residences on corner sites are exposed to more traffic noise and provide less security. Owners of corner sites may pay higher costs for front-footage sidewalks and assessments, and the side street setback may affect the permitted size of the building. Usually owners of residences on corner lots have to maintain a larger landscaped area that may, in fact, be public property.

Plottage

Sometimes highest and best use results from assembling two or more parcels of land under one ownership. If the combined parcels have a greater unit value than they did separately, plottage value is created. Plottage is an increment of value that results when two or more sites are combined to produce a larger site with greater utility.

corner influence
The effect on value produced by a property's location at or near the intersection of two streets; the increment of value or loss in value resulting from this location or proximity.

assemblage
The combining of two or more parcels, usually but not necessarily contiguous, into one ownership or use; the process that creates plottage value.

plottage
The increment of value created when two or more sites are combined to produce greater utility.

For example, there may be great demand for one-acre lots in an industrial park where most of the subdivided lots are of one-half acre. By itself, a half-acre lot has a value of $1.00 per square foot. However, when combined with an adjacent half-acre lot, the value may increase to $1.50 per square foot. The value difference may be offset by the premium a developer often has to pay to combine adjacent properties, or the reverse may occur if the lots are very large and assemblage yields a lower value per square foot in the marketplace due to negative economies of scale. Plottage value may also apply to an existing site of a special size or shape that has greater utility than more conventional, smaller lots. The appraiser analyzes neighbouring land uses and values to determine whether an appraised property has plottage value.

Plottage is significant in appraising agricultural land. Properties of less-than-optimum size have lower unit values because they cannot support the modern equipment needed to produce maximum profits. In an urban area, plottage of commercial office and retail sites and of residential apartment sites may increase the unit values of the lots assembled. For example, some cities wanting to encourage larger mixed-use developments will establish zoning policies that allow higher densities for larger sites. If a 66-foot wide lot can only achieve a 1.0 FSR, plottage will exist and developers will endeavour to assemble adjacent 66-foot lots.

Although the assemblage of land into a size that permits a higher and better use may increase the land's unit value (dollars per square foot or acre), the reverse may also occur. Land that must be divided or subdivided to achieve a higher and better use is commonly sold in bulk at a price less than the sum of the retail prices of its components. The lower unit price for the bulk sale reflects market allowances for risk, time, management, development, costs, sales costs, profit, and other considerations associated with dividing and marketing the land.

Excess Land and Surplus Land

A given land use has an optimum parcel size, configuration, and land-to-building ratio. Any extra or remaining land not needed to support the specific use may have a different value than the land area needed to support the improvement. The portion of the property that represents an optimal site for the existing improvements will reflect a typical land-to-building ratio. The appraiser can identify and quantify the land area needed to support the existing or ideal improvement. Any remaining land area is either *excess land* or *surplus land*.

Excess land is land that is not needed to serve or support the existing or proposed improvement. The highest and best use of the excess land may or may not be the same as the highest and best use of the improved parcel. Excess land has the potential to be sold separately and must be valued separately.

Surplus land is not currently needed to support the existing improvement and cannot be separated from the property and sold off. Surplus land does not have an independent highest and best use and may or may not contribute value to the improved parcel.

As an example, consider a residential property comprising a one-unit home and two standard-size lots in a fully developed subdivision. If the house was situated within the boundaries of a single lot and the normal land area for properties in the neighbourhood is a single lot, then the second, vacant lot would most likely be considered excess land, which could be separated from the lot of the existing

> **excess land**
> Land that is not needed to serve or support the existing improvement. The highest and best use of the excess land may or may not be the same as the highest and best use of the improved parcel. Excess land has the potential to be sold separately and must be valued separately.

> **surplus land**
> Land that is not currently needed to support the existing improvement but cannot be separated from the property and sold off. Surplus land does not have an independent highest and best use and may or may not contribute value to the improved parcel.

structure for future development to that parcel's highest and best use. If land values in the neighbourhood were $1.00 per square foot, then the excess land in this situation would probably add the full $1.00 per square foot to the value of the subject property, i.e., the house and the two lots. If the typical land area for properties in the neighbourhood were a double lot, regardless of building placement, then the same property would have neither excess land nor surplus land.

Now consider an industrial park where floor space ratios for warehouse properties range from 0.28 to 0.35 and land value is $2.00 per square foot. The subject property is a 20,000 square foot warehouse on a 100,000 square foot site, which results in floor space ratio of 0.20, well below the market area norm. If the additional land not needed to support the highest and best use of the existing property were in the back portion of the site, lacking access to the street, that land would probably be considered surplus land because it could not be separated from the site and does not have an independent highest and best use. In this situation, the surplus land would probably still contribute positively to the value of the subject property (because the existing improvements could still be expanded onto the surplus land), but it would most likely be worth less than the $2.00 per square foot price commanded by vacant land elsewhere in the industrial park.

Topography

Topographical studies provide information about land's contour, grading, natural drainage, soil conditions, view, and general physical usefulness. Sites may differ in value due to these physical characteristics. Steep slopes often impede building construction. Natural drainage can be advantageous, or, if a site is downstream from other properties or is a natural drainage basin for the area, it may have severely limited usefulness. Adequate drainage systems can offset the topographic and drainage problems that would otherwise inhibit the development of such a site. Upland land area (i.e., land above the mean high water line) and land with good drainage can typically support uses that are more intensive.

> Topographical characteristics, surface soil and subsoil quality, grade, drainage, and the bearing capacity of the soil determine the suitability of a land parcel for an agricultural use or a proposed improvement.

In describing topography, an appraiser must employ the terminology used in the area. What is described as a steep hill in one part of the country may be considered a moderate slope in another. In some instances, descriptions of a property's topography may be taken from published sources such as topographic maps (see Figure 10.1).

Geodetic Survey Program

Topographic maps prepared under the direction of the Geodetic Survey Division of Natural Resources Canada are referred to as quadrangles or quads They provide information that is useful in land descriptions (see Figure 10.2). Base lines, principal meridians, and township lines are shown along with topographic and man-made features. The topographic features commonly depicted on these maps include land elevations (represented by contour lines at specified intervals), rivers, lakes, inter-

Figure 10.1: Topographic Map

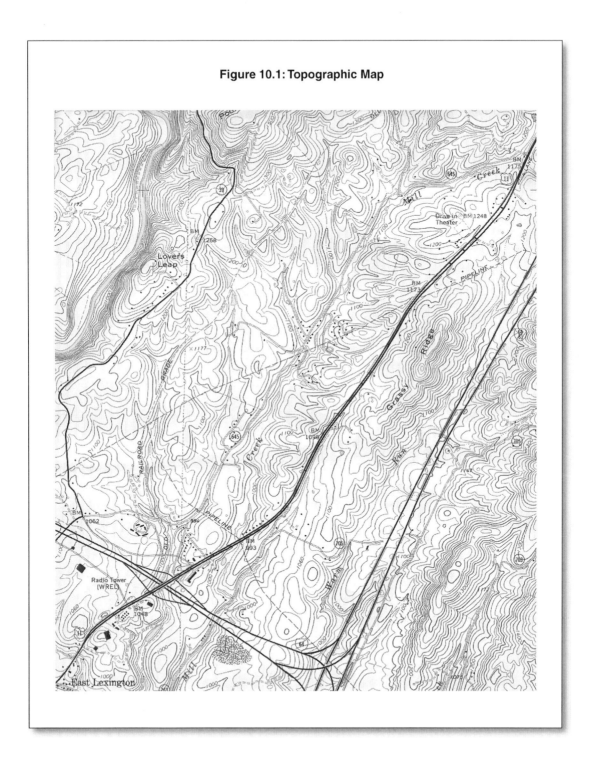

WHERE TO FIND – TOPOGRAPHIC MAPS

Topographic maps are available at most local and regional government offices and their websites.
The Centre for Topographic Information produces topographic maps of Canada at scales of 1:50,000 and 1:250,000. They are known as the National Topographic System (NTS). A government proposal to discontinue publishing of all hardcopy or paper topographic maps in favor of digital-only mapping data was shelved in 2006 after intense public opposition. National Resources Canada maintains the centre, and makes topographic maps and data available in print from regional offices and on the web. For more information, see: www.nrcan.gc.ca. Topographic and other maps are available online at *atlas.nrcan.gc.ca/site/english/maps/topo/index.html*

---

mittent streams and other bodies of water, poorly drained areas, and forest. The man-made features identified include improved and unimproved roads, highways, bridges, power transmission lines, levees, railroads, airports, churches, schools, and other buildings. Quadrangle maps also show surface geology.

Soil Analysis

Surface soil and subsoil conditions are important for both improved properties and agricultural land. A soil's suitability for building or for accommodating a septic system is important for all types of improved property, and it is a major consideration when the construction of large, heavy buildings is being contemplated. The need for special pilings or floating foundations has a major impact on the adaptability of a site for a particular use. Soil conditions affect the cost of development and therefore the property value.

Agronomists and soil scientists measure the agricultural qualities of soil and capacity of soil for specific agricultural uses. Engineers trained in soil mechanics test for soil consistency and load-bearing capacity. Local builders, developers, and others frequently know subsoil conditions, but if there is any doubt about the soil's bearing capacity, the client should be informed of the need for soil studies. All doubts must be resolved before the land's highest and best use can be successfully analyzed, or a description of any special assumptions must be included in the appraisal report.

WHERE TO FIND – SOILS DATA

Soils surveys conducted by Agriculture and Agri-Food Canada in aggregate are called the National Soil Database (NSDB). The NSDB is the set of computer readable files which contain soil, landscape, and climatic data for all of Canada. It serves as the national archive for land resources information that was collected by federal and provincial field surveys, or created by land data analysis projects.
For more information, see *www.agr.gc.ca*

Figure 10.2: US Department of the Interior Geological Survey

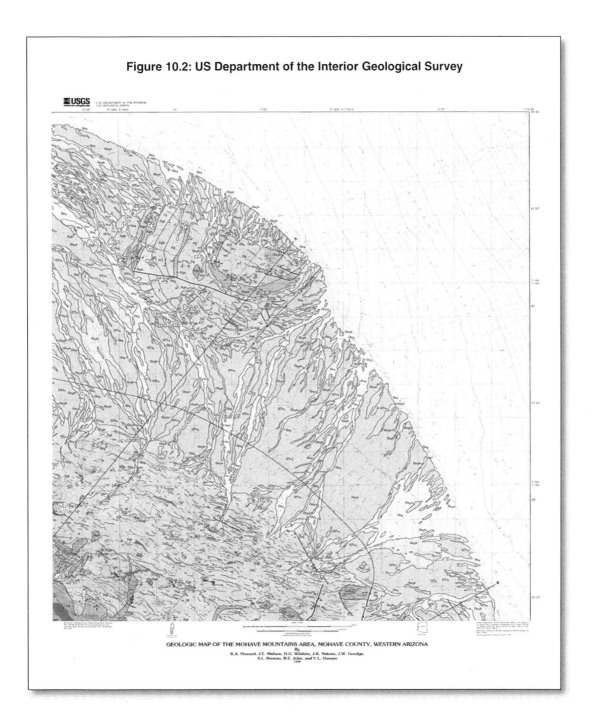

GEOLOGIC MAP OF THE MOHAVE MOUNTAINS AREA, MOHAVE COUNTY, WESTERN ARIZONA
By
K.A. Howard, J.E. Nielson, H.G. Wilshire, J.R. Nakata, J.W. Goodge,
S.L. Reneau, B.E. John, and V.L. Hansen
1999

Floodplain and Wetlands Analysis

Wetlands are lands that are seasonally or permanently covered by shallow water, including lands where the water table is at or close to the surface. The presence of abundant water causes the formation of hydric soils (lacking air) and favours the dominance of either hydrophytic plants (adapted to aquatic environments) or water-tolerant plants. Wetlands are characterized by plants adapted to saturated-soil conditions. The five major types of wetlands are marshes, swamps, bogs, fens, and shallow open waters.

Wetlands are the only ecosystem designated for conservation by international convention because they absorb the impact of hydrologic events, filter sediments and toxic substances, supply food and essential habitat for many species, provide products for food, energy, and building material, and are valuable recreational areas. Some wetlands help recharge groundwater, while others receive groundwater discharge. Wetlands are vulnerable to climatic variations and extreme events.

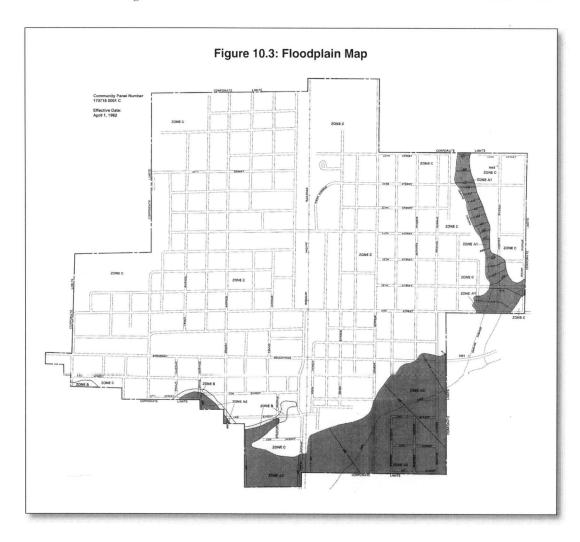

Figure 10.3: Floodplain Map

Wetlands occur across most of Canada; their location usually depends on local factors such as drainage, topography, and surface material.

The appraiser should check floodplain maps prepared by local governments and review any available surveys or topographical data provided by the client. Proximity to any flood zones may be determined by studying maps published by provincial and territorial agencies, pursuant to federal-provincial agreements that provide for the mapping of floodplains. Information is available through Environment Canada, and the relevant provincial and territorial agency.

The definition of what constitutes a wetland varies. Most laws describe wetlands in terms of three possible characteristics:

> **floodplain**
> The flat surfaces along the courses of rivers, streams, and other bodies of water that are subject to flooding.
>
> **wetlands**
> Areas that are frequently inundated or saturated by surface or groundwater and support vegetation typically adapted for life in saturated soil conditions; generally include swamps, marshes, bogs, and similar areas, but classification may differ in various jurisdictions.

1. Soils
2. Hydrology, i.e., the study of movement, distribution, and quality of water
3. Vegetation

There is no specific wetlands legislation in Canada. Wetlands receive indirect protection through a variety of national, provincial, and territorial legislation, for example see the Federal Fisheries Act.

Swamps, bogs, fens, marshes and estuaries are subject to varying degrees of influence from local, provincial, and federal governments. To value wetlands, appraisers must understand the unique features of the land, the evolving laws protecting these areas, the niche market for such properties, and the proper application of the approaches to value.

WHERE TO FIND – FLOODPLAIN MAPS

National Resources Canada publishes maps of wetlands; local, territorial, and provincial agencies often adapt this data for local wetland mapping and GIS systems.
For more information, see: *www.atlas.nrcan.gc.ca/site/english/maps/freshwater/distribution/wetlands*

Utilities

An appraiser investigates all the utilities and services available to a site. Off-site utilities may be publicly or privately operated, or there may be a need for on-site utility systems such as septic tanks and private water wells. The major utilities to be considered include the following:

- Sanitary sewers
- Domestic water, i.e., potable water, for human consumption
- Types of raw water for commercial, industrial, and agricultural uses
- Natural gas

- Electricity
- Storm drainage/sewer
- Telephone service
- Cable television

Although market area analysis describes, in general, the utility systems that are available in an area, a site analysis should provide a detailed description of the utilities that

> The cost of installing utilities is considered in the highest and best use conclusion and may be reflected directly or indirectly in the analysis, depending on the selection of comparable sales used in the valuation.

are available to the appraised site. An appraiser should determine the location and capacity of the utilities and note any unusually high connection fees. The appraiser should also identify and analyze atypically high or low service costs. It is not sufficient simply to establish which utilities are available. Any limitations resulting from a lack of utilities are important in highest and best use analysis, and the appraiser should investigate all available, alternative sources of utility service.

The appraiser should also consider the rates for utility service and the burden of any bonded indebtedness or other special utility costs. Of particular concern to residential, commercial, and industrial users are the following:

- Quality and quantity of water and its cost
- Costs and dependability of energy sources
- Adequacy of sewer facilities
- Any special utility costs or surcharges that might apply to certain businesses
- Impact of special or local improvement districts (SIDs or LIDs) on tax rate and repayment methods, e.g., special assessment

---

WHERE TO FIND – DATA ON UTILITIES

Accurate information on public utilities can be obtained from:
- Local public works departments
- Providers of on-site water and sewage disposal systems

- Local public works departments
- City/county planning departments

Site Improvements

In a site description, an appraiser describes off-site and on-site improvements. Then the appraiser analyzes how the site improvements affect value. On-site improvements include grading, landscaping, fences, curbs, gutters, paving, drainage and irrigation systems, walks, and other improvements to the land. Off-site improvements include access roads, utility hook-ups, remote water retention ponds, and sewer and drainage lines. An appraiser typically considers the value of off-site improvements in the site valuation process.

An appraiser must also describe and analyze the location of existing buildings on a site. Many appraisers make approximate plot plan drawings that show the placement of major buildings in relation to lot lines, access points, and parking or driveway areas. Land-to-building ratios and overall site configuration are usually quite important to a site's appeal and ability to support specific uses. The space allotted for parking influences a site's value for business and commercial use; therefore, the appraiser must analyze the parking space-to-building ratio in a commercial and industrial property. Zoning codes and parking by-laws will specify the minimum number of spaces required.

The appraiser considers any on-site improvements that add to or detract from a property's optimal use or highest and best use. For example, a lot zoned for multi-unit residential use might be improved with an 18-unit apartment building that is too valuable to demolish. If the site as vacant could accommodate a 24-unit building but the location of the present structure blocks the ability to add additional units, the appraiser may conclude that the site is underimproved and not developed to its highest and best use.

Accessibility

Site analysis focuses on the time-distance relationships between the subject site and other sites that serve as common origins and destinations. An appraiser describes and analyzes all forms of access to and from the property and the neighbourhood. In most cases, adequate parking area and the location and condition of streets, alleys, connector roads, freeways, and highways are important to land use. Industrial properties are influenced by rail and freeway access and the proximity of docking facilities. The location of airports, freeways, public transportation, and railroad service all affect industrial, commercial, and residential areas.

Traffic volume may be either advantageous or disadvantageous to a site, depending on other conditions that affect its highest and best use. High-volume local traffic in commercial areas is usually an asset; heavy through traffic may hurt retail stores, except those that serve regional travelers. Heavy traffic within residential areas is usually detrimental for single-unit residential neighbourhoods, but high-traffic streets that provide access to a subdivision or development are advantageous.

WHERE TO FIND – TRAFFIC VOLUME DATA

The volume of traffic passing a property is determined by a traffic count, which can usually be obtained from municipal engineering departments or provincial departments of transportation. Traffic counts indicate average daily traffic, peak hours, and direction. Observing the speed and turning movements of actual vehicles helps an appraiser judge how traffic affects a property's highest and best use.

The noise, dust, light, and fumes that come from a heavily travelled artery or freeway are not desirable for most low-density, residential lots. On the other hand, the advertising value of locations on major arteries can benefit offices and shopping centres, unless congestion restricts the free flow of traffic. The visibility of a commercial property from the street (commercial exposure) is an advertising asset; this asset is most valuable when the driving customer can easily exit the flow of traffic and enter the property.

Median strips, turning restrictions, one-way streets, and access restrictions can limit the potential uses of a parcel. In site analysis, the appraiser should test the probable uses of the site in relation to the flow of traffic. The appraiser must verify planned changes in access with the appropriate authority and consider these in the appraisal.

Environment

Appraisers also analyze land use in light of environmental conditions. Environmental considerations include factors such as the following:

- Local climate
- Availability of adequate and satisfactory water supply
- Pattern of drainage
- Quality of air
- Presence of wildlife/endangered species habitats
- Location of earthquake faults and known slide or avalanche zones
- Proximity to streams, wetlands, rivers, lakes, or oceans

Air and water pollution are by-products of increased population and urbanization. Public concern over pollution has prompted political action and legislation to protect the environment. In areas subject to extreme air pollution, regulations may exclude certain industries and limit the volume of traffic; such restrictions affect land use in these jurisdictions. In some jurisdictions, pollution rights have also become a saleable commodity. In locations near natural water sources, industrial uses may be prohibited while recreational uses are promoted. An appraiser must analyze environmental and climatic advantages and constraints to determine the proper land use for a site. Future land uses must be compatible with the local environment.

A site in a specific location may be influenced by its exposure to sun, wind, or other environmental factors. A very windy location can be disastrous to a resort but beneficial to a fossil-fuel power plant. The sunny side of the street is not always the most desirable for retail shops. In hot climates, the shady side of the street often gets more pedestrian traffic and greater sales, thus producing higher rents and higher land values. Ski resorts usually have slopes facing north for snow retention, and buildings facing south are desirable.

Analysis of a site's environment focuses on the interrelationships between the appraised site and neighbouring properties. An appraiser must consider the effects of any hazards or nuisances caused by neighbouring properties.. Of particular importance are safety concerns, e.g., the safety of employees and customers, of occupants and visitors, or of children going to and from school.

A site's value is also influenced by nearby amenities and developments on adjoining sites, such as parks, fine (or landmark) buildings, and compatible commercial buildings. The types of structures surrounding the property being appraised and the activities of those who use them can greatly influence site value.

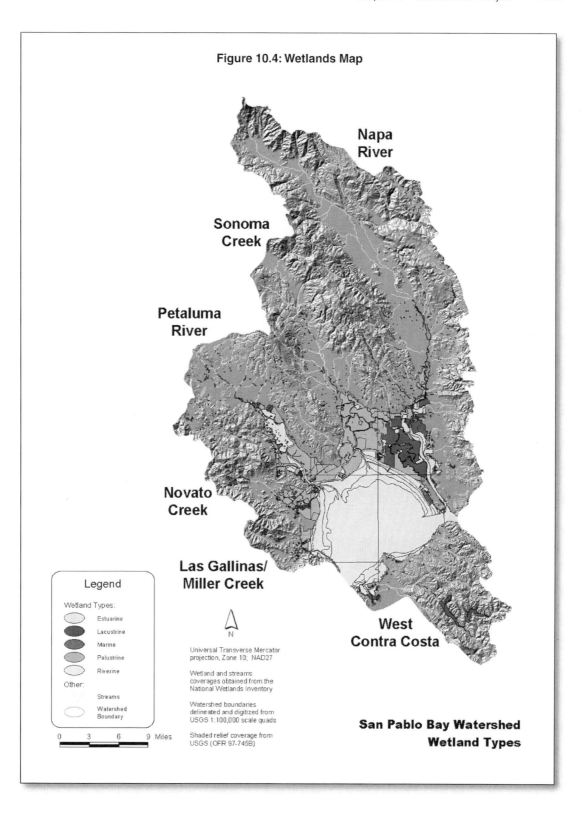

Figure 10.4: Wetlands Map

Federal and provincial environmental agencies have issued many environmental regulations that affect the use of land and may affect the value of land and improved properties. A complex network of regulations defines the environmental responsibilities and potential liabilities of property owners and investors, and these responsibilities and liabilities can adversely affect the value of real property interests. On one hand, environmental regulations can limit the use of land through protection of natural areas such as wetlands, aquifer recharge zones, and habitat areas for endangered or threatened species. On the other hand, real property interests may be impacted due to man's use or misuse of the land. Man-made environmental issues may be indicated by the presence of hazardous materials such as asbestos, PCBs, or petroleum hydrocarbons from leaking underground storage tanks (LUSTs). The existence of one or more adverse environmental conditions can reduce the market value of real property interests in a site.

Appraisers are not expected to have the knowledge or experience needed to detect the presence of hazardous substances or to measure their quantities. Like buyers and sellers in the real estate market, the appraiser must often rely on the advice of others, such as engineers or technical personnel with training in the detection and analysis of hazardous substances. However, depending on their knowledge and experience in the appraisal field, appraisers could reasonably be expected to estimate the impact of environmental contamination on property value. The consideration of environmental contamination in the appraisal process has been specifically addressed in professional appraisal standards, with topics addressed including relevant property characteristics

---

Figure 10.5: Relevant Property Characteristics

Professional standards discuss the relevant property characteristics that an appraiser should consider in an assignment involving a contaminated property:

- Whether the contamination discharge was accidental or permitted
- The status of the property with respect to regulatory compliance requirements
- The remediation lifecycle stage (before, during, or after cleanup) of the property as of the appraisal date
- The contamination constituents, e.g., petroleum hydrocarbons, chlorinated solvents
- The contamination conveyance, e.g., air, groundwater, soil
- Whether the property is a source, non-source, adjacent, or proximate site
- The cost and timing of any site remediation plans
- Liabilities and potential liabilities for site cleanup
- Potential limitations on the use of the property due to the contamination and its remediation
- Potential or actual off-site impacts due to contaminant migration (for source sites)

These characteristics may be used to describe the site and its environmental history and condition. They can also form the base of information from which to value a contaminated site and estimate the impact of the contamination on its value using one or more specialized valuation methods that have emerged in recent years for this purpose.

Figure 10.6: Specialized Terms and Definitions

Professional standards set forth the following key terms and definitions for use by appraisers who may be involved in the valuation of environmentally impacted properties:

- Diminution in Value (Property Value Diminution): The difference between the unimpaired and impaired values of the property being appraised. This difference can be due to the increased risk or costs (or both) attributable to the property's environmental condition.
- Environmental Contamination: Adverse environmental conditions resulting from the release of hazardous substances into the air, surface water, groundwater, or soil. Generally, the concentrations of these substances would exceed regulatory limits established by the appropriate federal, provincial, or local agencies.
- Environmental Risk: The additional or incremental risk of investing in, financing, buying, or owning property attributable to its environmental condition. This risk is derived from perceived uncertainties concerning: 1) the nature and extent of the contamination; 2) estimates of future remediation costs and their timing; 3) potential for changes in regulatory requirements; 4) liabilities for cleanup (buyer, seller, third party); 5) potential for off-site impacts; and 6) other environmental risk factors, as may be relevant.
- Environmental Stigma: An adverse effect on property value produced by the market's perception of increased environmental risk due to contamination (see Environmental Risk above).
- Impaired Value: The market value of the property being appraised with full consideration of the effects of its environmental condition and the presence of environmental contamination on, adjacent to, or proximate to the property. Conceptually, this could be considered the "as-is" value of a contaminated property.
- Remediation Cost: The cost to cleanup (or remediate) a contaminated property to the appropriate regulatory standards. These costs can be for the cleanup of on-site contamination as well as mitigation of off-site impacts due to migrating contamination.
- Remediation Lifecycle: A cycle consisting of three stages of cleanup of a contaminated site: before remediation or cleanup, during remediation, and after remediation. A contaminated property's remediation lifecycle stage is an important determinant of the risk associated with environmental contamination. Environmental risk can be expected to vary with the remediation lifecycle stage of the property.
- Source, Non-source, Adjacent, and Proximate Sites: Source sites are the sites on which contamination is, or has been, generated. Non-source sites are sites onto which contamination, generated from a source site, has migrated. An adjacent site is not contaminated, but shares a common property line with a source site. Proximate sites are not contaminated and not adjacent to a source site, but are in close proximity to the source site.
- Unimpaired Value: The market value of a contaminated property developed under the hypothetical condition that the property is not contaminated.

Source: Canadian Uniform Standards, 2010, 12.22 to 12.26 and Advisory Opinion 9 of Uniform Standards of Professional Appraisal Practise (USPAP), originally adopted in 1992 and substantially revised in 2002, Appraisal Foundation, Washington

(see Figure 10.5), specialized terms and definitions, and issues involved in valuing potentially impacted properties as if unimpaired and as impaired.[2]

The appraisal profession has arrived at a common set of specialized terms and definitions that pertain to contaminated properties and their valuation. Figure 10.6 lists terms, definitions, and concepts relevant to an appraisal assignment involving a site that might be potentially impacted by environmental contamination.

---

[2] Canadian Uniform Standards of Professional Appraisal Practise, 2010, 12.22 to 12.26.

The relevant property characteristics in Figure 10.5 and the valuation concepts, definitions, and terms in Figure 10.6 lead to a valuation framework that focuses on the potential effect of contamination on the hypothetical unimpaired value of the property.

These effects can reduce the unimpaired value to what has been referred to as the property's impaired value. For the appraiser, the key consideration involves the assembly of relevant market evidence of the reduction in value. Appraisers must avoid substituting their judgment for that of the marketplace. In recent years, contaminated properties have become more marketable and have begun to change hands with increasing frequency. Such transactions will usually provide sufficient basis for valuing or analyzing a site that may be impacted by environmental contamination.

SPECIAL CHARACTERISTICS OF RURAL, AGRICULTURAL, OR RESOURCE LAND

Rural or agricultural resource lands have specific characteristics that appraisers should investigate to describe these properties adequately:

- **Soil.** Precise soil surveys that indicate the soils found on properties, appropriate crops, and expected production are often available (see Figure 10.7). These surveys are useful in comparing agricultural properties.

- **Water rights, drainage, and irrigation.** The legal right to water is as important to the value of a property as the physical source of the water. Unlike the United States, the owners of property in Canada that abuts a waterway have reasonable rights to the water and to physically access the water. The provinces control water rights and regulate water usage, usually through their environmental ministry. Various provincial agencies determine the permissibility of large-scale use such as irrigation. Water export is a matter of some sensitivity that the federal government regulates.[3]

- **Climate.** General climatic conditions and growing seasons can affect crop production and, therefore, land value.

- **Potential crops.** The crops grown on a property are related not only to climate, soil, and irrigation, but also to the availability of labour, transportation, and access to the markets that make, transport, and sell the products produced from crops.

- **Environmental controls.** Cropping patterns are influenced by regulations on herbicides, insecticides, fertilizers, air and water pollution, and wildlife protection. Lead-based paint, underground storage tanks, asbestos in farm buildings, and cattle vats are common environmental liabilities.

- **Mineral rights.** The presence of precious metals, oil and gas, sand and gravel, quarry red rock such as building stone, clay deposits, or gemstones on a plot of land can affect its value. As with water rights, the legal right to extract

3   For more information on water rights in Canada, see *www.wsc.ec.gc.ca/hydrology/main_e.cfm?cname=hydro_e.cfm* and *www.watergovernance.ca*

ENVIRONMENTALLY IMPACTED PROPERTIES

The effects of environmental contamination on the value of real property can be categorized as follows:

- Cost effects: deductions for costs to remediate a contaminated property to appropriate regulatory standards, recognizing that not all costs are recognized by the market as having an effect on value.
- Use effects: limitations on the highest and best use of properties that may be impacted by environmental contamination, recognizing that these effects would be meaningful only if they limited the use of the site or property that would be the highest and best use without the effect of the contamination, and would otherwise meet the four highest and best use criteria (physically possible, legally permissible, financially feasible, and maximally productive).
- Risk effects: the effects on value due to increased perceptions of environmental risk by relevant market participants.

These factors influence the value of a potentially impacted site according to the following formula:

Impaired Value = Unimpaired Value
  – Cost Effects (Remediation and Related Costs)
  – Use Effects (Effects on Site Usability)
  – Risk Effects (Environmental Risk/Stigma)

In measuring the three potential effects on value (cost, use, and risk), cost effects are derived from remediation costs, which are usually estimated by environmental specialists. Assuming the market recognizes these costs, the appraiser can usually deduct them as a lump sum from the unimpaired value in the same way that a capital expenditure is deducted for deferred maintenance. When a discounted cash flow analysis is used, the anticipated costs can be deducted from the projected cash flows in the periods in which they are projected to occur.

Uncertainty regarding cost estimates, projection, and timing would be reflected in the environmental risk premium added to the unimpaired property or equity yield rate (risk effect). Use effects can be analyzed by evaluating the highest and best use of the subject contaminated property in an impaired and unimpaired condition. Risk effects, on the other hand, are derived from the perceived environmental risk and uncertainty related to the property's environmental condition. Measuring this element usually requires more sophisticated, less direct techniques.

Contamination may also have no effect on value. The influence of environmental impairment on real property value must always be found in the marketplace. Appraisers should be cautioned that, while formulaic approaches exhibit a structural logic and may be easy to explain, the market does not always respond in the same manner.

For further information, see Thomas O. Jackson, "Appraisal Standards and Contaminated Property Valuation", The Appraisal Journal (April 2003); Thomas O. Jackson, "Methods and Techniques for Contaminated Property Valuation", The Appraisal Journal (October 2003); William N. Kinnard Jr. and Elaine M. Worzala, "How North American Appraisers Value Contaminated Property and Associated Stigma", The Appraisal Journal (July 1999); Richard J. Roddewig, editor, Valuing Contaminated Property: An Appraisal Institute Anthology (Chicago: Appraisal Institute, 2002), Larry O Dybvig, Contaminated Real Estate; Implications for Real Estate Appraisers; Appraisal Institute of Canada, 1992.

all minerals contained in or below the surface of a property is as important as ownership of the land itself. Mineral rights may be granted with surface rights or without surface entry because the mineral estate is the dominant tenant in most provinces. Various lease and ownership relationships may be in effect and should be investigated. Since subsurface minerals can never be fully and absolutely quantified until they are extracted, and their extent and quality are subject to many variations, appraisers should recognize the risks and uncertainties associated with mineral properties. It is also important to remember that the activity of mineral extraction is a business activity and that real property interests must be separated from those of a business.

- **Unapparent environmental hazards.** Although the environmental liabilities associated with industrial plants are well known, many of the same liabilities may be present in other properties. Investors and analysts cannot assume that green rural properties that appear clean are actually free of environmental liabilities. In the 1940s and 1950s, farmers commonly used cattle vats, i.e., trenches filled with fuel oil through which cattle were led to rid them of mites and small insects. The fuel oil was often treated with DDT and other pesticides. When this practice fell into disuse, the trenches were simply filled in. In addition, farms often have aging underground storage tanks that held gasoline used to fuel farm vehicles. Farmland may also be contaminated by the accumulation of fertilizers and pesticides. Old railroad

Figure 10.7: Soil Map

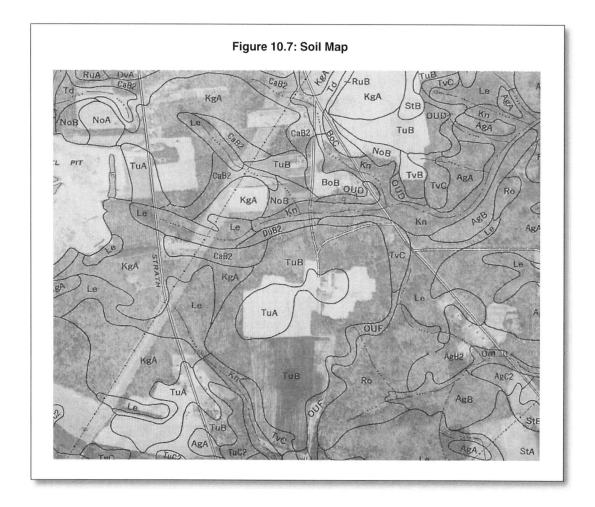

beds can constitute an environmental hazard because railroad ties were commonly soaked in creosote-filled trenches dug on site when tracks were laid. Timberlands are not free of contaminants either. Old turpentine stills are often found in areas where forests were once harvested.

- **Other considerations.** The appraiser must consider and analyze the location of wildlife habitats, the distances from populated areas, and the potential for recreational land uses in valuing agricultural land. An appraiser should also study special tax provisions, such as reduced taxes on agricultural or resource properties.[4] In October of 2006, the Government of Canada tabled the Canada's Clean Air Act. This act would create a new Clean Air Part in the Canadian Environmental Protection Act to strengthen the government's ability to reduce air emissions, regulate indoor and outdoor air pollutants and greenhouse gases, and require the establishment of national air quality objectives. However, these proposed changes would not allow for the creation and sale of pollution rights. In contrast, the US Clean Air Act of 1990 regulated the tonnage of acid-rain emissions that smokestack industries may release in proportion to plant size. Industries that do not use their full legal allowance can transfer or sell their pollution rights to other industries. Since 1993 pollution rights have been sold on both the Chicago Board of Trade and in the off-exchange pollution rights market.

---

[4]   For a thorough discussion of the methods used to describe and analyze the significant characteristics of land used for agricultural production, see American Society of Farm Managers and Rural Appraisers and Appraisal Institute, *The Appraisal of Rural Property*, 2nd ed. (Denver and Chicago, 2000).

CHAPTER 11

IMPROVEMENT ANALYSIS

An important part of every appraisal is the description of the type, quality, and condition of the building or buildings on the site and the analysis of the structure's design. The process of improvement analysis encompasses three interrelated tasks:

1. Property inspection
2. Building description
3. Analysis of architectural style and functional utility

In the valuation process, the appraiser gathers much of the information needed to adequately describe and analyze the improvements in the firsthand inspection of the real estate. Improper or inadequate inspection of the physical characteristics and features of the subject and comparable properties can create difficulties for an appraiser in later phases of the appraisal. For example, an overlooked structural problem could make the conclusions of the three approaches to value meaningless.

Accurate building descriptions are essential to all valuation assignments. In the description and analysis of the site and improvements, the appraiser should address all pertinent strengths and weaknesses, expand on any problem areas, and interpret the significance of the data to lay a foundation for the discussion of highest and best use. The appraiser needs a thorough understanding of the physical characteristics of the subject property to identify and select suitable comparables. A thorough building description helps the appraiser identify the extent and quality of building improvements, calculate their cost, and determine most forms of depreciation. Therefore, the accuracy of building descriptions directly affects the opinion of value produced by applying the three approaches to value.

Architectural style and *functional utility* are interrelated; appraisers must analyze their combined effect on property value. Architectural style is the character of a building's form and ornamentation. Functional utility is the ability of a property or building to be useful and to perform the function for which it is intended, according to current market tastes and standards. Functional utility also relates to the efficiency of a building's use in terms of architectural style, design and layout, traffic patterns, and the size and type of rooms. Both architectural style and functional utility influence human lives by providing or withholding beauty, comfort, security, convenience, light, and air. They may also ensure reasonable maintenance expenditures, preserve valuable traditions, or indicate the need for change.

Considerations of style and functional utility are integral to an appraisal. They are noted along with other physical characteristics during property inspection. Using comparable data, an appraiser can analyze how style and function influence a property's market value. Style and functional utility are examined in terms of the following:

1. The use for which a particular improvement was designed
2. Its actual or contemplated use
3. Its most productive use

These three uses may or may not be the same.

The ultimate goals of improvement analysis are the following:

• Proper identification of the important building components for the appraisal analysis

• Sound judgment of the quality and condition of improvements and components

• Convincing support for conclusions in the highest and best use analysis and application of the approaches to value

This chapter focuses on the structural elements and features that an appraiser will rate in the quality and condition survey, which is the groundwork for the analyses that follow improvement analysis in the valuation process.

PROPERTY INSPECTION

Sometimes consumers equate appraisal with the inspection of the subject real estate, but inspection is just one of the many tasks performed in an appraisal. Professional property inspectors are specialized contractors with expertise in uncovering defects in the structure and materials of various types of properties. Appraisers must be familiar with the property inspection process, but the aim of an appraiser in the field is not to comprehensively research the subject real estate. Rather, an appraiser observes the components and characteristics of the subject property that will influence value in the marketplace.

The importance of property inspection should not be underestimated. Much of the primary data an appraiser collects comes from the property inspection process. The real estate being appraised must be understood in the context of its immediate surroundings and the effect of other nearby improvements and land uses. Comparison of the subject and comparables is crucial for the direct comparison and income approaches, and estimating building costs in the cost approach is impossible without an accurate inventory of the building components in the subject. In addition,

> **property inspection**
> The act or process of inspecting firsthand the typical improvements and building components of the real estate involved in an appraisal assignment, either the subject property or comparable properties. Property inspection is the most visible step in improvement analysis.

comparison of the quality and condition of building components can be essential in making adjustments.

Many appraisers learn how to inspect a property through on-the-job training. Increased scrutiny from clients and appraisal regulators has reminded appraisers of their professional obligation to understand construction methods and materials, to judge condition and serviceability of building materials and components, and to assess functionality. The property inspection can be one of the longest periods of face-to-face interaction between the appraiser and the client; fundamental mistakes in the performance of the property inspection and in interactions with the client can be embarrassing and even costly, damaging the relationship between appraiser and client and jeopardizing any future business between them. Failure to disclose defects in an improvement because those defects were missed in the property inspection, or failure to verify information gathered through other means are flaws of an appraisal report that can result in litigation against an appraiser.

Sometimes an appraiser will not have the expertise to judge the quality and condition of specialized equipment or atypical building materials and may have to rely on the judgment of other professionals.[1] For a complex property, such as a manufacturing plant containing sophisticated equipment and mechanical systems, an appraiser may find blueprints provided by the developer/owner to be helpful.

BUILDING DESCRIPTION

In the valuation process, an appraiser describes the design, layout, and construction details of the subject improvements, which include the structural components, materials, and mechanical systems of each building under investigation. The appraiser also determines building size and the function, condition, and serviceability of each element described.

It is also important that the appraiser describe what does not constitute a building improvement, such as personal property items that should be expressly excluded from the appraisal. In some instances, this will require special analysis to determine whether items of machinery and equipment are personal property or qualify as fixtures. The building description provides the basis for comparing the subject property's improvements with improvements that are typically considered in the subject property's market and with the ideal improvements as determined in highest and best use analysis.

> **building description**
> The analysis of a building's design, layout, construction details, size, condition, and current use that provides the basis for comparing the subject property's improvements and the improvements typically accepted in the subject property's market.

To analyze the quality and condition of improvements, appraisers need a general understanding of the building construction process and the operation of essential

---

[1] Ethics Rule 4.2.7 of CUSPAP forbids an appraiser from undertaking an appraisal assignments if his or her inspection skills are inadequate. CUSPAP 12.29 provides that an appraiser's inspection should, at the minimum, be thorough enough to (a) adequately describe the real estate the appraisal report, (b) develop an opinion of highest and best use when such an opinion is necessary and appropriate, and (c) make meaningful comparisons in the valuation of the property.

building systems.[2] The typical construction materials and techniques used in a region can change over time for a variety of reasons:

- New building technologies evolve
- The prices of materials fluctuate significantly
- Rising or falling energy prices make a particular building material more desirable
- The dictates of fashion affect the demand for a certain building material or feature

With experience and thorough observation of market trends, appraisers will gain insight into how building components are perceived and valued in a particular market.

Elements of a Building Description

An appraiser prepares a building description by considering a variety of specific information in sequence. Primary concerns include the following items:

1. The type of use represented by the existing building
2. The codes and regulations affecting this use
3. Building size, plan, and construction
4. Details of the building's exterior and interior and its equipment and mechanical systems, both those included in the original construction and subsequent improvements

An appraiser must view a building objectively and analytically, paying careful attention to all components that ultimately contribute to the determination of the building's highest and best use as improved and any alternative uses to be considered in the assignment. The sheer number of components listed in a comprehensive building description should not be misinterpreted in the application of the approaches to value. The market's reaction to the presence or absence of structural components in a property is a more important consideration than the simple fact that those components exist.

Some improvements feature such unique or specialized design, materials, or construction features that distinguish them and may limit their marketability. For example, a chemical plant or a wharf facility may have special locational characteristics that complement the unique features of the improvements. The differences from the features of other properties with broader marketability do not necessarily suggest that the real estate is without value, rather that more specialized analyses are necessary. Furthermore, some properties may have special importance to their owner or user that does not reflect the value the property may have to its market. Appraisers must take care to value property in accordance with the disclosed scope of work and to be consistent with the definition of value in the assignment. However, many appraisals may also be used in financial reporting circumstances that might require

---

[2]   For an up-to-date and easy-to-read guide to construction materials and techniques, see Francis D.K. Ching and Cassandra Adams, Building Construction Illustrated, 3rd ed. (New York: John Wiley & Sons, Inc., 2000).

the user's consideration of the special relationship of the property to its owner or user, and the appraisal report will be more meaningful if this special nature is discussed in the report. In some financial reporting circumstances, it may be necessary to develop two appraisals: one of market or fair value and the other a use value for its owner.

Use Classification

Land uses can be divided into any number of types, depending on market norms and personal preferences. Traditionally, most appraisers have divided land uses into five major groups:

1. Residential
2. Commercial
3. Industrial
4. Agricultural
5. Other specialized uses

Each of these groups can be broken down into increasingly specific subgroups.

Systems of use classification may vary from market to market. For example, in some markets hotels and motels are considered a major property classification, whereas in other markets they are considered a subset of commercial properties. Appraisers should be familiar with the types of property defined by the market they are working in and employ a system of use classification that their clients will understand.

Zoning regulations establish the permitted uses of real estate. Existing and potential land uses must be checked against zoning regulations to determine if they are conforming or nonconforming uses. When the present use does not conform to current zoning regulations, the appraiser should consider how this fact might affect property value.

Building Codes and Ordinances

In addition to any use restrictions imposed by zoning, the planning and construction of buildings are restricted by various laws, codes, and regulations enacted at all levels of government to protect the health, safety, and welfare of the public. Provinces and territories have codes that control the kinds of buildings that are constructed within their borders. Governments establish regulations to ensure occupational health and safety, environmental protection, pollution control, and consumer protection. Local and regional building codes establish requirements for the construction and occupancy of buildings, and the codes contain specifications for building materials, methods of construction, and mechanical systems. These codes also establish standards of performance and address considerations such as structural strength, fire resistance, and adequate light and ventilation.

Building codes establish a form of standard, but the ordinances enacted for their application often vary from codes or place special terms or conditions on how the codes will be applied in a given jurisdiction. Note that national building codes do not always translate into local ordinances; however, local codes can add to but not take away from standards imposed by higher levels of government.

Size

Determining the size of a building may seem like the easiest step in preparing a building description, but it can be a formidable task for an appraiser who is not prepared for its inherent difficulties. The methods and techniques used to calculate building size vary regionally, differ among property types, and may reflect biases that significantly affect opinions of value. The appraiser must know the measurement techniques used in the area where the building is located as well as those used to describe properties elsewhere. Failure to apply measurement techniques and report building dimensions consistently within an assignment can impair the quality of the appraisal report.

An appraiser uses the system of measurement commonly employed in the area and includes a description of the system in the appraisal report. *Gross building area* is usually calculated. Measurements taken from plans should be checked against actual building measurements because alterations and additions are often made after plans are prepared. The areas of attached porches, freestanding garages, and other minor buildings are always calculated separately.

> Systems for measuring residential and non-residential properties vary. Gross building area is measured for all property types other than one-unit residential. Gross living area and gross leasable area are other common measurements.

No mandated Canadian standards exist for building measurement. The Appraisal Institute of Canada has published guidelines for measuring a house; however, these are not mandatory. A widely accepted measurement standard for residential properties is *Square Footage – Method for Calculating: ANSI Z765-2003*, developed by the National Association of Home Builders (NAHB) Research Centre with the American National Standards Institute (ANSI). The Canadian Real Estate Association (CREA) has recommended its members use this standard. Table 11.1 describes common building measurement standards.

Office buildings present special problems for appraisers because they are measured differently in different regions. The Building Owners and Managers Association International (BOMA) has established a method for measuring office building floor area. This widely used method is described in BOMA's publication *Standard Method for Measuring Floor Area in Office Buildings*, which is updated periodically. The description of an office building should include measurements of the following.

- Gross building area
- Finished building area
- Leasable building area

Some methods of office measurement allocate a pro rata portion of the restrooms, elevator lobbies, and corridors to each tenant; one variation also includes a pro rata portion of the ground floor main lobby in each tenant's leased area. Office building

Table 11.1: Building Measurement Standards

Gross living area (GLA)

Definition	Total area of finished, above-grade residential space; calculated by measuring the outside perimeter of the structure and includes only finished, habitable, above-grade living space. Finished basements and attic areas are not generally included in total gross living area. Local practices, however, may differ.
Use	Used by federal agencies to measure single-unit residential properties

Gross building area (GBA)

Definition	Total floor area of a building, excluding unenclosed areas, measured from the exterior of the walls; includes both the superstructure floor area and the substructure or basement area
Use	Used by federal agencies to measure multi-family properties; also the standard of measurement for industrial buildings

Gross leasable area (GLA)

Definition	Total floor area designed for the occupancy and exclusive use of tenants, including basements and mezzanines; measured from the centre of joint partitioning to the outside wall surfaces.
Use	Commonly used to measure shopping centres.

Note that the acronym GLA can stand for two different area measurements. Residential appraisers use GLA for gross living area; non-residential appraisers use it to refer to gross leasable area.

management may measure single-tenant and multi-tenant floors in the same building in different ways. Since these measurements vary with occupancy, the appraiser must apply a consistent method in calculating the floor-by-floor rentable area of a building.

The appraiser should not accept a statement about the size of a subject or comparable property without knowing the basis for the calculation. Unverified size information can cause the resulting opinion of value to be erroneous or misleading.

Format

A complete building description includes information about the details and condition of a building's exterior, interior, and mechanical systems. Although there is no prescribed method for describing all buildings, the outline in Figure 11.1 may be used to establish a format for building descriptions and can be adapted to the special needs of particular assignments.

Other formats can be useful in different circumstances, depending on the type of property concerned and the nature of the appraisal assignment. The level of detail required in the building description varies according to the assignment's scope of work.

> A building description includes a description of the exterior, the interior, and the equipment and mechanical systems.

Figure 11.1: Elements of a Building Description

A. Substructure
1. Footings
2. Slabs
3. Piles
4. Columns
5. Piers
6. Beams
7. Foundation Walls

B. Exterior Description
1. Framing
2. Insulation
3. Ventilation
4. Exterior Walls
5. Exterior Doors
6. Windows, storm windows and screens
7. Facade
8. Roof and drain system
9. Chimneys, stacks, and vents
10. Special features

C. Interior description
1. Interior walls, partitions, and doors
2. Division of space
   a. Storage areas
   b. Stairs, ramps, elevators, escalators, and hoists
3. Interior supports
   a. Beams, columns, and trusses
   b. Flooring system (subflooring)
   c. Ceilings

4. Painting, decorating, and finishing
   a. Basements
   b. Floor coverings
   c. Walls, partitions, and ceilings
   d. Molding and baseboards
   e. Fireplaces
5. Protection against decay and insect damage
6. Miscellaneous and special features

D. Equipment and mechanical systems
1. Plumbing system
   a. Piping
   b. Fixtures
   c. Hot water system
2. Heating, ventilation, and air-conditioning systems
   a. Heating systems
      (1) Warm or hot air
      (2) Hot water
      (3) Steam
      (4) Electric
   b. Air-conditioning and ventilation systems
3. Electrical systems
4. Miscellaneous equipment
   a. Fire protection
   b. Elevators, escalators, and speed ramps
   c. Signals, alarms, and call systems
   d. Loading facilities
   e. Attached equipment (process-related)

DESCRIPTION OF EXTERIOR MATERIALS AND DESIGN

An exterior description provides information on the following:

- Substructure, i.e., foundation
- Framing
- Insulation
- Ventilation
- Exterior walls, doors, and windows
- Roofs and drains
- Chimneys
- Special features

Substructure: A building's entire foundational structure, which is below grade and provides a support base or footings on which the superstructure rests

Footings

Type	Perimetric base
Materials	Concrete
Characteristics/Use	Most common type of footing; a concrete base rests on undisturbed earth below the frost line and distributes the load of the walls over the subgrade
Type	Plain footing
Materials	Concrete
Characteristics/Use	Unreinforced and designed to carry light loads
Type	Reinforced footing
Materials	Concrete and steel
Characteristics/Use	Contain steel to increase their strength
Type	Column
Materials	Concrete
Characteristics/Use	Long, relatively slender pillars
Type	Spread footing
Materials	Concrete
Characteristics/Use	Frequently used where the soil has poor load-bearing capacity

Foundations

Type	Slab-on-ground
Materials	Poured concrete
Characteristics/Use	Concrete or cinder block walls on concrete footings
	Cut stone or stone and brick (in older buildings)
	Most common type of foundation
Type	Mat and raft (floating foundation)
Materials	Concrete slab heavily reinforced with steel
Characteristics/Use	Used over soils that have poor load-bearing capacity; steel reinforcing makes the entire foundation function as a unit

Piles

Type	Columnar units
Materials	Concrete, Metal, Wood
Characteristics/Use	Piles serve as substitutes for footings, transmitting loads through soil with poor load-bearing capacity to lower levels where the soil's load bearing capacity is adequate

Columns, piers, and beams

Materials	Concrete
	Steel
Characteristics/Use	Foundation supports that can be used separately or in combination

Substructure

Substructure usually refers to a building's entire foundational structure, which is below grade and includes such foundation supports as footings, slabs, piles, columns, piers, and beams. To evaluate the quality and condition of footings (and other items of concealed construction throughout a building), which are visible only when a building is under construction, an appraiser must look for evidence of structural problems. Footings that are improperly designed and constructed often cause settling and wall cracks.

Superstructure

Superstructure usually refers to the portion of the building above grade. In multi-purpose buildings, however, components such as parking garages that are above grade but not used for habitable space are often considered part of the substructure.

Framing

The structural frame is the load-bearing skeleton of a building to which the exterior and interior walls are attached. The structural frames of most houses in Canada are made of wood. Many commercial and industrial buildings have steel or concrete frames.

A wood framing system that is defective can cause walls to crack, exterior walls to bulge, windows to stick, and doors to open or close improperly. Steel framing is

---

Superstructure: The portion of a building that is above grade

Framing

Type	Platform
Materials	Wood
Characteristics/Use	Vertical framing members (studs) are cut to the ceiling height of one floor, horizontal plates are laid on top, then more studs are cut for the next floor
Type	Post-and-beam
Materials	Wood
Characteristics/Use	Heavier and larger framing members support widely spaced beams; fewer interior load-bearing walls
Type	Precast concrete
Characteristics/Use	Prefabricated walls and floors are "tilted up" at the construction site
Type	Steel framing
Characteristics/Use	For functional, single-storey industrial plants with increasing large bays between columns; usually less expensive that precast or reinforced concrete and easier and faster to erect
Type	Solid masonry exterior walls with steel beam or reinforced concrete interior framing (newer buildings) or interior framing of wood beams and posts (older buildings)

usually less expensive than precast or reinforced concrete and it is easier and faster to erect. However, steel framing has one major disadvantage. Unless it is encased in heat-resistant, fireproof material such as plaster or concrete, the steel will buckle and bend in a fire, pulling adjacent structural members out of position and greatly increasing fire damage to the building. Reinforced and precast concrete framing is the most expensive and difficult to construct, but it is highly resistant to fire damage.

Insulation

Insulation not only helps economize on fuel and ensure the comfort of occupants in both warm and cold climates, but it also reduces noise transmission and impedes the spread of fire. The ability of an insulation material to resist the flow of heat is measured in R or RSI values. R value is derived by measuring the British thermal units (BTUs) that are transmitted in one hour through one layer of the insulation (RSI is a metric measure that is one-seventh of the R value). The higher the R or RSI value, the better the insulation.

There is no universal standard for the amount of insulation required in a structure because the amount varies with the climate and the type of building. For example, over-ceiling or under-roof insulation with an R value of 13 might be satisfactory in a mild climate if there is gas or oil heat and no air-conditioning. In cold or hot climates and in structures with electric heat or air-conditioning, insulation with an R value of 24 might be necessary. There has been a growing trend to superinsulate structures using insulation with much higher insulation values.

Insulation	
Type	Loose-fill
Materials	Mineral wool (rock, slag, or glass wool) or cellulosic fibre (recycled newsprint, wood chips, or other organic fibres)
Characteristics/Use	Poured or blown by a machine into a building's structural cavities
Type	Flexible
Characteristics/Use	Generally used where it is not practical to install loose-fill insulation or where the foil or kraft paper facing is needed as a vapour barrier
Type	Rigid
Characteristics/Use	Structural wall insulation
	Fibreboard
	Structural deck insulation
	Rigid board insulation
Type	Reflective
Materials	Foil
Characteristics/Use	Used to reflect heat transferred by radiation
Type	Foamed-in-place
Materials	Polyurethane

ASBESTOS IN BUILDINGS

Asbestos is a non-flammable, natural mineral material that separates into fibres. Asbestos-containing materials (ACMs) were widely used in structures built between 1945 and 1980 as thermal and acoustical insulation or for fireproofing and soundproofing. Other ACMs were used in siding and roofing shingles. Asbestos has also been found in many products around the house: it has been used in clapboard; shingles and felt for roofing; exterior siding; pipe and boiler covering; compounds and cement, such as caulk, putty, roof patching, furnace cement, and driveway coating; wallboard; textured and latex paints; acoustical ceiling tiles and plaster; vinyl floor tiles; appliance wiring; hair dryers; irons and ironing board pads; flame-resistant aprons and electric blankets; and clay pottery. Loose-fill vermiculite insulation may contain traces of "amphibole" asbestos.

Asbestos fibres pose a threat to human health when they are distributed in the air. The potential of any ACM to release fibres depends on its degree of friability, i.e., how easily it is crumbled or pulverized. Dry, sprayed-on thermal insulation over structural steel is highly friable. Densely packed, nonfibrous ACMs such as vinyl asbestos floor covering and pipe insulation are not considered friable under normal conditions. Nevertheless, these materials will become friable if they are broken, sawed, or drilled.

Encapsulation or enclosure of asbestos is effective as a short-term solution. The provincial and territorial occupational health and safety standards exist for the removal of asbestos when a building is being demolished or renovated.

Health Canada has encouraged provincial occupational health authorities to adopt stringent workplace exposure limits for asbestos. The sale of pure asbestos and certain high risk consumer products that are composed of or contain asbestos fibres is strictly regulated under the Hazardous Products Act. In addition, the emissions of asbestos into the environment from mining and milling operations are subject to the Canadian Environmental Protection Act.

The use of asbestos is not illegal. While alternative products are being developed to replace asbestos, products sold today containing asbestos are regulated under the Hazardous Products Act. Asbestos can be used safely, and public concern has led to improved product design and manufacture. Asbestos is now better encapsulated and sealed to reduce the escape of fibres. Asbestos is valuable in many applications because it has been difficult to find comparable substitute materials. For example, it is still an important component of brake lining and clutch facings.

One market's reaction to the effect asbestos has on the value of income-producing properties may differ from the reaction of other markets. There is little evidence, however, that investors are willing to sell properties at sharp discounts, or any at all, because of the problem.

For additional discussion of the influence of asbestos on real estate value, see Jeffrey D. Fisher, George H. Tse, and K.S. Maurice, "Effects of Asbestos on Commercial Real Estate: A Survey of MAI Appraisers", The Appraisal Journal (October 1993): 587–599; Robert Simons, "How Clean is Clean?" The Appraisal Journal (July 1994): 424–438; and Daniel F. Ryan, "A Lender's View of Hazardous Substances. . . And Appraiser Responsibility", Real Estate Appraiser & Analyst (Fall 1989): 10–12.

Ventilation

All buildings need ventilation to reduce heat buildup beyond tolerances in closed-off areas such as attics and spaces behind walls. Ventilation also prevents the condensation of water, which collects in unventilated spaces and causes building materials to rot and decay. When condensation seeps into insulation, it reduces its R rating. Ventilation can be accomplished with holes that range from one inch to several feet in diameter. These holes should be covered with screening to keep out vermin. Also, ventilation can be increased by using fans.

Exterior Walls and Doors

Exterior walls are either load-bearing or nonload-bearing. When the quality of the exterior walls is below the standard for buildings in the same market, the property may suffer a loss in value. An appraiser should note the presence or absence of energy-conserving material such as weatherstripping around doors. Door shoes, weatherproof thresholds, and sweeps will prevent air from leaking through cracks at the bottom of a door.

Exterior Walls	
Type	Load-bearing
Materials	Solid masonry (cement block, brick, or a combination)
	Poured concrete
	Pre-stressed concrete
	Steel beams covered with siding material
	Wood framing
Characteristics/Use	May be strengthened with masonry pilasters attached to the exterior of the wall
Type	Nonload-bearing
Materials	Porcelain enamel
	Steel
	Aluminum
	Pre-cast aggregate concrete
	Glass
	Corrugated iron, tilt-up precast concrete asbestos board, fibreglass and metal sandwich panels for industrial buildings
Characteristics/Use	Commonly used in larger buildings; attached to the framing system
Exterior Doors	
Type	Standard
Materials	Wood
	Metal
	Glass
Characteristics/Use	Exterior doors are usually solid; hollow exterior doors are a sign of poor-quality construction
Type	Large truck doors (commercial and industrial buildings)
Materials	Steel
Type/Components	Special-purpose doors with automatic door openers
Materials	Wood
	Metal
	Glass

Windows, Storm Windows, and Screens

In describing a building, the appraiser notes the type of window, its material or manufacture, and any energy-saving features. Since windows are a major source of heat and cooling loss, their design and installation is important. In commercial and industrial buildings, builders generally install windows of double or triple glazing and occasionally use casement windows.

Facade

Many houses, stores, office buildings, and industrial buildings have a facade, or front, that differs from the design and construction of the rest of the building. Special facades may cost extra and thus affect the property's value.

Windows

Types	Single and double-hung
	Casement
	Horizontal sliding
	Clerestory
	Fixed
	Awning
	Centre pivot
	Jalousie
Materials	Glass with wood framing (usually for houses) or aluminum or steel framing (often in residential, commercial, and industrial buildings)
Characteristics/Use	Windows should be tightly sealed, with caulking at the joints and between the wall and the window. The use of insulated glass, multiple glazing, and storm sashes helps keep cold air out and heat in.
	In most parts of the country, screens are needed for all windows that open. Most screens have aluminum frames, and in residences, screens are often combined with storm windows.

Facade

Types	Multi-family
	Retail
	Industrial, office, etc.
Materials	Masonry veneer or contrasting siding
	Glass or other decorative material
	More elaborate facade than exterior walls
Characteristics/Use	In modern industry and commerce, public image is important. An attractive store, warehouse, industrial plant, or office building has both advertising and public relations value to the occupant. Ornamentation, identifying, signs, lighting, and landscaping all contribute to a building's aesthetics.

Roof and Drainage System

A roof is designed and constructed to support its own weight and the pressure of snow, ice, wind, and rain. The roof covering prevents moisture from entering the structure. The water that falls on a roof must be directed to the ground or into a drainage system. Even so-called "flat" roofs may be slightly pitched to direct water to drains and gutters.

Most roofs need to be replaced several times during a building's life; therefore, an appraiser must investigate a roof's condition and age to determine its remaining useful life.

Roof	
Types	Flat
	Lean-to (saltbox)
	Gable
	Gambrel
	Hip
	Mansard
	Monitor
	Sawtooth
Materials	Wood trusses, joists or horizontal beams, joists and rafters, or posts and beams in residential construction
	Steel or wood trusses, glued wood beams, or steel or concrete frame with wood joists or purlins or with steel bar joists in commercial and industrial construction
Characteristics/Use	Flat roofs are used extensively in industrial and commercial buildings but are less common in residences. Lean-to roofs, often called shed roofs, are used on saltbox houses, and gambrel roofs are popular for barns and Cape Ann and Dutch Colonial houses. Monitor and sawtooth roofs are sometimes used in industrial construction.
Drain System	
Components	Gutters and downspouts
Materials	Galvanized steel
	Aluminum
	Copper
Characteristics/Use	Channel water from roofs to prevent damage and protect the appearance of walls when roof overhangs are not provided
Components	Gutters or eave troughs
Materials	Galvanized steel
	Aluminum
	Copper
Characteristics/Use	Catch rainwater at the edge of the roof and carry it to downspouts or leaders

Drain System, *continued*

Components	Downspouts or leaders
Materials	Galvanized steel
	Aluminum
	Copper
Characteristics/Use	Vertical pipes that carry the water to the ground or into sewers, dry wells, drain tiles, or splash pans
Components	Roof drains (in large buildings)
Materials	Galvanized steel
	Aluminum
	Copper
Characteristics/Use	Connected to storm drains by pipes in the building

Roof Covering

Materials	Asphalt shingles (prevalent in residential construction)
	Wood, asbestos, fiberglass, or cement shingles or shakes
	Metal
	Clay tile
	Slate
	Built-up layers of felt or composition material covered with tar and then gravel or another surfacing material (most common on flat roofs of commercial and industrial buildings)
	Single-membrane roof assembly
Characteristics/Use	Joints in roofs are created where two different roof slopes meet or where the roof meets adjoining walls or projections such as chimneys, pipes, and ventilation ducts. All joints must be flashed. Flashing is usually accomplished by nailing strips of galvanized metal, aluminum, or tin across or under the point, applying a waterproofing compound or cement, and securing the roofing material over the edges to hold it permanently in place.

Roof sheathing

Materials	Plywood
	Steel roof deck
	Lightweight precast concrete slabs
	Reinforced concrete slabs
	Insulated sheathing in large sheets

Chimneys, Stacks, and Vents

Exhaust systems range from simple metal vents and flues to complex masonry fireplaces, industrial chimneys, and ventilation systems. The efficiency of any fuel-burning heating system depends on its chimney, stack, or vent. Chimneys and stacks with cracked bricks, loose mortar joints, or other leaks may be serious fire and health hazards.

Chimneys, stacks, and vents	
Materials	Brick
	Metal
Characteristics/Use	Should be structurally safe, durable, and smoketight; should also be able to withstand the action of flue gases

Special Features

Special features that must be carefully described and considered in the valuation process might include the following:

- Artwork that is attached to the real estate and is not personal property
- Ornamentation
- Exterior elevators
- Solar and wind equipment
- Unique window installation
- Special masonry work and exterior materials
- Items required for the commercial or industrial use of buildings

Unique building features can present a valuation problem. The appraiser must decide if the items increase the property's market value or are valuable only to the current user. In the latter case, the items may add use value but little or no market value. If such items are expensive to remove, they may not appeal to a prospective buyer and the property could therefore lose value.

DESCRIPTION OF INTERIOR MATERIALS AND DESIGN

An interior description provides information about the following:

- Interior walls, partitions, and doors (including how the space is divided)
- Interior supports
- Stairways
- Painting, decorating, and finishing (including floor and ceiling coverings)
- Protection against decay and pests

Interior Walls, Partitions, and Doors

Like exterior walls, interior walls and partitions can be either load-bearing or nonload-bearing. In general, having fewer load-bearing interior walls allows for greater flexibility in the division of space within the structure.

Interior Supports

A building description includes consideration of the building's internal supports, which include the following:

- Beams, columns, and trusses
- The flooring system
- Ceilings

GREEN BUILDING AND SUSTAINABILITY

In the 21st century, widespread public concern over environmental "climate change" and the use of natural resources has focused attention on the built environment and the products of industry. The concept of sustainability has different meanings for different constituencies, and has particular resonance in the real estate industry because of the size and impact of the industry on national and global economies. In 2007, representatives of the valuation, building, and investment communities met at the Vancouver Valuation Accord to discuss sustainability and value using the United Nation's definition of sustainability: "a development that meets the needs of the present without compromising the ability of future generations to meet their own needs." Green building is the most widely recognized method for creating and fostering sustainable real estate.

Green building encompasses a wide range of renewable construction materials and energy- and resource-efficient building techniques along with an overriding philosophy of sustainable development. The most significant green building practices relate to the following:

- Sustainability of land, e.g., development density, stormwater management, brownfield redevelopment
- Water efficiency, e.g., water use reduction, landscaping
- Energy and atmosphere, e.g., renewable sources, ozone depletion
- Materials and resources, e.g., reuse, recycling, renewable materials
- Indoor environmental quality, e.g., air quality, emissions, passive heating
- Innovation and sustainable design

Measuring the effectiveness of green building efforts is difficult, and the process of creating and evaluating benchmarks is in its early stages. Sustainability is not always readily measurable at the property level, and many experimental materials and methods have not proven to be physically or economically sustainable. Many local governments have created sustainability plans with incentive programs to reward owners and developers of green buildings. A recognized professional standard is the Leadership in Energy and Environmental Design (LEED) standard for sustainable development. A group of real estate organizations including the National Multi Housing Council, International Code Council, and National Association of Home Builders is developing a new National Green Building Standard that will be certified by the American National Standards Institute. Consultants in private practice have examined the triple bottom line* as a tool to account for social and environmental influences as well as the traditional economic impact of industry.

Appraisers will have to gather and analyze more data on the impact of green building on cost as well as value before a systematic methodology for dealing with these special-design properties can be tested in the marketplace. Examples of possible impacts on the valuation process include the following:

- The financial feasibility and productivity of sustainable construction and design elements could affect highest and best use analysis.
- The higher cost (perceived or actual) of sustainable building materials and more efficient equipment and systems can add to the cost of construction indicated in the cost approach. R.S. Means currently publishes a green building project planning and cost estimating manual (see *www. rsmeans.com/bookstore/booksearch.asp*). The distinction between cost and value becomes a critical consideration when green building materials and systems are involved because of the debate over the benefit of green building, i.e., is the added expense worth the perceived additional cost to a typical property owner or investor in the marketplace? Furthermore, an argument could be made that a lack of sustainable features in a new building is a functionally obsolete design in a market that expects green building features. Likewise, the perceived lifespan of sustainable building components may need to be accounted for in cost estimates if the market participants expect the sustainable features to last longer than traditional components.

> **GREEN BUILDING AND SUSTAINABILITY, *continued***
>
> - In the income approach, the reduced operating expenses of a building with energy-efficient, low-maintenance features may positively affect effective gross income, and thereby value.
> - As green building becomes accepted and then expected in a market, the presence or lack of green building features in a subject or comparable property could affect the selection of comparable properties, adjustment for physical characteristics, and other aspects of the application of the direct comparison approach.
>
> In a market value appraisal assignment, the appraiser has a professional obligation to provide an independent and objective opinion of value and so must distinguish the social and governmental influences on value of sustainable improvements from the value the market ascribes to those improvements.
>
> Additional Resources
>
> US Green Building Council (*www.usgbc.org*)
>
> Green Building Initiative (*www.thegbi.org*)
>
> Energy Star (*www.energystar.gov*)
>
> Krisandra Guidry, "How Green is Your Building?: An Appraiser's Guide to Sustainable Design", The Appraisal Journal (Winter 2004): 57-68.
>
> * John Elkington, Cannibals with Forks: The Triple Bottom Line of 21st Century Business (Stony Creek, Conn.: New Society Publishers, 1998).

Beams, Columns, and Trusses

Beams and columns are used in many residential, commercial, and industrial buildings with basements or crawl spaces that are too wide for the first-floor joists or subfloor systems and cannot be supported by the foundation walls alone. As interior support systems, traditional joist construction is being replaced by both roof and floor truss systems.

Flooring System

Subflooring provides safe support for floor loads without excessive deflection and an adequate base for the support and attachment of finish floor material. Bridging stiffens the joists and prevents them from deflecting.

Ceilings

In some structures, the underside of the upper storey is an adequate ceiling. Appraisers must measure and consider ceiling height.

Stairs, Ramps, Elevators, Escalators, and Hoists

Designing and constructing even the simplest staircase is complicated. Local building codes dictate the minimum and maximum tread and rise of stairs, which should be consistent within a building. The National Building Code of Canada, supplemented by provincial building codes, have established accessibility guidelines, and public buildings that do not meet those regulations may suffer a value penalty based on the cost of necessary changes.

DIVISION OF SPACE

A building description provides a complete list of the number of rooms in the structure and their uses. Room sizes may also be stated. The number of bedrooms and bathrooms in a residential property usually influences the market for the property and its value. The number of units in an apartment building and the types and sizes of the rooms within the units significantly influence the property's income-producing potential. Similarly, the amount of office space in an industrial property and the partitioning of office suites may affect property value.

In certain parts of the Canada, many types of buildings have basements. In these areas, buildings without basements may have substantially less value than similar buildings with basements. If basements are not common in the area, a basement may add little or no value to a building.

Storage Areas

Home owners often complain about a lack of adequate storage space, especially in kitchens. Ample cabinets, closets, and other storage areas are important, particularly in homes without basements. Storage is particularly important in multi-family residential buildings. The value of apartment and condominium projects is often enhanced by the availability of storage space. Frequently, mini-storage facilities are located near apartment complexes because apartment units often have inadequate storage space. Storage problems can also exist in commercial and industrial buildings.

Interior Description

Walls

Type	Residential buildings
Materials	Wood studs covered with drywall materials, e.g., gypsum board, wood panels, ceramic tile, plywood, hardboard
	Plaster (less popular now)
	Masonry (in masonry houses)
Characteristics/Use	Interior walls can be painted, papered, or decorated in other ways
Type	Commercial buildings
Materials	Wire partitions
	Glass
	Wood
	Plywood
	Hardboard
	Metals
	Tile
	Concrete
	Solid masonry walls for fire protection
Characteristics/Use	Interior walls can be painted, papered, or decorated in other ways

Partitions

Materials	Various materials
Characteristics/Use	Generally nonload-bearing and movable.

In multi-storey buildings, appraisers must evaluate how efficiently the elevators and escalators in a building move people and freight. The elevators and escalators in many multi-storey buildings are inadequate and fall short of current market standards. Curing these deficiencies is often expensive or impossible; hydraulic elevators usually have lift posts with oil lines and cylinders in the ground, and leaks can go undetected into the ground.

Special elevators and hoists are often considered part of a building, although they may be studied under the equipment category.

Painting, Decorating, and Finishing

Most buildings are decorated many times during their useful lives. An appraiser reports the condition of the painting and decorating in a structure and notes when they will need to be redone. The attractiveness of painting and decorating is subjective. Many new owners and tenants will redecorate to suit their personal tastes. Unusual decorations and colours may have limited appeal and, therefore, may detract from a building's value. The quality of decoration is sometimes an important consideration in valuing a restaurant, store, or other commercial building.

PEOPLE WITH DISABILITIES, AND IMPROVEMENT ANALYSIS

In Canada, regulations as diverse as the Canadian Charter of Rights and Freedoms, building codes, and human rights legislation ensure people with disabilities have reasonable access to public facilities and private facilities such as shopping centres that serve the public. An improvement that does not conform to these requirements can suffer from obsolescence and thus value penalties. An appraiser cannot assume that improvements comply with the requirements of people with disabilities. Enforcement of these requirements can be triggered by a change in use or a title transfer. Owners of older properties may have to add ramps, elevators, or other special equipment to comply with regulations, which can impact value greatly.

A real estate appraiser is not required to become an expert in the field of access-for-the-disabled requirements; however, ethical standards (CUSPAP Ethics Rule 4.2.7) require an appraiser to be able to identify such issues and assess their significance.

For an overview of specific requirements of access and building design, see the websites for federal and provincial Human Rights Commissions; see also Randall Bell, "Appendix 2: Americans with Disabilities Act (ADA) Overview", Real Estate Damages: An Analysis of Detrimental Conditions (Chicago: Appraisal Institute, 1999), 268-272. For further discussion of considerations in the valuation process, see Richard W. Hoyt and Robert J. Aalberts, "Appraisers and the Americans with Disabilities Act", The Appraisal Journal (July 1995): 298-309 and Robert J. Aalberts and Terrence M. Clauretie, "Commercial Real Estate and the Americans with Disabilities Act: Implications for Appraisers", The Appraisal Journal (July 1992): 53-58.

Some considerations of interior finishes and decorating include the following:

- If finished basements are used for purposes other than storage and these uses are accepted and typical in the area, they can add significantly to the property's value.

Doors

Types	Simple hollow-core doors in most residential construction
	Solid-core doors in older buildings and office buildings
	Complex, self-closing, fire-resistant doors in commercial and industrial buildings
	Specialty, self-opening and self-closing doors in offices and commercial buildings
	Special-purpose doors, e.g., doors to bank vaults
Characteristics/Use	Hanging a door is complicated and often done improperly. Most poorly hung doors close improperly or fail to touch an edge of the frame when closed.

Interior Supports

Types	Beams
	Columns
	Trusses
Materials	Wood, masonry, concrete, or steel
Characteristics/Use	Designed to support heavy loads. Cracked or sagging beams may be an early indication of more serious problems in the future.
Type	Flooring system
Materials	Generally wood or concrete
Characteristics/Use	Serves as a base for floor covering
Type	Ceiling
Materials	Same material as interior walls (e.g., gypsum), tile, or underside of upper floor
Characteristics/Use	Ceilings that are too high or low for the property's current highest and best use as improved may be considered items of functional obsolescence and decrease the property's value.

Stairs and Ramps

Type	Residential buildings
Characteristics	Provides for safe ascent and descent, with adequate headroom and space for moving furniture and equipment. Railings should be installed on the sides of all interior stairways, including stairways in attics and basements, where they are often omitted.
Type	Public buildings
Characteristics	Codes often regulate where stairs are located, how they are designed and constructed, and how they are enclosed for fire protection. Public buildings may also have to be barrier free to provide access for handicapped people as mandated by Human Rights legislation and applicable building codes, such as requiring that ramps be installed both inside and outside the structure.

- The types and finishes of various wall and ceiling components should be differentiated.

- A wide variety of flooring is available, and some flooring materials are selected primarily for their low cost and durability. An appraiser should consider whether floor coverings can endure wear and tear and how they conform to a building's design and decoration.

- Unique, restored moulding can add value to older houses, but the use of mouldings is decreasing.

Most fireplaces in homes and commercial buildings such as restaurants, inns, and specialty stores do not provide the building's primary source of heat. In fact, because of their design, many have little heating power. Because fireplaces are difficult to construct, many are badly made and function poorly. One common problem is downdraft, whereby smoke is blown into the building by the wind outside. This can happen if the chimney does not extend at least two feet above any part of the roof within 10 feet of the chimney.

Protection Against Decay and Insect Damage

All wood is susceptible to decay and insect damage. When wood is consistently exposed to moisture and water, destructive organisms propagate on or beneath its surface. Insects damage wood more rapidly and visibly than decay does. Although several species of insects destroy wood, termites are by far the most destructive to both damp and dry wood. They colonize in moist soil or in dry wood and create infestations that are extremely difficult to eradicate.

Builders employ various techniques to protect against decay and insect damage:

- Sloping the ground away from foundations for good drainage and putting vapour barriers on the interior sides of exposed walls

- Using polyethylene as a soil cover in crawl spaces

- Flashing gutters, downspouts, and splash blocks to carry water away from foundation walls

- Using poured concrete foundation walls, concrete caps over unit masonry foundations, wood treatments, soil treatments, or metal termite shields

Building with dry, naturally durable woods and conducting regular maintenance inspections can also help prevent insect infestation and damage. Poorly aimed lawn irrigation systems can be a serious problem for improvements if the water collects against the foundation or is directed at exterior walls or windows. An improperly installed irrigation system can rot a window assembly or cause a mould problem in only a few years.

Miscellaneous and Special Features

In valuing industrial and commercial properties, an appraiser may find it helpful to distinguish between two categories of equipment:

Interior Painting, Decorating, and Finishing

Basement Finishes

Types	Unfinished, used for storage
	Finished (in residences and some commercial buildings), used for storage and other purposes
Characteristics	Dampness, which is often a problem in basements, may be caused by poor foundation wall construction, excess groundwater that is not properly drained by ground tiles, poorly fitted windows or hatches, poor venting of equipment, or poorly constructed or operating roof drains that allow water to enter. Signs that may indicate a wet basement include a powdery white mineral deposit a few inches off the floor, stains near the bottom of walls and columns or equipment that rests close to the floor, and the smell of mildew.

Flooring and Floor Coverings

Components	Sand, compressed dirt, bituminous paving, brick, stone gravel, concrete, and similar products
Characteristics	Suitable for many industrial buildings, warehouses, garages, and basements. In many commercial and industrial buildings, floors must be especially thick or reinforced to support heavy equipment.
Components	Terrazzo flooring
Characteristics	Made of coloured marble chips that are mixed into cement and ground smooth; used for high traffic areas such as the lobbies of public buildings.
Components	Wood in various forms
Characteristics	Continues to be a popular material for floors. Planks and blocks are used for industrial floors, and many commercial buildings use wood floors to conform to the design and overall decoration. Wood planks and hardwood strips are found in many residences, although other types of flooring have become more popular.
Components	Resilient, ceramic, and quarry tiles
Characteristics	Used in all types of buildings.
Components	Resilient flooring
Characteristics	Usually a combination of vinyl and asphalt; produced as sheet goods
Components	Carpeting
Characteristics	Once considered a luxury in residences, offices, stores, and commercial buildings, but today is widely used in all types of buildings

Interior Wall Coverings and Ceilings

Types	Walls and partitions
Characteristics	May be painted, papered, or panelled; supplemental finishings include ceramic tile and wainscot panelling.
Types	Ceilings
Characteristics	Can be drywall, plaster, or suspended panel (drop ceilings)
Types	Partitions
Characteristics	Can be wood or metal

- Equipment and mechanical systems that provide for human comfort, e.g., plumbing, heating, air-conditioning, and lighting
- Fixed building equipment that is process-related, e.g., air hoses, process piping, craneways, bus ducts, heavy electrical lines, and freezer equipment[3]

Since different users of structures and related improvements frequently adapt them for their own particular needs, some elements may not be suited for other users and therefore will not contribute to market value. Limited-market properties may require additional research because there is less data to support the estimate of utility and market acceptance of extra or unusual elements of the improvements.

Some properties with specialized functions and design features that may require additional research include the following:

- Steel mills
- Oil refineries and ethanol plants
- Chemical plants
- Concrete factories
- Mines
- Commercial establishments with unique design features (e.g., drive-in restaurants) or special facilities (e.g., the cooling room in a furrier's shop)
- Amusement parks
- Sports complexes
- Wharves and docks
- Transportation terminals
- Television and `radio transmission towers, studios, and theatres

EQUIPMENT AND MECHANICAL SYSTEMS

Most buildings cannot perform the functions for which they were designed and constructed unless their equipment and mechanical systems are in working order. Major equipment and mechanical systems include the following:

- The plumbing system
- The heating, ventilation, and air-conditioning (HVAC) system
- The electrical system

Plumbing System

Plumbing is an integral part of most buildings. It consists of supply, waste, and vent piping (which is usually covered or hidden except in industrial buildings) and fixtures and fittings (which are visible). Laundries, laundromats, and certain industrial buildings have elaborate plumbing systems.

> Equipment and mechanical systems provide for human comfort; industrial buildings also contain process-related equipment.

---

[3]   For discussion of the distinction between fixtures, personal property, and real estate, see Tables 1.1 and 1.2 in Chapter 1.

Plumbing System

Piping

Types	Supply pipes
	Waste pipes
	Vent pipes
Materials	Copper, cast iron, or plastic
Characteristics/Use	Galvanized steel, lead, or brass pipes in older buildings may need to be replaced.

Bathroom Fixtures

Types	Lavatories (or washbasins)
	Bathtubs
	Showers
	Toilets (or water closets)
	Bidets
	Urinals
Materials	Cast iron covered with acid-resistant vitreous enamel or porcelain; fiberglass or other materials are also used in lower-quality fixtures
Types	Sinks (or double sinks)
Materials	Monel® metal, stainless steel, enamelled steel, or cast iron covered with acid-resistant enamel

Kitchen Fixtures

Types	Sinks (or double sinks)
	Garbage disposals
	Dishwashers
Materials	Monel® metal, stainless steel, enamelled steel, or cast iron covered with acid-resistant enamel

Other Fixtures

Types	Instant hot water units
	Laundry tubs
	Wet bars
	Swimming pools or saunas
	Janitor sinks
	Drinking fountains
	Handwashing and eyewashing fountains

Fittings

Types	Faucets
	Spigots
	Drains
	Shower heads
	Spray tubes
	Floor drains in industrial buildings
Characteristics/Use	The water in an area may be hard, i.e., it contains minerals that react unfavorably with soap and make it difficult to rinse from clothing, hair, and skin. Often hard water cannot be used until it is treated, either with simple equipment or with automatic, complex, multi-stage systems.

Plumbing System, *continued*	
Hot Water System	
Types	Self-standing heater (in residential buildings)
	Large cast iron or steel boiler and storage tanks (in commercial and industrial buildings)
Characteristics/Use	Generally powered by electricity, gas, or oil.

Piping

Much of the cost of a plumbing system may be due to piping. The quality of the materials used, the way the pipes were installed, and how easily they can be serviced are significant considerations in estimating how long the pipes will last and how much they will cost to maintain. In many areas and for many building types, a high-quality piping system will last as long as the building.

Fixtures and Fittings

The appraiser must decide which building fixtures are part of the real estate and which are personal property. The design of bathroom fixtures can change substantially over time, and old fixtures may become obsolete during a building's economic life. An appraiser should report the need for modernization, but old fixtures of good quality, such as porcelain pedestal basins and footed tubs, are often rehabilitated and valuable.

Hot Water System

All homes and many commercial and industrial buildings need an adequate supply of hot water. Buildings with inadequate hot water systems suffer from functional obsolescence, e.g., when ongoing change, caused by technological advances and economic and aesthetic trends, renders building layouts and features obsolete. The size of the hot water storage tank needed is determined by the number of occupants and their water-using habits and by the recovery rate of the tank. The size and recovery rate of a storage tank may be limited to what the market will pay for. Commercial and industrial buildings often require much more hot water than homes.

Heating Systems

Most heating systems use warm or hot air, hot water, steam, or electricity and are powered by fuel oil, natural gas, electricity, or coal. The heating capacity required relates to the cubic content, exposure, design, and insulation level of the structure to be heated and appropriate standards for the local market area. The appraiser cannot assume that a building's heating system contributes maximum value to a property. A heating system installed at the time of construction may not be acceptable to potential buyers today. New technology continues to reduce energy consumption for large heating systems. Many industrial users who once depended on gas alone now install more efficient oil or electric systems to provide heat when the gas supply is curtailed. Electric heat has become so expensive in some areas that buildings using it sell for

> **cogeneration**
> The simultaneous production of electrical energy and low-grade heat from the same fuel.

substantially less than similar properties using other types of fuel. Cogeneration, the simultaneous production of electrical energy and low-grade heat from the same fuel, is also being used in some parts of the country.

Buyers are sensitive to energy costs. In some markets, apartments in which the owner supplies heat and hot water will sell for less than similar properties in which tenants pay for utilities. Buildings that have high ceilings, many openings, and poor insulation may be at a disadvantage in the market.

Air-Conditioning and Ventilation Systems

The most common type of air-conditioning system consists of an electrically powered compressor that compresses a coolant from gas into liquid outside the area being cooled. The heat released in this process is either blown away or carried away by water. Air-conditioners range from small, portable units to units that provide many tons of cooling capacity.

Commercial and industrial air-conditioning and ventilation systems are more complex. Some simply bring in fresh air from the outside and distribute it throughout the building; others merely remove foul air. Still others combine these two functions, but do not have any cooling or heating capacity. More complex systems wash, filter, and add or remove humidity from the air. The most complex systems perform all of

---

Heating Fuels: The type of fuel used in a building's heating system should be explained in the building description. Depending on the area and the type of building, one type of fuel may be more desirable than another. Nevertheless, many building heating systems do not use the most economical fuel. For any specific use, different fuels have different advantages and disadvantages, which are subject to change.

Type	Characteristics
Fuel oil	In spite of its high cost, fuel oil is a popular energy source that is easy to transport and store. On-site, 275-gallon tanks are used in millions of houses, and tanks that hold thousands of gallons of fuel oil are buried on industrial and commercial sites.
Natural gas	Natural gas is a convenient type of fuel because it is continuously delivered by pipelines; no storage tank is needed. In many parts of Canada, natural gas is the most economical fuel. Liquid petroleum gas, such as butane and propane, is used in many rural areas. It requires on-site storage tanks and is usually more expensive, but in other respects it is similar to natural gas.
Electricity	Like oil, gas, or coal, electricity can be used to produce heat in a furnace or to heat water in a boiler. In most areas electrical heating costs are high, but good insulation and control can eliminate waste.
Coal	In the past, coal was the most popular fuel for heating; it is still used in electrical generating plants and to generate power for some industrial and commercial uses. Coal is also used in residences for stoves and fireplaces, but the burning of certain types of coal creates environmental pollution.

these functions and also heat and cool air through a complex system of ducts and fans. In larger systems that use less electricity, water cools the pipes in which the gas has been compressed. The water is then conserved in towers that cool it for reuse.

HVAC System

Heating System	Heating is rated in British thermal units (BTUs).
Types	Warm or hot air
Characteristics/Use	Air heated in a furnace and circulated by a pressure blower or relying on the force of gravity. May include thermostats, filters, humidifiers, air cleaners, and air purification devices.
Types	Hot water (or hydronic systems)
Characteristics/Use	Hot water pumped by a circulator through pipes to radiators and cold water is returned to the boiler to be reheated. In radiant heating systems, hot water is pumped through narrow pipes embedded in floors, walls, and ceilings rather than through radiators.
Types	Steam
Characteristics/Use	Produced by a boiler, distributed through a one-pipe gravity system (identical to the piping used in hot water systems), and transferred through radiators. More complex and expensive two-pipe systems are found in larger, high-quality structures. In many provinces, licenses are required for certain classes of steam boilers; appraisers must be familiar with local boiler license laws and ascertain whether boilers have current, valid licenses.
Types	Electric
Characteristics/Use	Includes heat pumps, wall heaters, baseboard units, duct heating units, heating units installed in air-conditioning ducts, and radiant heat produced by electric heating elements embedded in floors, walls, and ceilings. The automatic regulation of a heating system helps it operate efficiently. A multiple-zone system with separate thermostats is more efficient than a single zone system with one thermostat. Complex systems provide an individual temperature control for each room. The efficiency of certain systems can be increased by putting a thermostat on the outside of the building. This helps building operators anticipate how much heat the system will need to produce.

Air-Conditioning and Ventilation System

Types	Electrically powered compressor and non-ozone-depleting refrigerant Gas-powered compressor and ammonia as coolant Combination with water-cooled pipes in which gas is compressed
Characteristics/Use	Standards depend on climate. Capacity is rated in tons of refrigeration. In some buildings the central air-conditioning equipment uses the same ducts as the hot air heating system. This is not always possible, however, because the air-conditioning may require ducts of a different size. Furthermore, heating registers should be placed low on the walls, while air-conditioning registers should be higher up or in the ceiling.

Electrical Systems

In an electrical system, power is distributed from the electrical service station through branch circuits, which are wires located throughout the building, to electrical outlets. Each branch circuit starts at a distribution box, where it is separated from the main service by a protection device such as a fuse or circuit breaker.

In commercial and industrial buildings, the wiring between the distribution boxes and the outlets is usually a rigid or flexible conduit. In most houses, BX or armoured cable is used. Plastic-coated wire is used in certain areas, and the old knob-and-tube wiring is still found in rural areas and older buildings, although it is considered obsolete.

Electrical System

Components	Rigid or flexible conduit BX or armored cable
Characteristics/Use	Most electrical wire is copper. A typical residential electrical system is a single-phase, three-wire system that provides a minimum of 100 amperes of electricity. Ampere services of 150, 200, 300, and 400 are needed when electric heating and air-conditioning are used. Most of these services can provide up to 220 volts by connecting three wires to the outlet.
Components	Power wiring
Characteristics/Use	Used in commercial and industrial buildings to operate utility systems, appliances, and machinery. The electrical power is generally carried at higher voltages (e.g., 240, 480, 600 volts or more) and higher amperages (e.g., 400, 800, 1,200 amperes or more). Power wiring is usually three-phase or three-phase-four-wire, which allows both lighting and three-phase power loads to be delivered by the same supply. It is carried in conduit or by means of plug-in bus ducts. Overhead bus ducts are frequently found in manufacturing plants where flexible service is needed.
Components	Switches and lighting fixtures
Characteristics/Use	Since lighting fixtures are stylized and styles change, they are often obsolete before they wear out. Fluorescent lighting, which may be suspended, surface-mounted, or recessed, is used extensively in commercial and industrial buildings. Often continuous rows are used in large spaces. Incandescent fixtures may be used for smaller rooms, accents, or special purposes. Sodium, mercury vapor, halogen, and halide lights are often installed in industrial buildings.
Components	Outside, yard, and parking lot lighting
Characteristics/Use	Usually downlighting of some kind; often mercury vapor, halogen, or halide lights
Components	Floor outlets or floor duct systems
Characteristics/Use	Used extensively in commercial and office buildings; provide convenient electrical outlets for office machines and telephone outlets at desks using a minimum number of cords
Components	Low-voltage switching systems
Characteristics/Use	In some houses and commercial buildings; allow many outlets and lights to be controlled from one place

Large-capacity power wiring may contribute to the value of an industrial improvement. However, if the wiring is an uncommon type and adds to a building's operating costs or will be expensive to remove, it may result in functional obsolescence. Similarly, any building with insufficient electrical service or wiring suffers from functional obsolescence.

Miscellaneous Equipment

In the building description, the appraiser must also consider miscellaneous equipment, such as the following:

- Fire protection
- Elevators, escalators, and speed ramps
- Signals, alarms, and call systems
- Loading facilities
- Attached equipment

ANALYSIS OF ARCHITECTURAL STYLE AND FUNCTIONAL UTILITY

A building may have functional utility but lack architectural style, such as a multipurpose precast concrete warehouse near a highway interchange, or it may have admirable style but little utility, such as a cavernous 1920s vintage movie palace in a declining urban neighbourhood. Form and function work together to create successful

---

Miscellaneous Equipment

Fire Protection

Components	Fire escapes
	Standpipes and hose cabinets
	Alarm services
	Automatic sprinklers
Characteristics/Use	A wet sprinkler system must have adequate water pressure to ensure that the pipes are always filled. A dry system has pressurized air in the pipes. When a sprinkler head opens, the pressure is relieved and water enters. Dry systems are used on loading docks, in un-heated buildings where there is a danger of water freezing, and in areas where there is no city water (usually because a well cannot supply sufficient pressure to operate a wet system).

Elevators

Type	Passenger
Characteristics/Use	Generally electric; most modern elevators are high-speed and completely automatic
Type	Freight
Characteristics/Use	Electric or hydraulic; hydraulic elevators are suitable for low-speed, low-rise operations

---

Miscellaneous Equipment, *continued*

Escalators and Speed Ramps

Type	Passenger
Characteristics/Use	Used to move large numbers of people up and down or along horizontal or gradual slopes; must be adequate to accommodate those who use the building

---

Signals, Alarms, and Call Systems

Components	Smoke detectors
Characteristics/Use	Required by law in many areas
Components	Security alarm systems
Characteristics/Use	Available for residential, commercial, and industrial use to warn occupants of forced entry, fire, or both
Components	Clocks, pneumatic tube systems, mail chutes, and incinerators
Components	Telephone wiring
Characteristics/Use	In small buildings the telephone company supplies the wiring and equipment. Larger buildings may have extensive systems of built-in cabinets, conduits, and floor ducts for telephone service. The telephone service in a building may be suitable for the current occupant but unsuitable for a potential buyer.

Loading Facilities

Type	Open loading docks
Characteristics/Use	May be important in commercial and industrial buildings. Off-street loading docks are usually required by zoning regulations. Many older buildings have loading doors only or substandard loading facilities. The floor of an efficient, one-storey industrial building may be built above grade at freight car or truck-bed level.
Type	Covered loading docks
Characteristics/Use	In some buildings, docks are enclosed for trucks and freight cars, and levelling devices are provided to assist in loading or unloading. A properly designed industrial building has space in front of truck docks so that vehicles can manoeuvre.

Attached Equipment

Components	Air hoses
	Process piping
	Industrial wiring for heavy electrical capacity
	Bus ducts
	Freezer equipment
Characteristics/Use	Often considered in terms of use value

---

architecture. Functional utility is not necessarily exemplified by minimal space or form; people's need for comfort and pleasure must also be considered in the design of offices, stores, hospitals, and houses. An appraiser must recognize and rank market preferences regarding style and functional utility and then relate these preferences to market value.

Good design meets the following criteria:

- Functions well – fitness of intended use
- Looks good – appeals to aesthetic sense
- Feels good – carries meaning, recreates feeling from another time or place
- Balance – sense of correct proportion, compatibility
- Affordable – consistent with market expectations for price range

Social and economic issues have the greatest impact on residential design. Governmental issues have a greater impact on non-residential design through zoning and building codes. Environmental issues affect the site more than the improvements, although topography and other factors may impact the placement of the improvements on the site.

Architectural Style

Architecture is the art and science of building design and construction. Architectural style affects the market value of property, so it is important for appraisers to understand its nature. Two basic types of styles are distinguished in American architecture: formal architecture and vernacular architecture. Figures 11.2 and 11.3 illustrate formal and vernacular architectural styles.

Formal architecture refers to the art and science of designing and building structures that meet the aesthetic and functional criteria of those trained in architectural history. Formal architectural styles are identified by common attributes of expression and are frequently named in reference to a geographic region, cultural group, or time period, e.g., the Italianate, Second Empire, and Prairie School styles.[4]

To a degree, the distinction between formal and vernacular architecture is analogous to the difference between fine art and folk art. Vernacular architecture identifies structures designed and built without reference to the aesthetic and functional criteria of architectural history, often buildings with an emphasis on function over form. Vernacular architecture reflects custom and responds to the environment and contemporary lifestyles. Vernacular styles share common attributes and may be technologically simple or sophisticated. These styles are usually unnamed because they are not formally studied by architectural historians. The traditional barn, the mass-produced homes constructed in modern subdivisions, and multi-tenant industrial park buildings are examples of vernacular styles.

> **architectural style**
> The character of a building's form and ornamentation.
>
> **formal architecture**
> Architecture identified by its conformity to aesthetic and functional criteria recognized by persons trained in architectural history.
>
> **vernacular architecture**
> Architecture designed and built by individuals according to custom and for its adaptive response to the environment and contemporary lifestyles, without reference to the aesthetic and functional criteria of architectural history.

> Market preferences are influenced both by the desire to maintain tradition and by an expectancy of innovation.

---

4   Literature on American architectural history is abundant. For a description of architectural styles in a real estate appraisal context, see Judith Reynolds, *Historic Properties: Preservation and the Valuation Process*, 3rd ed. (Chicago: Appraisal Institute, 2006) and Carole Rifkind, *A Field Guide to American Architecture*, rev. ed. (New York: Dutton, 1998). Additional sources are cited in the bibiliography.

Figure 11.2: Formal Architecture

Figure 11.3: Vernacular Architecture

Architectural style is influenced by market standards and tastes, which are influenced both by the desire to preserve tradition and by the desire for change, variety, and efficiency. The market's desire for change provides the impetus for developing new elements of architectural design. Changes in architectural trends are caused by the market's reaction to current styles. When a style becomes too extreme, a shift to elements of past styles frequently occurs. A reactive shift, then, provides contrast to the preceding, dominant architectural style. Such changes also produce avant-garde or experimental building styles, which are tested in the market and ultimately accepted or discarded.

Changes in architecture can also be generated by external forces. For example, in the 1970s, rising energy costs prompted new developments in the heating, ventilation, and air-conditioning systems used in office buildings. These developments include the trend toward stand-alone HVAC systems and the use of new exterior materials that conserve energy.

Architectural styles are modified over periods that are loosely related to the economic life cycles of buildings. Newly constructed buildings usually contrast in style with buildings of the previous period. Newly constructed buildings of all architectural styles enjoy broad market appeal, whether they are professionally designed or not. However, when a building is no longer new it is compared with other buildings in terms of the quality and usefulness of its architectural style. Form and structure, the most basic components of architectural style, limit and define a building's potential uses (and changes in use). These factors become more influential as time passes.

Functional Utility

To be functional, an item must work and be useful. However, the definition of functional utility is subject to changing expectations and standards. Optimal functional utility implies that the design and engineering of a building are considered to best meet perceived needs at a given time.

Functional inutility is an impairment of the functional capacity of a property or building according to market tastes and standards. It qualifies as functional obsolescence when ongoing change, caused by technological advances and economic and aesthetic trends, renders building layouts and features obsolete. Chapter 19 discusses the concept of functional obsolescence in detail. Functional inutility must be judged in terms of market standards of acceptability, specifically the standards of buyers who make up the market for a particular type of building within a particular period of time. Certain design elements of "smart office buildings", such as extra cooling capability, more flexible cabling systems, and additional power to run more sophisticated computer systems, may have been superadequate when they were originally constructed, but changing market desires have made some of those items standard.

> **functional utility**
> The ability of a property or building to be useful and to perform the function for which it is intended according to current market tastes and standards; the efficiency of a building's use in terms of architectural style, design and layout, traffic patterns, and the size and type of rooms.
>
> **functional inutility**
> Impairment of the functional capacity of a property or building according to market tastes and standards; equivalent to functional obsolescence because ongoing change makes layouts and features obsolete.

> In architecture, style and functional utility are necessarily interrelated because form and function work with design and construction to create a successful product.

Standards of functional utility vary with the type and use of property. Specific considerations for different types of property are discussed in the remainder of this chapter. Some general standards of functional utility considered by appraisers include the following:

- Compatibility
- Suitability or appropriateness
- Comfort
- Efficiency
- Safety
- Security
- Accessibility
- Ease and cost of maintenance
- Market standards
- Attractiveness
- Economic productivity

Design and Functional Utility by Property Type

Marketability is the ultimate test of functional utility. Generally, a building is functional if it successfully serves the purpose for which it was designed or adapted. Specific design considerations that affect the functional utility of residential, commercial, industrial, agricultural, and special-purpose buildings are discussed below.

Residential

Trends in single-unit and apartment design change, and building components such as porches, balconies, fireplaces, dining rooms, large kitchens, entry halls, and family rooms may be included or excluded. Housing standards vary widely for different income levels and in different regions. Historic houses are often less functional, but they may be in great demand due to their preservationist appeal. To evaluate the functional utility of residential buildings, appraisers should analyze standard market expectations. The functional utility of a single-unit or multi-family dwelling results primarily from its layout, accommodation of specific activities, adequacy, and ease and cost of maintenance.[5]

In general, more people have better housing today than they had in the past. Many amenities are now considered necessities and their inclusion is taken for granted. Even in periods of high construction and financing costs when average houses are smaller, the tendency is to retain extra bathrooms, labour-saving devices, and fireplaces.

In apartment buildings, amenities tend to be more important than space. Occupants often prefer a fireplace or an extra bathroom to an additional 200 square

---

EMERGING TRENDS IN RESIDENTIAL DESIGN

Remodelling: Becoming as common as new construction

Great room: Importance to the functions of the residence increasing

Floors: Wood or wood-look floors gaining popularity

Tile counters: Tile is a typical material; Corian® countertops may be an overimprovement in all but the highest-priced residences

Windows: Often retrofitted with vinyl coverings on frames for ease of maintenance.

Recessed ceiling lights: High ceilings are currently popular despite the energy costs, and recessed lighting increases the feeling of space

Electrical, plumbing, and heating systems: Often replaced with more efficient systems in resale homes

Cabinet finishes: Subject to the whims of fashion

Doors: Heavy, solid-core doors are replacing standard, hollow-core doors

---

[5]   For further discussion of single-unit home design and functional utility, see Henry S. Harrison, *Houses – The Illustrated Guide to Construction, Design & Systems*, 3rd ed. (Chicago: Real Estate Education Company, a division of Dearborn Financial, 1998) and Appraisal Institute, *Appraising Residential Properties*, 4th ed. (Chicago: Appraisal Institute, 2007). For discussion of apartment analysis, see Arlen C. Mills, Richard L. Parli, and Anthony Reynolds, *The Valuation of Apartment Properties*, 2nd ed. (Chicago: Appraisal Institute, 2007) and Daniel J. O'Connell, *The Appraisal of Apartment Buildings* (New York: John Wiley & Sons, Inc., 1990).

feet of area. Smaller kitchens and bathrooms tend to be more acceptable to the market for apartments than the market for houses. A dining area that is a part of the living room or kitchen is generally acceptable. Family rooms and living rooms may be spacious to offset the smallness of other rooms, and closet space must be plentiful.

The layout of a residential property relates to traffic patterns, i.e., where kitchens and bathrooms should be located for convenience and how private and non-private areas should be separated (see Table 11.2). A layout has functional inutility if it causes awkward traffic patterns. For example, inutility may result if people have to cross the living room to get to a bedroom, if the dining area is not next to the kitchen, or if groceries have to be brought through the living room to the kitchen.

Standards of adequacy vary. For the most part, the market will not accept a one-bathroom house, although one-bedroom apartments and condominium units remain popular. New kitchens and baths are larger, better equipped, and more expensively finished than the small, utilitarian kitchens and baths of the recent past. Dishwashers, garbage disposals, and wall ovens are usually standard in new construction and their absence may create a value penalty. Ceramic tile in baths and more elegant fixtures are becoming commonplace. The master bedroom frequently has its own compartmentalized bath with a spa tub and a separate dressing area. Closets are abundant in new apartments and houses. Some examples of functional obsolescence in residential property are listed in Table 11.3.

Table 11.2: Residential Layout Considerations

Poor floor plans are easily recognized by those who make up the market for houses, but standards often vary with current trends in a region and neighborhood. The location of various rooms in relation to the site can increase or diminish a dwelling's privacy and comfort.

Single-Unit Homes
- Bedrooms and living rooms are increasingly found in the rear of residences, often accessible to the garden or backyard. Formerly it was considered desirable for the living room and largest bedroom to be at the front of the house, oriented to the street.
- Kitchens, which were once relegated to the rear, are now just as likely to be on one side of a hall in the middle or at the front of a residence.
- Full bathrooms are most convenient, accessible, and private when they are near the bedrooms. They should be accessed directly or through a hall, not through a bedroom. Powder rooms should be located off a hall and near, but not too near, the living room or dining room.

Multi-Family Units
- Two-storey, two-unit residences with vertical access from within the unit, rather than from public space, have strong market appeal.
- Multi-unit housing is also built in stacked configurations with access on more than one level to minimize stair climbing.
- Low-rise, multi-family housing projects can be designed in a great many ways.
- Elevator apartment buildings tend to have more standardized, predictable floor plans to make the best use of space within a simple rectangular configuration.
- Structures designed for other uses are now being converted to apartments. Silos, breweries, warehouses, and schools have been successfully converted into multi-unit projects.
- As housing costs increase, multi-unit floor plans have become more compact, with smaller rooms and more efficient layouts

Table 11.3: Examples of Functional Obsolescence in Residential Improvements

- Interior and exterior finishes that require extensive maintenance can make a structure less competitive.
- In most markets a house that wastes fuel and electricity suffers major functional obsolescence. Energy-conserving features are particularly important in multi-family dwellings and often make the difference between a profitable operation and an unprofitable one.
- The mix of units in an apartment project (e.g., two-bedroom units and three-bedroom units) should meet market demands. An improper unit mix may indicate functional inutility.

Commercial

Commercial buildings are used for offices, stores, hotels, banks, restaurants, and service outlets. Frequently, two or more commercial uses are combined in a single building, e.g., a high-rise office building with ground-level retail space or a hotel with a retail arcade off the lobby. The structural and design features of commercial buildings are constantly changing. Developers want the most competitive building possible, within the cost constraints imposed by economic pressures. Therefore, they incorporate technological changes to meet the demand for innovation whenever possible.

The efficiency of commercial construction today is much greater than it was in the past. Greater utility can be observed both in the portion of the total area enclosed by the structure, which produces direct income in the form of rent, and in the structural facilitation that has evolved from new materials and construction methods. No single method of commercial building construction predominates. Methods vie with one another, and one may surpass others in a given area at a particular time.

Important considerations of functional utility in commercial properties include the following:

- Column spacing
- Bay depth
- Live-load floor capacity
- Ceiling height
- Module width
- Elevator speed, capacity, number, and safety
- Level of finish
- Energy efficiency
- Parking

Functional Utility in Shopping Centres

Functional utility can be extremely significant in shopping centres. Trends in shopping centres change so rapidly that many structures become functionally obsolete before they deteriorate physically. Since retail space is relatively easy to renovate, many centres are streamlined and modernized when they lose their market appeal. Some enclosed malls developed in the 1980s have been adapted to other uses or have been levelled and redeveloped as big-box power centres for value-oriented shoppers or lifestyle-oriented centres for high-end consumers. Many modern community shopping centres are designed with the power centre concept, incorporating a larger number of smaller anchors and a higher ratio of anchor space to minimize risk.[6]

Visibility and access are the primary considerations in the analysis of retail improvements. Other building amenities that can contribute to the functional utility of shopping centres include the following:

- Attractive public areas
- Well-kept grounds
- Adequate, well-located restroom facilities
- Suitable traffic patterns for shoppers
- Adequate column spacing
- Sufficient number of escalators
- Durable and easily maintained surface and finish elements
- Areas for shoppers and workers to rest
- Strong lighting and attractive, coordinated signs

EMERGING TRENDS IN SHOPPING CENTRE DESIGN

Individuality: In contrast to the trend of branding a product to promote consumer loyalty, shopping centre developers are emphasizing regional differences in architectural style to avoid homogeneity. Strong brand names within a shopping centre are still desirable, but the shopping centre itself should not be seen as a carbon copy of another property in a chain.

Entertainment retailing: Entertainment functions such as movie theatres, restaurants, and themed retailers are becoming increasingly common in "destination" shopping centres. Research has yet to demonstrate conclusively that the presence of movie theatres increases overall sales within a shopping centre, but properties that lack entertainment options may be at a competitive disadvantage in the investment market.

Themed districts within a shopping centre: In the past, the tenant mix was often adjusted so that competitors would be in different areas of a shopping centre. To foster convenience, comfort, and control for consumers with limited time, shopping centre owners are starting to cluster related retailers, e.g., wings of a mall focusing on fashion boutiques, sports-oriented retailers, and family-oriented stores. The effectiveness of the tenant mix of a shopping centre remains a good indicator of the competency of leasing and management.

Functional Utility in Office Buildings

Modern office buildings are often able to fulfill their primary function – accommodating the activities of office workers – longer than any other property type, with the possible exception of residential property. Although trends in office construction move more slowly than trends in retail and hotel design, the flexibility of office space is increasingly important to an office building's viability. Older office buildings that cannot be retrofitted to contemporary standards for wiring, HVAC capacity, and other essential systems will suffer in competition with more functional office space.

---

[6]   For a discussion of the spatial analysis of a shopping centre, see M. Gordon Brown, "Design and Value: Spatial Form and the Economic Failure of a Mall", *Journal of Real Estate Research*, vol. 17, no. 1/2 (1999): 189-225.

Office tenants are more likely to pay higher rents for space in an attractively designed building or for a prestigious address, but tenants are unlikely to renew their leases if the office space is unable to adapt to their changing needs. Even if a developer plans to rent full floors of a new office building, there may come a time when the owner must subdivide floors and rent space to smaller tenants.

Functional considerations for office buildings include the following:

- Appropriate density (low-, medium-, or high-rise structure) for market area
- Building shape and size
- Flexible and efficient use of space (larger floorplates are desirable)
- Expansion capabilities, including potential vertical expansion
- HVAC, plumbing, electrical, security, and communications systems
- Floor-to-floor heights
- Facade and interior and exterior signage
- Access to lobbies and public space
- Vertical transportation
- Amenities, e.g., retail and restaurants, fitness centres, day care facilities

Access to retail and support services is an important amenity in suburban office parks because these services may not be within easy driving distance; this is unlike urban office districts that have a concentration of diverse uses.

EMERGING TRENDS IN OFFICE BUILDING DESIGN

Office-hotel concept: As an alternative to negotiating 10- to 20-year office leases, some office building owners are experimenting with providing short-term or temporary space and services as needed by tenants.

Panel systems: Panel systems for separating workspaces are replacing traditional methods of dividing space in offices for several reasons:
1. Cost – the cost of the technology needed for the average office worker is rising
2. Flexibility – more diverse work teams need adaptable meeting space
3. Private office spaces can be arranged with new panel systems

Data and power infrastructure: Raised floors and carpet tile allow greater access to data and power cabling as well as denser bundling. (Carpet tile helps muffle the hollow sound of raised floors.) Sufficient space for telecommunications closets is important for long-term flexibility.

Indoor air quality: The Environmental Protection Agency has ranked indoor air pollution among the top five environmental risks to public health. Poor indoor air quality can be reduced using proper ventilation and air exchange rates.

Functional Utility in Hotels

Hotels range from tiny inns with fewer than a dozen rooms to huge convention hotels with more than a thousand rooms.[7] All hotels and motels were once measured against standard, current designs. This tendency continues for medium-priced hotels and the various extended-stay and limited-service categories, but appraisers must consider

---

[7]   For a thorough discussion of hotels, see Stephen Rushmore and Erich Baum, *Hotels and Motels: Valuations and Market Studies* (Chicago: Appraisal Institute, 2001) and Stephen Rushmore, Dana Michael Ciraldo, and John Tarras, *Hotel Investments Handbook* (Boston: Warren, Gorham & Lamont, 1997).

variation in architectural styles and interior finish in appraising older facilities and luxury hotels.

The type of patrons a hotel services determines the physical configuration of a hotel or motel. A motel must be oriented to the needs of drivers who wish to spend a minimum amount of time on the premises. On the other hand, a resort hotel must provide a variety of entertainment facilities for its guests.

The amount of hotel space devoted to guest rooms varies. A hotel that is a major meeting and entertainment centre has a much lower proportion of guest rooms to public areas than an extended-stay hotel. Many extended-stay hotels consist entirely of suites with small equipped kitchens, living rooms, and separate bedrooms. These hotels usually have small lobbies and restaurants. Since few hotels contain lodging facilities alone, appraisers must often consider multiple, mixed uses when analyzing the functional utility of the improvements.

EMERGING TRENDS IN HOTEL DESIGN

Needs of the business traveler: Access to communications technology (wireless internet connectivity and fax machines either in guest rooms or in a business centre) is increasingly important to business travelers. At a minimum, hotels catering to business travelers should have a health club in addition to a business centre.

Product types: All-suite, extended-stay, and hard budget hotels are the newest lodging concepts. The hard budget category avoids "amenity creep", i.e., renovation that is beyond typical maintenance and upkeep and that over time has turned limited-service hotels into mid-priced hotels.

Industrial

The most flexible design for industrial buildings, and the one with the greatest appeal on the open market, is a one-storey, square, or nearly square structure that complies with all local building codes.[8] Even for the simplest industrial buildings, though, the factors listed in Table 11.4 must be considered.

The combination of old and new industrial space may create substantial functional obsolescence if the new construction contributes less than its cost to the value of the whole. The layout of industrial space should allow operations to be carried out with maximum efficiency. Typically, receiving functions are performed on one side of the building, shipping functions on the other, and processing or storage functions in the middle.

Some industrial buildings include special features such as sprinkler systems, scales, loading dock levellers, cranes and craneways, refrigeration areas, conveyor systems, process piping (for compressed air, water, and gas), power wiring, and employee lockers and lunchrooms. These features may be standard equipment for certain industrial operations but not standard for the local real estate market.

---

[8]   See also Douglas McKnight, "A Practical Guide to Evaluating the Functional Utility of Warehouses", *The Appraisal Journal* (January 1999): 29-36 and Donald Sonneman, "Challenges in Appraising 'Simple' Warehouse Properties", *The Appraisal Journal* (April 2001): 174-181.

Table 11.4: Functional Utility of Industrial Improvements

Surplus land	In new construction surplus land on the site is frequently allocated for future expansion.
Clear span	Anywhere from 21 to 35 feet. Many smaller warehouses can be operated with a clear span of 15 to 20 feet, but higher ceilings might be standard in the market.
Percentage of office space	Varies widely depending on specific operation. If potential alternate uses of an existing property do not require as much finished office space, the excess may be an overimprovement.
Loading facilities	Multiple load facilities can reduce delays in incoming deliveries and outgoing orders. Overhead doors are less efficient loading facilities than loading docks, dock high floors, and truck wells.
Floor thickness and loading capacity	Typically, 5 to 8 inches of reinforced concrete. Live-load capacity – the ability to support moving or movable objects in the building at a certain weight – is a minimum 125 pounds per square foot for light warehouse space and manufacturing buildings and 250 pounds per square foot for heavy warehouses.
Power service	Manufacturing plants generally require more electrical service than warehouses.
Land-to-building ratio or floor space ratio (FSR)	Typically, 1.8 to 3.5 land-to-building area (0.28 to 0.55 floor space ratio). Many older facilities have less land and thus higher ratios. The ratio must allow plenty of space for parking, truck maneuvering, yard storage, and expansion. Floor area ratio (FSR) is also known as building-to-land ratio.
Size relative to typical building size	Big-box warehouses can be significantly larger than competitive buildings in the market. The cost of reconfiguring a large industrial building for multi-tenant use is a measure of functional inutility.
Slope of access to the site	Steep inclines can reduce loading efficiency.

Functional Utility in Manufacturing Plants

Manufacturing plants and other buildings used for industries that involve bulky or volatile materials and products have specialized equipment and building designs, so they have few potential users. Facilities for industries such as food processing or manufacturing computer chips must maintain prescribed levels of cleanliness. For example, the "clean rooms" needed for silicon wafer production may not contribute as much value as they cost to construct if used for alternative industrial uses. Buildings used for light manufacturing and processing have fewer limitations and greater appeal in the market.

Functional Utility in Warehouse and Distribution Facilities

Storage and distribution facilities range from simple cubicles, known as mini-warehouses, to huge regional warehouses with more than a million square feet. For optimal functional utility, warehouses should have adequate access, open areas, ceiling height, floor load capacity, humidity and temperature controls, shipping and receiving facilities, fire protection, and protection from the elements.

The primary consideration in warehouse location is good access. Just-in-time inventory practices require a distribution facility to be accessible to a greater variety of vehicles and cargo containers, making more frequent and often smaller pick-ups and deliveries. As a result, docks and dock areas must be designed with greater flexibility. Trucking is the most common means of transporting goods, but certain warehouse operations also need access to rail, water, and air transportation. If electric trucks are used, a battery-charging area should be included.

Forklifts, conveyor belts, and automatically guided vehicle conveyor systems are used to move materials inside warehouses. Pallets, or portable platforms, are used for moving and storing materials in most distribution operations. Therefore, ceiling heights in warehouses should accommodate the stacking of an ideal number of pallets. Newly constructed high-cube warehouses may be more efficient than older buildings with larger footprints and fewer automated systems for moving materials. Since wide spans provide maximum flexibility, a square structure generally is the most cost-effective.

Sprinkler systems are needed in warehouses where flammable goods are stored. The nature of the stored material determines whether the system should be wet or dry, using water or chemicals.

EMERGING TRENDS IN INDUSTRIAL BUILDING DESIGN

Automation: Industrial operations are less labour-intensive and more equipment-intensive than they once were, and the buildings that house those operations can devote more space to machinery and systems than to break rooms, locker rooms, etc. For example, telecom hotels, internet switching centres, and data centres often consist of bare storage space for computer equipment and are rarely visited by the people who own the equipment. Also, automated inventory operations increase efficiency, particularly when dealing with small electronic components or other products that are difficult to distinguish by the naked eye.

Just-in-time manufacturing and inventory practices: Manufacturers do not want to be burdened with the cost of storing large quantities of the products they produce, so their suppliers and the warehouse operators who serve them focus less on the long-term storage of inventory and more on the movement of inventory.

Buildings on Agricultural Properties

As the small, family farm has given way to fewer, larger farms, the contribution of farm buildings to the total value of farm real estate has been steadily decreasing. The number of farm buildings per acre of farmland has also decreased. Farms are increasingly operated by large, specialized business concerns, and the equipment and management needed to run agricultural operations have become increasingly specialized.[9]

Farm buildings must accommodate the type of machinery and equipment currently used in farming (see Table 11.5). To be useful, each farm building must contribute to the operating efficiency of the entire farm. Each building's usefulness relates to the type and size of the farm. Functional inutility can result from having too many farm buildings when fewer would be more efficient.

Table 11.5: Characteristics of Improvements on Agricultural Land

Type of Building	Characteristics
Barns	• Some barns have traditionally been multi-functional, providing animal shelter, grain storage, and a threshing floor. Other structures, such as tobacco barns and modern farm buildings, serve a single, specialized purpose. • The traditional North American barn is 60 feet long and 30 feet wide, with two gable ends, a loft, and double doors. • Most barns are built of wood, but some are made of stone, logs, or brick. • Old barns are suitable for modern, general-purpose farming if they are sufficiently adaptable. Virtually all newer barns have pre-engineered pole construction, which is less expensive and can accommodate more farming activities than older, multi-storey barns can.
Silos	• Silos have become more prevalent and larger. The use of baled, rather than loose, hay and the increased use of ensilage have lessened the need for barn storage.
Animal shelters	• Animal shelters should be dry and clean, provide protection from the wind and sun, and be adaptable to equipment storage.
Machine sheds	• Sheds are needed to house tractors, combines, discs, plows, harrows, cultivators, pickers, trucks, and other equipment.
Shop	• Most farms have an area for maintenance of mechanical equipment. Often the shop is a pole barn with concrete floors that has been modified. In winter, this may be the most important building on the property. • Usually heated, cooled, and insulated.
Dairy production facilities	• Pipeline milking machines and overhead feed bins dictate the requirements for milking parlors and loafing sheds where livestock are sheltered.

Special-Purpose Buildings

Although most buildings can be converted to other uses, the conversion of special-purpose buildings generally involves extra expense and design expertise. Special-purpose structures include the following:

• Houses of worship
• Theatres
• Sports arenas

---

[9] For additional information on improvements to rural land, see American Society of Farm Managers and Rural Appraisers and Appraisal Institute, *The Appraisal of Rural Property*, 2nd ed. (Denver and Chicago, 2000).

The functional utility of a special-purpose building depends on whether or not there is continued demand for the use for which the building was designed. When there is demand, functional utility depends on whether or not the building conforms to competitive standards. For example, there is a continued demand for movie theatres, but their design has changed due to high maintenance and utility costs. Ornate movie theatres are still used, but newly constructed theatres are generally simple, unembellished structures containing a larger number of smaller screens.[10]

The design and materials used in houses of worship are simpler today to keep maintenance and utility costs down. The functional utility of these structures, like sports and concert arenas, is primarily related to seating capacity. The structure's support facilities, general attractiveness, and appeal must also be considered.[11]

The adaptive-use movement has generated public interest in the conversion of special-purpose buildings to preserve architecturally significant structures that have outlived their function. Railroad stations, schools, firehouses, and grist mills are popular structures for conversion. The functional utility of these buildings relates to how much they deviate from building codes and how the cost of rehabilitation compares with the potential economic return. A typical item of functional inutility in adaptive-use projects is an insufficient number of staircases to meet building codes. By contrast, a high ceiling in a specialty property does not indicate functional inutility if it is considered a desirable architectural feature. Compliance with contemporary accessibility and fire codes is an additional consideration in evaluating the adaptive use of older buildings.

EVALUATING FUNCTIONAL UTILITY IN SPECIAL-PURPOSE BUILDINGS

To investigate the functional utility and value of building components designed specifically to serve the use of a special-purpose property, the appraiser can employ several strategies:

- Review appraisal literature pertaining to properties in a similar product category
- Search for market data on similar – i.e., not directly comparable – or related facilities
- Interview the current or recent occupant and other operators in that particular field
- Interview brokers or other appraisers specializing in that product or with experience in that segment of the market
- Interview the project architects and engineers
- Review building plans with a cost estimator or with architects or engineers experienced in that product type
- Review taxation case studies for pertinent precedents

The appraiser should also consider the Competency Rule of Canadian Uniform Standards of Professional Appraisal Practice in assignments relating to special-purpose property.

Source: David Paul Rothermich, "Special-Design Properties: Identifying the 'Market' in Market Value", The Appraisal Journal (October 1998): 410-415.

---

[10] See also Arthur E. Gimmy and Mary G. Gates, *The Business of Show Business: The Valuation of Movie Theaters* (Chicago: Appraisal Institute, 2000).

[11] For more information on houses of worship, see Martin H. Aaron and John H. Wright, Jr., *The Appraisal of Religious Facilities* (Chicago: Appraisal Institute, 1997).

Mixed-Use Buildings

Many buildings successfully combine two or more revenue-producing uses:

- Research and development facilities often combine office, laboratory, and industrial space within a single structure.
- Office buildings often contain ground-level retail space and restaurants.
- Hotels can be combined with retail, office, or residential uses.

In mixed-use buildings, each type of use reflects a number of design criteria, which must be analyzed separately. The structure must also be considered as a whole to determine how successfully it combines uses. The uses combined should be compatible, but minor incompatibilities can be alleviated with separate entrances, elevators, and equipment. In a mixed-use building without separate entrances and elevators, the residential units on upper floors and the office units below would both suffer. Only in a rather large building can the extra expense of separate features be justified. A hotel located in an office building should have its own entrance and elevators. Security and privacy should characterize a building's residential area, while a professional, prestigious image is desirable for the office portion of the structure.

Mixed-use developments (MUDs) are characterized by the physical and functional integration of their components. They are often sprawling structures built around centrally located shopping galleries or hotel courtyards. Walkways, plazas, escalators, and elevators provide an interconnecting pedestrian thoroughfare with easy access to parking facilities located underground, at street level, or above-ground. Since mixed-use developments bring together diverse participants, they require extensive, extraordinarily coherent planning.[12]

QUALITY AND CONDITION SURVEY

The building description and analysis of architectural style and functional utility culminate in the quality and condition survey. A structure can have a functional layout and an attractive design but be built with inferior materials and poor workmanship. These deficiencies increase maintenance and utility costs and adversely affect the property's marketability. Conversely, a building can be built too well or at a cost that cannot be justified by its utility. Most purchasers will not pay for these excess costs and only part of the original investment can be recaptured by the original owner through reduced maintenance expenses.

Practical or reasonable economy of construction results in an improvement that will produce rental income or value commensurate with its cost. Maintenance and operating expenses for an economically constructed building may be slightly higher than minimum expenses, but it is usually better to pay those expenses than to invest in a building of superior construction that will have higher taxes. To achieve the desired level of construction quality and cost, building materials and construction

---

[12] For a comprehensive analysis of mixed-use developments, see Dean Schwanke, *Mixed-Use Development Handbook* (Washington, D.C.: Urban Land Institute, 1987).

methods must be chosen and used properly. An appropriate combination of elements results in a building that is adequate for its intended purpose.

The character, quality, and appearance of building construction are reflected in each of the three approaches to value. The quality and condition of building components greatly influence the cost estimate, the depreciation estimate, the ability of the property to produce rental income, and the property's comparability with other properties. Analysis of the quality of construction and the methods and materials used complements the appraiser's analysis of the building's structural design and architecture.

> In the condition component of a quality and condition survey, the appraiser distinguishes among items in need of immediate repair (deferred maintenance items), short-lived items that can be replaced at a later date, and long-lived items expected to last for the remaining economic life of the building.

When a contractor takes shortcuts and fails to meet the advertised or contracted quality level of new construction, property owners and lenders can find themselves embroiled in litigation with aggrieved occupants. Because of the growing complexity of building design and construction, the quality of building components and construction is often best judged by a consulting engineer. The engineer can monitor the construction process to ensure that the work conforms to approved drawings and that the workmanship is satisfactory. An experienced appraiser may be able to relate evidence of construction problems – sagging floors, leaks, drafts, etc. – gathered in the property inspection to materials of poor quality or shoddy workmanship.

In the condition component of a quality and condition survey, the appraiser generally distinguishes among three types of building components:

1. Items in need of immediate repair on the date of the appraisal, i.e., deferred maintenance items
2. Items that may be repaired or replaced at a later time, i.e., short-lived items
3. Items that are expected to last the full economic life of the building, i.e., long-lived items

Examples of each type of building component are shown in Table 11.6.

Items in Need of Immediate Repair

Although a building may be in excellent condition, the appraiser usually finds some items in need of repair on the date of the appraisal. Repairing these items will normally add as much or more value to the property than the cost of their repair. When the cost approach to value is applied, these are considered items of curable physical deterioration.

The appraiser's repair list should include items that constitute a fire or safety hazard. Many clients request that these items be listed separately in the report. Sometimes the appraiser is asked to estimate the cost of each repair, which is called the cost to cure. Chapter 19 discusses techniques for estimating the cost to cure.

Table 11.6: Sample Items Considered in the Quality and Condition Survey

Poor floor plans are easily recognized by those who make up the market for houses, but standards often vary with current trends in a region and neighborhood. The location of various rooms in relation to the site can increase or diminish a dwelling's privacy and comfort.

Deferred Maintenance Items
- Touch-up exterior paint on buildings and the removal of graffiti
- Minor carpentry repairs on stairs, molding, trim, floors, and porches
- Redecorating interior rooms
- Fixing leaky or noisy plumbing
- Loosening stuck doors and windows
- Repairing torn screens and broken windows
- Rehanging loose or damaged gutters and leaders
- Replacing missing shingles, tiles, and slates and repairing leaky roofs
- Fixing cracked sidewalks, driveways, and parking areas
- Doing minor electrical repairs
- Replacing rotten floor boards
- Exterminating vermin
- Fixing cracked or loose tiles in bathrooms and kitchens
- Repairing septic systems
- Eliminating safety hazards such as windows that have been nailed shut
- Eliminating fire hazards such as paint-soaked rags in a storage area

Short-Lived Items
- Interior paint and wallpaper
- Exterior paint
- Floor finishes
- Shades, screens, and blinds (often considered personal property)
- Waterproofing and weatherstripping
- Gutters and leaders
- Roof covering and flashing
- Water heater
- Furnace
- Air-conditioning equipment
- Carpeting
- Kitchen appliances (considered short-lived items only if built-in)
- Sump pump
- Water softener system (often rented, not owned)
- Washers and dryers (often considered personal property)
- Ventilating fans

Long-Lived Items
- Hot and cold water pipes
- Plumbing fixtures (may also be considered functional components)
- Electric service connection (may also be considered functional components)
- Electric wiring
- Electric fixtures
- Ducts and radiators

Short-Lived Items

During the building inspection, an appraiser usually encounters other items that show signs of wear and tear but would not be economical to repair or replace on the date of the appraisal. The economic life of a building is the period over which the improvements contribute to property value. Many building components have to be repaired at some time during the economic life of the building. If the remaining life of the component is shorter than the remaining economic life of the structure as a whole, the component is identified as a short-lived item. Chapter 19 discusses age-life concepts such as economic life and remaining economic life in more detail.

The appraiser must decide if an item needs immediate repair or replacement or whether this work can be done later. If the repair or replacement will add less to the value of the property than it will cost, the maintenance should usually be delayed. For example, a building with a sound, 10-year old roof may hold up well for at least another five years. Although the roof has suffered some deterioration, replacing it probably would not add more value to the property than the cost of a new roof.

The appraiser should consider whether repairing an item is necessary to preserve other components. For example, sometimes the roof cover must be replaced or the economic life of the other components will be reduced. The appraiser should note whether the condition of the short-lived item is better or worse than the overall condition of the building.

> **short-lived items**
> A building component with an expected remaining economic life that is shorter than the remaining economic life of the entire structure.
>
> **long-lived items**
> Building components with an expected remaining economic life that is the same as the remaining economic life of the entire structure.

Long-Lived Items

The final step in a quality and condition survey is to describe the condition of those items that are not expected to require repair or replacement during the economic life of the building, assuming they are not subject to abnormal wear and tear or accidental damage. A building component with an expected economic life that is the same as the remaining economic life of the structure is called a long-lived item. Repair may not be required because the component has been built to last and has been well maintained. All the long-lived components of a building are rarely in the same condition. The items that are not in the same condition as the rest of the building are the important ones in the appraisal analysis.

Some defective long-lived items are not considered in need of repair because the cost of their replacement or repair is greater than the amount these items contribute to the value of the property. A serious crack in a foundation wall, for example, would probably be considered incurable physical deterioration. Incurable depreciation that results from problems in the original design of a structure is considered incurable functional obsolescence.

CHAPTER 12

HIGHEST AND BEST USE ANALYSIS

The analysis of relevant data to develop a market value opinion requires two important steps in the valuation process before the applicable approaches to value are applied. Market/marketability analysis begins the process of narrowing the focus from a broader macro view to data that is especially pertinent to the appraised property. Highest and best use relies on that analysis to identify the most profitable, competitive use to which the subject property can be put. The highest and best use is shaped by the competitive forces within the market where the property is located and provides the foundation for a thorough investigation of the competitive position of the property in the minds of market participants.

An understanding of market behaviour developed through market analysis is essential to the concept of highest and best use. Market forces create market value, so the interaction of market forces that identifies the highest and best use is of crucial importance.

FUNDAMENTALS OF HIGHEST AND BEST USE

Highest and best use may be defined as follows:

> The reasonably probable and legal use of vacant land or an improved property that is physically possible, appropriately supported, and financially feasible and that results in the highest value.

The theoretical focus of highest and best use analysis is on the potential uses of the land as though vacant. In practice, however, the contributory value of the existing improvements and any possible alteration of those improvements are also important in determining highest and best use and, by extension, in developing an opinion of the market value of the property.

In the analysis of highest and best use of land as though vacant, the appraiser seeks the answers to several questions:

- Should the land be developed or left vacant?
- If left vacant, when would future development be financially feasible?
- If developed, what kind of improvement should be built?

In the analysis of the highest and best use of the property as improved, the appraiser must answer additional questions:

- Should the existing improvements on the property be maintained in their current state, should they be altered in some manner to make them more valuable, or should they be demolished to create a vacant site for a different use?
- If renovation or redevelopment is warranted, when should the new improvements be built?

> To determine highest and best use, the appraiser must analyze data, not just compile it. As an analogy, in applying the direct comparison approach the appraiser does not just compile a list of comparable sales from the market data; he or she analyzes the relevant sales. It is critical that a careful highest and best use analysis precede the application of the approaches to value. Otherwise, there is a high likelihood that serious errors will be made in the valuation process.

In general, if the value of a property as improved is greater than the value of the land as though vacant, the highest and best use is the use of the property as improved. However, a property's existing use may represent an interim use, which begins with the land value for the new highest and best use and adds the contributory value of the current improvements until the new highest and best use can be achieved. In practice, a property owner who is redeveloping a parcel of land may remove an improvement even when the value of the property as improved exceeds the value of the vacant land. The costs of demolition and any remaining improvement value are taken into consideration in the test of financial feasibility for redevelopment of the land. Likewise, if an improved property has value but may have greater value if modified in some way, the cost of modifying the improvements and the value gained in that modification are accounted for in the determination of highest and best use.

The Four Tests

As market/marketability analysis progresses to highest and best use analysis, appraisers first consider the reasonably probable uses of a site that can be legally undertaken. In the analysis of pertinent data, four steps are implicit and are applied in the following order to develop adequate support for the appraiser's highest and best use opinion.

1. Legally permissible
2. Physically possible
3. Financially feasible
4. Maximally productive

An appraiser generally considers these criteria sequentially. The tests of physical possibility and legal permissibility can be applied in either order, but they both must be applied before the tests of financial feasibility and maximum productivity.

A use may be financially feasible, but this is irrelevant if it is legally prohibited or physically impossible.

> Highest and best use is the reasonably probable and legal use of vacant land or an improved property that is legally permissible, physically possible, appropriately supported, financially feasible, and that results in the highest value.

The six-step market analysis process described in Chapter 9 provides the data required for the four test criteria (see Figure 12.1). The initial analysis of the market and land use regulations (i.e., property productivity) usually limits the number of property uses to a few reasonably probable choices. For example, market analysis may suggest that there is demand for a large office building in a community. However, if modern, single-unit residential developments surround the subject site, a large, multi-storey office building would probably not be a reasonably probable use, even if it were legally permitted. Similarly, a housing development for the elderly might be a permissible use for a site, but, if most residents of the area are under 40-years old, this use is most likely not reasonably probable and would not be tested for financial feasibility. Consideration of whether a use is reasonably probable should continue throughout the analysis of highest and best use as the appraiser learns more about the potential use of the property. Reasonable probability is both a tentative starting point and a conclusion for the use or uses that are ultimately deemed probable. Appraisers constantly evaluate and reconcile what develops through competent application of the steps in the valuation process. Many of the considerations and discoveries that are made through their analyses become important points not only for the development of their own value conclusions, but also for inclusion in their reports to clients.

There may be a significant demand for a use in the market area of the subject property and the subject may be suited for this use, but a number of other sites may be equally or more appropriate. The appraiser must test the highest and best use conclusion to ensure that existing and potential competition from other sites has been fully recognized.

An appraiser must also consider the competition among various uses for a specific site. For example, competition for available sites along a commercial strip development may be intense. Developers of community garden uses, retail office uses, and fast food franchises may bid against one another for these sites, and the prices they pay for these sites will reflect this competition. Market demand is not

LAND AS THOUGH VACANT AND THE PROPERTY AS IMPROVED

The highest and best use of land as though vacant and the highest and best use of the property as improved are connected but distinctly different concepts. To clarify the distinction, consider a single-unit residential property located in an area zoned for commercial use. If there is market demand for a commercial use, the maximum productivity of the land as though vacant will most likely be for a commercial use. In this case, the residential improvements may contribute little, if any, to the value of the property as a whole except as an interim use during the transition between land uses. If, however, the market value for residential use is greater than the market value for the permitted commercial use less costs to demolish the residential improvements, then the highest and best use of the property as improved will be for continued residential use.

infinite. Even though the subject may be physically and locationally suited for that use, better-located sites may satisfy the market demand completely before the subject property can realize its development potential.

The same observation may be applied to central business districts (CBDs). The market may define the highest and best use of land in the CBD simply as high-rise development, which often includes a mix of uses such as office, retail, hotel,

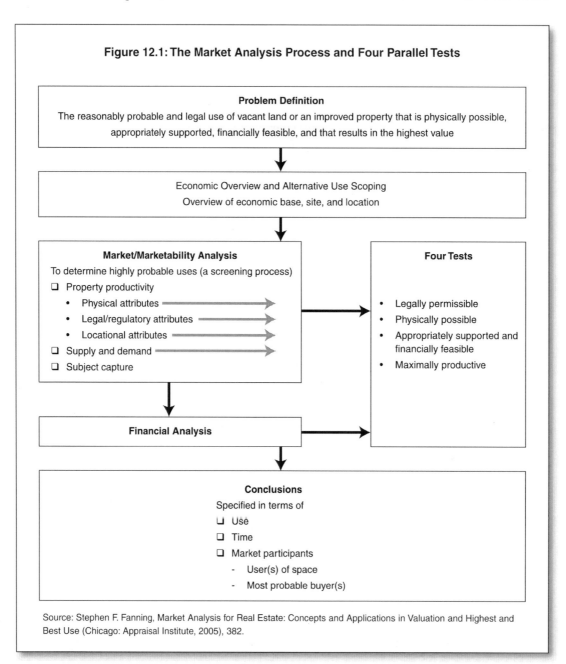

Figure 12.1: The Market Analysis Process and Four Parallel Tests

Problem Definition
The reasonably probable and legal use of vacant land or an improved property that is physically possible, appropriately supported, financially feasible, and that results in the highest value

Economic Overview and Alternative Use Scoping
Overview of economic base, site, and location

Market/Marketability Analysis
To determine highly probable uses (a screening process)
❑ Property productivity
- Physical attributes
- Legal/regulatory attributes
- Locational attributes
❑ Supply and demand
❑ Subject capture

Four Tests
- Legally permissible
- Physically possible
- Appropriately supported and financially feasible
- Maximally productive

Financial Analysis

Conclusions
Specified in terms of
❑ Use
❑ Time
❑ Market participants
- User(s) of space
- Most probable buyer(s)

Source: Stephen F. Fanning, Market Analysis for Real Estate: Concepts and Applications in Valuation and Highest and Best Use (Chicago: Appraisal Institute, 2005), 382.

and residential apartment or condominium use. At times the highest and best use conclusion for a CBD site does not indicate a specific highest and best use, but rather a class of uses that is supported by market area trends and reflects a consistent density of development.

APPLICATION OF HIGHEST AND BEST USE ANALYSIS

Highest and best use analysis builds on the conclusions of market/marketability analysis. The analysis of land as though vacant focuses on alternative uses, with the appraiser testing each reasonably probable use for legal permissibility, physical possibility, financial feasibility, and maximum productivity. In contrast, the appraiser applies the four tests in the analysis of the property as improved, but the focus is not on alternative uses but on three possibilities: continuation of the existing use, modification of the existing use, or demolition and redevelopment of the land.

Highest and Best Use of Land as though Vacant

Land is generally valued as though vacant. When land is already vacant, the appraiser values the land as it exists. However, when land is not vacant its contribution to the value of the property as improved depends on how it can be put to use. Therefore, the highest and best use of land as though vacant must be considered in relation to its existing use and all potential uses. A conclusion of the highest and best use of land as though vacant is required in nearly all appraisal assignments. However, the level of study will be significantly greater when a larger proportion of the total property value is in the land. The level of study will be significantly less when only a small proportion of the total property value is in the land. Appraisers explain in the appraisal report why a lower level of study may have been applied so that others can understand the justifications and the data on which they are based.

> The highest and best use of land as though vacant is concluded after the four criteria have been applied and various alternative uses have been eliminated. The remaining use that fulfills all four criteria is the highest and best use.

Testing the Legal Permissibility of Land as though Vacant

Private restrictions, zoning, building codes, historic district controls, and environmental regulations may preclude many potential uses. The appraiser must also consider whether there is a reasonable probability that the zoning or other restrictions could be changed in order for the highest and best use of the property to be realized.

In applying the test of legal permissibility, the appraiser determines which uses are permitted by current zoning, which uses could be permitted if a zoning change were granted, and which uses are restricted by private restrictions on the site. Private restrictions, title or deed restrictions, and long-term leases may prohibit certain uses or specify building setbacks, heights, and types of materials. If deed restrictions conflict with zoning laws or building codes, the more restrictive guidelines usually prevail, but this may pose a legal question that the appraiser cannot answer without assistance from a professional with the appropriate legal expertise. A long-term lease may affect the highest and best use because lease provisions may limit use over the remaining term of the lease. For example, if a property is subject to a land lease that has twelve years to run, it may not be economically feasible for the tenant to construct and move to a new building with a longer remaining economic life. In such a case, the appraisal report should state that the determination of highest and best use as leased is influenced by the lease's impact on utility over the remaining lease term.

In addition to analyzing zoning and private restrictions, testing the legal permissibility of a land use also requires the appraisers to investigate other applicable codes and ordinances, including building codes, historical district ordinances, and environmental regulations.

Building codes can prevent land from being developed to what would otherwise be its highest and best use by imposing burdensome restrictions that increase the cost of construction. For example, the additional cost of a water retention pond with excess capacity that is required by local ordinance could impact the size of a proposed community shopping centre. Less restrictive codes typically result in lower development costs, which attract developers; more restrictive codes tend to discourage development. In some areas, more restrictive building codes are used to slow new construction and limit growth. Historical ordinances, such as historic facade easements, and overlay districts may be so restrictive that they preclude development.

Concerns over the long-range effects of certain land uses sometimes result in increased environmental regulation and stricter development controls. Appraisers must be familiar with environmental regulations pertaining to clean air, clean water, and wetlands, and they should be sensitive to the public's reaction to proposed development projects. When resistance from local residents and the general public occurs, it can pressure public officials to stop or limit certain real estate developments or change the density or character of a specific plan.

As with zoning ordinances, if there are any limitations inherent in other applicable codes, ordinances, and regulations, the appraiser should investigate whether there is a reasonable probability of a change relative to the subject property.

Testing the Physical Possibility of Land as though Vacant

The test of physical possibility addresses the physical characteristics associated with the site that might affect its highest and best use. The size, shape, terrain, and accessibility of land and the risk of natural disasters such as floods or earthquakes affect the uses to which land can be put. The utility of a parcel may also depend on its frontage and depth. Irregularly shaped parcels can cost more to develop and, after development, may have less utility than regularly shaped parcels of the same size.

Ease of access enhances the utility of a site. For certain property types, visibility is an important feature. For other property types, the privacy provided by the lack of a view is a benefit. It is also important for the appraiser to consider the capacity and availability of public utilities. If a sewer main located in front of a property cannot be tapped because of a lack of capacity at the sewage disposal plant, the property's use might be limited. When topography or subsoil conditions make development difficult or costly, the land's utility may be adversely affected. If the cost of grading or constructing a foundation on the subject site is higher than is typical for sites in the area competing for the same use, the subject site may be economically infeasible for the highest and best use that would otherwise be indicated.

PROBABILITY OF A ZONING CHANGE

In investigating the reasonable probability of a zoning change, the appraiser must consider trends and the history of zoning requests in the market area as well as documents such as the community's comprehensive or master plan. Uses that are not compatible with the existing land uses in the area (such as a gas station in the middle of an exclusive single-family residential subdivision) and uses for which zoning changes have been requested but denied in the past (such as an industrial use where several industrial zoning changes have been turned down in the past two years) can usually be eliminated from consideration as potential highest and best uses. On the other hand, a zoning change from residential to commercial may be reasonable if other properties in the market area have received a similar zoning change recently or if a community's comprehensive plan designates the property for a use other than its current use. For example, consider a site zoned single-family residential in a transitional neighborhood where the zoning on several similar sites has been changed recently to commercial. Also, the city's comprehensive plan designates the property as lying within a future commercial corridor. Both of these factors may support an appraiser's conclusion that there is a reasonable probability of rezoning the subject site for commercial use.

Additional evidence of the possibility of new zoning includes land assemblage, removal of structures, and new construction in an area. This evidence may be supported by zoning change applications, zoning hearings, actions by municipalities, and interviews with planning and zoning officials. Even if there is no current market evidence of a zoning change, documented interviews with officials and discussion of zoning practices and histories can be helpful in evaluating the possibility of a zoning change. However, these interviews may not be a "proof" of a change or the denial of a change. Elected officials make decisions on zoning ordinances, and the processes are often heavily contested, with the outcomes not known until official actions are taken.

The probability of a zoning change may not be 100%, and the challenge is to determine whether market participants will pay a premium over the property's current value as zoned in anticipation of a potential zoning change and to document the conclusion. Because developers are frequently risk-averse, most buy "subject to" rezoning approval rather than "as is". Many sales never close because they are subject to rezoning that could not be obtained or could not be obtained within the developer's desired time frame. Appraisals involving a projected or assumed zoning change are subject to an extraordinary assumption or hypothetical condition, depending on the situation, and must be addressed as such. If, for the purposes of the appraisal, the appraiser concludes from research that the probability of a zoning change is likely, the appraisal is subject to an extraordinary assumption because although the appraiser believes the statement to be true, if it is not, the value opinion would be affected significantly.

Testing the Financial Feasibility of Land as though Vacant

In determining which uses are legally permissible and physically possible, an appraiser eliminates some uses from consideration. Only those uses that meet the first two criteria are analyzed further. As long as a potential use has value commensurate with its cost and conforms to the first two tests, the use is financially feasible. Some economic uses of land such as housing may not be income-producing in the sense of a commercial property, and economic feasibility is weighed by considering prices and price trends. For income-producing properties, the income analysis for financial feasibility must be supported with the six-step market/marketability study. The level of analysis may vary with assignments, but the economic demand for the subject is a prerequisite to the financial testing of alternatives.

If the physically possible and legally permissible uses are income-producing, the analysis of financial feasibility will often focus on which potential uses are likely to produce an income (or return) equal to or greater than the amount needed to satisfy operating expenses, financial obligations, and capital amortization of the investment. If the uses are not income-producing, the analysis will determine which uses are likely to create a value or result in a profit equal to or greater than the amount needed to develop and market the property under those uses. Appraiser's need to do analyses of supply and demand in order to identify those uses that are financially feasible and, ultimately, the use that is maximally productive.

A crucial element in highest and best use analysis is the timing for a specific use. Timing refers to when the improvements would be built as well as the future expectations of occupancy and rent levels. Land and location may suggest a parcel is a prime retail corner at some point in time, but if the retail potential is some years in the future, another use – for example, apartments – that can be developed immediately would make the land more valuable today.

To determine the financial feasibility of an income-producing use, the appraiser estimates the future gross income that can be expected from each use. Vacancy and collection losses and operating expenses are then subtracted from each gross income to obtain the likely net operating income (NOI) from each use. A rate of return on the invested capital can then be calculated for each use. If the net revenue capable of being generated from a use is sufficient to satisfy the required market rate of return on the investment, the use is said to be financially feasible.

To determine the financial feasibility of a use that will not generate income, the appraiser performs an economic analysis by comparing the value benefits that accrue from the use against the costs involved. If the value benefits exceed the costs, the use is considered feasible. If the value benefits fall below the costs or exceed costs by only a marginal amount, the use may not be financially feasible.

Successful application of the financial feasibility test to land as though vacant relies on interpretation of relevant and credible market evidence collected and analyzed in the market area and in the subject property's competitive market. Risk is an important consideration and must be weighed along with other feasibility factors. Any external obsolescence related to a specific use should be incorporated into the test of financial feasibility.[1]

---

[1]   For more information on financial feasibility and maximum productivity, see also Stephen F. Fanning, *Market Analysis for Real Estate: Concepts and Applications in Valuation and Highest and Best Use* (Chicago: Appraisal Institute, 2005), 389; and Richard Parli, "What's Financial Feasibility Got to Do With It?" *The Appraisal Journal* (October 2001): 419-423.

Testing the Maximum Productivity of Land as though Vacant

The test of maximum productivity is applied to the uses that have passed the first three tests. Of the financially feasible uses, the highest and best use is the use that produces the highest residual land value consistent with the market's acceptance of risk and with the rate of return warranted by the market for that use given the associated risk. To determine the highest and best use of land as though vacant, rates of return that reflect the associated risks are often used to capitalize income from different uses into their respective values. These are developed from previous research and reflect the rates that market participants apply to the range of uses being considered. Alternatively, land sales to users can be used to test which alternative is maximally productive. For example, if the subject site has current demand for apartments and demand for retail is estimated at five years in the future, the highest and best use can be tested by applying user sales data. Suppose apartment land is selling for $3.50 per square foot today to users and retail land is selling for $7.50 per square foot to users. If the land is held for five years at a discount rate of 20%, the present value of the retail land is $3.00 per square foot, which suggests that the highest and best use today is to develop apartments on the site. The use that produces the highest residual land value is the highest and best use.

An appraiser can find the residual land value by estimating the value of the proposed use (land and improvements) and subtracting the cost of the labour, capital, and entrepreneurial coordination expended to create the improvements. Alternatively, an appraiser can estimate the land value by capitalizing the residual income to the land. The land income that is capitalized into value is the residual income remaining after operating expenses and the return attributable to the improvements have been deducted from the income to the total property.[2] In testing alternate uses with the land residual technique, the process of capitalization magnifies any differences in the residual income attributable to the land . Therefore, the appraiser should take special care in considering the conclusions or data input into the highest and best use analysis. While the land residual technique can be used in the development of one indication of land value, it is more useful in highest and best use analysis because the relative residual land values of alternate uses can be compared to determine the use that yields the highest value. Chapter 22 discusses the land residual technique and other types of residual techniques in more detail.

The Conclusion of Highest and Best Use as though Vacant

The conclusion of highest and best use should be clearly stated in terms of the following:

1. Use(s)
2. Timing for use(s), i.e., absorption, rents, occupancy, and other considerations
3. Market participants
   a. Users
   b. Most probable buyers/tenants

---

[2] According to traditional economic theory, income attributable to the three other agents of production (labour, capital, and entrepreneurial coordination) is paid, and then the remaining income – i.e., the residual – is attributable to the land.

The conclusion of the highest and best use of a parcel of land should be as specific as the appraiser's research allows and the assignment requires. Available data might only support general conclusions as to use. General categories such as "an office building", "a commercial building", or "a one-unit residence" may be adequate in some situations, but in others the particular use demanded by market participants must be specified, such as "a suburban office building with 10 or more floors" or "a three-bedroom residence with at least 2,500 square feet." Sometimes there is ample sales evidence available on highly similar sites, so it is unnecessary to refine the highest and best use conclusion. In any case, the appraiser should provide market evidence that leads to an understanding of the use or uses, the timing for those uses, and the probable users and buyers.

The intensity of a use is an important consideration in highest and best use analysis. The present use of a site may not be its highest and best use. The land may be suitable for a much higher, or more intense, use. For instance, the highest and best use of a parcel of land as though vacant may be for a 10-storey office building, while the office building that currently occupies the site has only three floors. Conversely, it is possible the highest and best use could be less dense than the current use, perhaps due to a downturn in demand.

The timing of a specified use is another important consideration. In many instances, a property's highest and best use may change in the foreseeable future. For example, the highest and best use of a farm in the path of urban growth could be for interim use as a farm, with a future highest and best use as a residential subdivision. If the land is ripe for development at the time of the appraisal, there is no interim use. If the land has no subdivision potential, its highest and best use would be for continued agricultural use. In such situations, the immediate development of the land or conversion of the improved property to its future highest and best use is usually not financially feasible.

Another important consideration is who among the market participants would be attracted to the highest and best use. In the market delineation step of the market

---

THE IDEAL IMPROVEMENT

If the appraiser concludes that a building improvement is the highest and best use of a parcel of vacant land, the appraiser then determines and describes the type and characteristics of the ideal improvement to be constructed. The ideal improvement should meet the following criteria:

- Takes maximum advantage of the site's potential market demand
- Conforms to current market standards and the character of the market area
- Contains the most suitably priced components

If a new improvement is considered to be the highest and best use of the land as though vacant, it presumably will have no physical deterioration or functional obsolescence – i.e., it would be neither an underimprovement nor an overimprovement. Thus, any difference in value between the existing improvement and the ideal improvement would be attributable to these forms of depreciation. The appraiser must still consider external obsolescence, which may affect both the existing improvement and the ideal improvement.

analysis process (Step 2), the appraiser determines the probable users for the specified use as well as probable buyers. The development of those conclusions in market analysis is integral to highest and best use analysis.

Highest and Best Use of Property as Improved

Highest and best use of a property as improved pertains to the use that should be made of an improved property in light of the existing improvements and the ideal improvement described at the conclusion of the analysis of highest and best use as though vacant. With any improved property, there are three possibilities that must be considered:

1.   Demolish the existing improvements and redevelop the site
2.   Continue the existing use
3.   Modify the existing use

The analysis of highest and best use as improved also applies when proposed improvements are being valued. For example, consider an assignment in which the land is vacant at the time the appraisal is prepared, and the appraiser develops a market value opinion that is either:

1.   Subject to the hypothetical condition that the improvements are built as of the current date

     or

2.   Subject to the extraordinary assumption that the improvement will be built as of a future date.

In such a case, the appraiser must analyze the highest and best use of the property as if *improved as proposed*.

If an extraordinary assumption such as this is made, the appraiser bases the assumption on a conclusion developed from the appraiser's research and data. Because readers of the appraisal report may confuse the appraiser's opinion that the construction is likely with the fact that the improvements do not factually exist at present, appraisers must take care to distinguish these differences and the effect of differences in time frames between the effective date of the value opinion and the date that improvements are forecast to exist.

> The highest and best use of a property as improved may be continuation of the existing use, renovation or rehabilitation, expansion, adaptation or conversion to another use, partial or total demolition, or some combination of these alternatives.

Testing Continuation of the Existing Use of the Property as Improved

The existing use of the property as improved is often implicitly legally permissible and physically possible. If the existing use will remain financially feasible and is more profitable than modification or redevelopment, the existing use will remain the highest and best use of the property as improved.

An appraiser may need to address deferred maintenance in the analysis of the financial feasibility of the existing use. The property may require repairs for the existing improvements to achieve the best competitive position in the marketplace. The costs of curing physical deterioration or functional obsolescence, redesigning a building, or converting the existing improvements into an alternative use (including a provision for profit) must be analyzed in light of the value created in the market. The effect of the changes on value is more important than simply how much the changes will cost. If the changes will not be economically feasible, the expenditures would not be made – a point that the appraiser would be wise to incorporate into the highest and best use analysis.

Testing Modification of the Existing Use of the Property as Improved

Modification of the existing improvements must meet all four tests of highest and best use. The study of property productivity in the market analysis process is likely to show what changes to the existing use are physically possible and legally permissible. Determining the financially feasible modification that is more profitable than either the existing use or any other modifications is a matter of weighing the costs of modification and the benefit to the property, e.g., an adequate increase in rent as a result of the modification. Failing to adequately test for the possibility of modification of the existing use can be a serious flaw in an appraisal.

For nonconforming properties or properties with improvements that differ significantly from the ideal improvement, the appraiser must determine whether the codes, ordinances, or private restrictions allow modification of the improvements that would bring them into conformity. This may involve analysis of the reasonable probability of a change in zoning as was conducted in testing the highest and best use of the land as though vacant. Again, the appraiser should report any evidence supporting a reasonable probability that a change could be made to bring the improvements into conformity with a particular code, ordinance, or restriction. Such evidence could include trends in the market area, historical changes to codes or ordinances in the area, or a community's master plan. The appraiser should incorporate the costs of obtaining the changes, the time necessary to achieve the changes, and the risk of achieving the changes into the analysis of financial feasibility of modification of the existing use of the property as improved.

Testing Demolition of the Property as Improved and Redevelopment

Demolition can be considered the most extreme form of modification of the existing use of the property as improved. When an alternative use of the site is legally permissible, physically possible, financially feasible, and more profitable (less the cost of demolition and redevelopment of the site) than the continuing use of the existing improvements, then the alternative use will be the highest and best use of the property as improved. Many buildings are torn down and their sites left vacant or devoted to an interim use for a variety of reasons: property taxes, liabilities, avoidance of criticism about an "eyesore", and others.

SPECIAL SITUATIONS IN HIGHEST AND BEST USE ANALYSIS

In identifying and testing highest and best use, special considerations are required to address the following situations:

- Single uses
- Legally nonconforming uses
- Interim uses (including land held for investment purposes)
- Uses that are not the highest and best use
- Multiple uses
- Special-purpose uses

Single Uses

The highest and best uses of land as though vacant and property as improved are often consistent with surrounding uses. For example, in an industrial district, a single-unit home would usually stand out as an inconsistent – and inappropriate – land use. Sometimes, however, a property's highest and best use may be unusual or even unique. For example, market demand may be adequate to support one large, multi-storey office building in a community, but the market may not support more than one. As another example, a limited-market or special-use property such as a specialized industrial facility may be unique and highly beneficial to its site, but it might

> Single uses, interim uses, legally nonconforming uses, uses that are not the highest and best use, multiple uses, and special-purpose uses all require special consideration.

> single use
> A special case of highest and best use; a unique or special-purpose land use that may not be consistent with surrounding uses.

not be supported by surrounding land uses or comparable properties. Regardless of what improvement is currently on a site, the highest and best use of the site as though vacant should be the land use that meets all four tests. Therefore, the ideal improvement might be significantly different than the existing improvements, and the highest and best use of the site as though vacant for a single-use property might be to develop it differently than it is currently developed.

If an existing single-use property is being appraised, the appraiser should perform some level of market analysis to determine whether the single use should be continued or discontinued. If the analysis reveals that the single use should be discontinued, the appraiser should then ask what, if anything, should be done with the improvements? If the improvements do not contribute to value and the assignment involves an opinion of market value, then the highest and best use would probably be something other than maintaining the existing use. Also, the improvements might contribute to value but still not qualify as the highest and best use because modification of the existing improvements would create a higher value. For a proposed single-use property, the appraiser should carefully analyze the market to determine whether any other such properties already exist and, if so, if the market demand is strong enough to support another.

Legally Nonconforming Uses

A legally nonconforming use is a use that was lawfully established and maintained but no longer conforms to the land use regulations of the zone in which it is located. Some legal nonconformities can be created by governmental action such as a partial taking in an expropriation proceeding. Consider a gas station property with 20,000 square feet of land, which is the minimum amount of land area required by zoning for gas station use. If the city acquired 1,000 square feet of the land for an intersection improvement, the site would then contain 19,000 square feet and would no longer conform to the zoning require-ments for site size. Other legally nonconforming use situations can be created when codes and ordinances are changed. For example, a single-unit residence on a 7,500 square foot site in the core residential district of a community zoned R-1 requires at least 7,500 square feet of land area. If the city adopts a new zoning ordinance in which the minimum site size for a lot zoned R-1 is increased to 10,000 square feet, the existing property will no longer conform. In both instances, the nonconforming use situations are considered legal nonconformances because they were caused by an action of a governmental body. Some communities also differentiate between legally nonconforming uses and properties that are legal but do not conform to development standards. In the former, the use is nonconform-ing, but in the latter the property is still used in accordance with the zoning but the site (or the house) may be too small. Most zoning ordinances have special sections that deal with nonconforming use situations; appraisers must be familiar with these sections when appraising legally nonconforming uses.

> **legally nonconforming use**
> A use that was lawfully established and maintained, but no longer conforms to the use regulations of the current zoning in the zone where it is located; also known as a *grandfathered use.*

Zoning changes may create underimproved or overimproved properties. A one-unit residence located in an area that is subsequently zoned for commercial use may be an underimproved property. In this case, the residence will most likely be removed so that the site can be improved to its highest and best use, or the residence will be considered an interim use until conversion to commercial use is financially feasible. A legally nonconforming property can become overimproved when zoning changes reduce the permitted intensity of property use. For example, the site of an older apartment building with eight units in a fully built-up neighbourhood might be downzoned to a less intense use. That is, if the vacant site were developed now, the new zoning restrictions would only allow six units to be built. Nonconforming uses may also result from changes in development standards that affect features such as landscaping, parking, setbacks, and access.

Zoning ordinances vary with the jurisdiction. They usually permit a pre-existing, or grandfathered, use to continue but prohibit expansion or major alterations that support the nonconforming use. Some jurisdictions specify a time period for phasing out legally nonconforming uses. In many jurisdictions when a nonconforming use is discontinued, it usually cannot be reestablished. In most jurisdictions, a nonconform-ing use must be eliminated if the property suffers major damage or if the property is abandoned for a statutory period of time. In some instances, a nonconforming use can be rebuilt to the same intensity of use that it had prior to its destruction, provided it has no more impact on the market area than it did before.

When valuing land with a legally nonconforming use, an appraiser must recognize that the current use may be producing more income, and thus have more value, than the property could produce with a conforming use. The legally nonconforming use may also produce more income and have a higher value than comparable properties that conform to the zoning. Therefore, when the value of the legally nonconforming use of the property is developed by comparing similar, competitive properties to the subject in the direct comparison approach, the appraiser should consider the higher intensity of use allowed for the subject property and also consider the risks and limitations associated with the nonconformity. In the case of the eight-unit apartment building in an area downzoned to six-unit developments, for example, the appraiser will have to determine whether sales of properties with six units are appropriate comparable transactions in applying the direct comparison and income approaches.

Legally nonconforming uses that correspond to the highest and best use of the property as improved are often easy to recognize. However, sometimes it is not clear whether an existing nonconforming use is the site's highest and best use. The question can only be answered by careful analysis of the income or selling price produced by the nonconforming use and the incomes or selling prices that would be produced by alternative uses if the property were brought into conformity with existing regulations.

Interim Uses

The use to which a site or improved property is put until it is ready for its future highest and best use is called an interim use. Thus, interim use is a current highest and best use that is likely to change in a relatively short time, say, five to seven years. Buildings that are nearing the end of their physical lives, farms, parking lots, and temporary buildings may be interim uses. Mining and quarry operations may be considered special cases of interim uses that usually continue until depletion of the resource.

The appraiser must identify the interim uses of the property being appraised and all comparable properties. The appraiser mutst take into account differences in the interim uses of comparable properties even though their future highest and best uses are identical. Differences in the prices paid for such properties may be due to different return requirements and different anticipated demolition costs.

An interim use may or may not contribute to the value of the land or the improved property. If an old building or other use cannot produce gross revenues that exceed reasonable operating expenses, it does not contribute to property value. If the net return of the improvements is less than the amount that could be earned by the vacant land, the buildings do not have contributory value (although in some markets property owners may prefer to retain a single-unit dwelling on commercial land in transition rather than leave the land vacant). Indeed, the value

> **interim use**
> The temporary use to which a site or improved property is put until it is ready to be put to its future highest and best use.

of an improved property may be less than the value of the land as though vacant when demolition costs and real estate taxes are considered. The value of the land is based entirely on its potential highest and best use.

The principle of consistent use, which holds that land cannot be valued based on one use while improvements are valued based on another, must be considered when properties are devoted to temporary, interim uses. The use value of a site under an interim use may differ substantially from the market value of the same site as though vacant and available for development to its long-term highest and best use. Many outmoded improvements clearly do not resemble the ideal improvement, but they do create increments of value over the value of the vacant land. These improvements may appear to violate the principle of consistent use, but in fact, the market simply acknowledges that during the transition to a new use the value contributed by old improvements make the land and the existing improvements worth more than the vacant land.

Land that is held primarily for future sale, with or without an interim use, may be regarded as a *speculative investment*.[3] The purchaser or owner may believe that the value of the land will increase, but there is a risk that the expected appreciation will not occur while the investor holds the land. Nevertheless, the current value of the land is a function of its future highest and best use, so the appraiser should discuss its potential highest and best use. The appraiser may not be able to predict the exact future highest and best use, but the general type of future use and the timing for the use can be forecast based on its site, legal, locational, and market demand characteristics compared to competitive vacant tracts. The timing for such a use is usually in a range. The range can be broad in areas of long-term growth and tighter in areas with more current development potential.

Use That Is Not the Highest and Best Use

According to the concept of consistent use, an improvement must be valued based on a use that is consistent with the property's highest and best use (if the value sought is market value). However, many existing buildings and other improvements are inconsistent with the ideal improvements for their sites and are developed differently than they would be if the land were vacant. Nevertheless, the highest and best use may be in the same category as the existing use. For example, the highest and best use of a site improved with a 10-year-old apartment building may be for a new, more functional apartment building. Similarly, the highest and best use of a residential site improved with a 20-year-old house may be for a new, more modern one-unit residence.

For certain sites the general category of highest and best use may have changed, e.g., from apartment to industrial use or from one-unit residential to commercial use. If the improvements on these sites existed prior to the change in the market area, they suffer from external obsolescence and are likely to have less value than similar improvements on more appropriate sites. It would be incorrect to value such

---

[3]   In general usage, the term speculative investment can carry pejorative implications of high risk or uncertainty. In the language of real estate appraisal, speculation is defined as the purchase or sale of property motivated by the expectation of realizing a profit from a rise in its price.

improvements as if they were located on an appropriate site. The appraiser would need to find comparable sales on similarly inappropriate sites or determine an adjustment for the external obsolescence. Similarly, comparable rental properties ought to reflect or be adjusted to reflect similar deficiencies in location. The cost approach value indication would also be affected by external obsolescence.

Mixed Uses

Highest and best use often comprises more than one use for a parcel of land or an improved property. A large tract of land might be suitable for a planned unit development with a shopping centre in front, condominium units around a golf course, and

> mixed use
> A combination of compatible land uses in an area or in a single building.

one-unit residential sites on the remainder of the land. Business parks often have sites for retail stores in front and warehouse or light manufacturing structures in the rear.

One parcel of land may serve many functions. Timberland or pastureland may also be used for hunting, recreation, and mineral exploration. Land that serves as a right of way for power lines can double as open space or a park. Public streets with railroad sidings are also considered multiple-use land.

A single building can have multiple uses as well. A hotel may include a restaurant, a bar, and retail shops in addition to its guest rooms. A multi-storey building may contain offices, apartments, and retail stores. A "single-family", owner-occupied home may have an apartment upstairs.

If the highest and best use of a property is for more than one use on the same parcel or in the same building, the appraiser must estimate the contributory value of each use. If, for example, the market value of a timber tract that can be leased for hunting is compared on a unit basis with the value of another timber tract that cannot, the difference should be the value of the hunting rights. In the opinion of market value, the appraiser would have to account for both the value of the hunting rights and the value of the timber operation on the site. In oil-producing areas, appraisers are often asked to segregate the value of mineral rights from the value of other land uses; properties with mineral rights value can be compared with properties that do not have such rights. In multiple-use assignments, the sum of the values of the separate uses may be less than, equal to, or greater than the value of the total property.

Special-Use Properties

Since special-use properties are appropriate for only one use or for a very limited number of uses, appraisers may encounter practical problems in specifying highest and best use. The highest and best use of a special-use property as improved is probably the continuation of its current use if that use remains viable. For example, the highest and best use of a plant currently used for heavy manufacturing is probably continued use for heavy manufacturing, and the highest and best use of a grain elevator is probably continued use as a grain elevator, as long as there is sufficient market demand for such use. The highest and best use conclusions in both examples would likely include some forecast of continued economic demand. If the current use of a special-use property is physically, functionally, or economically obsolete and no alternative uses are feasible, the highest and best use of the land may be realized by demolishing the structure and possibly selling the remains for their scrap or salvage value. This may be true even if the improvements are still relatively new and even if they were costly to build.

Sometimes assignments involving special-use properties require two valuation scenarios to address the appraisal problem:

1. A market value based on the property's highest and best use
2. A use value that presumes the existing use

When this is the case, the appraiser must be careful to develop each value opinion appropriately and to be very clear in reporting the assignment results. An opinion of market value requires there be a market for the property. If there are no buyers for the subject property in its current use, an alternative use must be considered. Using the cost approach to value a special-use property where no market exists will usually overstate the market value of the property.

Table 12.1: Highest and Best Use Statements in Appraisal Reports

If . . .	The land is already improved to the highest and best use.
Then the report should include . . .	A discussion of this analysis and conclusion.
If . . .	The highest and best use of an improved property is different from its existing use.
Then the report should include . . .	Justification for this conclusion in a market value appraisal report.
If . . .	The property is improved but a separate estimate of land value is presented in the appraisal.
Then the report should include . . .	Discussion of the highest and best use of the land as though vacant as well as the highest and best use of the property as improved.
If . . .	A separate estimate of land value is not presented, and continued use of the property as improved is an appropriate limiting condition of the appraisal.
Then the report should include . . .	Discussion of only the highest and best use of the property as improved, unless the highest and best use of the land as though vacant is relevant to the analysis of highest and best use as improved.
If . . .	The highest and best use of the land as though vacant and highest and best use of the property as improved are different.
Then the report should include . . .	Discussion of the analysis of each highest and best use separately.

COMMON ERRORS AND ISSUES IN HIGHEST AND BEST USE

- One misconception is that it is acceptable to simply state the highest and best use conclusion. Appraisals typically require some analysis of highest and best use. Solely providing data is not addressing highest and best use – the data must be analyzed.
- Another misconception is that it is unnecessary to discuss excess land or functional issues relating to highest and best use.
- Sections of appraisal reports are related. The market analysis and other sections of the report must support highest and best use conclusions as well as the valuation sections.
- When the existing use is legal but nonconforming and is obviously the highest and best use, it is appropriate to acknowledge in the report that highest and best use is the current use, which is legal but nonconforming.

REPORTING HIGHEST AND BEST USE CONCLUSIONS

When an appraisal report includes a market value opinion, the report must address highest and best use. Highest and best use as though vacant must be addressed in reports that include a market value opinion for the site as though vacant. Highest and best use as improved must be addressed in reports that include a market value opinion for the property as improved. A logically structured highest and best use study of the four tests forms the foundation for the opinion of value. Certain conditions of an appraisal assignment may alter the information that should appear in the appraisal report regarding highest and best use, as illustrated in Table 12.1.

As illustrated earlier in the chapter, much of the information required to perform highest and best use analysis is developed using the six-step market analysis process. An appraiser may need to include a discussion of or reference to a separate marketability study (either inferred or fundamental) prior to the discussion of the highest and best use determination.

In addition, highest and best use analysis often incorporates techniques and data from the application of all three approaches to value. In many appraisal assignments, the final tests of financial feasibility and maximum productivity require information that is obtained from the application and development of the approaches. Therefore, even though the discussion of highest and best use traditionally precedes the approaches to value in an appraisal report, the conclusion of highest and best use often can be finalized only after a preliminary analysis of alternative land uses has been performed. The conclusions reported in the highest and best use section of a report should be consistent with conclusions and applications in the other parts of the report.

CHAPTER 13

THE DIRECT COMPARISON APPROACH

In the direct comparison approach, the appraiser develops an opinion of value by analyzing closed sales, listings, or pending sales of properties that are similar to the subject property. The comparative techniques of analysis applied in the direct comparison approach are fundamental to the valuation process. Estimates of market rent, expenses, land value, cost, depreciation, and other value parameters may be derived in the other approaches to value using comparative techniques. Similarly, conclusions derived in the other approaches are often analyzed in the direct comparison approach to estimate the adjustments to be made to the sale prices of comparable properties.

In the direct comparison approach, an opinion of market value is developed by comparing properties similar to the subject property that have recently sold, are listed for sale, or are under contract, i.e., for which purchase offers and a deposit have been recently submitted. A major premise of the direct comparison approach is that an opinion of the market value of a property can be supported by studying the market's reaction to comparable and competitive properties.

Comparative analysis of properties and transactions focuses on similarities and differences that affect value, which may include variations in property rights, financing terms, market conditions, and physical characteristics, among others. Elements of comparison are tested against market evidence using paired sales, trend analysis, statistics, and other techniques to identify which elements of comparison within the data set of comparable sales are responsible for value differences.

direct comparison approach
The process of deriving a value indication for the subject property by comparing similar properties that have recently sold with the property being appraised, identifying appropriate units of comparison, and making adjustments to the sale prices (or unit prices, as appropriate) of the comparable properties based on relevant, market-derived elements of comparison. The direct comparison approach may be used to value improved properties, vacant land, or land being considered as though vacant when an adequate supply of comparable sales is available.

This chapter focuses on the theory and concepts underlying the direct comparison approach. Chapters 14 and 15 further the discussion with a deeper examination of the methodologies employed by appraisers to analyze comparable sales.

RELATION TO APPRAISAL PRINCIPLES

The concepts of anticipation and change, which underlie the principles of supply and demand, substitution, balance, and externalities, are basic to the direct comparison approach. Guided by these principles, an appraiser attempts to consider all issues relevant to the valuation problem in a manner that is consistent and reflects local market conditions.

Supply and Demand

Property prices result from negotiations between buyers and sellers. In a market with many buyers and sellers acting in their own interests, buyers constitute market demand and the properties offered for sale make up the supply.[1] To estimate demand, appraisers consider the number of potential users of a particular type of property, their purchasing power, and their tastes and preferences. To analyze supply, appraisers focus on existing properties on the market, either unsold or vacant, as well as properties that are being constructed, converted, or planned. Shifts in any of these factors may cause the prices of properties in the market area to vary. Sales activity is also influenced by lenders because most real estate purchases involve some form of financing, which is directly related to purchasing power. When interest rates drop, market activity tends to accelerate and prices tend to rise because more buyers qualify for higher mortgage amounts. When interest rates rise, market activity tends to slow down and prices tend to fall. When loan money becomes scarce, either due to high interest rates or restrictive underwriting standards, market activity can be severely reduced. The ability of buyers to obtain financing is the real impediment to additional demand in most markets.

Substitution

The principle of substitution holds that the value of property tends to be set by the price that would be paid to acquire a substitute property of similar utility and desirability within a reasonable amount of time. This principle implies that the reliability of the direct comparison approach is diminished if substitute properties are not available in the market. For example, if a buyer does not have adequate choices in the marketplace, the buyer may have to pay a higher price given the lack of a suitable substitute and as a result of the conditions of sale, i.e., one of the elements of comparison. The conditions of sale will affect both the price paid for that imperfect comparable property and the credibility of that transaction in the subsequent analysis.

---

[1]   Market value is based on conventional economic theory, which predicts a unique market-driven price at the point where supply equals demand in a competitive market. Even in a *monopoly*, with only one seller, or a *monopsony*, with only one buyer, a unique price is predictable. But as soon as the market consists of only one seller and one buyer, called *bilateral monopoly*, economic theory can no longer predict a unique price. Bilateral monopoly theory predicts a minimum sale price and a maximum sale price, but no unique price, and suggests that any observed transaction price depends not on supply and demand but on the negotiating or bargaining skills of the buyer and the seller.

Balance

The forces of supply and demand tend toward equilibrium, or balance, in the market, but absolute equilibrium is almost never attained. Due to shifts in population, purchasing power, and consumer tastes and preferences, demand varies greatly over time. The construction of new buildings, conversion of existing buildings to other uses, and demolition of old buildings cause supply to vary as well.

The principle of balance also holds that both the relationship between land and improvements and the relationship between a property and its environment must be in balance for a property to achieve its optimum market value. For example, a property that has too much land in relation to its improvements (known as an *underimprovement*) or too many expensive amenities for its location (known as an *overimprovement*) is out of balance. Appraisers must watch for imbalances in the market and within specific properties because they can cause the market to ascribe different prices to otherwise comparable properties. Overimprovements and underimprovements can lead to functional obsolescence that may need to be accounted for in direct comparison, income, and cost approach analyses, albeit differently in each approach.

Externalities

External forces affect all types of property in positive or negative ways. Periods of economic growth and economic decline influence property values. An appraiser analyzes the market area of the subject property to identify all significant external influences. To a great extent, the adjustments made to the sale prices of comparable properties for differences in location reflect these external forces. That is, two competitive properties with identical physical characteristics may have quite different market values if one of the properties has less attractive surroundings. The condition and lighting of streets, the convenience of transportation facilities, the adequacy of police protection, the enforcement of municipal regulations, real estate tax burdens, and the proximity to shopping and restaurant facilities can all vary with location, making one location more or less attractive than another.

Market Analysis and Highest and Best Use

The conclusions of market analysis and highest and best use analysis are fundamental to the direct comparison approach. The analysis of the subject property's highest and best use and market area helps the appraiser identify and analyze the competitive supply and demand factors that influence value in the market. In addition, an adequately supported determination of the subject property's highest and best use provides the basis for the research and analysis of comparable sales, answering questions such as the following:

- Which comparable properties match the highest and best use of the subject property?
- Do the improvements contribute value to the comparable property?
- Is the comparable property as improved an interim or transitional use?
- Does excess land have a different highest and best use than the improved portion of the comparable property?

APPLICABILITY AND LIMITATIONS

The direct comparison approach is applicable to all types of real property interests when there are sufficient recent, reliable transactions to indicate value patterns or trends in the market. For property types that are bought and sold regularly, the direct comparison approach often provides a supportable indication of market value. When data is available, this is the most straightforward and simple way to explain and support an opinion of market value.

If the appraisal assignment is to develop an opinion of market value but no sales are available, the appraiser must question whether a market for the subject property exists at all. The common definitions of *market value* all assume a sale of the subject property, which implies the existence of a market. The market for a specific property may not be for the property as it is currently improved or configured. For example, in most markets a parcel of land improved with a provincial jail is unlikely to attract a buyer as presently improved, so the market value would be what a buyer would pay for the land (less demolition costs) or what, if any, economic use the building could be converted to.

Typically, the direct comparison approach provides the most credible indication of value for owner-occupied commercial and industrial properties, i.e., properties that are not purchased primarily for their income-producing characteristics. These types of properties are amenable to direct comparison because similar properties are commonly bought and sold in the same market.

Buyers of income-producing properties usually concentrate on a property's economic characteristics and put more emphasis on the conclusions of the income approach. Thoroughly analyzing the leased fee interest in comparable sales of large, complex, income-producing properties can be difficult because information on the economic factors influencing the decisions of buyers may not be readily available from public records or interviews with buyers and sellers. For example, an appraiser may not have sufficient knowledge of all the existing leases applicable to a neighbourhood shopping centre that is potentially comparable to the subject. The sale of a property encumbered by a lease involves rights other than the complete fee simple estate, and valuation of those rights requires knowledge of the terms of all leases and an understanding of the tenant or tenants occupying the premises. Some transactions may include sales of other physical assets or business interests. In each instance, if the sale is to be useful for comparison purposes, it must be dissected into its various components. Even when the components of value can be allocated, the sale may be less reliable as an indicator of the subject's real property value because of the complexity of the mix of factors involved.

At times the use of the direct comparison approach is limited, but comparable sales analysis remains a

> The direct comparison approach is applicable when sufficient data on recent market transactions is available. If no sales are found, the appraiser may have to use other approaches to value but only after the appraiser is convinced there is actually a market for the property. Essential information on income-producing properties derived through income comparison is used in the income capitalization and cost approaches.

significant and essential part of the valuation process. Although appraisers cannot always properly identify and quantify how the factors affecting property value are different, they can still analyze comparable sales to support the conclusions of the other approaches, i.e., develop a value bracket for the value indications derived from the cost and income approaches. In addition, comparable sales analysis can provide information used in the other approaches such as overall capitalization rates for the income approach or depreciation estimates for the cost approach. Income multipliers, capitalization rates, and yield rates are applied in the income approach to value, but appraisers extract such rates and factors from comparable properties in direct comparison analysis.

PROCEDURE

To apply the direct comparison approach, appraisers follow a systematic procedure:

1. Research the competitive market for information on properties that are similar to the subject property and that have recently sold, are listed for sale, or are under contract. Consider the characteristics of the properties such as property type, date of sale, size, physical condition, location, and land use constraints. The goal is to find a set of comparable sales as similar as possible to the subject property to ensure the comparable sales reflect the actions of similar buyers. Market analysis and highest and best use analysis set the stage for the selection of appropriate comparable sales.

2. Verify the information by confirming that the data obtained is factually accurate and that the transactions reflect arm's-length market considerations. Verification should elicit additional information about the property and the market so that comparisons are credible.

3. Select the most relevant units of comparison in the market (e.g., price per acre, price per square foot, price per front foot) and develop a comparative analysis for each unit. The appraiser's goal is to define and identify a unit of comparison that explains market behaviour.

4. Look for differences between the comparable sale properties and the subject property using all appropriate elements of comparison. Then adjust the price of each sale property, reflecting how it differs, to equate it to the subject property or eliminate that property as a comparable. This step typically involves using the most similar sale properties and then adjusting for any remaining differences. If a transaction does not reflect the actions of a buyer who would also be attracted to the subject property, the appraiser should be concerned about comparability.

5. Reconcile the various value indications produced from the analysis of comparables to a value bracket and then to a single value indication.

Researching Transactional Data

In the first step of the direct comparison approach, an appraiser gathers data on sales, listings, contracts, offers, refusals, and options of properties considered competitive with, and comparable to, the subject property. Data from completed transactions is considered the most reliable value indicator. The appraiser thoroughly researches the prices, real property rights conveyed, financing terms, motivations of buyers and sellers, expenditures made immediately after purchase, and dates (i.e., the market conditions) of the property transactions. The appraiser must also consider details on each property's location, physical condition, functional utility, economic characteristics, use, and non-realty components of value. Since conclusions must be market-derived, the appraiser will rely heavily on interviews, personal contacts, and proprietary research.

Regardless of the number of sales analyzed, the appraiser must understand each sale used for comparison to draw credible conclusions from comparisons. For example, the conditions of sale in a transaction of real property between parent and child may not be consistent with the definition of market value. It may be possible to determine the relationship between the reported sale price and market value only after the sale, the comparable property, and its market are researched and understood. Many sales that cannot be effectively used for direct comparison are still part of the market at large and can be used for bracketing, understanding general market activity, and other analytical purposes. Thus, market data is classified and weighted for its importance, relevance, and reliability.

Changing market conditions may reduce the validity or applicability of older sales that do not reflect the market's changes. Trends indicated by changing market conditions can be useful, but appraisers must be careful not to project trends without current, reliable market support. Historical sales may be valuable to retrospective valuations and may assist in time series analysis. However, significant changes in market conditions make the use of historical sales less reliable for current valuations. Legal changes comprise a broad array of possibilities including new tax laws, zoning, moratoriums, and buildings codes. The appraiser must look for a series of possible changes that may be imposed upon the market, thus changing the applicability of historical data. Also, some sales may reflect anticipations of such changes and may be evidence of market attitudes in advance of the actual change. Financing is also important in the analysis of comparable sale properties in the market.

Data Sources

Potential sources of sales data are many and varied. Primary sources include the following:

- Public records, e.g., land titles or land registry records
- Commercially available data from electronic reporting, multiple listing, and subscription services
- Published news articles in local newspapers or real estate periodicals
- Interviews with market participants, e.g., the parties to transactions, attorneys, appraisers, counsellors, brokers, property managers, lenders

All "raw" data obtained from a general source (e.g., assessors' records, data services) will need further research and verification with a party to the transaction.

An appraiser should exercise caution when sales data is provided by someone who is not a party to the transaction. Incorrect conclusions may result if the appraiser relies on such data without considering the motivation of the parties to the transaction.

> To apply the direct comparison approach, the appraiser first gathers data from sales, listings, contracts, offers, and refusals of competitive properties. Sources of this information include public records, multiple listing services, subscription services, real estate brokers, real estate periodicals, and interviews with the parties involved in market transactions.

Sometimes brokers will be able to provide more reliable information than the buyer or seller. Similarly, errors can result if anticipated income and expense schedules are inaccurate or if potential changes in use are not considered.

Much property and transaction information is available online and in easily accessed public records, but appraisers still maintain data files with the details of important and unique market transactions and add information as new transactions occur.

The geographic limits of the appraiser's search for sales data depend on the nature and type of real estate being valued and the available sales information. Certain types of properties have regional, national, and even international markets. For example, a hotel with an identifiable brand name may sell in a regional or national market, but a hotel with a less-recognized name may need to be compared to completely different properties. Using the brand-name and less-recognized hotels as comparable properties may be inappropriate. As another example, little comparable data may be found for the first property to be renovated in an area of deteriorated buildings or for the only property of a given type in a market area. In such a situation, the appraiser must establish the comparability of other areas and the competitiveness of the properties located there with the subject property. Similarly, an appraiser may gather data from a wide geographic area to find competitive properties for a regional shopping mall, large office building, resort hotel, large multi-use complex, or large industrial property.

In addition to sales of competitive properties, prior sales of the subject property must be considered in market value appraisals. Canadian Uniform Standards of Professional Appraisal Practice (CUSPAP) require appraisers to analyze and report

INBREEDING DATA

When the appraiser derives all adjustments from within a limited data set, a single erroneous sale price or figure can cause errors in the adjusted sale prices of all the comparable sales, leading to an erroneous indication of value for the subject property. This sort of situation in which the independence of the sales data is lost is known as *inbreeding*.

Verification of transactional and property data is the best method to prevent inbred adjustments from affecting the conclusions of the sales comparison approach. Another practical technique is developing adjustment amounts from a larger data set. The larger the number of adjustments made within a data set, the greater the probability that the results of the analysis will be affected by small data collection errors within the data set.

all agreements of sale, options, and listings of the subject property current as of the effective date of the appraisal and to analyze sales that occurred within the prior three years. If the information is not available, the analyst must explain the efforts taken to uncover it. This analysis is particularly significant when the comparable sales are limited and are either vastly superior to or inferior to the subject property.

It is imperative that the appraiser identify and analyze the strengths and weaknesses of the quantity and quality of the data compiled and the extent of the comparative analyses undertaken in the direct comparison approach. All relevant facts and opinions must be considered in the analysis and reported in the amount of detail required given the intended use of the appraisal as identified in the scope of work. The reliability of the data, the analyses performed, and the final conclusion of value should be presented in both the direct comparison approach and, where appropriate, the final opinion of value.

Verifying Transactional Data

Appraisers should verify information with a party to the transaction to ensure its accuracy and to gain insight into the motivation behind each transaction. The buyer's and seller's views of precisely what was being purchased at the time of sale are important. Sales that are not arm's-length market transactions (in accordance with the definition of market value used in the appraisal) should be identified and rarely, if ever, used. To verify sales data, the appraiser confirms statements of fact with the principals to the transaction, if possible, or with the brokers, closing agents, or lenders involved. Owners and tenants of neighbouring properties may also provide helpful information.

> **arm's-length transaction**
> A transaction between unrelated parties under no duress. The common definitions of market value usually set out the criteria for an arm's-length sale in detail.

Sometimes income and expense data for income-producing properties is unobtainable. If data on a particular sale is unavailable, assigning rents and expenses "based on market parameters" may be improper, especially for properties with existing leases. Nevertheless, market-derived rental and expense information may be useful in developing income and expense statements and appropriate capitalization rates for comparable properties. This sort of analysis can serve as a test of reasonableness for data developed in other ways.

Referencing public records and data services does not verify a sales transaction. It simply confirms that a transaction was recorded. Similarly, referencing the source of secondary data only confirms its existence and does not verify the transaction. Generally, secondary sources do not provide adequate information about sale concessions, whether the sale was an arm's-length transaction, if multiple properties were involved in the sale, if personal property was included, and other factors influencing value.

Selecting Units of Comparison

After sales data has been gathered and verified, systematic analysis begins. Since like units must be compared, each sale price should be stated in terms of appropriate units of comparison. The units of comparison selected depend on the appraisal problem and nature of the property, as illustrated in Table 13.1.

Appraisers use units of comparison to facilitate comparison of the subject and comparable properties. The sales should be analyzed to determine which unit of comparison has the closest correlation with the comparable

> **units of comparison**
> The components into which a property may be divided for purposes of comparison, e.g., price per square foot, front foot, cubic foot, room, bed, seat, apartment unit. These units usually facilitate analysis even when the properties are not very comparable.

sales. This analysis will identify the proper unit of comparison to be used, such as price per acre or price per square foot, which is especially important for properties in markets in transition.

Prices of comparable properties are not usually adjusted on the basis of differences in net operating income (NOI) per unit because rents and sale prices tend to move in relative tandem. A value indication developed using NOI per square foot as a unit of comparison is not independent of a value indication developed using direct capitalization, which negates the checks and balances provided by using more than one approach to value. In effect, the results suffer from circular logic.

Nevertheless, the appraiser should consider why the income per unit varies among the sale properties. Sensitivity and trend analyses may be performed to gain an understanding of this variance. For example, an appraiser may analyze sales of income-producing properties to derive potential and effective gross income multipliers, overall and equity capitalization rates, and even total property yield rates. These factors are not adjusted quantitatively. Instead, the appraiser considers their ranges and the similarities and differences between the subject and comparable sale properties that cause the multipliers and rates to vary. The appraiser then selects the rate from within the refined value bracket that is most appropriate to the property being appraised for use in the income approach.[2]

Analyzing and Adjusting Comparable Sales

Ideally, if all comparable properties are identical to the subject property, no adjustments will be required. However, this is rarely the case, especially for non-residential properties. After researching and verifying transactional data and selecting the appropriate unit of comparison, the appraiser adjusts for any differences.

---

[2]   While a superior property ought to sell and lease for more than an inferior one, in some cases that may not be true. Tenants and landlords alike will pay more for a property that is in a better location with newer improvements and more building area. However, if tenants are not responsible for the replacement of, say, the roof covering, they are not likely to pay more or less for a property with a roof that will need recovering soon. A buyer surely will pay less because of the needed roof, but tenants may not care. This will cause inconsistency in the multipliers and capitalization rates, which can be compensated for with adjustments to the sale prices of comparable sales used to extract the capitalization rates as discussed in Chapters 22 and 23.

Table 13.1: Typical Units of Comparison

Property Type	Typical Units of Comparison
Single-unit residential property	Total property price Price per square foot of gross living area
Apartment properties	Price per room Price per square foot of gross building area
Warehouses	Price per square foot of gross building area Price per cubic foot of gross building volume
Factories	Price per square foot of gross building area Price per machine unit
Office properties	Price per square foot of gross building area Price per square foot of net rentable area Price per square foot of usable area
Hotels and motels	Price per guest room
Restaurants, theatres, and auditoriums	Price per seat
Hospitals	Price per square foot of gross building area Price per bed
Golf courses	Price per round (annual number of rounds played) Price per membership Price per hole Price per acre
Tennis and racquetball facilities	Price per playing court
Mobile home parks	Price per parking pad
Marinas	Price per slip
Automobile repair facilities	Price per bay Price per square foot of gross building area
Agricultural properties	Price per acre Price per animal unit (for pastureland) Price per board foot (for timberland)
Vacant land	Price per front foot Price per square foot Price per acre Price per buildable square foot

After sales information has been collected and confirmed, it can be organized in a variety of ways. One convenient and commonly used method is to arrange the data on a *market data grid* (see Table 13.2). Each important difference between the comparable properties and the subject property that could affect property value is considered an element of comparison. Each element of comparison that is found to affect sale prices in the market is assigned a row on the grid, and total property prices or unit prices of the comparable properties are adjusted to reflect the value of these differences. The use of the grid is a way for appraisers to model typical buyer actions and to analyze sales data to quantify the impact of certain characteristics on value. Grids are also a good way to communicate the appraiser's logic clearly and efficiently to readers of the appraisal report.

Identification and Measurement of Adjustments

A sale price reflects many different elements that affect a property's value in varying degrees. *Quantitative* and *qualitative techniques* are employed to estimate the relative significance of these factors. Appraisers employ mathematical applications to derive quantitative adjustments. When sufficient market data to support a quantitative adjustment is not available, appraisers investigate qualitative relationships, also using mathematical applications to identify market trends. Only when the market data is insufficient to apply mathematical applications should the appraiser resort to direct or relative comparisons.

Quantitative adjustments are developed as either dollar or percentage amounts. Factors that cannot be quantified are dealt with in qualitative analysis. Table 13.3 shows various techniques used in quantitative adjustments and qualitative analyses and Chapter 14 discusses these concepts in more detail.

> **quantitative techniques**
> Techniques used to derive quantitative adjustments to comparable sale prices in the direct comparison approach.
>
> **qualitative analysis**
> In the direct comparison approach, the process of accounting for differences between comparables that are not quantified; usually follows quantitative adjustment.

> Quantitative adjustments may be applied to comparable sales prices as percentage or dollar amounts.

> **dollar adjustments**
> Adjustments for differences between the subject and the comparable properties expressed in monetary terms, rather than as a percentage.
>
> **percentage adjustments**
> Adjustments for differences between the subject and comparable properties expressed as a percentage of the sale price (or adjusted sale price); percentage adjustments are often used to reflect changes in market conditions and differences in location.

Adjustments can be made either to total property prices or to appropriate units of comparison. Often the "transactional" adjustments – property rights conveyed, financing, conditions of sale (motivation), expenditures made immediately after purchase, and date of sale (market conditions) – are made to the total sale price. The adjusted price is then converted into a unit price and adjusted for the "property"-related elements of comparison such as physical and legal characteristics.

Table 13.2: Market Data Grids

The sample market data grid below reflects the initial elements of comparison in a typical sequence. Blank lines are provided for additional property-related adjustments. If the comparable properties are similar to the subject property in regard to a specific element of comparison, no adjustment is required for that element. The sample grid includes separate lines for each element of comparison and adjustment to ensure that adjustments are made in a consistent manner.

Sample Market Data Grid: Comparison and Adjustment of Market Data

Element	Subject	Sale 1	Sale 2	Sale 3
Sale price	unknown			
Real property rights conveyed adjustment				
Adjusted price*				
Financing adjustment				
Adjusted price†				
Conditions of sale adjustment				
Adjusted price‡				
Expenditures made immediately after purchase				
Adjusted price§				
Market conditions adjustment				
Adjusted price¶				
Final adjusted sale price				
For reconciliation purposes:				
Net adjustment				
Net adjustment as % of sale price				
Gross adjustment				
Gross adjustment as % of sale price				

* Sale price adjusted for property rights conveyed
† Sale price further adjusted for financing
‡ Sale price further adjusted for conditions of sale
§ Sale price further adjusted for expenditures made immediately after purchase
¶ Sale price further adjusted for market conditions

The section labelled "For reconciliation purposes:" is provided to help the appraiser analyze the comparability of each sale, which indicates the relative reliability of the separate value indications derived. The final adjusted sale price of each transaction is a possible value indication for the subject property. Together the adjusted sale prices of the comparable properties may indicate a range of values within which the value of the subject property will likely fall. Each adjusted sale price can be analyzed to show the total, or absolute, adjustment made to the sale price of the comparable property and the percentage of the sale price that is reflected by this total adjustment. With these value estimates, the appraiser can rank the comparability of the sales to the subject and select an appropriate opinion of value, assuming the value conclusion is to be reported as a point estimate. The sale that requires the least significant or lowest total adjustment (i.e., the absolute adjustment based on the sum of the adjustments regardless of sign) is often the most comparable and generally should be given the most weight in reconciling the value indications from the sales comparison approach. Simply averaging the results of the adjustment process to develop an averaged value fails to recognize the relative comparability of the individual transactions as indicated by the size of the total adjustments and the reliability of the data and methods used to support the adjustments.

Table 13.3: Techniques Used in Quantitative and Qualitative Analysis

Quantitative Analysis	Qualitative Analysis
• Paired data analysis, e.g., sales and resales of the same or similar properties • Grouped data analysis • Secondary data analysis • Statistical analysis including graphic analysis and scenario analysis* • Cost-related adjustments, e.g., cost-to-cure, depreciated cost • Capitalization of income differences	• Trend analysis • Relative comparison analysis • Ranking analysis

* Note that forms of statistical analysis can also serve as qualitative techniques.

Elements of Comparison

Elements of comparison are the characteristics of properties and transactions that help explain the variances in the prices paid for real property. The appraiser determines the elements of comparison for a given appraisal through market research and supports those conclusions with market evidence. When properly identified, the elements of comparison describe the factors that are associated with the prices paid for competing properties. The market data, if analyzed properly, will identify the elements of comparison within the comparable sales that are market-sensitive.

The basic elements of comparison that should be considered in direct comparison analysis are as follows:

> elements of comparison
> The characteristics or attributes of properties and transactions that cause the prices of real estate to vary; include real property rights conveyed, financing terms, conditions of sale, expenditures made immediately after purchase, market conditions, location, physical characteristics, other characteristics such as economic characteristics, use, and non-realty components of value. Elements of comparison are analogous to the lines of adjustment shown on a direct comparison adjustment grid.

1. Real property rights conveyed
2. Financing terms, i.e., cash equivalency
3. Conditions of sale, i.e., motivation
4. Expenditures made immediately after purchase
5. Market conditions, i.e., time
6. Location
7. Physical characteristics, e.g., size, soils, access, construction quality, condition
8. Economic characteristics, e.g., expense ratios, lease provisions, management, tenant mix
9. Use, e.g., zoning, water and riparian rights, environmental, building codes, flood zones
10. Non-realty components of value, e.g., business value, chattel, franchises, trademarks

In most cases, the elements of comparison cover all the significant factors to be considered, but on occasion additional factors may be relevant. Other possible elements of comparison include governmental restrictions such as conservation or preservation easements and off-site improvements required for the development of a vacant site.

Often a basic element of comparison is broken down into subcategories that specifically address the property factor being analyzed. For example, physical characteristics may be broken down into subcategories for age, condition, size, and so on. Chapter 14 illustrates adjustment techniques for each of the standard elements of comparison. There is no limit to the number of elements of comparison that may be found in a market; therefore, it is important to remember that another line can always be added to an adjustment grid for an additional item recognized in the market. For example, an appraiser may need to add "roof colour" as an element of comparison if the market makes distinctions in sale price based on the colour of the roof. However, note that adding elements of comparison for adjustment may lead to multiple adjustments for the same factor, a common error that is discussed in Chapter 14.

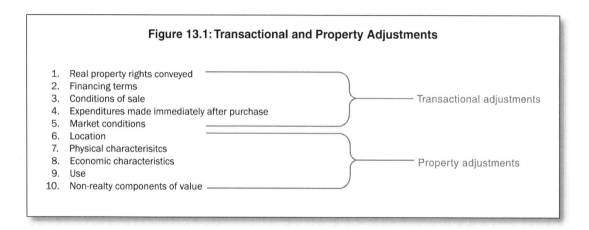

Figure 13.1: Transactional and Property Adjustments

1. Real property rights conveyed
2. Financing terms
3. Conditions of sale
4. Expenditures made immediately after purchase
5. Market conditions
— Transactional adjustments
6. Location
7. Physical characterisitcs
8. Economic characteristics
9. Use
10. Non-realty components of value
— Property adjustments

Sequence of Adjustments

The sequence in which adjustments are applied to the comparable sales is determined by the market data and the appraiser's analysis of that data. The first five elements of comparison in the list are considered "transactional" adjustments, while the latter five are considered "property" adjustments (see Figure 13.1). The transactional adjustments are generally applied in the order listed. The property adjustments are usually applied after the transactional adjustments, but in no particular order.

The sequence can vary depending on the availability and reliability of sales information. For example, resales supporting a market conditions adjustment may then allow a pairing of data to extract a financing terms adjustment. The sequence presented in Table 13.4 is provided for purposes of illustration. This sequence is often

Table 13.4: Sequence of Adjustments

Element of Comparison	Market-Derived Adjustment	Adjustment Applied to Sale Price of Comparable Property
Sale price*		$400,000
Transactional adjustments		
Adjustment for property rights conveyed	+ 5%	+ 20,000
Adjusted price		$420,000
Adjustment for financing terms	– 2%	– 8,400
Adjusted price		$411,600
Adjustment for conditions of sale†	+ 5%	+ 20,580
Adjusted price		$432,180
Adjustment for expenditures immediately after purchase	+ $20,000	+ $20,000
Adjusted price		$452,180
Adjustment for market conditions	+ 5%	+ 22,609
Adjusted price		$474,789
Property adjustments		
Adjustment for		
Location	+ 3%	+ 14,244
Physical characteristics	– 5%	– 23,739
Economic characteristics	– 5%	– 23,739
Use	+ 2%	+ 9,496
Non-realty components	+ 3%	+ 14,244
Indication of value		$465,295

* In the market data grid, the sale price could be converted into a unit price, such as price per square foot of leasable area, and adjustments made to the unit price rather than the sale price.
† The effect of the conditions of sale on the adjusted sale price may already be reflected in the adjustment for financing terms, depending on how the adjustments are extracted from the market.

applicable when percentage adjustments are calculated and added, either in conjunction with other percentage adjustments or in combination with dollar adjustments. The sequence of adjustments shown in Figure 13.1 is not the only order in which quantitative adjustments can be made. Adjustments may be applied in other sequences if the market and the appraiser's analysis of the data so indicate. Using the adjustment sequence, the appraiser applies successive adjustments to the prices of comparable properties.

Most property types other than one-unit residences are adjusted on a unit price basis. Property adjustments for location, physical characteristics, economic characteristics, use, and non-realty components are typically applied to a unit price.

Reconciling Value Indications in the Direct Comparison Approach

Reconciliation is necessary in nearly all sales analyses because the appraiser will usually analyze many sales that may lead to several different conclusions.[3] These value indications are resolved into a range of value or a single value indication, i.e., a point estimate. It is important that the appraiser consider the strengths and weaknesses of each comparable sale, examining the reliability and appropriateness of the market data compiled and the analytical techniques applied in the comparative analysis. The appraisal report should clearly communicate how the appraiser arrived at the value indication using the direct comparison approach.

In reconciling value indications in the direct comparison approach, the appraiser evaluates the number and magnitude of adjustments and the importance of the individual elements of comparison in the market to judge the relative weight a particular comparable sale should have in the comparative analysis. For example, for some properties, location is the most important element of comparison and other factors are of lesser importance; therefore, comparable sales that required less adjustment for differences in location are likely to be given more weight in the reconciliation than comparables sales that may have had fewer adjustments for other, less-important elements of comparison.

If one or two comparable transactions require fewer total adjustments than the other comparable transactions, an appraiser may attribute greater accuracy and give more weight to the value indications obtained from these transactions, particularly if the magnitude of the adjustments is approximately the same. Although the number of adjustments made to the sale prices of the comparable properties may be similar, the gross dollar amount of the total adjustments might vary considerably. For example, suppose an appraiser analyzes five comparable properties, each of which requires several adjustments. However, the gross dollar amount of adjustments for one comparable property totals 15% of the sale price, while the gross dollar adjustment for each of the other four properties is less than 5% of the sale price. If the sales are similar otherwise, less accuracy may be attributable to the comparable property that required the larger adjustment.

Usually the magnitude of net adjustments is a less reliable indicator of accuracy. The net adjustment is calculated by totalling the positive and negative adjustments. A net adjustment figure may be misleading because the appraiser cannot assume that any inaccuracies in the positive and negative adjustments will cancel each other out. For example, if a comparable property is 20% superior to the subject in some characteristics and 20% inferior in others, the net adjustment is zero but the gross adjustment is 40%. Another comparable sale may require several adjustments, all positive or all negative, resulting in a net adjustment of 6%. This property may well be a more accurate indicator of the subject's value than the comparable sale with the 0% net adjustment, which had large positive and negative adjustments that cancel each other out mathematically.

---

[3]   In addition to reconciliation within the direct comparison approach, reconciliation is also required when value indications are derived using two or more approaches to value. At that point in the valuation process, reconciliation results in the opinion of value identified in the definition of the appraisal problem. Chapter 25 discusses reconciliation of the final opinion of value.

Figure 13.2: Reconciliation Checklist

In the reconciliation process, the appraiser often asks several questions about the data and techniques used in the direct comparison approach:

- Is the comparable property similar in terms of physical characteristics and location?
- Does the comparable property have the same highest and best use?
- Was it developed, rented, or sold in the same market as the subject property?
- Are the characteristics of the transaction similar to those expected for the subject property?
- Would a potential buyer of the subject property consider the comparable property as a reasonable alternative to the subject?

In some cases the appraiser may ask additional questions:

- Are the expenses of the comparable properties appropriate indicators of the expenses of the appraised property?
- Are the estimates of depreciation in the appraised improvements justified by the comparison of comparable costs and comparable sales?
- Is one method preferred over another given the data available for each analysis?

It is also good practice in the reconciliation process to reexamine the major elements of comparison for which no adjustments were made and to explain why these elements of comparison did not require any adjustments.

Even when adjustments are supported by comparable data, the adjustment process and the values indicated reflect human judgment. Small inaccuracies can be compounded when several adjustments are added or multiplied. For this reason, the precise arithmetic conclusions derived from adjusted data should support, rather than control, the appraiser's judgment.

Units of Comparison and Real Property Interests in the Reconciliation Process

Two related points should be stressed in any discussion of the reconciliation process. In arriving at a final value indication in the direct comparison approach, the appraiser must ensure that the value concluded is consistent with the intended use of the appraisal and the value indications derived from the other approaches to value. This is especially important in regard to the date of the opinion of prospective value. For example, an appraiser may seek an opinion of the market value of an income-producing property at two different points in the future, e.g., upon project completion and upon stabilized occupancy. However, the only market data available may pertain to comparable properties at or near stabilized occupancy. Typically, this data is appropriate only for an analysis of the market value of the subject property at the point of stabilized occupancy. As a result, the appraiser has to reconcile the prospective value indication based on this data with value indications derived from the other approaches for the corresponding date of stabilized occupancy. This data should not be used to derive a value indication for the date of completion unless other, truly comparable sales can be identified with similar occupancy characteristics and leaseup potential.

The appraiser must also consider any differences in the property rights appraised between the comparable properties and the subject property because the comparable sales may include the transfer of a leased fee interest. If the data is not properly analyzed in the direct comparison approach, the value indication concluded for the leased fee interest in the subject property upon the achievement of stabilized occupancy might be lower or higher than the value for the fee simple interest. This value indication would not be compatible with the corresponding value indications derived from the cost and income approaches for the fee simple interest in the subject property unless adjustments have been made. Failure to recognize that the value indications may apply to different property rights would likely result in an inaccurate value conclusion.

CHAPTER 14

COMPARATIVE ANALYSIS

Comparative analysis is the general term used to identify the process in which an appraiser applies quantitative and qualitative techniques to comparable sales to derive a value indication in the direct comparison approach. An appraiser may use both quantitative adjustments and qualitative analysis in comparative analysis. Generally, an appraiser makes quantitative adjustments before he or she performs qualitative analysis.

The process of researching and applying quantitative adjustments involves a thorough analysis of the comparable sales to identify the elements of comparison that affect the value of the type of property being appraised. Quantitative adjustments derived in comparative analysis and applied to the sale prices of the comparable properties may be expressed in numerical amounts (e.g., dollars, percentages), or the conclusions of qualitative analysis may be described in terms that clearly convey the magnitude of the difference between the comparable property and the subject in regard to each element of comparison. The reader of the appraisal report must readily understand the source of dollar or percentage adjustments.

After the appraiser identifies quantitative differences, the appraiser uses qualitative analysis to determine which comparable sales are inferior, similar, or superior to the subject property for a specific element of comparison. The adjusted prices of the inferior and superior groups bracket the value of the subject and indicate a probable range of values. The appraiser can conclude a single value indication for the subject property from this range of values.

A value indication derived with qualitative analysis alone will usually require more narrative explanation in an appraisal report than an indication derived with quantitative adjust-

> **comparative analysis**
> The process by which a value indication is derived in the direct comparison approach. Comparative analysis may employ quantitative or qualitative techniques, either separately or in combination.

ments. In applying either technique, appraisers must ensure that their reasoning is clear and adequately explained. The extent of narrative explanation required also depends on the complexity of the property being appraised. The more complex the property, the more factors that must be considered in the analysis and then explained to intended users of the appraisal.

QUANTITATIVE ADJUSTMENTS

Several techniques are available to quantify adjustments to the sale prices of comparable properties:

- Data analysis techniques such as paired data analysis, grouped data analysis, and secondary data analysis
- Statistical analysis, including graphic analysis and scenario analysis
- Cost-related adjustments, i.e., cost-to-cure, depreciated cost
- Capitalization of income differences

Appraisers can usually find some logic to support most quantitative adjustments given the number of tools available to them. Of course, the value indication supported by quantitative adjustments may differ from the results of cost or income capitalization analysis, and the appraiser will have to reconcile the results of the sales adjustment process with the results of the other approaches to value. Above all, the appraiser must be careful to ensure that mathematical adjustments reflect the reactions of market participants.

Data Analysis Techniques

Paired data analysis is based on the premise that when two properties are equivalent in all respects but one, the value of the single difference can be measured to indicate the difference in price between the two properties. For example, two residential properties are similar in all respects except for location, e.g., one property has a corner lot while the other is on an interior lot. If both properties sell at a similar time so that there is no difference in market conditions, the difference in sale price can be attributed to the different locations of the properties, and that identifiable difference can be used in the adjustment process. If the home on the corner lot sold for $15,000 more than the home on the interior lot, that difference could be used to adjust the sale prices of other comparable sales in the market for location on a corner lot or an interior lot.

A related technique, *grouped data analysis*, involves grouping data by an independent variable such as date of sale and calculating equivalent typical values. The appraiser studies the grouped sales in pairs to identify the effect on a dependent variable such as the unit price of comparable properties. To apply this technique to the market used in the example described above, the appraiser would compare a group of comparable homes all on interior lots to a different group of residences all on corner lots rather than comparing just one property of each type.

Paired data and grouped data analysis are variants of *sensitivity analysis*, which is a method used to isolate the effect of individual variables on value. Often associated with risk analysis, sensitivity analysis studies the impact of variables on different measures of return.

Although paired data analysis is a theoretically sound method, it may be impractical when only a narrow sampling of sufficiently similar properties is available. This is particularly true for commercial and industrial properties and properties that do not sell frequently in the market. A lack of data can make quantifying the adjustments attributable to all the variables a difficult process. An adjustment derived from a single pair of sales is not necessarily indicative, just as a single sale does not necessarily reflect market value.

When sufficient data is available for "pure" pairings (i.e., pairs of sales that are identical except for the single element being measured), paired data analysis is the foundation for quantitative adjustments. When few pure pairings are available, the appraiser should use other analytical procedures or secondary data to test the reasonableness of the adjustment derived from the pure pairings.

An appraiser must take special care when relying on pairs of adjusted values because the difference measured may not represent the actual difference in value attributable to the characteristic being studied. The difference may include other aspects of the property, not just the one characteristic being studied. An appraiser should analyze pure pairings first. For example, an appraiser may compare data on a sale and resale of the same property to derive a market conditions adjustment. An appraiser should only use pairings of adjusted sales as an analytical tool when pure pairings are unavailable. When more than one element of comparison is involved, additional pairs can be studied to isolate and extract the differing elements of comparison.[1]

Grouped data analysis extends the logic of paired data analysis to larger data sets. In this technique, comparable sales are grouped by an independent variable such as date of sale and then the groups are studied as pairs. For example, sales of units in an industrial park that occurred in 2009 are grouped together, and the average sale price for that year is compared to the average sale price of another group of sales that occurred in 2010. Analyzing the pairs of average sale prices gives a measure of the forecast change in sale prices from 2009 to 2010.

> **paired data analysis**
> A quantitative technique used to identify and measure adjustments to the sale prices or rents of comparable properties; to apply this technique, sales or rental data on nearly identical properties is analyzed to isolate a single characteristic's effect on value or rent.

A third form of data analysis, *secondary data analysis*, is used to support adjustments derived by other methods. This technique makes use of data that does not directly pertain to the subject or comparable properties. This secondary data describes the general real estate market and is usually collected by a research firm or government agency.

---

[1] Comparable properties that contain different unit or inventory mixes should be adjusted for this difference before pairing analysis is conducted. Examples of properties with different unit or inventory mixes include apartment buildings with one-, two-, and three-bedroom units and agricultural lands with different types of soil. A unit or inventory mix adjustment is required to ensure that the comparables and subject are commensurate. The appraiser may be able to extract this adjustment by investigating the value relationships among the different classes of properties within the same property type.

Statistical Analysis

An appraiser can sometimes apply statistical methods to calculate adjustments to comparable sales. To use any form of statistical analysis, the appraiser must understand (and properly apply) fundamental statistical concepts as well as the particular methodology selected.[2] In applying statistical analysis, the appraiser must be careful not to develop a result that is mathematically precise yet logically meaningless or inappropriate for the particular appraisal. As with other adjustment techniques, statistical analysis must reflect the thought processes and conclusions of market participants to serve as a useful, persuasive valuation tool.

As an example of a common application, the appraiser can develop a series of adjustment factors for different tract sizes by creating a simple linear regression model and then use the results of the *regression analysis* as a means of inferring the size adjustment for properties within the range of the data. If there is a reasonable pattern, the appraiser can apply the model to a group of sales with differing land sizes to test its accuracy, although the process might also demonstrate that the adjustments compared are incorrect. Statistical analysis may not necessarily be the sole source of an adjustment amount. Often the technique provides market support for an adjustment derived by other means.

Appraisers should recognize the differences between statistical processes in the collection and description of data and should be able to distinguish between descriptive and inferential statistics. Without an understanding of these issues, any use of statistical calculations is dangerous or ill-advised. For example, some appraisers extract adjustments for direct comparison processes directly from multiple regression analyses, without recognizing that regression studies do not develop indications of causation, but rather of associations, between and among independent variables and a dependent (or predicted) variable such as sale price. It is improper to mix a value of a single regression coefficient that is developed for a given statistical model with other market adjustments developed from paired sales analysis or other market data comparison techniques.[3]

Scenario analysis is a form of modelling in which the outcomes of future events are forecast to test the probability or correlation of alternative outcomes. In the adjustment

> **statistical analysis**
> Quantitative techniques used to identify and measure adjustments to the sale prices of comparable properties; techniques include statistical inference and linear and multiple regression analysis.
>
> **graphic analysis**
> Quantitative techniques used to identify and measure adjustments to the sale prices of comparable properties; a variant of statistical analysis in which an appraiser interprets graphically displayed data visually or through curve fit analysis. Graphs can also be used to support and exhibit value trends for comparison elements in qualitative analysis.

---

[2] Full discussion of the statistical methods applicable to the direct comparison approach is beyond the scope of this text. Chapter 28 provides a review of basic statistical techniques. In addition, *The Appraisal Journal, Assessment Journal, The Journal of Real Estate Research, Real Estate Economics*, and other scholarly journals have published many articles on advanced statistical applications.

[3] The difficulty in applying regression analysis to real estate appraisal is discussed in Gene Dilmore, "Appraising with Regression Analysis: A Pop Quiz", *The Appraisal Journal* (October 1997): 403–404.

process, alternative scenarios can be created and then modelled to test the influence of changes in various elements of comparison on sale price. The technique allows the appraiser to forecast best, most-likely, and worst-case scenarios (such as the potential performance of proposed improvements) or to create other scenarios testing a range of values rather than a single point estimate. An appraiser often uses scenario analysis to measure the risk associated with certain market events and investment decisions.

Graphic Analysis

Graphic analysis is a form of statistical analysis in which the appraiser arrives at a conclusion by visually interpreting a graphic display of data and applying statistical curve fit analysis. A simple graphic display of grouped data may illustrate how the market reacts to variations in the elements of comparison or may reveal sub-market trends. In curve fit analysis, an appraiser may employ different formulas to determine the best fit for the market data being analyzed. The appraiser can plot the most reliable equation for the best-fitting curve, or the appraiser can identify the most appropriate equation of those commonly used to solve for an adjustment.

Cost Analysis/Cost-Related Adjustments

In *cost analysis*, adjustments are based on cost indicators such as depreciated building cost, cost to cure, or permit fees. *Cost-related adjustments* are most persuasive in markets with limited sales activity. The appraiser should be able to provide market support for cost-related adjustments because cost and value are not necessarily synonymous.

Buyers are clearly conscious of the cost of repairs, additions, or conversions as seen in the application of the cost approach (see Chapters 17, 18, and 19), but the cost of an improvement does not always result in a one-to-one increase in value for the property as a whole. For example, adding a swimming pool to a residential property at a cost of $50,000 may only add $25,000 to the sale price of the property if swimming pools are not a desirable amenity in that market. On the other hand, the swimming pool might be worth more to the property than the $50,000 cost to install it if few existing residential properties have swimming pools and the demographics in the market support the addition of that sort of luxury amenity. As another example, a potential buyer of a refrigerated warehouse may also look for buildings without refrigeration that can be converted into refrigerated space and factor in the cost of conversion into an offer (as well as other factors such as the time the building would be unavailable for use during the conversion).

Capitalization of Income Differences

An appraiser can use capitalization of differences in net operating income to derive an adjustment when the income loss incurred by a comparable property reflects a specific deficiency in the property, e.g., the lack of an elevator in a low-rise office building or inadequate parking facilities for a convenience store. Alternatively, a comparable property may enjoy a competitive advantage over the subject property, in which case the adjustment to the sale price of the comparable property would reflect the income premium the property enjoys. For example, an investor may decide to purchase a building with an elevator or one without an elevator based on the difference in potential rental rates.

Capitalization of income differences is easier to support than many other methods of quantifying adjustment amounts, and investors recognize this technique as a valid method of comparison. An appraiser commonly uses this method in expropriation assignments to illustrate a loss in value, e.g., the difference between the rental income the property generates before and after an event such as a government taking.

QUALITATIVE ANALYSIS

Qualitative analysis recognizes the inefficiencies of real estate markets and the difficulty in expressing adjustments with mathematical precision. Therefore, it is essential that the appraiser explains the analytical process and logic applied in reconciling the value indications using qualitative analysis techniques such as the following:

- Trend analysis
- Relative comparison analysis
- Ranking analysis

Statistical analysis and graphic analysis may serve as qualitative techniques when the results of those analyses do not support a precise adjustment amount but do support qualitative conclusions about value trends.

Trend Analysis

Trend analysis is applicable when a large amount of market data is available; it is especially useful when there is a limited number of closely comparable sales but a broad database of properties with less similar characteristics. An appraiser can test the various elements of comparison influencing a sale price to determine their market sensitivity. Once the appraiser has determined which elements of comparison show market sensitivity, the appraiser can analyze price patterns to support other analyses.

> **trend analysis**
> A qualitative technique used to identify and measure trends in the sale prices of comparable properties; useful when sales data on highly comparable properties is lacking, but a broad database on properties with less similar characteristics is available. Market sensitivity is investigated by testing various factors that influence sale prices.

Relative Comparison Analysis

Relative comparison analysis is the study of the relationships indicated by market data without recourse to quantification. Many appraisers use this technique because it reflects the imperfect nature of real estate markets. To apply the technique, the appraiser analyzes comparable sales to determine whether the comparable properties' characteristics are inferior, superior, or similar to those of the subject property.

In relative comparison analysis, one key issue concerns comparable properties with a similar highest and best use that compete in a similar market as the subject. Significant differences in highest and best use may exclude a potential comparable sale from consideration in qualitative analysis, just as it would be excluded in the quantitative adjustment process.

Reliable results can usually be obtained by *bracketing* the subject between comparable properties that are superior and inferior to it. However, if the comparable properties are either all superior or all inferior, only an upper or lower limit is set and no range of possible values for the subject can be defined. In this situation, the only conclusion the appraiser can draw for the subject is either that its value is more than the highest comparable indication (if all that comparable property's qualitative factors are inferior) or less than the lowest comparable indication (if all that comparable property's qualitative factors are superior). The appraiser must search the market diligently to obtain and analyze sufficient pertinent data to bracket the value of the subject property. If the available comparable sales do not bracket the subject's value, the appraiser should consider employing other analytical techniques to establish such a bracket. Quantitative adjustments to the comparable sales can often serve this purpose.

Ranking Analysis

Ranking analysis is used to sort the comparable data for differences in specific elements of comparison, e.g., size, corner or interior lot, frontage. An appraiser can use the technique to test the specific elements of comparison for their market sensitivities. The appraiser ranks the comparable sales according to overall comparability or by some other element of comparison so that the relative position of each comparable sale to the subject property is clear. Therefore, specific value trends can be established for elements of comparison that are market-sensitive, and those that show no discernable or reasonable trends will be discarded.

ELEMENTS OF COMPARISON

An appraiser should analyze each of the basic elements of comparison to determine whether an adjustment is required. If sufficient information is available, the appraiser

bracketing
A process in which an appraiser determines a probable range of values for a property by applying qualitative techniques of comparative analysis to a group of comparable sales. The array of comparables may be divided into three groups, i.e., those superior to the subject, those similar to the subject, and those inferior to the subject. The adjusted sale prices reflected by the sales requiring downward adjustment and those requiring upward adjustment refine the probable range of values for the subject and identify a value bracket in which the final value opinion will fall.

relative comparison analysis
A qualitative technique for analyzing comparable sales; used to determine whether the characteristics of a comparable property are inferior, superior, or similar to those of the subject property. Relative comparison analysis is similar to paired data analysis, but quantitative adjustments are not derived.

ranking analysis
A qualitative technique for analyzing comparable sales; a variant of relative comparison analysis in which comparable sales are ranked in descending or ascending order of desirability and each is analyzed to determine its position relative to the subject.

may make a quantitative adjustment. If there is insufficient support for a quantitative adjustment, the element of comparison may be better addressed using qualitative analysis.

An appraiser makes adjustments for differences in the elements of comparison to the price of each comparable property. An appraiser may make adjustments to the total property price, to a common unit price, or to a mix of both, but the appraiser must apply the unit prices consistently to the comparable properties at the appropriate points in the adjustment process. The magnitude of the adjustment made for each element of comparison depends on how much that characteristic of the comparable property differs from the subject property.

Appraisers should consider all appropriate elements of comparison and avoid double-counting adjustments for the same difference reflected in multiple elements of comparison. This requires an awareness of situations in which the influence of differences in one element of comparison may have an effect on an adjustment derived for a different element of comparison. For example, an adjustment made to the sale of a comparable property between two family members (i.e., so that the transaction is equivalent to an arm's-length sale) may include some or all of the influence of atypical financing terms negotiated between the parties and already be accounted for in a cash-equivalency adjustment.

PERSONAL INTERVIEWS

Personal interviews can reveal the opinions of knowledgeable individuals participating in the subject's market, e.g., trends in sale prices. Although data gathered through personal interviews is primary data, the opinions of market participants should not be used as the sole criterion for estimating adjustments or reconciling value ranges if an alternative method that relies on direct evidence of market transactions can be applied.

Transactional Adjustments

The transactional adjustments are generally applied in a specific sequence:

1. Real property rights conveyed
2. Financing terms
3. Conditions of sale
4. Expenditures made immediately after purchase
5. Market conditions

Real Property Rights Conveyed

When real property rights are sold, they may be the sole subject of the contract or the contract may include other rights, less than all of the real property rights, or even rights to another property or properties. Before a comparable sale property can be used in direct comparison analysis, the appraiser must first ensure that the sale price of the comparable property applies to property rights that are similar to those being appraised. This may require one or more adjustments to the price of the comparable property before the appraiser can compare specific differences in the physical real estate. For example, a particular marketplace might include both fee simple properties and those where tenure had been obtained through prepaid land leases with substantial remaining terms, e.g., 99 years. If a comparable sale involves a prepaid land lease, the appraiser will determine the terms of the lease, examining such factors as the remaining term, prepayment of rent, and rights to renew. An appraiser might interview the buyer and seller to ascertain how they considered the implications of the prepaid lease tenure and seek other supporting evidence before using the transaction for the appraisal of the fee simple interest in a subject property. It is possible that the transaction cannot be used for direct comparison purposes at all because there is no way to make an adjustment for the difference in rights. Some long-term land leases entail restrictions not found on fee simple properties; such limitations may also limit the transaction's use to a general market indicator or render the transaction unusable for direct market comparison because the real property rights conveyed are less than fee simple, and the appraiser cannot reliably quantify an adjustment.

Income-producing real estate is often subject to an existing lease or leases encumbering the title. By definition, the owner of real property that is subject to a lease no longer controls the complete bundle of rights, i.e., the fee simple estate. If the sale of a leased property is to be used as a comparable sale in the valuation of the fee simple interest in another property, the appraiser can only use the comparable sale if reasonable and supportable market adjustments for the differences in rights can be made. For example, consider the appraisal of the fee simple interest of real estate that is improved with an office building. A comparable improved property was fully leased at the time of sale, the leases were long-term, and the credit ratings of the tenants were good. To compare this leased fee interest to the fee simple interest in the subject property, the appraiser must determine if the contract rent of the comparable property was above, below, or equal to market rent. If the market rent for office space is $25 per square foot net and the average contract rent for the comparable property is $24 per square foot net, then the difference between market and contract rent is $1 per square foot.

The comparable property in question is improved with a 100,000 square foot office building. Analysis of market data indicates that an appropriate overall capitalization rate (R_o) is 10%, the vacancy and bad debt rate for the market in which the subject property is located is 5%, and a reasonable management expense is 4% of effective gross income.[4] The effective difference between the market rent of $25 per square foot and the contract rent of $24 per square foot is estimated by deducting the vacancy allowance (5%) and management expense (4%) from the actual difference between these rents ($1). This amount is then multiplied by the total area of the sale property to derive the annual rent loss for the remaining term of the lease:

$1.00 – 0.05 (5% vacancy and collection loss) = $0.95
$0.95 – 0.04 (4% management, rounded = $0.91
$0.91 × 100,000 sq. ft. = $91,000/year[5]

---

[4]   The appraiser should ensure that the operating expenses of the properties are comparable. The more services the landlord provides, the higher the rent the tenant usually pays, and often the property will have higher vacancy.

[5]   The calculations can also be made as follows:
    $1.00 × 0.95 × 0.96 = $0.91 (rounded)
    $0.91 × 100,000 sq. ft. = $91,000/year

Other expenses are not considered in this case because the leases are net leases and expenses do not constitute percentage charges against income. The annual rent loss is then discounted over the remaining term of the lease. Suppose that the lease on the office building in the example has 10 more years to run and market evidence supports an annual discount rate of 15%. Discounting the $91,000 annual loss in income over 10 years at 15% indicates an upward adjustment of $457,000 (rounded) to the comparable sale.[6] Note that these calculations are based on lease payments being made at the end of each period. If payments are instead made in advance, as is the market norm, the PV changes to $525,000.

PV of a payment of $91,000 per year for 10 years at a rate of j_1=15% = $456,700

Chapter 23 and 24 discusses present value calculations in more detail.

The calculation is based on the expectation that the $1.00 difference between market rent and contract rent remains constant over the 10-year period.

Calculating an adjustment for differences in real property rights is also necessary when just the leasehold interest is conveyed in a comparable sale. Although it is usually not recommended that the sale of a leasehold interest be compared to a fee simple interest, the limited availability of sales of directly comparable interests sometimes makes this necessary. For example, consider an office building that is owned and sold separately from its site, which is subject to a 99-year ground lease. The 100,000 square foot building, which is leased at market rent, sold for $7.5 million, or $75.00 per square foot. To develop an indication of the value of the fee simple interest in the total property, the value indication for the leased fee interest (the land) must be added to that of the leasehold interest (the building).

One method of developing a value indication for the leased fee interest (land only) is to capitalize the rent that accrues to the land. Suppose that the annual ground rent is $200,000, which is consistent with current market rents, and that market evidence supports a land capitalization rate of 8%. The value of the leased fee interest is $2,500,000 ($200,000 ÷ 0.08). Typically, the capitalization rate for the land will be lower than the rate for the building because the building incurs physical deterioration or obsolescence. In this case, an upward adjustment of $2.5 million for property rights conveyed would be shown in the direct comparison grid.

In comparing properties that are encumbered by long-term leases or are essentially fully leased with quality tenants, the appraiser must recognize that these leased properties may have significantly less risk than a competitive property that has shorter-term tenants at market rental rates. On the other hand, the reverse may be true in expanding markets. The ability to demand higher rental rates and the ready availability of tenants may favour the shorter-term lease strategy. The market position of a fully leased building is clearly different from that of a building with no leases at all. The buyer of a multi-tenant property that has a good cash flow in place may not be the same buyer who is interested in a property that is only one-third occupied. In the case of the property with two-thirds vacancy, the buyer may need a 20% down payment and another 20% to cover the shortfalls created by the lease-up period. It is

[6]   The calculator steps for the HP10BII financial calculator are shown in Appendix C at the end of end of the book

quite common for buyers of nearly empty buildings to have to invest capital for many years until the properties reach stabilized occupancy. The period of property lease-up to a stabilized level is easily reflected in the income capitalization approach but often needs to be adjusted for in the direct comparison approach.

Financing Terms

The transaction price of one property may differ from that of an identical property due to different financing arrangements. For example, the purchaser of a property may have assumed an existing mortgage at a favourable interest rate. In another case, a developer or seller may have arranged a buydown, paying cash to the lender so that a mortgage with a below-market interest rate could be offered. In both cases, the buyers probably paid higher prices for the properties to obtain below-market financing.

Other non-market financing arrangements include instalment sale contracts, or agreements-for-sale, in which the buyer pays periodic instalments to the seller and obtains legal title only after the contract is fulfilled, and wraparound loans or blended rate mortgages, which combine new financing with an existing mortgage in order to preserve the original mortgage's lower interest rate. These loans effectively afford a borrower/purchaser with below-market interest rates, which again must be accounted for. As well, below-market rates are sometimes extended to individuals who have substantial bank accounts and are therefore especially creditworthy.

In cash equivalency analysis, an appraiser investigates the sale prices of comparable properties that appear to have been sold with non-market financing to determine whether adjustments are needed to reflect typical market terms at the time of sale. Sales with non-market financing are compared to other sales transacted with market financing to determine whether an adjustment for cash equivalency can be made.

The typical definition of market value recognizes cash equivalent terms provided that the calculation of these terms reflects the market. Conditions of sale may reveal other, non-economic interests on the part of buyers or sellers. Confirmation of the intent of buyers and sellers is one way to verify a cash equivalency adjustment.

Cash equivalency calculations vary depending on the kind of financing arrangement that requires adjustment. Appraisers may calculate adjustments for atypical financing by analyzing sales and resales of the same property (e.g., a sale is negotiated at a price subject to the buyer securing new market financing and, while still under contract, the deal is renegotiated at a different face value with the seller providing terms), using paired data sets, or by discounting the cash flows (e.g., payments and balloons) created by the mortgage contract at market interest rates. If discounting is used, the appraiser should not assume that the buyer will always hold the property for the life of the mortgage. Market evidence often indicates otherwise. A mortgage is often discounted for a shorter term, but the balloon payment or outstanding balance must still be included. In addition, the benefit of a lower interest rate loan may not be as significant in future years as it is now. In other words, buyers who are able to arrange favourable financing may claim that the lower rate mortgage obtained through the sale will only benefit them until the mortgage interest rates come back down.

When an appraiser uses paired data analysis to derive a cash equivalency adjustment, the calculations for discounting and adjusting for atypical conditions of sale are often combined. In other words, the adjustments for financing and conditions of sale can be represented by a single figure.

For example, consider a house that sells for $250,000 with a down payment of $50,000 and a seller-financed $200,000 mortgage at an interest rate of 5.5% per annum, compounded semi-annually (j_2 = 5.5%). The mortgage is amortized over 25 years with a balloon payment due in 8 years. To determine the appropriate discount, the appraiser checks the market for sales of similarly financed notes and finds that in several instances similar $150,000, 5.5% notes had sold for near $125,000. The discount for these notes is calculated as follows:

($150,000 – $125,000) ÷ $150,000 = 0.1666 or 16.67%

The note that had a contract amount of $150,000 actually sold for $125,000. As a result, the seller of the property received the down payment plus $125,000 for the note, not $150,000 as it would imply on the surface. This discount may be applied to the $200,000 loan to arrive at an indicated cash equivalent value of the mortgage.

$200,000 – ($200,000 × 0.1666)	$166,667
Plus down payment	+ $50,000
Sale price adjusted for financing	$216,667

Calculating a cash equivalency adjustment by discounting cash flows can be accomplished in different ways. When a seller finances a mortgage at a below-market interest rate, the appraiser can estimate the present value of the mortgage by discounting the monthly mortgage payments at the market interest rate for the stated term of the mortgage.

For example, an appraiser might find a comparable sale of a one-unit residence that was sold for $220,000 with a down payment of $50,000 and a seller-financed mortgage of $170,000 for a 20-year term[7] at j_2 = 7.0% interest where the market-derived rate is assumed to be j_2= 9%. The cash equivalency adjustment is calculated as follows:

PV of monthly payments of $1,307.83 for 20 years at a market rate of j2 = 9%	
PV of mortgage = $147,081.13	
PV of mortgage, rounded	$147,100
Plus down payment	+ $50,000
Sale price adjusted for financing	$197,100

Calculator steps are shown in Appendix C.

---

[7]   Canadian mortgages are rarely fully amortized, instead typically having terms of five-years or less. Assuming a five-year term here, the market value of the mortgage increases to $157,524 and the adjusted sale price to $207,524. This is because the vendor is accepting a below-market interest rate for only five years, instead of 20 years of lost interest. This is also illustrated in the calculations in Appendix C

Figure 14.1: Mortgage Balance Calculations

Stated sale price	$250,000
Down payment	$50,000
Mortgage loan amount	$200,000
Mortgage loan interest rate	$j_2 = 5.5\%$
Monthly payments	
Amortization period	25 years
Mortgage term	8 years
Market interest rate	$j_2 = 7\%$

The present value of the contract payment of $1,220.79 and the outstanding balance owing at the end of the 8-year term of $162,285.85 discounted at a market rate of j_2=7% is $183,461.71. The amount the seller theoretically received, i.e., the present value of the mortgage plus the present value of the equity (down payment) is $233,460.71. Calculator steps are shown in Appendix C.

Discounting cash flows to calculate a cash equivalency adjustment may also take into account the expectation of a balloon payment. The following example incorporates the fact that the mortgagor (borrower) holds the mortgage for only eight years.[8] In the following example, the present value of the mortgage is computed as the sum of two components as shown in Figure 14.1:

1. The present value of the mortgage payments at the market interest rate for the expected life of the mortgage

2. The present value of the future mortgage balance at the market interest rate

Transactions involving mortgage assumptions can be adjusted to cash equivalency with the same method applied to seller-financed transactions. Other atypical mortgage terms include payments of interest only, followed by payments that include the repayment of the principal. This type of mortgage can also be adjusted to its cash equivalent value using the same adjustment procedure described here.

An appraiser must rigorously test financing adjustments derived from precise, mathematical calculations for analyzing cash equivalency against market evidence. Strict mathematical calculations may not reflect market behaviour. Market evidence must support whatever adjustment is made. If the cash discount indicated by the calculations is not recognized by buyers and sellers, the adjustment is not justified.

Appraisers must make sure that cash equivalency adjustments reflect market perceptions. It is necessary for the appraiser to talk with the buyers and sellers to determine if the financing terms affect value. In selecting an appropriate adjustment

---

[8]   The average mortgage life for loans of different types of properties can be ascertained from sales data on loans that were paid off or refinanced rather than assumed by a buyer. The buyer may only see a few years' benefit in favourable interest rates before the market mortgage interest rates fall and the benefit of the favourable financing disappears because others in the market can then obtain the favourable rate.

for use in cash equivalency analysis, the appraiser should give greater emphasis to the market-derived adjustment than to one derived by calculation.

Appraisers should also recognize that in some situations, financing and conditions of sale are interdependent, and they should be careful not to "double count" the influence of these factors when making quantitative adjustments.

Conditions of Sale

The definition of market value used in most assignments requires "typical motivations of buyers and sellers" where there is no duress on either party to consummate the sale. An adjustment for conditions of sale usually reflects the motivation of either a buyer or a seller who is under duress to complete the transaction. In many situations, the conditions of sale significantly affect transaction prices. These atypically motivated sales are not considered arm's-length transactions. For example, a developer may pay more than market value for lots needed in a site assemblage because of the plottage value expected to result from the greater utility of the larger site. A sale may be transacted at a below-market price if the seller needs cash in a hurry. A financial, business, or family relationship between the parties to a sale may also affect the price of property. Interlocking corporate entities may record a sale at a non-market price to serve their business interests. One member of a family may sell a property to another at a reduced price, or a buyer may pay a higher price for a property because it was built by his or her ancestors.

When an appraiser detects non-market conditions of sale in a transaction, the sale can be used as a comparable sale but only with care. The appraiser must thoroughly research the circumstances of the sale before an adjustment is made, and the appraiser must also adequately disclose the conditions in the appraisal. Any adjustment should be well supported with data. If the adjustment cannot be supported, the appraiser will diminish the weight given to it, or discard it.

Although conditions of sale are often perceived as applying only to sales that are not arm's-length transactions, some arm's-length sales may reflect atypical motivations or sale conditions due to unusual tax considerations, lack of exposure on the open market, or the complexity of expropriation proceedings. If the sales used in the direct comparison approach reflect unusual situations, the appraiser should make an appropriate adjustment (supported by market evidence) for motivation or conditions of sale. Again, the appraisal report should explain the circumstances of the sale.

In some markets with limited data, the appraiser cannot discard any sales and must use comparable sales with unusual conditions of sale; the intended use of the appraisal becomes an important consideration in this situation. Appraisers should always ask if they are giving the client the value opinion that reflects the intended use. As an example, suppose the appraiser finds that all the comparable sales were reported to have sold with the sellers under duress to sell because of high foreclosures; too much competition or a poorly performing market could cause a similar situation. The client, a lender, asked the appraiser to value the property as collateral. If the appraiser discards the sales made under duress and uses the cost approach as the only indication of value, the analysis may ignore the possibility that the client would have to sell the subject property in the current depressed market if the borrower defaults.

CONCESSIONS

Often a seller may give some sort of financial incentive to induce a buyer to make an offer on the seller's property rather than on a competitor's property. Some appraisers will identify this sort of financial "concession" offered by the seller as an adjustment to be made under the "conditions of sale" element of comparison, but other appraisers will label concessions as "financing terms." The label itself is less important than recognizing the effect of concessions on the sale price of a comparable sale, compensating for that effect, and not double counting the effect of the concession.

A concession is a financial payment, special benefit, or non-realty item included in the sale contract or rental agreement as an incentive to the sale or lease. Concessions occur when the seller or lessor agrees to pay an inducement or to give some credit or property to a buyer or lessee, who agrees to pay a higher price than the seller or lessor would normally pay in return for the inducement or credit. Concessions usually result in artificially inflated sale prices or lease rates. Often concessions allow financing that would otherwise not be possible. Concessions may be disclosed as part of the sale or lease, but often they are not. Examples include the following items:

- A sale that includes personal property items such as automobiles, motorcycles, cruise tickets, or furnishings.
- A sale in which the seller contributes to the buyer's portion of the closing costs. This lowers the amount of money a buyer needs at closing. The seller usually raises the selling price by the amount of the extra costs.
- A transaction in which the seller of the real property purchases a piece of personal property from the buyer at an inflated price. For example, the buyer has a used car worth $2,000, but the seller buys it for $20,000 (as part of the real property transaction), in effect giving the buyer a down payment. The price (but not the value) of the real property is increased by $18,000.
- A sale in which the seller subsidizes the buyer's mortgage, e.g., buys down the interest rate, pays the buyer's mortgage payments for a stated number of months, or provides some other arrangement. If the interest rate of the new loan is lower, some lenders will underwrite the loan at the discounted rate, which allows the buyer to take out a larger loan.
- A seller-financed sale in which the seller takes back a mortgage at a below-market rate, which will give the buyer lower payments unless the seller raises the sale price to compensate.
- The payment by the vendor of all or a part of the value added tax, i.e., GST or HST
- A free month's rent as part of a one-year apartment lease.
- A new lease in which the landlord pays the tenant's moving costs.
- Points paid by the seller.*
- Personal property, furniture, fixtures, and equipment (FF&E), or other non-realty items included in the sale.
- Payment of past due taxes. Delinquent taxes can impact not only the sale price due to added payments but can also be a motivating factor in the sale.

Verification is key to assessing the impact of concessions. Appraisers should adjust for these items because concessions are usually not in compliance with commonly used definitions of *market value*.

*Points: a percentage of the loan amount that a lender charges a borrower for making a loan; may represent a payment for services rendered in issuing a loan or additional interest to the lender payable in advance; also called *loan fee* or *bonus*.
Source: Appraisal Institute, *The Dictionary of Real Estate Appraisal*, 5th ed. (Chicago: Appraisal Institute, 2010).

The appraiser may be able to estimate an adjustment through paired sales analysis. For example, a comparable sale might entail a new housing unit on which the vendor (a developer) paid the net GST or HST as a sales incentive; an appraiser can compare that transaction to typical sales of similar properties in the market where the purchaser paid the net GST, and develop an indication of the premium paid by the buyer under the extraordinary motivation arising from the tax "saving".

Making direct comparisons is more difficult when the motivations of market participants are atypical. If the buyer is related to the seller, the sale price paid may not reflect the price that would be paid on the open market. Likewise, if a seller needs the proceeds of the sale quickly to avoid bankruptcy, a shrewd buyer may be able to purchase the property for less than what it would bring if it were on the market for a reasonable exposure time, allowing more potential buyers to participate in negotiations.

Interviewing the participants involved in the transaction may provide an indication of the magnitude of the adjustment, but sometimes the direction of an adjustment for conditions of sale may be all that can be determined. In the case of a distressed seller, an upward adjustment would probably be necessary to reflect the value the seller is not recapturing by accepting an expedient offer. The direction of a conditions of sale adjustment in transactions involving related parties may be more difficult to determine. Parents may accept a below-market price for a property to help their children pay for their first home, which would necessitate an upward adjustment if that sale were used as a comparable sale. Alternatively, younger members of a family may offer to purchase a property belonging to an older relative at a price higher than the market level so that they can keep the property in the family, which would suggest a downward adjustment is necessary. If the details of the transaction are too difficult to verify, an appraiser might not be able to develop an adjustment for conditions of sale.

Expenditures Made Immediately After Purchase

A knowledgeable buyer considers expenditures that will have to be made upon purchase of a property because these costs affect the price the buyer agrees to pay. Such expenditures may include the following:

- Costs to cure deferred maintenance
- Costs to demolish and remove any portion of the improvements
- Costs to petition for a zoning change
- Costs to remediate environmental contamination

These costs are often quantified in price negotiations and can be discovered through verification of transaction data. The relevant figure is not the actual cost that was incurred but the cost that was anticipated by both the buyer and seller.

Generally an adjustment for expenditures made immediately after purchase is simple to quantify when transaction data is being verified with the market participants. For example, consider a 150,000 square foot warehouse that is comparable to the property being appraised and was recently sold for $850,000. The new owner-occupant expected to spend $65,000 to install an additional door and loading dock, which was a market-driven decision. In an interview with the new owner of the comparable property, the appraiser learns that the demolition and new construction actually cost $105,000. The value indication for that comparable property would be

$915,000 ($850,000 + $65,000) rather than $955,000 ($850,000 + $105,000) because the $65,000 expenditure anticipated by the buyer was deducted from the price the property would command in the market if no expenditures were necessary. If the actual cost of the renovation had been $40,000, the buyer would have enjoyed a $25,000 savings ($65,000 - $40,000) from the expected cost, but those savings would not be reflected in the price the buyer was willing to pay, which is already an established fact.

Adjustments for deferred maintenance can be handled similarly, but the appraiser should make sure that the buyer and seller were aware of any items needing immediate repair. If the seller was not required to disclose that the roof of the warehouse had a leak and needed repairs, the buyer may not have anticipated those expenditures after the purchase, and there would be no adjustment to the recorded sale price for that item of deferred maintenance. Other expenses immediately after purchase that a buyer may need to budget for include the following:

- Cost of obtaining entitlements, e.g., development approvals, such as rezoning or approvals for utility, servicing, or road construction
- Demolition and removal costs
- Environmental remediation costs
- Large capital improvements needed at the time of sale

In direct comparison analysis, costs incurred by the new owners of comparable properties are reflected as positive adjustments to the sale prices of those properties. If the subject property requires some expenditure immediately after the purchase to reach its full utility, the adjustment amount is subtracted from the sale prices of all comparable sales that do not require a similar expenditure to adjust those transactions for differences from the subject property.

An adjustment for expenditures made immediately after purchase is distinct from an adjustment for the physical condition of a property. The expenditures adjustment is included among the transactional adjustments because it reflects those items that a buyer would have considered part of the price at the time of the sale. For example, a buyer bought a property that included a 6.75 acre site improved with a 122,000 square foot industrial building with many environmental problems. The buyer told the appraiser the cost of removing the environmental problems was $750,000. The sale price of the property was only $225,000. The appraiser is considering using this as a comparable land sale, but the buyer actually has $975,000 ($750,000 + $225,000) invested in the property, not just the $225,000 sale price. In the sequence of adjustments, an adjustment for expenditures made immediately after purchase is shown above the market conditions line, which means the market conditions adjustment would be made on the $975,000 price, not the $225,000 price.

Another application of this adjustment is for items that would affect the sale price but not necessarily the rental income. For example, the subject property is a 55,000 square foot three-storey office building that has a new roof covering and three new HVAC units. The cost of these items is $252,000. A nearly identical property just sold for $5 million, but this property needed a new roof covering and three new HVAC units. The rental rates of both buildings are the same, but the maintenance expense

for the comparable property is much higher. The adjustment for the deferred maintenance items found in the comparable property could be made on the condition line of
an adjustment grid or on the expenditures made immediately after purchase line. An
adjustment made on the condition line would affect the capitalization rate that might
be extracted from this sale. In other words, the capitalization rate would be a reflection of a sale with good income levels but deferred maintenance. If this adjustment
is made prior to extracting the capitalization rate, the result would be an "apples to
apples" comparison rather than the skewed amount that would result if the capitalization rate were extracted from a sale with the needed repairs.

Market Conditions

Comparable sales that occurred under market conditions different from those applicable to the subject on the effective date of value require adjustment for any differences
that affect their values. An appraiser makes an adjustment for market conditions if
general property values have increased or decreased since the transaction dates.

   Although the adjustment for market conditions is often referred to as a "time"
adjustment, time is not the cause of the adjustment. Market conditions that change
over time create the need for an adjustment, not time itself. In other words, increases
or decreases in property values in the market are the cause of the adjustment and
time is the measure of the adjustment. If market conditions have not changed, no
adjustment is required even though considerable time may have elapsed.

   Changes in market conditions may result from changes in income tax laws,
building moratoriums, and fluctuations in supply and demand. Sometimes several
economic factors work in concert to cause a change in market conditions. A recession tends to deflate all real estate prices, but specific property types or sub-markets
may be affected differently. A decline in demand may affect only one category
of real estate. If the demand for a specific type of property falls during a period of
inflation, sales transacted during that period may not provide a reliable indication
of the value of a similar property in a different period unless the appraiser makes
appropriate adjustments. In a depressed economy, recent sales are often difficult to
find. Older sales, occurring prior to the onset of the depressed economy, should be
used with great caution because they may not reflect the problems associated with
the depressed economy. In some instances when current sales do not exist, upward or
downward shifts in rent and rent terms may help the appraiser ascertain the direction
of market activity.

   Appraisers must also recognize that the sale of a property may be negotiated
months or even years before its final disposition. The buyer and the seller agree as
of the contract date, but the agreement does not become effective until the closing
date, often with changes to the agreement in the interim. An adjustment for changes
in market conditions between the date the contract is signed and the effective date
of value may be appropriate. Also, sometimes appraisers are called on to develop an
opinion of retrospective or prospective value, which requires a close study of changes
in market conditions.[9]

---

[9]   For guidance on the development of retrospective and prospective value opinions, see CUSPAP 6.25, 7.6. and the
      related Practice Notes

An appraiser usually measures an adjustment for changes in market conditions as a percentage of previous prices. While change is continuous, it is typically measured and quoted in discrete intervals. If the physical and economic characteristics of a property remain unchanged, analyzing two or more sales of the same property over a period of time will indicate the percentage of price change. In other words, an appraiser can measure the difference in sale prices of the same or similar properties over time to extract the rate of change, which can be used as the basis for adjustment in the direct comparison analysis. An appraiser should always attempt to examine several sets of sales to arrive at an appropriate adjustment. An adjustment supported by just one set of sales may be unreliable.

Sales and resales of the same properties often provide a good indication of the change in market conditions over time. If data on resales is unavailable, an appraiser can use sales of similar properties in the same market. In either case, an appraiser must examine the sale transactions very carefully. Analysis of sale and resale data from the same property may indicate that non-market conditions were involved in the transactions. Consider a 10,000 square foot strip shopping centre that sold five years ago for $600,000 and then sold again recently for $675,000. The indicated average annual appreciation of the shopping centre would be 2.5% ([($675,000 - $600,000) ÷ $600,000] ÷ 5 years).

In the same market area, a 12,000 square foot shopping centre with similar characteristics sold for $650,000 five years ago, and another 12,000 square foot property sold last year for $730,000. The average annual change per unit for those comparable properties is 3.08% per year ([($730,000 - $650,000) ÷ $650,000] ÷ 4 years). The results of additional calculations made using sale and resale data and paired sales of comparable properties can be reconciled to support the estimated market conditions adjustment. The transactions used in these additional calculations should be similar in terms of markets, land-to-building value ratios, and other elements of comparability.

Appraisers must remember that supply and demand are dynamic forces, and periods of decline are just as probable as periods of growth in real estate markets. For example, in the early 1990s many property markets saw falling prices, and negative market conditions adjustments were needed in direct comparison analysis involving sales data from that period of market decline. Also, in volatile markets, an adjustment for market conditions may be needed to account for periods of time in which sale prices go up and down. For example, an appraiser studying mid-rise office building sales in a metropolitan market finds that stable prices between 2003 and 2005 were followed by a decline in 2006 and a quick rebound to previous levels in 2007 followed by another period of stability. Comparable sales that occurred between 2005 and 2007 will require scrutiny because of the changing market conditions during that period, whereas comparable sales occurring before and after the temporary dip in the market may not require a market conditions adjustment at all.

The appreciation or depreciation of average sale prices in a market does not necessarily follow a linear pattern. Changes in sale price can also be irregular or stepped, or they can increase or decrease on a compounded basis. Statistical tools such as regression analysis and extrapolation are useful in determining precise mathematical relationships. However, any statistical model generated from the available data must reflect market thinking to be useful in the adjustment process.

Sorting and plotting sale and resale or paired sales data on a graph is another way to determine patterns of change. The reliability of such analyses is affected by the number of market transactions studied. With sufficient data, unit prices can be graphed over time to indicate the trend in the market. Rents can also be plotted on scatter diagrams to show differences over time (see Figure 14.2).

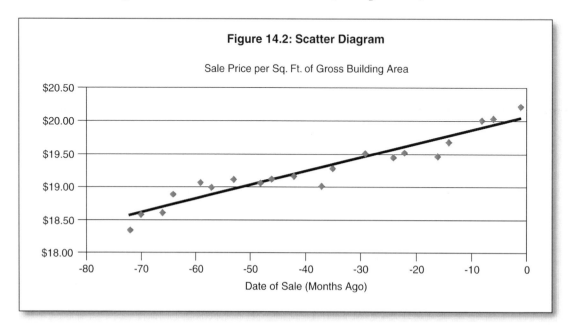

Figure 14.2: Scatter Diagram

If sales of comparable properties are not available, other evidence of shifting market conditions may include changes in the following:

- The ratio between sale prices and listing prices or between lease contracts and lease offering rates
- Exposure time
- Listing prices
- Trends in rents
- The number of offers a seller receives and the frequency of backup offers
- The proportion of accepted offers that actually close
- The number of foreclosures
- The number of available properties
- The number of building permits issued and their aggregate value
- Terms of available institutional financing
- Use of seller financing
- Changing market demographic patterns
- Demolition and new construction

Property Adjustments

Unlike the transactional adjustments, the appraiser does not need to apply property adjustments in a specific sequence. The typical property adjustments include the following items:

- Location
- Physical characteristics
- Economic characteristics
- Use/zoning
- Non-realty components of value

Location

An adjustment for location within a market area may be required when the locational characteristics of a comparable property are different from those of the subject property. Excessive locational differences may disqualify a property from use as a comparable sale.

Most comparable properties in the same market area have similar locational characteristics, but variations may exist within that area of analysis. Consider, for example, the difference between a residential property with a pleasant view of a park and one located two blocks away with a less attractive view. An appraiser may also need to make an adjustment for location to reflect the difference in demand for various office suites within a single building, the retail advantage of a corner location, the privacy of the end unit in a residential condominium project, or the value contribution of an ocean view. The comparison can also be shown with statistical and graphical analysis. For example, consider the 21 industrial sales shown in Figure 14.3 as a scatter plot and in Figure 14.4 as a set of linear regression lines sorted by location within the metropolitan area. The regression lines in Figure 14.4 are more descriptive and clearly show trends in sale price over time for each of the four locations. The vertical intercepts along the regression lines also illustrate differences in sale price attributable to locational differences that can be used to support adjustments for location.

As another example of the analysis of locational differences, consider the ordered array of data in Table 14.1, which illustrates a definite value trend difference between the interior and corner locations of comparable convenience stores in a market. The trend analysis shows the market reacting differently than expected. The common perception is that corner locations are superior to interior locations, but the table shows otherwise and the appraiser must investigate why the data contradicts conventional wisdom. In this case, intersection congestion seems to be restricting access to corner locations. The appraised property has an interior location, so comparable sales with corner locations would require upward adjustments. Comparable sales with interior locations would require no location adjustment.

To take the analysis further, suppose the unit sale prices in Table 14.1 are also affected by other elements of comparison that could not be measured by quantitative analysis. Trend analysis does not measure those differences, but does reflect discernible value trends for different elements. The same comparable sales are tested

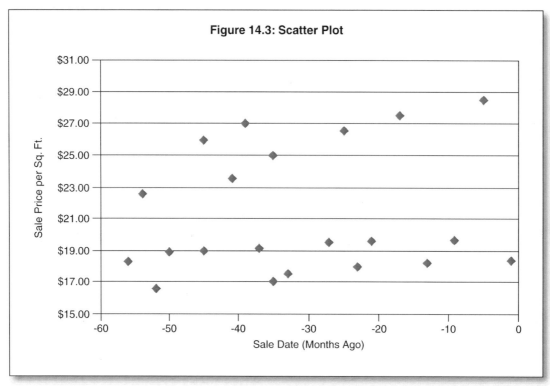

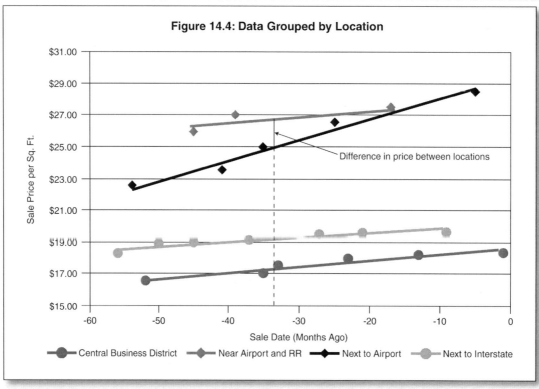

Table 14.1: Ranking Analysis of Location

Sale No.	Location	
	Interior	Corner
1	$15.00	
2		$10.00
3	$13.00	
4	$14.00	
5		$12.00
6		$11.00
7		$12.50
8	$13.00	
Mean:	$13.75	$11.38
Subject:	Interior	
Comparison:	Similar	Inferior

for value differences attributable to lot size in Table 14.2. The properties with 10,000 to 20,000 square feet require downward adjustment to the subject property, while the properties with 41,000 to 43,000 square feet require upward adjustment. The sales with 25,000 to 30,000 square feet require no adjustment. A linear regression plot (Figure 14.5) shows the market trend. The process can then be continued to test and apply additional adjustments for other physical, economic, and legal elements of comparison.

Physical Characteristics

If the physical characteristics of a comparable property and the subject property differ, each of the differences may require comparison and adjustment. Physical differences include differences in size, soils, site access, topography, quality of construction, architectural style, building materials, age, condition, functional utility, attractiveness, amenities, and other characteristics.

Table 14.2: Trend Analysis of Lot Size

Sale No.	Size		
	10,000–20,000 sq. ft.	25,000–30,000 sq. ft.	41,000–43,000 sq. ft.
1	$15.00		
2			$10.00
3	$13.00		
4	$14.00		
5		$12.00	
6			$11.00
7		$12.50	
8		$13.00	
Mean:	$14.00	$12.50	$10.50
Subject:		26,000 sq. ft.	
Relative comparison:	Superior	Similar	Inferior

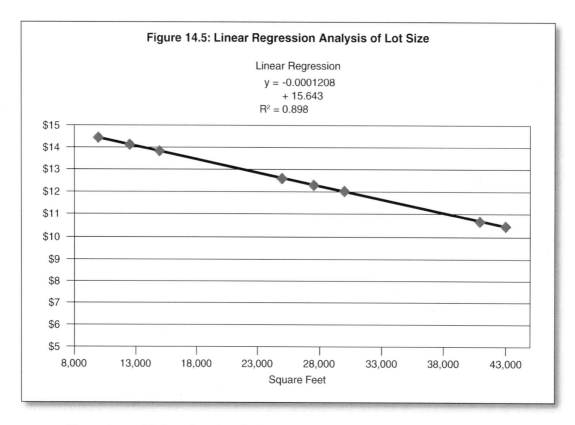

Figure 14.5: Linear Regression Analysis of Lot Size

Linear Regression
$y = -0.0001208 + 15.643$
$R^2 = 0.898$

The value added or lost by the presence or absence of an item in a comparable property may not equal the cost of installing or removing the item. The market dictates the value contribution of individual components to the value of the whole. Buyers may be unwilling to pay a higher sale price that includes the extra cost of adding an amenity. Conversely, the addition of an amenity sometimes adds more value to a property than its cost. In other cases, there may be no adjustment to value for the existence or absence of an item. For example, an extra bathroom in an apartment unit may contribute an additional $15 per month to market rent, and this amount could be capitalized to reflect the value attributable to the extra bathroom and an appropriate adjustment to comparable sales without an extra bathroom. The cost of adding a new bathroom to an existing apartment unit could be quite different.

Table 14.3. Comparable Apartment Properties

Comparable Property	One-Bedroom Unit	Two-Bedroom Unit	Incremental Rent for Second Bedroom
A	$650	$700	$50
B	$675	$728	$53
C	$700	$752	$52
D	$710	$760	$50
E	$714	$766	$52
F	$720	$771	$51

As an additional example, consider an apartment complex with both one-bedroom and two-bedroom units. Table 14.3 shows average monthly rents for competitive apartment properties. If the apartment buildings are otherwise comparable, the incremental rent attributable to a second bedroom could be reconciled at approximately $51 per month. Given a 5% annual vacancy and collection loss, operating expenses of 35% of rent collections, and a market-derived overall capitalization rate of 9% per year, the value of a second bedroom can be calculated as follows:

Rent per month	$51
Gross income per year ($51 × $12)	$612
Less 5% vacancy and collection loss	– $31
Subtotal	$581
Less operating expenses (35%)	– $203
Annual income attributable to second bedroom	$378
Capitalized @ 9%	$4,200

Based on this analysis, an adjustment could be applied to sales of comparable properties with unit mixes that differ from the subject property. Note that an extra bedroom also increases the overall size of a unit. Appraisers often adjust for the size of the unit, which may be all that is needed to compensate for the extra bedroom. Adjusting for both size and configuration may be appropriate, but adjusting for the size of the unit and then also for the extra area included in an extra room would likely be double counting the influence of the larger unit.

Economic Characteristics

Economic characteristics include all the attributes of a property that directly affect its income. An appraiser usually applies this element of comparison to income-producing properties. Characteristics that affect a property's income include operating expenses, quality of management, tenant mix, rent concessions, lease terms, lease expiration dates, renewal options, and lease provisions such as expense recovery clauses. Appraisers must take care not to attribute differences in real property rights conveyed or changes in market conditions to different economic characteristics.

Paired data analysis may provide the only persuasive support for adjustments for differences in the attributes of a property that affect its income such as operating expenses, management quality, tenant mix, rent concessions, and other characteristics. Some of these characteristics may already be reflected in the adjustment for location. For example, a warehouse in a municipality with low property tax rates may have a higher value than a comparable warehouse in a neighbouring community with higher tax rates, but the difference in value attributable to the tax rates will likely already be reflected in the adjustment for location.

Some appraisers analyze net operating income per unit to account for differences in economic characteristics, but the technique is not widely used because it essentially duplicates the techniques used in direct capitalization, which is discussed in Chapter 22. The ratio of the subject property's net operating income to a comparable property's net operating income is calculated and applied to the unit price of the comparable property to calculate a value indication for the subject property. For example, the subject property has net operating income of $100,000 and a comparable property has net operating income of $125,000. The comparable property's unit price of $30 per square foot is multiplied by the net operating income ratio of 0.8 ($100,000 ÷ $125,000), which results in a value indication of $24 per square foot. An appraiser can also calculate income ratios for other comparable properties; those results are reconciled into an indication of a unit price for the subject property.

Critics of net income multiplier analysis point out that the algebraic manipulation of sales and income data ultimately repeats the calculations used in direct capitalization. So when an appraiser uses net income multiplier analysis in the direct comparison approach and direct capitalization in the income capitalization approach, potential errors are duplicated in two of the three approaches to value and these errors will be hard to identify in the final reconciliation of the value indications.[10]

Given the problems associated with net income multiplier analysis and the possibility of double-counting for value influences reflected in other elements of comparison, appraisers must take great care in estimating and supporting adjustments for economic characteristics.

Use/Zoning

To qualify as comparable properties, the highest and best use of the properties should be very similar, if not the same, as that of the subject property. If comparables sales are scarce, an appraiser may need to make an adjustment to the sale prices of comparable properties with a different current use or highest and best use.

In the valuation of vacant land, zoning is one of the primary determinants of the highest and best use of the property because it serves as the test of legal permissibility. Thus, zoning or the reasonable probability of a zoning change is typically a primary criterion in the selection of market data. When comparable properties with the same zoning as the subject are lacking or scarce, parcels with slightly different zoning but a highest and best use similar to that of the subject may be used as comparable sales. An appraiser may have to adjust these sales for differences in utility if the market indicates that this is appropriate. On the other hand, a difference in the uses permitted under two zoning classifications does not necessarily require an adjustment if the parcels have the same use.

Sometimes differences in sale prices reduced to compatible units such as price of land per square foot of permissible building area can be attributed to the different zoning classification requirements. For example, because of differences in parking requirements or landscaping requirements, site development costs for two parcels under different zoning classifications may differ even if the parcels have the same highest and best use. Potential buyers will consider these dissimilarities and therefore they should be considered by the appraiser. Other legal considerations may include environmental requirements, access, easements, and flood zones.

Although it may be impossible to support a quantitative adjustment for different highest and best uses of otherwise comparable sites, an appraiser can use market data to support qualitative analysis of different intensities of use allowed by zoning.

---

[10] For further discussion of the applicability and limitations of net operating income multiplier analysis, see Mark W. Galleshaw, "Appropriate Uses of Economic Characteristics in the Sales Comparison Approach," *The Appraisal Journal* (January 1992): 91-98, the letters to the editor in the July 1992 issue of *The Appraisal Journal;* and Mark Rattermann, "Considerations in Gross Rent Multiplier Analysis," *The Appraisal Journal* (Summer 2006): 226-231.

Table 14.4: Recent Land Sales

Sale	Sale Price	Price per Sq. Ft.	Size (Sq. Ft.)	Maximum FSR	Maximum Building Area	Price per Sq. Ft. Building Area
A	$738,000	$22.00	33,541	1.00	33,541	$22.00
B	$450,000	$10.87	41,382	0.50	20,691	$21.75
C	$690,000	$11.31	60,984	0.50	30,492	$22.63
D	$2,100,000	$20.96	100,188	1.00	100,188	$20.96
E	$2,810,000	$19.97	140,699	1.00	140,699	$19.97
Subject			130,680	0.77	100,000	
Standard deviation:		5.46473				1.025757581

Table 14.5: Trend Analysis for Office Building

Sale	Size 20,691–30,492 sq. ft.	100,188 sq. ft.	140,699 sq. ft.
A	$22.00		
B	$21.75		
C	$22.63		
D		$20.96	
E			$19.97
Mean:	$22.13	$20.96	$19.97
Subject:		100,000 sq. ft.	
Comparison:	Superior	Similar	Inferior

For example, consider a 100,000 square foot office building on a 3.0 acre site where the current zoning allows for a maximum floor space ratio (FSR) of 0.50. The existing improvements predate a zoning change. The zoning regulations allow for improvements of equal size to be built if the existing improvements are razed or destroyed. Most of the comparable properties are in areas zoned for a maximum FSR of 1.0. A quantitative adjustment may be difficult to calculate using paired data analysis, but if a strong relationship between the zoning and sale price can be determined, the appraiser can still analyze the comparable sales. The recent land sales in the subject's market area listed in Table 14.4 are already adjusted for other elements of comparison.

The price per square foot of building area has a smaller standard deviation (1.03) than the price per square foot of site area (5.47). The market evidence supports use of the price per square foot of building area as the unit of comparison. The primary remaining difference is size. The trend analysis shown in Table 14.5 illustrates a value difference attributable to size. The ranking analysis supports a value estimate similar to the value of Sale D, or $20.96 per square foot of buildable area.

Non-Realty Components of Value

Non-realty components of value include personal property, business concerns, and other items that do not constitute real property but are included in either the sale price of the comparable or the ownership interest in the subject property. These components should be analyzed separately from the realty.[11] Furniture, fixtures, and equipment in a hotel or restaurant are typical examples of personal property.

---

[11] Appraisal Standard Rule 6.2.22 and Comment 7.23 requires that an appraiser must analyze the effect on value of any personal property, including tangible or intangible items that are not real property but that are included in the appraisal. This analysis may be omitted when not relevant to the assignment; otherwise competence in personal property appraisal is required when it is necessary to allocate the overall value.

In appraisals of properties in which the business operation is essential to the use of the realty, the appraiser must analyze the value of the non-realty component. In most cases the economic lives, associated investment risks, rate of return criteria, and collateral security for such non-realty components differ from those of the realty. In such situations, the non-realty components should be removed at the start of the adjustment analysis, so that the appraiser can work with a net purchase price of the real property alone.

If the value of the non-realty component cannot be separated from the value of the property as a whole, the appraiser should make clear that the value indication using the direct comparison approach reflects both the value of the real property and the value of the business operation.

Properties such as hotels and timeshare condominiums, which have high expense ratios attributable to the business operation, may include a significant business enterprise value component.

CHAPTER 15

APPLICATIONS OF THE DIRECT COMPARISON APPROACH

Chapters 13 and 14 described the basic theory and procedures of the direct comparison approach and introduced a number of specific techniques. This chapter illustrates the most commonly used techniques of direct comparison in the examples presented. An appraiser may employ both quantitative and qualitative techniques in the application of the direct comparison approach. If adjustments can be derived by quantitative techniques, they are generally applied first. Differences in specific elements of comparison that elude precise mathematical adjustment are subsequently considered in qualitative analysis. The two methodologies are complementary and are often used in combination.

An appraiser may also use other techniques to identify and estimate adjustments. The appraiser should consider all applicable techniques to determine which ones are most appropriate to the appraisal. Generally, the more complex the property being appraised, the greater the number of techniques that may be applied to its valuation.

OFFICE BUILDING EXAMPLE

The property being appraised is the leased fee interest in a five-year old, multi-tenant office building with 36,000 square feet of gross building area (GBA) and 31,800 square feet of rentable area (88% of GBA). Its occupancy rate is 90%, which is considered stable in the subject market area. The amount of space occupied by individual tenants ranges from 2,500 square feet to 7,000 square feet. The building is of average construction quality and is in average condition. The ratio of rentable area to gross building area is low in comparison to the average for the subject market area, which is approximately 93%. The site is appropriately landscaped. The open-space parking provided is both adequate and in compliance with the zoning code. The location, which may also be considered average, is an interior site accessed from a major arterial highway.

Current base rents range from $12.00 to $13.00 per square foot of rentable area. Rent for the overall building averages $12.60 per square foot and the quality of the tenants is good. With the exception of telephone service, the landlord pays all expenses, including janitorial and electrical. Operating expenses are typical for the market. The leases have three- and four-year terms. They contain an option to renew for three more years at the then-current market rent. All leases are less than 18 months old, and the rents and terms they specify are standard for the current market. Leasehold positions in the subject property do not have any particular advantage. The leased fee interest in the property is the interest to be appraised.

Five comparable sales are used in the analysis. All the comparable properties are mid-rise, multi-tenant office properties located in the subject's market area, and all were financed at market rates with conventional loan-to-value ratios. All the transactions involved the sale of a leased fee interest. The unit of comparison employed in this analysis is price per square foot of rentable area. The five comparable sales are described below (as of the date of sale), and the analysis is summarized in Table 15.1.

- Sale A was sold nine months ago for $2,930,000. The improvements are six years old and in average condition. The building contains 40,000 square feet of gross building area and 37,600 square feet of rentable area (94% of GBA). The indicated price per square foot of rentable area is $77.93. Average rent is $12.80 per square foot of rentable area. The landlord pays all expenses, and occupancy is 87%. The rents, lease terms, and expenses of the property are at market terms. The site is located at the intersection of a major arterial highway and a collector road. Parking is adequate. The ratio of parking spaces to rentable area in Sale A is approximately the same as that of the subject.

- Sale B was sold four months ago for $2,120,000. The building is four years old and contains 32,000 square feet of gross building area and 29,700 square feet of rentable area (93% of GBA). Its unit price is calculated to be $71.38 per square foot of rentable area. Site improvements are average, and the ratio of parking area to rentable area is similar to that of the subject property. The property is in average condition. The leases provide tenants with full services. Occupancy is 85% and the average base rent is $11.80 per square foot of rentable area, which is slightly below the market rate. The lengths of the leases are considered to be at market terms. However, the total expenses for the building are slightly higher than is typical for the market because two tenants who occupy 15% of the total space use excessive electricity. They do not pay additional rent to compensate for the extra expense. The property is located on an interior site accessed from a collector street. Parking is adequate.

- Sale C was sold five months ago for $2,450,000. The building contains 35,000 square feet of gross building area and 32,200 square feet of rentable area (92% of GBA). Its unit price is $76.09 per square foot of rentable area. The improvements were constructed five years ago and are in average condition. Rent averages $12.60 per square foot of rentable area. All tenant services are

Table 15.1: Market Data Grid

	Subject Property	Sale A	Sale B	Sale C	Sale D	Sale E
Sale price/	—	$2,930,000	$2,120,000	$2,450,000	$2,160,000	$2,470,000
Unit price (rentable area)		$77.93	$71.38	$76.09	$80.90	$73.08
Age	5 years	6 years	4 years	5 years	6 years	4 years
Gross building area	36,000	40,000	32,000	35,000	30,000	38,000
Rentable area	31,800	37,600	29,700	32,200	26,700	33,800
Rental area ratio	88%	94%	93%	92%	89%	89%
Occupancy rate	90%	87%	85%	90%	95%	90%
Elements of comparison						
Property interest conveyed	Leased fee	Leased fee —	Leased fee —	Leased fee —	Leased fee —	Leased fee —
Financing terms	Conventional	Conventional —	Conventional —	Conventional —	Conventional —	Conventional —
Conditions of sale	Arm's-length sale	Arm's-length sale —	Arm's-length sale —	Arm's-length sale —	Arm's-length sale —	Arm's-length sale —
Expenditures immediately after purchase	—	None —	None —	None —	$50,000 in deferred maintenance +1.87	None —
Adjusted unit price	—	$77.93	$71.38	$76.09	$82.77	$73.08
Date of sale	—	9 months ago +6.00%	4 months ago +2.67%	5 months ago +3.33%	2 months ago +1.33%	6 months ago +4.00%
Adjusted unit price	—	$82.61	$73.29	$78.62	$83.87	$76.00
Construction quality and condition	Average	Average	Average	Average	Average	Average
Ratio of parking spaces to rental area	Adequate	Similar	Similar	Similar	Inferior	Similar
Average rent per sq. ft. of rentable area	$12.60	$12.80	$11.80	$12.60	$13.00	$12.30
Location	Average	Superior	Inferior	Superior	Superior	Inferior
Expense ratio	Market norm	Similar	Inferior	Similar	Similar	Similar
Overall comparability	—	Superior	Inferior	Superior	Superior	Inferior

provided by the landlord. The building has an occupancy rate of 90%, and all rents, lease terms, and expense categories are considered to be at market terms. The property's location is at the intersection of a collector road and a major arterial highway. The property has a parking ratio similar to that of the subject.

- Sale D was sold two months ago for $2,160,000. The building is six years old and in average condition. It contains 30,000 square feet of gross building area and 26,700 square feet of rentable area (89% of GBA). The unit price is $80.90 per square foot of rentable area. The rent averages $13.00 per square foot of rentable area, and the lease terms and building expenses are at market levels. The occupancy rate is 95%. The site is located at the intersection of two major arterial highways and has a lower ratio of parking area to rentable area than the subject property.

- Sale E was sold six months ago for $2,470,000. The building was constructed four years ago and is in average condition. It contains 38,000 square feet of gross building area and 33,800 square feet of rentable area (89% of GBA). Its unit price is $73.08 per square foot of rentable area. The location is an interior site accessed by a collector street. The occupancy rate for the building is 90%. Rents average $12.30 per square foot of rentable area. Full tenant services are provided by the landlord. Rents, lease terms, and property expenses are at market terms. The property has adequate parking, and the parking ratio is similar to that of the subject property.

The appraiser first analyzes the market data and determines that all of the office building sales involved the transfer of a leased fee interest. Thus, no quantitative adjustments for differences in property rights conveyed are necessary. (The below-market rent of Sale B will be considered later as part of the economic characteristics of the comparable properties.) All sales were transacted with conventional market financing, so no adjustments for this element of comparison are required either. Since all of the transactions were conducted at arm's length, no adjustments for conditions of sale are necessary.

The buyer of the property in Sale D invested an additional $50,000 in repairs immediately after the sale for deferred maintenance on the building's HVAC system. The appraiser confirmed with both the buyer and the seller in the transaction that both parties considered the $50,000 cost of those repairs in their negotiations. As a result, the appraiser adjusted the reported unit price by $1.87 ($50,000/26,700 rentable square feet). The other sales required no adjustments for expenditures made immediately after purchase.

Prices in the local office property market had been stable for several years as the market absorbed excess supply, according to the appraiser's market analysis. Two years ago, sale prices began to rise quickly as demand for office space increased. The market research revealed that sale prices of similar properties rose at a rate of 5% over the first year, with that rate jumping up to an 8% increase over the course of the current year. Although the comparable sales used were generally recent transactions, all occurring within nine months of the date of valuation, this time period saw active market growth. Individual adjustments for differences in market conditions were based on the 8% annual rate of increase in the current year, e.g., 6.00% for Sale A (8% × 9/12), 2.67% for Sale B (8% × 4/12), and so on.

After the application of the quantitative adjustments for transactional elements of comparison, the appraiser examined the physical elements of comparison to determine if market evidence supported additional quantitative adjustments. Additional information on the sale of comparable properties revealed general value trends but did not support quantitative adjustments for the physical elements of comparison.

The relative comparison analysis of the physical elements of comparison is described below.

- Sale A has an adjusted unit price of $82.61 per square foot of rentable area. Its location at the intersection of a major arterial highway and a collector road is superior to the location of the subject property. The building has an average rentable area ratio, but it is a more efficient building than the subject. The building occupancy rate for Sale A is slightly lower than the subject's and lower than the rate considered typical for stabilized occupancy in the market. In short, Sale A has more superior than inferior attributes and these attributes are considered more significant. This sale indicates a unit value for the subject property of less than $82.61 per square foot of rentable area.

- Sale B has an indicated unit price of $73.29 per square foot of rentable area. Effective contract rent is lower than market rent. The location of this property on a collector street is inferior to the subject property's location on a major arterial highway. Sale B has a superior rentable area ratio, indicating that the property will yield a higher net income. The occupancy rate for the comparable property is below the market rate for stabilized occupancy, and the expense ratio for the property is slightly higher than typical, resulting in a lower net income. In all, more of the attributes of Sale B are inferior than superior and these inferior factors are also considered more significant. In this particular case, the difference in the rentable area ratios may be considered to have the least impact on value. Therefore, the analysis of Sale B indicates that the subject should have a unit value greater than $73.29 per square foot of rentable area.

- Sale C has a unit price of $78.62 per square foot of rentable area. The location of the property is similar to that of the subject, but the comparable property has a superior rentable area ratio. Sale C is superior to the subject, and the value for the subject should be less than $78.62 per square foot of rentable area.

- Sale D indicates a unit price of $83.87 per square foot of rentable area. Because it is situated at the intersection of two major arterial highways, the property has a significantly superior location compared to that of the subject. The availability of parking is more limited. Sale D has a higher occupancy rate than the stabilized occupancy rate that characterizes the market for this type of property. The superior location and higher occupancy outweigh the limited parking. Overall, this property is superior to the subject and an appropriate value for the subject would be less than $83.87 per square foot of rentable area.

- Sale E has an indicated unit price of $76.00 per square foot of rentable area. The location of the property on a collector street is inferior to that of the subject. The property is similar to the subject in all other elements of comparison. Since Sale E has an inferior location, the price of the subject should be greater than $76.00 per square foot of rentable area.

The value indications derived from the comparable sales are reconciled into a value bracket by arranging the five sales in an array relative to the subject (Table 15.2). The value bracket for the subject property is between $76.00 and $78.62 per square foot of rentable area. Sale C is the property most similar to the subject and therefore may be given the greatest weight.

Reconciliation

Based on the indicated range of value and the weight placed on Sale C, the market evidence supports an estimate of value of $78.00 per square foot of rentable area, which is in the upper mid-range of the value bracket. The market value of the subject property would then be calculated as follows:

$78.00 × 31,800 square feet = $2,480,400

Table 15.2: Bracketing the Subject Property's Value

Sale	Inferior	Superior
D		$83.87
A		$82.61
C		$78.62
E	$76.00	
B	$73.29	

INDUSTRIAL BUILDING EXAMPLE

The property being appraised is a 15-year old warehouse containing 25,000 square feet of gross building area and 2,500 square feet of finished office area. The ceiling height is 18 feet. The quality of construction is good and the building's condition is average.

The five comparable sales described below were used in the analysis. All of the properties are warehouses located in the subject property's market area.

- Sale A was sold one year ago for $622,000. The seller provided advantageous financing that resulted in the buyer paying $63,000 more than if the buyer had paid cash, i.e., a "vendor-take-back" or "purchase-money" mortgage. The property is a 28,000 square foot warehouse with an 18 foot ceiling height and 2,750 square feet of finished office area. It was 14 years old at the time of the sale. The quality of construction is good, but at the time of sale the warehouse exhibited excessive deferred maintenance. The buyer budgeted for expenses of $35,000 to upgrade the property.

Table 15.3: Quantitative Adjustments

	Subject	Sale A	Sale B	Sale C	Sale D	Sale E
Price	—	$622,000	$530,000	$495,000	$554,000	$626,000
Area in square feet	25,000	28,000	27,000	22,000	25,000	26,000
Ceiling height	18 ft.	18 ft.	18 ft.	17 ft.	19 ft.	18 ft.
Age	15 years	14 years	13 years	13 years	16 years	16 years
Construction quality	Good	Good	Average	Good	Good	Good
Office area	2,500	2,750	2,200	3,000	2,500	2,100
Elements of comparison						
Property rights conveyed	Fee simple	Fee simple —	Fee simple —	Leased fee +$27,681	Fee simple —	Leased fee −$75,087
Adjusted sale price		$622,000	$530,000	$522,681	$554,000	$550,913
Financing terms	Cash	Purchase-money mortgage −$63,000	Cash 0	Loan assumption −$9,000	Cash —	Cash —
Adjusted sale price		$559,000	$530,000	$513,681	$554,000	$550,913
Conditions of sale	Arm's length	Arm's length —	Arm's length —	Arm's length —	Arm's length —	Arm's length —
Expenditures made immediately after purchase	None	Excessive deferred maintenance $35,000	None —	None —	None —	None —
Adjusted sale price		$594,000	$530,000	$513,681	$554,000	$550,913
Market conditions	Current	One year × 1.04	6 mos. × 1.02	Current —	3 mos. × 1.01	Current —
Adjusted sale price		$617,760	$540,600	$513,681	$559,540	$550,913
Condition of improvements	Average	Average (after repairs) —	Average —	Average —	Average —	Average —
Adjusted sale price		$617,760	$540,600	$513,681	$559,540	$550,913
Adjusted price per sq. ft.		**$22.06**	**$20.02**	**$23.35**	**$22.38**	**$21.19**

- Sale B was sold six months ago for $530,000 in a cash payment to the seller. This 27,000 square foot warehouse has 18 foot ceilings and 2,200 square feet of finished office area. It was 13 years old at the time of sale. The quality of construction and condition are average.

- Sale C is a current sale transacted for $495,000. The buyer assumed an existing loan at below-market rates. This favourable financing resulted in the buyer paying $9,000 more than if the buyer had obtained financing at market terms. This 22,000 square foot warehouse has 17 foot ceilings and 3,000 square feet of finished office area. The property is 13 years old. The quality of construction is good and its condition is average. This warehouse is subject to a long-term lease at a below-market rate.

- Sale D was sold three months ago for $554,000. This 25,000 square foot warehouse has a 19 foot ceiling height and 2,500 square feet of finished office area. It is 16 years old. The quality of construction is good and the condition is excellent.

- Sale E is a current sale for $626,000 paid in cash to the seller. This 26,000 square foot warehouse has 18 foot ceilings and 2,100 square feet of finished office area. The building is 16 years old. The quality of construction is good and its condition is average. The property is subject to a long-term lease that is above market levels

Quantitative Adjustments

The quantitative adjustment procedure is summarized in Table 15.3 and described below.

Property Rights Conveyed

Sales C and E were sold subject to long-term leases, so both require an adjustment for property rights conveyed. At the time of sale, the lease on the property in Sale C had seven years remaining at a rate that was $0.25 below the market rate. Capitalizing the annual lost income of $5,500 at a market-derived rate of $j_1 = 9\%$ indicates an upward adjustment of $27,681 to the sale price of Sale C. The property sold in Sale E, on the other hand, was leased at a rate $0.45 above the market rate with 10 years remaining in the lease term. The present value of the $11,700 annual difference between contract and market rent is $75,087. This present value amount is subtracted from the price of Sale E to adjust that transaction for the favourable leasing terms in place at the time of the sale. Note that these present value calculations are based on lease payments being made at the end of each period. If payments are made in advance, as is the market norm, the PV of the lease differences for Sale C changes to $30,173 and Sale E changes to $81,844. Calculator steps for these lease calculations are provided in Appendix C.

Financing Terms

Sales A and C require adjustment for financing terms. The seller of Sale A provided advantageous financing that resulted in the buyer paying $63,000 more than the buyer would have paid in a cash transaction. Therefore, a downward adjustment of

$63,000 is made to Sale A. The buyer of Sale C assumed an existing, below-market loan. The buyer paid a $9,000 premium above the price that would have been paid under market terms, so a downward adjustment of $9,000 is made to Sale C.

Conditions of Sale

Since all the comparable sales were arm's-length transactions, none requires an adjustment for conditions of sale.

Expenditures Made Immediately After Purchase

Sale A suffered from excessive deferred maintenance. At the time of sale, the buyer anticipated spending $35,000 to upgrade the building to average condition.

Market Conditions

The sales occurred over a 12-month period. Market analysis shows that properties in this market have been appreciating at 4% annually. Sales A, B, and D require an upward adjustment for change in market conditions.

Condition of Improvements

The subject property is in average condition. Recall that Sale A was adjusted upward by $35,000 for expenditures made immediately after purchase to bring it in line with the subject property's condition. Another adjustment would not be made for the property's condition at the time of sale because, after correcting for deferred maintenance, the property was considered to be in average condition.

Adjusted Unit Prices

After applying all known quantitative adjustments, the comparable sales indicate a value range from $20.02 to $23.35 per square foot.

Qualitative Analysis

After quantitative adjustments are made, the sales may be analyzed for qualitative differences that will help in the reconciliation process. Table 15.4 shows a value trend within the comparable properties for the ratio of office area to total building area. The properties with a higher percentage of office space had a higher average unit price than did the properties with a smaller percentage of office space.

After relative comparison analysis, the value bracket has tightened to $21.19 to $23.35 per square foot with Sales A and D ($22.06 and $22.38 per square foot, respectively) most similar to the subject property. If the bracket of values were broader – for example, if the adjusted unit prices of Sales A and D ranged from $19.00 to $24.00 – the appraiser could analyze the comparables sales further to determine if the subject is more similar to the sales in the upper or lower ends of the bracket.

Other elements of comparison may affect the adjusted unit prices of comparable sales to some degree. The appraiser could prepare data arrays for each of the other physical characteristics that may have an effect on unit price (see Tables 15.5, 15.6, and 15.7), but if the market evidence does not show discernible trends for those elements of comparison individually or as a group, then no additional analysis would be necessary. For the five comparable sales, no clear trends in value can be discerned from the relative comparison analysis of construction quality, age of improvements, or ceiling height.

Table 15.4: Relative Comparison: Ratio of Office Area to Total Building Area

	8%	10%	14%
Sale A		$22.06	
Sale B	$20.02		
Sale C			$23.35
Sale D		$22.38	
Sale E	$21.19		
Mean	**$20.61**	**$22.22**	**$23.35**
Subject property		10%	
Relative comparison	Inferior	Similar	Superior

Table 15.5: Relative Comparison: Construction Quality

	Poor	Average	Good	Excellent
Sale A			$22.06	
Sale B		$20.02		
Sale C			$23.35	
Sale D			$22.38	
Sale E			$21.19	
Mean		$20.02	$22.50	
Subject property			Good	
Relative comparison	Inferior	Inferior	Similar	Superior

Table 15.6: Relative Comparison: Age of Improvements

	13–14	15	16
Sale A	$22.06		
Sale B	$20.02		
Sale C	$23.35		
Sale D			$22.38
Sale E			$21.19
Mean	$21.81		$21.79
Subject property		15	
Relative comparison	Inferior	Similar	Superior

Table 15.7: Relative Comparison: Ceiling Height

	17 feet	18 feet	19 feet
Sale A		$22.06	
Sale B		$20.02	
Sale C	$23.35		
Sale D			$22.38
Sale E		$21.19	
Mean	$23.35	$21.09	$22.38
Subject property		18 feet	
Relative comparison	Inferior	Similar	Superior

The range of adjusted unit prices for inferior or superior sales may overlap the range set by sales of different overall comparability (see Table 15.8). For example, suppose Sale D had an adjusted unit price of $20.75 per square foot, which is less than the unit price of Sale E, an "inferior" property. In that situation, the appraiser should address the causes for the overlapping and refine the value bracket. Comparing the ranges of inferior, similar, and superior properties can help the appraiser identify statistical outliers, i.e., observations that are extreme and often evidence of an error. An outlier may have an inordinate effect on a statistical model if the reason for its departure from the typical range cannot be explained.

Table 15.8: Overall Comparability

	Sale A	Sale B	Sale C	Sale D	Sale E
Percentage of office space	Similar	Inferior	Superior	Similar	Inferior
Construction quality	Similar	Inferior	Similar	Similar	Similar
Age of improvements	Superior	Superior	Superior	Inferior	Inferior
Ceiling height	Similar	Similar	Inferior	Superior	Similar
Overall comparability	Similar	Inferior	Superior	Similar	Inferior
Adjusted unit price	$22.06	$20.02	$23.35	$22.38	$21.19

Reconciliation

The value indications of the comparable sales with the highest overall comparability to the subject property – Sales A and D – are in a tight range, from $22.06 to $22.38. The comparable sales that are inferior (Sales B and E) or superior (Sale C) overall also bracket the two sales with similar overall comparability and further support a value indication of $22.25 per square foot. The market value of the subject property would then be calculated as follows:

$22.25 × 25,000 square feet = $556,250

CHAPTER 16

LAND AND SITE VALUATION

Land has value because it provides potential utility as the site of a structure, recreational facility, agricultural tract, or right of way for transportation routes, water storage, and many other uses. It may also have value because the owner can extract valuable components such as oil, coal, gravel, sand, or iron ore from it. In areas with little water, the ability to extract water from a site is very valuable, and that right could dwarf all other forms of utility. If land has utility for a specific use and there is demand for that use, the land has value to a particular category of users. Beyond the basic utility of land, however, there are many principles and factors that an appraiser must consider in land valuation. Although it is sometimes considered the simplest of appraisal tasks, the valuation of land requires analysis of a complex variety of factors and can, in practice, be the most difficult of all appraisal procedures.

RELATION TO APPRAISAL PRINCIPLES

Value Concepts and Principles

Anticipation, change, supply and demand, substitution, and balance are appraisal principles that influence land value. Anticipation means that the expectation of benefits to be derived in the future creates value. For example, if buyers anticipate that raw land in a certain location will be in demand for office use within the next five years, they may be motivated to acquire land for future development even though the development of office space is not presently tenable. The competition among the buyers who make up the market for raw land creates a price level for the land that may have little to do with the current use. In such circumstances, the highest and best use of the land could be an interim use while the land is held for future office development.

> **land**
> The earth's surface, both land and water, and anything that is attached to it whether by the course of nature or human hands; all natural resources in their original state, e.g., mineral deposits, wildlife, timber, fish, water, coal deposits, soil.
> **site**
> Land that is improved so that it is ready to be used for a specific purpose.

The supply of land is relatively stable. Although vast changes have occurred in the earth's surface over the ages and slight modifications in the supply and quality of land may occur over a lifetime, these natural events rarely affect the land that appraisers are concerned with. However, there are a few notable exceptions to the permanence of land, such as the accretion or erosion of land along a shoreline, the pollution of land with harmful wastes, the exhaustion of agricultural land through improper farming methods, and the transformation of arable land into desert due to ecological imbalances or climate change. Earthquakes may change the surface of the earth and faults beneath the surface can create vast sinkholes. Old underground mines can cause subsidence. Fortunately, these occurrences that change the supply of land are rare.

Land value is substantially affected by the interplay of supply and demand, but it is the economic use of a parcel of land that determines its value in a particular market. (When a parcel of land becomes an economic unit, it is commonly referred to as a site.) As an example, the price that a developer can afford to pay for a warehouse site is determined by the net income that the warehouse will earn and the cost of constructing the improvements. Intense competition for choice lots or for the last remaining lots in a particular location can cause prospective owners or owner-occupants to pay more for a particular site than is indicated by the broad spectrum of market activity and the highest and best use of the site. No object, including real property, can have value unless scarcity is coupled with utility.

The principle of substitution, which holds that a buyer will not pay more for one parcel of land than for an equivalent parcel, applies to land and site values. The principle of substitution indicates that the greatest demand will be generated for the lowest-priced site with similar utility. The principle of balance is also applicable to land and site values. When the various elements of a particular economic mix or a specific environment are in a state of equilibrium, land value is sustained; when the balance is upset, values change. If, for example, a district has too much industrially zoned land and a declining number of industrial users, then the value of industrial land will probably fall or remain the same over a period of time. On the other hand, if the industrial district is in transition to other uses and there is a reasonable probability of a zoning change, the value of a particular site could be higher than sales of comparable industrial sites would indicate.

Property Rights and Public Controls

The appraisal of land focuses on valuing the physical parcel and the accompanying property rights. These rights may include the right to do the following:

- Develop the land to its highest and best use
- Lease the land to others
- Farm the land
- Mine the land
- Alter the land's topography
- Subdivide the land
- Assemble the parcel of land with other parcels
- Hold the land for future use
- Construct or alter building improvements

Whenever possible, an appraiser should consult title reports, public records, or available survey information to identify easements, rights of way, and private or public restrictions that affect the subject property.

In an effort to encourage planned growth and compatibility among different land uses, governments regulate how land can be used. Most municipalities and regional governments have some form of zoning regulations that specify how a parcel of land can be developed. In addition to zoning, many jurisdictions now have master plans or official community plans that specify long-term development goals. Frequently, developers must have amenities such as open space, streets, and off-site public improvements in place or dedicated before a proposed development receives approval from the appropriate public agency. Usually developers will proceed with development only after they have submitted detailed development plans and obtained building department approval. In many areas, citizen groups will protest a development they do not like, and their objections frequently influence the type of development that is finally approved. Site value can increase substantially after site plan approval has been achieved and permitting has been obtained. At that point, the site has full entitlements for immediate development.

Through the power of expropriation, the government can acquire land from the private sector to be used for public and sometimes non-public projects, to augment the supply of public land, and to encourage economic development or eliminate blight. The taking of private land for economic development, and particularly for private sector development, has come under public scrutiny since the US Supreme Court decision in *Kelo v. City of New London*.

In some jurisdictions, land value is based on development rights, which may be transferable. For example, in some rural jurisdictions governmental agencies compensate farmers for retaining land in agricultural use and shift or sell the benefit of those development rights to other locations. Lower ad valorem taxes on agricultural land also affect rural land use. This form of tax subsidy tends to extend the duration of agricultural uses.

A relatively recent trend in Canada and elsewhere has been the acquisition of land for open space or conservation purposes that are held in perpetuity by qualified agencies.[1] Some jurisdictions conserve open space or natural lands through permanent title encumbrances that limit or prohibit the development potential of land. The use of land subject to perpetual open space or conservation easements is usually restricted, as specified in the deed of easement or land title. These deeds are vested in preservation or conservation trusts. Another way to preserve open space is through donation of specified easement rights to a qualified recipient such as a land trust.

Water, mineral, and air rights can be important in the appraiser's consideration of property rights.[2] Water rights cover the flow of water, usually for stated times and in stated quantities, for irrigation and hydroelectric power generation. Water rights can also take the form of riparian rights that, under common law, grant a landowner the ownership of waters that share a border with the parcel of land. In certain areas of

---

[1]   For example, see *www.natureconservancy.ca*

[2]   See also Appendix G of American Society of Farm Managers and Rural Appraisers and Appraisal Institute, *The Appraisal of Rural Property*, 2nd ed. (Denver and Chicago, 2000).

the country, these rights are critical to real estate valuation. The valuation of mineral rights requires specialized research, but appraisers should be aware if mineral rights are excluded from land ownership. Mineral rights cover the underground portion of the land and usually refer to the right to extract underground minerals or to use underground caverns or reefs for storage. Real estate developments established on air rights, usually over railways, can be found in urban areas, particularly where density is high and less land is available for new construction.

Physical Characteristics and Site Improvements

A parcel of land becomes a site when it is improved and ready to be used for a specific purpose. The physical characteristics of land, the utilities available, and the site improvements affect land use and value. The physical characteristics of a parcel of land that an appraiser must consider include size, shape, frontage, topography, location, view, and topographical characteristics such as contour, grade, and drainage.

> **off-site improvements**
> Improvements such as streets, sidewalks, curbing, traffic signals, and water and sewer mains, located off the property itself but necessary to facilitate development.
> **on-site improvements**
> Improvements such as grading, landscaping, fences, gutters, paving, drainage and irrigation systems, walks, and other physical enhancements to the land.

A site may have both on-site and off-site improvements that make it suitable for its intended use or for new construction. Off-site improvements such as controlled access by turn lanes or traffic signals are typically considered with land value and are included in the market value for the site. The availability of water, sewers, electricity, natural gas, and telephone and data lines also influences the use and development potential of a parcel of land (see Chapter 10). Only rarely are off-site improvements valued with other property improvements. In contrast, on-site improvements are subject to physical deterioration and functional obsolescence like buildings and other structures and are often valued with property improvements.

Highest and Best Use

Site value must always be considered in terms of highest and best use. Even if the site has improvements, the site value is based on its highest and best use as though vacant and available for development to its most economic use. Consideration of the site as though vacant is a commonly accepted procedure that facilitates the orderly analysis and solution of appraisal problems, which often require land to be valued separately. The comparability of competitive sites is based on their highest and best use on the date of sale. Regardless of how physically similar the potential comparable site is to the subject site, the sale property is not truly comparable if it does not have a similar highest and best use as the subject and should be dismissed from further consideration in the analysis of the subject property.

Highest and best use is also affected by how much the existing improvements contribute to property value. Site value may be equal to, or even greater than, total property value, even when substantial improvements are located on the site. The contribution of the improvements is estimated by subtracting the market value of the site from the market value of the total property as improved. When improvements do not contribute to the overall property value, demolition is usually appropriate. In most cases, the cost of converting the property into vacant land is a penalty to be deducted from the value of the site.

In some circumstances, the appraisal of a property may require that the site be considered in terms of a use other than its highest and best use. In an appraisal to develop an opinion of use value or a legal, nonconforming use value of an improved site, an appraiser may need to value the site according to its specified use, which is not its highest and best use. However, the appraiser may want to state what the highest and best use is so that the conclusions are not misleading.

Possibility of Assemblage

Certain parcels can achieve their highest and best use only as a part of an assemblage. In such a case, the appraiser must either determine the feasibility and probability of assembly or base the highest and best use determination and other appraisal decisions on the assumption that such an assembly would be made. For example, a large petrochemical plant may be constructed on a site that has been created by assembling several smaller tracts. The individual tracts may not have had the potential for such a large-scale industrial use separately and, therefore, may have had much lower unit values for alternative uses.

If the appraiser concludes that the highest and best use can be achieved through an assemblage, the costs and timing of achieving the assemblage and the economic demand for the assembled property must be taken into consideration. In the example of the petrochemical plant, assembling the site might take more than two years. Although the assemblage would allow the smaller parcels to accommodate the plant, the time delay may be too long for the developer of the proposed petrochemical plant. The appraiser must also recognize that frequently a higher-than-market price might have to be paid to assemble a tract of land, particularly for properties acquired near the end of the assemblage period. An appraiser must reflect these costs in the resulting land value estimate and in the appraiser's conclusions as to the reasonable probability of assemblage. Appraisers should avoid summing the cost of the parts (smaller parcels) to develop an opinion of the market value of the whole (larger assembled) parcel, and conversely they should avoid assigning the unit value of the larger parcel to the components without other market evidence to support those conclusions. It is always advisable to keep in mind that the opinion of market value assumes someone would buy the property for the amount of the appraisal; sometimes in assemblage situations that is the most difficult concept.

> An appraiser begins the valuation of a parcel of land by identifying the real estate and property rights to be valued, any encumbrances on those property rights (e.g., easements, rights of way, use restrictions on title or in deeds, and zoning ordinances), the land's physical, functional, and economic characteristics, and the available utilities and site improvements. Comparable data on similar parcels is collected and the highest and best use of the subject site is analyzed.

APPLICABILITY AND LIMITATIONS OF VALUATION TECHNIQUES

The site value analysis in an appraisal report can appear as a separate stand-alone section or as a subsection of the cost approach. Typically, site value analysis is a separate section when the property being appraised is vacant land or an agricultural property with minimal improvements. In the model of the valuation process described in Chapter 7, site value is a separate analysis, performed before the application of the three approaches to value. This placement emphasizes the importance of site value in developing the highest and best use analysis and in assignments conducted primarily to derive the value of underlying land in its present use. Sometimes a property is appraised without a separate site value conclusion such as in the valuation of a condominium interest. The land for condominium projects is usually held as a common tenancy with each owner having rights to a portion of the land.

The direct comparison approach is usually the preferred methodology for developing a site value conclusion for many types of appraisals. When this approach is used, most of the techniques described in Chapter 13, with respect to selecting comparable sales and the adjustment process, can be applied to site valuation. When sales of similar parcels are not plentiful enough for the application of direct comparison, alternative techniques such as market extraction, allocation, and various income capitalization techniques may be used. The income capitalization techniques can be divided into direct capitalization techniques such as land residual and ground rent capitalization and yield capitalization techniques such as discounted cash flow analysis/subdivision development analysis; these methods are particularly useful for specialized assignments such as development lands. All these land valuation procedures, which are summarized in Table 16.1, are derived from the three traditional approaches to value.

Table 16.1: Applicability and Limitations of Land Valuation Techniques

Direct Comparison

Procedure	Sales of similar, vacant parcels are analyzed, compared, and adjusted to provide a value indication for the land being appraised.
Applicability	Direct comparison is the most common technique for valuing sites, and it is the preferred method when comparable sales are available.
Limitations	A lack of sales and the comparability of the available data may weaken support for the value estimate

Market Extraction

Procedure	An estimate of the depreciated cost of the improvements is deducted from the total sale price of the property to arrive at the land value.
Applicability	This technique is most applicable when: • The contribution of the improvements to total property value is generally small and relatively easy to identify. (The technique is frequently used in rural areas.) • The improvements are new, their value is known, and there is little or no depreciation from any causes.

Table 16.1: Applicability and Limitations of Land Valuation Techniques, *continued*

Limitations	The appraiser must be able to determine the value contribution of the improvements, estimated at their depreciated cost.

Allocation

Procedure	A ratio of site value to property value is extracted from comparable sales in competitive locations and applied to the sale price of the subject property to develop the site value.
Applicability	This technique is applicable when: • Valuing one-unit residential lots where ample sales of both lots and improved homes are available for comparison purposes. This method tends to be less accurate for commercial properties, especially when the number of vacant land sales is inadequate. • For commercial properties or where relatively few sales are available, allocation can provide a check for reasonableness rather than a formal opinion of site value.
Limitations	The allocation method does not produce conclusive value indications unless ample sales data is available. The method is rarely used as the primary land valuation technique for properties other than residential subdivision lots. Also, land-to-property value ratios can be difficult to support.

Income Capitalization Techniques

Direct Capitalization: Land Residual Technique

Procedure	The net operating income attributable to the land is capitalized at a market-derived land capitalization rate to provide an estimate of value.
Applicability	This technique is most applicable in testing the feasibility of alternative uses of a particular site in highest and best use analysis or when land sales are not available.
Limitations	The following conditions must be met: 1. Building value is known or can be accurately estimated. 2. Net operating income to the property is known or can be estimated. 3. Both building and land capitalization rates are available from the market.

Direct Capitalization: Ground Rent Capitalization

Procedure	A market-derived capitalization rate is applied to the ground rent of the subject.
Applicability	This method is useful when • comparable rents, rates, and factors can be developed from an analysis of sales of leased land.
Limitations	An adjustment to the value indication for property rights may be necessary when current rent under the existing contract does not match market rent.

Yield Capitalization: Discounted Cash Flow Analysis – Subdivision Development Analysis

Procedure	Direct and indirect costs and entrepreneurial incentive are deducted from an estimate of the anticipated gross sales price of the finished lots, and the net sales proceeds are discounted to present value at a market-derived rate over the development and absorption period. If entrepreneurial incentive is not deducted as a line-item expense, then the discount rate must reflect the full effect of any profit.
Applicability	This technique is applicable when • subdivision development is the highest and best use of the land.
Limitations	Discounted cash flow analysis requires significant amounts of data such as development costs, profit margins, sales projections, and the pricing of developed lots.

Note: some legal rulings do not recognize subdivision development analysis as a valid valuation technique for litigation valuation or other purposes.

DIRECT COMPARISON

The direct comparison approach may be used to value land that is actually vacant or land that is being considered as though vacant for appraisal purposes. Direct comparison is the most common technique for valuing land, and it is the preferred method when comparable sales are available. To apply this method, data on sales of similar parcels of land is collected, analyzed, compared, and adjusted to provide a value indication for the site being appraised. In the comparison process, the similarity or dissimilarity of the parcels is considered.

The appraiser must perform several tasks in developing an opinion of site value:

- Gather data on actual sales as well as listings, offers, and options based on highest and best use.

- Identify the similarities and differences in the data.

- Identify the highest and best use of each potential comparable sale and then choose the appropriate sales for analysis.

- Identify units of comparison that explain market behaviour.

- Adjust the appropriate unit prices of the comparable sales to account for the dissimilar characteristics of the site being appraised.

- Form a conclusion as to the market value of the subject site.

The goal of the direct comparison approach is to select the most comparable sales and then adjust the comparable sales for differences that cannot be eliminated within the selection process. Elements of comparison include property rights, financing terms, conditions of sale (motivation), expenditures immediately after purchase, market conditions (changes over time), location, physical characteristics, available utilities, and zoning. The physical characteristics of a parcel of land include its size, shape, frontage, topography, soil conditions, location, and view. For a detailed discussion of elements of comparison, see Chapter 14. Unit prices may be expressed as price per square foot, front foot, acre, lot, dwelling unit, floor space ratio (FSR), or other unit prices used in the market.

> Direct comparison is the most commonly used and preferred method of valuing land. Data on sales of similar parcels of land is collected, analyzed, compared, and adjusted to reflect the similarity or dissimilarity of those parcels to the site of the subject property.

If sale prices have been changing rapidly over the past several years and an adequate amount of sales data is available, the sales selected for comparison should take place as close as possible to the effective appraisal date. When current data on local sales is not available, the appraiser may need to expand the search to another market area, which usually calls for an adjustment for location, or extend the search back in time in the same market area, which usually calls for an adjustment for market conditions. The decision to use sales from another market area or older sales should be based on which adjustment has more support, the location adjustment or the market conditions adjustment.

Among generally similar sales, size may be less important as an element of comparison than date and location. Most land uses have an optimal site size; if the site is too large, the value of the surplus land tends to decline at an accelerating rate. Since sales of different sizes may have different unit prices, appraisers ordinarily give more weight to comparables that are approximately the same size as the subject property.

Zoning is often the most basic criterion in selecting comparables. Sites zoned the same as the subject property generally have the same or a similar highest and best use and are the most appropriate comparables. However, zoning can be less important than utility or highest and best use in areas that are in transition or targeted for redevelopment. If sufficient sales in the same zoning category are not available, appraisers can use data from similar zoning categories and make adjustments, if necessary. As a general rule, the greater the difference between the subject and the comparables, the more potential there is for distortion and error in direct comparison.

In addition to recorded sales and signed contracts, appraisers should consider offers to sell (listings) and offers to purchase. However, offers provide less reliable data than signed contracts and completed sales. Often the final sale price is lower than the initial offer to sell but higher than the initial offer to buy. Negotiations can take place in several stages.

Additionally, many appraisers will also update a prior sale of the subject to the effective date of valuation. For example, if the subject site sold 18 months ago for $545,000 in a market that is increasing at 3% per year, the appraiser would draw an indication of market value by adjusting the prior sale for the changes in the market:

$$\$545,000 \times [1 + (1.5 \times .03)] = \$569,525$$

This assumes that the property has not changed since the prior sale, the prior sale meets all the requirements of a market sale, the prior sale occurred within a reasonable period from the effective date of value, there have been no material physical changes to the property during the intervening period, that applicable zoning and land use regulations have not changed, and economic conditions prevailing on the date of sale and the effective date of appraisal have not changed. Updating a prior sale of the subject property is not a simple process and should be performed with extreme care.

Data on land sales is available from sources such as electronically transmitted and printed data services, newspapers, and title and assessment records. Interviews with the parties involved in transactions – i.e., the buyers, sellers, lawyers, and brokers – can provide more direct information and may reveal adjustments that should be made for conditions of sale or sale concessions. These interviews should also identify the intended use and the status of approvals and entitlements. After an appraiser collects and categorizes comparable data and the appraiser examines and describes comparable properties, sales data can be assembled in an organized, logical manner. Sales are commonly arrayed in a market data grid that identifies the elements of comparison that may require adjustments. An appraiser may make appropriately developed adjustments to the sale or unit prices of the comparables for significant differences between the subject property and the comparable properties using a variety of techniques. Chapter 14 discusses techniques for making adjustments in direct comparison analysis.[3]

---

[3]   See also James H. Boykin, *Land Valuation Adjustment Procedures and Assignments* (Chicago: Appraisal Institute, 2001).

Generally, an appraiser makes separate adjustments to the comparable sales for each element of comparison. The magnitude of each adjustment is indicated by the data and the judgment of the appraiser. Land parcels of different sizes sell at different unit prices because the optimal size of a parcel depends on its use. Unit prices also vary with the date of sale and location. If the data selected is not sufficient to support the required adjustments, the appraiser should gather and analyze additional comparable data.

A sale price adjustment may be simply an acknowledgment of a property's superiority or inferiority; alternatively, it may be a precise dollar amount or percentage developed from market evidence. Adjustments can also be totalled and factored into the comparable sale prices as part of the initial data gathering process. Typically, adjustments are made in a preferred order, i.e., transaction adjustments for property rights, financing, and sale and market conditions are made before property adjustments for location and physical characteristics. All adjustments should be presented in the appraisal report in a logical and understandable manner.

ALTERNATIVE TECHNIQUES

Vacant parcels of land in densely developed urban locations may be so rare that their values cannot be estimated reliably by direct comparison. Similarly, sales of vacant parcels of land in remote areas may occur so seldom that sufficient comparable data is not available. In such cases, land value can be estimated by market extraction, allocation, or one of the income capitalization techniques.

Market Extraction

Market extraction is a technique in which land value is extracted from the sale price of an improved property by deducting the contributory value of the improvements, often estimated at their depreciated cost. The remaining value represents the value of the land. An appraiser frequently analyzes improved sales in rural areas in this way because the building and site improvements contribute little value in comparison to the underlying land value. The improvement contribution is typically small and relatively easy to identify.

To apply the extraction method, an estimate of the depreciated cost of the improvement(s) – i.e., contributory improvement value – is deducted from the total sale price of the property to arrive at the land value. Extraction is used to estimate the land value of improved properties in rural areas and properties in which the improvements contribute little to total property value.

Given the necessary market data, the application of the market extraction technique is a straightforward process. As an example, consider a vacant subject site in an area where few sales of comparable sites have occurred recently. The sales summarized in Table 16.2 involve sites that are similar to the subject property except for the improvements. The reported value of the improvements is subtracted from each sale price to calculate value indications for the sites of the comparable properties (see Table 16.3). Those value indications can, in turn, be analyzed using direct comparison techniques and reconciled into a value indication for the subject site. In this case, the value indications range from $407,000 to $435,000.

Table 16.2: Comparable Sales for Market Extraction

Sale	Sale Price	Description
1	$450,000	Includes storage building that contributes $15,000
2	$465,000	Includes 1,500 square foot building valued at $32 per square foot
3	$432,000	Includes permits and approvals for construction worth $25,000
4	$448,000	Includes a temporary sales building that contributes $32,000

Table 16.3: Market Extraction of Site Value

	Sale 1	Sale 2	Sale 3	Sale 4
Sale price	$450,000	$465,000	$432,000	$448,000
Less contribution of improvements	– $15,000	– (1,500 × $32)	– $25,000	– $32,000
Value indication	$435,000	$417,000	$407,000	$416,000

Allocation

The allocation method is based on the principle of balance and the related concept of contribution. Both affirm that there is a normal or typical ratio of land value to property value for specific categories of real estate in specific locations. An appraiser may derive meaningful support for an allocation ratio from a variety of sources:

- Mass appraisals prepared by assessors
- Observed patterns over time in an area
- Consultation with developers who sell improved properties and can allocate sale prices between the land and the improvements based on their costs

The allocation method has its greatest benefit and accuracy when estimating the value of residential subdivision lots. This is the most common application of this technique and can produce accurate results if sufficient sales data is available. In situations where there are limited sales data, the allocation method does not produce conclusive value indications, but it can be used to establish approximate land value when the number of vacant land sales is inadequate.

For example, the appraiser could use allocation to value the site for a new one-unit home in a large, newly developed subdivision where few sales of vacant land have occurred, but data from several recent sales of improved properties is available. The sale prices of new homes in the development range from $275,000 to $315,000, and site values range from 15% to 20% of sale prices. Based on these figures, site values may range from $41,250 to $63,000.

Because of the relatively large number of sales needed to support a credible value opinion, an appraiser rarely uses allocation as the primary method of site valuation for commercial properties. Its most common application is in subdivision lot sales analysis, where the appraiser can directly measure the ratio of lot value to total property value. The technique is not used often for commercial properties because parcel size and intensity of use vary widely, particularly for industrial properties. It is also difficult for appraisers to use allocation to value parcels that have more land than is necessary for the existing improvements.

The allocation method and sometimes the extraction method can be difficult to use in markets where the highest and best use and land value ratios of comparable parcels are not similar to the subject. For example, the subject site is zoned commercial but is improved with a residence; the commercial land value is $500,000 and the improved property value is $550,000. In this case, if the comparable sites did not have similarly high land value ratios, the allocation and extraction methods may give a false indication of value. An appraiser should use the allocation and extraction methods with extreme care and only when lack of market data prevents application of more direct methods and procedures.

Income Capitalization Procedures

The various income capitalization procedures used to estimate land values rely on information that is often difficult for an appraiser to obtain, e.g., reliable capitalization rates for the land residual technique. Therefore, these techniques are generally not used as primary valuation techniques except in special situations such as subdivision development analysis. Chapters 22, 23, and 24 discuss direct capitalization and yield capitalization techniques in more detail.

Direct Capitalization: Land Residual Technique

Historically, an appraiser used the land residual technique to estimate land value when sales data on similar parcels of vacant land was not available. Techniques like extraction and allocation have superseded the land residual technique in land valuation because these other techniques rely on fewer variables subject to an appraiser's judgment and expertise and thus are more persuasive. In current practice, the land residual technique is used almost exclusively in highest and best use analysis to test the productivity of alternate uses of the site as though vacant as shown in Chapter 12.

> The land residual technique is a method of estimating land value in which the net operating income attributable to the land is isolated and capitalized to produce an indication of the land's contribution to the total property.

The land residual technique requires that the following conditions be met:

1. Building value is known or can be accurately estimated. Chapter 18 discusses procedures for estimating building costs.

2. Net operating income to the property is known or can be estimated. Chapter 21 discusses the development of income and expense estimates.

3. Both building and land capitalization rates can be extracted from the market. Chapter 22 discusses the extraction of land and building capitalization rates.

Small variations in any of these variables can result in a dramatic change in the land value estimate.

To apply the land residual technique, an appraiser first determines what actual or hypothetical improvements represent the highest and best use of the site as though vacant. Then the net operating income of the property is estimated from market rents and operating expenses as of the date of the appraisal. Next, the appraiser calculates how much of the income is attributable to the building and subtracts this amount from the net operating income. The remainder is the residual income attributable to the land, which is capitalized at a market-derived land capitalization rate to provide an estimate of site value.

Direct Capitalization: Ground Rent Capitalization

Ground rent is the amount paid for the right to use and occupy the land according to the terms of a ground lease. It can be used in estimating the value of the landowner's interest in the land, i.e., the leased fee interest. Market-derived capitalization rates are used to convert ground rent into market value.

> Market-derived capitalization rates are used to convert ground rent into an indication of land value.

The ground rent capitalization procedure is useful when an analysis of comparable sales of leased land indicates a range of rents and capitalization rates. If the current rent corresponds to market rent, the value indication obtained will be equivalent to the market value of the fee simple interest in the land. If the ground rent paid under the terms of the existing contract does not correspond to market rent, the value estimate given the current ground rent must be adjusted for the difference in property rights (i.e., the leased fee interest versus the fee simple interest) to obtain an indication of the market value of the fee simple interest.

Ground leases can have different terms and escalation clauses, so the appraiser should consider all the benefits to the lessor during the term of the lease and any option periods and forecast when the reversion of the property will take place.

If information on sales of comparable sites subject to land leases is unavailable, the appraiser can investigate sales of comparable plots of land that are not leased. Analysis of these transactions may yield an estimate of the rate of return an investor expects from comparable sites, i.e., a market-derived capitalization rate that can be applied to the ground rent of the subject property.

Yield Capitalization: Discounted Cash Flow Analysis (Subdivision Development Analysis)

An appraiser can use the subdivision development method, using discounted cash flow analysis, to value vacant land that has the potential for subdivision development. The land must support a highest and best use for immediate development purposes at the time of appraisal or have short-term market demand to support financially feasible subdivision development.

Valuing finished lots in a subdivision is a common assignment for real estate appraisers, but subdivision development analysis is a complex procedure. When there is sufficient reliable market data, the subdivision development method provides credible results. The technique is most useful for reporting the market value for a group of subdivision lots, whether existing or proposed. The method uses what is known as a *bulk sale* scenario to develop the value of all lots to one purchaser. The value indication is most persuasive when the direct comparison method provides additional support..

In essence, the subdivision development method uses yield capitalization techniques in the income approach to perform a discounted cash flow analysis. To use discounted cash flow analysis to estimate raw land value, the appraiser must thoroughly understand the land development process and all the factors influencing the subject property's market area.

The development of any project considers three phases of development:

1. The permitting stage
2. The construction stage
3. The absorption stage

Data on sales and costs for the developed lots must be available. The developer usually provides the necessary project information, including the subdivision plan and the costs of development. The developer might also provide a feasibility, marketability, or absorption study, and a schedule of lot prices, or the appraiser might undertake this work as part of the assignment. When the developer supplies the information, the appraiser has a responsibility to compare this information with other relevant market data. The market data and all conclusions in the analysis are the responsibility of the appraiser.

> An appraiser applies subdivision development analysis when subdivision and development represent the highest and best use of the land and when sales data on finished lots is available. The number and size of the finished lots, their likely sale prices, the length of the development and marketing periods, and the absorption rate are estimated. Gross income and expenses are projected when they are expected to occur. The resulting sales proceeds are then discounted back to arrive at an indication of land value.

Subdivision development analysis may involve tracts of residential, commercial, or industrial land (or a mix of land uses) that are large enough to be subdivided into smaller lots or parcels and sold to builders or end users. A planned subdivision can create a higher, better, and more intense use of the property when zoning, available utilities, access, and other influential elements are favourably combined.

The appraiser must consider the proposed development of the raw land and all costs associated with permitting, construction, and absorption of the finished lots over the entire three phases of development. To develop an "as is" value, the property must have current zoning or land use permissions in place to support the development proposal. If current zoning is not in place, the value estimate is subject to a hypothetical condition, i.e., the value depends on a condition that the favourable rezoning will be approved by appropriate governmental authorities, which is contrary to known facts.

To estimate raw land value using this technique, an appraiser is required to do the following:

- Accurately estimate the highest and best use of the site, e.g., mix and intensity of uses
- Create or affirm a supportable subdivision development plan
- Determine the timing and cost for approval and development (including environmental mitigation needs and costs of obtaining development approvals during the permitting stage)
- Forecast a realistic lot price or schedule of values over the absorption stage
- Accurately forecast the lot absorption rate and price mix using inferred or fundamental demand and supply analysis (including properly supported projections of community or market growth over the absorption period)
- Estimate a market-supported timeline for the permitting, construction, and absorption phases
- Forecast marketing and related holding and sales expenses over the permitting, construction, and absorption period
- Estimate the annual real estate taxes and any other miscellaneous expenses over the three stages of development
- Consider management supervision or administrative costs as part of development expenses
- Choose an appropriate yield capitalization method using either a property yield rate excluding a line item for entrepreneurial incentive[4] or a matched pair analysis of discounted rate and line-item entrepreneurial incentive

In simplified form, an appraiser begins the analysis of a subdivision development by determining the number and size of the lots that can be created on the appraised parcel of land physically, legally, and economically. The proposed lots must conform to jurisdictional and zoning requirements with regard to size, frontage, topography, soil quality, and off-site improvements, e.g., water facilities, drainage, sewage, streets, curbs, and gutters. The lots must also meet the demands of the market in which the property is located. Without surveys and engineering studies, an appraiser cannot know exactly how many lots can be created from a particular parcel of land. However, this analysis is often significant to the scope of work of the appraisal assignment. The extent of the analysis required should be reflected in the cost of the appraiser's services, especially if the information is not readily available. A reasonable estimate of the number of potential lots can often be deduced from zoning information, subdivision ordinances, or, preferably, the number of lots or typical unit density reflected in similar subdivision developments in the subject's market area. An appraiser must also make allowances to account for the land needed for streets, green space, water retention facilities, and any common areas.

If available, a preliminary development plan for the hypothetical subdivision of the vacant land being appraised will specify much of the data the appraiser needs:

---

[4]   Entrepreneurial incentive, entrepreneurial profit, and other forms of profit are discussed in more detail in Chapter 17.

- Number and size of the lots
- Construction work to be accomplished
- Direct (hard) and indirect (soft) construction costs
- Probable time required to subdivide the land and construct the on-site and off-site infrastructure
- Expenses and holding costs that will be incurred during the three stages of development

The appraiser then undertakes a preliminary marketability analysis to assess the supply and demand situation and probable capture and absorption rates to produce a supportable absorption forecast for the lot inventory. Accurate forecasts of product demand and competitive supply can reduce development risk and are critical to the analysis because the raw land value can vary widely depending on the rate at which lots are absorbed over time.[5] The appraiser estimates the projected retail prices of the lots by applying the direct comparison method.

Two methods may be used to allocate entrepreneurial incentive in subdivision analysis. First, entrepreneurial incentive can be accounted for in the selection of the discount rate used in the present value calculation (Chapter 23 discusses the process of discounting). In this scenario, all income and expenses flow through into the calculation of net proceeds, and a property yield rate is applied in the capitalization process. This scenario represents a true internal rate of return. The other method is sometimes known as the *split-rate method*. In the second method, the appraiser allocates a portion of the profit a typical developer would require to develop the land as a line-item expense in the list of subdivision development expenses and applies an appropriate discount rate. Both methods can accurately measure entrepreneurial incentive if applied competently.

The next step in subdivision development analysis requires the appraiser to forecast the income and expenses associated with the permitting, construction, and eventual sellout or absorption of the lots over time. The time period used for the analysis ends when the last lot is sold. Depending on the project size and sales velocity, annual, semi-annual, or quarterly discounting periods are used. The projection period begins with the property in its current "as is" condition and, if permitting is required, will include the time frame needed to achieve permitting, construction, and the absorption of all lots. If permitting is already in place as of the date of valuation, then the time period considered in the discounting calculation consists of the construction and absorption phases only. For a raw land value conclusion, the net cash flows from each period are discounted to time period zero to arrive at a present value of the net proceeds.

The following example illustrates how discounted cash flow analysis is applied in subdivision analysis to estimate raw land value. A 20-acre tract of vacant land is being considered for development as a residential subdivision with 48 lots. It will take six months to plot the subdivision, achieve entitlements, and construct the infrastructure for the entire site. After permitting and construction are completed, the developer anticipates a two-year absorption period to market the entire lot inventory.

---

5   Robert W. Owens, "Subdivision Development: Bridging Theory and Practice", *The Appraisal Journal* (July 1998): 274-281.

Discounting will be conducted over all five semi-annual phases. The market supports an average retail price of $40,000 per lot in the first semi-annual marketing period. Average lot prices will increase $2,000 in each succeeding six-month period. Expenses are projected as follows:

- Survey, site plan, and development fees over the permitting stage are estimated to be $35,000 in the first semi-annual period. Holding costs over the permitting and construction stage are estimated at about $1,300.

- On-site construction costs, including infrastructure improvements within the subdivision as well as soft costs, are $10,500 per lot for a total cost of $504,000 spread over periods 1, 2, and 4.

- Off-site development costs are also required as part of the subdivision approval by local authorities. This adds $5,000 per lot for a total of $240,000 for off-site road and other improvements. The holding costs and taxes over the construction period are considered as part of the $1,300 cost of the permitting phase. The absorption costs include marketing at 7% of gross sales and legal and closing costs at 2% of gross sales.

- After the lots are built, taxes are accounted for in the holding costs over the remaining absorption period. Taxes are estimated at $400 per year for each developed lot in inventory in each period (calculated for the average number of lots in inventory in each period at $200 per lot). Miscellaneous costs over the absorption period are $3,000 per period.

- Administration costs and supervision costs (sometimes referred to as the developer's fee) are $10,000 per period, which is appropriate given the relatively small size of this project.

Table 16.4 shows a discounted cash flow analysis of the income and expenses associated with the projections for the hypothetical project over the 2½ year permitting, construction, and absorption period. The DCF analysis anticipates that lot sale prices will increase and expenses will reflect the pattern shown in the 30-month projection. A yield rate of 23% (or 11.5% over each six-month period) based on market-derived rates from similar subdivision development sales is used with no line-item entrepreneurial incentive. (Published surveys from national data providers are also used as sources of yield rates.) Accordingly, all the entrepreneurial incentive associated with the project is accounted for in the selection of the yield rate. After applying the yield rate to the net proceeds, the indicated land value for the raw land in "as is" condition at the time of the appraisal can be rounded to $572,000.

Some market participants may prefer to have a separate allocation for entrepreneurial incentive as a line-item expense in the list of development expenses. When the split-rate method is used, the discount rate is selected in conjunction with the line-item incentive used for the calculation. Line-item incentive is a percentage of gross sales, not an interest rate. In Table 16.5, an 8% line-item entrepreneurial incentive is included in the DCF analysis. The appropriate yield rate is 15.5% (or 7.75% over each six-month period) with the given line-item entrepreneurial incentive of 8% of gross lot sales each period. The total present value is rounded to $572,000, the same as the land value conclusion derived using the true yield rate method with no line-item entrepreneurial incentive.

The application of DCF analysis is useful as a method for checking the reasonableness of value indications derived from other methods applied to estimate the

Table 16.4: DCF Analysis (with No Line-Item Entrepreneurial Incentive)

Description		Semi-annual Period					
		1	2	3	4	5	Total
Beginning lot inventory		0	48	36	24	12	
Number of developed lots		48	0	0	0	0	48
Lots sold		0	12	12	12	12	48
Ending lot inventory		48	36	24	12	0	
Cumulative lots sold		0	12	24	36	48	
Average lot price			$40,000	$42,000	$44,000	$46,000	
Gross lot sales income		$0	$480,000	$504,000	$528,000	$552,000	$2,064,000
Less: Permitting stage costs							
	Survey, site plan, and fees	$35,000					
	Holding costs during permitting and construction	$1,300					$1,300
Less: Construction stage costs							
	On-site direct and indirect construction costs	$384,000	$95,000		$25,000		$504,000
	Off-site construction costs	$240,000					$240,000
Less: Absorption phase costs							
	Marketing		$33,600	$35,280	$36,960	$38,640	$144,480
	Legal/closing		$9,600	$10,080	$10,560	$11,040	$41,280
	Miscellaneous		$3,000	$3,000	$3,000	$3,000	$12,000
	Holding costs during absorption		$8,400	$6,000	$3,600	$1,200	$19,200
Less: Administrative/ supervision costs		$10,000	$10,000	$10,000	$10,000	$10,000	$50,000
Less: Line-item entrepreneurial incentive							$0
	Percent of gross sales 0.00%	$0	$0	$0	$0	$0	$0
Subtotal expenses		$635,300	$159,600	$64,360	$89,120	$63,880	$1,012,260
Net proceeds		-$635,300	$320,400	$439,640	$438,880	$488,120	$1,051,740
Present value calculation							
Annual discount rate 23.00%							
Present value per period		-$569,776	$257,717	$317,156	$283,953	$283,238	$572,288
Indicated land value		$572,288					
Rounded		$572,000					

$$PV = -\$635{,}300(1+i_{sa})^{-1} + \$320{,}400(1+i_{sa})^{-2} + \$439{,}640(1+i_{sa})^{-3} + \$438{,}880(1+i_{sa})^{-4} + \$488{,}120(1+i_{sa})^{-5}$$

Where i_{sa} = 11.5% (23%/ 2)

PV = -$569,776 + $257,717 + $317,156 + $283,953 + $283,238

PV = $572,288, rounded to $572,000

Calculator steps are shown Appendix C.

value of vacant land with development potential. Comparing the value indication derived from DCF analysis with a value indication derived from direct comparison allows an appraiser to test the feasibility of a proposed project and solve for the appropriate discount rate and associated line-item profit allocation. If the value

Table 16.5: DCF Analysis (with Line-Item Entrepreneurial Incentive)

Description	Semi-annual Period					
	1	2	3	4	5	Total
Beginning lot inventory	0	48	36	24	12	
Number of developed lots	48	0	0	0	0	48
Lots sold	0	12	12	12	12	48
Ending lot inventory	48	36	24	12	0	
Cumulative lots sold	0	12	24	36	48	
Average lot price		$40,000	$42,000	$44,000	$46,000	
Gross lot sales income	$0	$480,000	$504,000	$528,000	$552,000	$2,064,000
Less: Permitting stage costs						
Survey, site plan, and fees	$35,000					
Holding costs during permitting						
and construction	$1,300					$1,300
Less: Construction stage costs						
On-site direct and indirect						
construction costs	$384,000	$95,000		$25,000		$504,000
Off-site construction costs	$240,000					$240,000
Less: Absorption phase costs						
Marketing		$33,600	$35,280	$36,960	$38,640	$144,480
Legal/closing		$9,600	$10,080	$10,560	$11,040	$41,280
Miscellaneous		$3,000	$3,000	$3,000	$3,000	$12,000
Holding costs during						
absorption		$8,400	$6,000	$3,600	$1,200	$19,200
Less: Administrative/						
supervision costs	$10,000	$10,000	$10,000	$10,000	$10,000	$50,000
Less: Line-item						
entrepreneurial incentive						
Percent of gross sales 8.000%	$0	$38,400	$40,320	$42,240	$44,160	$165,120
Subtotal expenses	$635,300	$198,000	$104,680	$131,360	$108,040	$1,177,380
Net proceeds	-$635,300	$282,000	$399,320	$396,640	$443,960	$886,620
Present value calculation						
Annual discount rate 15.500%						
Present value per period	-$589,606	$242,893	$319,205	$294,257	$305,673	$572,422
Indicated land value	$572,422					
Rounded	$572,000					

$PV = -\$635{,}300(1+i_{sa})^{-1} + \$282{,}000(1+i_{sa})^{-2} + \$399{,}320(1+i_{sa})^{-3} + \$396{,}640(1+i_{sa})^{-4} + \$443{,}960(1+i_{sa})^{-5}$

Where i_{sa} = 7.75% (15.5%/ 2)

$PV = -\$589{,}606 + \$242{,}893 + \$319{,}205 + \$294{,}257 + \$305{,}673$

PV = $572,422, rounded to $572,000

Calculator steps are shown in Appendix C.

indication from the DCF analysis is less than the value indication from the direct comparison approach, the appraiser may judge the proposed project to be infeasible. Developers who are also home builders may perform a subdivision analysis that begins with the sale prices of the finished homes. Appraisers may also use this type of analysis to develop land value. However, the cost of constructing the homes must be deducted, and care must be taken in selecting the discount rate and in allocating the entrepreneurial incentive between land and improvements in accordance with market practices. In this scenario, the yield rates are typically higher than yield rates for vacant lots only.

CHAPTER 17

THE COST APPROACH

It is important to note that the cost approach is a theoretical breakdown of the property into land and building components. It is theoretical because market participants sell rights, not land and buildings. The breakdown into land and building components is important because it creates many issues that would not be relevant in the other approaches where the land is not separated from the buildings. For example, the allocation of external obsolescence is an issue for the cost approach, but not for the income and direct comparison approaches.

Like the direct comparison and income approaches, the cost approach to value is based on market comparisons. The appraiser estimates the cost of the subject improvements by comparison to the construction cost of substitute properties with the same utility as the subject. The estimate of development cost is adjusted for market-extracted losses in value caused by the age, condition, and utility of the subject improvements or for locational problems. Next, the land value is added based on comparison with comparable land sales. The sum of the value of the land and the improvements is adjusted for

> In the cost approach, a property is valued based on a comparison with the cost to build a new or substitute property. The cost estimate is adjusted for the depreciation evident in the existing property.

the rights included with the subject based on market comparisons. The cost approach reflects market thinking because market participants relate value to cost. Buyers tend to judge the value of an existing structure not only by considering the prices and rents of similar buildings, but also by comparing the cost to create a new building with optimal physical condition and functional utility. Moreover, buyers adjust the prices they are willing to pay by estimating the costs to bring an existing structure up to the physical condition and functional utility they desire.

To apply the cost approach, an appraiser estimates the market's perception of the difference between the property improvements being appraised and a newly constructed building with optimal utility, i.e., the ideal improvement. In its classic form, the cost approach produces an opinion of the value of the fee simple interest in the real estate. If the purpose of the appraisal is to estimate the value of an interest other than fee simple, an adjustment may be required. For example, an appraiser could make a property rights adjustment as a lump-sum adjustment at the end of the cost approach. This would be particularly important when the interest appraised is the leased fee encumbered by a long-term lease.

In applying the cost approach, an appraiser must distinguish between two cost bases – *reproduction cost* and *replacement cost* – and use one of the two consistently throughout the analysis. The market and physical condition of the appraised property usually suggest whether an exact replica of the subject property (reproduction cost) or a substitute property of similar size and use (replacement cost) would be the basis of a more suitable comparison.

The appraiser estimates the cost to construct the existing structure and site improvements (including direct costs, indirect costs, and an appropriate entrepreneurial profit or incentive) using one of three traditional techniques:

> **cost approach**
> A set of procedures through which a value indication is derived for the fee simple interest in a property by estimating the current cost to construct a reproduction of (or replacement for) the existing structure, including an entrepreneurial incentive; deducting depreciation from the total cost; and adding the estimated land value. Adjustments may then be made to the indicated fee simple value of the subject property to reflect the value of the property interest being appraised.

1. Comparative-unit method
2. Unit-in-place method
3. Quantity survey method

The appraiser then deducts all depreciation in the property improvements from the cost of the new structure as of the effective appraisal date. The amount of depreciation present is estimated using one or more of three fundamental methods:

1. Market extraction method
2. Economic age-life method
3. Breakdown method

When the value of the land is added to the cost of the improvements less depreciation, the result is the value of the fee simple interest in the real estate.

This chapter provides an outline of the cost approach (see Figure 17.1) and explains the fundamental appraisal concepts that support this approach to value. Chapters 18 and 19 discuss the specifics of cost and depreciation estimates, i.e., the essential techniques applied to render a convincing opinion of value using the cost approach.

RELATION TO APPRAISAL PRINCIPLES

Substitution

The principle of substitution is basic to the cost approach. This principle affirms that a knowledgeable buyer would pay no more for a property than the cost to acquire a similar site and construct improvements of equivalent desirability and utility without undue delay. In the cost approach, existing properties can be seen as substitutes for the property being appraised, and their value is also measured relative to the value of a new, optimal property. In short, the cost of property improvements on the effective

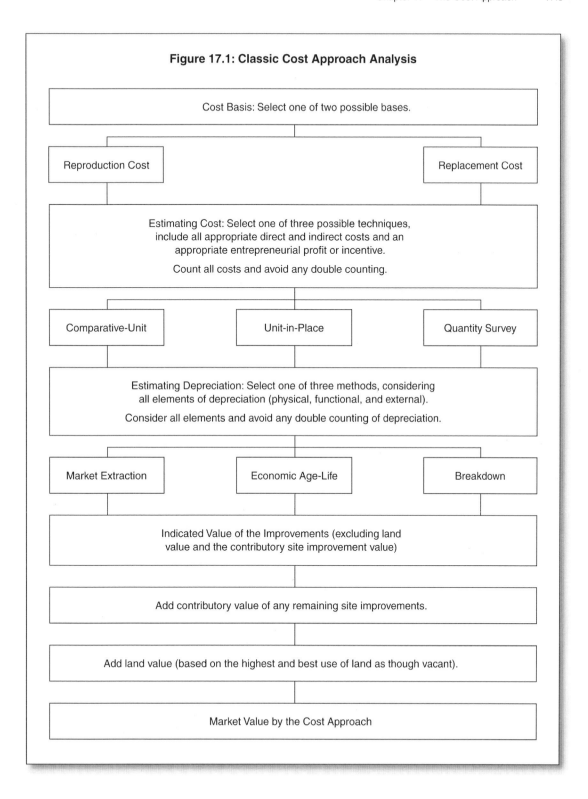

Figure 17.1: Classic Cost Approach Analysis

Cost Basis: Select one of two possible bases.

Reproduction Cost

Replacement Cost

Estimating Cost: Select one of three possible techniques, include all appropriate direct and indirect costs and an appropriate entrepreneurial profit or incentive.

Count all costs and avoid any double counting.

Comparative-Unit

Unit-in-Place

Quantity Survey

Estimating Depreciation: Select one of three methods, considering all elements of depreciation (physical, functional, and external).

Consider all elements and avoid any double counting of depreciation.

Market Extraction

Economic Age-Life

Breakdown

Indicated Value of the Improvements (excluding land value and the contributory site improvement value)

Add contributory value of any remaining site improvements.

Add land value (based on the highest and best use of land as though vacant).

Market Value by the Cost Approach

date of the appraisal plus the accompanying site value provides a measure against which prices for similar improved properties may be judged.

Supply and Demand

Shifts in supply and demand cause prices to increase or decrease. As a result, a single property may have different values over time. If costs do not shift in proportion to price changes, the construction of buildings will be more or less profitable and the value of existing buildings will increase or decrease commensurately. If costs of production increase faster than values, new construction will be less profitable or may not be financially feasible. In other words, the incentive for developers to build is directly tied to supply and demand.

Contribution

The principle of contribution, which holds that the value of an individual component of a property is measured in terms of how much it contributes to the value of the property as a whole, is integral to the application of the cost approach. The various methods of estimating building costs are based on the contributions of the various components of a property. Conversely, the principle of contribution implies that the value of a component may be measured as the amount its absence would detract from the value of the property as a whole. From this perspective, the estimation of depreciation can be seen as an application of the principle of contribution.

In the application of the cost approach, an appraiser measures the amount each component contributes to the value of the property as a whole in relation to the highest and best use of the property. For example, if the highest and best use of the property is for the conversion of the existing improvements to an alternative use, items that must be changed for the property to achieve its highest and best use would suffer from some form of depreciation.

In the cost approach, the effect on value of a deficiency or superadequacy is addressed in the estimate of a form of depreciation known as *functional obsolescence*. An appraiser can identify the deficiency or superadequacy by comparing the existing improvements with the ideal improvement and then treat it by making a deduction from the cost of the improvements. As the improvements depreciate, the site often contributes a higher percentage of total property value. As the ratio of site value to total property value approaches 100%, it becomes more likely that the improvements will be demolished and the property redeveloped to a new highest and best use.

Externalities

The construction cost and market value of a property may be affected differently by conditions that are external to the property. Externalities such as inflation or natural disasters may increase material and labour costs without a corresponding increase in market values. Real estate values do not always run parallel with other economic trends. On the other hand, an external event such as the completion of a sewer line may increase the value of a property but have no impact on its cost. Gains or losses in value caused by externalities may accrue to the land, the site, the building, or the property as a whole. Rising construction costs can significantly affect the market value of new construction and, in turn, the demand for and market value of older, substitute properties.

In the cost approach, a loss in building value due to external causes is attributed to external obsolescence. Externalities can be temporary and may work in positive and negative directions over the life of a building improvement.

Highest and Best Use

In the first series of tests of highest and best use, the appraiser analyzes the site as though vacant and available to be developed to its highest and best use and identifies an ideal improvement or course of development. If the site is improved, the appraiser performs a second highest and best use analysis comparing the existing improvements to the ideal. Thus, a parcel of land may have one highest and best use as though vacant, and the existing combination of the site and improvements may have a different highest and best use as improved. Existing improvements have a value equal to the amount they contribute to the site, or they may penalize the property value if they have outlived their usefulness. This penalty is often measured by the cost to remove the obsolete improvements from the site.

Existing improvements are rarely identical to the ideal improvements, unless they are new construction, and even then they may be an overimprovement or underimprovement by comparison with the ideal. For example, a new building that is poorly designed for the market is worth less than its cost because of the functional obsolescence in its design, which is discussed in more detail later in this chapter. An accurate and detailed analysis of highest and best use is critical to the cost approach because the comparison of the existing improvement and the ideal improvement identifies any forms of depreciation that are present in the building.

Stabilization

The value of a property indicated by the cost approach is a fee simple value. For properties that are leased, the cost approach assumes stabilized occupancy and income. An appraiser considers the holding costs that accrue during the leasing phase of property development along with other indirect costs such as leasing commissions, marketing costs, and rent concessions. Tenant finish costs may also be necessary to achieve stabilized occupancy and, if so, they must be added as a direct cost. Also, a property with rents that are higher or lower than market rents may be stabilized in terms of occupancy, but the value developed by the cost approach may still require an adjustment.

APPLICABILITY AND LIMITATIONS

In any market, the value of a building can be related to its cost. The cost approach is particularly important when a lack of market activity limits the usefulness of the direct comparison approach and when the property to be appraised is not amenable to valuation by the income approach – e.g., a single-unit residence. Since cost and market value are usually more closely related when properties are new, the cost approach is important in estimating the market value of new or relatively new construction. The approach is especially persuasive when land value is well supported and the improvements are new or suffer only minor depreciation and, therefore, approximate the ideal improvement that is the highest and best use of the land as though vacant. An appraiser can also apply the cost approach to older properties given adequate data to measure depreciation.

The cost approach may be used to develop an opinion of market value (or some other value such as use value or fair value, if the appraisal assignment requires) and is frequently applied to proposed construction, special-purpose or specialty properties, and other properties that are not frequently exchanged in the market such as public buildings. Buyers of these properties often measure the price they will pay for an existing building against the cost to build minus depreciation or against the cost to purchase an existing structure and make any necessary modifications. If comparable sales are not available, they cannot be analyzed to develop an opinion of the market value of such properties. Therefore, current market indications of depreciated cost or the costs to acquire and refurbish an existing building are the best reflections of market thinking and, thus, of market value (or use value or fair value).

> The cost approach is most applicable in valuing new or proposed construction when the improvements represent the highest and best use of the land and land value is well supported.

> Depending on the purpose of the appraisal assignment, the cost approach can be used to develop an opinion of the market value or use value of special-purpose properties and properties that are not frequently exchanged in the market.

When the physical characteristics of comparable properties differ significantly, the relative values of these characteristics can sometimes be identified more precisely with the cost approach than with direct comparison. Because the cost approach starts with the cost to construct a replica or a substitute property with optimal physical and functional utility, it can help an appraiser determine accurate adjustments for physical differences in comparable sale properties. If, for example, an appraiser must make an adjustment for inadequate elevators in a comparable property, the cost to cure the deficiency can be used as a basis for this adjustment. Thus, the cost approach provides the appraiser with data to use in estimating depreciation and in deriving an adjustment to apply in the direct comparison approach.

The cost approach is especially useful when building additions or renovations are being considered, a key issue in highest and best use analysis. An appraiser can use the approach to estimate whether the cost of an improvement, including an entrepreneurial incentive, will be recovered through an increased income stream or in the anticipated sale price. This analysis can help identify and prevent the construction of overimprovements.

Since the cost approach requires that land and improvements must be valued separately, it is also useful in appraisals for insurance purposes, when uninsurable items must be segregated from insurable items. In valuation for financial reporting (i.e., accounting purposes), the cost approach is applied to estimate depreciation for income tax purposes. In cases where site value tends to make up a considerable portion of overall property value (such as agricultural properties or high-exposure commercial outparcels), the cost approach can take on greater significance because it is the only approach requiring a separate conclusion of site value.

Finally, an estimate of probable building and development costs is an essential component of feasibility studies, which test the investment assumptions on which land use plans are based. A proposed development is considered financially feasible when market value exceeds total building and development costs plus a reasonable, market-supported estimate of entrepreneurial incentive, i.e., the anticipated profit necessary for an entrepreneur to proceed with the project.

If the cost approach yields a higher value than the direct comparison or income approaches, it may be an indication that the development is not economically feasible. If the cost approach yields a higher value for an existing building, then the appraiser may need to take a closer look at one or more of the inputs – land value, current cost, depreciation, or entrepreneurial incentive. In an improving market, the actual profit may be higher than market-derived estimates of entrepreneurial incentive, resulting in a lower value by the cost approach. For older properties or properties in fluctuating markets, an inaccurate estimate of the remaining economic life could result in depreciation being understated, resulting in a higher value by the cost approach. When an appraiser produces a higher or lower value in the cost approach, the appraiser usually compares the value against the results of one or more of the other approaches and explains the differences in reconciliation.

When improvements are considerably older or do not represent the highest and best use of the land as though vacant, the physical deterioration, functional obsolescence, and external obsolescence may be more difficult to estimate. Furthermore, relevant comparable data may be lacking or the data available may be too diverse to indicate an appropriate estimate of entrepreneurial profit, i.e., the profit actually earned from a completed project. These conditions may render the cost approach less reliable.

One of the weaknesses of the cost approach from an investment perspective is the assumption that newly constructed improvements are immediately available on the date of the appraisal. An investor looking at options for an immediate purchase may consider the months or years required to develop and construct a new property to be an undue and unacceptable delay. From the perspective of that investor, the cost approach would have no relevance.

Appraisers must remember that the cost approach results in an indication of the value of the fee simple interest in a property. To value real estate held in leased fee or property subject to other partial interests, appraisers must make adjustments to reflect the specific real property rights being appraised such as a leased fee interest.

PROCEDURE

After gathering all relevant information and analyzing data for the market area, site, and improvements, an appraiser follows a series of steps to derive a value indication by the cost approach. The appraiser will do the following:

1. Estimate the value of the site as though vacant and available to be developed to its highest and best use.

2. Determine which cost basis is most applicable to the assignment: reproduction cost or replacement cost.

3. Estimate the direct (hard) and indirect (soft) costs of the improvements as of the effective appraisal date.

4. Estimate an appropriate entrepreneurial profit or incentive from analysis of the market.

5. Add the estimated direct costs, indirect costs, and entrepreneurial profit or incentive to arrive at the total cost of the improvements.

6. Estimate the amount of depreciation in the structure and, if necessary, allocate it among the three major categories:

    ◦ Physical deterioration
    ◦ Functional obsolescence
    ◦ External obsolescence

7. Deduct estimated depreciation from the total cost of the improvements to derive an estimate of their depreciated cost.

8. Estimate the contributory value of any site improvements that have not already been considered. (Site improvements are often appraised at their contributory value – i.e., directly on a depreciated-cost basis – but may be included in the overall cost calculated in Step 2 and depreciated if necessary.)

9. Add site value to the total depreciated cost of all the improvements to develop the market value of the property.

10. Adjust the value conclusion if any personal property (e.g., furniture, fixtures, and equipment) or intangible assets are included in the appraisal assignment. If necessary, this value, which reflects the value of the fee simple interest, may be adjusted for the property interest being appraised to arrive at the indicated value of the specified interest in the property.

Site Value

In the cost approach, the estimated market value of the site is added to the depreciated cost of the improvements. The value of the site depends on its highest and best use. Site value can be estimated using various techniques, which are discussed in Chapter 16. Appraisers must remember that the site value estimates produced with these techniques reflect the value of the fee simple interest. If a land lease is involved and it is not at market terms, this could have a positive or negative effect on value.

Reproduction Cost versus Replacement Cost

The cost to construct an improvement on the effective appraisal date may be developed as the estimated reproduction cost or replacement cost of the improvement. The theoretical base (and classic starting point) for the cost approach is reproduction cost, but replacement cost is commonly used because it may be easier to obtain and can reduce the complexity of depreciation analysis. An important distinction must be made between the terms.

- Reproduction cost is the estimated cost to construct, as of the effective appraisal date, an exact duplicate or replica of the building being appraised, insofar as possible, using the same materials, construction standards, design, layout, and quality of workmanship and embodying all the deficiencies, superadequacies, and obsolescence of the subject improvements.

- Replacement cost is the estimated cost to construct, as of the effective appraisal date, a substitute for the building being appraised using contemporary materials, standards, design, and layout. When this cost basis is used, some existing obsolescence in the property may be cured. Replacement cost may be the only alternative if reproduction cost cannot be estimated.

> **replacement cost**
> The estimated cost to construct, at current prices as of the effective appraisal date, a substitute for the building being appraised using modern materials and current standards, design, and layout.
>
> **reproduction cost**
> The estimated cost to construct, at current prices as of the effective date of the appraisal, an exact duplicate or replica of the building being appraised, using the same materials, construction standards, design, layout, and quality of workmanship and embodying all the deficiencies, superadequacies, and obsolescence of the subject building.

> Cost may be estimated on two different bases: replacement cost or reproduction cost. Specific types of obsolescence would be precluded by using a replacement cost estimate.

The decision to use reproduction cost or replacement cost is often dictated by the age of the structure, its uniqueness, and any difference between its intended use at the time of construction and its current highest and best use. In theory, the use of either reproduction cost or replacement cost should yield the same indication of value after proper application, but in practice both cost estimates and depreciation estimates may be different. If reproduction cost or replacement cost is used inconsistently, double counting of items of depreciation and other errors can be introduced into the analysis. An appraiser must clearly identify the cost basis selected for a particular appraisal in the report to avoid misunderstanding and must consistently apply the cost basis throughout the cost approach to avoid errors in calculating an estimate of value.

The use of replacement cost can eliminate the need to measure many, but not all, forms of functional obsolescence such as poor design and superadequacies (over-built or excessive construction). Replacement structures usually cost less than identical structures (i.e., reproductions) because they are constructed with materials and techniques that are more readily available and less expensive in the current market. Also, correcting deficiencies may result in lower costs. Thus, a replacement cost figure is usually lower and may provide a better indication of the existing structure's contribution to value. A replacement structure typically does not suffer functional obsolescence resulting from superadequacies. However, if functional problems persist in the hypothetical replacement structure, an amount must be deducted from the replacement cost. Estimating replacement cost generally simplifies the procedure for measuring depreciation in components of superadequate construction. An example of functional obsolescence would be the absence of a desirable feature such as air-conditioning in an existing improvement in a market where this feature is standard. This form of obsolescence would be corrected in a replacement building.

Estimating reproduction cost can be complicated because the improvements may include materials that are now unavailable and construction standards may have changed. Nevertheless, reproduction cost usually provides a basis for measuring depreciation from all causes when such measurement is necessary.

Cost Estimates

To develop cost estimates for the total building, appraisers must consider direct (hard) and indirect (soft) costs. Both types of cost are essential to a reliable cost estimate. Chapter 18 discusses the traditional data sources and appraisal techniques used to estimate building costs.

Direct construction costs include the costs of material and labour as well as the contractor's profit required to construct the improvement on the effective appraisal date. The overhead and profit of the general contractor and various subcontractors are usually part of the construction contract and therefore represent direct costs that should always be included in the cost estimate. In more complex projects, where multiple contractors, construction staging, or other complications are involved, a management fee may be required. Indirect costs are expenditures or allowances that are necessary for construction but are not typically part of the construction contract. Since the entrepreneur provides the inspiration, drive, and coordination necessary to the overall project, the cost approach should include an appropriate entrepreneurial profit or incentive, which will be discussed later in this chapter.

> **direct costs**
> Expenditures for the labor and materials used in the construction of improvements; also called *hard costs*.
>
> **indirect costs**
> Expenditures or allowances for items other than labor and materials that are necessary for construction but are not typically part of the construction contract. Indirect costs may include administrative costs; professional fees; financing costs and the interest paid on construction loans; taxes and the builder's or developer's all-risk insurance during construction; and marketing, sales, and lease-up costs incurred to achieve occupancy or sale; also called *soft costs*.

Because the quality of materials and labour greatly influences costs, the appraiser should be familiar with the costs of the materials used in the subject property. A building can cost substantially more than is typical if items such as walls and windows are overinsulated or thicker slabs are used to accommodate greater floor loads. Many newer structures contain elements that may not be found in older buildings with which they compete. At one time, the market may have considered features such as internet connectivity, networking and telecommunications capabilities, and adequate, reliable power in "smart" office buildings to be high-tech overimprovements. Such features may not have contributed as much value as they cost then, but as demand for these building materials and features continues to increase so does their contribution to value.

The competitive situation in the local market can also affect cost estimates. Actual contractor bids based on the same set of specifications can vary substantially. A contractor who is working at capacity is inclined to make a high bid, while one who needs the work is likely to submit a lower figure. The items cited in the right-hand column of Table 17.1 reflect typical indirect costs incurred in a balanced market. In markets that are out of balance, higher costs may result from a prolonged absorption period, e.g., additional marketing or carrying costs, tenant improvements, leasing commissions, and administrative expenses. The increase in costs can contribute to external obsolescence.

Some indirect costs, such as architectural fees and property taxes, are generally related to the size and cost of the project; these are often estimated as a percentage of direct costs. Other costs, such as leasing and sales commissions, are related to the type of property or market practice. Still others, such as fees for appraisals and environmental studies, are a function of the time required to accomplish the task. The indirect costs of carrying an investment during and after construction are a combination of all of the above. Although total indirect costs are sometimes estimated as a percentage of direct costs, more detailed studies of these costs are recommended. When using a cost estimating service, it is important to know which costs are included in the cost estimates and which need to be added by the appraiser.

Table 17.1: Direct Costs and Indirect Costs

Direct Costs	Indirect Costs
• Building permits • Materials, products, and equipment • Labor used in construction • Equipment used in construction • Security during construction • Contractor's site office and temporary fencing • Material storage facilities • Power line installation and utility costs • Contractor's profit and overhead, including job supervision; coordination and management (when appropriate); worker's compensation; and fire, liability, and unemployment insurance • Performance bonds	• Architectural and engineering fees for plans, plan checks, surveys to establish building lines and grades, and environmental studies • Appraisal, consulting, accounting, and legal fees • The cost of carrying the investment in land and contract payments during construction* • All-risk insurance expense and ad valorem taxes during construction • The cost of carrying the investment in the property after construction is complete but before stabilization is achieved • Supplemental capital investment in tenant improvements and leasing commissions • Marketing costs, sales commissions, and any applicable holding costs to achieve stabilized occupancy in a normal market • Administrative expenses of the developer

*If the property is financed, the points, fees or service charges, and interest on construction loans are indirect costs.

Entrepreneurial Incentive and Entrepreneurial Profit

Entrepreneurs (developers, contractors, investors, and others) compete against each other in the real estate marketplace, and any building project will include an economic reward (above and beyond direct and indirect costs) sufficient to induce an entrepreneur to incur the risk associated with that project in that market. For a new building that is the highest and best use of the site, the difference between the market value and the total cost of development (i.e., the sum of site value and direct and indirect costs) is the profit (or loss) realized:

> Market Value
> – Total Cost of Development
> Profit (or Loss)

Whether or not a profit is actually realized depends on how well the entrepreneur has analyzed the market demand for the property, selected the site, and constructed the improvements. In the case of income-producing properties, the profit realized will also depend on the entrepreneur's ability to obtain the proper tenant mix and negotiate leases.

The term *entrepreneurial incentive* refers to the amount an entrepreneur expects or wants to receive as compensation for providing coordination and expertise and assuming the risks associated with the development of a project. In contrast, *entrepreneurial profit* refers to the difference between the total cost of development and marketing and the market value of a property *after* completion and achievement of stabilized occupancy and income.[1] In short, incentive is anticipated while profit is earned.

As a market-derived figure, an estimate of entrepreneurial profit or entrepreneurial incentive is only as reliable and precise as the available market data warrants. Nevertheless, an estimate of profit is a fundamental component of total cost, and most market areas have a typical or appropriate range of profit that can be determined through market research, usually through interviews with developers and other market participants about anticipated, acceptable, and actual levels of profit achieved in the market. The range of profit will vary for different types of structures and with the nature or scale of a given project. The entrepreneurial incentive for a proposed development may be higher where creative concepts, greater risk, or unique opportunities have market acceptance. Less risky, more standard competitive projects may merit a lower measure of profit. For example, the first speculative high-rise office park in a suburban market is likely to require greater entrepreneurial incentive than a new residential subdivision development in a community with demonstrable population growth.

Also, the amount of profit earned can relate to the stage of development and the different levels of risk and expertise that may be required at different stages. For

---

> **entrepreneurial incentive**
> A market-derived figure that represents the amount an entrepreneur expects to receive for his or her contribution to a project and risk.
>
> **entrepreneurial profit**
> A market-derived figure that represents the amount an entrepreneur receives for his or her contribution to a project and risk; the difference between the total cost of a property (cost of development) and its market value (property value after completion), which represents the entrepreneur's compensation for the risk and expertise associated with development.

---

[1]   Historically, *entrepreneurial profit* has been the more common term in general usage and serves as a broader term in the discussion of the cost approach. In this text, the term *entrepreneurial incentive*, which is a more recent addition to the appraisal lexicon, is used specifically in reference to a situation that calls for a forecast of the reward an entrepreneur expects to receive at the completion of a real estate development.

example, an entrepreneur can start earning a reward from the start of the project. This reward can increase as land is acquired, plans are drawn up, permits are approved, financing is secured, contracts are signed, construction is completed, and units are sold off or leased. It can be difficult to estimate exactly how much profit would be earned at each stage of construction, although lenders may require interim values that reflect financing costs and taxes during the construction and leasing phases.

Contributions of the Entrepreneur, Developer, and Contractor

In analyzing the components of reward and compensation received (or anticipated) by an entrepreneur, the appraiser may choose to further distinguish between the concepts of project profit, entrepreneurial profit, developer's profit, and contractor's profit:

- Project profit is the total amount of reward for entrepreneurial coordination and risk.
- Entrepreneurial profit refers to the portion of project profit attributable to the efforts of the entrepreneur, distinct from the efforts of the developer, if one is present. In projects in which the entrepreneur and the developer are one and the same, the entrepreneurial profit is equivalent to total project profit.
- Developer's profit represents compensation for the time, energy, and expertise of an individual other than the original entrepreneur – usually, in large projects, the person responsible for managing the overall development process.
- Contractor's profit (including subcontractors' fees) is essentially a portion of the project's overhead and is not usually reflected in the entrepreneurial reward.

The measure of project profit used in cost approach calculations usually includes both a developer's profit and an entrepreneurial profit. The profit a contractor receives is often already reflected in the fee a contractor charges and would therefore be included in the direct costs.

In practice, separating the value impact of the entrepreneurial coordination from other market influences can be difficult. To ensure the reasonableness of an estimate of entrepreneurial incentive or entrepreneurial profit, appraisers should carefully examine the source of additional property value over and above the total cost of development and the effects of supply and demand for properties of that type in the subject market area. For example, some appraisers point out that the value associated with the amenities of a property may be such that the sale price of the property could significantly exceed the sum of the costs of the land, building, and marketing, e.g., in an overheated seller's market where sale prices are inflated.

Some appraisers also observe that entrepreneurial incentive often represents an intangible asset in build-to-suit, owner-occupied properties. The owner-occupant may consider any additional operating profit due to the property's efficient design to be an incentive. However, the entrepreneurial profit might only be realized years after the property is built when a similar owner-occupant pays a premium for the property's immediate suitability. In this case, entrepreneurial profit is likely to become obscured over time by changing market conditions. For certain types of specialized owner-occupied improvements, such as public buildings, no entrepreneurial profit may ever be recorded because the owner neither anticipates nor wants a profit.

The way in which comparable properties have been developed affects the availability of data. Appraisers are sometimes able to calculate entrepreneurial profit from comparable costs for speculatively built properties such as condominiums and multi-family developments. In the value estimate of a speculatively built property, entrepreneurial profit represents a return to the entrepreneur for the skills employed and the risks incurred, although the actual return may differ from the anticipated return. However, in large-scale developments, the issue is complicated because the entrepreneurial profit may not reflect the proportionate contributions of the improved site and the improvement to the overall property value. For example, developers of tract subdivisions might realize most of their profit on the value of the houses built on the finished lots, not necessarily the value of the lots.

Data on entrepreneurial profit for custom-built properties may not be available if the property owner who contracted the actual builders was acting as the developer. The prices of upscale, custom-built properties often reflect the attractiveness of these amenity-laden properties as well as the high costs of the materials used. Thus, the breakdown of costs for custom-built properties may not be comparable to the breakdown for speculatively built properties, which further complicates the task of estimating a rate of entrepreneurial profit. Theoretically, however, the value of custom-built properties should also reflect an entrepreneurial profit.

The appraiser must also scrutinize the cost data on which the value estimate is based to determine whether or not an allowance for entrepreneurial profit has already been made. If this is not done, the entrepreneurial profit could be included twice. Data derived from sales of comparable sites often includes a profit for the land developer. Cost-estimating services quote direct costs (e.g., contractor's profit) and indirect costs (e.g., sales costs), but they may or may not provide estimates of entrepreneurial profit. Because different sources of data reflect costs in different ways, the appraiser should identify where the entrepreneurial profit is considered in the estimate, i.e., whether it is an item already included in the sum of total cost and land value or a stand-alone item added to the sum of total cost and land value.

Depreciation

Depreciation[2] is the difference between the contributory value of an improvement and its cost at the time of appraisal:

> Reproduction or Replacement Cost of Improvement
> - <u>Contributory Value of Improvement</u>
> Depreciation

By estimating the depreciation incurred by an improvement and deducting this estimate from the improvement's reproduction or replacement cost, an appraiser can conclude the depreciated cost of the improvement. This depreciated cost approximates the improvement's contribution to the property's market value as illustrated

---

[2]   Many of the terms appraisers use are also used by accountants, economists, and other real estate professionals. The term *accrued depreciation*, which appeared in earlier editions of *The Appraisal of Real Estate*, was originally borrowed from accounting practice. In accounting, accrued depreciation (or alternatively *accruals for depreciation*) refers to the total depreciation taken on an asset from the time of purchase to the present, which is normally deducted from an asset's account value to derive net book value. While accrued depreciation has long been used in an appraisal context, the simpler and more concise term *depreciation* is equally suitable and has been used throughout this edition. The term *total depreciation* also remains in use by appraisers, although depreciation is used without modification in this textbook in most cases to refer to estimates of both the total amount of depreciation that a property suffers from and the amount of depreciation attributable to a particular form of depreciation, i.e., a part of the whole.

in Figure 17.2. Chapter 19 discusses techniques for estimating depreciation.

Depreciation in an improvement can result from three major causes operating separately or in combination:

> Depreciation is the difference between the market value of an improvement and its reproduction or replacement cost at the time of appraisal. The depreciated cost of the improvement can be considered an indication of the improvement's contribution to the property's market value

- Physical deterioration – wear and tear from regular use, the impact of the elements, or damage.

- Functional obsolescence – a flaw in the structure, materials, or design that diminishes the function, utility, and value of the improvement.

- External obsolescence – a temporary or permanent impairment of the utility or saleability of an improvement or property due to negative influences outside the property. (External obsolescence may result from adverse market conditions. Because of its fixed location, real estate is subject to external influences that usually cannot be controlled by the property owner, landlord, or tenant.)

The sum of all these components is total depreciation. The market recognizes the occurrence of depreciation and the appraiser interprets how the market perceives the effect of depreciation.

Theoretically, depreciation can begin in the design phase or the moment construction is started, even in a functional building that represents the highest and best use of a site. Improvements are rarely built under ideal circumstances and their construction takes considerable time. During the construction process, physical deterioration can be temporarily halted or even corrected, but physical deterioration tends to persist throughout the life of the improvements. Moreover, as time goes on and a building's features become dated in comparison to new buildings, functional obsolescence sets in. Consider, for example, an industrial building that was built in the early 1970s. The structure's 12 foot ceilings, which were the market standard then, might be considered totally inadequate now that greater clear heights are the norm. New buildings can have functional obsolescence even before they are constructed, which is usually attributable to a design that does not meet market standards.

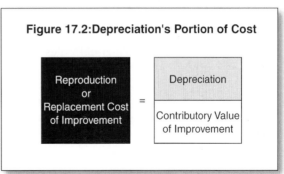

Figure 17.2:Depreciation's Portion of Cost

In the cost approach, the depreciation attributable to all causes is extracted from the market, or calculated when market extraction is not possible, and deducted from the current cost to arrive at the depreciated cost:

    Current Cost
-   Total Depreciation Applicable
    Depreciated Cost

Depreciation in Appraising and Accounting
The term depreciation is used in both accounting and appraisal, so it is important to distinguish between the two usages. Book depreciation is an accounting term that refers to the amount of capital recapture written off for an asset on the owner's books for income tax or financial reporting purposes. Under the current Generally Accepted Accounting Principles (GAAP), the term has typically been used in income tax calculations to identify the amount allowed as accruals for the retirement or replacement of an asset under the federal tax laws. Book depreciation may also be estimated using a depreciation schedule set by the Canada Revenue Agency (CRA). Traditionally, book depreciation has not been market-derived like the depreciation estimates developed by appraisers. Instead, various formula-based techniques (e.g., the straight-line method, units of production method, declining balance method, sum-of-the-years'-digits method) have been used to calculate scheduled depreciation.

The depreciated cost of the site improvements (or their contribution to value) and the site value are added together to provide an indication of the market value of the property:

> Depreciated Cost
> + Site Value
> Market Value

Depreciation is a penalty only insofar as the market recognizes it as causing a loss in value. For some older buildings, the value loss due to apparent depreciation may be offset by a temporary scarcity relative to demand or by an improvement's historical or architectural significance. In these situations, an appraiser should exercise caution not to penalize a property unduly in the cost approach.

As mentioned earlier, an appraiser's use of reproduction cost rather than replacement cost to derive a current cost estimate will affect the estimation of depreciation. Some forms of functional obsolescence are eliminated when replacement cost is used, but other forms remain unaffected. Consider an industrial building with poor access for trucks and with a 28 foot ceiling height in a market where 24 foot ceiling heights are the norm. A replacement cost estimate could be based on a building with a 24 foot ceiling height, while a reproduction cost estimate would be based on a building with a 28 foot ceiling height. By using replacement cost instead of reproduction cost, the appraiser eliminates the superadequacy attributable to the ceiling height but not the deficiency caused by poor access to the street. Moreover, any additional costs of ownership caused by the superadequacy would not be eliminated in the replacement cost estimate. If the excess ceiling height were the cause of additional heating, cooling, insurance, or property taxes, the superadequacy would also cause additional depreciation. An appraiser using replacement cost would have to consider any excess operating costs associated with the superadequate construction.

> The difficulty of estimating depreciation in older properties may diminish the reliability of the cost approach in valuing these properties.

CHAPTER 18

BUILDING COST ESTIMATES

To apply the cost approach to value, an appraiser must prepare an estimate of the cost of the improvements as of the effective date of appraisal. Such an estimate can be prepared by an appraiser who understands construction plans, specifications, materials, and techniques and can access a variety of data sources or computer programs available for this purpose. Alternatively, the work can be done with the assistance of expert cost estimators. In either case, the appraiser is responsible for the result. All individuals who are delegated to estimate costs should carefully review and describe existing improvements.

Proposed improvements may be valued based on plans and specifications provided that the appraiser discloses that the improvements have not yet been built and that their completion as specified is an extraordinary assumption of the appraisal. Residential appraisers are commonly asked to provide an opinion of prospective value under the extraordinary assumption that a property will be completed as planned. Non-residential appraisers are also asked to value property that has not yet been completed, and sometimes two prospective values are called for: the value at the time of completion and the value at the time stabilized occupancy and income are achieved. The values may be based on the extraordinary assumptions that the improvements will be completed as proposed on a future date (for the value upon completion) and the property will be stabilized (for the value upon reaching stabilization).

COST DATA SOURCES

Construction contracts for buildings similar to the building being appraised provide a primary source of comparable cost data. Some appraisers maintain comprehensive files of current cost data, including current costs for completed houses, apartments, hotels, office buildings, retail buildings, and industrial buildings. These costs can provide a basis for calculating the cost to construct an existing or proposed building. Contract-reporting services may indicate building areas or a general building description, the low bids, and the contract award. The appraiser can then obtain any missing information, such as the breakdown of office and warehouse space in an industrial property, and classify the building type for filing purposes. When an appraiser carefully develops and manages cost comparable files, they can supply authentic square foot costs on buildings of all types for use in appraisal assignments.

> Cost data may be obtained from construction contracts, building contractors, and published or computer-assisted cost-estimating services.

In the absence of construction contract data, local building contractors and professional cost estimators can be reliable data sources. In an active market, an appraiser can also obtain cost information by interviewing local property owners who have recently added building or land improvements similar to those found on the subject property. If work contracts and accounting records of recently improved properties are available, they can provide significant details.

Cost-Estimating Services

Many cost-estimating services publish data for estimating the current cost of improvements. These services include the following:

- Marshall and Swift Publication Company: *www.marshallswift.com*
- F. W. Dodge Corporation: *www.fwdodge.com*
- R. S. Means Company, Inc.: *www.rsmeans.com*

Published cost manuals usually include direct unit costs and some indirect costs. (Appraisers should be aware that published cost estimates may or may not include indirect costs such as loan interest during construction or real estate brokerage fees.) An appraiser must research the market to determine which costs are most applicable to the appraisal assignment. National cost services list the costs of many site improvements separately, rather than as part of building costs. This data includes the costs of roads, storm drains, rough grading, soil compaction, utilities, and jurisdictional utility hookup fees and assessments. Published cost services do not usually provide demolition costs; more often they are obtained from actual costs or from demolition contractors. Also, cost service data does not usually include entrepreneurial profit. The appraiser usually estimates such costs separately and includes them in the estimate of total cost.

Although buildings can be measured in several ways, appraisers should measure buildings according to local custom. To use cost service data effectively, an appraiser must understand the measurement technique used by the service. Several cost-estimating services publish manuals or maintain electronic databases that break down costs into square foot increments. Unit costs for building types usually start with a building of a certain size (i.e., a base area), which serves as a benchmark. Then additions or deductions are made to account for the actual number of square feet and building components in the subject property. Data provided by cost-estimating services can be used to confirm estimates developed from local cost data.

Cost Index Trending

Cost manuals and electronic databases are updated periodically by including cost index tables that reflect changes in the cost of construction over a period of years. Cost indexes convert a known cost as of a past date into a current cost estimate. Sometimes cost index tables can be used to adjust costs for different geographic areas. Cost index trending is also useful for estimating the current cost of one-of-a-kind items when standard costs are not available. However, there are practical limitations in applying this procedure because, as the time span increases, the reliability of the current cost indication tends to decrease.

> Cost index trending may be used to convert historical data into a current cost estimate.

As an example of cost index trending, suppose the contract cost for constructing a building in January 2000 was $1,000,000. The index for January 2000 is 285.1 and the current index is 327.3. To trend the historical cost into a current cost, the current cost index is divided by the historical cost index and the result is multiplied by the historical cost. In this case, the current cost is calculated as follows:

Current cost index = 327.3 ÷ 285.1 = 1.148
Current cost estimate = 1.148 × $1,000,000 = $1,148,000

Problems can arise when cost index data is used to estimate current cost. The accuracy of the figures cannot always be ascertained, especially when it is not clear which components are included in the data, i.e., only direct costs or direct costs and some indirect costs. Furthermore, historical costs may not be typical for the time period, and the construction methods used at the time of the historical cost may differ from those used on the effective appraisal date. Although cost index trending may be helpful in confirming a current cost estimate, it is not a reliable substitute for the cost estimating methods described in the following section.

COST-ESTIMATING METHODS

The three traditional cost-estimating methods are the following:

1. The comparative-unit method
2. The unit-in-place method
3. The quantity survey method

The quantity survey method produces a cost estimate based on a detailed inventory of the labour, materials, and equipment used in the subject improvements. The comparative-unit and the unit-in-place methods provide less detail, but they are the primary bases for the cost estimates used in most appraisals.

Comparative-Unit Method

The *comparative-unit method* is used to derive a cost estimate in terms of dollars per unit of area. The method employs the known costs of similar structures adjusted for market

ESTIMATING ENTREPRENEURIAL INCENTIVE

Regardless of the general cost-estimating method applied, estimates of entrepreneurial profit or incentive should be derived through market analysis and interviews with developers to determine the expectations of entrepreneurial reward required as motivation to undertake a particular development. The actual entrepreneurial profit earned is a record of results and can differ from the anticipated profit (i.e., the incentive) that originally motivated the entrepreneur to proceed. The typical level of anticipation or incentive should be used in the cost estimate.

Depending on market practice, entrepreneurial profit or incentive may be estimated in different ways:

- As a percentage of direct costs
- As a percentage of direct and indirect costs
- As a percentage of direct and indirect costs plus land value
- As a percentage of the value of the completed project

Presumably, the amount of entrepreneurial profit would be the same regardless of how it is calculated – e.g., as 22%, 20%, 15%, or 13% of the appropriate base cost selected, as shown below.

In the following example, the appraiser investigated the dollar amount of certain costs and ratios (or relative percentages) of entrepreneurial incentive attributable to the same set of costs and then calculated entrepreneurial incentive:

Base Cost	% Applied	Entrepreneurial Incentive
Direct costs	22% × $545,000	= $120,000 (rounded)
Direct costs + indirect costs	20% × ($545,000 + $55,000)	= $120,000
Direct costs + indirect costs + land value	15% × ($545,000 + $55,000 + $200,000)	= $120,000
Completed project	13% × ($545,000 + $55,000 + $200,000 + $120,000)	= $120,000 (rounded)

Note that in the calculation of entrepreneurial incentive as a percentage of the value of the completed project, a figure for the variable being solved for (i.e., entrepreneurial incentive) appears in the equation. The final calculation of entrepreneurial incentive as a percentage of the value of the completed project would actually be expressed as follows:

[($545,000 + $55,000 + $200,000) × 0.13] ÷ (1 - 0.13) = $120,000 (rounded)
entrepreneurial incentive   = [(direct costs + indirect costs + land value)
                                                           × (market-derived percentage of value of the completed project)]
                                                           ÷ [1 – (market-derived percentage of value of the completed project)]

In depressed markets the appraiser should focus on whether diminished entrepreneurial incentive or entrepreneurial loss represents a form of external obsolescence. Considering entrepreneurial coordination as a component of cost in a depressed market helps establish a basis for estimating the level of rent required to induce new construction, which may in turn provide some insight into problems of absorption and stabilized occupancy. Estimating an appropriate amount of entrepreneurial incentive remains a challenge for appraisers because expectations of profit vary with different market conditions and property types. Consistent relationships between profit and other costs are difficult to establish.

conditions and physical differences. Indirect costs may be included in the unit cost or computed separately. If the comparable properties and the subject property are in different markets, the appraiser may need to make an adjustment for location.

Unit costs vary with size; all else being equal, unit costs decrease as buildings increase in area. This reflects the fact that plumbing, heating units, elevators, doors, windows, and similar building components do not usually cost proportionately more in a larger building than in a smaller one.

The comparative-unit method is relatively uncomplicated, practical, and widely used. Unit cost figures are usually expressed in terms of gross building dimensions converted into square or cubic feet. Total cost is estimated by comparing the subject building with similar, recently constructed buildings for which contract prices are available. The trend in costs between the date of the contract (or construction) and the effective appraisal date must be factored into the comparison.

> Building costs may be estimated using one of three methods: the comparative-unit method, the unit-in-place method, or the quantity survey method.

> comparative-unit method
> A method used to derive a cost estimate in terms of dollars per unit of area or volume based on known costs of similar structures that are adjusted for time and physical differences; usually applied to total building area.

In the absence of contract prices, an indication of the total cost of a building can be extracted from sales of similar, newly constructed buildings as long as the following tests are met:

1. The improvements reflect the highest and best use of the site
2. The property has reached stabilization
3. Supply and demand are in balance
4. Site value can be reasonably ascertained

The value of the site is subtracted from the sale price of each comparable property, and the residual indicates the cost of the improvements.

Most appraisers using the comparative-unit method apply unit cost figures developed using data from a recognized cost service. Unit costs for the benchmark buildings found in cost-estimating manuals usually start with a base building of a specified size. Adjustments or refinements are then made to the base cost for any differences between the subject building and the benchmark building. If the subject building is larger than the benchmark building, the unit cost is usually lower; if the subject building is smaller, its unit cost will probably be higher.

Since few buildings are identical in terms of size, design, and quality of construction, the benchmark building is often different from the subject building. Different roof designs, interior design characteristics, and irregular perimeters and building shapes can affect comparative-unit costs substantially. Figure 18.1 illustrates this situation. Most cost services include adjustment criteria to alter or adjust the base cost to the specific characteristics of the subject structure. However, the cost service may not address all elements and a more "building-specific" cost analysis developed by the unit-in-place method may be needed.

To develop a reliable estimate with the comparative-unit method, an appraiser calculates the unit cost from similar improvements or adjusts the unit cost figure to reflect variations in size, shape, finish, and other characteristics. The unit cost applied should also reflect any changes in cost levels between the date of the benchmark unit cost and the effective appraisal date. The ratio between the costs of mechanical equipment and the basic building shell has increased consistently through the years.

Equipment tends to increase unit building costs and depreciate more rapidly than other building components.

To use area cost estimates, an appraiser assembles, analyzes, and catalogues data on actual building costs. These costs should be divided into general construction

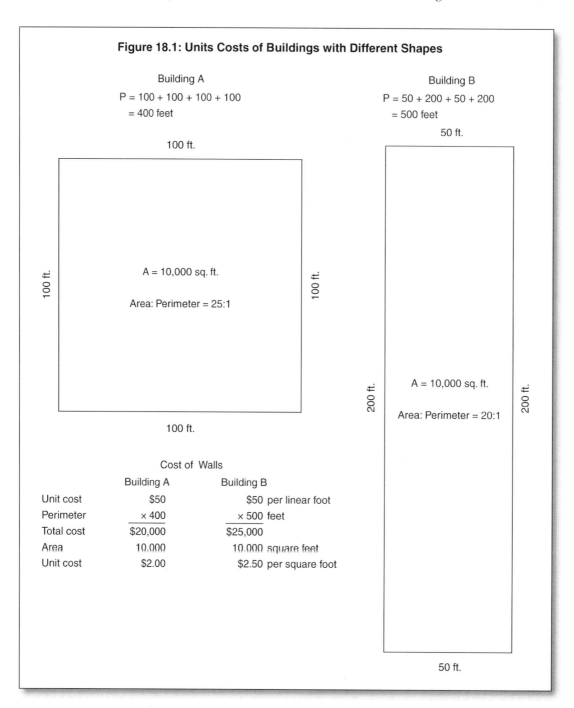

Figure 18.1: Units Costs of Buildings with Different Shapes

	Building A	Building B
Unit cost	$50	$50 per linear foot
Perimeter	× 400	× 500 feet
Total cost	$20,000	$25,000
Area	10,000	10,000 square feet
Unit cost	$2.00	$2.50 per square foot

categories, and an appraiser should use separate figures to account for special finishes or equipment. The overall area unit cost can then be broken down into its components, which may help the appraiser adjust a known cost for the presence or absence of items in later comparisons.

The apparent simplicity of the comparative-unit method can be misleading. To develop dependable unit cost figures, an appraiser must exercise judgment and carefully compare the subject building with similar or standard structures for which actual costs are known. Errors can result if an appraiser selects a unit cost that is not comparable to the building being appraised. However, when it is correctly applied, the method produces reasonably accurate estimates of cost.

The warehouse shown in Figure 18.2 will be used to illustrate the comparative-unit method (and later the unit-in-place, or segregated-cost method and the quantity survey method).

Table 18.1 shows how comparative-unit costs from a published cost manual can be applied to the warehouse building. Calculations such as those shown can be used to confirm a cost indication obtained from construction contracts for similar properties in the same market as the property being appraised on or about the effective appraisal date. An appraiser can use published data independently when no local cost data is available.

In Table 18.1, an adjustment for the warehouse's sprinkler system was made using a square foot unit cost. In other cases, similar adjustments may be appropriate for observed physical differences in the amount of office area, construction features, or specific equipment.

Cost manuals rarely include all indirect costs or an allowance for entrepreneurial profit, so adjustments must often be made to obtain an indication of the total cost. In Table 18.1 adjustments are made for the following items:

1. Indirect costs not included in the base price quoted in the cost manual

2. Indirect costs after construction needed to achieve typical stabilized occupancy[1]

3. Entrepreneurial profit calculated as a percentage of total direct and indirect costs

The estimate of the value of the site and site improvements was derived through direct comparison.

Table 18.1 indicates the cost of the warehouse building plus the site value, but the result shown is more likely to represent the value of a close substitute than a duplicate structure. Cost services use typical buildings for their base cost, so an appraiser can apply the comparative-unit method, develop reliable adjustment amounts and factors, and produce a reasonable property value estimate.

Construction contracts normally include other improvements to the land such as auxiliary buildings, driveways, water retention basins, underground drainage facilities, rail sidings, fences, and landscaping. The possible combinations and varied value contributions of these improvements can cause a wide divergence in unit cost if the total contract is related to the size of the major improvement only. Therefore, when

---

[1]   The cost to achieve stabilized occupancy may be nominal for a single-tenant building or a typical owner-occupied building. However, large multitenant warehouse, office, or apartment properties can have substantial lease-up costs, promotional expenses, or other costs (or loss in income) that must be considered.

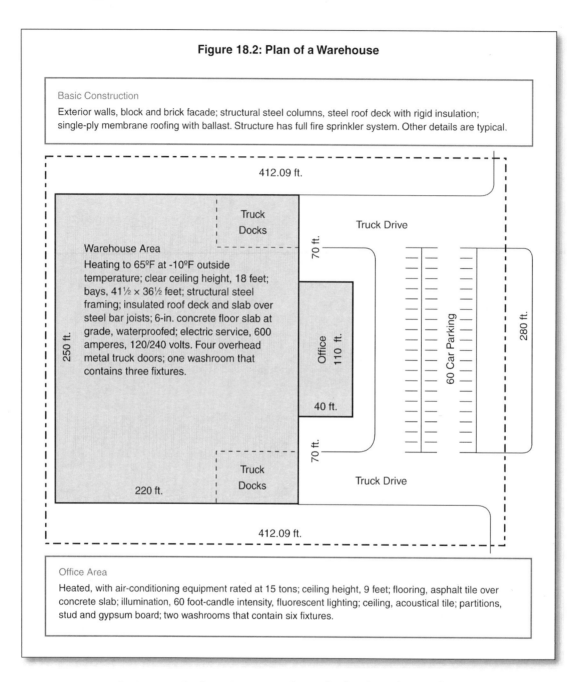

Figure 18.2: Plan of a Warehouse

Basic Construction

Exterior walls, block and brick facade; structural steel columns, steel roof deck with rigid insulation; single-ply membrane roofing with ballast. Structure has full fire sprinkler system. Other details are typical.

Office Area

Heated, with air-conditioning equipment rated at 15 tons; ceiling height, 9 feet; flooring, asphalt tile over concrete slab; illumination, 60 foot-candle intensity, fluorescent lighting; ceiling, acoustical tile; partitions, stud and gypsum board; two washrooms that contain six fixtures.

an appraiser uses actual contract costs from the local market in the comparative-unit method, it is imperative that the costs of these other improvements be excluded from the determination of the base price so that these costs are not counted twice – first implicitly in the base unit cost and then again explicitly as an adjustment based on actual costs.

Table 18.1: Warehouse Property – Comparative-Unit Method

Base cost per sq. ft.		$27.22
Add for sprinkler system per sq. ft.	+	1.14
Subtotal		$28.36
Adjustment for ceiling height variations	×	1.086
Subtotal		$30.80
Adjustment for area/perimeter	×	0.895
Subtotal		$27.57
Current cost multiplier	×	1.120
Subtotal		$30.88
Local cost multiplier	×	0.980
Total cost per sq. ft.		$30.26
Indirect costs not included in cost manual*	×	1.050
Subtotal		$31.77
Indirect costs from completion to stabilized occupancy*	×	1.070
Subtotal		$33.99
Entrepreneurial profit at 10% of total direct and indirect costs		
$33.99 x 0.10	+	3.39
Subtotal		$37.38
Total cost for warehouse building:		
59,400 sq. ft. @ $37.38 per sq. ft.		= $2,220,372
	(rounded)	$2,220,000
Site value and site improvements per sq. ft. of building		
59,400 sq. ft. @ $10.94 per sq. ft.	(rounded) +	650,000
Total value indicated by the cost approach		$2,870,000

Source: Marshall Valuation Service

*Note: Contractor's overhead and profit and some other indirect costs are included in these base costs and adjustments. The source of published cost data should be studied for a complete understanding of what is included in quoted costs. For purposes of simplicity, a percentage was applied to account for indirect costs.

Unit-in-Place Method

In the unit-in-place (or segregated-cost) method, an appraiser applies individual unit costs for various building components to the various subcomponents in the structure or to linear, area, volume, or other appropriate measures of these components. Using this method, the appraiser computes a unit cost based on the actual quantity of materials used plus the labour of assembly required for each square foot of area. For example, the cost can be applied based on the square feet of floor area or linear feet of wall of a certain height. The same procedure is applied for other structural components.

> **unit-in-place method**
> A cost-estimating method in which total building cost is estimated by adding together the unit costs for the various building components as installed; also called the *segregated-cost method*.

Unit-in-place cost estimates are made using specific cost data for standardized structural components as installed, such as those shown in Table 18.2.

Table 18.2: Specific Cost Data for Structural Components

Structural Component	Unit
Excavation	Dollars per cubic yard
Foundation	Dollars per linear foot of foundation or cubic yard of concrete
Floor construction	Dollars per square foot
Interior partitions	Dollars per linear foot
Roofing	Dollars per square (i.e., 100 square feet of roof area)

The unit-in-place concept is not limited to cubic, linear, or area units. The measure on which the cost is based may be the measure employed in a particular trade, such as the cost per ton of air-conditioning. An appraiser may also apply the unit-in-place concept to the cost of complete, installed components such as the cost of a roof truss that is fabricated off site, delivered, and erected.

All unit costs are totalled to provide the estimated direct cost of the entire improvement. Unit-in-place cost estimates may be based on an appraiser's compiled data, but they are usually obtained from a cost-estimating service that provides updated monthly figures. An appraiser may include contractor's overhead and profit in the unit cost figures provided by some cost services, or they may be computed separately. The appraiser must know exactly what is included in any unit price quoted. Indirect costs are usually computed separately. The objective is to count all appropriate costs and to avoid any double counting.

The following example shows how the cost of a brick veneer wall would be calculated on a unit-in-place basis. Costs such as these vary with market conditions and location; the figures shown are used only for purposes of illustration.

Table 18.3: Example of Unit-in-Place Method for Brick Veneer Wall

Description	Cost	Unit
4 in. face brick, installed: common bond, ½-in. struck joints, mortar, scaffolding, and cleaning included	$460.00	per 1,000
Dimension lumber, erected: 2 in.- -4 in. wood stud framing, 16 inches on center	$360.00	per 1,000 bd. ft.
Sheathing, installed: impregnated 4 ft. 8 ft., ½ in.	$0.42	per sq. ft.
Insulation, installed: 2½ in., foil backing on one side	$0.22	per sq. ft.
Gypsum board: ½ in. with finished joints	$0.30	per sq. ft.
Paint: primer and one coat flat	$0.25	per sq. ft.

From this data the cost per square foot of wall can be estimated as follows:

Table 18.4: Unit Cost Per Square Foot of Brick Veneer Wall

Description	Cost	Unit
Bricks	$3.45	per 7½*
Wood stud framing	$0.24	per 7½*
Sheathing.	$0.42	per sq. ft.
Insulation	$0.22	per sq. ft.
½-in. gypsum board	$0.30	per sq. ft.
Paint	+ $0.25	per sq. ft.
Total for finished wall	$4.88	per sq. ft.

*To calculate a total unit cost, the unit cost of certain construction elements must be converted to the unit measure of the total cost. In this example, each square foot of wall requires 7½ bricks and 2⁄3 board feet of wood stud framing.

After calculating the unit cost of $4.88 per square foot, the appraiser can estimate the total cost of a veneer wall that meets these standards without detailing the quantities of material and labour. In practice, a cost analyst would refine the procedure by adjusting for waste and for extra framing for windows and doors, which require wall openings, lintels, and facing corners.

The unit costs for all components can be calculated in a similar fashion and, once these are established, the appraiser can estimate the cost of an entire building. When fully developed, the unit-in-place method provides a substitute for a complete quantity survey and produces an accurate cost estimate with considerably less effort. Table 18.5 illustrates how the unit-in-place method can be used to estimate the reproduction cost of the warehouse shown in Figure 18.2.

In Table 18.5 adjustments are made for the following:

1.   Indirect costs not included in the cost manual's base price

2.   Indirect costs after construction needed to achieve typical stabilized occupancy

3.   Entrepreneurial profit calculated as a percentage of total direct and indirect costs

Note the difference in total adjustments for indirect costs in Tables 18.1 and 18.5. As the cost of the property is broken down into more precise increments using the unit-in-place method, a smaller portion of the total indirect costs is included in the base price quoted in the cost manual for each building component. The single figure of cost per square foot that is used in the comparative-unit method accounts for more of the total indirect costs than the individual cost figures for excavation, site, foundation, framing, and so on. Therefore, the adjustment for "indirect costs not included in cost manual" in the comparative-unit method is smaller than the adjustment for "indirect costs not included in cost manual" in the unit-in-place method.

In the unit-in-place method, an appraiser may estimate the value of site improvements separately on a depreciated-cost basis and add them to the depreciated cost of the improvements. More typically, the value of site improvements, estimated either on a depreciated-cost basis or extracted from market data, may be added as a contributory amount to total property value.

Quantity Survey Method

The most comprehensive and accurate method of cost estimating is the *quantity survey method*, which will more often be applied by a contractor or professional cost estimator than an appraiser. A quantity survey reflects the quantity and quality of all materials used in the construction of an improvement and all categories of labour required. Unit costs are applied to these figures to arrive at a total cost estimate for materials and labour. Then the contractor adds a margin for contingencies, overhead and profit.[2]

> quantity survey method
> A cost-estimating method in which the quantity and quality of all materials used and all categories of labour required are estimated and unit cost figures are applied to arrive at a total cost estimate for labour and materials.

Depending on the size of the project and the resources of the contractor, the quantity survey and cost calculations may be prepared by a single cost estimator or

----

[2]   See *www.CIQS.org*

by a number of subcontractors whose bids are compiled by a general contractor and submitted as the final cost estimate. In either case, the analysis details the quantity, quality, and cost of all materials furnished by the general contractor or subcontractor and the appropriate cost allowances.

Table 18.5: Warehouse Property – Unit-in-Place Method

Excavation	59,400 cu. ft. @	$0.24 per cu. ft. =	$14,256
Site	115,385 sq. ft. @	$0.17 per sq. ft. =	19,615
Foundation	59,400 sq. ft. @	$1.79 per sq. ft. =	106,326
Framing	59,400 sq. ft. @	$4.82 per sq. ft. =	286,308
Floor (concrete)	59,400 sq. ft. @	$3.12 per sq. ft. =	185,328
Floor (asphalt tile)	4,400 sq. ft. @	$1.02 per sq. ft. =	4,488
Plumbing (three rooms)			
Fixtures	9 fixtures @	$2,525 per fixture =	22,725
Drains	6 units @	$380 per unit =	2,280
Sprinkler system	59,400 sq. ft. @	$1.48 per sq. ft. =	87,912
HVAC	55,000 sq. ft. @	$0.84 per sq. ft. =	46,200
	4,400 sq. ft. @	$4.20 per sq. ft. =	18,480
Electrical and lighting	59,400 sq. ft. @	$1.70 per sq. ft. =	100,980
Exterior wall			
Concrete block	15,180 sq. ft. @	$12.09 per sq. ft. =	183,526
Brick facade	5,060 sq. ft. @	$13.80 per sq. ft. =	69,828
Partition			
Walls	8,650 sq. ft. @	$3.70 per sq. ft. =	32,005
Doors	10 sq. ft. @	$103 per sq. ft. =	1,030
Overhead doors (10 ft. × 12 ft. × 4)	480 sq. ft. @	$18.25 per sq. ft. =	8,760
Roof joists and deck	59,400 sq. ft. @	$6.86 per sq. ft. =	407,484
Roof cover and insulation	59,400 sq. ft. @	$2.18 per sq. ft. =	129,492
Miscellaneous specified items			+ 30,000
Subtotal			$1,776,163
Current cost multiplier			× 1.030
(different base from Table 18.1)			
Subtotal			$1,829,448
Local cost multiplier			× 0.980
Total cost (from manual – $30.18 per sq. ft.)			$1,792,859
Indirect costs not included in cost manual*			× 1.100
Subtotal			$1,972,145
Indirect costs from completion to date of stabilized occupancy*			× 1.050
Subtotal			$2,070,752
Entrepreneurial profit at 10.0% of total direct and indirect costs			
$2,070,752 × 0.10			+ 207,075
Total cost ($38.35 per sq. ft.)			$2,277,827
		(rounded)	$2,278,000
Plus site value and site improvements			+ 650,000
Total project value			$2,928,000

Source: Marshall Valuation Service

*   Note: Contractor's overhead and profit and some indirect costs are included in the base costs. Architect's fees and other indirect costs are not.

The source of published cost data should be studied for a complete understanding of what is included in the quoted costs.

    For purposes of simplicity, a percentage was applied to account for indirect costs.

A general contractor's cost breakdown for the warehouse shown in Figure 18.2 is summarized in Table 18.6. This is only a summary; the specific quantities and costs are not indicated.

Contractor bids do not usually include indirect costs or entrepreneurial profit. The analysis illustrated in Table 18.6 reflects indirect costs and the calculation of entrepreneurial profit as a percentage of total direct and indirect costs. In the examples presented, indirect costs are considered in various stages of the cost-estimating procedure. A breakdown of the costs that make up these estimates is preferred to the percentage adjustment, and the appraiser should provide a breakdown to support the percentages applied. Note that when the direct costs of the individual elements of construction are broken down into discrete amounts, as shown in Table 18.6, less of the indirect costs are accounted for in those cost figures than in the figures for other cost-estimating methods and thus the percentage adjustment for total indirect costs is higher.

Table 18.6: Warehouse Property – Contractor's Breakdown

General conditions of contract	$7,854
Excavating and grading	24,781
Concrete	182,053
Carpentry	25,473
Masonry	194,231
Structural steel	280,343
Joist, deck, and deck slab	329,827
Roofing	57,494
Insulation	32,378
Sash	5,256
Glazing	11,329
Painting	7,611
Acoustical material	5,803
Flooring	3,335
Electric	75,334
HVAC	67,560
Piping	6,458
Plumbing and sprinkler system	+ 77,461
Subtotal	$1,394,581
Contingencies @ 5.0%	69,729
Contractor's overhead and profit @ 12.0%	+ 167,350
Total proposed contract costs ($27.46 per sq. ft.)	$1,631,660
(rounded)	$1,631,700
Indirect costs before, during, and after construction*	× 1.27
Subtotal	$2,072,259
Entrepreneurial profit ($2,072,259 × 0.10)	+ 207,226
Total reproduction cost	$2,279,485
Plus site value and site improvements	+ 650,000
Total project value	$2,929,485
(rounded)	$2,929,000

*   For purposes of simplicity, a percentage was applied to account for indirect costs.

Although site improvements such as parking facilities, landscaping, and signage are commonly included in a general contractor's bid, they are not detailed in Table 18.6. They should be included in a cost estimate of all improvements. In a cost estimate of an existing building, a separate itemization of site improvements facilitates the consideration of depreciation. Because the quantity survey method usually produces a cost estimate of a duplicate building, Table 18.6 indicates the reproduction cost of the warehouse building as of the effective appraisal date.

In recent years the percentage of a construction contract that is subcontracted out has increased. Subcontractors have become more efficient in their specializations. Subcontractor unit-in-place costs compare favourably with the cost of work done by employees of the general contractor, and the general contractor can operate with reduced overhead. To produce a quantity survey estimate, each contractor and subcontractor must provide a breakdown of materials, labour, overhead, and profit. The contractor's profit may depend on the volume of work that the contractor has lined up.

Although the quantity survey method produces a complete cost analysis of the improvements being appraised, it is time-consuming, costly, and frequently requires the services of an experienced cost estimator. For these reasons, this method is seldom used in routine appraisal assignments.

CHAPTER 19

DEPRECIATION ESTIMATES

An appraiser may use several methods to estimate depreciation. Each is acceptable and should result in roughly the same value as long as the appraiser applies the method consistently and logically. The method used should reflect the reaction of an informed and prudent buyer to the condition and quality of the property and the market in which the property is found. The primary goals of depreciation analysis are to identify all forms of depreciation recognized by the market, to treat all these forms of depreciation, and to charge only once for each form of depreciation, i.e., to avoid double counting items of depreciation. An appraiser may use the various methods of estimating depreciation in combination to solve specific problems or the appraiser may apply each method separately to test the reasonableness of the estimates derived from other methods.

The three principal methods for estimating depreciation are the following:

- The market extraction method
- The economic age-life method
- The breakdown method

Most appraisers use market extraction and economic age-life calculations as the primary methods to estimate the total depreciation in a property. The market extraction and economic age-life methods are applied to the whole property and are easier to understand and use. The elements of depreciation are implicit, not explicit. Both methods are limited in that they assume lump-sum depreciation from all causes can be expressed in an overall estimate, do not always distinguish between short-lived and long-lived items, and rely on the appraiser's forecasts of effective age and remaining economic life. The economic age-life and market extraction methods are further limited in that they

> The three methods used to estimate depreciation are the market extraction, economic age-life, and breakdown methods.

typically reflect a straight-line pattern of depreciation. Of the two, the market extraction method is the better method to demonstrate changes in the rate of depreciation over time.

The breakdown method is a more comprehensive method that identifies specific elements of depreciation and treats each element separately. It enumerates the components of total depreciation – i.e., physical deterioration, functional obsolescence, and external obsolescence – and separates physical deterioration into three categories – deferred maintenance, short-lived components, and long-lived components.

> **short-lived item**
> A building component with an expected remaining economic life that is shorter than the remaining economic life of the entire structure.
>
> **long-lived item**
> A building component with an expected remaining economic life that is the same as the remaining economic life of the entire structure.

Regardless of the method applied, the appraiser must ensure that the final estimate of depreciation reflects the loss in value from all causes and that no form of depreciation has been considered more than once. Double charges for depreciation may produce approach. Also, the analysis of depreciation must be internally consistent, using either reproduction cost or replacement cost as the cost basis throughout. As explained in Chapter 17, replacement cost eliminates the need to consider certain forms of obsolescence. Switching between reproduction and replacement cost within the analysis of depreciation greatly increases the chances of double counting items of depreciation.

AGE AND LIFE RELATIONSHIPS

All three methods of estimating depreciation consider age and life relationships either directly or indirectly. The age and life relationships relate to the entire improvement and also to its various components. Depreciation occurs over the life of an improvement or a component; in theory, an improvement or component loses all of its value over its life. For example, suppose that the typical life expectancy of a freestanding retail store in a given market is 40 years. Theoretically, when the building is 40 years old, it will have reached the end of its life expectancy and will have lost all of its value to depreciation, with no contributory value remaining to add to the value of the vacant site. Short-lived building components may go through this cycle several times over the same 40-year period. For example, the life expectancy of a water heater installed in the building will be much shorter than 40 years, and some components may have to be replaced several times over the building's 40-year life.

> **curable or incurable?**
> Items of physical deterioration or functional obsolescence are economically feasible to cure if the cost to cure is equal to or less than the anticipated increase in the value of the property. If the cost to cure is more than the anticipated increase in value, the item is incurable.

In estimating the total depreciation of an improvement, the age-life concepts most important to market extraction are actual age, total depreciation, annual rate of depreciation, and the implied total economic life that can be estimated. In the economic age-life method, the concepts most important are total economic life, effective age, and remaining economic life.

The concepts of economic life, effective age, and remaining economic life expectancy consider all elements of depreciation in one calculation. Therefore, the effective age estimate considers not only physical wear and tear, but also any loss in value for functional and external considerations. This type of analysis is characteristic of the market extraction and economic age-life depreciation methods. However, the economic age-life method can be modified to reflect the presence of any known items of curable physical deterioration or incurable deterioration in short-lived building components. With the market extraction method, the actual age is preferred, and it is important to use comparable properties that have the same physical, functional, and external characteristics as the subject. Typically the market extraction method is not modified to reflect depreciation of short-lived building components. However, a lump-sum adjustment may be made if the subject property suffers from curable depreciation in the form of deferred maintenance.

> Age-life relationships used to develop an estimate of total depreciation in the market extraction and economic age-life methods include total economic life, effective age, and remaining economic life. Age-life relationships used to estimate deterioration in individual physical components in the breakdown method include useful life, actual age, and remaining useful life.

When estimating physical deterioration in the breakdown method, the most important age-life concepts are the following:

- Actual age
- Useful life
- Remaining useful life

The use of these terms in the breakdown method emphasizes the separation of physical deterioration from functional and external obsolescence. The economic age-life method uses economic life, which considers all three components of depreciation in one calculation. The breakdown method employs useful life for physical deterioration, which is separated into short-lived and long-lived building components. The useful life of a building (i.e., the life of structural or long-lived items) is typically longer than its economic life, while the short-lived components have a useful life that is shorter than that of the whole building. In spite of that difference, the application of useful life in the breakdown method and economic life in the market extraction and economic age-life methods should yield the same approximate estimate of total depreciation.

Actual Age and Effective Age

Actual age, which is sometimes called *historical age* or *chronological age*, is the number of years that have elapsed since building construction was completed. Actual age serves two purposes in depreciation analysis. First, it is the initial element analyzed in the estimation of effective age. Second, in the application of the breakdown method, it is fundamental to the age-life analysis needed to estimate physical deterioration in the short-lived and long-lived components of an improvement.

Effective age is the age indicated by the condition and utility of a structure and is based on an appraiser's judgment and interpretation of market perceptions. Even in the same market, similar buildings do not necessarily depreciate at the same rate. The maintenance standards of owners or occupants can influence the pace of building depreciation. If one building is better maintained than other buildings in its market area, the effective age of that building may be less than its actual age. If a building is poorly maintained, its effective age may be greater than its actual age. If a building has received typical maintenance, its effective age and actual age may be the same.

As an example, consider a 23-year old strip retail centre that has been redecorated on the inside but has not been modernized. The original roof and HVAC components are still in place. The building would probably have an effective age of about 23 years. The small amount of work done in redecorating is usually not sufficient to reduce the effective age. Now suppose that, in addition to the redecorating, the building's roof and HVAC system have been replaced. In this case, the building would probably have an estimated effective age of less than 23 years. If the same 23-year old building were in poor condition, had not been redecorated, had a defective HVAC system, and had below-average occupancy because of poor maintenance, it would probably have an estimated effective age greater than 23 years. An appraiser must also take into account the condition and functional utility of an improvement as well as market and locational factors in estimating an improvement's effective age.

Total Economic Life and Useful Life

An improvement's total *economic life* begins when it is built and ends when the improvement no longer contributes value for the use for which it was originally intended and is no longer the highest and best use of the underlying land. This period is usually shorter than the improvement's physical life expectancy, which is the total period the improvement can be expected to exist physically. At the end of a building's economic life, there are several options available to the property owner:

- Renovation or conversion to a new use
- Rehabilitation
- Remodelling
- Demolition and replacement with a suitable new structure

> **economic life**
> The period over which improvements to real property contribute to property value.
>
> **useful life**
> The period of time over which a structure or a component of a property may reasonably be expected to perform the function for which it was designed.

Both economic life and useful life acknowledge that market forces operate in such a way that buildings are either renovated, converted to a new use, rehabilitated, remodelled, or torn down long before they physically wear out.

An appraiser must consider all aspects of a property and its market, including the quality and condition of the construction, the functional utility of the improvements, and market and locational externalities, in the estimation of a property's economic life. The economic life of an improvement is shaped by a number of factors, including the following:

- Physical considerations, i.e., the rate at which the physical components of an improvement wear out, given the quality of construction, the use of the property, maintenance standards, and the region's climate

- Functional considerations, i.e., the rate at which construction technology, tastes in architecture, energy efficiency, and building design change; these factors can render an improvement functionally obsolete, regardless of its age or condition

- External considerations, i.e., short-term and long-term influences such as the stage of a neighbourhood's life cycle, the availability and affordability of financing, and supply and demand factors

Many functional and external considerations may have no discernable effect on the value of an improvement as recognized by the market on the date of the opinion of value but may have a profound effect at some future time – say, in 20, 50, or even 100 years. Changes in market preferences and locational attributes are not typically predictable or, for that matter, curable. Although it is difficult to forecast economic life expectancy, market study and analysis of historical trends and neighbourhood life cycles may provide important information.

To estimate an improvement's economic life, an appraiser studies the typical economic life expectancy of recently sold improvements similar to the subject in the market area. The techniques used to develop total economic life include the following:

- Extracting depreciation from comparable sales (market extraction method)

- Observing real estate cycles and changes in market preferences to establish the length of time that similar properties are in demand and improvements are contributing to market value

- Consulting with owners and developers regarding the feasibility of improvements that extend a building's economic life

- Considering the investment horizon used by buyers and sellers, to the extent that it might be influenced by their anticipation of remaining economic life

- Interviewing property managers, leasing agents, and real estate brokers regarding market preferences

- Reviewing published cost services that report average economic lives by property type

- Considering the impact that appreciating land values will have on the remaining economic life of the improvements

To calculate total economic life expectancy as of the date of sale, an appraiser takes the reciprocal of the average annual depreciation rate. For example, consider a residential subdivision where recent sales indicate an average annual rate of depreciation of 2% for properties that are very comparable to the subject property, i.e., all built in the same phase of the subdivision's development and sold near the time of the sale of the subject. Calculating the reciprocal of 2% results in a total economic life expectancy for the subject property of 50 years (100%/2%) as of the date of the opinion of value. This does not mean that the total economic life expectancy of the subject has always been and will always be 50 years. Rather, at the time the property was sold, its average annual rate of depreciation indicated a total economic life expectancy of 50 years. Likewise, it should not be assumed that the property will have an economic life of only 50 years. The total economic life expectancy of 50 years is a value that helps explain the total depreciation in a property at a given point in time.

Renovation and modernization can effectively extend a building's life expectancy by "resetting the clock". For example, consider a building with a 50-year economic life expectancy. If at the 10-year mark the property was substantially modernized, bringing the physical components up to current market standards for new construction, then the effective age of the property could be reset to zero and the remaining economic life expectancy (before the renovation) of 40 years would be reset to the original 50 years – or to some other figure, depending on the extent of modification to the property. Many historic properties have an economic life equal to or greater than the physical life of the building materials because of continued renovation and restoration.

Useful life, as used in age-life calculations in the breakdown method, is the period of time over which the components of the improvement may reasonably be expected to perform the functions for which they were designed. Although the physical life expectancy of some components, such as structural elements made of concrete and steel, may be hundreds of years, the useful life recognizes the economic influences acting on the improvements that contain these components. Accordingly, if a 40-year old industrial building is being demolished so that its site can be redeveloped, it is probable that all components of the building will be demolished, regardless of their remaining physical utility.

The useful life of short-lived physical components (HVAC components, roof covering, interior decorating, floor finishes, etc.) is shorter than the life expectancy of the entire building. Conversely, long-lived components (usually the structural components of a building, such as the foundation, framing, and underground piping) have a life expectancy that is longer than the building's economic life expectancy. Distinguishing between short-lived and long-lived components is important when breakdown techniques are applied and gives the appraiser flexibility in estimating component depreciation that is not available with the market extraction and economic age-life methods.

Remaining Economic Life and Remaining Useful Life

Remaining economic life is the estimated period over which existing improvements are expected to continue to contribute economically to property value. The concept is applied in the economic age-life method. Usually improvements can be regarded as investments designed to contribute to value over a long period of time. Some depreciation occurs between the date when the improvements begin to contribute to value and the date of the opinion of value; wear and tear can take their toll even during construction, which is usually a long process. The remaining economic life extends from the date of the opinion of value to the end of the improvement's economic life. An improvement's remaining economic life is always less than or equal to its total economic life, but never more than its total economic life as long as the highest and best use of the property does not change. In the breakdown method, remaining useful life is the estimated period from the actual age of a component to the end of its total useful life expectancy. The remaining useful life of any long-lived component is greater than its remaining economic life, unless there are no short-lived components or the short-lived components are already completely depreciated.

The total economic life of similar structures minus the effective age of the improvement will approximate the remaining economic life of the subject property improvements. As an example, consider a 15-year old subject property. The appraiser searches the market area and finds three sales of properties that are very comparable in size, layout, and other physical characteristics:

- Property 1, an 8-year old building, has an annual depreciation rate of 2.0% and a total economic life expectancy of 50 years (100%/2%). Its remaining economic life expectancy is therefore 42 years (50 – 8 = 42).

- In contrast, Property 2, a 19-year-old building, has an annual depreciation rate of 1.51% and a total economic life expectancy of 66 years (100%/1.51%). Its remaining economic life expectancy is 47 years (66 – 19 = 47).

- Property 3, a 14-year-old building, has an annual depreciation rate of 1.75% and a total economic life expectancy of 57 years (100%/1.75%). Its remaining economic life expectancy is 43 years (57 – 14 = 43).

A pattern can be observed. As a building ages, the total depreciation increases but the average annual depreciation rate may also change. The remaining economic life expectancy would increase as the effective age decreases over time due to periodic repairs and maintenance. In other words, total economic life and its components do not always remain constant. Reconciliation should be based on the improvement that is most similar in age to the subject property. Of the three sales, the improvement closest to the subject property in age is Property 3. In light of this similar sale and the pattern indicated by the market data, the appraiser could reasonably reconcile the total economic life expectancy for the subject property at 60 years. Using the economic age-life method, which will be discussed in detail later in this chapter, the total depreciation would equal 25% (15/60) of the property's cost.

Figure 19.1 illustrates a pattern that might be exhibited by many types of buildings. As the building ages, the average annual rate of depreciation decreases, resulting in a downward curve, until total depreciation eventually levels off and the value of the improvement stabilizes at its salvage value. The economic life may be extended as routine maintenance occurs and the building continues to be used, unless or until a competing use for the site raises the land value high enough to support demolition and redevelopment of the site. The building might also be redeveloped with another use, supporting the concept that useful life may continue long after economic life has ended. Conversely, the opposite situation could occur in markets that are changing rapidly. As land value increases and as market preferences change to different designs or property types, average annual depreciation accelerates and both economic life and useful life are shortened. Both situations may occur over the life of the same improvement, which is why economic life and useful life estimates apply to a specific point in time. Figure 19.2 depicts the depreciation curve in a market that is changing rapidly and exerting upward pressure on land values.

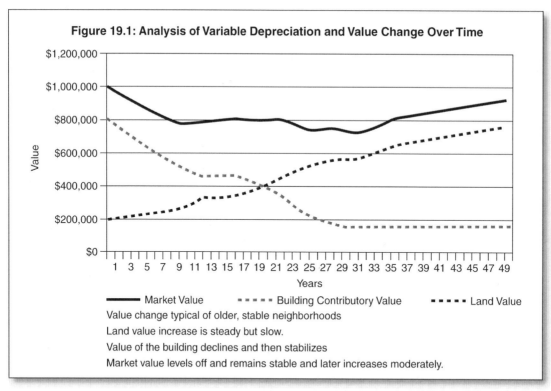

Figure 19.1: Analysis of Variable Depreciation and Value Change Over Time

Value change typical of older, stable neighborhoods
Land value increase is steady but slow.
Value of the building declines and then stabilizes
Market value levels off and remains stable and later increases moderately.

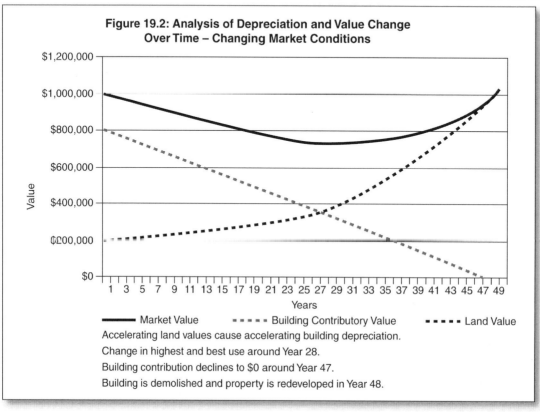

Figure 19.2: Analysis of Depreciation and Value Change Over Time – Changing Market Conditions

Accelerating land values cause accelerating building depreciation.
Change in highest and best use around Year 28.
Building contribution declines to $0 around Year 47.
Building is demolished and property is redeveloped in Year 48.

MARKET EXTRACTION METHOD

The *market extraction method* relies on the availability of comparable sales from which depreciation can be extracted. It makes use of direct comparisons with market sales. While easy to understand and explain, an appraiser should use this method only if sufficient data exists and if the quality of that data is adequate to permit meaningful analysis. By considering all elements in one calculation, market extraction can be an oversimplification of the complex interplay of physical, functional, and external causes of depreciation. The technique is primarily used to extract total depreciation, to establish total economic life expectancy, and to identify other types of obsolescence or excess physical deterioration. The market extraction method includes the following steps:

1. Find and verify sales of similarly improved properties that are similar in terms of age and utility to the subject property. Although it is desirable, it is not essential that the comparable sales be current sales. They should be from the subject property's market area, but they can be from a market that is comparable, i.e., with similar tastes, preferences, and external influences.

2. Make appropriate adjustments to the comparable sale prices for certain factors, including property rights conveyed, financing, and conditions of sale. A market conditions adjustment is not made because the appraiser is estimating cost and depreciation at the time of the sale. No adjustments are made for physical, functional, or external impairments because these factors are the source of the depreciation that is being measured.

3. Subtract the value of the land at the time of sale from the sale price of each comparable property to obtain the contributory value of the improvements.

4. Estimate the cost of the improvements for each comparable property at the time of its sale. The cost estimates should have the same basis, i.e., reproduction cost or replacement cost. Typically, an appraiser will use replacement cost because he or she may not have sufficient information on all the sales to develop a credible opinion of reproduction cost. Also, the cost estimate should include all improvements.

5. Subtract the contributory value of all improvements from the current construction cost to determine the total dollar amount of depreciation of the improvements as of the date the sale occurred. The extracted depreciation includes all forms of depreciation.

6. Convert the dollar estimates of depreciation into percentages by dividing each estimate of total depreciation by the current construction cost. If the ages of the sales are relatively similar to the age of the subject property, the percentages of total depreciation can be reconciled into a rate appropriate to the subject property. This rate is applied to the subject's cost to derive an estimate of the subject's total depreciation.

7. If the ages of the comparable properties are different than the subject property, then develop an annual depreciation rate. This step expands the analysis to calculate annual rates of depreciation and to support an estimate of the total economic life expectancy of the subject property.

Consider the sales in Example 1 (Table 19.1). All are of fee simple interests and the ages, function, and external influences of the sale properties are similar to the subject property. In this case, the percentage range of total depreciation is so narrow that it is not necessary to annualize the calculations. The cost of the subject improvements is $240,000 (more than the price of Sale 1 but much less than the price of Sale 3), so the percentage of depreciation can be reconciled to 33% of cost. The total lump-sum dollar depreciation estimate comes to approximately $80,000 ($240,000 × 33%).

Table 19.1: Example 1

	Sale 1	Sale 2	Sale 3	Step in Procedure
Sale price	$215,000	$165,000	$365,000	1, 2
Less value of land	− 60,000	− 40,000	− 127,750	3
Depreciated cost of improvements	$155,000	$125,000	$237,250	3
Cost of improvements	$230,000	$195,000	$375,000	4
Less depreciated cost of improvements	− 155,000	− 125,000	− 237,250	5
Total depreciation in dollars	$75,000	$70,000	$137,750	5
Total depreciation percentage	$75,000/$230,000	$70,000/$195,000	$137,500/$375,000	6
	32.61%	35.90%	36.73%	

If there are differences between the sales (e.g., location, remodelling, functional utility, degree of maintenance), total depreciation may show greater variation, and further analysis will be needed to understand the total depreciation. The appraiser converts total depreciation to an annual depreciation rate by dividing each percentage by the actual age of the sale property. An appraiser may use effective age but this requires specific knowledge about the quality of construction and physical characteristics of the improvements. Actual age is preferred because it is a fact that is readily available, whereas effective age is based on the appraiser's judgment. Whether actual or effective age is used, the same age basis must be applied consistently to all sales. Then the appraiser analyzes the calculated depreciation rates and compares the comparable sale properties to the subject in order to select an appropriate annual depreciation rate for the subject improvements. Finally, the annual depreciation rate is multiplied by the age of the subject to develop an estimate of total depreciation.

The comparable sales in Example 2, shown in Table 19.2, have a wider range of ages. Suppose again that all the sales are of a fee simple interest and that no major functional or external obsolescence is evident.

In Example 2, the range of total percentage depreciation estimates is wide because of the age differences between the comparable sales. In this case, comparing annual depreciation rates provides more credible support for the depreciation estimate. Assuming that the subject improvements are 15-years old, which is closest to the actual age of Sale 2, a reasonable estimate of annual depreciation would be 1.4% per

Table 19.2: Example 2

	Sale 1	Sale 2	Sale 3	Step in Procedure
Actual age of comparable property	8	14	19	
Sale price	$998,000	$605,000	$791,000	1, 2
Less value of land	− 140,000	− 100,000	− 125,000	3
Depreciated cost of improvements	$858,000	$505,000	$666,000	3
Cost of improvements	$950,000	$627,000	$934,000	4
Less depreciated cost of improvements	− 858,000	− 505,000	− 666,000	5
Total depreciation in dollars	$92,000	$122,000	$268,000	5
Total depreciation percentage	9.68%	19.46%	28.69%	6
Actual age of comparable property	8	14	19	
Average annual depreciation rate	1.21%	1.39%	1.51%	7
Total economic life expectancy	100%/1.21%	100%/1.39%	100%/1.51%	
	82.6 years	71.9 years	66.2 years	

year, which is within the calculated range of 1.21% to 1.51% for the comparable sales. Applying this rate to the subject's age, total depreciation for the subject improvements is calculated at 21% (15 × 1.4%).

The model can be further expanded to support an estimate of the total economic life expectancy for the subject property. The average annual depreciation for the subject improvements equates to a total economic life of 71.4 years (100%/1.4%). This falls within the range of the total economic life expectancies of the comparables sales, 66.2 to 82.6 years, and appears reasonable for the subject property.

Applicability and Limitations

When sales data is plentiful, the market extraction method provides a reliable and convincing estimate of depreciation. However, the appraiser must be able to develop an accurate site value estimate for each of the comparable sales and a defensible estimate of replacement cost for each sale. Additionally, the comparable properties should have physical, functional, and external characteristics similar to the subject, and they should have incurred similar amounts and types of depreciation.

When the comparable properties differ in design, quality, or construction, it is difficult to ascertain whether differences in value are attributable to these characteristics or to a difference in age, and thus depreciation. The market extraction method is difficult to apply when the type or extent of depreciation varies greatly among the comparable properties due to characteristics other than age. Locational differences are assumed to be removed with the subtraction of land value. However, external conditions may affect building values as well, which is why it is important to select sales that are subject to the same (or similar) market influences. If the sales analyzed are affected by special financing or unusual motivation, the problem is further complicated.

The usefulness of the method depends heavily on the accuracy of the site value estimates and the cost estimates for the comparable properties. If the sales are located in market areas that are not comparable to the subject's, the method may not be appropriate. Market extraction considers all types of depreciation in a lump sum and does not break down the estimate into the various components of depreciation. However, this depreciation method is truly market-based and easy to understand, and for these reasons should be considered when it can be appropriately supported.

ECONOMIC AGE-LIFE METHOD

The effective age and total economic life expectancy of a structure are the primary concepts used by an appraiser in measuring depreciation using age-life relationships. In the *economic age-life method*, an appraiser estimates total depreciation by calculating the ratio of the effective age of the property to its economic life expectancy and applying this ratio to the property's total cost. The formula is as follows:

(Effective Age ÷ Total Economic Life) × Total Cost = Depreciation

Although it is not always as accurate as other techniques, the economic age-life method is the simplest way to estimate depreciation.

The method is applied in the following steps:

1. Conduct research to identify the anticipated total economic life of similar structures in the market area and estimate the effective age of the subject building. The data used in the market extraction method would also be applicable in the economic age-life method.

2. Divide the estimated effective age of the subject by the anticipated total economic life of similar structures. The resulting ratio is then applied to the subject's cost to estimate total lump-sum depreciation.

3. Subtract the lump-sum estimate of depreciation from the cost of the subject improvement to arrive at the improvement's contribution to property value.

As an example, market research (Step 1) yields the following information about the subject and comparable properties:

Total cost of subject	$668,175
Subject's land value	$180,000
Estimated effective age of subject	18 years
Total economic life expectancy of comparables	50 years

The total percentage of depreciation (36%) is determined by dividing the estimated effective age of 18 years by the total economic life expectancy of 50 years (Step 2). Thus, the economic age-life formula indicates total depreciation of 36%. When this rate is applied to the cost of $668,175, the total depreciation indicated is $240,543 (Step 3). The cost approach is applied as follows:

Total cost	$668,175
Less total depreciation	– 240,543
Depreciated cost	$427,632
Plus land value	+ 180,000
Indicated value by the cost approach	$607,632

Applicability and Limitations

The economic age-life method is simple, easy to apply, and easy to understand. It allows an appraiser to determine total depreciation, which can subsequently be allocated among its various causes using breakdown procedures. Although this method is usually the simplest way to estimate depreciation, it does have certain limitations.

First, because the percentage of depreciation is represented by the ratio of effective age to total economic life, this method assumes that every building depreciates on a straight-line basis over the course of its economic life. The straight-line pattern of depreciation is only an approximation of the total depreciation of a property at a specific point in time.

Second, the economic age-life method, like the market extraction method, does not divide depreciation into its various categories – physical, functional, and external. All forms of depreciation are included in one depreciation estimate. In market areas where comparable properties incur types and amounts of depreciation that differ from the subject property, the economic age-life method may be difficult to justify.

Finally, the economic age-life method, again like the market extraction method, does not recognize the difference between short-lived and long-lived items of physical deterioration. Because a single figure is assumed to reflect all the depreciation in the structure as a whole, varying amounts of deterioration in short-lived items are not directly indicated in the age-life method. For example, a structure as a whole may be estimated to be 20% depreciated except for the roof, which, unlike other roofs in the neighbourhood, is estimated to be 90% depreciated. In this situation, the breakdown method would allow an appraiser to make a more refined analysis.

Variations of the Economic Age-Life Method

In some situations, the impact of certain items of depreciation on value is known or can be easily and accurately estimated, so an appraiser can apply a variation of the economic age-life method and deduct those items from total cost before applying the age-life ratio. Such variations combine techniques from the market extraction and breakdown methods with the traditional economic age-life method.

In the most common variation of the economic age-life method, known as the *modified economic age-life method*, the appraiser knows the *cost to cure* the curable items of depreciation (both physical and functional). If an appraiser deducts curable items of depreciation from the cost of improvements before he or she applies the age-life ratio, this mirrors what typical purchasers consider when deciding on whether to invest in a property. This procedure is most meaningful when the subject property has curable depreciation not typically found in the market data at the time of appraisal. If the cost to cure is known, it can simply be deducted from the total cost. When the curable items are dealt with first, the appraiser may have to consider using a lower effective age or a longer remaining economic life expectancy in calculating the modified economic age-life ratio.

For example, consider a 20-year old property with a total cost of $892,000. The interior needs to be completely refurbished at a documented cost of $82,500. Sales of similar buildings that were sold after being refurbished were used to extract a total economic life expectancy of 50 years. In deriving a total economic life expectancy for each comparable building, the appraiser used an effective age that was 25% lower than the building's actual age because investors in the market feel that the effective age of a building will be lower than its actual age once the interior has been refurbished. This avoids any double counting of depreciation. After the completion of the refurbishment, the subject's effective age is assumed to be 15 years, i.e., 25% lower than its actual age of 20 years. Dividing 15 years by the market-extracted total economic life expectancy of 50 years indicates total depreciation (excluding the interior) of 30%. This ratio is applied to the subject's cost less the cost of interior refurbishment ($892,000 – $82,500, or $809,500) to derive a depreciation estimate of $242,850. Assuming a land value estimate of $100,000, the cost approach can be applied as follows:

Total cost	$892,000
Less cost to refurbish interior	– 82,500
Remaining cost	$809,500
Less depreciation	
(Remaining cost × economic age-life ratio: $809,500 × 30%)	– 242,850
Depreciated cost	$566,650
Plus land value	+ 100,000
Indicated value by cost approach	$666,650

In situations where external obsolescence is present, an appraiser can apply another variation of the economic age-life method. If external obsolescence is affecting the subject property and there are sales of properties in the subject market that have incurred the same external obsolescence, the appraiser should use the total economic life extracted from these sales in the economic age-life ratio. However, where there are no sales in the subject market similarly affected, the appraiser can use market extraction or economic age-life to estimate total depreciation and economic life without the external obsolescence and then estimate external obsolescence using the breakdown method. The estimated depreciation from the economic age-life method and the estimated external obsolescence from the breakdown method would be added together to arrive at an estimate of total depreciation.

As an example, consider a property in a district where there is an oversupply of competitive properties. This glut of competitive space has resulted in a 10% reduction in rents, which the appraiser equates to a 10% loss in building value. Land value has not been affected at this point. Until the oversupply is corrected through the natural interaction of supply and demand, the property will continue to be affected. The cost of the 10-year old building improvement is $696,000, and the land value is estimated at $255,000. The market extraction method, applied to comparables in the subject's market a year earlier when there was no oversupply, indicated a total economic life expectancy of 50 years. Using the economic age-life method, depreciation is thus estimated at 20% (10 ÷ 50).

The physical and functional depreciation estimated for the subject improvements by the economic age-life method is $139,200 ($696,000 × 20%) and the additional external obsolescence for the building is estimated to be $69,600 ($696,000 × 10%). Total depreciation, therefore, is allocated as follows:

Depreciation attributable to all causes except external obsolescence	$139,200
Depreciation attributable to the external obsolescence	+ 69,600
Total depreciation	$208,800

Note that the external obsolescence is caused by an oversupply in the market, and it is unlikely that such a situation will be permanent. As supply and demand again approach equilibrium, the oversupply will probably disappear.

In this example, the appraiser has determined that the reduction in value is entirely attributable to the improvements. If market data indicated that land values had also declined by 10%, then a portion of the reduction in overall value would be accounted for in the land value. In this case, the appraiser calculates the ratio of improvement value to total property value ($696,000 ÷ $951,000 or 73%) and weights the calculation of external obsolescence by this percentage ($696,000 × 10% × 73% or $50,808) before it is deducted in the cost approach. This procedure ensures that the reduction in total property value is correctly allocated between land and improvements, and not double-counted.

The modified economic age-life techniques work best when relatively few adjustments need to be made to the economic age-life method of estimating total depreciation. Usually, relatively nominal adjustments are made for curable physical items or for a functional or external influence. If more than one atypical element exists in a property, it may be advisable to use the more detailed breakdown method.

BREAKDOWN METHOD

The *breakdown method* is the most comprehensive and detailed way to measure depreciation because it segregates total depreciation into individual component parts:

- Physical deterioration
- Functional obsolescence
- External obsolescence

Each step calculates one type of depreciation. The process is cumulative, with each subsequent step building on the results of the prior step until all forms of depreciation have been considered. Alternatively, the depreciation calculation may begin with the estimation of total depreciation by the market extraction or economic age-life method and then apply the breakdown method to allocate total depreciation into more precise components. In other words, the appraiser can start from either the top or the bottom of the flowchart shown in Figure 19.3 and use the breakdown method to work toward the other end for a more complete understanding of all the forms of depreciation present in a property.

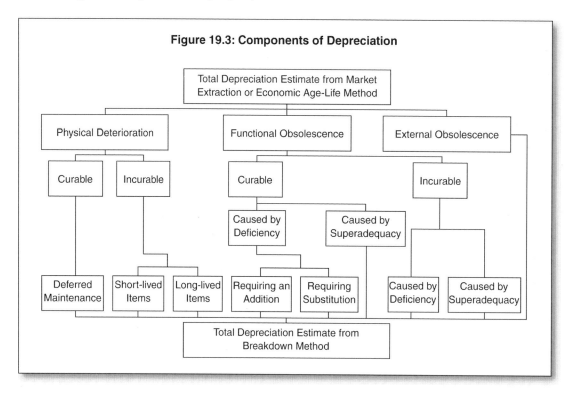

Figure 19.3: Components of Depreciation

The primary techniques used to calculate the different types of depreciation include the following:

- Estimation of cost to cure, which is a measure used for curable physical deterioration (deferred maintenance) and curable functional obsolescence
- Application of an economic age-life ratio to measure curable physical deterioration and incurable physical deterioration for both short-lived and long-lived components
- Application of the functional obsolescence procedure to estimate all types of functional obsolescence
- Analysis of market data (paired sales or other techniques), which may be used to identify and estimate functional obsolescence caused by a deficiency or superadequacy as well as external obsolescence

- Capitalization of income loss[1] or excess operating costs, which may be used to estimate incurable functional obsolescence as well as external obsolescence

Table 19.3 shows how the breakdown method can be applied to allocate an estimate of total depreciation among its various components or to develop a conclusion of total depreciation by adding together estimates of each item of depreciation.

Applicability and Limitations

The breakdown method is primarily used when the appraisal assignment requires that each form of depreciation be accounted for in the appraisal report. In addition to allocating lump-sum estimates of total depreciation among their various components, an appraiser uses the breakdown method when the market extraction and economic age-life methods cannot be applied. This usually occurs when the multiple elements of depreciation that exist in the subject property are not accurately reflected in available sales data and a closer analysis of these elements of depreciation is required. An appraiser may also use the breakdown method when the economic age-life method is too simplistic to account for the varied forms of depreciation present.

When using the breakdown method, several cautions and considerations should be kept in mind. First, if the sum of all items of physical deterioration estimated using the breakdown method is equivalent to the total depreciation derived from

Table 19.3: Procedures for Applying the Breakdown Method

Purpose To allocate a known estimate of total depreciation developed with the market extraction or economic age-life methods among its various components

Procedure 1. Estimate total depreciation using the market extraction or economic age-life method.
2. Calculate all items of physical deterioration, add them up, and subtract the total from the lump-sum depreciation estimate. The residual amount, if any, represents depreciation attributable to functional and external obsolescence.
3. Calculate all items of functional obsolescence, add them up, and subtract that total from the total amount of obsolescence.
4. Any residual represents the depreciation attributable to external obsolescence.

Purpose To develop an estimate of total depreciation one item at a time

Procedure 1. Calculate all items of physical deterioration, including deferred maintenance, if present, using the appropriate techniques, and then add up all estimates to arrive at total physical deterioration.
2. Calculate all items of functional obsolescence, again using appropriate techniques, and add these estimates together to arrive at total functional obsolescence.
3. Calculate external obsolescence. When external obsolescence cannot be allocated from a lump-sum estimate, it is calculated either through analysis of paired data or by capitalization of income loss. The estimate of external obsolescence may have to be allocated between the site and the improvements, depending on how it is derived.
4. Add together all physical deterioration (including cost to cure deferred maintenance), functional obsolescence, and external obsolescence to arrive at an estimate of total depreciation.

---

[1] In previous editions of *The Appraisal of Real Estate*, the term *rent loss* had been used to denote the loss of income from rent. The term *income loss*, which is used in this edition, denotes lost rent as well as other income that may be lost to depreciation.

the market extraction or economic age-life methods, then no functional or external obsolescence is present. Second, if the sum of all items of physical deterioration and functional obsolescence estimated with breakdown techniques is equivalent to the total depreciation derived from the market extraction or economic age-life methods, then no external obsolescence is present.

Finally, if the sum of the items of depreciation estimated by the breakdown method substantially differs from the total depreciation derived from the market extraction or economic age-life methods, the appraiser should review all the methods applied as a test of reasonableness. A difference in the results obtained from the breakdown method and the market extraction or economic age-life methods may result for numerous reasons:

- The total depreciation derived from the market extraction or economic age-life methods may have been estimated incorrectly or does not reflect the characteristics of the depreciation in the subject property.

- The subject property may suffer from an element of depreciation that is indicated in the breakdown method but not in the market extraction or economic age-life methods, possibly due to dissimilarities in the comparable data.

- One or more of the breakdown techniques may have been applied incorrectly. For example, an incorrect application of the breakdown method may have resulted in double counting some element of depreciation. As another example, one of the most common errors in applying the breakdown method is selecting a physical or useful life for the long-lived components that is the same as the economic life of the property overall. Unless there are no short-lived items, it is mathematically impossible for the useful life of long-lived components and the economic life of the property as a whole to be the same.

> Components of physical deterioration include items of deferred maintenance, short-lived items, and long-lived items.

Physical Deterioration

In the breakdown method, all physical building deterioration or depreciation falls into one of three categories:

- Deferred maintenance
- Short-lived physical deterioration
- Long-lived physical deterioration

Deferred maintenance is curable, whereas short-lived and long-lived items of physical deterioration are not curable, usually because it is not physically possible or economically feasible to cure them. Elements of total depreciation that are not physical deterioration must be some form of obsolescence (either functional or external).

Curable Physical Deterioration – Deferred Maintenance

Curable *physical deterioration*, also known as *deferred maintenance*, applies to items in need of immediate repair on the effective date of the appraisal. Some examples include broken windows, a broken or inoperable HVAC system, carpet needing immediate replacement, a leaking roof, or inoperable restrooms. For most properties, deferred maintenance involves relatively minor items that are 100% physically deteriorated, i.e., broken. The item must be replaced or repaired for the building to continue to function as it should and to be marketable to potential buyers. Since these repairs must be performed for the building to continue to function, they are considered curable items.

There are two major tests of the curability of a physically deteriorated item:

- First, if spending the money to "cure" the item will result in a value increment equal to or greater than the expenditure, the item is normally considered curable.

- Second, if spending the money to cure the item will not result in a value increment equal to or greater than the expenditure but will allow other existing items to maintain their value, then the item is normally considered curable.

Deferred maintenance (deterioration) is measured as the cost to cure the item or to restore it to a new or reasonably new condition. The cost to cure may exceed the item's cost when it is installed new. Cost to cure is analogous to an age-life procedure because the age of a curable item equals (or exceeds) its total useful life expectancy, resulting in 100% deterioration. All deferred maintenance items are completely deteriorated, and therefore they may all be treated together in the breakdown method.

For example, suppose that during the inspection of an office the appraiser notes that the exterior walls need to be scraped, primed, and painted. A painting contractor quotes a price of $5,000 to do the work. However, according to the appraiser's cost manual, the job performed at the present time – i.e., as part of an original construction project – should only cost $3,500. In this instance, the correct measure of cost to cure is $5,000. If the painting work was done during the original construction, the walls would not have had to be scraped. The contractor could have just primed and painted them. The extra cost is the difference between the cost to cure and the total cost. The higher amount should be used by the appraiser as the cost to cure and the appropriate measure of curable physical deterioration for this building component.

Appraisers should note also that deferred maintenance items typically require a lump-sum adjustment in the direct comparison and income approaches because these problems are specific to the subject property and would not be reflected in the values provided by comparable sale or comparable rental properties.

Incurable Physical Deterioration – Short-lived Items

Once any curable physical deterioration is estimated, the remaining physical deterioration is allocated to either short-lived or long-lived building components. Short-lived items are those that are not ready to be replaced on the date of the opinion of value but will probably have to be replaced in the foreseeable (i.e., "short-term") future. Examples include the roof covering, interior floor finish, furnaces, and water heaters. A short-lived item is not 100% physically deteriorated, so it does not yet need to be cured. However, the appraiser draws the same conclusions that market participants do, i.e., that the items will be 100% deteriorated before the end of the building's total useful life expectancy and will have to be replaced. When those items reach the point of 100% physical deterioration, they become curable items. The same tests of curability that are applied to items of deferred maintenance are applied to short-lived items. Unlike items of deferred maintenance, which have lasted beyond their useful life expectancy and need to be replaced immediately, the short-lived items have generally not reached the end of their total useful life expectancy and are not completely deteriorated, but they are substantially depreciated in comparison with the overall structure.

The deterioration in short-lived items is measured by estimating a separate age-life ratio and applying it to the current cost of each short-lived item. Because each short-lived item usually has a different age and a different total useful life expectancy, a separate age-life ratio or schedule must be calculated for each item.

As an example, consider a 20-year old boiler in an apartment building. According to a boiler contractor, the total useful life expectancy of a boiler such as this is 25 years. On the date of the opinion of value, the boiler is operative and there is no need to replace it. However, a prudent purchaser or owner would anticipate that the boiler will have to be replaced within a few years. The replacement cost of the boiler is $30,000. The age-life ratio is used to estimate a depreciation rate of 80% (20 ÷ 25 = 0.80). When this ratio is applied to the cost to replace the boiler ($30,000), the deterioration (curable, short-lived depreciation) indicated is $24,000 ($30,000 × 0.80). The boiler would not be considered a short-lived item if its remaining useful life were equal to or greater than the remaining economic life of the overall property.

The age of short-lived items may be the actual age or their effective age. Effective age is less commonly used than actual age because effective age relies on the appraiser's judgment. However, in some circumstances effective age could be more appropriate depending upon the degree of maintenance or amount of wear and tear. The useful life may be developed from a variety of sources, including observation, historical data, published cost surveys, manufacturer's warranties, discussions with builders and property managers, and others.

Many lenders and investors rely on property condition surveys to help them plan for future replacements. These surveys can be useful to appraisers as well because they are usually prepared by an engineer and provide all of the detail required to

DAMAGE/VANDALISM

Damage or vandalism requires special treatment in the estimation of depreciation. The measure of damage is the cost to cure. Damage or vandalism must be treated separately from other forms of physical deterioration because it is not considered in the estimate of cost. By curing damage or vandalism, the life of the damaged component is neither renewed nor prolonged. It simply is restored to its condition prior to the damage.

As an example, consider a brick wall that has been spray painted with graffiti. The cost of sandblasting the wall to remove the graffiti is $5,000. Nowhere in the overall cost is there a provision for the removal of graffiti. The measure of damage in this instance would be $5,000, the full cost to cure.

Typically, the cost to cure damage is added to the curable physical deterioration and included among the items of physical deterioration in the breakdown method. However, the $5,000 cost to cure is not subtracted from cost when calculating long-lived physical deterioration.

complete a breakdown depreciation analysis, including identification and allocation of long- and short-lived components and the calculation of current age and remaining useful life. Property condition surveys include replacement cost estimates and a 10- to 20-year schedule that indicates exactly when replacements will be required. They tell the property owner what expenditures are needed immediately, what replacements will be needed in future years, and how much they will cost.

Incurable Physical Deterioration – Long-lived Items

Long-lived items include all items that were not treated as items of deferred maintenance or as short-lived items. Long-lived items are assumed to have the same age and life expectancy; therefore, they are all treated together. Examples of long-lived items include exterior walls, structural framing, the roof structure, underground piping, foundation walls, and insulation. The cost of the long-lived items is the remainder after subtracting the cost of the short-lived items and any deferred maintenance from the cost of the entire structure. A long-lived item is not 100% physically deteriorated. Therefore, it does not need to be cured. In addition, such an item is not normally replaced except under extraordinary circumstances – e.g., if a foundation wall is damaged. In that case, the long-lived component becomes an element of deferred maintenance, and the same tests of curability that are applied to the other physical components are applied to the long-lived items. The deterioration of long-lived items is measured by estimating an age-life ratio and applying it to all components of cost that have not already been treated for physical deterioration.

As an example, consider a small industrial building with a total cost of $700,000. It is 35 years old and has a total useful life expectancy of 100 years. The cost to cure the curable items (deferred maintenance) is $10,000 – as discussed earlier, the cost to cure for deferred maintenance is considered equal to the associated replacement cost new. Short-lived building components include the boiler, roof cover, and floor covering. The cost to replace the boiler is $40,000, the cost to replace the roof covering is $60,000, and the cost to replace the floor finish is $20,000. There are no other short-lived items. The age-life ratio is calculated to be 35% (35-year actual age / 100-year useful life). The replacement cost of the long-lived items is estimated by deducting the cost to cure the curable items and the sum of the costs to replace the short-lived items from the cost of the structure:

Total replacement cost – long- and short-lived items		$700,000
Short-lived items	Replacement Cost	
Deferred maintenance – replace restroom	$10,000	
Boiler	40,000	
Roof covering	60,000	
Floor finish	+ 20,000	
Subtotal – replacement cost of short-lived items		– $130,000
Remaining replacement cost attributed to long-lived items		$570,000

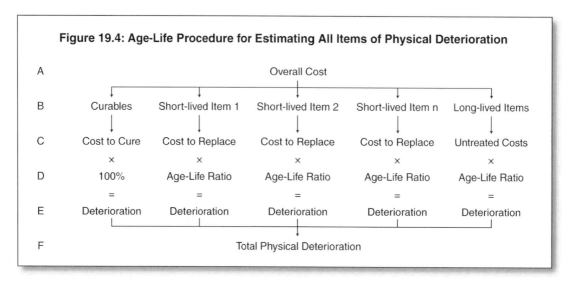

Figure 19.4: Age-Life Procedure for Estimating All Items of Physical Deterioration

The age-life ratio is then applied to the untreated costs (35% × $570,000), and the resulting amount of deterioration attributable to the long-lived items is calculated to be $199,500.

A common mistake in estimating the replacement cost of long-lived components is to first calculate the depreciation of the short-lived components and then deduct the depreciation of the short-lived components, rather than their cost, to develop the replacement cost of the long-lived components. Although the deferred maintenance shown in the preceding table will appear as depreciation on the cost approach summary, it is also the replacement cost of a fully depreciated item, and it must be included with the short-lived replacement costs before it can be deducted as depreciation.

> The age-life procedure is a useful model for ensuring that all forms of physical deterioration are correctly estimated and dealt with only once.

Understanding Age-Life Relationships and the Breakdown Method

Figure 19.4 illustrates an age-life procedure that can be used to estimate all forms of physical deterioration, both curable and incurable. In addition to showing the correct relationship between all items of physical deterioration, the diagram is designed to ensure that all types of physical deterioration are considered and no items of physical deterioration are treated more than once. This age-life procedure works whether the breakdown method is being used to allocate a known total depreciation amount among its components or to develop an estimate of total depreciation.

The procedure has four steps. First, the total cost is allocated among the curable items, the incurable short-lived items, and the incurable long-lived items (Step C in Figure 19.4). Second, an age-life ratio is calculated for each allocated cost item (Step D). Third, the appropriate age-life ratio is applied to the estimated cost of each item (Step E). Finally, the individual items of physical deterioration are added together to develop an estimate of total physical deterioration (Step F).

Reading across the top row of the diagram to Row A, the appraiser enters the overall cost of the improvement. Note the arrows leading from Row A to Row B. Row B is used to separate the various building components into curables, short-lived components, and long-lived components. The first column on the left is for the curable items, which are grouped together because they are all 100% physically deteriorated. The last column on the right is for the long-lived items, which are also grouped together because they all have incurred the same amount of physical deterioration. In the centre of the diagram, there are separate columns for each short-lived item because each typically has a different age and a different total useful life. The number of interior columns depends on the number of short-lived items observed by the appraiser. An appraiser calculates depreciation of short-lived items for each individual item.

Row C is used to allocate the improvement's overall cost, recorded in Row A, among the individual items. The sum of the cost to cure all curable items is entered in the left column. The cost to replace each of the short-lived items is entered in the appropriate column in the central portion of the diagram. The cost to cure the curable items and the individual costs to replace all short-lived items in Row C are added up and the total is deducted from the cost in Row A. The result is entered in the column on the right, which represents the remaining costs attributable to the long-lived items. All of the items in Row C, when added together, should equal the overall cost in Row A. By allocating costs before estimating the deterioration in any item, the appraiser is assured that all items will be treated for physical deterioration and none will be treated more than once.

The appraiser enters the age-life ratio of each item in Row D. All curable items are completely deteriorated, so 100% should be entered in the left-hand column of Row D. A separate age-life ratio is calculated for each short-lived item, using the effective age and economic life expectancy of the specific item. Total useful life for short-lived

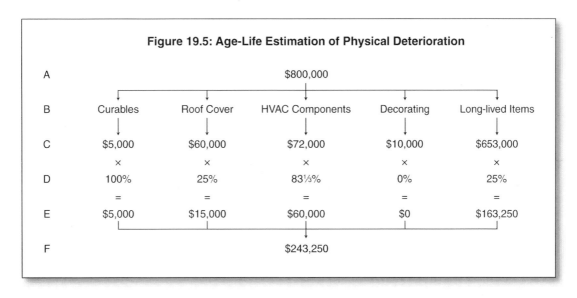

Figure 19.5: Age-Life Estimation of Physical Deterioration

	Curables	Roof Cover	HVAC Components	Decorating	Long-lived Items
A			$800,000		
B	Curables	Roof Cover	HVAC Components	Decorating	Long-lived Items
C	$5,000	$60,000	$72,000	$10,000	$653,000
	×	×	×	×	×
D	100%	25%	83⅓%	0%	25%
	=	=	=	=	=
E	$5,000	$15,000	$60,000	$0	$163,250
F			$243,250		

items may be obtained from the actual age of a component at the time of its replacement, analysis of manufacturer warranties, and information from property managers, contractors, and suppliers, i.e., building equipment stores and lumber yards.

Also, an age-life ratio is calculated based on the actual age of the long-lived items, which is usually equivalent to the chronological age of the building, and the total useful life expectancy of the long-lived items, which is usually extracted from the market. The age-life ratio calculated for long-lived items is entered in the right-hand column of Row D. The appraiser should recognize that the total useful life expectancy of long-lived items is longer than the economic life of the building overall, unless there are no short-lived components. Moreover, regardless of how long physical components may last (e.g., concrete might last indefinitely), an economic factor must also be considered, which is why the term *useful life* is used rather than *physical life*. Economic reasons will prevail when a building reaches the end of its economic life and is torn down. An appraiser can estimate total useful life for long-lived components using neighbourhood data, information from structural engineers, analysis of demolition permits, or direct market extraction. If a building is torn down and the site is redeveloped with a use similar to the use of the building that was torn down, the age of the building at the time it was torn down may be indicative of the building's useful life.

Physical deterioration estimates are calculated in Row E. The age-life ratio in each column of Row D is applied to the corresponding cost in Row C. The result is the physical deterioration for each item. The deterioration estimates in Row E should be less than the costs in Row C for all columns except the first, where the deterioration estimate in Row E should equal the cost in Row C. An appraiser calculates the total physical deterioration for the subject property by adding up all of the items in Row E and recording the sum in Row F.

As an example of these calculations, consider a 25-year old industrial building in average condition. Its overall cost is $800,000 (see Figure 19.5). On the date of inspection, the appraiser found one overhead door damaged beyond repair, which will cost $5,000 to replace. The roof was replaced five years ago and has a 20-year guarantee, which indicates that it is 25% depreciated. The cost to replace it is $60,000. The original HVAC components should last another five years, which indicates they are 83⅓% deteriorated (25/30). The cost to replace the HVAC components is $72,000. The offices were just completely redecorated at a cost of $10,000. The appraiser estimates that they will not have to be redecorated for another five years. Based on an analysis of demolition permits, the appraiser concludes that the total useful life expectancy of the long-lived items is 100 years.

In this example, the total physical deterioration is the sum of the individual deterioration calculations, $5,000 + $15,000 + $60,000 + $163,250, or $243,250. On an age-life basis, the total depreciation is 30% ($243,240/$800,000). The average annual depreciation is 1.2% per year (30%/25 years) and the overall economic life is 83 years (1/1.2% per year). The total depreciation of short-lived items is $80,000 ($5,000 + $15,000 + $60,000) and the current cost of these items is $147,000 ($5,000 + $60,000 + $72,000 + $10,000). The total depreciation of the short-lived items is 54.42%

($80,000/$147,000) over 25 years, or roughly 2.18% per year. The overall economic life of the short-lived components is 46 years (1/2.18% per year). A summary of the depreciated cost of the improvements is shown below:

Total current cost of all improvements		$800,000
Less depreciation		
Short-lived components	80,000	
Long-lived components	+ 163,250	
Total depreciation		− 243,250
Depreciated value of building improvements		$556,750

Functional Obsolescence

Functional obsolescence is caused by a flaw in the structure, materials, or design of the improvement when compared with the highest and best use and most cost-effective functional design requirements at the time of appraisal. A building that was functionally adequate at the time of construction can become inadequate or less appealing as design standards, mechanical systems, and construction materials change over time. Functional obsolescence is attributable to defects within the property, in contrast with external obsolescence, which deals with conditions outside the property. Functional obsolescence, which may be curable or incurable, can be caused by a deficiency, which means that some aspect of the subject property is below standard in respect to market norms. It can also be caused by a superadequacy, which means that some aspect of the subject property exceeds market norms.

In some cases, functional obsolescence is created by a developer or owner who incorporates special features at the request of the occupant, i.e., features that would not appeal to the market in general. An example of a superadequacy is an expensive, in-ground swimming pool in a neighbourhood of relatively low-cost homes. Equally common is functional obsolescence that occurs as a result of changing tastes or market preferences. Too few bathrooms or ceiling heights that are below current standards are examples of functional obsolescence due to deficiencies.

There are five types of functional obsolescence:

- Curable functional obsolescence caused by a deficiency requiring an addition (installation) of a new item

> Functional obsolescence may be caused by a deficiency or a superadequacy. Some forms are curable and others are incurable.

- Curable functional obsolescence caused by a deficiency requiring the substitution (replacement) of an existing item, i.e., "curing a defect"

- Curable functional obsolescence caused by a superadequacy that is economically feasible to cure

- Incurable functional obsolescence caused by a deficiency

- Incurable functional obsolescence caused by a superadequacy

Characteristics of the different types of functional obsolescence are illustrated in Table 19.4. Elements of total depreciation not identified as physical deterioration or as functional obsolescence must be external obsolescence.

Table 19.4: Types of Functional Obsolescence

Type	Characteristics/Measure
Curable deficiency requiring an addition	The subject suffers functional obsolescence because it lacks something that other properties in the market have. Since the item is not present, the property cannot be penalized for any deterioration the item may have incurred. However, because it usually costs more to add an item to an existing property than to include it when the property was originally built, the excess cost to cure is the appropriate measure of functional obsolescence.
Curable deficiency requiring substitution or modernization	A curable deficiency requiring substitution or modernization is caused by something that is present in the subject property but is either substandard compared to other properties on the market or is defective and thereby prevents some other component or system in the property from working properly. The measure is the excess cost to cure. In addition, the depreciated or remaining cost of the existing item, now worthless, must be deducted.
Curable superadequacy	A superadequacy is a type of functional obsolescence caused by something in the subject property that exceeds market requirements but does not contribute to value an amount equal to its cost. The superadequacy may have a cost to carry (i.e., higher operating costs) that must be considered. A superadequacy is only curable if it can be removed and value is added (or costs reduced) to the property – including any salvage value – from its removal. Note that in most applications of the cost approach, the need to estimate the functional obsolescence attributable to an incurable superadequacy is eliminated by using replacement cost instead of reproduction cost. Superadequacies are not replicated in a replacement cost estimate. Nevertheless, whether replacement or reproduction cost is used, any extraordinary expense of ownership associated with the superadequacy must be quantified and deducted as a penalty from the value of the property.
Incurable deficiency	The subject suffers functional obsolescence because it is missing a building component or design feature (e.g., a building with unusually low ceilings) that is not economically feasible to correct.
Incurable superadequacy	A property component that exceeds market requirements is incurable functional obsolescence caused by a superadequacy. It represents a cost without any corresponding increment in value or a cost that the increment in value does not meet. Because the component is incurable, the property must suffer the loss or added costs of ownership over time. However, if the cost of ownership increases over time, the obsolescence may become curable.

Like the curability of physical deterioration, there are two major tests of curability for functional obsolescence caused by a deficiency or superadequacy:

- If spending the money to cure the item will result in a value increment equal to or greater than the expenditure, the item is normally considered curable.

- If spending the money to cure the item will not result in a value increment equal to or greater than the expenditure but will allow existing items to maintain their value, the item is again considered curable.

If the cost to cure the item will not result in a value increment greater than the loss in value caused by the item or building component, then the item is considered incurable.

Functional obsolescence can be corrected in two ways:

- The functional obsolescence is cured by the property owner when this is economically feasible (and sometimes when it is not economically feasible)

- Market norms change, eliminating the cause of the functional obsolescence

Problem-Solving for Functional Obsolescence

A simple process can be used to identify and select the appropriate treatment for a functional problem. The first step is to identify the functional problem (see Figure 19.6). In many cases, this is readily apparent from the property inspection and information from the highest and best use analysis or other analyses in the valuation process. Once the functional problem has been identified, the next step is to determine which building components are causing the problem and identify possible corrective measures (and associated costs to cure).

In many cases there will be only one cost to cure program to fix or improve a functional problem. Often, especially for superadequate components, there may be no economically feasible or practical method to cure the problem. In this case, the component is incurable and the property must endure the loss in value. If there are multiple cost-to-cure scenarios to cure a particular problem, the appraiser should select the most appropriate or cost-effective measure.

The cost to cure must consider the cost to tear out or replace the existing component, plus the cost of the correct replacement component, plus any other costs above and beyond the total cost if the component was included in the initial construction, less any salvage value. Essentially, the final measure is total cost to cure offset by any salvage value:

```
    Cost to tear out or remove existing component
  + Cost of correct replacement component
  + Any costs above and beyond total cost if included in initial construction
  − Salvage value (if any)
    Cost to cure
```

The next step is to quantify the loss caused by the functional problem associated with the building component. The value loss could be caused by a loss in income, an increase in expenses or operating costs, or a combination of both. Alternatively, the value loss might be quantified by market evidence such as paired sales analysis. By definition, the loss cured will equal the value added once the cure is accomplished. If the value added is equal to the cost, it may still be desirable to cure the problem to remain competitive in the market.

Figure 19.6: Analyzing a Functional Problem

1. Identify the functional problem.
2. Identify the component(s) in the facility or lack of component(s) associated with the problem.
3. Identify possible corrective measure(s) and the related cost to cure.
4. Select the most appropriate corrective measure.
5. Quantify the loss caused by the functional problem, which results in added value if the problem is corrected.
6. Determine if the item is curable or incurable. (If the value added is equal to or greater than the cost to cure, the functional problem is curable.)
7. Apply the functional obsolescence procedure.

Now the cost to cure is compared with the quantified loss. If the value added (once the cure is accomplished) is greater than the cost to cure, then the functional problem is curable. Otherwise, the functional problem is incurable. The next step is to solve for the dollar amount of depreciation using the functional obsolescence procedure.

Using the Functional Obsolescence Procedure

Figure 19.7 diagrams a procedure that can be used to calculate all forms of functional obsolescence caused by a deficiency or a superadequacy, whether the obsolescence is curable or incurable. Use of this model ensures that all components of functional obsolescence will be treated in a consistent manner, that none of the items will be treated more than once, and that no double charges will be made for items that have already been depreciated (i.e., charged under physical deterioration), which is particularly important for superadequacies.

> The functional obsolescence procedure ensures that all items of functional obsolescence will be treated consistently, that none will be considered more than once, and that double depreciation charges will not be made.

First, the cost of the existing item is identified. If the item is a form of functional obsolescence caused by a deficiency requiring an addition, there will be no cost for the item and zero will be entered on this line. Also, when replacement cost, rather than reproduction cost, is used for the cost basis, there typically will be no cost allotted for any superadequate items. As stated earlier in the text, all forms of functional obsolescence present in the subject property would be included in a reproduction of that property, whereas a replacement structure is built to contemporary standards and would not have certain forms of obsolescence present in the subject improvement.

In the second step, any depreciation that has already been charged for the item is deducted. In nearly all instances, this depreciation will be physical deterioration. As in the first step, if the item does not already exist in the building, no depreciation will have been charged and zero will be entered on this line. The net effect of the first two steps is to completely remove the total cost of the item, i.e., physical deterioration already taken plus remaining cost not depreciated in the first two steps.

Regardless of the type of functional obsolescence, the appraiser must investigate a cost to cure to determine whether the item is curable or not. If the functional obsolescence is curable, the third step is to add up all the costs associated with curing

---

Figure 19.7: Procedure for Estimating All Forms of Functional Obsolescence

Step 1.	Cost of existing item	$xxx,xxx
Step 2.	Less depreciation previously charged	− xxx,xxx
	plus	
Step 3.	Cost to cure (all costs)	+ xxx,xxx
	or	*or*
	Value of the loss	+ xxx,xxx
Step 4.	Less cost if installed new	− xxx,xxx
Step 5.	Equals depreciation for functional obsolescence	$xxx,xxx

---

the item. This includes the cost of purchasing and installing a new item, the cost of removing the old item, less any salvage value. If the functional obsolescence is incurable, the third step is to add the value of the loss attributable to the obsolescence. This value can be obtained by capitalizing an income loss (using an income multiplier or a capitalization rate) or through analysis of market data such as paired sales.

The fourth step is to enter a deduction for the cost of the item as though installed new on the date of the value opinion, if appropriate. When the third step involves a curable item, the combination of the third and fourth steps essentially yields the excess cost to cure. As the final step, the appraiser adds up all of the entries to derive the total functional obsolescence attributable to each factor. The model described here works for all types of functional obsolescence. The following examples demonstrate how the procedure is used to estimate different types of functional obsolescence.

Curable Functional Obsolescence Caused by a Deficiency Requiring an Addition

Consider a small office building without air-conditioning in a market where this feature is standard. Because of retrofit requirements, it is more costly to install the air-conditioning now than it would have been as a part of the original construction. The current cost to install the air-conditioning is $12,000; if the work had been done as a part of new construction, the cost would have been only $10,000. Installing air-conditioning would allow the property owner to raise rents, and effective gross income would increase an estimated $2,000 per year. The current effective gross income multiplier (EGIM) is 7.0. The functional obsolescence is curable because the value increase ($2,000 × 7.0 = $14,000) is greater than the cost to cure ($12,000).

1.	Cost of existing item	$0
2.	Less depreciation previously charged	0
	plus	
3.	Cost to cure (all costs)	+ 12,000
	or	
	Value of loss	−
4.	Less cost if installed new	− 10,000
5.	Equals depreciation for functional obsolescence	$2,000

Note that because the air-conditioning is not present in the existing improvement, no cost is shown as total cost and no deterioration was charged (Steps 1 and 2). The cost to install the air-conditioning as a part of new construction on the date of the opinion of value is $10,000 (Step 4), but the actual cost to retrofit and install the air-conditioning is $12,000 (Step 3). The curable functional obsolescence is the excess cost to cure, or $2,000 (Step 5).

Incurable Functional Obsolescence Caused by a Deficiency

Now suppose that installing an air-conditioning system in the office is not economically feasible – e.g., the current cost of the necessary renovations (say, $20,000) is greater than the value gained by adding the item ($14,000). For each building component in the functional depreciation area, two elements must be identified:

- The cost to cure
- The amount of loss caused by the component or lack of the component

When the loss is cured, the amount of the loss essentially becomes the value added. In this case, the cost to cure is $20,000. If the item is cured, the value added (or reduction in loss) is only $14,000, which means the item is incurable. The depreciation charged is the amount of the loss, over and above the cost if installed new. In the previous example, the item was curable and the measure of depreciation was the excess cost to cure.

1.	Cost of existing item	$0
2.	Less depreciation previously charged	0
	plus	
3.	Cost to cure (all costs)	–
	or	
	Value of loss 14,000	
4.	Less cost if installed new	– 10,000
5.	Equals depreciation for functional obsolescence	$4,000

Again, because the air-conditioning is not present in the existing improvement, no deterioration was charged. The value of the loss is equivalent to the lost income attributable to the deficiency. The effect of this loss is partially offset by the $10,000 that would have been expended to install air-conditioning as part of new construction. The incurable functional obsolescence is $4,000.

Costs to cure and losses sustained by a component can and do change over time. Items identified as incurable at one point in time can become curable and vice versa over the life of the property.

Curable Functional Obsolescence Caused by a Deficiency Requiring Substitution or Modernization

Now suppose that the office building has an outdated air-conditioning system that does not meet market standards and needs to be retrofitted. The reproduction cost of the existing air-conditioning system is $8,000, and the item is 25% physically deteriorated ($8,000 × 0.25 = $2,000). The cost to remove the existing air-conditioning is

$4,500, the salvage value of that equipment is $3,000, and the current cost of install-ing an appropriate air-conditioning system is $12,000 ($10,000 to install the correct component plus $2,000 to retrofit the space). The property can still be expected to increase effective gross income by $2,000 per year (with an EGIM of 7.0) if an appro-priate air-conditioning system is installed, so the extra income generated ($14,000) would exceed the cost to cure ($4,500 - $3,000 + $12,000 = $13,500) and the item is therefore curable. If the correct air-conditioning system had been installed as part of new construction, the cost would have been $10,000.

1.	Cost of existing item	$8,000
2.	Less depreciation previously charged	− 2,000
	plus	
3.	Cost to cure (all costs)	+ 13,500
	or	
	Value of loss	−
4.	Less cost if installed new	− 10,000
5.	Equals depreciation for functional obsolescence	$9,500

In this case, application of the formula essentially removes the existing component from cost (the $8,000 cost of the existing equipment less physical depreciation of $2,000 already charged) in the first two steps and penalizes cost by the excess cost to cure of $3,500 ($13,500 − $10,000) in the third and fourth steps.

Suppose that the existing equipment had no salvage value. The cost to cure the deficiency ($4,500 for removal of existing equipment plus $12,000 for installation of the new system, or $16,500) would exceed the value gained by replacing the air-condi-tioning system ($14,000), and the item of functional obsolescence would be incurable. Incurable functional obsolescence caused by the deficiency (i.e., the inadequacy of the existing air-conditioning system) would be $10,000 as shown below.

1.	Cost of existing item	$8,000
2.	Less depreciation previously charged	− 2,000
	plus	
3.	Cost to cure (all costs)	−
	or	
	Value of loss	+ 14,000
4.	Less cost if installed new	− 10,000
5.	Equals depreciation for functional obsolescence	$10,000

Curable Functional Obsolescence Caused by a Superadequacy

Consider a warehouse built for an owner-occupant with an HVAC system providing excess cooling capacity for the storage of perishable goods. When the property goes on the rental market, the HVAC system will be superadequate in relation to most typical warehouse uses. The current reproduction cost of the existing HVAC system is $40,000, and the component is 30% depreciated. Removing the superadequate item would cost $5,000, the salvage value is $8,000, and installing an HVAC system with typical capacity for the market would cost $22,000 for a total cost to cure of $19,000

($5,000 - $8,000 + $22,000). If a lower-capacity HVAC system had been installed as part of new construction, the item would have only cost $16,000. The lower-capacity HVAC would save the property owner $200 per month in electricity and maintenance expenses. Capitalized at an annual rate of 12% (a building capitalization rate derived from analysis of comparable sales), the value of the cost savings would be $20,000 ($200 x 12/12%), which exceeds the cost to cure. The item is therefore curable.

1.	Reproduction cost of existing item	$40,000
2.	Less depreciation previously charged	– 12,000
	plus	
3.	Cost to cure (all costs)	+ 19,000
	or	
	Value of loss	–
4.	Less cost if installed new	– 16,000
5.	Equals depreciation from functional obsolescence	$31,000

If the replacement cost of the appropriate HVAC system is used as the cost basis rather than reproduction cost, the superadequate item would not be included in the substitute property, so there would be no charge for the existing item, nor for the item as installed new. The measure of depreciation due to curable functional obsolescence caused by a superadequacy would be the cost to cure, i.e., the cost to remove the superadequate item less salvage value plus the cost to install the appropriate item.

1.	Replacement cost of existing item	$0
2.	Less depreciation previously charged	0
	plus	
3.	Cost to cure (all costs)	+ 19,000
	or	
	Value of loss	–
4.	Less cost if installed new	0
5.	Equals depreciation from functional obsolescence	$19,000

Note that the depreciation estimate when replacement cost is used as the cost basis ($19,000) is less than the depreciation estimate when reproduction cost is used ($31,000). As stated in earlier chapters, the corresponding estimates of total cost using replacement cost would probably be lower than the estimate provided by reproduction cost figures because replacement cost would not include an oversized, atypical HVAC system. Therefore, less depreciation would be subtracted from the replacement cost estimate than from the reproduction cost estimate to arrive at the same figure (or a similar figure) for both cost bases.

Incurable Functional Obsolescence Caused by a Superadequacy

A superadequacy is often difficult to cure. Consider an industrial building with 24 foot ceiling heights where the market norm is 18 foot ceilings. The cost of a building with 24 foot ceilings is $1.2 million, whereas the cost of a building with 18 foot ceilings is $1.0 million. The subject building costs $5,000 more per year to heat and cool than comparable properties in the subject's market. The extra $200,000 spent in the original construction on the extra six feet of ceiling height adds no value to the property and there is no reasonable cost to cure, so the superadequacy is incurable.

In this market, the higher ceiling would not be installed in a substitute property. Therefore, in the calculation of functional obsolescence, the amount entered as cost if installed new is zero. Note also that if replacement cost is used, the $200,000 cost of the superadequacy will be eliminated and the measure of functional obsolescence would be only the capitalized additional costs of ownership. The extra ceiling height costs the subject property $5,000 more per year than the costs incurred by competitive buildings, and analysis of income and expense data for comparable buildings yields a building capitalization rate of 12.5% in this market. The incurable functional obsolescence is estimated to be $40,000 ($5,000/0.125). Because the item is superadequate, it does not belong in the structure and there is no correct replacement component, so there is no entry in Step 4. The replacement cost calculation is as follows:

> When estimating functional obsolescence caused by a superadequacy, the appraiser must remember whether the cost basis in the calculations is reproduction cost or replacement cost. A superadequacy in an existing improvement would not be installed in a replacement structure, so the cost of that item would not be included in the estimation of functional obsolescence when replacement cost figures are used.

1.	Replacement cost of existing item	$0
2.	Less depreciation previously charged	0
	plus	
3.	Cost to cure (all costs)	–
	or	
	Value of the loss	+ 40,000
4.	Less cost if installed new	0
5.	Equals depreciation from functional obsolescence	$40,000

If reproduction cost is used, the additional $200,000 cost of the superadequacy will not be eliminated. The incurable functional obsolescence would be measured as the cost of the superadequate item less the physical deterioration already charged plus the capitalized additional costs of ownership. Assuming that a 10% charge has already been levied for incurable physical deterioration due to the extra ceiling height, the incurable functional obsolescence would be the cost of the superadequate item ($200,000 for the extra six feet of ceiling height) less the physical deterioration already charged ($20,000) plus the added costs of ownership ($40,000). The resulting depreciation estimate is $220,000.

1.	Reproduction cost of existing item	$200,000
2.	Less depreciation previously charged	– 20,000
	plus	
3.	Cost to cure (all costs)	–
	or	
	Value of the loss	+ 40,000
4.	Less cost if installed new	0
5.	Equals depreciation from functional obsolescence	$220,000

External Obsolescence

External obsolescence is a loss in value caused by factors outside a property. It is often incurable. External obsolescence can be either temporary (e.g., an oversupplied market) or permanent (e.g., proximity to an environmental disaster). External factors frequently affect both the land and building components of a property's value. The current land value considers the effect of external factors. External obsolescence usually has a market wide effect and influences a whole class of properties, rather than just a single property. However, external obsolescence may affect only one property when its cause is location, e.g., proximity to negative environmental factors or the absence of zoning and land use controls.

> External obsolescence may be caused by economic or locational factors. It may be temporary or permanent, but it is not usually considered curable on the part of the owner, landlord, or tenant.

> External obsolescence may be estimated by allocation of market-extracted depreciation, market data analysis, or capitalization of income loss.

When an appraiser studies market data to develop an estimate of external obsolescence, it is important to isolate the effect of the obsolescence on land value from the effect on the value of the improvements. In some situations, external obsolescence may be attributed entirely to the land; in other situations, it may be attributed entirely to the improvements. Often external obsolescence can be allocated between land and improvements. This is critical if external obsolescence is already reflected in the estimate of land value. A building-to-property-value ratio derived through market area analysis may be used to determine the loss in value to be allocated to the building.

The three primary methods of measuring external obsolescence are the following:

- Allocation of market-extracted depreciation
- Analysis of market data
- Capitalization of an income loss

External Obsolescence Estimated by Allocation of Market-Extracted Depreciation

When a lump-sum figure of total depreciation is estimated through market extraction, that amount can be allocated between the three major types of depreciation to generate an estimate of external obsolescence. As an example, consider an industrial property with a reproduction cost of $1 million in a market where similarly depreciated buildings have sold for $800,000. Total physical deterioration is calculated at $80,000, and total functional obsolescence is calculated at $10,000. The remaining portion of total depreciation, $110,000, can be allocated to external obsolescence.

Total cost		$1,000,000
Sale price (excluding land value)		− 800,000
Depreciation from all sources		$200,000
Allocation		
Physical deterioration		
Curable	$10,000	
Incurable	+ 70,000	
Total physical deterioration	$80,000	

Functional obsolescence	
Curable	$2,500
Incurable	+ 7,500
Total functional obsolescence	$10,000
Total physical deterioration and functional obsolescence	− 90,000
Allocation to external obsolescence	$110,000

External Obsolescence Estimated by Market Data Analysis

Using paired data analysis, consider a subject property that is a 12-unit apartment building located downwind of a relatively new asphalt batching plant. Sale A is a vacant lot adjacent to the subject that is zoned for a 12-unit apartment building and was just sold for $36,000 ($3,000 per unit). Sale B is a vacant site on the other side of town that is also zoned for a 12-unit apartment building and was recently sold for $48,000 ($4,000 per unit). Sale C is a 9-unit apartment building in the subject's neighbourhood that was recently sold for $459,000 ($51,000 per unit). Sale D is a 10-unit apartment building on the other side of town that was sold for $540,000 ($54,000 per unit). Using Sales C and D, the external obsolescence attributable to the property as a whole is estimated at $3,000 per unit (the difference between $54,000 and $51,000, the sale prices per unit). The subject property would thus incur $36,000 in external obsolescence (12 units × $3,000). Sales A and B indicate that $12,000 of this external obsolescence ($1,000 per unit, calculated as the difference between $4,000 and $3,000, the sale prices of the land per unit) is recognized in the land value. The remaining $24,000, therefore, is attributable to the building.

External Obtsolescence Overall:

	Sale C – down-wind	Sale D – up-wind
Sale Price	$459,000	$540,000
Sale price per unit	$51,000	$54,000
External obsolescence per unit	$3,000	
External obsolescence for subject (12 unit) = $36,000		

External Obsolescence for Vacant Land:

	Sale A – down-wind	Sale B up-wind
Sale Price	$36,000	$48,000
Sale price per unit (according to zoning)	$3,000	$4,000
External obsolescence per unit	$1,000	
External obsolescence for subject (12 unit) = $12,000		

External Obsolescence for Building:

$36,000 − $12,000 = $24,000

External Obsolescence Estimated by Capitalization of Income Loss

When a property produces income, the income loss caused by the external obsolescence can be capitalized into an estimate of the loss in total property value. This procedure is applied in two steps. First, the market is analyzed to quantify the income loss. Next, the income loss is capitalized to obtain the value loss affecting the property as a whole. If the income loss is anticipated to be permanent, it can be capitalized by applying either a gross income multiplier to a gross income loss or an overall capitalization rate to a net income loss. If the income loss is not anticipated to be permanent, it can be estimated using discounted cash flow analysis.

For example, consider a 4,000 square foot retail establishment in an oversupplied market. In a normal market, net operating income would be $8.00 per square foot. However, since the oversupply began, net operating income has fallen to $6.25 per square foot. The oversupply, which is unique to the subject's market, was caused by overbuilding. The overall capitalization rate indicated by the market is 10%. Since the oversupply is anticipated to continue indefinitely, the external obsolescence can be calculated by direct capitalization. The total income loss of $7,000 ([$8.00 – $6.25 = $1.75] × 4,000 square feet) is capitalized by the overall capitalization rate of 10%. The resulting external obsolescence of $70,000 would probably be attributed entirely to the improvements (if land value is not impacted).

If the oversupply were anticipated to continue for a relatively short period of time, the external obsolescence could be calculated by discounted cash flow analysis. Suppose that the $7,000 income loss will only last three years and that the appropriate discount rate is 13%. The external obsolescence could be calculated as the present value of $7,000 per year for three years, discounted at $j_1 = 13\%$, or $16,528 (calculator steps found in Appendix C). As in the previous example in which direct capitalization was used, it is likely that the entire amount of external obsolescence would be attributable to the improvement.

CHAPTER 20

THE INCOME APPROACH

Income-producing real estate is typically purchased as an investment, and from an investor's point of view, earning power is the critical element affecting property value. One basic investment premise holds that the higher the earnings, the higher the value, provided the amount of risk remains constant. An investor who purchases income-producing real estate is essentially trading present dollars for the expectation of receiving future dollars. The income approach to value consists of methods, techniques, and mathematical procedures that an appraiser uses to analyze a property's capacity to generate benefits (i.e., usually the monetary benefits of income and reversion) and convert these benefits into an indication of present value.

The analysis of cost and sales data is often an integral part of the income approach, and an appraiser frequently employs capitalization techniques in the cost and direct comparison approaches. An appraiser commonly uses capitalization techniques to analyze and adjust sales data in the direct comparison approach; in the cost approach, an appraiser often measures obsolescence by capitalizing an estimated income loss. The income approach is described here as part of the systematic valuation process, but the various methods, techniques, and procedures used in the approach are general-purpose analytical tools applicable in the valuation and evaluation of income-producing properties.

This chapter provides a broad overview of the income approach and discusses the rationale and methods behind it. Chapters 21 through 24 continue this discussion with detailed explanations of the specific methods, techniques, and procedures used to project and capitalize future benefits.

> In the income approach, an appraiser analyzes a property's capacity to generate future benefits and capitalizes the income into an indication of present value. The principle of anticipation is fundamental to the approach. Techniques and procedures from this approach are used to analyze comparable sales data and to measure obsolescence in the cost approach.

RELATION TO APPRAISAL PRINCIPLES

Anticipation and Change

Anticipation is fundamental to the income approach. All income methods, techniques, and procedures attempt to consider anticipated future benefits and estimate their present value. This may involve either forecasting the anticipated future income or estimating a capitalization rate that implicitly reflects the anticipated pattern of change in income over time.

The approach must also consider how change affects the value of income-producing properties. To provide sound value indications, the appraiser must carefully address and forecast investors' expectations of changes in income levels, the expenses required to ensure income, and probable increases or decreases in property value. The defined income of a real estate investment may differ according to the type of investor. The ongoing securitization and globalization of real estate investment has brought new participants into the market. The income streams that real estate investment trusts (REITs) and pension funds look to are different from the net incomes on which more traditional investors have focused.[1]

The capitalization process must reflect the possibility that actual future income, expenses, and property value may differ from those originally anticipated by an investor on the date of appraisal. The more uncertainty there is concerning the future levels of these variables, the riskier the investment. Investors expect to earn a higher rate of return on investments that are riskier. This should be reflected in the support provided for the discount rate and capitalization rate obtained from market research.

Supply and Demand

The principles of supply and demand and the related concept of competition are particularly useful in forecasting future benefits and estimating rates of return in the income approach. An appraiser determines both income and rates of return in the market. The rents charged by the owners of a shopping centre, an office building, an apartment building, or any income-producing property usually do not vary greatly from those charged by owners of competing properties.

If the demand for a particular type of space exceeds the existing supply, owners may be able to increase rents. Vacancy rates may fall and developers may find new construction profitable. Property values may increase until supply satisfies demand. On the other hand, if the demand for space is less than the existing supply, rents may decline and vacancy rates may increase. Therefore, to estimate rates of return and forecast future benefits, appraisers consider the demand (both present and anticipated) for the particular type of property and how the demand relates to supply.

---

[1]   For a discussion of how pension fund managers and other institutional investors analyze income and cash flow to property, see the discussion of the securitization of real estate markets in Chapter 5.

APPLICABILITY AND LIMITATIONS

Any property that generates income can be valued using the income approach. When an appraiser uses more than one approach to value to develop an opinion of value for an income-producing property, the value indication produced by the income approach might be given greater weight than that of the other approaches in the final reconciliation of value indications.

INTERESTS TO BE VALUED

Income-producing real estate is usually leased, which creates legal estates of the lessor's interest (i.e., the leased fee) and the lessee's interest, i.e., the leasehold. There are also hybrid situations involving partially leased buildings. Federal or provincial law often requires appraisers to value leased properties as fee simple estates, not leased fee estates, e.g., for expropriation and ad valorem taxation.

When an appraisal assignment involves the valuation of the fee simple interest in a leased property (whether due to government regulations or the desires of the client), the valuation of the entire bundle of rights may or may not require the valuation of the separate parts. The value of a leasehold estate may be positive, zero, or negative, depending on the relationship of market rent and contract rent, as explained in Chapter 6. The difference between the market rent and contract rent may be capitalized at an appropriate rate or discounted to present value to produce an indication of leasehold value, if any, without consideration of the value of the leased fee estate.

Although the market values of leased fee and leasehold positions are often said to be "allocated" between the two (or more) interests, each interest must be valued on its own merit. An appraiser can then compare the results with the valuation of an unencumbered fee simple interest. This comparison is particularly important when contract benefits or detriments are substantial.

Appraisers should not necessarily conclude that leasehold and leased fee values are additive and always equal fee simple value. It is possible that both the leaseholder and the leased fee owner are disadvantaged because of the terms of the lease. Also, there may be an apparent advantage of one party over the other when compared with other leases. However, the existence of the advantage may result in problems that outweigh its benefits and ultimately are disadvantageous to that party.

Like all contracts, a real estate lease depends on the actual performance of all parties to the contract. A weak tenant with the best of intentions may still be a high risk. The same is true of a financially capable tenant who is litigious and willing to ignore lease terms, break a lease, and defy lawsuits. If the tenant defaults or does not renew a lease, the value of the underlying property does not change, but the value of the leased fee may be seriously affected.

Since a leasehold or a leased fee is based on contract rights, the appraiser needs special training and experience to differentiate between what is generally representative of the market and other elements of a contract that are not typical of the market. An understanding of the risks associated with the parties and the lease arrangement is also required. A lease never increases the market value of real property rights to the fee simple estate. Any potential value increment in excess of a fee simple estate is attributable to the particular lease contract, and even though the rights may legally "run with the land", they constitute contract rather than real estate rights. Conversely, detrimental aspects of a lease may result in a situation in which either or both of the parties to the lease, and their corresponding value positions, may be diminished.

An appraiser can use income capitalization to simulate investor motivations. For example, investors in small residential income properties might typically purchase on the basis of *gross income multipliers* (GIMs) or *effective gross income multipliers* (EGIMs). Thus, the appraiser could develop an opinion of the value of a subject property using EGIMs. Similarly, investors in large office buildings with numerous tenants might project future cash flows by analyzing each lease and considering the impact of lease renewals and the anticipated sale of the property at the end of a projection period. The appraiser could simulate this process by conducting a similar discounted cash flow analysis for the subject property.

Income capitalization techniques do not always rely on comparable sales, but some appropriate form of market support is needed. Yield capitalization does require selection or development of an appropriate *yield rate*. The yield rate should reflect what investors expected to earn on comparable sales as well as other real estate investment alternatives with similar risk currently available in the market.

DEFINITIONS

The income approach employs more specialized terminology than any of the other approaches to value, and the meanings of the various terms sometimes overlap. Table 20.1 shows the relationships between different rates used in the approach and the real property interests that can be valued. Table 20.2 lists synonymous terms and symbols commonly used in the income approach.

Table 20.1: Rates, Ratios, and Relationships

Property Interest	Net Income or Cash Flow	Forecast Reversion	Capitalization Rate	Yield Rate
Total property (V_O)	Net operating income (*NOI* or I_O)	Proceeds of resale (*PR or REV*), property reversion Net proceeds of disposition (V_N or REV_N)	Overall capitalization rate (R_O)	Risk rate, discount rate (Y_O)
Debt, mortgage loan (V_M)	Debt service (I_M), monthly – DS, annual – ADS	Balance, balloon (V_M or OSB), book value (*b*)	Mortgage capitalization rate (R_M)	Yield rate to mortgage (Y_M), interest rate
Equity (V_E)	Equity dividend (I_E)	Equity reversion ATER	Equity capitalization rate (R_E)	Equity yield rate (Y_E)
Land, site (V_L)	*NOI* to land (NOI_L or I_L)	Land reversion (*LR*) rate (R_L)	Land capitalization	Land yield rate (Y_L)
Building, improvements (V_B)	NOI to building (NOI_B or I_B)	Building reversion (*BR*)	Building capitalization rate (R_B)	Building yield rate (Y_B)
Leased fee (V_{LF})	NOI to lessor (NOI_{LF} or I_{LF})	Property reversion (*PR*) or proceeds of resale	Leased fee capitalization rate (R_{LF})	Leased fee yield rate (Y_{LF})
Leasehold (V_{LH})	NOI to lessee (NOI_{LH} or I_{LH})	None or proceeds of resale of leasehold estate	Leasehold capitalization rate (R_{LH})	Leasehold yield rate (Y_{LH})

Table 20.2: Terms and Synonyms Used in the Income Approach

Category	Preferred Term	Synonym/Symbol
Lease	Flat rental lease	Level payment lease
	Variable rental lease	Index lease
	Step-up or step-down lease	Graduated rental lease
	Revaluation lease	
	Lease with an annual increase	
	Percentage lease	
Rent	Contract rent	
	Market rent	Economic rent
	Scheduled rent	
	Pro forma rent	
	Effective rent	
	Excess rent	
	Deficit rent	
	Percentage rent	
	Overage rent	
Future benefits	Potential gross income	*PGI (or GPI)*
	Effective gross income	*EGI*
	Gross Realized Income	*GRI (same as EGI)*
	Net operating income	NOI or I_O*
	Equity dividend	Income to equity (I_E)
	Reversion	Reversionary benefits, resale value, property reversion
Operating expenses	Fixed expense	
	Variable expense	
	Replacement allowance	Replacement reserve, capital items, tenant improvements, leasing commissions
Rates of return	Overall capitalization rate	R_O
	Equity capitalization rate	Cash flow rate, cash on cash return, equity dividend rate, R_E
	Terminal capitalization rate	Residual capitalization rate, R_T or R_N
	Land capitalization rate	R_L
	Building capitalization rate	R_B
	Discount rate	Risk rate
	Safe rate	Riskless rate, relatively riskless rate
	Internal rate of return	*IRR*
	Overall yield rate	Property yield rate, Y_O
	Equity yield rate	Y_E
	Mortgage capitalization rate	Mortgage constant, annual loan constant, R_M
Income multipliers	Potential gross income multiplier	*PGIM*
	Effective gross income multiplier	*EGIM*
Vacancy	Frictional vacancy	
Stabilization	Stabilized occupancy	
	Stabilized income	

* The traditional abbreviation NOI is commonly used in accounting, finance, economics, and other professional disciplines. The abbreviation IO is used in Appraisal Institute educational materials to maintain a consistent set of variables and subscripts throughout income capitalization calculations. The abbreviations can be used interchangeably.

> ## MARKET VALUE AND INVESTMENT VALUE
>
> An important distinction is made between market value and investment value. Investment value is the value of a certain property use to a particular investor. Investment value may coincide with market value, which was defined in Chapter 2, if the client's investment criteria are typical of successful buyers in the market. In this case, the two opinions of value may be the same number, but the two types of value and their concepts are not interchangeable.
>
> Market value is objective, impersonal, and detached. Investment value is based on subjective, personal parameters. To develop an opinion of market value with the income approach, the appraiser must be certain that all the data and forecasts used are market-oriented and reflect the motivations of a typical investor who would be willing to purchase the property as of the effective date of the appraisal. A particular investor may be willing to pay a price different from market value, if necessary, to acquire a property that satisfies other investment objectives unique to that investor.

Leases

The income to various lease interests transferred by the landlord to the tenant is generally derived through the conveyance and operation of leases. A lease is a written[2] document in which the rights to use and occupy land or structures are transferred by the owner to another for a specified period of time in return for a specified rent. An appraiser begins the income approach by studying all existing and proposed leases that apply to the subject property. These leases provide information on the base rent, any other income, and the division of expenses between the landlord and the tenant.

Although a lease can be drawn to fit any situation, most leases[3] fall into one of several broad classifications:

> **lease**
> A written document in which the rights to use and occupy land or structures are transferred by the owner to another for a specified period of time in return for a specified rent.

- Flat rental
- Variable rental
- Step-up or step-down
- Revaluation
- Annual increase
- Percentage

Leases may be negotiated on a gross rental basis, with the lessor paying most or all operating expenses of the real estate (or the increase above the base-year expenses), or on a net rental basis, with the tenant paying all expenses. When leases are negotiated on a modified gross rental basis, lease terms fall between these extremes and specify the division of expenses between the lessor and the lessee. Leases can also be categorized by their terms of occupancy:

- Month-to-month
- Short-term (generally five years or less)
- Long-term (generally more than five years)

---

[2] Land titles matters are the jurisdiction of Canada's provinces and territories and can vary by locale.

[3] Other lease types are defined in accounting practice, e.g., capital or financing leases and operating or service leases. These leases often involve equipment.

LEASES AND EXPENSES

The terms gross lease, modified gross lease, and net lease do not always mean the same thing in different markets. The expenses that are included in each type of rent vary from market to market. In general, the following distinctions can be made:

- Gross lease, tenant pays rent and landlord pays expenses
- Modified gross lease, tenant and landlord share expenses
- Net lease, landlord passes on all expenses to tenant

Sometimes real estate professionals will refer to a triple net lease, in which the tenant pays utilities, taxes, insurance, and maintenance and the landlord pays for structural repairs only.

To analyze income and expenses based on market observation, the appraiser must understand how these terms are used in the market and clearly communicate that information to the intended user in the appraisal report. Furthermore, the appraiser must consistently account for the same expenses in the analysis of the income generated by a certain type of lease. For example, the available market data for five comparable office properties supports an estimate of market rent in the range of $27.50 to $31.00 per square foot, all quoted on a net rental basis. The rents for four of the properties range from $27.50 to $29.00 per square foot, and the tenants in those buildings pay for all expenses. The owner of the fifth comparable property, for which net rents are quoted at $31.00 per square foot, actually pays for insurance, i.e., that owner defines net rent differently than the other property owners. Consequently, the rent of the net lease of the fifth property, which would be equivalent to a modified lease in the other buildings, is noticeably higher.

An extreme form of net lease is commonly referred to as a bondable lease (or sometimes as an absolute triple net lease). In effect, the tenant is responsible for all expenses for the entire duration of the lease term, and is even obligated to continue to pay rent after a casualty or condemnation. The shifting of risk from landlord to tenant creates a lease with the obligations equivalent to a bond. Bondable leases are most often used in credit tenant leases.

Flat Rental Lease

A *flat rental lease* specifies a level of rent that continues throughout the duration of the lease. In a stable market, this type of lease is typical and acceptable. Flat rental leases are also prevalent in net rent situations where changes in expenses are the responsibility of the tenant(s). However, in a changing economy, leases that are more responsive to fluctuating market conditions are preferred. When flat rental leases are used in inflationary periods, they tend to be short-term such as apartment leases. Some assignments require the appraiser to express the estimate of market rent on a "levelled" basis. This requires forecasting any change in market rent over a projection period and converting the total income generated by that lease over the projection period into an annual level equivalent.

> **flat rental lease**
> A lease with a specified level of rent that continues throughout the lease term.
>
> **index lease**
> A lease, usually for a long term, that provides for periodic rent adjustments based on the change in an economic index.

Variable Rental Lease

A *variable rental lease* is quite common, particularly when an owner anticipates periodic changes in market rent. Sometimes this type of lease may specify a periodic percentage change; at other times, the change may be tied into a specific index such as the national or local Consumer Price Index. Often those leases are called *index leases*. At other times, the lease may specify that the rent change will be tied to the higher or lower of the two, the period percentage or the index. This is particularly prevalent in gross and modified gross leases where an owner needs periodic income adjustments to offset increases in expenses.

Step-Up or Step-Down Rental Lease

Step-up or step-down leases (also known as *graduated rental leases*) provide for specified changes in the amount of rent at one or more points during the lease term. A step-up lease, which allows for smaller rent payments in the early years, can be advantageous to a tenant establishing a business in a new location. This type of lease can also be used to recognize tenant expenditures on a property that are effectively amortized during the early years of the lease. Long-term ground leases may include provisions for increasing the rent to reflect the expectation of future increases in property value and protect the purchasing power of the landlord's investment. Since property value is usually expected to increase, tenants are expected to pay commensurately higher rents.

> **step-up (step-down) lease**
> A lease that provides for a certain rent for an initial period, followed by an increase (or decrease) in rent over stated periods.

Step-down leases are less common than step-up leases. They are generally used to reflect unusual circumstances associated with a particular property such as the likelihood of reduced tenant appeal in the future or capital recapture of interior improvements during the early years of a long-term lease. Also, a step-down lease may be used when initial tenant improvements are recaptured over the first lease period by the landlord and when the second lease period has a lower income level.

Lease with an Annual Increase

One of the most common types of leases simply increases the rent annually by a dollar amount specified in the lease.

Revaluation Lease

Revaluation leases provide for periodic rent adjustments based on revaluation of market rent under prevailing market conditions. Although revaluation leases tend to be long-term, some are short-term with renewal option rents based on revaluation of market rent when the option is exercised. When the parties to a lease cannot agree on the value or rent, revaluation through appraisal or arbitration may be stipulated in the lease.

> **revaluation lease**
> A lease that provides for periodic rent adjustments based on the market rental rate of the space.

Percentage Lease

In *percentage leases,* some or all of the gross income is based on a specified percentage of the volume of business, productivity, or use achieved by the tenant. Percentage leases may be short- or long-term and are most frequently used for retail properties. A straight percentage lease may have no minimum rent, but most specify a guaranteed minimum rent and an overage rent, which is defined in the next section.

Rent

The income to investment properties consists primarily of rent. Different types of rent affect the quality of property income. Appraisers use several categories to analyze rental income:

- Market rent
- Contract rent
- Effective rent
- Excess rent
- Deficit rent
- Percentage rent
- Overage rent

Market Rent

Market rent is the rental income a property would probably command in the open market. It is indicated by the current rents that are either paid or asked for comparable space with the same division of expenses as of the date of the appraisal. Market rent is sometimes referred to as *economic rent.*

Rent for vacant or owner-occupied space is usually estimated at market rent levels and distinguished from contract rent in the income analysis. In fee simple valuations, all rentable space is estimated at market rent levels. Any rent attributed to specific leases is disregarded in the income analysis. In a leased fee analysis, current contract rents defined by any existing leases are used for leased space, and income for vacant space is estimated at market rent. In developing market rent and expense estimates, the appraiser should ensure that property management is competent.

Market data usually provides evidence of a range of market rents. For example, if the market for industrial space shows a rent range of $4.00 to $5.00 per square foot of gross building area on a gross rental basis and the subject property is leased for $3.00 per square foot of gross building area, the appraiser could conclude that the actual rent is below market levels. However, if the actual rents were $3.90, $4.50, or $5.05 per square foot of gross building area, it would be reasonable to conclude that those rents are consistent with market rents. If market rents are on a gross rental basis and the subject is leased on a net rental basis, it may be difficult to compare market and contract rent.

> **market rent**
> The most probable rent that a property should bring in a competitive and open market reflecting all conditions and restrictions of the typical lease agreement, including the rental adjustment and revaluation, permitted uses, use restrictions, expense obligations, term, concessions, renewal and purchase options, and tenant improvements (TIs).

Contract Rent

Contract rent is the actual rental income specified in a lease. It is the rent agreed on by the landlord and the tenant and may be higher than, less than, or equal to market rent. Also, it is important to compare rents of properties with similar division of expenses, similar lease terms, or a similar level of finished space.

Effective Rent

In markets where concessions take the form of free rent, above-market tenant improvements, or atypical allowances, an appraiser must quantify the true *effective rent*. Effective rent (or actual occupancy cost) is an analytical tool used to compare leases with different provisions and develop an estimate of market rent. Effective rent may be defined as the total of base rent, or minimum rent stipulated in a lease, over the specified lease term minus rent concessions, e.g., free rent, excessive tenant improvements, moving allowances, lease buyouts, cash allowances, and other leasing incentives. Effective rent may be calculated in several different ways.

> **contract rent**
> The actual rental income specified in a lease.

Effective rent may be estimated based on rental income from existing leases at contract rates or rental income from leases at market rates. In calculating effective rent, an appraiser must allow for rent concessions in effect at the time of the appraisal, discounts, or other benefits that may have prompted a prospective tenant to enter into a lease.

The timing of the rent concessions may make analysis of effective rent a moot point. For example, consider a 10,000 square foot industrial property with a five-year lease at $4,000 per month, four months of rent concessions (the first two months of the first two years), and a date of value at the beginning of the third year of the lease. The concessions granted in the first two years of the lease are not an issue in the analysis of the income generated in the third year, and the actual and effective rent would be the same on the date of value.

Effective rent can be calculated as the average, annual rent net of rent concessions or as an annual rent that produces the same present value as the actual annual rents net of rent concessions. While these two methods are considered interchangeable, they do not produce the same results. The first method is a mathematical average, whereas the second is a discounting procedure in which the rent concessions are accounted for in the years that they actually occur.

> **effective rent**
> The rental rate net of financial concessions such as periods of no rent during the lease term and above- or below-market TIs.

As a simple example of effective rent calculations, consider a lease on a 10,000 square foot industrial building in which the rent is specified as $4,000 per month (or $48,000 per year) for a five-year term with level income throughout the lease term. When the lease was negotiated, the tenant received free rent for the first month of each year as a concession. The contract rent is $4.80 per square foot. However, the effective rent is only $4.40 per square foot:

$4,000 per month × 11 months = $44,000

$44,000 ÷ 10,000 square feet = $4.40 per square foot

There are options for the treatment of tenant improvement costs. The appraisal problem will dictate whether it is appropriate to deduct all tenant improvements or only deduct the additional actual tenant improvement costs over a market standard.

Excess Rent

Excess rent is the amount by which contract rent exceeds market rent at the time of the appraisal. Excess rent is created by a lease that is favourable to the lessor and may reflect superior management or a lease that was negotiated in a stronger rental market. Excess rent may be expected to continue for the remainder of the lease if the relationship of contract rent and market rent is expected to remain the same for the duration of the lease.

However, small tenants may not be able to succeed because of the rent disadvantage. Higher risk may also be present for a large, financially capable company with the power to break the lease. Due to the higher risk associated with the receipt of excess rent, an appraiser may calculate it separately and capitalize or discount it at a higher rate. Since excess rent is the result of the lease contract rather than the income potential of the underlying real property on the valuation date, the incremental value created by a lease premium can result in a leased fee value that exceeds the fee simple value. Such a situation is known as a *negative leasehold*.

Deficit Rent

Deficit rent represents the amount by which market rent exceeds contract rent at the effective date of the appraisal. It is created by a lease favourable to the tenant and may reflect uninformed parties, inferior management, or a lease executed in a weaker rental market. Similarly, when leased fee value is less than fee simple value, taxes may be based on the higher fee simple value. A leased fee value that is less than the fee simple value results in a positive leasehold interest for the tenant's position in the property. When there is a positive leasehold interest for a financially strong tenant, there is often reduced risk for the leased fee owner. This may reduce the capitalization rate that is appropriate for the leased fee position.

---

excess rent
The amount by which contract rent exceeds market rent at the time of the appraisal; created by a lease favorable to the landlord (lessor) and may reflect unusual management, unknowledgeable parties, or a lease execution in an earlier, stronger rental market. Due to the higher risk inherent in the receipt of excess rent, it may be calculated separately and capitalized at a higher rate in the income approach.

deficit rent
The amount by which market rent exceeds contract rent at the time of the appraisal; created by a lease favorable to the tenant, resulting in a positive leasehold, and may reflect uninformed parties, inferior management, or a lease executed in a weaker rental market.

percentage rent
Rental income received in accordance with the terms of a percentage lease; typically derived from retail store and restaurant tenants and based on a certain percentage of their gross sales.

Percentage Rent

Percentage rent is rental income received in accordance with the terms of a percentage clause in a lease. Percentage rent is typically derived from retail tenants and is based on a certain percentage of their sales revenue. It is usually paid at the end of each year and may be more difficult to collect than other forms of rent paid on a more regular basis.

The emergence of new competition in the area or the departure of an anchor tenant from a shopping centre may reduce or eliminate anticipated percentage rent. Also, as is true for excess rent, the conditions that create percentage rent may not extend for the duration of the lease. Furthermore, calculation of a store's sales revenue can be impacted by transactions involving a "virtual" or internet component. Depending on the tenant, percentage rent may involve more risk than other forms of rent and may be capitalized or discounted separately or at a different rate. Note that the risk is in the variability of the income, more than in the likelihood that collecting the rent will be difficult.

Overage Rent

Overage rent is percentage rent paid over and above the guaranteed minimum rent or base rent. The level of sales at which a percentage clause is activated is specified in a lease and called a *breakpoint*. The natural breakpoint is the level of sales at which the percentage rent exactly equals the base rent.

The breakpoint in a percentage lease does not necessarily have to be the natural breakpoint. For example, if the annual base rent was set in the lease at $400,000 and the percentage of retail sales specified in the lease was 20%, then the natural breakpoint would be a sales volume of $2,000,000, i.e., $400,000 ÷ 0.20 = $2,000,000. The breakpoint specified in the lease could be set at a sales volume of $2,250,000; in this case the tenant would pay the base rent of $400,000 until the percentage clause is activated, and the percentage rent jumps to $450,000 ($2,250,000 × 0.20 = $450,000). The breakpoint could also be set lower than the natural breakpoint – say, at a sales volume of $1,750,000 – but the actual rent paid is usually the higher of the two, base rent or percentage rent.

> **overage rent**
> The percentage rent paid over and above the guaranteed minimum rent or base rent; calculated as a percentage of sales in excess of a specified breakpoint sales volume.
>
> **base rent**
> The minimum rent stipulated in a lease.

Overage rent should not be confused with excess rent. Overage rent is a contract rent; it may be market rent, part market and part excess rent, or excess rent only.

Future Benefits

The benefits of owning specific rights in income-producing real estate include the right to receive all cash flows accruing to the real property over the holding or projection period (i.e., the term of ownership) plus any proceeds from disposition of the property at the termination of the investment.[4]

An appraiser considers various measures of future benefits in the income approach. Commonly used measures include the following:

- Potential gross income
- Effective gross income
- Net operating income
- Equity dividend
- Reversionary benefits

Potential Gross Income

Potential gross income (PGI or GPI) is the total potential income attributable to the real property at full occupancy before operating expenses are deducted. It may refer to the level of rental income prevailing as of the effective date of the appraisal or expected during the first full month or year of operation, or to the periodic income anticipated during the projection period.

Effective Gross Income

Effective gross income (EGI, or gross realized income) is the anticipated income from all operations of the real property adjusted for vacancy and collection losses. This adjustment covers losses incurred due to unoccupied space, turnover, and non-payment of rent by tenants.

Net Operating Income

Net operating income (NOI or I_O) is the actual or anticipated net income remaining after all operating expenses are deducted from effective gross income. Net operating income is customarily expressed as an annual amount. In certain income capitalization applications, a single year's net operating income may represent a steady stream of fixed income that is expected to continue for a number of years. In other applications, the income may represent the starting level of income that is expected to change in a prescribed pattern over the years or the appraiser may have to estimate the net operating income for each year of the analysis.

> **potential gross income (PGI or GPI)**
> The total income attributable to real property at full occupancy before vacancy and operating expenses are deducted.
>
> **effective gross income (EGI)**
> The anticipated income from all operations of the real property after an allowance is made for vacancy and collection losses and an addition is made for any other income (also known as gross realized revenue).
>
> **net operating income (NOI or I_O)**
> The actual or anticipated net income that remains after all operating expenses are deducted from effective gross income but before mortgage debt service and book depreciation are deducted.
> *Note*: This definition mirrors the convention used in corporate finance and business valuation for EBITDA, i.e., earnings before interest, taxes, depreciation, and amortization.
>
> **equity dividend (I_E)**
> The portion of net operating income that remains after total mortgage debt service is paid but before ordinary income tax on operations is deducted.

---

[4]   The *holding period* is a more broadly defined, market-oriented measure of how long investors typically retain ownership of real property, whereas the *projection period* is used in investment analysis to forecast the term of ownership given the reasonable expectation of certain market events occurring in the future.

Equity Dividend

Equity dividend (I_E) is the portion of net operating income that remains after debt service is paid. Like net operating income, a single year's equity dividend may represent a steady stream of fixed income, the starting level of a changing income stream, or the equity income for a particular year of the analysis.

Reversion

Reversion is a lump-sum benefit an investor receives upon termination of an investment or at an intermediate analysis period during the term of an investment (especially for appraisals). The reversionary benefit may be calculated before or after the mortgage balance is deducted. For example, the reversionary benefits for fee simple and leased fee estates are the net proceeds expected to result from resale of the property at the end of the investment projection period. For a mortgagee or lender, reversion consists of the balance of the mortgage when it is paid off or forecast to be paid off. Table 20.3 shows several possible investment positions in an income-producing property and identifies the income streams and reversions associated with each interest.

> reversion
>
> A lump-sum benefit that an investor receives or expects to receive upon the termination of an investment; also called *reversionary benefit*.

Reversionary benefits are usually estimated as anticipated dollar amounts or as relative changes in value over the presumed projection period. An appraiser may base a dollar estimate of the reversion on a lessee's option to purchase the property at the end of the lease. Alternatively, the appraiser may estimate the value of the reversion

Table 20.3: Summary of Incomes and Reversions Associated with Various Real Property Interests in Income-Producing Property

Fee Simple	
Income	Net operating income based on market rents (*NOI* or I_O)
Reversion	Net proceeds of disposition (REV_N or V_N)
Mortgagee (Lender's Position)	
Income	Mortgage debt service (PMT or I_M)
Reversion	Balance if paid prior to maturity or balloon payment if paid at maturity; none if loan amortizes fully (OSB_N or V_{MN})
Equity	
Income	Equity cash flow or equity dividend (I_E)
Reversion	Net equity proceeds of disposition ($ATER_N$ or V_{EN})
Leased fee	
Income	Net operating income based on contract rents
Reversion	Property reversion or net proceeds of disposition of leased fee estate
Leasehold	
Income	Rental advantage when contract rent is below market rent; rental disadvantage when contract rent is above market rent
Reversion	None if held to end of lease or net proceeds of resale of leasehold estate

at the end of the projection period by applying a capitalization rate to the income that a buyer expects to receive at the time of resale (or expected resale). Reversionary benefits may or may not require separate measurement, depending on the purpose of the analysis and the method of capitalization employed.

Operating Expenses

In the income approach, a comprehensive analysis of the annual expenses of property operation is essential whether the value indication is derived from estimated net operating income or equity dividend. Operating expenses represent the periodic expenditures necessary to maintain the real property and continue the production of the revenue.

> **reconstructed operating statement**
> A statement prepared by an appraiser to reflect the future performance of a property based on the historical income and expenses of an investment property. In preparing reconstructed operating statements, appraisers may consult accountants' financial balance sheets, comparable properties, auditors' statements, and historical data provided by the ownership entity.
>
> **operating expenses**
> The periodic expenditures necessary to maintain the real property and continue production of the effective gross income, assuming prudent and competent management.

An operating statement that conforms to this definition of operating expenses is used for appraisal purposes. This reconstructed operating statement may differ from statements prepared for an owner or by an accountant because these often include non-cash expenses such as depreciation or interest expenses. Operating statements are prepared on either a cash or accrual basis, and the appraiser must know the accounting basis used in the operating statements for the property being appraised. Operating statements provide valuable factual data and can be used to identify trends in operating expenses.

Operating expenses comprise three categories:

1. Fixed expenses
2. Variable expenses
3. Replacement allowance

These classifications have been used for a long time, but there are other valid systems that an appraiser can employ and different property types may require different formats.

Fixed Expenses

Fixed expenses are operating expenses that generally do not vary with occupancy and have to be paid whether the property is occupied or vacant. Real estate taxes and building insurance costs are typically considered fixed expenses. Although these expenses rarely remain constant, they generally do not fluctuate widely from year to year, do not vary in response to changing occupancy levels, and are not subject to management control.

> **fixed expenses**
> Operating expenses that generally do not vary with occupancy and that prudent management will pay whether the property is occupied or vacant.
>
> **variable expenses**
> Operating expenses that generally vary with the level of occupancy or the extent of services provided.

Therefore, an appraiser can usually identify a trend and accurately estimate these expense items.

Variable Expenses

Variable expenses are operating expenses that generally vary with the level of occupancy or the extent of services provided, though most variable expenses have some minimal fixed component regardless of occupancy. Specific expense items of this type may vary greatly from year to year, but similar types of property often reflect a reasonably consistent pattern of variable expenses in relation to gross income. Since fewer services are provided to the tenants of freestanding retail and industrial properties, these properties usually have a much lower ratio of expenses to gross income than do apartment and office buildings.

Replacement Allowance

A *replacement allowance* (reserves) provides for the periodic replacement of building components that wear out more rapidly than the building itself and must be replaced periodically during the building's useful life, i.e., capital items. Market participants may view replacement allowances differently from market to market, e.g., accounting for replacement allowance as a line item or implicitly in the capitalization or discount rate. Appraisers must deal with replacement allowances in a manner that is consistent with the method used in the relevant market for comparable properties.

> replacement allowance
> An allowance that provides for the periodic replacement of building components that wear out more rapidly than the building itself and must be replaced during the building's economic life; sometimes referred to as *reserves*.

Rates of Return

A prudent investor ultimately seeks a total return greater than or equal to the amount invested. Therefore, the investor's expected return consists of two components:

1. Full recovery of the amount invested, i.e., the return of capital
2. A reward for the assumption of risk, i.e., a return on invested capital

Because the returns from real estate may take a variety of forms, an appraiser uses many rates, or measures of return in capitalization. All measures of return can be categorized as either income rates, such as an overall capitalization rate (R_O) or equity capitalization rate (R_E), or discount rates, such as an effective interest rate (the rate of return on debt capital), yield rate (the rate used to convert future payments into present value, Y_O), or internal rate of return (IRR).

The term *discount rate* describes any rate used to convert future cash flows over time into a present value. Because investors expect their total return to exceed the amount

> An investor's total expected return includes the return of capital (recapture of capital) and a return on capital (compensation for use of capital until recapture). Rates of return may be income rates (ratios of annual income to value that are used to convert income into value) or yield rates (rates of return on capital).

invested, the present value of a prospective benefit is less than the expected future worth of that benefit – thus the "discount".[5] A yield rate, a specific type of discount rate, is the rate of return on capital. It considers all expected property benefits, including a reversion.

Under certain conditions, the yield rate for a property may be numerically equivalent to the corresponding income rate; nevertheless, the rates and their related concepts are not the same, nor are they interchangeable. An income rate is the ratio of one year's income to value.[6] A yield rate is applied to a series of individual incomes to obtain the present value of each and is calculated in the same way as an internal rate of return.

> **discount rate**
> A yield rate used to convert future payments or receipts into present value; usually considered to be a synonym for *yield rate*.

In the income approach, both income rates and yield rates can be derived for, and applied to, any component of real property rights or the underlying physical real estate. For example, an appraiser may analyze total property income in terms of income to the land and income to the building or in terms of income to the mortgage and equity interests in the property. Similarly, an appraiser may seek the total investment yield or analyze the separate yields to the land and the building or to the mortgage and the equity interests. Finally, an appraiser may want to know the value of the unencumbered fee simple, the leased fee, or the leasehold interest. Chapters 21 through 23 present practical examples of these applications and the relevant symbols, formulas, and procedures.

Return on and Return of Capital

The notion that an investor anticipates a complete recovery of invested capital – plus a payment for the use of capital – prevails in the real estate market just as it does in other markets. The term *return of capital* refers to the recovery of invested capital; the term *return on capital* refers to the additional amount received as compensation for use of the investor's capital until it is recaptured. Investors are concerned with both types of return. The rate of return on capital is analogous to the yield rate or the interest rate earned or expected.

> **return of capital**
> The recovery of invested capital, usually through income and/or reversion.
>
> **return on capital**
> The additional amount received as compensation (profit or reward) for use of an investor's capital until it is recaptured. The rate of return on capital is the yield rate or the interest rate earned or expected.

A typical example is the mortgage loan calculation in which return of and return on are considered in the level mortgage payment over time.

In real estate investments, capital may be recaptured in many ways.[7] Investment capital may be recaptured through annual income or it may be recaptured all or in part through disposition of the property at the termination of the investment. It may

---

[5]   For a thorough discussion of discounting, see Charles Akerson, *Capitalization Theory and Techniques: Study Guide*, 2nd ed. (Chicago: Appraisal Institute, 2000).

[6]   The rate is usually calculated with the income for the first year, although the income for the previous year may be used. In rare cases the incomes for several years might be averaged to obtain a representative income figure.

[7]   The term *recapture* was coined at a time when investors assumed that property values could only decline due to depreciation from physical or functional causes. Today appraisers use the term when some income provision must be made to compensate for the loss of invested capital.

also be recaptured through a combination of both. If the property value does not change between the time the initial investment is made and the time the property is sold, the investor can recapture all the initial capital invested at property resale at the end of the holding period. Thus, when initial value is equivalent to resale value, the annual income can all be attributed to the return on capital. If the income has remained level (or constant), the indicated income rate (i.e., the overall capitalization rate) will equal the return on capital.

In yield capitalization, the distinction between the return on and the return of capital is more explicit. The yield rate estimated for cash flows determines a specified return on capital. Direct capitalization, on the other hand, uses income rates such as overall capitalization rates, which must implicitly allow for both the return on and return of capital. When an appraiser applies the capitalization rate to the subject property's income, the indicated value must represent a price that would allow the investor to earn a market rate of return on the capital invested along with the recapture of the capital. Thus, the capitalization rate estimated and applied to value property must reflect or consider a market level of return of and return on the initial investment in one calculation.

> **yield rate (Y)**
> A rate of return on capital, usually expressed as a compound annual percentage rate. A yield rate considers all expected property benefits, including the proceeds from sale at the termination of the investment.
>
> **overall yield rate (Y_O)**
> The rate of return on the total capital invested, including both debt and equity. Also called the property yield rate. When applied to cash flows, it is called a discount rate.

Income Rates

An income rate expresses the relationship between one year's income and the corresponding capital value of a property.

An *overall capitalization rate* (R_O) is an income rate for a total property that reflects the relationship between a single year's net operating income and the total property price or value. It is used to convert net operating income into an indication of overall property value. An overall capitalization rate is not a rate of return on capital or a full measure of investment performance. It may be more than, less than, or equal to the expected yield on the capital invested, depending on projected income and value changes.

An *equity capitalization rate* (R_E) is an income rate that reflects the relationship between a single year's equity cash flow expectancy and the equity investment. When used to capitalize the subject property's cash flow after debt service into equity value, the equity capitalization rate is often referred to in the real estate market as the

> **income rate**
> A rate that reflects the ratio of one year's income to the value of the property; includes the overall capitalization rate (R_O), the equity capitalization rate (R_E), and the mortgage capitalization rate (R_M).
>
> **overall capitalization rate (R_O)**
> An income rate for a total real property interest that reflects the relationship between a single year's net operating income expectancy and the total property price or value.
>
> **equity capitalization rate (R_E)**
> An income rate that reflects the relationship between one year's equity cash flow and the equity investment.

cash flow rate, cash on cash return, or *equity dividend rate.* Like the overall capitalization rate, the equity capitalization rate is not a rate of return on capital. It may be more than, less than, or equal to the expected equity yield rate, depending on projected changes in income, value, and amortization of the loan.

Discount Rates

Various sorts of discount rates are used to discount cash flows applicable to a specific position or interest in defined real estate. Discount rates may or may not be developed in the same way as internal rates of return and may not necessarily consider all expected property benefits.

A yield rate is a rate of return on capital. It is usually expressed as a compound annual percentage rate. The yield rate considers all expected property benefits (both positive and negative over time), including the proceeds from disposition at the termination of the investment, if any. The term *interest rate* usually refers to the yield rate for debt capital, not equity capital.

An *internal rate of return* (IRR) is the yield rate that is earned for a given capital investment over the period of ownership. The internal rate of return for an investment is the yield rate that equates the present value of the future benefits of the investment to the amount of capital invested. The internal rate of return applies to all expected benefits, including the net proceeds from disposition at the investment's termination. It can be used to measure the return on any capital investment, before or after income taxes.

An *overall yield rate* (Y_O), or property yield rate, is a rate of return on the total capital invested. It considers all changes in income over the investment projection period as well as the reversion at the end of the projection period. It does not, however, consider the effect of debt financing. Rather, it is calculated as if the property were purchased with no debt capital. The overall yield rate can be viewed as the combined yield on both the debt and equity capital; it is calculated in the same way the internal rate of return is calculated.

An *equity yield rate* (Y_E) is a rate of return on equity capital. It may be distinguished from a rate of return on debt capital, which is usually referred to as an *effective mortgage interest rate.* The equity yield rate is the equity investor's internal rate of return. It is affected by the amount of financial leverage employed in securing mortgage debt.

Estimating Rates

Whether an income rate or a yield rate is applied, the conversion of income into property value should reflect the annual rate of return the market indicates is necessary to attract investment capital. This rate is influenced by many factors:

- The degree of perceived risk
- Market expectations regarding future inflation
- The prospective rates of return for alternative investments
- The rates of return earned by comparable properties in the past
- The availability of debt financing
- The prevailing tax law

Because the rates of return used in the income approach represent prospective rates, not historical rates, the market's perception of risk and changes in purchasing power are particularly important. Generally, higher overall capitalization rates are associated with less desirable properties, and lower overall capitalization rates are associated with more attractive properties.

The suitability of a particular rate of return cannot be proven with market evidence, but the rate estimated should be consistent with the data available. Rate estimation requires appraisal judgment and knowledge of prevailing market attitudes and economic indicators.

Typically, investors expect to receive a return on capital that represents the time value of money with an appropriate adjustment for perceived risk. The time value of money underlies the accrual of interest on investments. The minimum rate of return for invested capital is sometimes referred to as the *safe, riskless,* or *relatively riskless rate,* e.g., the prevailing rate on insured savings accounts or guaranteed government securities.[8] Theoretically, the difference between the total rate of return on capital and the safe rate may be considered a premium to compensate the investor for risk, the illiquidity of invested capital, and other investment considerations.

A discount rate reflects the relationship between income and the value that a market will attribute to that income. The financial and economic concepts implicit in a discount rate are complex and have been the subject of significant analysis for more than a century. Although four key components can be identified within a discount rate – the safe rate plus considerations of illiquidity, management, and various risks – a discount rate that is constructed by adding allowances for these components can be misleading or inaccurate. The band of investment concept can be helpful in understanding these components, especially in differentiating marginal risk considerations, but these band of investment methodologies should not be represented as developing a market discount rate.

> The rate of return on investment combines a safe rate with a premium to compensate the investor for risk, the illiquidity of invested capital, and management involvement. The rate of return on capital may incorporate inflationary expectations and should reflect the competition for capital among alternative investments of comparable risk.

> **time value of money**
> The concept underlying compound interest that holds that $1 (or another unit of currency) received today is worth more than $1 (or another unit of currency) received in the future due to opportunity cost, inflation, and the certainty of payment.
>
> **band of investment**
> A technique in which the capitalization rates attributable to components of a capital investment are weighted and combined to derive a weighted-average rate attributable to the total investment

Risk

The anticipation of receiving future benefits creates value, but the possibility of not receiving or losing future benefits reduces value and creates risk. Higher rewards are required in return for accepting higher risk. To a real estate investor, risk is the chance

---

[8]   For example, Government of Canada bonds. Note that the yields of GOC bonds vary with the term; when establishing risk free rates of return from bonds, it is necessary to match bond term with the anticipated term or investment horizon of the real estate investment under review.

of incurring a financial loss and the uncertainty of realizing projected future benefits. Most investors try to avoid excessive risk; they prefer certainty to uncertainty and expect a reward for taking a risk. Appraisers must recognize investors' attitudes in analyzing market evidence, projecting future benefits, and applying capitalization procedures. The appraiser must be satisfied that the income rate or yield rate used in capitalization is consistent with market evidence and reflects the level of risk associated with receiving the anticipated benefits.

Inflation

Appraisers should be aware of the difference between inflation and appreciation in real value. Inflation is an increase in the volume of money and credit, a rise in the general level of prices, and the consequent erosion of purchasing power. Appreciation in real value results from an excess of demand over supply, which increases property values beyond typical levels of inflation.

The amount of inflation expected affects the forecast of future benefits and the estimation of an appropriate income or yield rate. If inflation is anticipated, the desired nominal rate of return on invested capital will likely increase to compensate for lost purchasing power. The required nominal rate, then, will increase to offset the expected inflation. Most investors try to protect the real rate of return over time.

A distinction must be made between expected inflation and unexpected inflation. Expected inflation refers to changes in price levels that are expected at the time the investment is made or when the property is being appraised. However, actual inflation may differ from what was anticipated at the time the investment was made. Depending on how the investment responds to the actual change in price levels, its value may fluctuate over time at a different rate than originally anticipated. If the return on the investment does not increase with unexpected inflation, the investor's real rate of return will be less than originally projected.

PROCEDURE

The income approach supports two basic methodologies: *direct capitalization*, which uses the relationship of one year's income to conclude a value, and *yield capitalization*, which considers a series of cash flows over time together with any reversion value or resale proceeds (*discounted cash flow* or *DCF analysis*).

Initially, both methods require a comprehensive study of historical income and expenses for the subject property. This study is combined with an analysis of typical income and expense levels for comparable properties. The appraiser develops a reconstructed operating statement for the subject property. This statement must reflect the purpose of the appraisal, especially with respect to the property interest being appraised.

> The two methods of income capitalization are direct capitalization, in which a single year's income is divided by an income rate or multiplied by an income factor to reach an indication of value, and yield capitalization, in which future benefits are converted into a value indication by discounting them at an appropriate yield rate (discounted cash flow, or DCF analysis) or applying an overall rate that reflects the investment's income pattern, value change, and yield rate.

Leased fee value will reflect current leases and the associated expense structure, while fee simple value starts with an income based on market rent.

Yield capitalization will require a consideration of probable income and expenses over the designated projection period, often from 5 to 10 years. When this method is used, the appraiser must forecast income and expenses over time together with the eventual reversion or resale value of the property. Direct capitalization, on the other hand, requires a one-year cash flow estimate (date of valuation plus next 12 months) and application of an overall rate to estimate value. This method relies on sales of properties with income characteristics and future expectations similar to the subject property.

Although there are various income capitalization techniques available to the appraiser, certain steps are essential in applying the income approach. Before applying any capitalization techniques, an appraiser must work down from potential gross income to net operating income. To do this, the appraiser will do the following:

1. Research the income and expense data for the subject property and comparables.

2. Estimate the potential gross income of the property by adding the rental income and any other potential income.

3. Estimate the vacancy and collection loss.

4. Subtract vacancy and collection loss from total potential gross income to arrive at the effective gross income of the subject property.

5. Estimate the total operating expenses for the subject by adding fixed expenses, variable expenses, and a replacement allowance (where applicable).

6. Subtract the estimate of total operating expenses from the estimate of effective gross income to arrive at net operating income. (Deductions for capital items may also be necessary at various points in time through the projection period to calculate the cash flow used in discounted cash flow analysis.)

7. Apply one of the direct or yield capitalization techniques to this data to generate an estimate of value via the income approach.

Direct Capitalization, Yield Capitalization, and Discounting

Direct capitalization makes use of a single year's income and a market-derived factor or overall capitalization rate. Initially, the process appears rather simple. The practitioner only needs to estimate the income and the factor or overall capitalization rate. In this analysis, the most important consideration is choosing sales with similar income and expense expectations over time. In contrast, yield capitalization requires the practitioner to provide explicit forecasts of income, expenses, and changes in vacancy levels and expenditures over the projection period. The appraiser must also estimate the net sale price of the property at the end of the projection period. The concluded yield rate is then applied to convert anticipated economic benefits into present value. The appraiser must derive yield rates from properties with similar characteristics.

Practitioners who use direct capitalization must recognize that while an overall capitalization rate is only applied to one characteristic of the property (i.e., to a single year's net operating income), the overall capitalization rate is valid only if it accounts for all the other characteristics of the property. For example, suppose that annual increases of 3% are forecast in the net rent of a comparable sale property over the projection period and annual increases of 2% are forecast in the net rent of the subject. Applying the sale property's 10% overall capitalization rate to the subject's income would be a misapplication of the approach and would overstate the subject's value.

In yield capitalization, the practitioner must draw specific conclusions about changes in net income, cash flow, and property value over the projection period. These conclusions are provided in forecasts of future income and property reversion. The reader of the appraisal report can review the forecasts and examine each component of the future income and property value.

Also, specific investment goals for the return on and of invested capital can be considered in yield capitalization. The property's projected income and reversion are discounted to a present value by applying the investor's anticipated yield rate in the present value procedure. Yield rates can be calculated and applied with hand-held financial calculators or personal computers. An appraiser can use various software programs to discount cash flows.

Both direct capitalization and yield capitalization are market-derived, and when applied correctly they should result in similar value indications for a subject property. In applying the income approach, the appraiser need not be limited to a single capitalization method. With adequate information and proper use, direct and yield capitalization methods should produce similar value indications. If differences arise, the appraiser should check that the various techniques are being applied correctly and consistently and that the analysis reflects the actions of market participants.

CHAPTER 21

INCOME AND EXPENSE ANALYSIS

To apply any capitalization procedure, an appraiser must develop a reliable estimate of income expectancy. Although some capitalization procedures are based on the actual level of income at the time of the appraisal, all must eventually consider a projection of future income. An appraiser must consider the future outlook both in the estimate of income and expenses and in the selection of the appropriate capitalization methodology to use. Failure to consider future income would contradict the principle of anticipation, which holds that value is the present worth of future benefits.

Historical income and current income are significant, but the ultimate concern is the future. The earning history of a property is important only insofar as it is accepted by buyers as an indication of the future. Current income is a good starting point, but the direction and expected pattern of income change are critical to the capitalization process.

An appraiser can convert many types of first-year income into value estimates for different property interests using direct capitalization. Some examples are the following:

- Potential gross income (PGI)
- Effective gross income (EGI)
- Net operating income (NOI or IO)
- Equity cash flow (IE)

> In the direct capitalization approach, four income streams may be analyzed: potential gross income (PGI), effective gross income (EGI), net operating income (NOI or I_O), and equity cash flow (I_E).

In yield capitalization, an appraiser can use various cash flows and appropriate reversion values to estimate the value of different property interests:

- NOI and property reversion over a projection period for a leased fee or fee simple interest value

- Equity cash flow (I_E) and equity reversion over a projection period for an equity value (V_E)

- Property cash flow considering tenant improvements (TIs) and leasing commissions, and property reversion over the projection period for a leased fee or fee simple interest value

When using either direct or yield capitalization, reliable projections of income are important. Significant value differences can result when an appraiser uses the same overall capitalization rate or potential gross income multiplier to convert different income estimates into value. If, for example, a potential gross income multiplier of 6.0 is applied to potential gross income estimates of $50,000 and $55,000, values of $300,000 and $330,000 result. A $5,000 difference in potential gross income produces a $30,000 difference in value. Similarly, when an overall capitalization rate of 10% is applied to net operating income estimates of $35,000 and $40,000, values of $350,000 and $400,000 result. In this example, a $5,000 difference in net operating income results in a $50,000 value difference. Thus, income forecasting is a sensitive and crucial part of income capitalization because of the significant effect on value.

An appraiser may estimate income for a single year or series of years depending on the data available and the capitalization method employed. The analysis can be based on the following:

- The actual level of income at the time of the appraisal
- A forecast of income for the first year of the investment
- A forecast of income over a specified projection period
- A stabilized, average annual income over a specific projection period

If an appraiser seeks to determine an opinion of market value, the income forecast should reflect the expectations of market participants. In an assignment to develop an opinion of investment value, the appraiser may base the income forecasts on the specific ownership or management requirements of the investor.

If an investment in a partial interest, e.g., an equity interest in a fee simple or leased fee estate, is being valued, the equity dividend may be used. In this case, the equity income is determined by deducting annual mortgage debt service from net operating income to calculate equity dividend. Sometimes debt service is based on an existing mortgage and the amount is specified. In other cases, an appraiser must estimate debt service based on the typical mortgage terms indicated by current market activity and the property type being appraised.

Table 21.1 lists the key elements to investigate in developing income and expense estimates for various property types. The specific line items involved in the generation of income and the allocation of expenses may vary for different property types.

Estimating and Adjusting Market Rent

An investigation of market rent levels starts with the subject property. By examining financial statements and leases and interviewing selected tenants during property inspection, an appraiser can verify the subject property's current rent schedule. Further verification may be necessary if the owner's or manager's information is in doubt. An appraiser may compare the sum of current rents with previous totals using operating statements for the past several years. The appraiser should examine statements of rents, including the rent paid under percentage leases or escalation clauses for all building tenants. After analyzing the existing rent schedule for the subject property, the appraiser reduces all rents to a unit basis for comparison. The appraiser must describe and explain all differences in rents within the property.

Table 21.1: Characteristic Income and Expenses of Principal Property Types

Industrial Buildings

Lease and income	Medium- to long-term net or modified gross lease; contract rent.
Expenses	Tenants pay most operating expenses and sometimes prorated property taxes, insurance, and exterior maintenance; landlord pays management expenses; tenant improvement allowance sometimes provided by landlord; leasing commissions paid by landlord to agent or broker.

Retail Properties

Major (anchor) tenants

Lease and income	Long-term net lease; base and percentage (overage) rent.
Expenses	Tenants pay utilities, interior maintenance, and common area maintenance (such expense recoveries are prorated); tenants may share in advertising and management expenses; tenant improvement allowance provided by landlord; leasing commissions paid by landlord to agent or broker; tenant improvements and leasing commissions are typically treated as below-the-line items.

Smaller (local) tenants

Lease and income	Short- to medium-term net lease; base and percentage (overage) rent.
Expenses	Tenants pay utilities, interior maintenance, and common area maintenance (such expense recoveries are prorated); tenants may share in advertising and management expenses; tenant improvement allowance provided by landlord; leasing commissions paid by landlord to agent or broker; tenant improvements and leasing commissions are typically treated as below-the-line items.

Multi-Family Residential

Lease and income	Lease for one year or less; modified gross lease; contract rent.
Expenses	Tenants often pay own utility expenses; landlord pays property taxes, insurance, management, maintenance; replacement allowance treated as an above-the-line item; no tenant improvement allowance.

Office Buildings

Lease and income	Medium- to long-term lease; base rent may be adjusted upward on an escalation basis according to an index.
Expenses	Under a gross lease, landlord pays all operating expenses; under a net lease, tenants pay all expenses; leases may contain provisions to pass through any increase in certain expenses, over a specified base amount and customarily on a per square foot basis. Tenant improvement allowance provided by landlord; leasing commissions paid by landlord to agent or broker.

Note: The treatment of expenses described here is typical of many, but not all, markets.

Then the appraiser assembles rental data for comparable space in the market so that equivalent market rents can be estimated, if necessary, and reduces the data to a unit of comparison.

When a market rent estimate for the subject property is required, the appraiser gathers, compares, and adjusts comparable rental data. The appraiser should identify the parties to each lease to ensure that the party held responsible for rent payments is actually a party to the lease or, by endorsement, the guarantor. It is also important to ascertain that the lease represents a freely negotiated, arm's-length transaction. A lease that does not meet these criteria, such as a lease to an owner-tenant or a sale-leaseback, may not provide a reliable indication of market rent.

The rents of comparable properties can provide a basis for estimating market rent for a subject property once they have been reduced to the same unit basis applied to the subject property. An appraiser may adjust comparable rents just as the appraiser can adjust transaction prices of comparable properties in the direct comparison approach. Recent leases for the subject property may be a good indication of market rent, but lease renewals or extensions negotiated with existing tenants should be used with caution. Existing tenants may be willing to pay higher rents to avoid relocating. Alternatively, a landlord may offer existing tenants lower rent to avoid vacancies and the expense of obtaining new tenants.

The elements of comparison considered in rental analysis are the following:

- **Real property rights being leased and conditions of rental**. Rentals that do not reflect arm's-length negotiations most likely will have to be eliminated as comparables.

- **Market conditions**. Economic conditions change, so leases negotiated in the past may not reflect current prevailing rents.

- **Location.** Time-distance linkages and unit-specific location in project.

- **Physical characteristics.** Size, height, interior finish, functional layout, site amenities, etc.

- **Division of expenses stipulated in the lease and other lease terms.** Were concessions made? Who pays operating expenses? What are the provisions regarding changing the rent during the term for the lease?

- **Use of the property.** Market rents might have to be adjusted for the intended use or level of build-out of the subject property when it differs from that of the comparable.

- **Non-realty components.** For example, if a leasing or management company is involved, the income of a hotel that is part of a national chain may be higher than that of a hotel not in a chain. The higher income stems from the value associated with the name of the hotel franchise, not from any difference in the income potential of the real property.

The amount of data needed to support a market rent estimate for a subject property depends on the complexity of the appraisal problem, the availability of directly comparable rentals, and the extent to which the pattern of adjusted rent indications derived from the comparables differs from the income pattern of the subject property. When sufficient, closely comparable rental data is not available, the appraiser should include other data, preferably data that can be adjusted. If an appraiser uses proper judgment in making adjustments, a reasonably clear pattern of market rents should emerge.

INTERESTS

To a certain extent, the interest being appraised determines how rents are analyzed and estimated. The valuation of fee simple interests in income-producing real estate is based on the market rent the property is capable of generating. Therefore, to value proposed projects without actual leases, properties with unleased space, and owner-occupied properties, market rent estimates are used in the income approach.

To value the leased fee estate, the appraiser considers contract rent for leased space, which may or may not be at market levels, and market rent for vacant and owner-occupied space. When discounted cash flow analysis is used, an appraiser requires future market rent estimates to estimate income after existing leases expire. It should be emphasized that the discounting of contract rents usually does not result in an opinion of the market value of the fee simple interest. It results in an opinion of the market value of the leased fee interest.

To value a leased fee interest in a recently completed, income-producing property that has not achieved stabilized occupancy, an appraiser must forecast an appropriate vacancy and collection loss over an appropriate absorption or lease-up period. In appraising the value of a fee simple interest in a newly completed, 100% owner-occupied property, it may be appropriate to make a deduction in the forecast time for the market to achieve 100% use and occupancy of the building. (This is analogous to the lease-up time needed to achieve stabilized occupancy in tenanted properties.) Appraisals of proposed properties for lending purposes often require value estimates at different stages in the property's development:

- As is
- When completed
- At stabilization

The "as is" value is typically the current value of the vacant land. The other two values are hypothetical values assuming completion of construction (with various assumptions respecting the extent of lease-up, including the costs of placing tenants – commissions and tenant inducements) and assuming stabilized occupancy.

INCOME AND EXPENSE DATA

To derive pertinent income and expense data, an appraiser investigates comparable sales and rentals of competitive income-producing properties of the same type in the same market. For investment properties, an appraiser reviews current and recent incomes and studies vacancy and collection losses and typical operating expenses. Interviews with owners and tenants in the area can provide lease and expense data.

Appraisers try to obtain all income and expense data from the income-producing properties used as comparables. This data is tabulated in a reconstructed operating statement and filed by property type. A suggested format for reconstructed operating statements is illustrated later in this chapter.

Like expense data, rental information is difficult to obtain. Therefore, appraisers should take every opportunity to add rents to their rental databases. Although infrequently done, long-term leases may be filed in public records. Although increasingly less common, some tenants register their leases at the land titles or registry office, and appraisers can obtain copies of this data. Classified ads may also provide rental information. Many appraisers periodically check advertised rentals and recorded rental information by property type or area. It is convenient to file rental data under the same property use classifications used for sales data. Because sources of rental data vary, appraisers should take care to ensure the accuracy of this information.

Income and expense comparables should be filed chronologically and by property type so they can be retrieved easily and used to estimate the expenses for a similar type of property. An appraiser should convert income and expense figures to appropriate units of comparison for analysis. For example, an appraiser may report income in terms of rent per apartment unit, per room, per hospital bed, or per square foot. An appraiser can express expenses for insurance, taxes, painting, decorating, and other required maintenance in the same units of comparison used for income, or they can be expressed as a percentage of the effective gross income. The appraiser must use the unit of comparison selected consistently throughout the analysis of the subject property and the rental database information.

Rental property data may show vacancy rates as a percentage of potential gross income and operating expenses as a percentage of effective gross income. This data is essential in valuing income-producing property.

Lease Data

If written leases exist and the income estimate is based on the continuation of lease income, the appraiser examines lease abstracts for provisions that could affect the quantity, quality, and durability of property income. The appraiser may either read the leases or rely on the client or another authorized party to disclose all pertinent lease provisions through lease summaries or briefs. In any case, the appraiser should describe the source of information and level of verification in the scope of work section of the appraisal report. The appraiser also analyzes the leases of competitive properties to estimate market rent and other forms of income applicable to the market for competitive space.

> An income and expense forecast begins with lease analysis.

Typical lease data includes the following information:

- Date of the lease
- Reference information, if the lease is recorded
- Legal description or other identification of the leased premises
- Name of lessor, i.e., owner or landlord
- Name of lessee, i.e., tenant
- Lease term
- Occupancy date
- Commencement date for rent payment
- Rent amount, including any percentage clause, graduation, and payment terms
- Rent concessions, including any discounts or benefits
- Landlord's covenants, i.e., items such as taxes, insurance, and maintenance for which the owner or landlord is responsible

- Tenant's covenants, i.e., items such as taxes, insurance, maintenance, utilities, and cleaning expenses for which the tenant is responsible
- Right of assignment or right to sublet, i.e., whether the leasehold, or tenant's interest, may be assigned or sublet, under what conditions, and whether assignment relieves the initial tenant of future liability
- Option(s) to renew, including the date of required notice, term of renewal, rent, and other renewal provisions
- Expense caps and expense stops, escalation rent, and expense recoveries
- Options to purchase and any accompanying conditions
- Escape clauses, cancellation clauses, and kick-out clauses
- Continued occupancy contingency
- Security deposits, including advance rent, bond, or expenditures by the tenant for items such as leasehold improvements
- Casualty loss, i.e., whether the lease continues after a fire or other disaster and on what basis
- Lessee's improvements, including whether they can be removed when the lease expires and to whom they belong
- Noncompete and exclusive use clauses
- Condemnation, including the respective rights of the lessor and the lessee if all or any part of the property is appropriated by a public agency
- Revaluation clauses
- Special provisions

Special attention should be paid to lease data on rent, rent concessions, the division of expenses, renewal options, escalation clauses, purchase options, escape clauses, and tenant improvements.

Figure 21.1 shows a sample form for analyzing a typical office lease.

Rent

The amount of rent to be paid by the tenant is basic lease data. An appraiser considers rent from all sources, which may include base, or minimum, rent, contract rent, percentage rent, and escalation rent. An appraiser should clearly identify the sources of rental income.

Rent Concessions

When real estate markets are oversupplied, landlords may give tenants concessions such as free rent for a specified period of time or extra tenant improvements. In shopping centre leases, retail store tenants are sometimes given rent credit for interior store improvements. Rent concessions often result from imbalanced market conditions and the relative negotiating strengths of the landlord and the tenant. It is not unusual for free rent concessions to be given outside of the lease term so that the concessions do not appear on the written lease contract. In these situations, appraisers must still consider the lease concessions when calculating the effective rent being paid.

Figure 21.1: Office Space Rental Worksheet

Building _____

Suite No./Identifier _____   Floor _____

Lessor _____

Lessee _____   Guarantor _____

Rentable area _____   Usable area _____   Rentable/usable area ratio ___

Lease date _____   Commencement _____   Expiration _____

Base rent _____   CPI escalation   ☐ Yes   ☐ No

Graduations _____

_____

Tenant improvements (by owner) _____

Tenant improvements (by tenant) _____

Special provisions _____

_____

Who pays	Lessor	Lessee	Stop	Stop Amount per Sq. Ft.	Cap	Cap Amount per Sq. Ft.
Fixed expenses						
Real estate taxes	☐	☐	☐	_____	☐	_____
Property insurance (fire, storm, vandalism)	☐	☐	☐	_____	☐	_____
Variable expenses						
Tenant space utilities	☐	☐	☐	_____	☐	_____
Common area utilities	☐	☐	☐	_____	☐	_____
Tenant space HVAC	☐	☐	☐	_____	☐	_____
Common area HVAC	☐	☐	☐	_____	☐	_____
Tenant space cleaning (janitorial service)	☐	☐	☐	_____	☐	_____
Common area cleaning	☐	☐	☐	_____	☐	_____
Repairs and maintenance						
Exterior	☐	☐	☐	_____	☐	_____
Interior	☐	☐	☐	_____	☐	_____
Management	☐	☐	☐	_____	☐	_____
Other expenses (if any) ____	☐	☐	☐	_____	☐	_____
_____	☐	☐	☐	_____	☐	_____

Renewal options

How many _____   Years each _____

New rent _____

New escalation (and base year) _____

New tenant improvements _____

Comments _____

_____

Lessor/Lessee Division of Expenses

Most leases outline the obligations of the lessor and the lessee to delineate specifically who must pay for taxes, insurance, utilities, heat, janitorial service (if any), repairs, unit owner's or common area (CAM) expenses, and other expenses required to maintain and operate the leased property. The appraiser should identify the division of expenses in each lease analyzed and compare the rents and estimated rental value of the subject space to those of comparable space. Any required adjustments in the division of expenses in comparable properties should reflect the same lease terms and division of expenses as the subject property.

Renewal Options

Renewal options that allow a tenant to extend the lease term for one or more prescribed periods of time are frequently included in leases. A typical renewal option requires that the tenant provide advance notice of the intention to renew. The lease must also identify the length of the renewal period and the rent or method of determining the rent to be paid. The extension period rent may be set at the original rent or at a level determined when the lease was negotiated. Alternatively, it may be calculated with a procedure or formula specified in the lease when the option is exercised. Renewal options are binding on the landlord but allow the tenant to make a decision based on the circumstances at the time of renewal. Thus, renewal options tend to favour the tenant.

If the terms of the renewal option are favourable to the tenant, then an appraiser should note this fact in the appraisal report, and the appraiser may be justified in concluding that the tenant would exercise the option to renew. If the terms of the renewal option are not favourable to the tenant, however, this fact should still be pointed out, and the appraiser may conclude that the tenant would not exercise the option to renew. This is particularly important in discounted cash flow analysis and yield capitalization, where it might have a significant impact on the appraiser's selection of a projection period as well as projections of outlays for downtime between leases, tenant improvements, and leasing commissions.

Expense Cap and Expense Stop Clauses

Leases often include clauses that limit the expenses that either the landlord or the tenant will pay. With an expense cap, operating expenses are borne by the tenant to a specified level above which the landlord picks up additional expenses. The cap defines the tenant's maximum obligations and limits the tenant's exposure to the risk of increasing expenses. With an expense stop, the landlord meets defined operating expenses to a specified level above which increases in operating expenses become the responsibility of the tenant or lessee. This allows the landlord to pass through any increases above the specified level over time and protects the landlord against unforeseen increases in expenses. Often the level of expenses incurred during the first year of the lease is specified as the level of the stop, although a stated amount per square foot is sometimes used.

> expense cap
> A clause in a lease that limits a tenant's share of operating expenses.
> expense stop
> A clause in a lease that limits the landlord's expense obligation because the lessee assumes any expenses above an established level.

Expense stop clauses are often added to traditional gross or flat rental leases. In multi-tenant office buildings, increased expenses are usually prorated among the tenants in proportion to the area they occupy or on some other equitable basis. The prorated shares are then added to the tenants' rents; the owner normally pays the expenses allocated to vacant space.

Sometimes a single stop provision is used to cover all the expenses to be passed through to the tenants. Alternatively, an expense stop might be specified for individual expense items. For example, tax stop clauses provide that any increases in taxes over a specified level be passed on to the tenant.

Escalation Clauses

Escalation payments are frequently based on changes in a local wage rate or index such as the Consumer Price Index (CPI). In New York City, in a famous example, the porter wage escalation formula is frequently used. Each 1¢ increase in the porter wage rate – i.e., the hourly wage paid to office building workers who are members of the porters' union – produces a 1¢ to 1½¢ increase in expense charges per square foot of space. An escalation clause helps the landlord offset increases in operating expenses, which are passed on to tenants on a pro rata basis. Some escalation clauses are drawn so broadly that the lease is almost applied on a net rental basis.

> escalation clause
> A clause in an agreement that provides for the adjustment of a price or rent based on some event or index, e.g., a provision to increase rent if operating expenses increase.

Expense Recovery Clauses

An expense recovery clause stipulates that some or all operating expenses paid by the landlord are recoverable from the tenant. In different parts of the country, expense recoveries are known as additional rent, *reimburseables, billables,* or *pass-throughs.* Some of these items (e.g., common area maintenance charges) may be considered under operating expenses, while others may be considered under replacement allowances. Expense recoveries are usually treated as separate revenue items, and recoverable expenses are usually deducted as expenses in income and expense statements. The analysis should consider whether the recoverable items have historically been recovered and the probability of recovery in the future. Leases detail items that landlords can recover as additional charges to tenants, so appraisers must carefully read the landlord's responsibilities and tenant responsibilities sections of a rental agreement.

Purchase Options

Certain leases include a clause granting the lessee an option to purchase the leased property or match any offer to purchase. In some cases, this option must be exercised on the lease termination date or at some point or points during the lease term. In other cases, this option may be available at any time. The option price may be fixed or it may change periodically based on an empirical formula, depreciated book value, or revaluation of the property. In industrial and office build-to-suit situations, the option price may be the cost to construct improvements plus the interest through the option period. A purchase option may only give the lessee the right to purchase the property or make an offer if an offer to purchase is made by a third party. This provision is referred to as a *right of first refusal*. A purchase option can restrict marketability. Also, unless the property is being appraised in fee simple, the option price, if stated, may represent a limit on the market value of the leased fee estate.

Escape, Kick-Out, and Buyout Clauses

An escape clause permits a tenant to cancel a lease under circumstances that would not ordinarily be considered justification for lease cancellation. For example, an expropriation or casualty clause might allow the tenant to cancel the lease if the expropriation or casualty loss hinders operations. A casualty clause may stipulate that the landlord be allowed a reasonable amount of time to make necessary repairs and provide for appropriate abatement of rent in the interim. A landlord might include a demolition clause in a lease to preserve the prospects for sale or redevelopment of the site. This type of escape clause can affect rent levels and market value.

A kick-out clause written into a lease allows a landlord to cancel a lease upon the occurrence of a specific event, e.g., if sales have not achieved a predetermined level after a certain period of time. Co-tenancy clauses in retail leases permit tenants to terminate a lease if the landlord has not replaced an anchor tenant or other specified tenant or tenant types within a predetermined period. Kick-out clauses may create risk and warrant adjustments to discount rates or capitalization rates used in direct capitalization.

> **escape clause**
> A provision that allows a tenant to cancel a lease.
>
> **continued occupancy clause**
> A lease provision that conditions the continued occupancy of one tenant upon the occupancy of another, usually an anchor tenant in a multi-tenant retail centre

Buyout clauses provide for a payment by either a landlord or a tenant to the other to induce the cancellation of a lease. The amount of the payment may be set by the lease or be negotiated at the time of the cancellation.

Continued Occupancy Clauses

Multi-tenant properties may be subject to leases that condition the continued occupancy of one tenant on the occupancy of another tenant. An anchor tenant's decision to vacate during the lease term can precipitate the departure of other tenants as well. In appraising shopping centres, an appraiser must analyze the probability of an anchor tenant leaving at or before expiration of the current lease. This is true whether or not the satellite (i.e., non-anchor) stores have leases conditioning their occupancy on the continued occupancy of the anchor tenant. Small stores are often unable to continue operation if the anchor leaves the centre.

Tenant Improvements

Extensive tenant improvements (TIs) can influence contract rent or they may be built into the asking rent as a tenant improvement allowance. Yield capitalization and discounted cash flow analysis usually addresses consideration of tenant improvements because the costs accrued can be incorporated into the analysis at the appropriate points of the projection period. Ignoring the impact of TIs in direct capitalization may be a mistake. Stabilized net operating income should recognize the tenant improvements made to a property that are appropriate for the market.

> **tenant improvement allowance or tenant improvements (TIs)**
> A dollar amount (usually expressed as an amount per square foot) provided to the tenant by the landlord for the construction of tenant improvements, which may or may not equal the cost of remodeling.
>
> **above-the-line expense**
> An expense that is recorded "above" the net operating income line in a reconstructed operating statement and therefore is considered part of the total operating expenses for the property.
>
> **below-the-line expense**
> An expense that is recorded "below" the net operating income line in a reconstructed operating statement and therefore is not considered part of the total operating expenses for the property; tenant improvements and leasing concessions are the most common line items recorded below the net operating income line.

When the lessor makes capital expenditures not accounted for in the asking rent, reimbursement may be accomplished through marginally higher rent that amortizes the lessor's expenditures over all or part of the lease period. If the tenant makes capital expenditures, the lessor may reduce the tenant's rent for all or part of the lease term as compensation for such tenant expenditures. In many retail environments, the rents vary directly with the level of build-out provided to the tenant. When using these leases as comparable data, the level of build-out supplied with the rent is an important element of comparison.

Tenant improvements are driven by the market, i.e., they are only done if the market dictates it. Also, tenant improvements do not apply to all property types. The standard maintenance and upkeep of an apartment unit before renting the unit to a new tenant is not usually considered a tenant improvement, unless the cleaning and refurbishment exceed the typical levels needed to maintain the property's competitiveness in the market. If the TIs directly impact net operating income and are recorded above the NOI line item in a reconstructed operating statement, they are considered above-the-line expenses. More often, they are treated as below-the-line expenses.

A developer or owner may be responsible for a certain level of build out or tenant improvements and that will be reflected in the rent as defined in a tenant workletter. Improvements in excess of that level are the responsibility of tenants and are not reflected in the rent, or they may be provided by the landlord and amortized over the lease term. The level of build-out may be different for new space and for retrofitting an existing space, and the level of tenant improvements may be different for a renewal tenant and a new tenant.

Noncompete, Dark Store, and Exclusive Use Clauses

Leases may contain a provision that prohibits tenants from operating another similar business in a nearby, competing shopping centre. For example, a tenant who sells sporting goods may agree not to open another, competing sporting goods facility near the shopping centre. This is known as *radius restriction*.

In some jurisdictions, a lease may include a clause that states that the tenant must continue to occupy the site throughout the term of the lease and is barred from opening a competitive store within a certain period after the expiration date of the lease. A dark store clause protects a landlord, whose property could be put in a poor releasing position if a tenant moves out and opens another store within the same trade area. A dark store clause may be especially important in a percentage lease involving an anchor or other major tenant.[1]

An exclusive use clause may be written into a lease by a landlord who wishes to control the retail mix of the shopping centre. A tenant may also seek such a clause if they want to achieve some degree of monopoly status, e.g., a fast food retailer that wants to have the only restaurant of its type in the shopping centre.

> **exclusive use clause**
> A provision that limits the landlord from leasing to any other tenants in the property or in a defined area who are conducting a similar business.
>
> **dark store clause**
> A clause in a lease that states that the tenant must do business at the site throughout the full term of the lease and cannot open a competitive store within a specified time period prior to the expiration of the lease, which could put the subject property in a poor releasing position; may also affect the rent payments of other tenants; vital in a straight percentage lease involving a major tenant. This type of clause may not be legal in all jurisdictions.
>
> **non-compete clause**
> A provision that limits tenants from operating a similar business in a competing location, usually specified in terms of distance (a radius restriction)

DEVELOPING RECONSTRUCTED OPERATING STATEMENTS

Assessing the earning power of a property means reaching a conclusion regarding its net operating income expectancy. The appraiser estimates income and expenses after researching and analyzing the following:

- The income and expense history of the subject property
- Income and expense histories of competitive properties
- Recently signed leases, proposed leases, and asking rents for the subject and competitive properties
- Actual vacancy levels for the subject and competitive properties
- Management expenses for the subject and competitive properties

---

[1] A dark store clause may sometimes be referred to as a *go dark clause*, which is also sometimes used to describe the kickout clause discussed previously. The two should not be confused. A kickout clause protects the tenant while a dark store clause protects the landlord.

- Operating expense data and operating expenses at the subject and competitive properties

- Forecast changes in taxes, energy costs, and other operating expenses

Appraisers often present this information in tabular form to assist the reader of the report. Income and expenses are generally reported in annual or monthly dollar amounts and analyzed in terms of nominal dollar amounts, dollars and cents per unit of rentable area, or dollars and cents based on another unit of comparison. To show how historical and forecast data on operating expenses is commonly arrayed, Table 21.2 summarizes the operating expense history of a downtown office building with 60,000 rentable square feet of space. Table 21.3 summarizes the operating expenses of five comparable properties in the same market area and allows for easy comparison of the subject property and

> An appraiser develops income estimates by analyzing information on the subject and competitive properties, i.e., individual income and expense histories, recent transactional data (signed leases, rents asked and offered), vacancy levels, and management expenses. An appraiser should also investigate published operating data, tax assessment policies, projected utility rates, and market expectations.

the comparables. It is obvious that the total operating expenses of the subject, at $15.82 per square foot for the year being studied, are significantly higher than those of the comparables, which range from $13.73 to $15.07 per square foot. For most of the operating expenses listed, the per-unit expenses for the subject fall within the ranges set by the comparable properties, but the expenses for electricity, at $4.14 per square foot, and

Table 21.2: Subject Property Operating Expense History

	Year 1 Actual		Year 2 Actual		Year 3 Actual		Year 4 Budget	
	Dollars	Per Square Foot	Dollars	Per Square Foot	Dollars	Per Square Foot	Dollars	Per Square Foot
Fixed expenses								
Real estate taxes	$232,812	$3.88	$272,378	$4.54	$314,433	$5.24	$323,400	$5.39
Insurance	7,134	0.12	7,050	0.12	19,875	0.33	20,100	0.34
Variable expenses								
Electricity	$200,390	$3.34	$216,632	$3.61	$211,789	$3.53	$248,350	$4.14
Steam heat	79,211	1.32	71,390	1.19	72,675	1.21	85,250	1.42
Cleaning	117,102	1.95	109,775	1.83	128,987	2.15	136,750	2.28
Payroll	8,432	0.14	10,208	0.17	11,386	0.19	12,600	0.21
Repairs and maintenance	17,388	0.20	30,688	0.51	30,075	0.05	52,025	0.00
Water and sewer	3,010	0.05	3,030	0.05	2,412	0.04	4,800	0.08
Administrative, legal, and accounting	1,180	0.02	1,778	0.03	10,856	0.18	10,850	0.18
Management fees	47,570	0.79	49,300	0.82	50,100	0.84	53,500	0.89
Miscellaneous	3,031	0.05	88	0.001	610	0.01	600	0.01
Total operating expenses	$717,260	$11.95	$772,317	$12.87	$861,998	$14.37	$949,025	$15.82

Note: Figures have been rounded.

cleaning, at $2.28 per square foot, are higher than for any of the comparables. In the income and expense analysis, the appraiser will have to investigate the reasons for the higher costs of electricity and cleaning for the subject property.

After thoroughly analyzing property and lease data for the subject and comparable properties, the appraiser develops a net operating income estimate for the subject property. If the appraiser is focusing on the benefits accruing to the equity investment, he or she also estimates the equity dividend.

Potential Gross Income

Appraisers usually analyze potential gross income on an annual basis. Potential gross income comprises the following items:

- Rent for all space in the property, e.g., contract rent for current leases, market rent for vacant or owner-occupied space, percentage and overage rent for retail properties

- Rent from escalation clauses

- Reimbursement income

- All other forms of income to the real property, e.g., income from services supplied to the tenants, such as secretarial service, switchboard service, antenna connections, storage, garage space, and income from coin-operated equipment and parking fees

Because service-derived income may or may not be attributable to the real property, an appraiser might find it inappropriate to include this income in the property's potential gross income. The appraiser may treat such income as business income or as personal property income, depending on its source. If a form of income is subject to vacancy and collection loss, it should be incorporated into potential gross income, and the appropriate vacancy and collection charge should be made to reflect effective gross income.

Vacancy and Collection Loss

Vacancy and collection loss is an allowance for reductions in potential gross income attributable to vacancies, tenant turnover, and nonpayment of rent or other income. This line item considers two components:

- Physical vacancy as a loss in income

- Collection loss caused by concessions or default by tenants

The rents collected each year are typically less than annual potential gross income, so an allowance for vacancy and collection loss is usually included in the appraisal of income-producing property. The allowance is usually estimated as a

> **vacancy and collection loss**
> A deduction from potential gross income (PGI) made to reflect income reductions due to vacancies, tenant turnover, and nonpayment of rent; also called vacancy and credit loss or vacancy and contingency loss. Often it is expressed as a percent of PGI and should reflect the competitive market. Its treatment can differ according to the interest being appraised, property type, capitalization method, and whether the property is at stabilized occupancy.

percentage of potential gross income, which varies depending on the type and characteristics of the physical property; the quality of its tenants; the type and level of income streams; current and projected market supply and demand conditions; and national, regional, and local economic conditions.

Published surveys of similar properties under similar conditions may indicate an appropriate percentage allowance for vacancy and collection loss. An appraiser should survey the local market to support the vacancy estimate. The conclusion in the income approach may differ from the current vacancy level indicated by primary or secondary data because the estimate reflects typical investor expectations for the subject property only over the projection period. Other methods of measuring vacancy and collection loss include comparing potential gross income at market rates against the subject property's actual collected income.

Effective Gross Income

Effective gross income (or gross realized revenue) is calculated as the potential gross income minus the vacancy and collection loss allowance.

Operating Expenses

Operating expenses may be recorded in categories selected by the property owner. The records also may follow a standard system of accounting established by an association of owners or by accounting firms that serve a particular segment of the real estate market.

> operating expenses
> The periodic expenditures necessary to maintain the real property and continue production of the effective gross income, assuming prudent and competent management.
>
> fixed expenses
> Operating expenses that generally do not vary with occupancy and that prudent management will pay for whether the property is occupied or vacant.

Generally, operating expenses are divided into three categories:

1. Fixed expenses
2. Variable expenses
3. Replacement allowance

However operating expenses are organized, an appraiser analyzes and reconstructs expense statements to develop an estimate of the typical operating expense forecast for the property on an annual cash basis.

Fixed Expenses

Most reconstructed operating statements contain line items for real estate taxes and building insurance costs. An appraiser can find tax data in public records, and the assessor's office may provide information about projected changes in assessments or rates and their probable effect on future taxes. If a property is assessed unfairly, the appraiser may need to adjust the real estate tax expense in the reconstructed operating statement. If the subject property has an unusually low assessment compared to other, similar properties or appears to deviate from the general pattern of taxation in the jurisdiction, the appraiser must consider the most probable amount and trend of future taxes. An appraiser should study any past changes in the assessment of the subject property. If the assessment is low, the provincial assessment statute will require the assessor to raise it. If the figure is high, however, obtaining a reduction might require a formal appeal, success at which might not be easily obtained. In projecting real estate taxes, an appraiser tries to anticipate tax assessments based on past tax trends, present taxes, the municipality's future expenditures, and the perceptions of market participants. Since the concept of market value presumes a sale, the real estate tax projection should consider the impact of the presumed sale on the anticipated assessed value and taxes.

For proposed properties or properties that are not currently assessed, appraisers can develop operating statement projections without including real estate taxes. The resulting estimate is net operating income before real estate taxes, and a provision for real estate taxes is included in the capitalization rate used to convert this net income into property value. For example, assume that real estate taxes are typically 2% of market value and net operating income after real estate taxes would normally be capitalized at 11% to derive an opinion of market value for the subject property. In this case, the estimated net operating income before real estate taxes could be capitalized at 13% (11% + 2%, which is known as a *loaded capitalization rate*) to derive a property value indication. Alternatively, the appraiser may choose to estimate real estate taxes for a proposed project based on building costs or the taxes paid by recently constructed, competitive properties. Any unusual, unpaid special assessments or other mandatory, one-time expenses should be addressed as a lump-sum adjustment at the end of the analysis, if that is what market participants would do.

An owner's operating expense statement may show the insurance premiums paid on a cash basis. If the owner does not pay premiums annually, they must be adjusted to a hypothetical annual cash expense before they are included in the reconstructed operating statement. Typical insurance items include fire, extended coverage, and owner's liability insurance. Depending on the type of property, elevators, boilers, plate glass, or other items may also be insured. The appraiser must determine the amount of insurance and, if it is inadequate or superadequate, adjust the annual cost to indicate appropriate coverage for the property. As with all projected expenses, the insurance expense estimate must reflect dynamic changes in the market such as the increase in insurance costs following an event like a catastrophic hurricane.

Insurance on business inventory, business liability, and other business property is the occupant's responsibility and therefore should not be charged to the operation of the real estate. When questions concerning co-insurance or terms of coverage arise, an appraiser might need to obtain professional insurance counsel.

Variable Expenses

Operating statements for large properties frequently list many types of variable expenses such as the following:

- Management
- Leasing commissions
- Utilities, e.g., electricity, gas, water, and sewer
- Heat

- Air-conditioning
- General payroll
- Cleaning
- Maintenance and repair of structure
- Decorating
- Grounds and parking area maintenance
- Miscellaneous, e.g., administrative, security, supplies, rubbish removal, and exterminating

Management Charges

Management services may be contracted or provided by the property owner. The management expense may have two components: a professional property management fee and other expenses related to the operations of the asset. The property management fee is usually expressed as a percentage of effective gross income, which conforms to the local pattern of such charges for typical management.[2] For

> **variable expenses**
> Operating expenses that generally vary with the level of occupancy or the extent of services provided.

some property types, there may be additional management expenses such as on-site supervision and the cost of maintaining and operating on-site facilities such as offices or apartments for resident managers. These additional management expenses, in conjunction with other management expenses such as the cost of telephone service, clerical help, legal or accounting services, printing and postage, and advertising and promotion, may be accounted for elsewhere in the expense statement. Management expenses may be included among recoverable operating expenses in certain markets for some property types.

In some markets, standard retail leases contain a provision for levying administrative charges as a percentage of common area maintenance charges. These charges are typically treated as a mark-up to tenant reimbursements and may replace or be in addition to the management fee.

Leasing Commissions

Leasing commissions are fees paid to an agent for leasing tenant space. In direct capitalization, leasing commissions are either treated as a normalized annual expense or not included as an expense in the reconstructed operating statement, depending on local market convention. In discounted cash flow analysis, leasing commissions are typically included in the time period they are expected to occur. Leasing commissions may or may not be reflected in the operating statements provided by the owner. Initial leasing commissions, which may be extensive in a new development, are

---

[2]   Actual property management should be distinguished from asset management. Large, investment-grade properties are often held as part of a portfolio that includes both securities and real estate. The managers of these portfolios make critical decisions concerning when to acquire a real estate asset, how to finance or when to refinance, and when to reposition a property in the market. Though their roles are distinct, the functions of a property manager and an asset manager may sometimes be intertwined. Asset management fees should not be included among the items enumerated as operating expenses for real property. See *The Office Building: From Concept to Investment Reality*, John Robert White, ed. (Chicago: Counsellors of Real Estate, Appraisal Institute, and Society of Industrial and Office Realtors, 1993), 488-489, 529-530.

usually treated as part of the capital expenditure for developing the project. These initial leasing commissions are not included as ongoing periodic expenses.

A blended rate can be developed to reflect leasing commission costs for both existing leases and new leases. For example, if the tenant renewal ratio for a property is 70%, the leasing commission for existing tenants is 2.5%, and the leasing commission for new tenants is 6%, a blended rate can be developed as follows:

0.70 × 0.025 =	0.0175
0.30 × 0.060 =	+ 0.0180
Blended rate =	0.0355 (3.55%)

This blended rate is then applied to existing tenant leases as they expire.

Utilities

An appraiser usually projects utility expenses for an existing property based on an analysis of past charges and current trends. The subject property's utility requirements can be compared with known utility expenses per unit of measure – e.g., per square foot, per room, per apartment unit – for similar properties to estimate probable future utility expenses. Hours of tenant operation may prove to be significant in the analysis. For example, the number of nights per week that a shopping centre is open and the hours of after-dark operation will directly affect electricity consumption and may also affect expenses for maintenance and garbage removal. In analyzing utility expenses, appraisers recognize local circumstances and the current and expected future cost of all applicable utilities. Utilities may be paid entirely by the property owner, entirely by the tenant, or shared. Owners may recoup these expenses as part of common area reimbursements or through a different utility reimbursement plan, e.g., a ratio utility billing system (RUBS) in a multi-family property.

Although the cost of electricity for leased space is frequently a tenant expense, and therefore not included in the operating expense statement, the owner may be responsible for lighting public areas and for the power needed to run elevators and other common building equipment. Some regional shopping centres purchase electricity on a wholesale basis and resell it to the tenants on a retail basis, keeping the difference as profit.

Gas

When used for heating and air-conditioning, gas can be a major expense item that is either paid by the tenant or paid by the property owner and reflected in the rent.

Water

The cost of water is a major consideration for industrial plants that use processes that depend on water and for multi-family projects, in which the cost of sewer service is usually tied to the amount of water used. It is also an important consideration for laundries, restaurants, taverns, hotels, and similar operations. The leases for these properties may stipulate that the tenant pay this expense. If the owner typically pays for water, this charge should be included in the expense statement.

Sewer

In municipalities with sewer systems, the tenant or the owner of the real estate may pay a separate charge for use of the system. This total expense may be substantial, particularly for hotels, motels, recreational facilities, apartments, and office buildings.

Heat

The cost of heat is generally a tenant expense in single-tenant properties, industrial or retail properties, and apartment or office projects with individual heating units. It is a major expense item shown in operating statements for office buildings and centrally heated apartment properties. The fuel consumed may be oil, gas, electricity, or public steam. Certain accounting methods include heating supplies, maintenance, and workers' wages in this expense category.

Public steam suppliers and gas companies maintain records of fuel consumption and corresponding degree-days from year to year. (One degree-day is equal to the number of degrees, during a 24-hour day, that the mean temperature falls below a standard, usually about 65° Fahrenheit or 18° Celsius) An appraiser can use these records and fuel cost data to compare the property's heating expense for the most recent years with a typical year. An appraiser should reflect probable changes in the cost of the fuel used in his or her projection.

Air-Conditioning

Air-conditioning expenses may be charged under the individual categories of electricity, gas, water, payroll, and repairs, or heating and air-conditioning may be combined under the category of heating, ventilation, and air-conditioning (HVAC). The cost of air-conditioning varies with local climatic conditions and the type of system installed. An appraiser may base a projection of this expense on typical unit charges for the community or the property type. Most office buildings and many apartment buildings have central HVAC systems, and operating expenses are included in their annual statements. Most retail properties and some apartment buildings have individual ("package") heating and air-conditioning units that are operated by the tenants. The maintenance and repair of these units, particularly in apartments, may continue to be the property owner's obligation.

General Payroll

General payroll expenses include payments to all employees whose services are essential to property operation and management but whose salaries are not included in other specific expense categories. In some areas, the cost of custodial or janitorial service is based on union wage schedules; in others, the charge is negotiated based on local custom and practice. If a custodian or manager occupies an apartment as partial payment for his or her services, the apartment's rental value may be included as income and an identical amount deducted as an expense. In certain properties, additional expenses are incurred to pay the salaries of security personnel, porters, and elevator operators. Unemployment and social security taxes for employees may be included under general payroll expenses or listed in a separate expense category.

Cleaning

In office buildings, the cost of cleaning or janitorial services is a major expense and usually includes two elements: cleaning costs and cleaning supplies. An appraiser usually estimates cleaning costs in terms of cost per square foot of rentable area, whether the work is done by payroll personnel or by an outside cleaning firm. This expense is equivalent to maid service or housekeeping in hotels and furnished apartments. In hotels and motels, cleaning expenses are attributed to the rooms department and may be estimated as a percentage of the department's gross income. The percentage established reflects the property's previous experience and industry standards. Cleaning may be an owner or tenant expense, depending on the property type and lease provisions.

Maintenance and Repair of Structure

Maintenance and repair expenses are incurred during the year to maintain the structure and its major components and to keep them in good working order. These expenses may cover roof repair; window caulking; mortar repairs; exterior painting; and the repair of heating, lighting, and plumbing equipment. Typically, under triple net leases, tenants pay maintenance costs and the owner pays for repair costs. There may be a contract for elevator maintenance and repair, and often owners are still responsible for maintenance of the roof, HVAC system, and general structure. However, the comprehensiveness of these contracts varies, and the appraiser must determine any additional operating expenses not covered by the maintenance contract. For example, a contract covering air-conditioning equipment would probably be included in the air-conditioning expense category.

Alterations, including major replacements, modernization, and renovation, may be considered capital expenditures and therefore are not included as a periodic expense under repair and maintenance. If the lessor makes alterations in the rented space, the expense may or may not be amortized by additional rent; in some cases, the tenant may pay for alterations.

The total expense for property maintenance and repair is affected by the extent to which building component and equipment replacements are covered in the replacement allowance as well as the age, condition, and functional utility of the property. If an appraiser includes an extensive replacement allowance in the reconstructed operating statement, annual maintenance and repair expenses may be reduced. Similarly, if an owner cures items of deferred maintenance, the annual maintenance and repair expenses may be reduced.

For some properties, historical expense records may include typical repairs and even capital expenses in an overall category called repairs and maintenance. If this is the case, the reconstructed operating statement will need to show an adjustment to the historical data, especially where separate replacement allowances are included. The goal of the analysis is to consider all appropriate expenses over time as well as a replacement allowance to ensure the ongoing repair of major building components. Also, there may be some crossover in the tenant improvement category and the replacement allowance or repair category. An appraiser should apply the same methodology to any comparable sales information to ensure consistency when the appraiser extracts the various rates and ratios and then applies them to the subject property.

Decorating

Decorating expenses may include the cost of interior painting, wallpapering, or wall cleaning in tenant or public areas. Lease provisions may stipulate that the owner is only responsible for decorating vacant space to attract new tenants. Decorating expenditures may vary with local practice and the supply and demand for space.

Grounds and Parking Area Maintenance

The cost of maintaining grounds and parking areas can vary widely depending on the type of property and its total site area. The cost of snow removal may be substantial in cold areas, particularly for properties with outdoor parking in addition to sidewalks and driveways. Hard-surfaced public parking areas with drains, lights, and marked car spaces are subject to intensive wear and can be expensive to maintain. These expenses may be entirely or partly reimbursed through an increment added to the rents of tenants served by the facility. In this case, both the added income and the added expenses are included in the appraiser's reconstructed operating statement. This expense category also covers landscape and lawn maintenance.

Security

Certain types of buildings in some areas may require security provisions, the cost of which will vary according to the number of employees needed to control entry and exit and to circulate through the property. Maintenance and energy expenses may also be incurred if security provisions include electric alarm systems, closed circuit television, or flood lighting.

Supplies

The cost of cleaning materials, office supplies, and miscellaneous items not covered elsewhere may be included under supplies.

Rubbish Removal and Exterminating

Garbage and pest control services are usually contracted and their cost is included in the expense statement.

Miscellaneous

Expenses for miscellaneous items vary with property type. If this expense category represents a significant percentage of effective gross income, however, it may be wise to explain individual expense items or reallocate them to specific categories.

Replacement Allowance

A replacement allowance, sometimes referred to as *reserves*, provides for the periodic replacement of building components that wear out more rapidly than the building itself and must be replaced during the building's economic life. Depending on local practice, an appraiser may reflect the replacement allowance explicitly as an expense or implicitly in the capitalization or discount rate.

If reflected explicitly, the annual replacement allowance for each component of a property is usually estimated as the anticipated cost of its replacement prorated over its total useful life, provided this does not exceed the total useful life of the structure. Some appraisers use simple

> **replacement allowance**
> An allowance that provides for the periodic replacement of building components that wear out more rapidly than the building itself and must be replaced during the building's economic life; sometimes referred to as *reserves*.

averaging (with or without calculating a sinking fund payment), while others prefer to show the actual cost and timing of these replacements. New elevators or other components that are expected to have useful lives that equal or exceed the remaining useful life of the structure do not require an allowance for replacement, unless making replacements or installing new equipment increases the remaining useful life of the structure beyond that of the long-lived items. Examples of building components that may require a replacement allowance include the following:

- Roof covering
- Carpeting
- Kitchen, bath, and laundry equipment
- HVAC compressors, elevators, and boilers
- Specific structural items and equipment that have limited economic life expectancies
- Sidewalks
- Driveways
- Parking areas
- Exterior painting and weatherproofing windows

The scope of items to be covered in a replacement allowance is a matter of appraisal judgment based on market evidence. However, the appraiser must base the magnitude and coverage of the replacement allowance on the annual repair and maintenance expenses of the property for the specific components considered in the allowance. Historical operating statements prepared on a cash basis may include periodic replacement expenses under repair and maintenance. If the appraiser makes comprehensive provisions for replacements in the reconstructed operating statement, these charges may be duplicated unless the annual maintenance expense estimate is reduced.

In certain real estate markets, space is rented to a new tenant only after substantial interior improvements are made. If this work is performed at the landlord's expense and is required to achieve the estimated rent, the expense of these improvements may be included in the reconstructed operating statement as part of the replacement allowance, in a separate tenant improvements or capital expenditure category, depending on local practice.

A total expense estimate that provides for all items of repair, maintenance, and replacement may exceed the actual expenditures shown in the owner's operating statements for recent years. This is particularly common when the building being appraised is relatively new and the owner has not incurred many capital or repair expenses. In preparing a reconstructed operating statement for a typical year, an appraiser recognizes that replacements must be made eventually and that replacement costs affect operating expenses. These costs can be reflected in increased annual maintenance costs or, on an accrual basis, in an annual replacement allowance.

The appraiser must know whether or not a replacement allowance is included in any operating statement used to derive a market capitalization rate for use in the income approach. It is essential that the income statements of comparable properties be consistent. Otherwise, adjustments will be required. A capitalization rate derived from a comparable sale property is valid only if it is applied to the subject property on the same basis. Consequently, if an appraiser derives a rate from a sale with an expense estimate that does not provide for a replacement allowance, he or she should not apply this rate to an income estimate for a subject property that includes such an allowance without an adjustment that reflects the difference. Investor survey rates may or may not include deductions for replacement allowances, and the appraiser must exercise caution in applying capitalization and discount rates from surveys.

Total Operating Expenses

Total operating expenses are the sum of fixed and variable expenses and the replacement allowance cited in the operating expense estimate.

Net Operating Income

After total operating expenses are deducted from effective gross income, the remainder is the net operating income.

Additional Calculations

After the appraiser calculates net operating income, further calculations may be needed to determine the following items:

- Mortgage debt service
- Equity dividend
- Expense and income ratios

Mortgage Debt Service

Mortgage debt service is the annual sum of all mortgage payments. Mortgage debt service is deducted from net operating income to derive equity dividend, which is used in certain capitalization procedures. The definition of market value assumes financing terms compatible with those found in the market. Thus, in estimating market value, the mortgage debt service to be deducted from the net operating income must be based on market terms. In some cases, the appraiser may be asked to develop an opinion of the value of the equity investor's position based on existing financing. In this case, the debt service would reflect the terms specified in the existing mortgage(s).

Equity Dividend

Equity dividend is the income that remains after all mortgage debt service is deducted from net operating income.

Expense and Income Ratios

The ratio of total operating expenses to effective gross income is the *operating expense ratio* (OER). The complement of this ratio is the *net income ratio* (NIR), which is the ratio of net operating income to effective gross income. These ratios tend to fall within certain ranges for specific categories of property. Experienced appraisers recognize appropriate ratios, so they can identify statements that deviate from typical patterns and require further analysis.

> Operating expense ratios and net income ratios are used to identify income and expense statements that are not typical or to confirm those that are typical.
>
> net income ratio (NIR)
> The ratio of net operating income to effective gross income (NOI/EGI); the complement of the operating expense ratio, i.e., NIR = 1 – OER.
>
> operating expense ratio (OER)
> The ratio of total operating expenses to effective gross income (TOE/EGI); the complement of the net income ratio, i.e., OER = 1 – NIR.

An appraiser can often use North America wide studies of apartment and office building properties conducted by the Institute of Real Estate Management (IREM) and the Building Owners and Managers Association (BOMA) as general guides in assessing the reasonableness of operating expense ratios. Similar studies are also available for hotels, industrial properties, and mini-warehouses. Sometimes local BOMA or IREM chapters or real estate appraisal organizations and their chapters conduct and publish studies of operating expenses that an appraiser can use as market indicators. Published studies are useful, but the appraiser must still develop operating expense ratios from comparable properties in the subject property's market or verify the applicability of published ratios to this market. Appraisers must also consider the applicability of the survey data to the physical characteristics of the subject property. For example, an appraiser should probably not use an IREM survey of buildings with an average building size of 400 units in the analysis of a 30-unit apartment building.

SAMPLE ONE-YEAR INCOME AND EXPENSE FORECAST

The property being appraised, Southside Apartments, is a three-year old, 55-unit apartment project with total annual rent collections of $367,200 at 100% occupancy. Additional information needed for the income and expense forecast follows.

- Open parking is included in the rent.
- Additional income from coin-operated equipment averages about $1,380 per year at full occupancy so the total, annual potential gross income at 100% occupancy is $368,580.

EXCLUSIONS FROM RECONSTRUCTED OPERATING STATEMENTS

The operating statements prepared for real estate owners typically list all expenditures made during a specific year. An owner's statement may include nonrecurring items that should not be included in an expense estimate intended to reflect typical annual expenses. Such a statement may also include items of business expense or costs associated with the specific circumstances of ownership.

A reconstructed operating statement represents an opinion of the probable future net operating income of an investment.* Certain items included in operating statements prepared for property owners should be omitted in reconstructed operating statements prepared for appraisal purposes. These items include the following:

- Book depreciation
- Depletion allowances or other special tax considerations
- Income tax
- Special corporation costs
- Additions to capital
- Loan payments

Book Depreciation

The book depreciation for the improvements on a parcel of real estate is based on historical cost or another previously established figure that may have no relation to current market value. Moreover, book depreciation may be based on a formula designed for tax purposes. The capitalization method and procedure selected provide for the recapture of invested capital, so including depreciation in the operating expense statement would be redundant.

Depletion Allowances or Other Special Tax Considerations

A depletion allowance is an accounting process that allows for lower taxation of revenue generated by extracting natural resources from a property because there is less oil, coal, natural gas, or other minerals left in the ground. The concept of depletion is similar to the depreciation of assets, and including the depletion allowance in the operating expenses would be redundant for the same reasons given for book depreciation.

Income Tax

The amount of income tax varies with the type of property ownership, i.e., the property may be held by a corporation, a partnership, a public utility, or an individual. The expected or average income tax of the owner is not an operating expense of the property; it is an expense of ownership.

Special Corporation Costs

The expenses attributable to corporate operations also pertain to the type of ownership. Corporate expenses are not part of a reconstructed operating statement developed for appraisal purposes.

Additions to Capital

Expenditures for capital improvements usually do not recur annually and therefore should not be included in an estimate reflecting the typical annual expenses of operation. Capital improvements may enhance value by increasing the annual net operating income or economic life of the property, but the capital expenditure is not a periodic operating expense.

The exclusion of capital expenditures is specific to reconstructed operating statements, which are used to calculate net operating income. An average annual expectation may be included in the replacement reserve. When an appraiser estimates cash flows are for a discounted cash flow analysis, capital expenditures may be deducted from the net operating income in the year the expenditure is expected to occur and not averaged on an annual basis. This is particularly important when the property's future net operating income is based on the assumption that the capital expenditure will be made.

EXCLUSIONS FROM RECONSTRUCTED OPERATING STATEMENTS, *continued*

In this case, failure to account for the capital expenditure could result in an overstatement of value. Similarly, value may be understated if capital improvements are presumed to have been "written off" without appropriately considering their contribution to value or their additions to the total capital invested.

Loan Payments

Operating statements prepared by owners often reflect loan payments in the form of periodic debt service and may include a loan payoff. These payments are not included in the reconstructed operating statement because net operating income is defined to exclude mortgage debt service.

* Some practitioners use the term pro forma synonymously with reconstructed operating statement. Technically, a pro forma is a financial statement, e.g., a balance sheet or income statement used by a business developed "according to form." In appraisal practice, a reconstructed operating statement is developed to conform to the appraiser's definition of net operating income, which generally differs from the definition of income used by accountants. Thus, a reconstructed operating statement drawn up by an appraiser will usually differ from a typical pro forma income statement prepared by an accountant.

- Annual vacancy and collection loss is estimated at 4% and local management services are available for 5% of effective gross income.
- The part-time building superintendent receives an annual salary of $16,800, including fringe benefits.
- Last year's real estate tax bill was $17,875, but taxes are expected to be $18,700 by the end of this year.
- The owner carries $1 million in fire and extended coverage insurance and pays an annual premium of $1,567. The appraiser believes that this coverage should be increased to $1.2 million with a premium of $1,880 (1.2 × $1,567 = $1,880). The additional expense for other insurance coverage is $770 per year and is a typical requirement.
- The cost to cover site maintenance and snow removal averages $5,900 per year.
- Trash removal costs $45 per month and supplies are estimated at $1,100 per year.
- Pest control costs are $65 per month and miscellaneous expenditures are projected at $325 per year.
- Building tenants pay their own utilities, including gas and electricity for individual apartment heating and air-conditioning units. Based on the expenses of the comparables and anticipated rate changes, the electricity for public space is expected to cost $2,200 in the coming year. Expenses for other utilities, including water, consistently run about $1,000 each year.
- Historically, repair and maintenance expenses have ranged from $24,000 to $26,000 per year, including some capital expenditures.
- The appraiser anticipates that capital replacement will accelerate, and the reconstructed operating statement should include a separate replacement allowance for such capital items in addition to normal repair and maintenance expenses.

Table 21.5: Southside Apartments: Reconstructed Operating Statement

Income			
Potential gross annual income			
Rents	11 units @ $500/mo.	$66,000	
12 units @ $525/mo.		75,600	
16 units @ $575/mo.		110,400	
16 units @ $600/mo.		+ 115,200	
Subtotal		$367,200	
Other income		+ 1,380	
Total potential gross income @ 100% occupancy		$368,580	
Less vacancy and collection loss @ 4%		− 14,743	
Effective gross income			$353,837
Operating expenses			
Fixed			
Real estate taxes		$18,700	
Insurance			
Fire and extended coverage		1,880	
Other		+ 770	
Subtotal		$21,350	
Variable			
Management ($353,837 × 0.05)		$17,692	
Superintendent		16,800	
Site maintenance and snow removal		5,900	
Electricity		2,200	
Other utilities		1,000	
Repair and maintenance		25,000	
Trash removal ($45 × 12)		540	
Pest control ($65 × 12)		780	
Supplies		1,100	
Interior decorating*		10,000	
Other		+ 325	
Subtotal		$81,337	
Replacement allowance			
Exterior paint ($4,650 ÷ 3)		$1,550	
Kitchen and bath equipment ($1,300 × 55) ÷ 10		7,150	
Carpeting ($900 × 55) ÷ 6		8,250	
Roof ($18,000 ÷ 20 years)		+ 900	
Subtotal (5.04% of *FGI*)		$17,850	
Total operating expenses			− $120,537
Operating expense ratio ($120,537 ÷ $353,837) = 34.07%			
Total expenses per unit ($120,537 ÷ 55) = $2,192 per unit			
Net operating income			$233,300
Net operating income ratio ($233,300 ÷ $353,837) = 65.93%			

* 55 units × $500 = $27,500; $27,500 + $2,500 = $30,000; $30,000 ÷ 3 = $10,000

- Exterior painting, which is estimated to cost $4,650 in the present market, is scheduled to be done every three years.

- Most of the apartments are rented on one-year leases, with a typical redecorating cost of $500 per apartment every third year.

- Public space is minimal, and redecorating this space costs about $2,500 every third year.

- All the apartments have electric stoves, refrigerators, dishwashers, garbage disposals, and exhaust fans, so a replacement allowance of $1,300 per apartment is required. The economic lives of these items vary, but they are estimated to average 10 years.

- The replacement of carpeting costs the owner about $900 per unit, and the average economic life of carpeting is six years.

- The roof is considered to have a 20-year life and a replacement cost of $18,000.

The operating statement shown in Table 21.5 reflects these estimates. The precision of each entry is approximate, and in most cases the appraiser is rounding to the closest $5 or $10, which is well within the estimated accuracy of the data.

SAMPLE MULTI-YEAR INCOME AND EXPENSE FORECAST

The analysis shown in Table 21.6 is based on a six-year forecast of the income and expenses generated by the apartment building described in the preceding example. All the techniques described in this chapter are used to develop a net operating income estimate for the first year of the forecast. Estimates for the other years are based on existing lease provisions and expected forecasts regarding lease renewals and growth rates applied to other income and operating expenses. The following conclusions are reached:

- Market rents are anticipated to increase 3% annually as are the receipts from the coin-operated equipment in the property.

- Operating expenses are forecasted to increase 3% annually, with the exception of the superintendent's salary, which will increase an average of 5% per year, and the cost of electricity for common areas, which is expected to increase 7.5% annually.

- Note that leasing commissions and tenant improvements are included as a variable expense in the multi-year forecast for the apartment building. Leasing commissions are estimated at 3% of rent collections on average, while no tenant improvements are anticipated for the six-year projection period.

Table 21.6: Income and Expense Analysis (Multi-Year Forecast)

	Year 1	Year 2	Year 3	Year 4	Year 5	Year 6
Income						
Potential gross income	$367,200	$378,216	$389,562	$401,249	$413,286	$425,685
Other income	1,380	1,420	1,465	1,505	1,550	1,600
Vacancy and collection loss	(14,743)	(15,129)	(15,582)	(16,050)	(16,531)	(17,027)
Effective gross income	$353,837	$364,507	$375,445	$386,704	$398,305	$410,258
Operating expenses						
Fixed expenses						
Real estate taxes	$18,700	$19,261	$19,839	$20,434	$21,047	$21,678
Insurance						
Fire and extended coverage	1,880	1,936	1,994	2,054	2,116	2,179
Other	770	793	817	841	867	893
Variable expenses						
Leasing commissions	10,574	10,893	11,219	11,556	11,903	12,260
Tenant improvements	0	0	0	0	0	0
Management	17,692	18,223	18,769	19,333	19,913	20,510
Superintendent	16,800	17,640	18,522	19,448	20,421	21,442
Site maintenance and						
snow removal	5,900	6,077	6,259	6,447	6,641	6,840
Electricity	2,200	2,365	2,542	2,733	2,938	3,158
Other utilities	1,000	1,030	1,061	1,093	1,126	1,159
Repair and maintenance	25,000	26,250	27,037	27,849	28,684	29,545
Trash removal	540	556	573	590	608	626
Pest control	780	803	828	852	878	904
Supplies	1,100	1,133	1,667	1,202	1,238	1,275
Interior decorating	10,000	10,300	10,609	10,927	11,255	11,593
Other	325	335	345	355	366	377
Replacement allowance						
Exterior painting	1,550	1,550	1,550	1,550	1,550	1,550
Kitchen and bath						
equipment	7,150	7,150	7,150	7,150	7,150	7,150
Carpeting	8,250	8,250	8,250	8,250	8,250	8,250
Roof	+ 900	+ 900	+ 900	+ 900	+ 900	+ 900
Total operating expenses	$131,111	$135,445	$139,931	$143,564	$147,851	$152,289
Operating expense ratio	37.05%	37.16%	37.27%	37.13%	37.12%	37.12%
Total expenses per unit	$2,384	$2,463	$2,544	$2,610	$2,688	$2,769
Net operating income	$222,726	$229,062	$235,514	$243,140	$250,454	$257,969

CHAPTER 22

DIRECT CAPITALIZATION

Direct capitalization is a method used in the income approach to convert a single year's income expectancy into a value indication. This conversion is accomplished in one step, either by dividing the income estimate by an appropriate income rate or by multiplying it by an appropriate income factor.

Direct capitalization is widely used when properties are already operating on a stabilized basis and there is an ample supply of comparable sales with similar risk levels, incomes, expenses, physical and locational characteristics, and future expectations. This methodology may be less useful for properties going through an initial lease-up or when income or expenses are expected to change in an irregular pattern over time. However, investors often have minimum first-year rate of return (capitalization rate) requirements. Comparables with similar future expectations may not be available in these cases and one of the yield capitalization techniques may be more appropriate. The advantages of direct capitalization are that it is simple to use, easy to explain, often expresses market thinking, and provides strong market evidence of value when adequate sales are available.

Direct capitalization is applied using one of two basic methods:

- Applying an overall capitalization rate to relate value to the entire property income, i.e., net operating income

- Using residual techniques that consider components of a property's income and then applying market-derived capitalization rates to each income component analyzed

Direct capitalization is distinct from yield capitalization, which is discussed in Chapters 23 and 24, in that it does not directly consider individual cash flows beyond the capitalized year. Yield capitalization explicitly calculates the year-by-year effects of potentially

> **direct capitalization**
> A method used to convert an estimate of a single year's income expectancy into an indication of value in one direct step, either by dividing the net income estimate by an appropriate capitalization rate or by multiplying the income estimate by an appropriate factor. Direct capitalization employs capitalization rates and multipliers extracted from market data. Only one year's income is used. Yield and value change are implied, but not identified.

Table 22.1: Income Streams, Rates, and Factors for Direct Capitalization

Income Streams	Income Rates	Income Factors
Potential gross income	Overall (property) capitalization	Potential gross income
Effective gross income	rate, fee simple (R_O)	multiplier (*PGIM*)
Net operating income	Mortgage capitalization rate (R_M)	Gross rent multiplier (*GRM*)
Equity income	Equity capitalization, or equity	Effective gross income
Mortgage income	dividend, rate (R_E)	multiplier (*EGIM*)
Land income	Land capitalization rate (R_L)	
Building income	Building capitalization rate (R_B)	
Income to the landlord's leased	Capitalization rate for the leased	
fee interest	fee position (R_{LF})	
Income to the tenant's	Capitalization rate for the	
leasehold interest	leasehold position (R_{LH})	

The basic formulas for direct capitalization are:

$I = R \times V$ $R = I \div V$ $V = I \div R$

$V = I \times F$ $I = V \div F$ $F = V \div I$

where I is income, R is capitalization rate, V is value, and F is factor.

changing income patterns, changes in the original investment's value, and other considerations. In contrast, direct capitalization processes a single year's income into an indication of value. Either direct capitalization or yield capitalization may correctly produce a supportable indication of value when based on relevant market information derived from comparable properties, which should have similar income-expense ratios, land value-to-building value ratios, risk characteristics, and future expectations of income and value changes over a typical projection period. When this data is available, the choice of capitalization method does not affect the indication of value.

Direct capitalization may be based on various income flows and use various income rates and factors. Table 22.1 lists the types of information an appraiser will need to apply the income approach. The list in Table 22.1 is not all-inclusive.

DERIVATION OF OVERALL CAPITALIZATION RATES

Any interest in real estate that is capable of generating income can be valued by direct capitalization. For owner-occupied properties or properties not subject to a lease, it is most common to appraise the fee simple interest. However, if a property is subject to a lease, then the appropriate interest to appraise may be the leased fee interest.[1] The direct capitalization formula that applies to these types of valuation assignments is:

Value = Net Operating Income ÷ Overall Capitalization Rate

---

[1]   There are specific exceptions to appraisals of leased fee interests, such as assignments relating to real estate taxes and many litigation appraisal assignments. The property interest to appraise is determined based on the intended use and intended user of the appraisal.

Overall capitalization rates can be estimated with various techniques; the techniques used depend on the quantity and quality of data available.[2] When supported by appropriate market data, accepted techniques include the following:

- Derivation from comparable sales

- Derivation from effective gross income multipliers and net income ratios

- Band of investment, mortgage and equity components

- Band of investment, land and building components

- The debt coverage formula

- Yield capitalization techniques such as the general yield and change formula (R_O = yield - change in income and value) and the Ellwood method[3]

An appraiser can use the debt coverage formula and yield capitalization techniques to estimate an overall rate or support rates derived from market sales. However, they are not primary methods of direct capitalization.

> Overall capitalization rates may be derived from comparable sales, effective gross income multipliers and net income ratios, band of investment or weighted-average techniques (based on mortgage and equity components with R_M and R_E or land and building components with R_L and R_B), debt coverage ratios (DCRs), and yield capitalization techniques.

Derivation of R_O from Comparable Sales

Deriving capitalization rates from comparable sales is the preferred technique when sufficient data on sales of similar, competitive properties is available. An appraiser needs data on each property's sale price, income, expenses, financing terms, and market conditions at the time of sale. In addition, the appraiser must make certain that the net operating income of each comparable property is calculated and estimated in the same way that the net operating income of the subject property is estimated. Often the operating data available for comparable sale properties is from the year that ended just prior to the date of sale, so the appraiser may have to explain (or adjust for) the subsequent changes in market conditions. Both the income and expense data (on the date of valuation plus the next 12 months) and the structure of expenses in terms of replacement allowances and other components should be similar to those of the subject. Moreover, neither non-market financing terms nor different market conditions should have affected the prices of the comparables. If the objective of the appraisal is to value the fee simple interest, incomes for the comparables analyzed must be at or around the level of market rent or adjustments will be necessary. If the appraiser seeks to obtain the value of the leased fee interest, the comparables must be leased in the same manner as the subject property or adjustments will be required.

The overall level of risk associated with each comparable should be similar to that of the subject property. An appraiser can analyze risk by investigating the credit rating of the property's tenants, market conditions for the particular property, the

[2] Surveys of overall capitalization rates based on the market expectations of lenders and owners are available, but such data should be rigorously scrutinized.

[3] Readers interested in reviewing Ellwood mortgage-equity analysis may consult Appendix B or Charles B. Akerson, *Capitalization Theory and Techniques: Study Guide*, 2nd ed. (Chicago: Appraisal Institute, 2000).

stability of the property's income stream, the level of investment in the property by the tenant, and the property's upside or downside potential.

When these requirements are met, the appraiser can estimate an overall rate by dividing each property's net operating income by its sale price. Table 22.2 illustrates this procedure using data from four comparable sales. If all four transactions are equally reliable and comparable, the appraiser might conclude that an overall rate of 0.0941 to 0.0984 should be applied to the subject property. The final rate concluded depends on the appraiser's judgment as to how comparable each sale is to the subject property. For example, if Sales A and D are the most comparable, the concluded rate might be about 0.0960, or 9.6%.

Table 22.2: Derivation of Overall Capitalization Rates from Comparable Sales

	Sale A	Sale B	Sale C	Sale D
Net operating income	$35,100	$40,000	$30,500	$48,400
Price	$368,500	$425,000	$310,000	$500,000
Indicated R_O	0.0953	0.0941	0.0984	0.0968

If there are differences between a comparable property and the subject property that could affect the overall capitalization rate concluded, the appraiser must account for these differences. In such cases, the appraiser must decide whether the rate concluded for the subject property should be higher or lower than the rate indicated by a specific sale or group of sales. Appraisal judgment is also needed to determine whether the rate selected for the subject should fall within the range established by the sales or be set above or below the range, as it is in certain cases. If there are wide differences between a comparable property and the subject property that could affect the overall capitalization rate, the appraiser must explain the market behaviour or property characteristics that account for these differences.

When rates derived from comparable sales are used, the overall capitalization rate is applied to the subject property in a manner consistent with its derivation. In other words, if the market-derived capitalization rates are based on the properties' net operating income expectancies for the first year – i.e., date of sale through next 12 months – the capitalization rate for the subject property should be applied to its anticipated net operating income for the first year of operation.

The net income to be capitalized may be estimated before or after an annual allowance for specific replacement categories, e.g., the allowance for furniture, fixtures, and equipment for hotel properties and the replacement allowance for office properties.[4] Again, it is imperative that the appraiser analyze comparable sales and derive their capitalization rates in the same manner used to analyze the subject property and capitalize its income.

The following examples illustrate the importance of deriving and applying rates consistently. In the first example, the replacement allowance for the subject property

---

[4] In some markets, practitioners no longer deduct a replacement allowance as an above-the-line item in direct capitalization. Whenever this expense item is implicit in the capitalization rate, it should not be deducted in estimating the net operating income for a subject property.

is estimated to be $2,500. The overall rate indicated by comparable sales, in which a replacement allowance is not deducted as an operating expense, was 0.0850. In the second example, the replacement allowance is deducted as an operating expense, and the indicated overall rate becomes 0.0825. In the first calculation, the allowance is not included as an expense item for the subject property, so the net operating income there is $2,500 higher than in the second calculation. The valuation conclusions produced by the two calculations are identical because the appraiser derived and applied the rates consistently.

Allowance for Replacements Not Included in Operating Expenses

Net operating income	$85,000
Overall rate	0.0850
Capitalization: $85,000 ÷ 0.0850	$1,000,000

Allowance for Replacements Included in Operating Expenses

Net operating income	$82,500
Overall rate	0.0825
Capitalization: $82,500 ÷ 0.0825	$1,000,000

Whether net operating income is estimated with or without an allowance for replacements, the overall capitalization rate is calculated by dividing net operating income by a comparable property's sale price. An overall capitalization rate provides compelling evidence of value when a series of conditions are met:

1. Data must be drawn from properties that are physically similar to the property being appraised and from similar (preferably competing) markets. Where significant differences exist for a given comparable, its value indication may be afforded less weight or may be discarded entirely.

2. Sale properties used as sources for calculating overall capitalization rates should have current (date of sale) and future market expectations, including income and expense patterns and likely value trends, that are comparable to those affecting the subject property.

3. Income and expenses must be estimated on the same basis for the subject property and all comparable properties.

4. The comparable property's price must reflect market terms, or an adjustment for cash equivalency must be made.

5. If adjustments are considered necessary for differences between a comparable and the subject property, they should be made separately from the process of calculating the overall capitalization rate and should be based on market evidence.

Derivation of R_o from Effective Gross Income Multipliers

Sometimes an overall capitalization rate cannot be derived directly because the stringent data requirements cannot be met, but reliable transaction data and gross income data can be obtained from several comparable sales. In such cases, an *effective gross income multiplier* can be derived and used in conjunction with a net income ratio (NIR) to produce an overall capitalization rate. The NIR is the complement of the operating expense ratio (OER). Thus, NIR = 1 - OER. The derivation of income multipliers is discussed later in this chapter.

The net income ratio is the ratio of net operating income to effective gross income. Although effective gross income multipliers can be based on annual or monthly income, annual income is used unless otherwise specified. Monthly income is primarily used for one-unit or small multi-family properties. Frequently, an appraiser can obtain market-wide averages of operating expense ratios as well as the effective gross income multipliers indicated by comparable sales. If a property is truly comparable to the subject, it may be appropriate to use the subject's net income ratio and the comparable property's effective gross income multiplier to develop the rate.

> **effective gross income multiplier (EGIM)**
> The ratio between the sale price (or value) of a property and its effective gross income.

The formula for deriving an overall capitalization rate from a net income ratio and an effective gross income multiplier is:

$$R_o = NIR \div EGIM$$

Returning to Table 22.2, consider Sale A, which was recently sold for $368,500. Suppose the potential gross income of the property is $85,106 and its effective gross income is $80,000. The operating expense ratio of the property is 56.25%, so its operating expenses are $45,000 and its NOI is $35,000. The effective gross income multiplier is 4.6063 ($368,500 ÷ $80,000) and the net income ratio is 0.4375 ($35,000 ÷ $80,000). The overall capitalization rate extracted from the effective gross income multiplier of Sale A is:

$$R_o = 0.4375 \div 4.6063$$
$$R_o = 0.09498, \text{ or } 9.5\%$$

After this calculation is performed for all the comparables, an estimated overall capitalization rate can be reconciled from the overall capitalization rate indications derived.

Derivation of R_o by Band of Investment – Mortgage and Equity

Since most properties are purchased with debt and equity capital, the overall capitalization rate must satisfy the market return requirements of both investment positions. Lenders must anticipate receiving a competitive interest rate commensurate with the perceived risk of the investment or they will not make funds available. Lenders generally require that the loan principal be repaid through periodic amortization payments. Similarly, equity investors must anticipate receiving a competitive equity cash return commensurate with the perceived risk, or they will invest their funds elsewhere.

The *mortgage capitalization rate* (R_M) is the ratio of the annual debt service to the principal amount of the mortgage loan. The rate established at the inception of a mortgage is commonly called the *mortgage constant*. The annual mortgage constant for a new loan is calculated by multiplying each period's payment by the number of payments per year and then dividing this amount by the amount of the loan. A current mortgage constant may also be calculated on the basis of the outstanding mortgage amount once debt service payments have been made. It should be noted that the mortgage capitalization rate (R_M) differs from the mortgage interest rate (Y_M). The mortgage interest rate, or yield rate to the mortgage, is the internal rate of return that equates the present value of the mortgage payments with the principal balance of the loan, i.e., the rate used to calculate the mortgage payment.

The mortgage capitalization rate is a function of the interest rate, the frequency of amortization, and the amortization term of the loan. It is the sum of the interest rate and the sinking fund factor. When the loan terms are known, the mortgage capitalization rate can be calculated, using a financial calculator or any of a variety of computer software programs, by simply dividing annual debt service by the remaining mortgage balance, if known. Appraisers generally calculate mortgage capitalization rates with financial calculators or computer software.

The equity investor also seeks a systematic cash return. The rate used to capitalize equity income is called the *equity capitalization rate* (R_E); it is the ratio of annual equity dividend to the amount of equity investment. The equity capitalization rate may be more or less than the expected equity yield rate (Y_E) because the latter takes into account the effect of debt financing on the income received by the equity investor. For appraisal purposes, a property's equity capitalization rate is the anticipated cash flow to the equity investor for the first year of the projection period divided by the initial equity investment.

The overall capitalization rate must satisfy both the mortgage capitalization rate requirement of the lender and the equity dividend requirement of the equity investor. For mortgage-equity analysis, it can be viewed as a composite rate, weighted in proportion to the total property investment represented by debt and equity. The overall capitalization rate is a weighted average of the mortgage capitalization rate (R_M) and equity capitalization rate (R_E). The loan-to-value ratio (M) represents the loan or debt portion of the property investment; the equity ratio (E, which is sometimes shown as 1 - M) represents the equity portion of the property investment. The sum of E and M is 1, i.e., 100%.

---

band of investment
A technique in which the capitalization rates attributable to components of a capital investment are weighted and combined to derive a weighted-average rate attributable to the total investment.

---

mortgage capitalization rate (R_M)
The capitalization rate for debt; the ratio of the annual debt service to the principal amount of the mortgage loan. Also called *mortgage constant*, *annual constant*, or *loan constant*.

equity capitalization rate (R_E)
An income rate that reflects the relationship between one year's equity cash flow and the equity investment.

equity yield rate (Y_E)
An internal rate of return on equity capital.

equity ratio (E)
The ratio between the down payment paid on a property and its total price; the fraction of the investment that is unencumbered by debt.

loan-to-value ratio (M)
The ratio between a mortgage loan and the value of the property pledged as security, usually expressed as a percentage. Also called loan ratio.

An appraiser may obtain typical mortgage terms and conditions by surveying lenders active in the market area. Equity capitalization rates are derived from comparable sales by dividing the annual equity dividend of each sale by the equity investment. The equity capitalization rate used to capitalize the subject property's equity dividend ultimately depends on the appraiser's judgment as to how individual investors perceive the relationship between market value and investment value, especially in a market with fluctuating mortgage interest rates.

When the mortgage and equity capitalization rates are known, an overall rate may be derived with the band of investment, or weighted-average technique[5] using the following formulas:

Mortgage component $M \times R_M =$ _____
Equity component $+ \ E \times R_E =$ $+$ _____
                          $R_O =$ _____

To illustrate how the overall capitalization rate is calculated with the band of investment technique, suppose that the following characteristics describe the subject property.

Available loan   75% loan-to-value ratio, 7.0% interest per annum, compounded semi-annually, 25-year amortization period (monthly payment) = 8.4% mortgage capitalization rate (RM) (rounded, calculator steps shown in Appendix C)

Equity capitalization rate   6.5% (derived from comparable sales)

The overall rate is calculated as follows:

$R_O =$ 0.75×0.084 $M \times R_M$
          $+ \ \underline{0.25 \times 0.065}$ $+ \ \underline{E \times R_E}$
$=$ $0.063 + 0.0163$
$=$ 0.0793

Although this technique can be used to derive overall capitalization rates, appraisers should be extremely careful when using it for this purpose. The technique is only applicable when sufficient market data is available to estimate equity capitalization rates. Typically, where sufficient market data is available, the appraiser can calculate the overall rate directly, reducing the underlying usefulness of this technique. A capitalization rate used to develop an opinion of market value should be justified and supported by market data, but such data often is not available. When the available market data is scarce or not reliable, an appraiser may use mortgage-equity techniques to develop or test capitalization rates. Appraisers may develop information through interviews with market participants and from their own records, which can be pieced together for such tests. These indirect analyses are not substitutes for market data, but they can lead to valuable insights and understandings. The mortgage

---

[5]   The band of investment is similar to the weighted average cost of capital (WACC) used in finance.

yield rate (Y_M) should not be used in place of the mortgage capitalization rate (R_M), nor should an equity yield rate (Y_E) be substituted for an equity capitalization rate (R_E).

Derivation of R_O by Band of Investment – Land and Building

A band of investment formula can also be applied to the physical components of property, i.e., the land or site and the buildings. Essentially this methodology is the same as the mortgage-equity technique, except that the elements are the physical property components. Just as weighted rates are developed for mortgage and equity components in mortgage-equity analysis, weighted rates for the land and buildings can be developed if accurate rates for these components can be estimated independently and the proportion of total property value represented by each component can be identified. The formula is:

$$R_O = \begin{array}{l} L \times R_L \\ + B \times R_B \end{array}$$

where L = land value as a percentage of total property value, R_L = land capitalization rate, B = building value as a percentage of total property value, and R_B = building capitalization rate.

> **building capitalization rate (R_B)**
> The rate used in certain residual techniques or in a band of investment to convert building income into an indication of building value. The ratio of building income to building value.
>
> **land capitalization rate (R_L)**
> The rate used to convert land income into an indication of land value when certain residual or band of investment techniques are applied. The ratio of land income to land value.

As an example, assume the land represents 45% of the value of a property and the building represents the other 55%. The land capitalization rate derived from comparable sales data is 8.0%, and the building capitalization rate is 11.0%. The indicated overall rate is calculated as follows:

$$
\begin{array}{lll}
R_O = & 0.45 \times 0.08 & L \times R_L \\
 & +\ \underline{0.55 \times 0.11} & +\ \underline{B \times R_B} \\
 = & 0.036 + 0.0605 & \\
 = & 0.0965 &
\end{array}
$$

Land and building capitalization rates may be extracted by applying residual analysis to improved properties. Land and building residual techniques are illustrated later in this chapter.

Debt Coverage Formula

In addition to the traditional terms of lending – i.e., the interest rate, loan-to-value ratio, amortization term, maturity, and payment period – real estate lenders sometimes use another judgment criteria: the *debt coverage ratio* (DCR). This is the ratio of net operating income to annual debt service (I_M), or the

> **debt coverage ratio (DCR)**
> The ratio of net operating income to annual debt service (DCR = NOI ÷ I_M); measures the ability of a property to meet its debt service out of net operating income; also called debt service coverage ratio (DSCR).
>
> **debt service (I_M or PMT)**
> The periodic payment that covers the interest on, and retirement of, the outstanding principal of the mortgage loan; also called *mortgage debt service*.

payment (PMT) that covers interest on and retirement of the outstanding principal of the mortgage loan:

$$DCR = NOI \div I_M$$

The debt coverage ratio is frequently used by institutional lenders, who are generally fiduciaries who manage and lend the money of others, including depositors and policyholders. Because of their fiduciary responsibility, institutional lenders are particularly sensitive to the safety of loan investments, especially the safety of principal. They are concerned with safety and profit and are anxious to avoid default and possible foreclosure. Consequently, when they underwrite loans on income-producing property, institutional lenders try to provide a cushion so that the borrower will likely be able to meet the debt service obligations on the loan even if building income declines.

To estimate an overall rate, the debt coverage ratio can be multiplied by the mortgage capitalization rate and the loan-to-value ratio. However, the method should only be applied if the property is at stabilized occupancy. Lenders sometimes refer to overall capitalization rates derived by this method as *in-house capitalization rates*. The formula is:

$$R_O = DCR \times RM \times M$$

For a property with net operating income of $50,000 and annual debt service of $43,264, the debt coverage ratio is calculated as:

$$DCR = \$50,000 \div \$43,264$$
$$= 1.1557$$

If R_M equals 0.085 and M is 0.75, R_O is estimated as

$$R_O = 1.1557 \times 0.085 \times 0.75$$
$$= 0.0737$$

With this method, lenders can use market data to check on the reasonableness of capitalization rates derived from comparable properties and internal evaluation guidelines.

RESIDUAL TECHNIQUES

Residual techniques are based on the same basic premises that apply to direct capitalization rates. However, while an overall rate processes the entire net operating income into a value indication, the residual techniques separate net operating income into various components. These include the income attributable to physical components (land and building residuals) and financial components (mortgage and equity residuals). Although these components can be appraised by applying yield capitalization techniques, in direct capitalization only the first year's net operating income for each component is included in the analysis. The application of residual techniques is only justified if the inferences on which the techniques are based are reasonable.

Regardless of which known and unknown (residual) components of the property are being analyzed, the appraiser starts with the value of the known items and the net operating income, as shown in Table 22.3. The appraiser:

> **residual techniques**
> Procedures used to capitalize the income allocated to an investment component of unknown value after all investment components of known values have been satisfied; may be applied to a property's physical components (land and building) or financial interests (mortgage and equity).

1. Applies an appropriate capitalization rate to the value of the known component to derive the annual income needed to support the investment in that component

2. Deducts the annual income needed to support the investment in the known component from the net operating income to derive the residual income available to support the investment in the unknown component

3. Capitalizes the residual income at a capitalization rate appropriate to the investment in the residual component to develop the present value of this component

4. Adds the values of the known component and the residual component to derive a value indication for the total property

Residual techniques allow an appraiser to capitalize the income allocated to an investment component of unknown value after other investment components of known value have been satisfied. They can be applied to the physical components of a property (land and building) or to the financial components of a property (mortgage and equity) only when specific property information is available. The usefulness of the building residual and mortgage residual techniques is extremely limited.

Table 22.3: Known and Unknown Variables in Residual Calculations

Residual Technique	Known	Unknown
Land residual	Net operating income (NOI) Building value (V_B) Building capitalization rate (R_B) Land capitalization rate (R_L)	Land or site value (V_L)
Building residual	Net operating income (NOI) Land or site value (V_L) Land capitalization rate (R_L) Building capitalization rate (R_B)	Building value (V_B)
Mortgage residual	Net operating income (NOI) Amount of equity (V_E) Equity capitalization rate (R_E) Mortgage capitalization rate (R_M)	Mortgage amount (V_M)
Equity residual	Net operating income (NOI) Mortgage amount (V_M) Mortgage capitalization rate (R_M) Equity capitalization rate (R_E)	Amount of equity (V_E)

Prior to the publication of *The Ellwood Tables* in 1959, the physical residual techniques (land and building) were the dominant methods for valuing real estate. L. W. Ellwood's contribution to the income approach changed the practice of appraisal in several ways:

- Prior to *The Ellwood Tables*, appraisers generally considered all market value transactions to reflect cash transfers between the buyer and the seller with no provision for financing. Ellwood recognized that most market transactions involved cash to the seller but were financed in part with some form of debt or other financial consideration on the part of the buyer. His view was that each component – mortgage and equity – could be analyzed separately in the context of a given property.

- Ellwood promoted the simple understanding that choosing an alternate method – direct capitalization or yield capitalization – did not produce a different result; as long as market rates appropriate to the method were applied, the same result would be produced.

- Ellwood emphasized that the concept of the present worth of anticipated future benefits provides that if it is possible to construct a cash flow statement for any given time horizon, it is possible to use some form of discounting in the capitalization process. This realization permitted appraisers and investors to consider more precisely the anticipated benefits of a given property and to avoid using direct capitalization to analyze a single year's income, which might be less precise. Ellwood said, "Two years are better than just one", and that even a five-year analysis was feasible for most income-producing properties.

- Until *The Ellwood Tables*, most appraisers focused on land and building components (or, at times, on leases and the analysis of natural resources). Ellwood added the consideration of mortgage and equity components, not as a substitute, but to provide another dimension to the analysis.

- Ellwood did not limit his concept to market value alone. Instead, he provided an analytical framework in which specific anticipations or market expectations could be tested and the results applied to either opinions of market value or other aspects of property financial analysis.

- Although Ellwood is most often credited with adding new considerations to real property appraisal analysis, he also clarified, refocused, and brought new understanding to the fundamental appraisal methods and techniques that had been applied for many years. In this way, he helped overcome errors and abuses in traditional appraisal practices while adding new techniques.

The development of computerized discounted cash flow analyses in professional appraisal practice has largely supplanted the use of residual techniques, except when the data needed to apply more sophisticated techniques is not available. Today, residual techniques are used primarily in specialized situations, e.g., in highest and best use analysis as a test of financial feasibility. Nevertheless, residual analysis techniques remain a fundamental component of appraisal theory and well-rounded appraisers should be familiar with them.

Building Residual Technique

An appraiser who applies the building residual technique must be able to estimate land or site value independently. The technique is especially applicable when data on land values and land rents is available to establish land capitalization rates. The appraiser applies the land capitalization rate to the known land value to obtain the amount of annual net income needed to support the land value. Then this amount is deducted from the net operating income to derive the residual income available to support the investment in the building(s). The appraiser capitalizes this residual income at the building capitalization rate to derive an

> **building residual technique**
> A capitalization technique in which the net operating income attributable to improvements is isolated and capitalized by the building capitalization rate (R_B) to indicate the improvements' contribution to total property value. When the improvements' value is added to land value, a total property value opinion is produced.

indication of the present value of the building(s). Finally, the land value and the building value are added to derive an indication of total property value. In this way, the land and building capitalization rates derived from the market are applied to the subject property.

For example, consider a small warehouse with an estimated land value of $200,000. Analysis of several sales of comparable sites reveals a land capitalization rate of 6.5% and a 10% building capitalization rate. (Techniques for calculating capitalization rates for residual components are illustrated later in the chapter.) The net operating income of the subject property is estimated to be $67,500. Using the building residual technique, the value of the subject property is calculated as follows:

Estimated land value		$200,000
Net operating income	$67,500	
Less income attributable to land		
Land value × R_L ($200,000 × 0.065)	– 13,000	
Residual income to building	$54,500	
Building value (capitalized: $54,500 ÷ 0.10)		+ 545,000
Indicated property value		$745,000

This technique is simple, but its applicability and usefulness are limited. Depending on the particular market, the building residual technique may or may not reflect the way purchaser-investors regard investment real estate. It is also extremely difficult to apply when the income projection is shorter than the remaining economic life of the improvements, and the reversion consequently represents more than simply the value of the site.

When the required data is available, the building residual technique can be used to value properties with improvements that have suffered substantial depreciation. In fact, current reproduction or replacement cost minus the present value of the improvements provides an estimate of total depreciation. In addition, the building residual technique directly measures the contribution of the improvements to total property value, so it can help an appraiser determine when demolition or major renovation of property improvements is economically feasible or, if appropriate, help establish the tax basis for depreciation of the improvements.

Land Residual Technique

The land residual technique calls for a separate estimation of the value of the building (or buildings). In land residual applications, an appraiser will often consider a new highest and best use assuming a building that does not exist. Thus, an appraiser usually estimates building value as the current cost to construct a new building that represents the highest and best use of the land or site.

> **land residual technique**
> A method of estimating land value in which the net operating income attributable to the land is isolated and capitalized to produce an indication of the land's contribution to the total property.

The building capitalization rate is applied to the building value to obtain the amount of annual net income needed to support the value of the building. This amount is then deducted from net operating income to indicate the residual income available to support the investment in the land. The residual income is capitalized at the land capitalization rate to derive an indication of the value of the land. Finally, the building value is added to the land value to derive an indication of total property value.

Using the same data used in the building residual example but assuming that building value rather than land value is known, the problem is calculated from the opposite viewpoint. The land and building capitalization rates derived from the market are applied to the subject property as follows:

Estimated building value		$545,000
Net operating income	$67,500	
Less income attributable to the building		
Building value × R_B ($545,000 × 0.10)	− 54,500	
Residual income to land	$13,000	
Land value (capitalized: $13,000 ÷ 0.065)		+ 200,000
Indicated property value		$745,000

The land residual technique allows an appraiser to estimate land values when recent data on land sales is not available. In practice, an appraiser often uses the technique to test the highest and best use of the land or site for proposed construction. An appraiser can also use this technique to provide a value indication for new structures that do not suffer from depreciation. However, the land residual technique is not as applicable when the cost to produce a new building is inconsistent with the amount of value such a building would contribute to property value.

Equity Residual Technique

To apply the equity residual technique, an appraiser deducts annual debt service from net operating income to obtain the residual income to the equity interest. An appraiser who uses this technique must be able to obtain mortgage loan terms from the market and estimate the dollar amount of the debt.

To derive an equity capitalization rate from the market, the appraiser may apply the following process. Assume the loan is $375,000 with 7.0% interest per annum, compounded semi-annually, a 25-year term, and monthly payments. Calculator steps are shown in Appendix C.

Net operating income	$60,000
Less mortgage debt service	– 31,519 (*mortgage constant is thus*
	$13,519/$375,000, or 0.084051)
Residual income to equity	$28,481
Equity investment (known)	$212,000
Equity capitalization rate	
$28,481 ÷ $212,000	13.434%

For a similar property with comparable characteristics, the 13.434% equity capitalization rate can be divided into the equity income to develop an indication of equity value. When equity value is added to the mortgage amount, an indication of property value is produced.

Mortgage Residual Technique

When the mortgage residual technique is applied, the amount of available equity is the known component and the mortgage amount or value is unknown. The income needed to satisfy the equity component at the equity capitalization rate is deducted from the net operating income to obtain the residual income to the mortgage component. The residual mortgage income is then capitalized into value at the mortgage capitalization rate. The preceding example of equity residual capitalization can be approached from the opposite side of the equation to illustrate mortgage residual technique calculations:

Available equity		$212,000
Net operating income	$60,000	
Equity × R_E ($212,000 × 0.13434)	– 28,481	
Residual income to mortgage	$31,519	
Mortgage value		
(capitalized: $31,519 ÷ 0.08405)		+ 375,003
Indicated property value		$587,003

The mortgage residual technique works as a mathematical process, but it does not follow the customary logic of market participants. Its most common use is in determining the amount of mortgage available and the associated value requirement. However, the technique assumes that the amount of funds the equity investor is willing to invest in the property has already been determined and that the investor requires a specified equity dividend rate from the property. This implies that the loan amount depends on the residual cash flow available for mortgage debt service and the mortgage capitalization rate. Lenders generally will not make a loan unless net operating income exceeds the mortgage debt service by a specified amount. In addition, once the loan is made, the lender has the legal right to receive the agreed-upon debt service, but any residual cash flow goes to the equity investor. Even with below-market loans, the equity investor receives the income remaining after payment of the contract interest. Thus, the mortgage residual technique does not necessarily reflect market behaviour and would not normally be appropriate for estimating the value of a property subject to a specific mortgage.

Deriving a Building Capitalization Rate

The appraiser must find support for one or more of the rates used in each of the residual techniques and then must solve for the unknown rate. Consider the following examples of the extraction of a building capitalization rate:

Example 1

A nearby property with the same use as the subject property recently sold for $750,000. The land was purchased for $230,000 and the improvements were constructed within the past year. Based on its design and construction materials, the improvements are expected to have a remaining economic life of 50 years. First-year net operating income is expected to be $77,900. Rate extraction is performed as follows:

Sale price	$750,000
Less land value	− 230,000
Indicated building value	$520,000
Annual recapture with 50-year economic life	× 2%
Annual recapture in dollars	$10,400
Net operating income	$77,900
Less annual recapture	− 10,400
Annual interest earnings	$67,500
Interest rate on land and building investment	
$67,500 ÷ $750,000 =	0.09 or 9%
Building capitalization rate	
0.09 + 0.02 =	0.11 or 11%

Example 2

A comparable property in the same area just sold in a sale-leaseback transaction. After acquiring land and constructing a building for their own use, the sellers sold the completed property to a buyer, who then leased the property to its original owners for a 25-year term with options to renew. The land was acquired for $200,000 and a $400,000 building was constructed. The buyer paid $600,000 for the property and leased it back to the sellers for $59,000 per year, with the tenant paying all taxes, insurance, maintenance, and other costs. In the market, land leases of similar sites typically require an 8.5% rent rate for 25-year terms. The building is expected to have a 50-year economic life. Rate extraction is performed as follows:

Total rent		$59,000
Less land rent ($200,000 × 8.5%)		− 17,000
Indicated annual building rent		$42,000
Less indicated annual building recapture		
$400,000 × 2%		− 8,000
Indicated annual building income		$34,000
Annual land rent	$17,000	
Plus indicated annual building income	+ 34,000	
Total annual interest earnings		$51,000
Annual interest rate on land and building investment		
$51,000 ÷ $600,000 =		0.085 or 8.5%

Note that the appraiser must recognize that this procedure is actually a lease analysis, not an analysis of the land and building alone. For example, the lease calls for a renewal in 25 years. If there is no renewal, the buyer will receive an additional "income" in the amount of the value of the property in 25 years. If there is a renewal, the buyer will receive additional benefits that depend on the terms of the renewal. Thus, the 8.5% annual interest rate is actually a return on the terms of the lease contract and, in this instance, will probably underestimate the land and building rates. Although this calculation does not produce land and building rates for capitalization purposes, it may be used as an additional consideration in conjunction with more definitive market data.

Example 3

A comparable five-year-old building constituting leasehold improvements was just sold. The property is nearby and has a similar use to the property being appraised. The improvements at the time of construction had an expected remaining economic life of 50 years, and there have been no significant market changes or building alterations over the past five years. Market data indicates that if the property were owned by a single owner, it would likely have a market value of $700,000. An overall capitalization rate of 10.5% would apply to the land and building combined. The improvements sold for $485,000 at the same time that the business operating on the property was sold. The new owner must pay land rent of $19,350. Rate extraction is performed as follows:

Indicated property value		$700,000
Less sale price of the improvements		− 485,000
Indicated land value		$215,000
Sale price of the improvements		$485,000
Remaining economic life	45 years	
Recapture rate	$1 \div 45 =$	× 0.022
Annual recapture in dollars		$10,670
Indicated property value		$700,000
Overall capitalization rate		× 0.105
Indicated property income		$73,500
Less annual recapture in dollars		− 10,670
Annual interest on land and building		$62,830
Interest rate of land and improvements		
$62,830 \div $700,000 =		0.09 or 9%
Building capitalization rate		
0.09 + 0.022 =		0.112 or 11.2%

GROSS INCOME MULTIPLIERS AND GROSS RENT MULTIPLIERS

Gross income multipliers (GIMs) are used to compare the income-producing characteristics of properties. Potential or effective gross income may be converted into an opinion of value by applying the relevant gross income multiplier. This method of capitalization is mathematically related to direct capitalization because rates are the reciprocals of multipliers or factors. Therefore, it is appropriate to discuss the derivation and use of multipliers under direct capitalization.

To derive a gross income multiplier from market data, sales of properties that were rented at the time of sale or were anticipated to be rented within a short time must be available. The ratio of the sale price of a property to its known annual gross income at the time of sale or its projected income over the first year of ownership is the gross income multiplier. Gross income multipliers are typically calculated on an annual basis.

Appraisers who attempt to derive and apply gross income multipliers for valuation purposes must be careful for several reasons. First, the properties analyzed must be comparable to the subject property and to one another in terms of physical, locational, and investment characteristics. Properties with similar or even identical multipliers can have very different operating expense ratios and, therefore, may not be comparable for valuation purposes.

Second, the term *gross income multiplier* is used because some of the gross income from a property or type of property may come from sources other than rent. A gross rent multiplier applies to rental income only and can be calculated on a monthly or annual basis, consistent with market practices.

> The application of income multipliers is also a direct capitalization procedure. In developing an income or rent multiplier, it is essential that the income or rent of the properties used to derive the multiplier be comparable to that of the subject and that the specific multiplier derived be applied to the same income base.

Third, the appraiser must use similar income data to derive the multiplier for each transaction. For example, GIMs extracted from full-service rentals would not be applied to a subject property leased on a net basis. The sale price can be divided by either the potential or effective gross income, but the data and measure must be used consistently throughout the analysis to produce reliable results. However, different income measures may be used in different valuation studies and appraisals. The income measure selected is dictated by the availability of market data and the purpose of the analysis.

To illustrate the difference between various gross income multipliers, the following calculations are made using data for Sale A shown in Table 22.2. Note that in the discussion following Table 22.2, the potential gross income for Sale A was indicated to be $85,106 and the effective gross income was $80,000.

Potential gross income multiplier	= Sale Price ÷ Potential Gross Income
	= $368,500 ÷ $85,106
	= 4.33 (rounded)
Effective gross income multiplier	= Sale Price ÷ Effective Gross Income
	= $368,500 ÷ $80,000
	= 4.61 (rounded)

After the gross income multiplier is derived from comparable market data, it must be applied on the same basis it was derived. In other words, an income multiplier based on effective gross income can only be applied to the effective gross income of the subject property; an income multiplier based on potential gross income can only be applied to the potential gross income of the subject property. In addition, the timing of income must be comparable. If sales are analyzed using next year's income expectation, the multiplier derived must be applied to next year's income expectation for the subject property.

CHAPTER 23

YIELD CAPITALIZATION – THEORY AND BASIC APPLICATIONS

Yield capitalization is the more complex of the two fundamental methods used in the income approach to value. Various techniques are available within this methodology for converting a series of future cash flows received over time into an opinion of value.

Yield capitalization is used to convert future benefits into an indication of present value by applying an appropriate yield rate. To select an appropriate yield rate for a market value appraisal, an appraiser analyzes market evidence of the yields anticipated by typical investors, supported by market sales data, or both. When an appraiser seeks to determine investment value, the yield rate used should reflect the individual investor's requirements, which may differ from the requirements of typical investors in the market.

To perform yield capitalization, an appraiser:

1. Selects an appropriate projection period

2. Forecasts all future cash flows or cash flow patterns (including the reversion)

3. Chooses an appropriate yield rate

4. Converts future benefits into present value by discounting each annual future benefit or by developing an overall rate that reflects the income pattern, value change, and yield rate using one of the various yield capitalization formulas

> Yield capitalization is used to convert future benefits, typically a periodic income stream and reversion, into present value by discounting each future benefit at an appropriate yield rate or by applying an overall rate (extracted using one of the yield methods) that explicitly reflects the investment's income pattern, change in value, and yield rate.

Yield capitalization procedures include the application of capitalization rates that reflect an appropriate yield rate, the use of present value factors, and discounted cash flow analysis. An appraiser may use mortgage-equity formulas and yield rate or value change formulas to derive overall capitalization rates.

Like direct capitalization, yield capitalization should reflect market behaviour. To apply the discounting procedure, the appraiser must be familiar with the following concepts and techniques:

- Income patterns
- Capital return concepts
- The mathematics of the discounting process
- Investor requirements or expectations, i.e., projection period, anticipated market growth, and inflation
- The appropriateness of the selected yield rate

DISCOUNTING

Discounting is a general term used to describe the process of converting future cash flows into a present value. The discount rate is the rate used for the discounting process and may be a property yield rate, equity yield rate, or some other defined rate. In real estate appraisal practice, the most common total bundle of rights methodology used is the property yield rate (Y_O).

In the discounting process, periodic incomes and the final reversion are converted into present value through discounting, a procedure based on the concept that benefits received in the future are worth less than the same benefits received today. The return on an investment compensates the investor for foregoing present benefits – i.e., the immediate use of capital – and accepting future benefits and risks. This return is usually called *interest* by lenders and *yield* by property owners and equity investors. The discounting procedure includes the expectation that the return of capital will be accomplished through periodic income, the final reversion, or a combination of the two.

> **discounting**
> A procedure used to convert periodic incomes, cash flows, and reversions into present value; based on the concept that benefits received in the future are worth less than the same benefits received now.
>
> **cash flow**
> The periodic income attributable to the interests in real property

An investor seeks a total return that exceeds the amount invested. The present value of a prospective benefit must be less than its expected future benefits. A future payment is discounted to present value by calculating the amount that, if invested today, would grow with compound interest at a satisfactory rate to equal the future payment. The standard formula for discounting future value to present value is:

$$\text{Present Value} = \frac{\text{Future Value}}{(1+i)^n}$$

where i is the rate of return on capital per period (or the discount rate) that will satisfy the investor and n is the number of periods that the payment will be deferred. If a series of future payments is expected, each payment is discounted with the standard formula, and the present value of the payments is the sum of all the present values. The yield formula is expressed as:

$$PV = \frac{CF_1}{(1+Y)} + \frac{CF_2}{(1+Y)^2} + \frac{CF_3}{(1+Y)^3} + \dots + \frac{CF_n}{(1+Y)^n}$$

where PV = present value; CF = the cash flow for the period specified; Y = the appropriate periodic yield rate; and n = the number of periods in the projection. This standard discounting procedure is the foundation for all present value calculations.[1]

The formula for calculating the future value of a sum deposited today is:

Future Value = Present Value $\times (1 + i)^n$

Note that the formulas for the present value and future value of a single payment are reciprocals of each other. Growing an amount with interest and discounting a future amount to a present value are very much related.

The amount deposited or received can be in the form of a single lump sum, a series of periodic instalments such as rental income, or a combination of both. When amounts are compounded or discounted, the rate used is the effective interest rate; on an annual basis, this rate is identical to the nominal interest rate. If amounts are compounded or discounted more often than annually – e.g., semi-annually or monthly – the nominal interest rate is divided by the number of compounding or discounting periods. For example, a nominal rate of 12%, compounded semi-annually is a periodic rate of 6% per semi-annual compounding period, or a nominal rate of 12% compounded monthly is a periodic rate of 1% per monthly period. By law, Canadian amortizing mortgages may compound no more frequently than semi-annually, and this affects interest rate calculations.

Financial calculators and computers can be used to change interest rates into the appropriate conversion frequency, i.e., monthly, quarterly, or annually.

> **effective interest rate (i)**
> An interest rate, usually expressed as an annual rate, that includes the effect of compounding; also, the lender's yield to maturity, which in many instances is equivalent to the lender's internal rate of return; also called effective rate.
>
> **nominal interest rate (I)**
> A stated or contract rate; an interest rate, usually annual, that does not necessarily correspond to the true or effective rate of growth at compound interest; e.g., a true or effective 1% monthly interest rate may be called a nominal annual interest rate of 12%, although true growth with monthly compounding amounts to slightly more than 12.68% per year.
>
> **periodic interest rate**
> Interest rate over the period; e.g., rate per month, per day, per quarter, or per year.

> **discounted cash flow (DCF) analysis**
> The procedure in which a discount rate is applied to a set of projected income streams and a reversion. The analyst specifies the quantity, variability, timing, and duration of the income streams as well as the quantity and timing of the reversion and discounts each to its present value at a specified yield rate. DCF analysis can be applied with any yield capitalization technique and may be performed on either a lease-by-lease or aggregate basis.

All present value problems consider the following:

1. The initial starting cost, value, or investment
2. The amount of the periodic cash flows over time
3. The reversion or resale value
4. The yield rate that equates the cash flows and reversion to the initial starting value
5. The amount of time (number of periods) between the initial cash flow and the reversion

---

[1]   For formulas, tables, and sample applications of the six functions of one, see Appendix B.

Since each individual cash flow is considered separately, a discounted cash flow (DCF) analysis can be used to solve any problem when three of the four factors are known.

In DCF analysis, the quantity, variability, timing, and duration of cash flows are specified. Cash flow refers to the periodic income attributable to the interests in real property. Each cash flow is discounted to present value and all the present values are totalled to obtain the value of the real property interest being appraised. The future value of that interest, the reversion, is forecast at the end of the projection period and is also discounted. The cash flows discounted with the DCF process may be the net operating income to the entire property or the cash flows to specific interests, e.g., the cash flows to the equity interest (equity dividends), or debt service for the mortgage interest.

With the DCF process, an appraiser can discount each payment of income and the reversion separately and add all the present values together to obtain the present value of the property interest being appraised. The formula treats the reversion as a cash flow that can be valued separately from the income stream. The formula can be used to develop opinions of the following:

- Total property value (V_O)
- Loan value (V_M)
- Equity value (V_E)
- Leased fee value (V_{LF})
- Leasehold value (V_{LH})
- The value of any other interest in real property

PROJECTION PERIOD AND HOLDING PERIOD

The *holding period* of an investment is defined as the term of ownership of the investment, whereas the *projection period* is a presumed period of ownership. In other words, the projection period is a period of time over which expected net operating income is projected for purposes of analysis and valuation. Although these terms are often used interchangeably, appraisers are more often concerned with the projection period applicable to the analysis in question.

The projection period may vary with the investment and investor. The appraiser usually estimates a projection period that is consistent with investor expectations developed through surveys and interviews. In the selection of an appropriate projection period, the appraiser should consider lease expirations, vacancies, rollovers, anticipated capital improvements, and other atypical events that may cause cash flow aberrations.

Risk increases as the projection period of an investment increases for several reasons:

- Maintenance costs increase as a building ages.
- Remaining economic life declines as a building ages.
- Functional issues relating to competition from newer properties may force a property into a lower investment category.
- In general, as forecasts look farther into the future, the conclusions become more uncertain.

Any series of periodic incomes, with or without a reversion, can be valued with the basic DCF formula. A wide range of formulas are available for valuing level annuities and increasing and decreasing annuities, which are introduced later in this chapter. These formulas have two benefits. First, they can be used as shortcuts to solve for property value, although if used as shortcuts they may be harder for the appraiser to explain and for the client to understand. Second, and more importantly, they provide a systematic methodology to evaluate real estate and the interactions of current value, income flows, and future value in a single problem-solving framework.

Most often financial calculators or computer spreadsheets are used to solve discounting problems mathematically. To apply compounding or discounting procedures, the appraiser must know the following:

- The basic formulas
- How the various factors relate to one another
- How they may be used or combined to apply yield capitalization and develop an indication of value

Spreadsheets and calculators are useful in solving various yield capitalization problems. However, in the final analysis, an opinion of value and conclusions about time, amount, and yield reflect the appraiser's judgment based on appropriate research of the subject property and relevant market data.

Estimation of a Yield Rate for Discounting

The estimation of an appropriate yield rate is critical to DCF analysis. To select an appropriate yield rate, an appraiser must verify and interpret the attitudes and expectations of market participants, including buyers, sellers, advisers, and brokers. Although the actual yield, or internal rate of return, on an investment cannot be calculated until the investment is sold, an investor may set a target yield for the investment before or during ownership. Historical yield rates derived from comparable sales may be relevant, but they reflect past, not future, benefits in the mind of the investor and may not be reliable indicators of current yield. Therefore, the estimation of yield rates for discounting cash flows should focus on the prospective or forecast yield rates anticipated by typical buyers and sellers of comparable investments. An appraiser can verify investor expectations by interviewing the parties to comparable sales transactions or reviewing offering materials for comparable properties recently offered for sale.

The appraiser narrows the range of indicated yield rates and selects an appropriate yield rate by comparing the physical, economic, financial, and risk characteristics of the comparable properties with the property being appraised and assessing the competition for capital in other rival investments. In some situations, there may be reason to select a yield rate above or below the indicated range. The final estimation of a yield rate requires judgment, just as an appraiser uses judgment to select an overall capitalization rate or equity capitalization rate from the range indicated by comparable sales. In selecting a yield rate, the appraiser should analyze current conditions in capital and real estate markets and the actions, perceptions, and expectations of real estate investors.

Different Rates

Yield rates are primarily a function of perceived risks. Different portions of forecast future income may have different levels of risk and therefore different yield rates.[2] In lease valuation, for example, one rate might be applied to discount the series of net rental incomes stipulated in the lease and a different rate might be applied to discount the reversion. One rate reflects the creditworthiness of the tenant as well as the benefits, constraints, and limitations of the lease contract, while the other is subject to free, open-market conditions. The decision to apply a single yield rate to all benefits or to apply different rates to different benefits should be based on investors' actions in the market and the methodology used to extract the yield rate. In all cases, the yield rate should be applied in the same way it was extracted.

INCOME STREAM PATTERNS

After specifying the amount, timing, and duration of the cash flows to the property interest being appraised, the appraiser should identify the pattern that the income stream is expected to follow during the projection period. These patterns may be grouped into the following basic categories:

- Variable annuity (irregular income pattern)
- Level annuity
- Increasing or decreasing annuity

THE NATURE OF ANNUITIES

Although the word *annuity* means an annual income, the term is used to refer to a program or contract specifying regular payments of stipulated amounts. Payments need not be annual, but the interval between payments is usually regular. An annuity can be level, increasing, or decreasing, but the amounts must be scheduled and predictable. Income characterized as an annuity is expected at regular intervals and in predictable amounts. Obviously real estate income or rental income can have the characteristics of an annuity. Monthly mortgage payments are perhaps the best example of an annuity. The pattern of income expected from a real estate investment may be regular or irregular. Various capitalization techniques have been developed to apply to a wide range of income patterns.

Variable Annuity: Non-Systematic Change

In a variable annuity, payment amounts may vary in each period. To value a variable annuity, the present value of each income payment is calculated separately and these values are totalled to obtain the present value of the entire income stream. This procedure is discounted cash flow analysis.

---

[2] When future events that could profoundly impact the income-producing potential of a property may or may not occur, probability analysis may be appropriate. Probability analysis is frequently required when properties are subject to potential environmental hazards and compliance with environmental regulations is pending. For example, a site may require an undetermined level of environmental remediation, the remediation required may or may not be completed within a given time frame, or the environmental regulation(s) governing the remediation may be modified. In such situations, probability analysis can help an appraiser develop a yield rate.

Any income stream can be valued as if it were a variable annuity. Level annuities and annuities that change systematically are subsets or regular patterns of income that can also be handled with special formulas that reflect the systematic pattern of the income stream. These shortcut formulas can save time and effort in certain cases, but valuing an income stream as a variable annuity with a calculator or computer program may be just as easy and will result in the same conclusion.

> **variable annuity**
> An income stream in which the payment amounts vary per period. A variable annuity is characteristic of one kind of income model and one kind of property model.

Level Annuity

A level annuity is an income stream in which the amount of each payment is the same; it is a level, unchanging flow of income over time. The payments in a level annuity are equally spaced and regularly scheduled. Level annuities can be discounted in the same manner as variable annuities. There are two types of level annuities:

- Ordinary annuities
- Annuities payable in advance

> **level annuity**
> An income stream in which the amount of each payment is the same; a level, unchanging flow of income over time.
>
> **ordinary annuity**
> A type of annuity in which cash flows are paid at the end of each period. Also known as an *annuity in arrears*.
>
> **annuity payable in advance (annuity due)**
> A type of level annuity; similar to an ordinary annuity except that payments are received at the beginning of each period.
>
> **increasing annuity**
> An income stream of evenly spaced, periodic payments that is expected to increase in a systematic pattern.

Ordinary Annuity

An ordinary annuity, which is the most common type of level annuity, is distinguished by income payments that are received at the end of each period, often referred to as "in arrears". Standard fixed-payment mortgage loans, many corporate and government bonds, endowment policies, and certain lease arrangements are ordinary annuities.

Annuity Payable in Advance (Annuity Due)

An annuity payable in advance is a level annuity in which the payments are received at the beginning of each period. A lease that requires payments at the beginning of each month, such as most apartment leases, creates an annuity payable in advance.

Increasing or Decreasing Annuity

An income stream that is expected to change in a systematic pattern is either an increasing annuity or a decreasing annuity. Appraisers encounter three basic patterns of systematic change:

1. Step-up and step-down annuities
2. Straight-line (constant-amount) change per period annuities
3. Exponential-curve (constant-ratio) change per period annuities

Step-Up and Step-Down Annuities

A *step-up* or *step-down* annuity is usually created by a lease contract that calls for a succession of level annuities of different amounts to be paid in different periods of the lease term. For example, a lease might call for monthly payments of $500 for the first three years, $750 for the next four years, and $1,200 for the next six years. Over the 13-year term of the lease, there are three successive level annuities, one for three years, one for four years, and one for six years.

> **step-up or step-down annuity**
> A type of increasing or decreasing annuity, usually created by a lease contract that calls for a succession of level annuities of different amounts to be paid in different periods of the lease term.
>
> **straight-line (constant-amount) change per period**
> Refers to a type of annuity or income/property model that increases or decreases by a fixed amount per period; also called *constant amount change per period.*
>
> **exponential-curve (constant-ratio) change per period**
> Refers to a type of annuity or income/property model that increases or decreases at a constant ratio and, as a result, the increases or decreases are compounded.

Straight-Line (Constant-Amount) Change per Period Annuity

An income stream that increases or decreases by a fixed amount each period fits the pattern of a straight-line (constant-amount) change per period annuity. These income streams are also called *straight-line increasing* or *straight-line decreasing annuities.* For example, a property may have an estimated first-year net operating income of $100,000 that is forecast to increase by $7,000 per year. Thus, the second year's net operating income will be $107,000, the third year's net operating income will be $114,000, and so forth. Similarly, the income stream of a straight-line decreasing annuity is expected to decrease by a constant amount each period.

Exponential-Curve (Constant-Ratio) Change per Period Annuity

An income stream with an exponential-curve (constant-ratio) change per period is also referred to as an *exponential annuity.* This type of income stream increases or decreases at a constant ratio and therefore the increases or decreases are compounded. For example, a property with an estimated first-year equity dividend of $100,000 that is forecast to increase 7% per year over each preceding year's cash flow will have an equity dividend in the second year of $107,000 ($100,000 × 1.07). However, the third year's equity dividend will be $114,490 ($107,000 × 1.07) and the fourth year's equity dividend will be $122,504 ($114,490 × 1.07).

REVERSION

As mentioned previously, income-producing properties typically provide two types of financial benefits: periodic income and the future value obtained from a sale of the property or reversion of the property interest at the end of the projection period. The length of the projection period can usually be determined by reviewing the property's lease expiration date(s) or other significant, atypical events. The length of the projection period and the discount rate are interactive. Generally, the longer the projection period, the greater the risk and the higher the discount rate. This future cash flow is called a *reversion* because it represents the anticipated return of a capital sum at the end of the investment.

There are several ways to estimate a resale price or property reversion at the end of the projection period. A capitalization rate can be applied to the appropriate income for the year following the end

> **terminal capitalization rate (R_N)**
> The capitalization rate applied to the expected net income for the year immediately following the end of the projection period to derive the resale price or value of a property. Also called a *going-out*, *residual*, or *reversionary capitalization rate*.

of the forecast. When an overall capitalization rate is used to estimate a resale price, it is called a *terminal, going-out*, or *residual capitalization rate* (R_N). The rate is different from the *going-in capitalization rate*, i.e., the overall capitalization rate found by dividing a property's net operating income for the first year after purchase by the present value of the property. The terminal, or residual, capitalization rate forecast is generally, though not necessarily, higher than the going-in capitalization rate. The terminal capitalization rate must reflect the reduction in the remaining economic life of the property and the greater risk associated with estimating NOI at the end of the projection period. The balance of the mortgage could then be deducted to calculate the owner's net sale proceeds, or equity reversion, if an equity yield analysis is being performed.

A single property may include one or more property interests that have their own streams of periodic benefits and reversions. For example, a property may have an equity interest with equity dividends as the periodic benefit and the equity

> **balloon payment**
> The outstanding balance due at the maturity of a balloon mortgage.

reversion – i.e., property reversion minus the mortgage balance at loan maturity or property resale – as the reversionary benefit. The same property could have a mortgage with debt service as the periodic benefit and the mortgage balance (called a *balloon payment*) as the reversionary interest. A single property also comprises both building and land components. In situations involving long-term ground leases where the objective is to value the leasehold estate in the building, annual ground rent should be deducted before capitalizing net operating income attributable to the leasehold estate.

The reversion is often a major portion of the total benefit to be received from an investment in income-producing property. If the investor's capital is not recaptured through some combination of cash flow and reversion proceeds, the effective rate of return on the investment will always be negative. For certain investments, all capital recapture is accomplished through the reversion, indicating higher risk; for other investment properties, part of the recapture is provided by the reversion and part is provided by the investment's income stream.

To judge how much of the return of an investment will be provided by the reversion, an appraiser acknowledges that three general situations could result from the original investment:

1. The property may increase in value over the projection period

2. The property's value may not change, i.e., the value of the property at the end of the projection period may be equal to its value at the beginning of the period

3. The property may decline in value over the period being analyzed

Because these possible outcomes affect the potential yield of the investment and the amount of income considered acceptable, yield capitalization requires the appraiser to determine market expectations as to the change, if any, that will occur in the original investment or the property value over the projection period. For leveraged investments, equity build-up may also occur through periodic debt service payments that include amortization.

When a property is expected to be sold, the appraiser projects the reversion amount and considers the net proceeds of resale. The term *net proceeds of resale* refers to the net difference between the transaction price and the selling expenses, which may include brokerage commissions, legal fees, closing costs, transfer taxes, and possibly penalties for the prepayment of debt. An appraiser should carefully analyze the transaction price to determine if costs of repair, capital improvements, and environmental remediation, if any, have been appropriately reflected. The transaction price may have to be adjusted to reflect extraordinary costs incurred by either party.

> **net proceeds of resale**
> The net difference between the transaction price and the selling expenses of a property; refers to the property's reversion.

An appraiser establishes the likely value of the reversion in light of the expectations of investors in the market for the type of property being appraised. The appraiser may ask the following questions:

*   Do investors expect a change in the value of this type of property in this particular locale?

*   By how much will values change and in which direction? The appraiser analyzes and interprets the market and estimates the value of the future reversion based on the direction and the amount or percentage of change that investors expect. The use of personal computers and software to perform lease-by-lease analysis allows appraisers to make more accurate forecasts of future cash flows, which help establish or estimate the reversion.

DISCOUNTING MODELS

The present value of any increasing, level, or decreasing income stream or of any irregular income stream can be calculated with DCF analysis. Specific valuation models, or formulas, categorized as either income models or property models, have been developed for application to corresponding patterns of projected benefits. Income models are based on broad trends and require fewer specific cash flow inputs. When these models fit specific property expectations, they may be applied as shortcuts in place of more detailed DCF analysis and provide the same results.

Income models can be applied only to a stream of income. The present value of an expected reversion or any other benefit not already included in the income stream must be added to obtain the investment's total present value. When a property model is used, an income stream and a reversion are valued in one operation. Other present value models employ discounted cash flow analysis, which is discussed in Chapter 24.

> Specific valuation formulas, called *income* and *property models*, have been developed to solve and explain specific patterns of benefits without the need for a comprehensive DCF calculation.

Income Models

Valuation models can be applied to the following patterns of income:

> income model
>
> A spreadsheet formula developed to project a pattern of periodic income. Income models can reflect level income with no change in value, level income with changing value, income and value that change by fixed amounts per period (straight-line), income and value that change at a constant ratio (exponential-curve), variable or irregular income with changing value, or level-equivalent income.

- Variable or irregular income
- Level income
- Straight-line (constant-amount) change per period income, i.e., the J factor
- Exponential-curve (constant-ratio) change per period income, i.e., the K factor
- Level-equivalent income

These models are not necessarily real estate- or property-specific, but they can be used to solve a variety of financial asset valuation problems that involve real estate.

Variable or Irregular Income

As mentioned previously, the discounting process or formula can be used to solve any present value problem. The present value of an uneven stream of income is the sum of the discounted benefits treated as a series of separate payments or reversions. This model simply totals all present values using the standard discounting formula. The routine can be applied as a property valuation model as well as an income valuation model because it can be adapted to include the final reversion as part of the final cash flow expected at the end of the last, or *n*th, period.

Level Income

When a lease provides for a level stream of income or when income can be projected at a stabilized level, one or more capitalization procedures may be appropriate depending on the investor's capital recovery expectations. Capitalization can be accomplished using capitalization in perpetuity. In the past, the present worth of an income stream was also calculated using the Inwood premise or the Hoskold premise, which are discussed in Appendix B.[3]

---

3   Over time, the Hoskold premise has become less popular and rarely reflects the thinking of real estate investors. It is now considered appropriate only for certain types of investments, e.g., in calculating the replacement allowance for leasing equipment or personal property. A Hoskold capitalization rate can be easily constructed by adding the speculative rate to the sinking fund factor for the safe rate, e.g., the prevailing rate for insured savings accounts or government bonds.

Capitalization in perpetuity can be considered a property valuation model or an income valuation model. If, for example, a property is expected to generate level net operating income for a finite period of time and then be resold for the original purchase price, the property could be valued with capitalization in perpetuity simply by dividing the expected periodic income by an appropriate discount rate. In this model, the discount rate and the overall capitalization rate are the same because the original investment is presumed to be recovered at the termination of the investment.

> **capitalization in perpetuity**
> Capitalization in which the discount rate equals the overall capitalization rate. Capitalization in perpetuity is applicable when a property is expected to generate level net operating income for a finite period and then be resold at the original purchase price.

Straight-Line (Constant-Amount) Change per Period in Income

When income is expected to increase or decrease by a fixed amount per period, the periodic income over time can be graphically portrayed as a straight line; the term *straight-line* is used to describe this type of income pattern.

The formula for valuing straight-line income patterns should not be confused with direct capitalization with straight-line recapture. Although direct capitalization with straight-line recapture may be seen as a model for valuing a particular income stream, the procedure can also be applied to properties in which the expected change in value is commensurate with the expected change in income. Therefore, direct capitalization with straight-line recapture and related concepts are discussed with property models later in this chapter. Again, the formula applies to income streams only. [4]

Exponential-Curve (Constant-Ratio) Change per Period in Income

The constant-ratio model represents an income pattern that increases or decreases at the same rate per period. Many real estate income streams will increase following a pattern close to the constant-ratio premise, although typically on a short-term basis. Portrayed graphically, this type of income stream follows an exponential curve rather than a straight line. This income pattern is sometimes referred to as changing at a compound rate. Analysis of exponential-curve change is primarily accomplished with computers.

Level-Equivalent Income

All non-level income streams can be converted into a level-equivalent pattern. This is particularly useful when the assignment requires the conclusion be expressed as a level income amount but the market is performing on a non level basis, e.g., estimating market rent for federal government property. For budgeting purposes, the government requires that these rent estimates be reported as a level-equivalent amount. Few markets rent on this basis, however, and most leases include a provision for increases over time, usually in relation to an index such as the Consumer Price Index (CPI). Therefore, the appraiser needs to first estimate the rent as it is found in the market, then convert it into a level-income equivalent.

---

[4]   See James J. Mason, ed. and comp., *American Institute of Real Estate Appraisers Financial Tables*, rev. ed. (Chicago: American Institute of Real Estate Appraisers, 1982), Table No. 5, Ordinary Annuities Changing in Constant Amount.

Converting income into a level equivalent has two steps:

1. Calculate the present value of the irregular income stream at the appropriate yield rate.

2. Calculate the level payment that has the same present value.

The second step can be accomplished by multiplying the present value by the instalment to amortize one factor at the yield rate. Another way to adjust the income to a level equivalent is to calculate a factor that, when multiplied by the first year's income, results in the equivalent level income. When the income is forecast to change at a compound rate, the K factor can be used to adjust it to a level equivalent:

$$\text{Level income} = K \text{ factor} \times I_o$$

Of course, the calculation is also easily accomplished with any pattern of income using either a financial calculator or a computer.

Property Models

When both property value and income changes are expected to follow a regular or predictable pattern, one of the yield capitalization models for property valuation may be applicable. The common yield capitalization models employ a capitalization rate, R, which is also used in direct capitalization.

There is a difference, however, between direct capitalization and yield capitalization. In direct capitalization, R is derived directly from market data, without explicitly addressing the expected rate of return on capital or the means of recapture. In yield capitalization, R cannot be determined without taking into account the income pattern, the anticipated rate of return on capital, and the timing

> **property model**
> A short-cut formula to DCF analysis that converts a yield rate into a capitalization rate given certain specific patterns of income and a change in value over a projection period.

of recapture. This does not mean that yield capitalization procedures are not market-oriented. On the contrary, for some property types yield capitalization procedures may represent the most realistic simulation of decision making in the marketplace.

Real estate investors are greatly influenced by expectations of change in property values. When an investor looks forward to property appreciation as a component of the eventual investment yield, that investor is anticipating that the total yield rate will be higher than the initial year's expected rate of income, i.e., the overall capitalization rate. The total yield rate is a complete measure of performance that includes any property appreciation and increase in income or depreciation. The general formula for this relationship is:

$$Y = R + A$$

where Y is the yield rate, R is the capitalization rate, and A is the adjustment rate that reflects the total change or growth in income and value.

Thus, the capitalization rate for an appreciating property equals the total yield rate minus an adjustment for expected growth:

$$R = Y - A$$

Similarly, the capitalization rate for a depreciating property can be seen as the yield rate plus an adjustment for expected loss:

$$R = Y - (-A) \text{ or } R = Y + A$$

Because A is often expressed as a function of the total relative change in property income and value, the Greek letter delta (Δ) is used to denote change. To calculate A it is usually necessary to multiply Δ by a conversion factor, such as an annual sinking fund factor or an annual recapture rate, to convert the total relative change in income and value into an appropriate periodic rate of change. The symbol for the annualizer is a. The general formula for R may be expressed as:

$$R = Y - \Delta a$$

delta (Δ)
In mathematics, the symbol for percentage change.

conversion factor (a)
An element in yield and change formulas that converts the total change in capital value over the projection period into an annual percentage; varies with the pattern of the income stream and may be an annual sinking fund factor or an annual recapture rate; also called the *annualizer*.

where R is the capitalization rate, Y is the yield rate, Δ is the total relative change in income and value over the projection period, and *a* is the annualizer or conversion factor.

This general formula for the capitalization rate can be adapted and used with typical income/value patterns for the property as a whole or for any property components. In the general formula, R, Y, and Δ apply to the total property and are expressed without subscripts. However, if there is a possibility of confusing the total property with any of its components, subscripts should be used for clarification, e.g., R_O. Once the appraiser determines the appropriate capitalization rate, an indication of property value can be obtained by applying the following universal valuation formula:

$$\text{Value} = \text{Income} \div \text{Cap Rate or } V = I \div R$$

Level Income

Level Income with No Change in Value

When both income and value are expected to remain unchanged, a property may be valued by capitalization in perpetuity, which was explained in the discussion of income models. According to the general formula, $R = Y - \Delta a$, the capitalization rate (R) becomes the yield rate (Y) when there is no change in value because Δ equals zero.

Level Income with Change in Value

When level income with a change in value is projected over a period of n years, the general formula for R is adapted by substituting the sinking fund factor at rate Y over n years in place of the conversion factor *a*. For example, consider a commercial property that will generate a stable NOI of $25,000 per year for the next eight years. Total property appreciation of 40% is expected during this eight-year period because market rents are expected to exceed contract rents. The appraiser concludes that the appropriate yield rate is 11%. To solve this problem, the formula $R = Y - \Delta a$ is used with the sinking fund factor for 11% over eight years as a. The sinking fund factor is 0.084321, so R is calculated as follows:

$$R = 0.11 - (0.40 \times 0.084321) = 0.076272$$
$$\text{Value} = NOI \div R$$
$$\text{Value} = \$25{,}000 \div 0.076272 = \$327{,}774$$

Calculator steps are found in Appendix C.

Property models used in solving for value can also be used to manipulate or explain a given set of market data to determine other unknowns. For example, in the problem above only the NOI and rate of change or appreciation in property value are known. While DCF analysis may be used as proof of the solution, it is not feasible to apply DCF analysis to solve the problem. This is true because only the rate of appreciation is known from the market, and the dollar amount of the future reversion and the current present value are unknown and interdependent. This illustrates the most significant benefits of the property models, i.e., the ability to make value decisions based on broad trends as well as the ability to explain market behaviour.

Straight-Line (Constant-Amount) Changes in Income and Value

When income and value are expected to increase or decrease by fixed amounts per period according to the standard, straight-line pattern, property value can be estimated using direct capitalization with straight-line recapture. The general formula for the capitalization rate (R) can be adapted for use with the standard, straight-line income/value pattern by using the straight-line recapture rate as the conversion factor (a). The straight-line recapture rate is simply the reciprocal of the projection period. For example, if income is projected over a period of 25 years, the annual, straight-line recapture rate is 1/25, or 4%. Depreciation of 100% would indicate that the projection period is equal to the property's remaining economic life. The concept of a limited remaining economic life does not apply to appreciating properties, but 100% appreciation would indicate a projection period equal to the amount of time required for the pwroperty to double in value.

Classic Straight-Line Recapture

The straight-line capitalization procedure has historically been used to value wasting or waning assets, i.e., investments whose income is declining as their asset base wanes. This classic procedure has limited applicability due to its underlying expectations, but it should be thoroughly understood to ensure its proper use. The basis of the classic straight-line procedure is the expectation that capital will be recaptured in equal dollar amounts during the investment's economic life and that net income consists of a declining amount that represents the return of capital plus a declining return on the capital remaining in the investment. Total income, therefore, diminishes until the asset is worthless and all capital has been recovered.

The presumption that value and income will decline steadily is frequently inconsistent with market behaviour; nevertheless, the procedure has important uses. Straight-line recapture is appropriate whenever the projection of income and value in an investment corresponds with the expectations implicit in the procedure. Classic straight-line recapture is most easily understood when it is applied to an investment in a wasting asset such as a perishable structure, a stand of timber, or a mineral deposit. The procedure is inappropriate for valuing an investment in land or another asset that can sustain value indefinitely.

For example, consider an investment in a partial interest in real estate such as a leasehold in which all improvements must be written off during the term of the lease. If $50,000 is invested in a 10-year leasehold expected to earn 8% per year as a yield on capital, what flow of income to the investor would be required to return the entire amount of the investment on a straight-line basis during the 10-year period and, in addition, yield 8% per year to the investor?

Yearly recapture would be one-tenth of $50,000, or $5,000. The investor is entitled to a return on unrecaptured capital amounting to 8% of $50,000 in the first year, 8% of $45,000 in the second year, 8% of $40,000 in the third year, and so forth (see Table 23.1). The income flow starts at $9,000 the first year and drops $400 each year after that. The total income payable at the end of the tenth and final year would be $5,400, of which $5,000 would be the last instalment of the return of capital and the other $400 would be the interest due on the capital remaining in the investment during the tenth year. Thus, the investor achieves 100% capital recovery plus an 8% return on the outstanding capital, assuming non-level income.

Table 23.1: Periodic Return of and Return on Capital

End of Year	Invested Capital	Return of Capital	Return on Capital	Total Return	% of Previous Year's Invested Capital at 8%
0	$50,000	—	—	—	—
1	45,000	$5,000	$4,000	$9,000	18.00%
2	40,000	5,000	3,600	8,600	19.11
3	35,000	5,000	3,200	8,200	20.50
4	30,000	5,000	2,800	7,800	22.29
5	25,000	5,000	2,400	7,400	24.67
6	20,000	5,000	2,000	7,000	28.00
7	15,000	5,000	1,600	6,600	33.00
8	10,000	5,000	1,200	6,200	41.33
9	5,000	5,000	800	5,800	58.00
10	0	5,000	400	5,400	108.00

Note that the recapture rate amounts to 10% of the original investment and is simply the reciprocal of the economic life. Also, all income is presumed to be payable at the end of each year, and the yields are always computed at the end of the year on the amount of capital outstanding during the year. Based on the starting income, the capitalization rate in this example would be \$9,000/\$50,000, or 18%. The 18% capitalization rate could also be calculated by adding the 10% recapture rate to the 8% yield rate.

The straight-line capitalization procedure reflects some useful mathematical relationships:

first period return on investment = original value × yield rate
periodic change in value = original value × periodic rate of change
periodic change in income = periodic change in value × yield rate

When the decline in income and value reflects these relationships, the periodic rate of change is the recapture rate and the reciprocal of the recapture rate is the economic life.

Expanded Straight-Line Concept

The traditional concept of straight-line recapture can be expanded to remove some of its theoretical constraints and facilitate a broader range of practical applications. The expectation of a predictable decline in income can be expanded to include any predictable change, which allows the appraiser to consider growing assets as well as wasting assets. A predictable rate of change within the foreseeable future can also eliminate the need to consider the full economic life of a property. Although there are significant theoretical differences, the expanded straight-line concept corresponds mathematically to classic straight-line recapture.

Under both the expanded and classic straight-line concepts, changes in value and income are presumed to occur on a straight-line basis. The basic requirements for a satisfactory return on, and complete recovery of, invested capital are also preserved. However, the expanded concept does not require that capital be recaptured in annual instalments throughout the economic life of a property. Rather, the property could be resold for a predictable amount at some point during its economic life, thereby providing for partial or complete return of the invested capital at the time of resale.

The straight-line capitalization rate is simply a combination of the yield rate and the straight-line rate of change, which is expressed in the general formula $R = Y - \Delta a$, where Δ is the relative change in value in n periods and a is $1/n$. For example, consider a leasehold that will produce I_{LH} of \$19,000 the first year. This I_{LH} is expected to decline thereafter in the standard straight-line pattern and value is expected to fall 25% in 10 years. The anticipated income pattern must match up with the lease contract. To appraise the leasehold to yield 12%, use the formula $R_{LH} = Y_{LH} - \Delta_{LH} a$, where the subscript LH denotes the leasehold.

$R_{LH} = 0.12 - (-0.25 \times 0.1) = 0.145$
Value $= I_{LH} \div R$
Value $= \$19,000 \div 0.145 = \$131,034$

The classic and expanded straight-line concepts are popular because they are simple to use and do not require complex calculations. However, straight-line concepts have theoretical and practical limitations. The straight-line premise is not always a realistic reflection of investor expectations of changing income and value.

Exponential-Curve (Constant-Ratio) Changes in Income and Value

When both income and value are expected to change at a constant ratio, the capitalization rate can be determined using the general formula:

$$R = Y - \Delta a$$

where Δa is the relative change in value and income for one period. Thus, Δa can be replaced with the periodic compound rate of change (CR). The formula then becomes:

$$R = Y - CR$$

where Y is the yield rate per period and CR is the rate of change per period. An expected loss is treated as a negative rate of change, and the formula becomes:

$$R = Y - (\text{-CR})$$

or

$$R = Y + CR$$

If both income and value are expected to change at the same rate, the capitalization rate is expected to remain constant. Therefore, this pattern of growth or decline is sometimes referred to as the *frozen cap rate pattern*. For example, suppose an income-producing property is expected to produce NOI of $50,000 for the first year. Thereafter both NOI and value are expected to grow at a constant ratio of 2% per year. In other words, 2% is the expected ratio of the increase in income for any year to the income for the previous year. The ratio of the increase in value for any year to the value for the previous year is also 2%. To appraise the property to yield 11%, the formula is:

$$R_o = Y_o - CR_o$$
$$R_o = 0.11 - 0.02 = 0.09$$
$$\text{Value} = \$50,000 \div 0.09 = \$555,556$$

The elements in the above equation can be transposed so that:

$$Y_o = R_o + CR_o$$

The overall yield rate, therefore, is equal to the overall capitalization rate plus the periodic adjustment, provided the rate of change is anticipated to continue at the same rate into the foreseeable future. Property models based on an exponential pattern of change in income and value often reflect the thinking of investors in the market.

Variable or Irregular Income and Value Changes

When income and value are not expected to follow a regular pattern of change, the present value of a property can be obtained by applying the standard discounting formula separately to each projected benefit, including the final reversion. This is often done using discounted cash flow analysis rather than an income or property model. The next chapter provides examples of applications of discounted cash flow analysis.

Level-Equivalent Income

As noted previously, any pattern of income can be converted into a level-equivalent income. Therefore, the level income property model, $R = Y - \Delta a$, can be applied to solve for the value of any pattern of income once that income has been converted into its level equivalent. Suppose, for example, the appraiser is valuing a property with net operating income of $200,000, growing at 4% per year. If the value is expected to increase 15% over a five-year projection period ($\Delta_O = 15\%$) and the appropriate yield rate is 12%, the value can be calculated by first calculating the level-equivalent income and then dividing that income by an overall capitalization rate developed using the level income property model.

To calculate the level-equivalent income, first calculate the present value of the cash flows at the 12% yield rate:

Year	Net Income
1	$200,000
2	$208,000
3	$216,320
4	$224,973
5	$233,972

PV = $200,000(1.12)^{-1}$ + $208,000(1.12)^{-2}$ + $216,320(1.12)^{-3}$ + $224,973(1.12)^{-4}$ + $233,972(1.12)^{-5}$

Present value of the cash flows at j_1=12% is $774,096.
Calculator steps are shown in Appendix C.

CHAPTER 24

DISCOUNTED CASH FLOW ANALYSIS AND SPECIAL APPLICATIONS IN INCOME CAPITALIZATION

Discounted cash flow (DCF) analysis is appropriate for any pattern of regular or irregular income.[1] In many markets and for many property types, DCF analysis is the technique investors prefer. The proper application of DCF analysis identifies the market conditions investors are anticipating as of the date of value. DCF analysis is not a prediction by the appraiser. Basic computer technology makes DCF analysis a practical tool for everyday appraisal work.

APPLICABILITY OF DCF ANALYSIS

Discounted cash flow analysis can be used both to estimate present value and to extract a yield rate from a comparable sale. Generally, DCF analysis is used to solve for present value given the rate of return or for the rate of return given the purchase price. In typical appraisal work, the appraiser begins by developing detailed spread-sheets with computer software. These spreadsheets show itemized incomes, expenses, and cash flows year by year, or occasionally month by month, over the presumed period of ownership or another projection period that the market suggests. The cash flows, including the net resale price, are then discounted at a rate (or rates) to derive an indication of present value. In this way, the appraiser can account for all cash flows in and out of the real property interest being

> Discounted cash flow (DCF) analysis is a procedure in which a yield rate is applied to a set of income streams and a reversion to determine whether the investment property will produce a required yield given a known acquisition price. If the rate of return is known, DCF analysis can be used to solve for the present value of the property. If the property's purchase price is known, DCF analysis can be applied to find the rate of return.

[1] See 12.37 (2010 edition) of Canadian Uniform Standards of Uniform Appraisal Practise, which addresses criteria for proper DCF analysis as well as unacceptable practices.

appraised and estimate the timing of these cash flows so that the time value of money is properly recognized in the analysis.

Critics point out that projections not warranted by market evidence can result in unsupported market value indications and that the results of the analysis can change significantly due to even small changes in the projections. Other critics object to the uncertainty of forecasting financial results five or ten years into the future and cite this as a reason for not using or relying on the DCF technique. However, this argument ignores the reality of the real estate marketplace. Investors do make forecasts and rely on DCF analysis, particularly in regard to large, investment-grade, multi-tenant properties such as shopping centres and office buildings and properties with non-stabilized incomes such as new buildings undergoing lease-up.

When yield capitalization was first expanded in applications of the valuation process by L. W. Ellwood in the 1960s, there was initial confusion over mathematical processes and relationships that are now commonly understood. At first, many appraisers mistakenly believed that yield capitalization could only apply to long-term, dependable income streams. Ellwood held two positions that were considered novel at the time but were factual expressions of already accepted appraisal principles. First, he recognized that any form of capitalization was useless and potentially misleading unless the net income to be capitalized was accurately and supportably developed. Second, he established that the yield rate for capitalization should be the market yield rate that would relate that net income (over time) to market value. Ellwood believed that there were variations that could be used to test and understand market behaviour. For example, if the incomes including the reversion were expressed in a time frame as short as a five-year income statement, the effects of lesser uncertainty in the early property incomes and the greater uncertainty of the reversion amount could be mitigated in present value discounting processes. In capitalization, the contribution to present value decreases as time from the date of value increases, so greater weight is afforded to those "knowns" that are closest to the date of value. Although these processes required significant amounts of calculating time and the use of printed tables, modern practice of appraisers includes wide access to computer software that performs the calculations almost instantly. However, the use of software does not relieve the appraiser from understanding what is being performed by the computer.

In keeping with the principle of anticipation, market-supported forecasting is the essence of valuation. Hence, it must be approached in the same way that all market data extractions are accomplished, i.e., with diligent research and careful verification. Discounted cash flow analysis can only provide accurate results if the forecasts developed are based on accurate, reliable information. Unless a contractual level or patterned income is involved, most real estate incomes will vary from year to year. The ranges may increase over time, particularly with changes in business cycles or local property markets. It is most common for appraisers to develop a "stabilized" income stream, which may be level or some consistent rate of change, to represent a property's income for yield capitalization purposes. This practice follows common procedures applied by buyers and sellers, and should mirror their reasoning and behaviour.

FORECASTING

In making forecasts, an appraiser employs the same procedure applied by investors who use DCF analysis in their decision making. The procedural steps typically include forecasting income, vacancy, operating and capital expenses, and equity dividend (if appropriate) over ownership periods of five to fifteen years. In some markets and in some situations, ten years is cited as an average or standard projection period or typical ownership period; in others, the forecast period may be shorter or longer. When appropriate, debt service and after-tax cash flow may also be forecast. An appraiser also estimates the residual income from the sale of the property at the end of the forecast period.

> **forecasting**
> To estimate, calculate, or indicate in advance. Forecasts made by appraisers are based on past trends and the perceptions of market participants concerning the continuation of these trends and the realization of these perceptions in the future.

Typical forecast categories to be addressed in DCF analysis include the following:

- Current market rental rates, lease expiration dates, and expected rental rate changes
- Lease concessions and their effect on market rent
- Existing base rents and contractual base rent adjustments
- Renewal options
- Existing and anticipated expense recovery (escalation) provisions
- Tenant turnover
- Vacancy loss and collection allowance
- Operating expenses
- Net operating income
- Capital items including leasing commissions and tenant improvement allowances
- Reversion and any selling or transaction costs
- Discount rate(s)

APPLICATIONS

The two DCF analyses that follow concern a 10,000 square foot shopping centre. The first example provides an overview of the procedures used to forecast and discount cash flows into value. The second example shows how to extract a yield rate from a comparable sale.

Forecasting and Discounting Cash Flows into Value

The property being appraised is the leased fee interest in a small strip shopping centre consisting of five units of 2,000 square feet each. The following information is gathered for the DCF analysis:

- Market rents are currently $22.00 per square foot per year, and the appraiser's analysis of market rents over the past five years indicates that they have increased at a compound rate of 2.5% per year and that the market expects that pattern to continue.

- The lease on Store A will run for two more years at a rent of $1,825 per month. An interview with the tenant indicates that the tenant intends to renew the lease at the market rate when the lease expires.

- Store B has a 10-year lease with six years remaining. The rent is currently $3,223 per month and will increase at a rate of 5% per year or one-half the change in the Consumer Price Index (CPI), whichever is greater. The CPI is expected to increase 4% per year over the next five years.

- Stores C, D, and E were recently leased for 10 years. These leases and all new leases are set at market rent with provisions to keep the rents at market rates throughout the projection period.

- The landlord is responsible only for real estate taxes, exterior maintenance, management, and capital items. Tenants are responsible for all other expenses.

- Taxes are currently $7,000 per year. The tax assessor reviews and reassesses properties every three years. The subject property was reviewed one year ago and taxes are expected to increase by about $800 with each subsequent review.

Table 24.1: Five-Year DCF Analysis of a Shopping Centre

	Year 1	Year 2	Year 3	Year 4	Year 5	Year 6
Income						
Store A	$21,900	$21,900	$46,220	$47,380	$48,560	$49,780
Store B	38,676	40,610	42,640	44,772	47,011	49,362
Store C	44,000	45,100	46,220	47,380	48,560	49,780
Store D	44,000	45,100	46,220	47,380	48,560	49,780
Store E	44,000	45,100	46,220	47,380	48,560	49,780
Subtotal	$192,576	$197,810	$227,520	$234,292	$241,251	$248,482
Collection loss (0.5%)	$963	$989	$1,138	$1,171	$1,206	$1,242
Effective gross income	$191,613	$196,821	$226,382	$233,121	$240,045	$247,240
Expenses						
Taxes	$7,000	$7,000	$7,800	$7,800	$7,800	$8,600
Maintenance	2,400	2,640	2,880	3,120	3,360	3,600
Management	9,629	9,891	11,376	11,715	12,063	12,424
Replacement	0	30,000	0	0	0	0
Subtotal	$19,029	$49,531	$22,056	$22,635	$23,223	$24,624
Net cash flow	$172,584	$147,290	$204,326	$210,486	$216,822	$222,616

Net resale price (Year 6 net cash flow capitalized at a terminal capitalization rate of 7% less a sales expense of 3% of sale price) = $222,616/0.07 x 0.97 = $3,084,822

Present value is the PV of the cash flows plus the PV of the net resale price

$PV = \$172,584(1.11)^{-1} + \$147,290(1.11)^{-2} + \$204,326(1.11)^{-3} + \$210,486(1.11)^{-4} + \$216,822(1.11)^{-5} + \$3,084,822(1.11)^{-5}$

Present value of the cash flows and resale price at $j_1 = 11\%$ is $2,522,445.

Calculator steps are shown in Appendix C.

There is a market expectation that the change will probably remain the same over the next two reviews, i.e., the period of the income and expense analysis.

- General exterior maintenance, including cleanup and landscaping, costs $200 per month. This expense is expected to increase each year by $20 per month.

- Property management fees are set at 5% of the rents collected.

- A nominal collection loss of 0.5% of scheduled rent is anticipated.

- The roof should be replaced during the second year at a cost of $30,000 (see Table 24.1), but no other exterior repairs or replacements are expected during the projection period.

- Income for the sixth year of the investment is forecast to estimate the resale price of the property at the end of the five-year projection period. The income for Year 6 of this forecast is the income for the first year of operation under the new owner. The net resale price of the property in five years is expected to be approximately $3,085,000 (NOI for Year 6 capitalized at 7% less a sales expense of 3% of the sale price).

The appraiser has determined through diligent research that a leased fee yield rate of 11% is appropriate and is using the five-year discounted cash flow analysis shown in Table 24.1 to estimate the value of the leased fee estate ($2,522,445).

Extracting a Yield Rate from a Comparable Sale

In the subject property's market area, a 12,000 square foot strip shopping centre with four tenants was recently purchased for $817,000. Table 24.2 shows the buyer's projected income and expense data for the five-year expected holding period and for Year 6, which is used for the reversion calculation.

At the end of the five-year projection period, the investor expects to resell the property at a terminal capitalization rate of 6.4%, resulting in a forecast reversion of $948,672 ($60,715/0.064). To solve for a yield rate (in this case, an internal rate of return, or IRR), analysts use financial calculators and spreadsheet software. Calculator steps are in Appendix C.

Solving for the expected overall yield rate using a financial calculator and the cash flows shown in Table 24.3 produces a yield rate of 9.0% (rounded). As an additional check, other comparable sales could be analyzed and the resulting yield rates reconciled to provide additional market support for the overall yield rate estimate.

INVESTMENT ANALYSIS

In addition to developing an opinion of value or extracting a yield rate from comparable sales, analysts often use discounted cash flow analysis techniques to test the performance of real estate investments at a desired rate of return. Measures of investment performance include the following:

- Net present value
- Internal rate of return

Table 24.2: Buyer's Income and Expense Forecast

	Year 1	Year 2	Year 3	Year 4	Year 5	Year 6
Income						
Store 1	$10,000	$10,400	$10,816	$11,249	$11,699	$12,165
Store 2	17,676	18,210	18,888	19,453	19,941	20,835
Store 3	13,151	13,677	14,224	14,793	15,385	16,000
Store 4	19,726	20,515	21,348	22,189	23,077	24,000
Subtotal	$60,553	$62,802	$65,276	$67,684	$70,102	$73,000
Expenses						
Taxes	$6,600	$6,600	$6,600	$7,200	$7,200	$7,200
Maintenance	810	875	953	1,060	1,108	1,210
Management	3,020	3,133	3,256	3,374	3,515	3,625
Collection loss	300	257	243	240	264	250
Replacement	0	0	5,200	0	5,200	0
Subtotal	$10,730	$10,865	$16,252	$11,874	$17,287	$12,285
Net cash flow	$49,823	$51,937	$49,024	$55,810	$52,815	$60,715

Table 24.3: Projected Cash Flow in Each Year

Period	Cash Flow	
0	-$817,000	
1	$49,823	
2	$51,937	
3	$49,024	
4	$55,810	
5	$52,815	(cash flow)
	$948,672	(reversion)

IRR is the interest rate that equates the present value of the cash flows (+ reversion) with the initial investment

$-817,000 = \$49,823(1+IRR)^{-1} + \$51,937(1+IRR)^{-2} + \$49,024(1+IRR)^{-3} + \$55,810(1+IRR)^{-4} + \$52,815(1+IRR)^{-5} + \$948,672(1+IRR)^{-5}$

Calculator steps are shown in Appendix C. The yield on this investment is approximately 9%.

- Payback period
- Profitability index (or benefit/cost ratio)
- Time-weighted rate

Used alone, these measures are not perfect, but as a collection of tools they have proven their effectiveness. They reflect a common market understanding and are useful in typical real estate applications.

Net Present Value and the Internal Rate of Return

Net present value (NPV) and the internal rate of return (IRR) are two discounted cash flow models widely used to measure investment performance and develop decision-making criteria. Net present value (dollar reward) is the difference between the present value of all positive cash flows and the present value of all negative cash flows, or capital outlays. When the net present value of the positive cash flows is greater than the net present value of the negative cash flows or capital outlays, the investment exceeds the return requirements of the investor. If the reverse relationship exists, the investment is not considered feasible.

> Net present value (NPV) and the internal rate of return (IRR) are two discounted cash flow models widely used for measuring investment performance.

A net present value of zero indicates that the present value of all positive cash flows equals the present value of all negative cash flows or capital outlays. The rate of discount that makes the net present value of an investment equal zero is the internal rate of return. In other words, the IRR discounts all returns from an investment, including returns from its termination, to a present value equal to the original investment.

Applicability and Limitations of NPV

A number of decision rules for applying the NPV can be established. For example, suppose that a property with an anticipated present value of $1,100,000 for all investment returns over a 10-year projection period can be purchased for $1,000,000. If one investor's NPV goal is zero, this investment exceeds that criterion. It also meets a second investor's goal for an NPV of $100,000, but it would not qualify if the goal were $150,000.

> net present value (NPV)
> The difference between the present value of all expected investment benefits and the present value of the capital outlays:
>
> $$NPV = PV - CO$$
>
> internal rate of return (IRR)
> The annualized yield rate or rate of return on capital that is generated or capable of being generated within an investment or portfolio over a period of ownership.

Net present value does consider the time value of money, and different discount rates can be applied to different investments to account for general risk differences. However, this method cannot handle different required capital outlays. For example, it cannot differentiate between an NPV of $100,000 on a $1,000,000 capital outlay and the same NPV on a $500,000 capital outlay. Therefore, this technique is best used in conjunction with other measures.

A common example of the use of an NPV analysis is called a hurdle rate analysis. Some investors, particularly those involved in minerals property investments, use a stated yield rate, which is the minimum acceptable rate of return for that investor, to determine the extent to which a potential investment can exceed that minimum. If there is a surplus of NPV above zero to justify further attention, the investor can then spend the time and

> The IRR has notable limitations. Unusual combinations of cash flows may produce more than one IRR. The IRR must be viewed with suspicion when net cash flows to an investment at a zero rate of return have a negative cumulative value. A negative IRR may be interpreted as a rate of loss, but it is theoretically meaningless. Moreover, as a measure of return on invested capital, the IRR is not valid for investments that are "financed out" and require little or no equity capital.

resources to pursue a more precise estimate of potential investment yield if the investment otherwise appears to be worth the exercise.

Limitations and Pitfalls of the IRR

By understanding the limitations and pitfalls appraisers may encounter using the IRR, practitioners can avoid wasted effort and false conclusions. The search for a single IRR within a plausible range is not always successful. Unusual combinations of cash flows may produce strange results, and more than one IRR, or in rare cases no IRR, may be indicated.

More Than One IRR

Consider a real estate investment in which the investor puts down $2,300, borrows $10,000, and pays an effective rate of 10% interest only, with the principal to be repaid in a lump sum at the end of 10 years. The investor's net cash flows can then be tabulated as shown in Table 24.4.

The IRR for the net cash flows after financing can be obtained through graphic analysis. Net present values are calculated for even discount rates between 0% and 24% and plotted on a graph. Table 24.5 and Figure 24.1 indicate not one but two IRRs. Using a computer, the two IRRs are calculated as 4.50839% and 18.3931%.

Multiple rates like these are interesting theoretically, but it is difficult to accept more than one IRR as a useful measure of performance. In real estate investment analysis, the presence of multiple IRRs usually suggests that some other measure of performance would be more appropriate or that the cash flows or time frame should be adjusted to permit a more meaningful analysis. Close examination of the example presented here reveals some characteristics of the IRR that may not be apparent in more typical examples.

Negative Net Present Value at Zero Rate of Return

The cumulative value of the net cash flows in Table 24.4 is negative. Negative net cash flows total $4,300, while positive net cash flows total $4,000. Therefore, the net present value – i.e., the difference between the present value of expected benefits, or positive cash flows, and the present value of capital outlays, or negative cash flows – with no discounting or at a zero discount rate is -$300 (see Figure 24.1). This should be a warning sign to the analyst.

Under these conditions, the IRR cannot be positive unless the mixture of positive and negative cash flows over time is such that the net present value increases with increases in the discount rate until the net present value reaches zero. The preceding example illustrates this phenomenon. This type of reverse discounting is mathematically valid, but it is contrary to the practical notion of reducing net present value by increasing the discount rate. It is not surprising that the IRR in such cases is difficult to comprehend and of questionable use.

Negative IRR

If the net present value of an investment at a 0% rate of return is negative, a negative IRR may be indicated. The IRR is generally understood to be a positive rate of return,

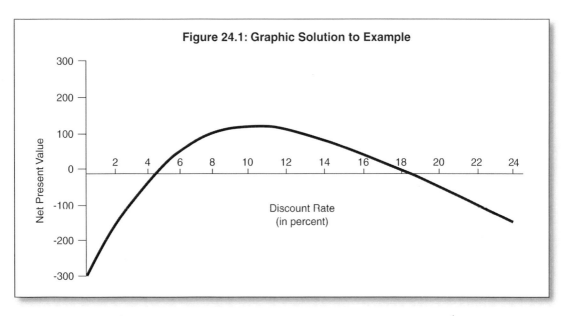

Figure 24.1: Graphic Solution to Example

Table 24.4: Net Cash Flow

Year	Cash Flow Before Loan/Interest	Loan	Interest	Net Cash Flow
0	−$12,300*	$10,000	$0	−$2,300
1	$2,000	0	−$1,000	$1,000
2	$2,000	0	−$1,000	$1,000
3	$2,000	0	−$1,000	$1,000
4	$2,000	0	−$1,000	$1,000
5	$1,000	0	−$1,000	0
6	$1,000	0	−$1,000	0
7	$1,000	0	−$1,000	0
8	$1,000	0	−$1,000	0
9	$1,000	0	−$1,000	0
10	$9,000†	−$10,000	−$1,000	−$2,000

* Initial cash outlay
† Income and proceeds from sale

but a negative IRR may be interpreted as a rate of loss. Any prospective rate of loss will normally discourage capital investment.

The concept of a negative IRR has theoretical, as well as practical, limitations. A glance at the IRR equation reveals that a negative IRR of 100% or more has no meaning because it involves division by zero or powers of a negative number.

Little or No Equity

Because the IRR is a measure of the return on invested capital, it cannot be used to measure the performance of opportunities that require no investment of capital. Some investments can be "financed out", i.e., financed with loans that cover 100% or more of the capital required. If the projected net cash flows are all positive, there is no IRR. Obviously, no discount rate can make a series of exclusively positive benefits equal zero.

Table 24.5: Table of Net Present Values

Discount Rate	Net Present Value
0	-$300
2	-$133
4	-$21
6	$48
8	$86
10	$99
12	$93
14	$74
16	$45
18	$8
20	-$34
22	-$80
24	-$128

The same rationale can be applied to investments calling for very low equity or a very small down payment in relation to expected returns. For example, a profit of $1 on an investment of $1 amounts to a 100% rate of return. A return of $100 on an investment of $1 indicates a 10,000% rate of return. When the investment is very small, slight changes in income can cause astronomical changes in the rates of return and loss. The IRR is an impractical yardstick for such investments.

However, the IRR can be a valuable indicator in analyzing investments that are 100% financed at the start and expected to operate at a loss for a period of time. In these arrangements, the early negative cash flows may represent a significant investment of equity capital and the prospective IRR may be the best measure of performance. It may also be useful to compare the prospective IRR before financing with an interest rate that reflects the cost of capital. The difference can be used as a measure of prospective leverage.

Reinvestment Concepts

The IRR is an internal rate of return on the capital within an investment. It can be applied to a single property or to an entire investment portfolio. No assumption is made as to how the investor actually employs funds that are received during the investment's ownership. The income from a real estate investment may be reinvested in another project at another rate of return, stored in a vault, or spent, but the IRR is not affected. Regardless of whether or not an investor in fact reinvests capital withdrawn from the investment at any given rate, a defining characteristic of the IRR is that it is mathematically consistent with reinvestment at the same rate of interest as the IRR. This establishes a framework for distinguishing between the IRR and other measures of investment return that make explicit reinvestment assumptions.

Incorporating a reinvestment concept in investment analysis is useful when viewing returns within the context of overall portfolio performance. It is a fundamental concept of finance that to calculate a rate of return on an investment and to compare two or more alternative investments, all of the dollars in an investment must be considered over the entire period of analysis. Although it is entirely possible to calculate the actual return in hindsight by considering what all of the dollars in the original investment produced over the analysis period, appraisers generally consider the opportunity returns of anticipated future cash flows. Income-producing real

> Reinvestment concepts may be incorporated into IRR analysis. The adjusted or modified IRR (AIRR or MIRR) is an IRR with reinvestment. The financial management rate of return (FMRR) is an IRR with a specified borrowing rate.

estate typically generates both a return on and a return of invested capital over the life of the investment. The rate of return can differ with various reinvestment assumptions. Although there are potential problems with the concept of an IRR, its use does not force any particular reinvestment assumptions, even though it is consistent with reinvestment at the same rate as the IRR.

As discussed above, one problem associated with the IRR is that certain situations can produce mathematical results that support more than one IRR. A different rate of return concept with a specific reinvestment premise is sometimes used to avoid multiple IRRs. Although the assumption of a specific reinvestment rate other than the IRR does not result in an IRR, reinvestment assumptions are applied to a number of rate of return concepts that make up a family of IRR-related measures.

IRR with reinvestment

The IRR with reinvestment is based on the expectation that all income from a project can be immediately reinvested at a specified rate and left to grow at that rate until the end of the investment projection period. The combined results of the investment's earnings and reinvestment are then reflected in one overall rate of return. The IRR with reinvestment traces the expected total performance of the original capital sum at work in more than one investment, rather than ignoring what occurs with portions of the capital investment during the ownership period. This measure can also be used to prevent multiple solutions to the IRR equation. The IRR with reinvestment is often called the adjusted or modified IRR (AIRR or MIRR). The formula for the MIRR appears in Appendix B.

IRR with a Specified Borrowing Rate

The IRR with a specified borrowing rate is another variation of the IRR that can be used to prevent multiple rates. It is sometimes called the IRR for investment or financial management rate of return (FMRR). The IRR for investment, or FMRR, specifies an interest rate for the borrowed funds needed during the period when the investment is producing negative cash flows. As with other rates derived from the IRR, it recognizes that there are different risks and potential earnings that apply to the funds withdrawn from the original investment. The concept of financial management is that lower rates will be paid on borrowings and risk management will permit the eventual earning of a higher rate of return on the real estate investment. And again, as is the case with other rates that assume reinvestment (AIRR and MIRR), to derive the FMRR the entire amount of invested capital is analyzed over the life of the real estate investment.

Applicability of IRR

The IRR can be as important to the real estate investor as the interest rate is to the mortgage lender; in fact, the two measures are equivalent. The interest rate on a mortgage is the same as the mortgagee's yield, or the IRR, unless points are involved. The IRR is not a meaningful measure of all investments and, even when it is meaningful, it is not the only possible criterion. It is, however, a fundamental and pure measure of a particular investment's financial performance. In general, the IRR is a valuable analytical tool if the decision maker understands its attributes and limitations and has access to complementary or alternative analytical techniques.

Other Measures of Performance

Popular alternative measures of financial performance or profitability include the following:

- Payback period
- Profitability index or benefit/cost ratio
- Time-weighted rate

These yardsticks do not measure performance or profit on the same scale or under the same assumptions as the IRR. Their usefulness depends on the situation and the user's preferences. Neither the IRR nor any alternative measure is superior in all situations.

Payback Period

As a measure of investment return, the payback period is seldom used alone; it is commonly employed in conjunction with other measures such as the internal rate of return. It is also sometimes used in evaluating risky investments overseas. The payback period (PB) is defined as the length of time required for the stream of net cash flows produced by an investment to equal the original cash outlay. The break-even point is reached when the investment's cumulative income is equal to its cumulative loss. The payback period can be calculated from either before-tax or after-tax cash flows, so the type of cash flow selected should be identified. The equation for payback period may be expressed as follows:

> **payback period (PB)**
> The length of time required for the stream of cash flows produced by the investment to equal the original cash outlay.

$$PB = \frac{\text{Equity Capital Outlay}}{\text{Annual Net Equity Cash Flows}}$$

Because real estate appraisers typically account for income as if received annually at the end of the period, full payback is not considered to occur until the end of a year. Therefore, the payback period indicated by the prior equation will be rounded up to a whole number, i.e., to the end of the next year.

This measure of performance is used by investors who simply want to know how long it will take them to recapture the dollars they have invested. In theory, an investment with a payback period of three years would be preferable to one with a payback period of five years, all else being equal. Similarly, an investment that will return the investor's capital in six years would be unacceptable to an investor who seeks investment payback within four years.

For an equity investment that is expected to produce equal cash flows, the payback period is simply the reciprocal of the equity capitalization rate (or equity dividend rate):

$$PB = \frac{1}{R_E \text{(rounded to the next whole number)}}$$

If annual equity cash flows are not expected to be equal over the payback period, the equity cash flows for each year must be added until the sum equals or exceeds the equity capital outlay; this point indicates the year in which payback occurs.

Although the payback period is simple and easily understood, it has a number of drawbacks. First, it measures the amount of time over which invested money will be returned to the investor, but it does not consider the time value of the money invested. A five-year investment payback for a $100,000 investment that pays $10,000 in Year 1 and $90,000 in Year 5 is not distinguished from the payback for a $100,000 investment that pays $90,000 in Year 1 and $10,000 in Year 5. The time value of money allows the first investment to use an additional $80,000 (i.e., the difference between the $90,000 paid in the second investment and the $10,000 paid in the first investment) from the second year through the fifth.[2]

Another shortcoming of the payback period is that it does not consider the effect of any gain or loss of invested capital beyond the break-even point and does not specifically account for investment risks. An investment with a three-year payback may be far riskier than another investment with a five-year payback, but the shorter period generally appears preferable. Thus, this measure of performance should only be used to compare investments with similar investment character- istics or in conjunction with other performance measures in carefully weighted applications.

> **profitability index (PI)**
> The present value of anticipated investment returns (benefits) divided by the present value of the capital outlay (cost); also called benefit/cost ratio.

Profitability Index

Although measuring the investment proceeds per dollar invested is too imprecise for general use, a refinement of this technique is commonly applied. The profitability index (PI), which is also called the benefit/cost ratio, is defined as the present value of the anticipated investment returns (benefit) divided by the present value of the capital outlay (cost). The formula is:

$$PI = \frac{\text{Present Value of Anticipated Investment Returns}}{\text{Present Value of Capital Outlay}}$$

This measure employs a desired minimum rate of return or a satisfactory yield rate. The present value of the anticipated investment returns and the capital outlay

---

[2]   A more sophisticated, but less popular, measure is the discounted payback period, which recognizes the time value of money at a stipulated rate of return. In this context the payback period is the amount of time required for the discounted benefits to equal the discounted costs.

are calculated using the desired rate as the discount rate. If, for example, the capital outlay is $12,300 and the present value of the benefits, based on a satisfactory yield rate of 10%, is $13,100, the profitability index is $13,100 ÷ $12,300 = 1.065.

A profitability index greater than 1.0 indicates that the investment is profitable and acceptable in light of the chosen discount rate. A profitability index of less than 1.0 indicates that the investment cannot generate the desired rate of return and is not acceptable. A profitability index of exactly 1.0 indicates that the opportunity is just satisfactory in terms of the desired rate of return and, coincidentally, the chosen discount rate is equal to the anticipated IRR. The discount rate used to compute the profitability index may represent a minimum desired rate, the cost of capital, or a rate that is considered acceptable in light of the risks involved.

This refined measure of investment performance considers the time value of money, which is not considered in calculating the proceeds per dollar invested. A profitability index is particularly useful in comparing investments that have different capital outlay requirements, different time frames for receiving income or other investment returns, and different risk characteristics. A profitability index is commonly used in conjunction with other measures, particularly with net present value. When combined, these measures provide special insights into the investments under consideration.

Time-Weighted Rate

A time-weighted rate is technically an average of all actual, instantaneous rates over a period of time. It is similar to the rate of growth for capital invested in a mutual fund in which all dividend income is automatically reinvested. The time-weighted rate, which is also known as the unit-method rate or the share-accounting rate, is used primarily to measure the performance of a portfolio manager, not the performance of the portfolio itself.

> **time-weighted rate**
> The average of all actual, instantaneous rates over a period of time; also called unit-method rate or share-accounting rate.

Analysis of Office/Retail Building Investment

The analysis that follows is based on a five-year forecast of the future benefits from an office/retail building investment.[3] Net operating income is estimated for each year. The proceeds from resale of the property at the end of the fifth year are also estimated.

Property Analysis

The subject property is a three-storey office/retail building with 32,100 square feet of gross building area. The property includes 10,000 square feet of floor rentable area on each level. The first level, at street grade, has 4,018 square feet of usable area allocated to a retail tenant, while the remainder of the building is designated office space. The building has a load factor of 12%.

---

[3]   The example was adapted from the Appraisal Institute seminar *Office Building Valuation: A Contemporary Perspective*.

The building was originally constructed about 20 years ago but underwent a major renovation about two years ago. Currently, three tenants occupy the building and a fourth tenant has just signed a lease. Lease terms and data on expenditures and other property and market information are described below and summarized in Tables 24.6, 24.7, and 24.8.

Rationale for the Forecast

The appraiser determines that investors in office buildings similar to the subject property typically forecast net operating incomes or equity dividends over a five-year projection period. To establish a purchase price that will justify the risk inherent in the proposed investment, the forecast net operating incomes or equity dividends and the reversion are discounted at an appropriate yield rate.

To simulate typical investor analysis, the appraiser:

1. Analyzes current income, establishes the market rent level for each tenant's space, and forecasts future income for each year of a six-year period based on existing leases, probable lease renewal at market rent, and expected vacancy experience.

2. Forecasts other income, including income from escalation clauses contained in existing leases and expected escalation provisions in new leases.

3. Forecasts future property expenses after analyzing historical operating expenses, the experience of competitive properties, and the current budget for the property.

4. Estimates net operating income.

5. Estimates property reversion.

6. Forecasts mortgage debt service based on existing or proposed financing terms.

7. When appropriate, estimates the equity dividends to be generated by the property in each year of the forecast projection period.

8. Estimates the reversionary benefits to be received at the end of the projection period (in this case, Year 6 NOI using an 8.5% terminal cap rate). If a significant capital expenditure or change in leases in the sixth year – i.e., the year of reversion – is expected, the projection period may be extended to incorporate this event. This will ensure that the analysis is not impacted by an unusual event in the reversion year used to calculate the reversion value.

In a market value appraisal, these steps must be applied in a manner that reflects the thinking of market participants. In this sample application, the appraiser begins by assembling pertinent information on comparable office buildings in the same market as the subject property. To verify the data, the appraiser interviews one of the participants, usually the buyer, to determine the NOI (or equity dividend) forecast associated with each comparable property.

Tenants and Leases in the Subject Property

Tenant 1, a national restaurant tenant, is located on the first floor (4,018 usable square feet). The tenant moved in shortly after renovation, two years ago, and pays $19.50 per square foot of rentable area per year on an absolute net lease basis fixed for 10 years. This tenant has the right to renew for another 10 years at market rent.

Tenant 2, a law firm, occupies 4,911 square feet of usable area on the first floor and 8,929 square feet of usable area on the second floor. This local firm has experienced considerable growth over the past 10 years and moved to the subject building to accommodate this expansion. The lease began two years ago and has a term of 10 years with an option to renew at market rents. The tenant is currently paying rent of $15.75 per square foot of rentable area per year, with an expense stop or cap of $4.25 per square foot. The lease calls for the rent to increase at 2% per year.

Tenant 3 occupies 6,786 square feet of usable area on the third floor and currently pays $17 per square foot of rentable area per year on a full-service basis. An escalation clause provides for a 3.5% annual increase in rent over the five-year term of the lease, which began two years ago. This tenant has an option to renew for another five years at a fixed rent of $20 per square foot of rentable area per year full service and has indicated an intention to do so. At the time of renewal, the owner will give the tenant a TI allowance of $4 per square foot of rentable area to refresh the space. The leasing commission at the time of renewal is estimated at 2% of total contract rent, and it is due in full at the time of renewal.

The remainder of the space, 2,143 square feet of usable area on the third floor, has just been leased to Tenant 4 at $16 per square foot of rentable area per year with rents escalating at 3.5% per year and an expense stop/cap of $5.00 per square foot. The term of the lease is seven years. For this new tenant, the TI allowance is $12 per square foot of rentable area and the leasing commission is 4% of total contract rent. The commission is paid during the first month.

Relevant lease information is summarized in Figure 24.2, and the rental income for each lease is forecast in Table 24.6.

Forecast Operating Expenses and Reimbursements

Property taxes are $64,000, due at the end of the year. Property insurance is $0.23 per square foot of rentable area per year. Property management is 4% of potential rental income. CAM is $3.25 per square foot of rentable area per year. Property taxes are expected to grow at 4% per year, while insurance and CAM are expected to grow at 3% per year over the next 10 years.

The total operating expenses for each year in the six-year projection period are calculated in Table 24.7, and operating expense reimbursements are summarized in Table 24.8.

Capital Expenses

At the time of renovation, the owners elected to postpone replacement of the roof. However, all parties agree that a capital expenditure of $40,000 will be required in four years to replace the roof. In Table 24.9, the leasing expenses and capital costs are listed in the year those charges are incurred.

Figure 24.2: Lease Abstracts

Tenant 1

Creditworthiness	High – national credit tenant
Usable area	4,018 sq. ft.
Rentable area	4,500 sq. ft.
Term of lease	10 years (began 2 years ago)
Escalation clause	None
Renewal clause	Yes – right to renew for another 10 years at market rental rate
Contract/forecast rent	$19.50 per sq. ft. per year (rentable)

Tenant 2

Creditworthiness	Good
Usable area	13,840 sq. ft.
Rentable area	15,500 sq. ft.
Term of lease	10 years (began 2 years ago)
Escalation clause	2% annually
Renewal clause	Yes – right to renew at market rental rate
Contract/forecast rent	$15.75 per sq. ft. per year (rentable)

Tenant 3

Creditworthiness	Average
Usable area	6,786 sq. ft.
Rentable area	7,600 sq. ft.
Term of lease	5 years (began 2 years ago)
Escalation clause	3.5% annually
Renewal clause	Right to renew for 5 additional years at $20 per sq. ft. per year fixed
Contract/forecast rent	3 years at $17 per sq. ft. per year, 5 years at $20 per sq. ft. per year (rentable)

Tenant 4

Creditworthiness	Average
Usable area	2,143 sq. ft.
Rentable area	2,400 sq. ft.
Term of lease	7 years
Escalation clause	3.5% annually
Renewal clause	None
Contract/forecast rent	$16 per sq. ft. per year (rentable)

Table 24.6: Summary of Forecast Contract Rental Income

	Year 1	Year 2	Year 3	Year 4	Year 5	Year 6
Tenant 1	$87,750	$87,750	$87,750	$87,750	$87,750	$87,750
Tenant 2	$244,125	$249,008	$253,988	$259,067	$264,249	$269,534
Tenant 3	$129,200	$133,722	$138,402	$152,000	$152,000	$152,000
Tenant 4	$38,400	$39,744	$41,135	$42,575	$44,065	$45,607
Potential rental income	$499,475	$510,224	$521,275	$541,392	$548,064	$554,891

Table 24.7: Total Forecast Operating Expenses Over Projection Period

	Year 1	Year 2	Year 3	Year 4	Year 5	Year 6
Property taxes	$64,000	$66,560	$69,222	$71,991	$74,871	$77,866
Property insurance	$6,900	$7,107	$7,320	$7,540	$7,766	$7,999
Property management	$19,979	$20,409	$20,851	$21,656	$21,923	$22,196
Common area maintenance	$97,500	$100,425	$103,438	$106,541	$109,737	$113,029
Total operating expenses	$188,379	$194,501	$200,831	$207,728	$214,297	$221,090

Table 24.8: Forecast Operating Expense Reimbursements Over Projection Period

	Year 1	Year 2	Year 3	Year 4	Year 5	Year 6
Tenant 1	$28,257	$29,175	$30,125	$31,159	$32,144	$33,163
Tenant 2	$31,454	$34,617	$37,888	$41,451	$44,845	$48,355
Tenant 3	$0	$0	$0	$0	$0	$0
Tenant 4	$3,070	$3,560	$4,067	$4,618	$5,144	$5,687
Total operating expense reimbursements	$62,781	$67,352	$72,080	$77,228	$82,133	$87,205

Table 24.9: Leasing Expenses and Capital Costs

	Year 1	Year 2	Year 3	Year 4	Year 5	Year 6
Leasing commissions	$11,949			$15,200		
Tenant improvements	$28,800			$30,400		
Capital costs				$40,000		

Other Research

Investors allocate a vacancy allowance of at least 5% of potential rental income even when a property is fully occupied. In addition, reversionary capitalization rates for similar buildings are approximately 8.5%, a five-year projection period is typically used for analysis, and selling expenses are estimated at approximately 3%. Investors are typically using a 9.5% discount rate when discounting the cash flows before debt service and the reversion to arrive at a value indication. Market participants are not deducting a replacement allowance before calculating net operating income (NOI or I_O), but they are deducting leasing fees and capital expenses before calculating cash flow before debt service. In Table 24.10, cash flow before debt service is calculated for each year of the six-year projection period.

Reversion Calculation

The resale price is forecast by applying an 8.5% overall capitalization rate to the net operating income for the year after the projection period (Year 6). The net operating income for Year 6 represents the projected income for Year 1 under the next owner. In this application, sales expenses of 3% are deducted to determine the net resale price:

$$\frac{6\text{th Year NOI}}{\text{Terminal Cap Rate}} = \text{Reversion Value}$$

$$\frac{\$393,261}{0.085} = \$4,626,600$$

Reversion Value	$4,626,600

$$\frac{<\text{Selling Expenses}>}{\text{Reversion}} = \frac{-138,798}{\$4,487,802}$$

The Investor's Desired Rate of Return

The value of the property can be estimated by calculating the present value of the net cash flow for each of the five-year projection period and adding the present value of the cash flow from the sale of the property in Year 6 (the net resale price). Suppose the typical investor requires an overall yield rate (YO) of 9.5%. At a 9.5% discount rate, the present value of the cash flow before debt service and reversion is $4,163,668 (see Table 24.10). This means that the investor would expect to earn a 9.5% rate of return if $4,163,668 is paid for the property.

Additional Analysis

Although property value was estimated by discounting the projected cash flow for each year rather than by applying a formula to develop an overall capitalization rate, an overall capitalization rate is implied in the solution. In this case the overall capitalization rate (R_O) for Year 1 is 8.38% ($348,903/$4,163,668). This overall capitalization rate is lower than the 8.5% capitalization rate applied to the estimated NOI for Year 6 to estimate the resale price.[4] The overall capitalization rate of 8.38% implied by a value estimate of $4,163,668 was calculated using the NOI for Year 1.

This example illustrates the need to carefully consider the anticipated pattern of NOI when selecting an overall capitalization rate to be used in direct capitalization or a property model for yield capitalization. Capitalization rates can differ significantly for properties with different patterns of NOI beyond the first year and different resale potential. The absence of a regular income pattern does not necessarily mean that detailed DCF analysis is the only method that should be considered. The appraiser may discover that one of the standard valuation models can be adjusted to compensate for a deviation from the regular income pattern or that a special valuation model can be devised to solve the problem at hand.

---

[4]   See D. Richard Wincott, "Terminal Capitalization Rates and Reasonableness", *The Appraisal Journal* (April 1991): 253-260. If, over the projection period, a substantial capital expenditure is allocated for the refurbishment or renovation of an aging property, R_N may equal or be less than R_O. Such a relationship between R_N and R_O is also likely when current income exceeds market levels or when current market conditions are inferior to those anticipated at the end of the projection period.

Table 24.10   Forecasting Cash Flows

	Year 1	Year 2	Year 3	Year 4	Year 5	Year 6
Income						
Tenant 1	$87,750	$87,750	$87,750	$87,750	$87,750	$87,750
Tenant 2	244,125	249,008	253,988	259,067	264,249	269,534
Tenant 3	129,200	133,722	138,402	152,000	152,000	152,000
Tenant 4	38,400	39,744	41,135	42,575	44,065	45,607
Potential rental income	499,475	510,224	521,275	541,392	548,064	554,891
Other income	0	0	0	0	0	0
Expense reimbursements						
Tenant 1	28,257	29,175	30,125	31,159	32,144	33,163
Tenant 2	31,454	34,617	37,888	41,451	44,845	48,355
Tenant 3	0	0	0	0	0	0
Tenant 4	3,070	3,560	4,067	4,618	5,144	5,687
Total expense reimbursements	62,781	67,352	72,080	77,228	82,133	87,205
Total income	562,256	577,576	593,355	618,620	630,197	642,096
Vacancy & collection allowance (5)%	24,974	25,511	26,064	27,070	27,403	27,745
Effective gross income	537,282	552,065	567,291	591,550	602,794	614,351
Operating expenses						
Property taxes	64,000	66,650	69,222	71,991	74,871	77,866
Property insurance	6,900	7,107	7,320	7,540	7,766	7,999
Property management	19,979	20,409	20,851	21,656	21,923	22,196
Common area maintenance	97,500	100,425	103,438	106,541	109,737	113,029
Total operating expenses	188,379	194,591	200,831	207,728	214,297	221,090
Net operating income	**348,903**	**357,474**	**366,460**	**383,822**	**388,497**	**393,261**
Leasing commissions	11,949			15,200		
Tenant improvements	28,800			30,400		
Capital costs				40,000		
Cash flow before debt service	**$308,154**	**$357,474**	**$366,460**	**$298,222**	**$388,497**	

Present value is the PV of the cash flows plus the PV of the reversion value of $4,487,802

$$PV = \$308,154(1.095)^{-1} + \$357,474(1.095)^{-2} + \$366,460(1.095)^{-3} + \$298,222(1.095)^{-4} + \$388,497(1.095)^{-5} + \$4,487,802(1.095)^{-5}$$

Present value of the cash flows and reversion at $j_1 = 9.5\%$ is $4,163,668.

Calculator steps are shown in Appendix C.

CHAPTER 25

RECONCILING VALUE INDICATIONS

In the valuation process, an appraiser usually applies more than one approach to value, and each approach typically provides a different indication of value. If two or more approaches are used, the appraiser must reconcile the value indications. Moreover, several value indications may be derived in a single approach. In the direct comparison approach, for example, the analysis of each comparable sale produces an adjusted sale price, which is an indication of value for the subject property. The various units of comparison applied to sales may also produce different value indications, e.g., apartment properties may be analyzed in terms of price per unit or price per room, and office buildings in terms of price per square foot of gross building area (GBA) or price per square foot of rentable area. In an analysis of income, different indications of value can result from applying income multipliers to specific types of income, directly capitalizing net income, and discounting cash flows.

The appraiser resolves multiple value indications derived within a single approach as part of the application of that approach. In addition, after all necessary approaches are applied, the appraiser resolves the multiple indications provided by each approach. Resolving the differences among various value indications is called reconciliation. Although the result of the final reconciliation process is usually the ultimate value conclusion, the reconciliation analysis may indicate that more research is needed or that new analyses must be performed. For example, reconciliation may reveal conflicts or unresolved questions. Thus, reconciliation provides an integral quality control assessment of the valuation process prior to the final opinion of value and also helps identify key factors that must be cited and explained, or explained further, in the appraisal report.

> **final opinion of value**
> The range of values or single dollar figure derived from the reconciliation of value indications and stated in the appraisal report.

Table 25.1: Questions Asked in Reconciling Value Indications

Regarding the direct comparison approach:
- Is there an adequate number of sales?
- Are the sales comparable?
- Are there prior sales of the subject property that need to be analyzed?
- Is there market support for the adjustments that were made?
- Were those factors that could not be supported by quantitative adjustment dealt with adequately using qualitative analysis in the reconciliation?
- Is the range of adjusted sale or unit prices within the range exhibited in the market?
- Are the conclusions of the approach consistent with the conclusions in the other approaches?

Regarding land valuation:
- Is there an adequate number of sales?
- Are the sales comparable?
- Is there market support for the adjustments that were made?
- Were those factors that could not be supported by quantitative adjustment dealt with adequately using qualitative analysis in the reconciliation?
- Is the range of adjusted sale or unit prices within the range exhibited in the market?

Regarding the cost approach:
- Is the land value well supported?
- Are the cost estimates reliable and market-based?
- Do the cost estimates account for all of the costs?
- Are the sales used to extract depreciation from the market reliable?
- Were physical, functional, and external depreciation estimated accurately?
- Are the conclusions of the approach consistent with the conclusions in the other approaches?

Regarding the income approach:
- Is there an adequate number of rental comparables?
- Are the rental properties comparable?
- Is there market support for the adjustments that were made?
- Were those factors that could not be supported by quantitative adjustment dealt with adequately using qualitative analysis in the reconciliation?
- Is there historical expense information available? If so, how reliable is it?
- Do the owner's income and expense statements include all income?
- Do the owner's income and expense statements include all expenses?
- Do the owner's income and expense statements include any expenses that are not typical?
- Are the expense projections in line with market estimates?
- Is there market support for the capitalization method?
- Is there market support for the capitalization or discount rate?
- Does the method of capitalizing income reflect market patterns?
- Are the conclusions of the approach consistent with the conclusions reached in the other approaches?

The final value opinion does not simply represent the average of the different value indications derived. No mechanical formula is used to select one indication over the others; rather, final reconciliation relies on the proper application of appraisal techniques and the appraiser's judgment. Table 25.1 illustrates the types of questions an appraiser asks when reconciling value indications within the approaches to value.

FINAL RECONCILIATION

In the final reconciliation, the appraiser reconsiders the entire appraisal, making sure that the data available and the analytical techniques and logic applied have led to consistent judgments. The appraiser checks the data to ensure that it is authentic, pertinent, and sufficient. The value definition, the identified property rights, and the qualifying conditions imposed are carefully reconsidered to ascertain whether the procedures used in the analysis specifically address each of these items. The appraiser examines the differences in the conclusions derived from the various approaches, applies tests of reasonableness to these primary conclusions, and resolves any inconsistencies.

> In final reconciliation, the appraiser reexamines the entire appraisal to confirm consistent application of the approaches applied (comparables used and adjustments calculated), the highest and best use conclusions upon which each approach is based, the defined value estimated in each approach, and the real property interests being appraised.

At this stage of the valuation process, the appraiser asks a variety of questions:

- Is the effective age of the property used in the cost approach consistent with the physical condition reported?

- Is the same physical condition assumed in making adjustments to rent comparables, expense comparables, and sales comparables in the income and direct comparison approaches?

- Are the results of all the approaches consistent with the appraiser's conclusion of highest and best use?

- Do the indications derived from the approaches applied reflect the same defined value? For example, a value indication derived from income capitalization that is higher than an indication based on the cost approach may or may not include a non-realty or business enterprise value component.

- Are the property rights appraised consistent throughout the appraisal? If the subject is the leased fee interest and the income approach is based on leased fee income, do the values indicated by the direct comparison and cost approaches also reflect the value of the leased fee interest?

- Is the market area analysis consistent with the direct comparison, income, and cost approaches? If values are increasing and there is good demand indicated in the neighbourhood description section of the report, is that description consistent with the market conditions illustrated in the application of the approaches to value?

All mathematical calculations should be checked, preferably by someone other than the person who performed them originally. Significant errors can lead to incorrect value indications, but even minor errors can diminish the client's confidence in the appraisal. Finally, the logic employed throughout the valuation process should be scrutinized, and the appraiser should ask these additional questions:

> Appraisal judgment and proper application of appraisal techniques are critical in final reconciliation.

- Do the approaches and methods applied consider all the available data and systematically lead to meaningful conclusions that relate directly to the intended use of the appraisal?

- Does the appraisal provide the information required to solve the client's problem? For example, if the client wants to establish a depreciation basis to compute income tax, does the appraisal allocate separate values to the improvements and the land? A client who contemplates remodelling will want information on the costs and benefits of this plan. If the client is considering whether to accept an offer to purchase, the appraiser must adequately analyze the terms of the proposed contract.

RECONCILIATION CRITERIA

Re-examining an appraisal helps ensure its accuracy, its consistency, and the logic leading to the value indications. An appraiser relies more on professional experience and judgment in reconciliation than in any other part of the valuation process. The appraiser weighs the relative significance, applicability, and defensibility of each value indication and relies most heavily on the approach that is most appropriate to the nature of the appraisal problem.

Reconciliation requires appraisal judgment and a careful, logical analysis of the procedures that lead to each value indication. Appropriateness, accuracy, and quantity of evidence are the criteria with which an appraiser forms a meaningful, defensible final opinion of value.

Appropriateness

The appropriateness of an approach to the intended use of the appraisal is usually directly related to property type. For example, an appraisal to develop an opinion of the market value of a 30-year-old community shopping centre will ordinarily employ procedures associated with the income approach, such as the derivation of an income multiplier, net income capitalization, or the discounting of cash flows. The cost approach might not be useful in valuing obsolete improvements, but it may be useful in an analysis of highest and best use to determine whether demolition of all or part of the improvements is appropriate. Where income data is scarce, in a market dominated by owner-occupants, the direct comparison approach can be used to obtain value information on a property.

> The appraiser uses reconciliation criteria to form a meaningful, defensible, and credible final value conclusion. The appropriateness of the approaches, the accuracy of the data and calculations, and the quantity or sufficiency of the evidence presented are considered relative to the specific appraisal problem.

Although the final value opinion is based on the approach or approaches that are most applicable, the final value opinion need not be identical to the value produced by the most applicable approach. If two approaches are applicable, the final opinion of value may be closer to one value indication than to the other. For example, the value indication derived from the income approach may be lower than the value indication derived from the direct comparison approach. If market participants are primarily interested in income-earning potential, the final opinion of value may be closer to the conclusion derived from the income approach than from direct comparison. However, if the property is an owner-occupied dwelling, the direct comparison approach would likely be of primary relevance.

Accuracy

The accuracy of an appraisal is measured by the appraiser's confidence in the accuracy of the data and the adjustments made to each comparable property analyzed. For example, how confident is the appraiser of the adjustments made to each cost comparable, each sale comparable, and each rent comparable? Similarly, how reliable is the data supporting depreciation and cost estimates, estimates of income and expenses, and the capitalization rate selected? An appraiser may have more confidence in the accuracy of the data and calculations used in one approach than in another.

The number of comparable properties, the number of adjustments, and the gross and net dollar amounts of adjustments may suggest the relative accuracy of a particular approach. If a large number of comparable properties are available for one approach and they seem to suggest a reasonably uniform pattern of market activity, greater accuracy may be indicated and the appraiser may place more reliance on this approach. For example, if there are many rental properties competitive with the appraised property, an appraiser may be able to extract current income, expense, and capitalization rate data from these properties and attribute greater accuracy and confidence to the income approach. If the appraiser finds several recently developed properties similar to the property being appraised, comparable data supporting land values and development costs may lend authority to the cost approach. Recent sales of similar properties may provide the data needed to estimate accurate unit values by direct comparison.

Quantity of Evidence

Appropriateness and accuracy affect the quality and relevance of the value indication derived from a comparable sale or an approach. Although these criteria are considered separately in reconciliation, both must be studied in relation to the quantity of evidence provided by the market data. Even if the data analyzed is accurate, if data is scarce the value conclusion may lack support.

For example, consider an appraiser who is attempting to extract an overall capitalization rate from three comparable sales. The properties are considered appropriate in terms of their physical and locational characteristics and the similarity of

> confidence interval
> In statistics, the specification of a zone within a population, based on a sample mean and its standard error, within which the true mean most probably lies.

the transactions. The available data for each sale is verified and considered reliable, and it appears that each comparable sale could produce an accurate estimate of the overall capitalization rate. However, the available data for one comparable property includes a detailed capital budget and an operating statement of the property's expenses and income for the preceding three years. The data on the two other comparable properties is less detailed. Only total gross and net income data for three years is available for one comparable property; for the other, detailed data is available for only one year. Because more data is available for the first comparable property, the appraiser will have greater confidence in the capitalization rate obtained from this sale than in the rates obtained from the other two sales.

In statistical terms, the confidence interval in which the indicated value lies may be narrowed by adding data to the statistical sample. Regardless of the quantity of evidence available, the appraiser is responsible for providing a market-supported value opinion consistent with the definition of value used in the assignment.

FINAL OPINION OF VALUE

In an appraisal report, the final opinion of value may be stated as a single figure, as a range of values, or in relation to a benchmark amount, e.g., "not more than" or "not less than". Traditionally an opinion of value is reported as a single dollar amount, i.e., a point estimate. A point estimate is required for many purposes:

- Real estate taxation
- Calculating depreciation deductions for income tax
- Estimating compensation in casualty, liability, and expropriation cases
- Determining value-based rent
- Making property transfer decisions

Because of legal or other requirements, most clients require a point estimate of value.

A point estimate should be rounded to reflect the degree of precision the appraiser can associate with the particular opinion of value. Often the manner in which the figure is rounded is a matter of convention, e.g., to two or three significant digits. For example, if the final value estimate is a six-digit number, the figure will likely be rounded to the nearest thousand or ten thousand dollars; if it is a seven-digit number, it will likely be rounded to the nearest ten thousand or hundred thousand dollars.

Even a rounded figure may imply greater precision than is warranted. Because an appraised value is an opinion, it implies a range in which the property value may fall. That value range usually reflects the range of value conclusions derived from two or more approaches, but the final value opinion need not fall within this range. For example, an appraiser may report an opinion of value of $9,400,000 to represent a conclusion drawn from two approaches with preliminary indications of $9,390,000 and $9,380,000. In this case, the conclusion of $9,400,000 is not statistically

---

The final opinion of value may be stated as a single figure (point estimate), as a range of value, or in relation to a benchmark amount, e.g., "not more than" or "not less than".

point estimate
A final value indication reported as a single dollar amount. A point estimate is typically regarded as the most probable number, not the only possible number, and is often required for revenue and compensation purposes.

rounding
Expressing an amount as an approximate number, i.e., exact only to a specified decimal place. An appraisal conclusion may be rounded to reflect the level of precision associated with the value opinion.

derived. It is outside the range indicated by the two approaches, but it may reasonably reflect the market value of the property based on the two approaches given other supporting evidence analyzed in the reconciliation process. In addition to the point value estimate, the appraiser might report the value range as "between $9,300,000 and $9,400,000".

> **range of value**
> In final reconciliation, the range in which the final market value opinion of a property may fall; usually stated as a variable amount between a high and low value limit.
>
> **probability range**
> The confidence level associated with a specific value opinion or set of value opinions.

When reporting a range, the appraiser indicates that the most probable value is no lower than the low end and no higher than the high end of the range. A wide range may be of no use to a client, but a narrow range may imply precision that is not warranted. When provided with a value range, clients or intended users might see the extreme that suits their purposes as a virtual guarantee. Accordingly, appraisers must take care to report their final value conclusions in a manner that does not mislead clients and intended users.

Separate from a range of value, an appraiser may report a probability range to suggest the confidence level associated with the opinion of value given an adequate amount of data to apply statistical analysis. The evidence considered in each approach should allow for such variation. For example, an appraiser may consider a more aggressive and a less aggressive market rent schedule for a proposed shopping centre. Different capitalization rates may be applied to the two income streams along with different discount rates and income multipliers. Any value differences resulting from the higher and lower projected rents in the income approach should be correlated with different levels of risk-related entrepreneurial incentive in the cost approach.

CHAPTER 26

THE APPRAISAL REPORT

The conclusions reached by appraisers in valuation analysis are communicated to the client in an appraisal report. An appraisal report may be written or oral. Most clients request written reports. Regardless of whether the appraisal report is written or oral, it leads the reader from the definition of the appraisal problem through analysis and relevant descriptive data to a specific conclusion. In a self-contained or summary appraisal report, the appraiser must present facts, reasoning, and conclusions clearly and succinctly. The length, type, and content of appraisal reports are dictated by the intended use and purpose of the appraisal, the nature and complexity of the problem to be solved, and (most importantly) the information needs of the intended user (or users).

PROFESSIONAL STANDARDS FOR APPRAISAL REPORTS

Each analysis, opinion, or conclusion that results from an appraisal must be communicated in a manner that is meaningful to the intended user and will not be misleading. Members of the Appraisal Institute of Canada are required to conduct their appraisal activities in compliance with the requirements of the Canadian Uniform Standards of Professional Appraisal Practice (CUSPAP). Appraisal Institute members must also adhere to the organization's Code of Professional Conduct and Code of Ethics.

The Foreword to the Canadian Uniform Standards of Professional Appraisal Practice states, "A member of the Appraisal Institute of Canada must develop and communicate his or her analysis, opinions and advice in a manner that will be meaningful to the client, that will not be misleading in the marketplace and that will be in compliance with these standards." The Appraisal Standard of CUSPAP sets forth the requirements for reporting an appraisal of real property. These are generally performance-related, for as the Practice Notes state, "These Standards do not dictate the form, format or style of reporting. These are functions of the needs of users and appraisers. The substantive content of a report determines its compliance."

However, the definitions section of the Standards provides guidance on the terminology that can apply to the report of an appraiser.

Appraisal Report: types include:

- Narrative – comprehensive and detailed
- Short Narrative – concise and briefly descriptive
- Form – a standardized format combining check-off boxes and narrative comments

The formal format requirements within the Standards do not extend beyond this definition. The Practice Notes provide further guidance, as discussed later in this chapter.

TYPES OF REPORTS

An appraisal report may be oral or written.[1] Written communications may be form or narrative reports. Usually a report is presented in the format requested by the intended user. However, even if a client asks for a report that does not include detailed documentation, the appraiser must undertake the analysis required by the assignment as set by the scope of work. In such a case, all material, data, and working papers used to prepare the appraisal are kept in the appraiser's file. Although the appraiser may never need to provide written substantiation for an opinion that is submitted in abbreviated form, he or she may be asked to explain or defend the opinion at a later time.

The extent of file documentation depends on the type of report prepared. A less detailed report will require more file documentation, while a more detailed report will require little external documentation. At one end of the spectrum is the narrative type of appraisal report, which includes detailed descriptions of the data, reasoning, and analyses used to arrive at the value conclusion. The short narrative appraisal report typically contains much less of this information, with additional support in the appraiser's files. At the other extreme is form appraisal report formats that contain some, but not all, of the descriptive information gathered in the appraiser's analysis; additional information is typically retained in the appraiser's files.

The discussion of some topics may be less extensive in reports that are less than a narrative appraisal report, but the report still must conform to CUSPAP and contain sufficient information to lead the reader to the appraiser's conclusions. The appraiser who prepares an oral report of an appraisal must keep all notes and data on file, along with a complete synopsis of the analysis, conclusions, and value opinion.

Oral Roporto

An appraiser may make an oral report when the circumstances or the needs of the intended user do not permit or warrant a written report. Expert testimony presented in an examination-for-discovery, a deposition, or in court is considered an oral report. In other situations, oral reports are communicated to the intended user in person or by telephone. Canadian Uniform Standards require that, to the extent that it is

---

[1]   An appraisal report sent to a client via e-mail or some other electronic medium qualifies as a written appraisal report.

both possible and appropriate, each oral real property appraisal report, including expert testimony that addresses value, must comply with the Appraisal Standard Rules.

Each oral report must include the underlying bases of the appraisal, especially any extraordinary assumptions or hypothetical conditions used. After communicating an oral report, the appraiser must keep on file all notes and data relevant to the assignment so that if asked at a later date (i.e., any time during the required record retention period), the appraiser could produce a report that would meet the requirements for an appraisal report suited for the intended user and the intended use.

This work file should include summaries of any oral reports or testimony, or a transcript of testimony, including the appraiser's signed and dated certification. Canadian Uniform Standards require that a work file must be in existence prior to and contemporaneous with the issuance of an oral (or written) report. The written summary of an oral report must be added to the work file within a reasonable time after the issuance of the oral report. The organization and composition of the appraiser's work file may vary so long as the file contents are retrievable by the appraiser during the required record retention period. The work file can reference information that is located elsewhere, e.g., stored electronically on a computer, in another file, or at some other location.

oral report
A report that is transmitted orally.

written appraisal report
Any written communication of an appraisal, appraisal review or appraisal consulting service that is transmitted to the client upon completion of an assignment (Dictionary of Real Estate Appraisal, 5th Edition).

written report
The results of a valuation communicated to a client in writing, which includes electronic communication. Written reports may be detailed narrative documents containing all pertinent materials examined and analyses performed to arrive at a value conclusion, or abbreviated narrative documents, including periodic updates of value, forms used by governmental and other agencies, or letters to clients. (IVS).

Written Reports

Form Reports

Form reports often meet the needs of financial institutions, insurance companies, and government agencies. They are required for the purchase and sale of most homes and for the related mortgage financing. Because these intended users review many appraisals, using a standard report form is efficient and convenient. When a form is used, those responsible for reviewing the appraisal know exactly where to find each category or item of data in the report. By completing the form, the appraiser ensures that no item required by the reviewer is overlooked. The Appraisal Institute of Canada has developed standardized forms for reporting an appraisal, which incorporate suggestions from

form report
An appraisal report presented on a form, such as those required by financial institutions, insurance companies, and government agencies. The reporting requirements for form reports, which are the same as for other types of reports, are set forth in the Appraisal Standard of the Canadian Uniform Standards of Professional Appraisal Practice. The form appraisal report entails a standardized format combining check-off boxes and narrative comments.

narrative report
A written report presented in narrative style.

users of appraisal reports.[2] Appendix 1 shows a Residential Appraisal Report form with the appropriate certification and limiting conditions.

Form reports, like all appraisal reports, must comply with the Appraisal Standard of CUSPAP. Due to their abbreviated and standardized nature, forms typically do not address all of the information required by professional standards for the variety of property types and appraisal requirements. To meet the needs of users of appraisal services and for standards compliance, appraisers usually need to provide supplemental information on form appraisal requirements.

RESPONSIBILITY FOR SIGNING AN APPRAISAL REPORT

1. A member signing a report assumes responsibility for the entire report including technical assistance in the form of factual information that is collected by an assistant. Technical assistance is not significant professional assistance unless it involves analysis, opinions and conclusions;

2. If the certification bears only one signature, then that individual is responsible for the entire report;

3. Members must disclose in the certification, any significant professional assistance in the preparation of the report;

4. Members must disclose in the certification, any significant consulting assistance in the preparation of the report;

5. If the certification bears the signature of the member and employer/supervisor/prime contractor, then both individuals are responsible for the entire report;

6. If the certification bears the signature of two or more members as joint authors, then each is responsible for the entire report, and a member cannot cosign a report with a student or non-member;

7. Another person with authorization may sign the certifying member's name, unless contrary to the law of the relevant jurisdiction.

CUSPAP, 11.13

NARRATIVE APPRAISAL REPORTS

The narrative appraisal report, the most elaborate and detailed format for reporting appraisal conclusions, gives appraisers the opportunity to support and explain their opinions and conclusions fully and to convince the reader of the soundness of the final opinion of value. In preparing a narrative appraisal report, the appraiser should keep descriptive sections separate from analysis and interpretation. Factual and descriptive data is usually presented in early

> A narrative appraisal report generally has four parts (introduction, premises of the appraisal, presentation of data, and analysis of data and conclusions) and an addenda.

---

[2]   Discussions of form reports and related issues regularly appear in Canadian Property Valuation, a quarterly publication of the Appraisal Institute of Canada. For an in-depth discussion of appraisal form reports, see the following guidebooks: Mark Rattermann, *Using the Individual Condominium Unit Appraisal Report Forms: Fannie Mae Form 1073 and Exterior-Only Form 1075* (Chicago: Appraisal Institute, 2006); Mark Rattermann, *Using Residential Appraisal Report Forms: URAR 2005 (Form 1004) and Exterior Inspection (Form 2005)* (Chicago: Appraisal Institute, 2005); and Mark Rattermann, *Using the Small Residential Income Property Appraisal Report (Fannie Mae Form 1025/Freddie Mac Form 72)* (Chicago: Appraisal Institute, 2006). The discussions pertain to forms that are different from, but similar to forms in common use in Canada.

sections of the report so that subsequent analysis and interpretation may refer to these facts and indicate how they influence the final opinion of value. Repetition and unnecessary duplication should be avoided, but the presentation of data may depend on the nature and length of the report.

The research presented in a well-prepared appraisal report can be detailed, and the report should exhibit logical organization and sound reasoning. These basic attributes are enhanced by good composition, a fluid writing style, and clear expression. An appraiser should avoid the use of technical jargon and slang. To communicate with the reader effectively, the contents of the report should be set forth as succinctly as possible.[3]

The appraiser may not be present when the report is reviewed or examined, so the report is his or her representative. A good report creates a favourable impression of the appraiser's professional competence. The following suggestions may help appraisers make a good impression:

- The paper, cover, and binding of the report should be of good quality.

- The size and style of the type used should be attractive and readable. Graphics such as photographs and charts should be carefully prepared. The style of headings and subheadings should be appropriate to the subject matter.

- Ideally, illustrations should be integrated within the text or presented on pages that face the material being discussed. For example, a photograph of the subject property may be placed on the page facing the identification of the property. A neighbourhood map could be included on a page facing the neighbourhood description to show the location of the subject property. Charts and graphs should be presented where they are discussed, but illustrations that are not directly related to the narrative should be placed in the addenda.

- The contents of the report should be presented in clearly labelled sections that are identified in the table of contents.

General Outline

Narrative appraisal reports will vary in content and organization, but they all contain certain elements. Essentially, a narrative appraisal report follows the order of steps in the valuation process.

Most narrative appraisal reports have four major parts. The contents of each section may be formally divided with subheadings or presented in a continuous narrative. In either case, the major divisions of the report should be identified with individual headings. The four basic parts of a report are the introduction, the premises of the appraisal, the presentation of data, and the analysis of data and conclusions. Many reports have a fifth section, the addenda, which includes supplemental information and illustrative material that would interrupt the text. The organization of narrative reports varies, but the outline in Figure 26.1 can be used as a general guide.

---

[3]   For further discussion of effective appraisal report writing, see: Larry Dybvig, Steven Thair, Michael Grover; *Handbook of Disclosure Guidelines*, Appraisal Institute of Canada 1996. Also see Alan Blankenship, *The Appraisal Writing Handbook* (Chicago: Appraisal Institute, 1998).

Figure 26.1: General Outline of Narrative Appraisal Report

Part One – Introduction
   Title page
   Letter of transmittal
   Table of contents
   Certification
   Summary of important conclusions

Part Two – Identification of the Appraisal Problem and Scope of Work
   Identification of type of appraisal and type of report
   Identification of the client
   Identification of any intended user(s) other than the client
   Statement of intended use
   Identification of the subject property
   Identification of property rights appraised
   Type and definition of value
   Effective date of opinion of value
   Extraordinary assumptions and hypothetical conditions
   General assumptions and limiting conditions
   Scope of work

Part Three – Presentation of Data
   Legal description
   Identification of any personal property or other items that are not real property
   History, including prior sales and current offers or listings
   Market area, city, neighborhood, and location data
   Land description
   Improvement description
   Taxes and assessment data
   Marketability study, if appropriate

Part Four – Analysis of Data and Conclusions
   Highest and best use of the land as though vacant
   Highest and best use of the property as improved
   Land value
   Cost approach
   Direct comparison approach
   Income approach
   Reconciliation and final opinion of value
   Estimate of exposure time
   Qualifications of the appraiser

Addenda
   Detailed legal description and title information, if not included in the presentation of data
   Detailed statistical data
   Leases or lease summaries
   Other appropriate information
   Secondary exhibits

The arrangement of items in this outline is flexible and can be adapted to almost any appraisal assignment and any type of real property. In practice, this outline would be adapted to the particular requirements of the assignment and to suit the personal preference of the appraiser and, more importantly, the client and other intended users, if any. Appraisals of certain types of property may require revisions in or additions to the basic framework presented here.

Part One – Introduction

Title Page

The title page lists the property address, the date of value, the name and address of the appraiser, and the name and address of the client.

Letter of Transmittal

The letter of transmittal formally presents the appraisal report to the client. It should be drafted in proper business style and be as brief as the character and nature of the assignment permit. A suitable letter of transmittal may include the following elements:

- Date of letter and salutation
- Street address of the property and a brief description, if necessary
- Statement identifying the interest in the property being appraised
- Statement that the property inspection and all necessary investigation and analyses were made by the appraiser
- Reference that the letter is accompanied by an appraisal report of a specified number of pages and identification of the type of appraisal and report format
- Type of value developed in the appraisal report
- Effective date of the appraisal
- Opinion of value[4]
- Any extraordinary assumptions and hypothetical conditions
- Appraiser's signature

Table of Contents

The various sections of the report are customarily listed in order in the table of contents. The major divisions of the report and any subheadings used in the report should be shown here.

---

[4]   Detaching of the letter of transmittal from the report can mislead the intended user of the report. If the appraiser deems it appropriate to include the opinion of value or another conclusion in the letter of transmittal, the conclusion should be qualified with a statement such as the following:

This letter must remain attached to the report, which contains n pages plus related exhibits, in order for the value opinion set forth to be considered valid.

See CUSPAP, Appraisal Standard

Certification

The certification usually follows the final opinion of value and must be signed by the appraiser. The certification states that the appraiser has personally conducted the appraisal in an unbiased, objective manner in accordance with CUSPAP.

Whether the certification is included as part of the introduction or presented on a separate, signed page, certification is important because it establishes the appraiser's position, thereby protecting both the appraiser's integrity and the validity of the appraisal. An appraiser who signs any part of the report, including the letter of transmittal, must also provide a signed certification and accept responsibility for the content of the report. See Figure 26.2 for an example.

Figure 26.2: Certification

CUSPAP 7.28 requires that each written real property appraisal report contain a signed certification that is similar in content to the following:

Re: (Property Identification)

I certify to the best of my knowledge and belief that:

- The statements of fact contained in this report are true and correct;
- The reported analyses, opinions, and conclusions are limited only by the reported assumptions and limiting conditions, and are my personal impartial, and unbiased professional analyses, opinions, and conclusions;
- I have no (or the specified) present or prospective interest in the property that is the subject of this report, and no (or the specified) personal interest with respect to the parties involved;
- I have no bias with respect to the property that is the subject of this report or to the parties involved with this assignment;
- My engagement in and compensation for this assignment were not contingent upon developing or reporting predetermined results, the amount of the value estimate, or a conclusion favouring the client;
- My analyses, opinions and conclusions were developed, and this report has been prepared, in conformity with the Canadian Uniform Standards;
- I have the knowledge and experience to complete the assignment competently;
- No one provided significant professional assistance to the person(s) signing this report. (If there are exceptions, the name of each individual providing significant professional assistance and the extent of that assistance must be stated.);
- As of the date of this report the undersigned has fulfilled the requirements of The Appraisal Institute of Canada Continuing Professional Development Program for members;
- The undersigned is (are all) members in good standing of the Appraisal Institute of Canada.
- I did not (did) personally inspect the subject property of the report;
- Based upon the data, analyses and conclusions contained herein, the market value of the interest in
- the property described, as at (insert date), is estimated at (insert value);

Signature and date of certification.

(If more than one person signs, this certification must clearly specify which individuals did and which individuals did not make a personal inspection of the appraised property.)

Summary of Important Conclusions

When an appraisal report is long and complex, a summary of the major points and important conclusions in the report may be useful. Such a statement, which is sometimes called an executive summary, is convenient for readers of the report and allows the appraiser to stress the major points considered in reaching the final opinion of value. The following list indicates the type of material that is frequently included in a summary. However, all of the following items do not apply to every appraisal assignment:

- Brief identification of the property
- Identification of the type of appraisal and report format
- Any extraordinary assumptions or hypothetical conditions
- Determinations of the highest and best use of the land as though vacant and of the property as improved
- Age of improvements
- Land value opinion
- Value indication from the cost approach
- Value indication from the direct comparison approach
- Value indication from the income approach
- Final opinion of defined value

Part Two – Identification of the Appraisal Problem and Scope of Work

Identification of Type of Appraisal and Report Format

The report type is often stated.

Identification of the Client

The report is usually addressed to the client, i.e., the person who engages the appraiser. As explained earlier in the text, the client can be a single person or entity or a number of people acting in concert.

Identification of Intended User(s) Other Than the Client

The client is not necessarily the only person (or entity) who will read the report. The appraiser is also responsible to report conclusions and analyses in a manner that is clear and understandable to all intended users identified at the onset of the assignment. As part of the scope of work decision, the appraiser determines who qualifies as an intended user of the report. The report must identify the intended user, by name or type.

Statement of Intended Use

The appraiser explains the intended use of the appraisal in the report so that the client and any other intended users understand the appraiser's intent.

Identification of Subject Property

A complete legal description is commonly used to identify the subject property. Depending on the nature of the subject property, the appraiser may need to provide more or less detail to identify the subject property clearly. For example, a parcel of raw land may need to be identified by a detailed metes and bounds description whereas an existing home might be identified simply by a street address.

Identification of Property Rights Appraised

In identifying the subject property, the appraiser must state and should define the particular rights or interests being valued. A thorough discussion is warranted in appraisals of partial interests in property or limited rights such as surface or mineral rights. Other encumbrances such as easements, mortgages, and special occupancy or use requirements should also be identified and explained in relation to the defined value to be developed.

Type and Definition of Value

An acceptable definition of the type of value being appraised is included in the report to eliminate any confusion in the mind of the intended user or other readers of the report. (Definitions of various types of value are cited in Chapter 2.) CUSPAP requires the appraiser provide the source of the value definition.

Effective Date

An appraisal assignment may call for one of the following:

- An opinion of current value
- An opinion of retrospective value
- An opinion of prospective value

It is essential to report the date as of which the value conclusion is applicable. Commonly, the date of the opinion of value and the date of the inspection of the property are the same for appraisals of current market value. If the date of inspection differs from the date of the opinion of value, then both dates should be noted in the appraisal report.

Extraordinary Assumptions and Hypothetical Conditions

When a value opinion is subject to an extraordinary assumption or hypothetical condition, the report must clearly and conspicuously disclose the assumption or condition and state that its use might have affected the value conclusion.

General Assumptions and Limiting Conditions

General assumptions and limiting conditions may be stated in the letter of transmittal, but they are usually included as separate pages in the report. These statements are used to help protect the appraiser and to inform the client and other intended users of the report. The general assumptions found in a typical appraisal report deal with issues such as legal and title considerations, liens and encumbrances, property management, information furnished by others (e.g., engineering studies, surveys),

---

Figure 26.3: Assumptions and Limiting Conditions

Appraisers need to consider the applicability of assumptions and limiting conditions on a case-by-case basis. Canadian Uniform Standards of Professional Appraisal Practice cites the following examples of ordinary assumptions and limiting conditions:

Ordinary Assumptions
- reliability of data sources;
- compliance with government regulations;
- normal financing;
- marketable title;
- no defects in the improvements;
- bearing capacity of soil;
- no encroachments
- diligence by intended user

Limiting Conditions:
- denial of liability to non-intended users and for any non-intended use;
- conclusions may be valid only at the date of valuation;
- responsibility denied for legal factors;
- fees for attendance at legal proceedings to be agreed;
- report must not be used partially;
- possession of report does not permit publication;
- disclosure for peer review may be required;
- cost estimates are not valid for insurance purposes;
- value conclusion is in Canadian dollars;
- denial of responsibility for any unauthorized alteration to a report;
- validity requires original signature.

(See Handbook of Disclosure Guidelines, AIC 1996 for a full inventory of clauses)

Examples of extraordinary assumptions and hypothetical conditions:
- an absence of contamination where such contamination is probable;
- the presence of municipal sanitary sewer where unknown or uncertain;
- assumed zoning where the zoning is unknown or uncertain;
- assumed condition where an interior inspection is not possible.

Other examples of extraordinary assumptions entail hypothetical conditions:
- repairs or improvements have been completed;
- execution of pending lease;
- rezoning has been achieved;
- an expropriation scheme is disregarded;
- a prospective appraisal; [see 6.2.5]
- municipal sanitary sewer when none is available;
- aggregate (retail) or bulk (wholesale) marketing of units.

concealment of hazardous substances on the property, and compliance with zoning regulations and local, provincial, and federal laws. General assumptions and limiting conditions are not boilerplate for the report, though they are typically applicable to nearly every assignment; neither are they a means of avoiding research or issues that are pertinent to a given appraisal.

Each assumption or condition must be reasonable and supportable in the context of the appraisal and must not conflict with the appraiser's other responsibilities such as the identification of extraordinary assumptions or hypothetical conditions. The appraiser must also be careful not to confuse assumptions and limiting conditions with scope of work issues. See Figure 26.3 for examples of typical general assumptions and limiting conditions.

Scope of Work

A clear and accurate description of the scope of work appropriate to the appraisal assignment protects those persons whose reliance on the appraisal may be affected. The level of detail and explanation must be sufficient to allow the intended users to understand the scope of work performed.

Providing a freestanding section of the appraisal report on the scope of work helps the intended user find the discussion of what the appraiser did to solve the appraisal problem, why the activities were performed, and who helped in the appraisal process. Alternatively, the scope of work of the assignment can be discussed throughout the appraisal report, within each respective section, e.g., discussion of the scope of the research and analysis of comparable sales in the direct comparison approach section of the report. Whether scope of work is discussed in its own section, throughout the appraisal report, or in some combination of the two, the requirement to be clear and not misleading remains.

Part Three – Presentation of Data

Legal Description

The subject real estate is identified so that it cannot be confused with any other parcel of real estate. This can be achieved by including a full legal description of the property in the report. When a copy of a registered subdivision plan is used, the appraiser may refer to it at this point and present it on a facing or following page. If the legal plan is unavailable, the appraiser can describe the property by name, specifying the side of the street on which the property fronts, the street address, and the lot and block number. A photograph of the subject property on a facing page can enhance this section of the report. Personal property and other items that are not real property should be identified if relevant to the assignment.

History

CUSPAP requires that current and prior sales of the subject property within three years of the effective date be analyzed and addressed in the appraisal report, along with agreements for sale, options, and listings within one year prior to the date of valuation.[5] Recent changes in the property's character of operating profile should be addressed.

Historical property data may include information on the following:

- Original assemblage, acquisition, or construction costs
- Expenditures for capital additions or modernization
- Financial data or transfers of ownership
- Casualty loss experience
- History and type of occupancy
- Developments or use of the property before construction of the present improvements
- Any other facts that may pertain to or affect the computations, estimates, or conclusions presented in the report

Market Area, City, and Neighbourhood Data

Relevant facts about the subject's market area, city, and neighbourhood should be discussed in the report. (The use and reliability of different types of data in relation to various classifications of property and specific appraisal problems are discussed in Chapters 4 and 8). An appraiser weighs and considers all pertinent factors in data analysis, but the report should discuss only the data that is found to be significant to the problem at hand. Both positive and negative aspects of the market area should be discussed. If the appraiser only provides data in support of either positive or negative factors, the report will be misleading, which is evidence of bias and a violation of the ethical rules for professional conduct.

If a considerable amount of supporting statistical data (e.g., population figures, cost of living indexes, family income figures) is needed, the appraiser may choose to incorporate this data into the body of the report or present it in tabular form on facing pages and reference it in the narrative. A separate section for market data is not needed in many reports. In fact, market data is often combined with neighbourhood data.

The amount of neighbourhood and location data required depends on the information needs of the intended user or users. For example, when an appraisal is prepared for an out-of-town client who is unfamiliar with the property and the community, it may be wise to include more community and neighbourhood data than a local client would need.

An appraiser should also note the presence of special amenities or detrimental conditions in the neighbourhood and provide reasons or data to support any conclusions about these factors. For example, if the appraiser states that the market area is growing, actual growth figures or building projections supporting that assertion should be included in the report. If a report states that a neighbourhood is in decline due to abnormal deterioration or poor maintenance, the appraiser might refer to specific properties that exhibit these detrimental conditions or use photographs to illustrate neighbourhood conditions.

---

[5] Tribunals and users of appraisal reports can be interested in sales and rental history regardless of when they occurred; the CUSPAP time requirements are minimum requirements.

Land Description

Pertinent facts about the subject site belong in the land description section. Land description involves three different aspects of the subject property's site:

- Physical characteristics
- Legal characteristics
- Economic characteristics

Physical Characteristics

Relevant physical site data may include descriptions of the following:

- The property's frontage, depth, site area, and shape
- Soil and subsoil conditions
- Utilities
- Any improvements that benefit or harm the site

In the land description section of an appraisal report, the appraiser should offer a conclusion as to the utility or adaptability of the site for existing or proposed improvements.

Legal Characteristics

When significant to the appraisal problem, zoning and private restrictions (such as easements) should be discussed in detail. The appraiser should provide sufficient land use data to help the reader understand the limitations that zoning regulations place on the use or development of the site. If the appraiser needs to explore the possibility of a zoning change, this analysis should also be addressed. Other existing public and private restrictions such as floodplain regulations, scenic easements, and wetland restrictions should be discussed and their effect on the utility and value of the property described.

Economic Characteristics

Economic characteristics of a property that may have an effect on its value and should be discussed in the appraisal report include the following:

- Real estate taxes
- Special assessments or development levies
- Facilities benefits districts or other public encumbrances affecting the site

These economic encumbrances differ from legal encumbrances such as easements and encroachments. The former are related to the governmental power of taxation whereas the latter arise from police power.

Improvement Description

In the description of improvements section, all building and improvement data relevant to the appraisal problem is presented and discussed. Although an appraiser considers and processes much data in the course of an appraisal, only significant property characteristics that influence the value conclusion are presented in the report. These characteristics may include the following:

- Actual and effective building age
- Building size
- Number and size of units
- Structural and construction details
- Mechanical equipment
- Physical condition
- Functional utility or inutility

Property information may be supported with drawings, photographs, floor plans, and elevations. If the description of structural details and mechanical equipment is long, an outline may be used in the body of the report to emphasize the important items.

Tax and Assessment Data

If relevant to the assignment analyses or conclusions, an appraiser should report current assessed values and ad valorem tax rates and include a calculation of the current annual tax load of the subject property in the appraisal report. An appraiser should also analyze existing assessment trends or prospective changes in tax rates. It may be appropriate to discuss the tax assessment or tax load on the subject in relation to the taxes on other properties, particularly if the difference is significant.

Marketability Study

In the appraisal of income-producing properties such as office buildings, shopping centres, and apartment buildings, a marketability study may be performed to find out how the subject property fits into the overall market in terms of rent levels and absorption rates. A marketability study is usually directly related to the conclusions presented in the appraisal report. Such a study may examine the following:

- The specific real estate market or submarket
- The supply of existing properties, e.g., inventory of space, construction trends, vacancy patterns, and absorption rates
- The demand forecast, e.g., projected expansion or shrinkage
- The current balance of supply and demand
- Competitive rent levels

Part Four – Analysis of Data and Conclusions

Market Analysis and Highest and Best Use

For an appraisal of market value, the appraisal report must address the highest and best use conclusion, including discussion of the effects on use and value of existing land use regulations, reasonably probable modifications of those regulations, economic supply and demand, the physical adaptability of the real estate, and market area trends, as outlined in Standards Rule 6.24 of CUSPAP. A discussion of the analyses leading to the highest and best use conclusion must also be provided in narrative appraisal reports.

The appraisal report must also present the conclusions of the appraiser's analysis of highest and best use of land as though vacant and highest and best use of the property as improved as dictated by the scope of work. That is, for appraisals of vacant land (or land valued as though vacant) the report must include the conclusion of highest and best use of the land as though vacant. The conclusion of the highest and best use of the property as improved must consider the possibilities of retaining, remodelling, or removing and redeveloping the improvements.

Ultimately the reported conclusion of highest and best use must answer this question: What would the most probable buyer of the subject property do with the property to maximize its value?

Land Value

If land is valued as though vacant, a section of the report must address this analysis. In the land value section, market data is presented along with an analysis of the data and reasoning that lead to the land value opinion. The factors that influence land value should be presented in a clear and precise manner and the narrative should lead the reader to the land value opinion.

Approaches to Value

An appraiser develops the approaches required to produce credible assignment results. The application of each approach is described and the factual data, analysis, and reasoning leading to the value indication are presented in the report.

If the intended users are not familiar with the mechanics of the three approaches to value, the appraiser should briefly explain the procedures applied. The extent of explanation required depends on the circumstances of the assignment and knowledge of the intended users. Simple statements that describe what is included in each of the three approaches (such as those provided in Figure 26.4) can help the reader better understand the report.

The three approaches are seldom completed independently. An appraisal is composed of a number of integrated, interrelated, and inseparable procedures that have a common objective: a credible opinion of value.

Reconciliation of Value Indications

CUSPAP requires reconciliation of the data within each approach as well as reconciliation of the approaches used. The reconciliation of value indications should lead the reader logically to the final opinion of value. The final opinion of defined value may be stated in many ways. The following is a simple example:

> As a result of my investigation and analysis, it is my opinion that the market value of the identified interest in the property, as of July 20, 2010, was: $400,000

Note that the date of the value opinion usually differs from the date of the report.

Exposure Time

Most market value definitions refer to exposure time. In an appraisal, the term means the estimated length of time the property interest being appraised would have been offered on the market before the hypothetical consummation of a sale at market value

---

Figure 26.4: Descriptions of the Approaches to Value

The approaches to value could be described in an appraisal report as follows:

In the direct comparison approach, properties similar to the subject property that have been sold recently or for which listing prices or offers are known are compared to the subject. Data from generally comparable properties is used and comparisons are made to demonstrate a probable price at which the subject property would sell if offered on the market.

In the cost approach, an estimated reproduction or replacement cost of the building and land improvements as of the date of appraisal is developed (including an estimate of entrepreneurial profit or incentive), and an estimate of the losses in value that have taken place due to wear and tear, design and plan deficiencies, or neighborhood influences is subtracted. An estimate of the value of the land is then added to this depreciated building cost estimate. The total represents the value indicated by the cost approach.

In the income approach, the rental income of the property is calculated and deductions are made for vacancy and collection loss and expenses. The prospective net operating income of the property is then estimated. To support this estimate, operating statements for the subject property in previous years and for comparable properties are reviewed. An applicable capitalization method and appropriate capitalization rates are developed and used in computations that lead to an indication of value.

Note that the description of the approaches to value may be more or less detailed depending on the level of detail required by the report format and the sophistication of the client.

---

on the effective date of the appraisal; a retrospective estimate based on an analysis of past events assuming a competitive and open market.

Exposure time is always presumed to have preceded the effective date of the appraisal. It may be expressed as a range, and should appear in that section of the report that presents the discussion and analysis of market conditions and with the final value conclusion. Exposure time is different for various types of real estate and under various market conditions. Rather than appear as an isolated estimate of time, it must refer to the property appraised, at the value estimated. The overall concept of reasonable exposure time encompasses not only adequate, sufficient, and reasonable time, but also adequate, sufficient, and reasonable marketing effort. The distinction between exposure time (i.e., past) and marketing time (i.e., future) must be made clear if the report refers to both.

Professional standards require that an opinion of exposure time accompany a market value opinion. The estimate needs to have a foundation in market analysis; in practice, exposure time can usually be estimated through reference to the sales time associated with the comparables used in the appraisal.

Qualifications of the Appraiser

The appraiser's qualifications may be included in the report as evidence of the appraiser's competence to perform the assignment. These qualifications may include facts concerning the following:

- Professional experience
- Educational background and training
- Business, professional, and academic affiliations and activities
- The types of properties appraised and the nature of the appraisal assignments undertaken

Misrepresentation of qualifications or presenting misleading information regarding qualifications would, of course, be a breach of professional ethics. The Ethics Standard of CUSPAP Ethics states, "It is unethical for a member to knowingly act in a manner that is misleading (4.2.3), to act in a manner that is fraudulent (4.2.4), to claim qualifications, including Continuing Professional Development credits, improperly (4.2.6)" and "to undertake an assignment lacking the necessary competence (4.2.7)."

Addenda

Depending on the size and complexity of the appraisal assignment, supplementary material may be added to the report to present information that would interrupt the narrative. The following items may be included in the addenda, if they have not already been incorporated into the body of the report:

- Plot plan
- Plans and elevations of buildings
- Photographs of properties referred to in the report
- City, neighbourhood, and other maps
- Charts and graphs
- Historical income and expense data
- Building specifications
- Detailed estimates of the reproduction or replacement costs of buildings
- Sales and listing data
- Leases and lease abstracts
- Marketability analysis data, e.g., information on construction trends, vacancy trends, and competitive rent levels

Appendix I: Residential Appraisal Report Form

RESIDENTIAL APPRAISAL REPORT

REFERENCE: .... FILE NO.: ....

CLIENT

CLIENT: ....
ATTENTION: ....
ADDRESS: ....
E-MAIL: ....
PHONE: ....   FAX: ....

APPRAISER

APPRAISER: ....
COMPANY: ....
ADDRESS: ....
E-MAIL: ....
PHONE: ....   FAX: ....

SUBJECT

NAME: ....
PROPERTY ADDRESS: ....   CITY: ....   PROVINCE: ....   POSTAL CODE: ....
LEGAL DESCRIPTION: ....
PURPOSE OF THE APPRAISAL: To estimate market value or ☐ Other ....
INTENDED USE OF THE APPRAISAL: ....
INTENDED USERS (by name or type): ....
REQUESTED BY: ☐ Client above   ☐ Other ....
THIS APPRAISAL REPORT REPRESENTS THE FOLLOWING VALUE: (if not current, see comments)   ☐ Current   ☐ Retrospective   ☐ Prospective
☐ Update of original report completed on ....   with an effective date of ....   File No. ....
PROPERTY RIGHTS APPRAISED: ☐ Fee Simple ☐ Leasehold ☐ Cooperative ☐ Condominium ☐ Strata Maintenance Fee: $ ....   ☐ See comments
IS THE SUBJECT A FRACTIONAL INTEREST, PHYSICAL SEGMENT OR PARTIAL HOLDING? ☐ No   ☐ Yes (if yes, see comments)
MUNICIPALITY AND DISTRICT: ....
ASSESSMENT: Land $ .... Imps $ .... Total $ ....   Assessment Date: ....   Taxes $ ....   Year ....
EXISTING USE: ....
OCCUPIED BY: ....
HIGHEST AND BEST USE OF SUBJECT PROPERTY: ☐ As Improved, or ☐ Other *Note: if highest and best use is not the existing use, or not the use reflected in the report, see additional comments.*

NEIGHBOURHOOD

NATURE OF DISTRICT:	☐ Residential	☐ Rural	☐ Commercial ☐ Industrial ☐
TREND OF DISTRICT:	☐ Improving	☐ Stable	☐ Transition ☐ Deteriorating ☐
BUILT-UP:	☐ Over 75%	☐ 25 - 75%	☐ Under 25% ☐
CONFORMITY Age:	☐ Newer	☐ Similar	☐ Older ☐
Condition:	☐ Superior	☐ Similar	☐ Inferior ☐
Size:	☐ Larger	☐ Similar	☐ Smaller ☐

AGE RANGE OF PROPERTIES: .... to .... years
MARKET OVERVIEW Supply: ☐ Good ☐ Average ☐ Poor
Demand: ☐ Good ☐ Average ☐ Poor
PRICE TRENDS: ☐ Increasing ☐ Stable ☐ Declining
PRICE RANGE OF PROPERTIES: $ .... to $ ....

SUMMARY: INCLUDES VALUE TRENDS, MARKET APPEAL, PROXIMITY TO EMPLOYMENT AND AMENITIES, APPARENT ADVERSE INFLUENCES IN THE AREA, IF ANY (e.g. railroad tracks, unkempt properties, major traffic arteries, Hydro facilities, anticipated public or private improvements, commercial/industrial sites, landfill sites, etc.)
....
....
....
....

SITE

SITE DIMENSIONS: ....
SITE AREA: ....   Source: ....
TOPOGRAPHY: ....
CONFIGURATION: ....
ZONING: ....
DOES EXISTING USE CONFORM TO ZONING? ☐ YES ☐ NO (see comments)
EASEMENTS: ☐ Utility ☐ Access ☐ Other ....

UTILITIES: ☐ Telephone ☐ Sanitary Sewer ☐ Septic System ☐ Municipal Water ☐ Well
☐ Natural Gas ☐ Storm Sewer ☐ Open Ditch
FEATURES: ☐ Paved Road ☐ Sidewalk ☐ Street Lights ☐ Gravel Road ☐ Curbs
☐ Cablevision ☐ Lane ☐
ELECTRICAL: ☐ Overhead ☐ Underground
DRIVEWAY: ☐ Private ☐ Mutual ☐ None ☐ Single ☐ Double
Surface: ....
PARKING: ☐ Garage ☐ Carport ☐ Driveway ☐ Street
LANDSCAPING: ☐ Good ☐ Average ☐ Fair ☐ Poor
CURB APPEAL: ☐ Good ☐ Average ☐ Fair ☐ Poor

COMMENTS: (includes any positive and negative features such as conformity with zoning, effects of known easements, known restrictions on title, such as judgments or liens, effects of assemblage, any known documentation of environmental contamination, etc.)
....
....
....
....

IMPROVEMENTS

CONSTRUCTION COMPLETE: ....   PERCENTAGE COMPLETE: ....
YEAR BUILT (estimated): ....   EFFECTIVE AGE: .... years   REMAINING ECONOMIC LIFE (estimated): .... years

FLOOR AREA ☐ Sq. M. ☐ Sq. Ft.   BUILDING TYPE: ....
MAIN ....   DESIGN/STYLE: ....
SECOND ....   CONSTRUCTION: ....
THIRD ....   BASEMENT: ....
FOURTH _____   BASEMENT AREA: .... ☐ Sq. M. ☐ Sq. Ft. .... % Finished
TOTAL _____   WINDOWS: ....
Source: ....   FOUNDATION WALLS: ....

ROOFING:
Condition: ☐ Good ☐ Average ☐ Fair ☐ Poor
EXTERIOR FINISH: ....
Condition: ☐ Good ☐ Average ☐ Fair ☐ Poor
UFFI APPARENT: ☐ Yes ☐ No ☐ Removed

BEDROOMS (#)   BATHROOMS (#)   INTERIOR FINISH: Walls Ceilings
☐ Large   ☐ 2-piece   ☐ Good   Drywall ☐ ☐
☐ Average   ☐ 3-piece   ☐ Average   Plaster ☐ ☐
☐ Small   ☐ 4-piece   ☐ Fair   Paneling ☐ ☐
   ☐ 5-piece   ☐ Poor   ☐ ☐
            ☐ ☐

CLOSETS: ☐ Good ☐ Average ☐ Fair ☐ Poor
INSULATION: ☐ Ceiling ☐ Walls ☐ Basement ☐ Crawlspace
Source: ....
PLUMBING LINES:
FLOOR PLAN: ☐ Good ☐ Average ☐ Fair ☐ Poor
BUILT-INS/EXTRAS: ☐ Garbage Disposal ☐ Central Air ☐ Swimming Pool ☐ Fireplace(s)
☐ Oven ☐ Air Cleaner ☐ Sauna ☐ Garage Opener ☐ Dishwasher
☐ Vacuum ☐ Solarium ☐ Security System ☐ Stove ☐ Whirlpool
☐ Skylights ☐ HR Ventilator ☐

FLOORING: ....
ELECTRICAL: ☐ Fuses ☐ Breakers
Estimated rated capacity of main panel: .... amps
HEATING SYSTEM: ....   Fuel type ....
WATER HEATER: Type ....
OVERALL INT. COND: ☐ Good ☐ Average ☐ Fair ☐ Poor

BASEMENT FINISHES/UTILITY: ....
GARAGES/CARPORTS: ....
DECKS, PATIOS, OTHER IMPROVEMENTS: ....
COMMENTS: (Building, appearance, quality, condition, services, extras, anticipated public or private improvements, etc.)
....
....
....

© APPRAISAL INSTITUTE OF CANADA   AIC FULL LEGAL 04/04

RESIDENTIAL APPRAISAL REPORT

ROOM ALLOCATION

LEVEL:	MAIN	SECOND	THIRD		BASEMENT
ENTRANCE					
LIVING					
DINING					
KITCHEN					
FULL BATH					
PART BATH					
BEDROOM					
FAMILY					
LAUNDRY					
OTHER					
TOTAL ROOMS					

COST APPROACH

SOURCE OF COST DATA: ☐ MANUAL   ☐ CONTRACTOR   ☐ OTHER

LAND VALUE: .... $ ....

	COST NEW	DEPRECIATED COST
BUILDING		
COST @ $	$	
GARAGE	$	$
BASEMENT FINISH		
	$	$
OTHER EXTRAS	$	$
	$	$
	$	$
	$	$
	$	$
TOTAL REPLACEMENT COST	$	
LESS: ACCRUED DEPRECIATION .... %	$	$
INDICATED VALUE	$	
VALUE BY THE COST APPROACH (rounded)	$	

NOTE: The construction cost estimates contained herein were not prepared for insurance purposes and are invalid for that use. The Cost Approach is not applicable when appraising individual strata/condominium type dwelling units.

DIRECT COMPARISON APPROACH

	SUBJECT	COMPARABLE NO. 1		COMPARABLE NO. 2		COMPARABLE NO. 3	
		Description	$ Adjustment	Description	$ Adjustment	Description	$ Adjustment
DATE OF SALE							
SALE PRICE	$	$		$		$	
LOCATION							
SITE SIZE							
BUILDING TYPE							
DESIGN/STYLE							
AGE/CONDITION							
LIVEABLE FLOOR AREA							

	Total	Bdrms	Baths		Total	Bdrms	Baths		Total	Bdrms	Baths		Total	Bdrms	Baths	
ROOM COUNT																
BASEMENT																
PARKING																

ADJUSTMENTS (Gross/Net)		%	% $	%	% $	%	% $
ADJUSTED VALUES		$		$		$	

CONCLUSIONS:

SALES HISTORY—ANALYSIS OF KNOWN CURRENT AGREEMENTS FOR SALE, PRIOR SALES, OPTIONS, LISTINGS OR MARKETING OF THE SUBJECT: (minimum of three years)

VALUE BY THE DIRECT COMPARISON APPROACH (rounded): $

EXPOSURE TIME

COMMENT ON REASONABLE EXPOSURE TIME:

RECONCILIATION

RECONCILIATION AND FINAL ESTIMATE OF VALUE:

AS A RESULT OF MY APPRAISAL AND ANALYSIS OF ALL APPLICABLE DATA AND RELEVANT FACTORS, IT IS MY CONCLUSION THAT THE MARKET VALUE OF THE INTEREST IN THE SUBJECT PROPERTY

AS AT .... (Effective Date of the Appraisal)   IS $ ....

THIS REPORT WAS COMPLETED ON: ....

© APPRAISAL INSTITUTE OF CANADA   AIC FULL LEGAL 04/04

RESIDENTIAL APPRAISAL REPORT

DEFINITIONS

DEFINITION OF MARKET VALUE: The most probable price which a property should bring in a competitive and open market as of the specified date under all conditions requisite to a fair sale, the buyer and seller each acting prudently and knowledgeably, and assuming the price is not affected by undue stimulus.

Implicit in this definition is the consummation of a sale as of a specified date and the passing of title from seller to buyer under conditions whereby: buyer and seller are typically motivated; both parties are well informed or well advised, and acting in what they consider their own best interests; a reasonable time is allowed for exposure in the open market; payment is made in terms of cash in Canadian dollars or in terms of financial arrangements comparable thereto; and the price represents the normal consideration for the property sold unaffected by special or creative financing or sales concessions granted by anyone associated with the sale.

(Source: Canadian Uniform Standards of Professional Appraisal Practice) *Note: If other than market value is being appraised, see additional comments.*

DEFINITION OF HIGHEST AND BEST USE: The reasonably probable and legal use of the property, that is physically possible, appropriately supported, and financially feasible, and that results in the highest value.

SCOPE

The scope of the appraisal encompasses the due diligence undertaken by the appraiser (consistent with the terms of reference from the client, the purpose and intended use of the report) and the necessary research and analysis to prepare a report in accordance with the Canadian Uniform Standards of Professional Appraisal Practice of the Appraisal Institute of Canada. The following comments describe the extent of the process of collecting, confirming and reporting data and its analysis, describe relevant procedures and reasoning details supporting the analysis, and provide the reason for the exclusion of any usual valuation procedures.

ASSUMPTIONS AND LIMITING CONDITIONS AND EXTRAORDINARY ITEMS

ORDINARY ASSUMPTIONS & LIMITING CONDITIONS
The certification that appears in this appraisal report is subject to the following conditions:
1. This report is prepared at the request of the client and for the specific use referred to herein. It is not reasonable for any other party to rely on this appraisal without first obtaining written authorization from the client, the author and any supervisory appraiser, subject to the qualification in paragraph 11 below. Liability is expressly denied to any person other than the client and those who obtain written consent and, accordingly, no responsibility is accepted for any damage suffered by any such person as a result of decisions made or actions based on this report. Diligence by all intended users is assumed.
2. Because market conditions, including economic, social and political factors change rapidly and, on occasion, without warning, the market value estimate expressed as of the date of this appraisal cannot be relied upon as of any other date except with further advice from the appraiser and confirmed in writing.
3. The appraiser will not be responsible for matters of a legal nature that affect either the property being appraised or the title to it. No registry office search has been performed and the appraiser assumes that the title is good and marketable and free and clear of all encumbrances including leases, unless otherwise noted in this report. The property is appraised on the basis of it being under responsible ownership.
4. The subject property is presumed to comply with government regulations including zoning, building codes and health regulations and, if it doesn't comply, its non-compliance may affect market value.
5. No survey of the property has been made. Any sketch in the appraisal report shows approximate dimensions and is included only to assist the reader of the report in visualizing the property.
6. This report is completed on the basis that testimony or appearance in court concerning this appraisal is not required unless specific arrangements to do so have been made beforehand. Such arrangements will include, but not necessarily be limited to, adequate time to review the appraisal report and data related thereto and the provision of appropriate compensation.
7. Unless otherwise stated in this report, the appraiser has no knowledge of any hidden or unapparent conditions of the property (including, but not limited to, its soils, physical structure, mechanical or other operating systems, its foundation, etc.) or adverse environmental conditions (on it or a neighbouring property, including the presence of hazardous wastes, toxic substances, etc.) that would make the property more or less valuable. It has been assumed that there are no such conditions unless they were observed at the time of inspection or became apparent during the normal research involved in completing the appraisal. This report should not be construed as an environmental audit or detailed property condition report, as such reporting is beyond the scope of this report and/or the qualifications of the appraiser. The author makes no guarantees or warranties, express or implied, regarding the condition of the property, and will not be responsible for any such conditions that do exist or for any engineering or testing that might be required to discover whether such conditions exist. The bearing capacity of the soil is assumed to be adequate.
8. The appraiser is not qualified to comment on environmental issues that may affect the market value of the property appraised, including but not limited to pollution or contamination of land, buildings, water, groundwater or air. Unless expressly stated, the property is assumed to be free and clear of pollutants and contaminants, including but not limited to moulds or mildews or the conditions that might give rise to either, and in compliance with all regulatory environmental requirements, government or otherwise, and free of any environmental condition, past, present or future, that might affect the market value of the property appraised. If the party relying on this report requires information about environmental issues then that party is cautioned to retain an expert qualified in such issues. We expressly deny any legal liability relating to the effect of environmental issues on the market value of the subject property.
9. The appraiser obtained information, estimates and opinions that were used in the preparation of this report from sources considered to be reliable and accurate and believes them to be true and correct. The appraiser does not assume responsibility for the accuracy of items that were furnished by other parties.
10. The opinions of value and other conclusions contained herein assume satisfactory completion of any work remaining to be completed in a good and workmanlike manner. Further inspection may be required to confirm completion of such work.
11. The contents of this report are confidential and will not be disclosed by the author to any party except as provided for by the provisions of the Canadian Uniform Standards of Professional Appraisal Practice ("The Standards") and/or when properly entered into evidence of a duly qualified judicial or quasi-judicial body. The appraiser acknowledges that the information collected herein is personal and confidential and shall not use or disclose the contents of this report except as provided for in the provisions of the Canadian Uniform Standards of Professional Appraisal Practice (the "Standards") and in accordance with the appraiser's privacy policy. The client agrees that in accepting this report, it shall maintain the confidentiality and privacy of any personal information contained herein and shall comply in all material respects with the contents of the appraiser's privacy policy.
12. The appraiser has agreed to enter into the assignment as requested by the client named in the report for the use specified by the client, which is stated in the report. The client has agreed that the performance of this appraisal and the report format are appropriate for the intended use.
13. Written consent from the author and supervisory appraiser, if applicable, must be obtained before any part of the appraisal report can be used for any purpose by anyone except the client and other intended users identified in the report. Where the client is the mortgagee, liability is extended to its insurer. Liability to any other party or for any other use is expressly denied regardless of who pays the appraisal fee. Written consent and approval must also be obtained before the appraisal (or any part of it) can be altered or conveyed to other parties, including mortgagees (other than the client) and the public through prospectus, offering memoranda, advertising, public relations, news, sales or other media.
14. If transmitted electronically, this report will have been digitally signed and secured with personal passwords to lock the appraisal file. Due to the possibility of digital modification, only originally signed reports and those reports sent directly by the appraiser, can be relied upon without fault.

Other:

EXTRAORDINARY ASSUMPTIONS & LIMITING CONDITIONS

An extraordinary assumption or limiting condition has been invoked in this appraisal report. ☐ YES ☐ NO   If yes, see attached addendum.

HYPOTHETICAL CONDITIONS

A hypothetical condition has been invoked in this appraisal report. ☐ YES ☐ NO   If yes, see attached addendum.

JURISDICTIONAL EXCEPTION

A jurisdictional exception has been invoked in this appraisal report. ☐ YES ☐ NO   If yes, see attached addendum.

CERTIFICATION

I certify that, to the best of my knowledge and belief:
1. The statements of fact contained in this report are true and correct.
2. The reported analyses, opinions and conclusions are limited only by the reported assumptions and limiting conditions and are my personal, impartial and unbiased professional analyses, opinions and conclusions.
3. I have no past, present or prospective interest or bias with respect to the property that is the subject of this report and no personal interest or bias with respect to the parties involved with this assignment, except as specified herein.
4. My engagement in this assignment is not contingent upon developing or reporting a predetermined result, upon the amount of value estimate, upon a direction in value that favours the cause of the client, upon the attainment of a stipulated result or the occurrence of a subsequent event.
5. My analyses, opinions and conclusions were developed, and this report has been prepared, in conformity with the Canadian Uniform Standards of Professional Appraisal Practice.
6. I have the knowledge and experience to complete this assignment competently. Except as herein disclosed, no other person has provided me with significant professional assistance in the completion of this appraisal assignment.
7. The Appraisal Institute of Canada has a mandatory Continuing Professional Development Program for all members. As at the date of this report, the requirements of this program have been fulfilled.

SUPERVISORY APPRAISER'S CERTIFICATION If a supervisory appraiser has signed this appraisal report, he or she certifies and agrees that "I directly supervised the appraiser who prepared this appraisal report and, having reviewed the report, agree with the statements and conclusions of the appraiser, agree to be bound by the appraiser's certification and am taking full responsibility for the appraisal and the appraisal report."

PROPERTY IDENTIFICATION

ADDRESS: CITY: PROVINCE: POSTAL CODE:

LEGAL DESCRIPTION:

AS A RESULT OF MY APPRAISAL AND ANALYSIS OF ALL APPLICABLE DATA AND RELEVANT FACTORS, IT IS MY CONCLUSION THAT THE MARKET VALUE OF THE INTEREST IN THE SUBJECT PROPERTY

AS AT   (Effective date of the appraisal)   IS $

APPRAISER	SUPERVISORY APPRAISER (if applicable)
SIGNATURE:	SIGNATURE:
NAME:	NAME:
DESIGNATION:	DESIGNATION:
DATE SIGNED	DATE SIGNED
DATE OF INSPECTION:	DATE OF INSPECTION:
LICENSE INFO (where applicable)	LICENSE INFO (where applicable)
NOTE: For this appraisal to be valid, an original or a password protected digital signature is required.	*NOTE: For this appraisal to be valid, an original or a password protected digital signature is required.*

ATTACHMENTS:
☐ ADDITIONAL SALES   ☐ EXTRAORDINARY ITEMS ADDENDUM   ☐ NARRATIVE ADDENDUM   ☐ PHOTO ADDENDUM   ☐ SKETCH ADDENDUM
☐ MAP ADDENDUM   ☐
☐

RESIDENTIAL APPRAISAL REPORT - ADDENDUM

CLIENT

CLIENT: ....
ATTENTION: ....
ADDRESS: ....
....
E-MAIL: ....
PHONE: ....   FAX: ....

APPRAISER

APPRAISER: ....
COMPANY: ....
ADDRESS: ....
....
E-MAIL: ....
PHONE: ....   FAX: ....

EXTRAORDINARY ITEMS ADDENDUM

EXTRAORDINARY ASSUMPTIONS & LIMITING CONDITIONS

An extraordinary assumption is a hypothesis, either supposed or unconfirmed, which, if not true, could alter the appraiser's opinions and conclusions (e.g. an absence of contamination where such contamination is possible, the presence of a municipal sanitary sewer where unknown or uncertain). An extraordinary limiting condition is a necessary modification or exclusion of a Standard Rule which must be explained and justified by the appraiser (e.g. exclusion of a relevant valuation approach.) The appraiser must conclude before accepting the assignment which involves invoking an Extraordinary Limiting Condition that the scope of the work applied will result in opinions and conclusions which are credible. Both must accompany statements of each opinion/conclusion so affected.

HYPOTHETICAL CONDITIONS

Hypothetical conditions may be used when they are required for legal purpose, for purposes of reasonable analysis or for purposes of comparison. Common hypothetical conditions include proposed improvements and prospective appraisals. For every Hypothetical Condition, an Extraordinary Assumption is required (see above). An analysis based on a hypothetical condition must not result in an appraisal report that is misleading or that relies on actions or events that would be illegal or improbable within the context of the assignment. Following is a description of each hypothetical condition applied to this report, the rationale for its use and its effect on the result of the assignment.

JURISDICTIONAL EXCEPTION The Jurisdictional Exception permits the appraiser to disregard a part or parts of the Standards determined to be contrary to law or public policy in a given jurisdiction and only that part shall be void and of no force or effect in that jurisdiction. The following comments identify the part or parts disregarded, if any, and the legal authority justifying these actions.

CHAPTER 27

APPRAISAL REVIEW AND APPRAISAL CONSULTING

The majority of appraisal assignments focus on market value and follow the procedures outlined in the valuation process. At some point in their careers, however, most appraisers will encounter an appraisal situation or receive a request for a valuation-related service outside their normal range of activities, many of which require specialized knowledge and skills. Some appraisers create profitable businesses out of these specialized assignments, but additional study and experience in these areas are required.

APPRAISAL REVIEW

According to the Canadian Uniform Standards of Professional Practice (CUSPAP), appraisal review is defined as the act or process of developing and communicating an opinion about all or part of an appraisal. The subject of an appraisal review assignment may be all or part of an appraisal report, the work file, or a combination of these. CUSPAP maintains a distinct Review Standard to govern appraisal reviews. The subject of an appraisal review can be an appraisal report, another appraisal review report, or a consulting report. The most common assignments involve the review of an appraisal report. To meet the defined objectives of an appraisal review assignment, the reviewer will examine the data, reasoning, analyses, and conclusions developed by another appraiser. Most appraisal reviews are performed to determine the credibility of the value conclusion and the adequacy of the supporting evidence provided. The reasonableness and necessity of any hypothetical conditions, extraordinary assumptions, or general limiting conditions are also often considered.

Appraisal reviews are performed by appraisers. However, appraisal reviews may be limited to specific issues. The extent and purpose of an appraisal review is a scope of work decision determined by the appraiser based on communication with the client. The type and extent of a review may vary with the training of the reviewer, the specific needs of the client, and other circumstances. The review requirements of lenders may be tailored to their specific policies and procedures, which include compliance with the requirements of primarily federal agencies. Mortgage insurers have unique appraisal requirements, as do federal and provincial agencies that conduct appraisal reviews as a normal part of their appraisal acceptance and audit procedures. Provincial and local government agencies such as highway departments conduct reviews in conjunction with the acquisition of rights of way and have specific appraisal requirements for expropriation proceedings. Appraisal reviewers also serve the corporate and private sectors by facilitating decisions pertaining to buying, selling, and leasing real property as well as decisions relating to the management of real properties as fixed assets.

Like those who prepare appraisals, appraisal reviewers must disclose the nature and extent of their work and carefully detail the contingent or limiting conditions that apply. If an appraiser accepts an assignment to conduct a review of an appraisal prepared by another appraiser, it may be wise for the appraisal reviewer to inform the client of the different levels of appraisal reviews available and to recommend the type of review appropriate to the client's needs.

The primary function of the appraisal reviewer is not to appraise the subject property but to examine the contents of a report and form an opinion as to its adequacy and appropriateness. The scope of work decision for the appraisal review assignment must take into account the function of the appraisal reviewer and of the appraisal review. In some instances, an appraisal reviewer may be called upon to form an opinion of property value based on the information contained in the appraisal report. When this occurs, the appraisal reviewer takes on another role, becoming an appraiser as well as an appraisal reviewer subject to all the requirements that apply to developing an appraisal and to performing an appraisal review.

Appraisal reviewers are commonly said to review the appraisal report of another appraiser. Although that statement is accurate, it can be misleading. Most appraisal reviews are performed to determine whether the valuation conclusion is credible, properly supported, and developed in accordance with generally accepted valuation principles and standards. Thus, a well-written and professionally presented appraisal report may be unacceptable if the valuation conclusion that it contains fails these tests. Sometimes a well-developed and supported valuation conclusion may be reported in an incomplete, confusing, or inadequate manner. The appraisal reviewer must be able to distinguish between the substance of the appraisal and the report that conveys the value opinion.

> **appraisal review**
> The act or process of developing and communicating an opinion about all or part of an appraisal. The subject of an appraisal review assignment may be all or part of an appraisal report, the work file or a combination of these (CUSPAP, 2010 ed.)

Usually an appraisal reviewer identifies and judges the reasoning and logic that underlie the work of another appraiser, but the reviewer does not substitute his or her own judgment for the judgment of that appraiser. The appraisal reviewer has the same obligations for objectivity, confidentiality, and independence in the valuation process as the appraiser whose work is reviewed.

Appraisal review is not the same as activities limited to factual verification of work performed by an appraiser. Appraisers are sometimes asked to verify or to comment on the accuracy of only a portion of the work of another appraiser. In many instances, the verification work may not permit the verifier to have access to the original report. Such functions may or may not need an appraiser. Verification is an important and necessary adjunct to due diligence studies that frequently relate to the information in an appraisal, rather than the conclusions of value. To avoid confusion, misrepresentation, or abuse of the verification process, the appraisal reviewer's report must identify the scope of work for verification as something different from an appraisal review. For example, an appraiser conducting an investigation of possible CUSPAP violations is specifically identified as an activity that does not constitute an appraisal review.[1]

Limitations of Appraisal Reviews

The distinction between an appraisal review and a second opinion of value is critical. An appraisal review by itself does not necessarily lead to an alternative value conclusion. The appraisal reviewer may disagree with the value opinion or the analytical process presented in the report, and the appraisal reviewer may recommend to the client that another appraisal be commissioned.

Also, the appraisal reviewer must distinguish between the review process and the appraisal process. An appraisal reviewer who suggests an alternative opinion of value has assumed the role of an appraiser and is no longer acting as an appraisal reviewer. In that event, the appraisal reviewer must follow the Appraisal Standard in developing the value opinion. If the reviewer's value opinion is expressed in a separate report, then the Review Standards must be followed.

To avoid any confusion concerning these different functions in the minds of market participants, appraisers who review appraisal reports should not sign the appraisal reports under review. Under Canadian Uniform Standards, a review appraiser who signs an appraisal report can become fully responsible for the contents of that report.

Scope of Work in Appraisal Reviews

Applicable appraisal review procedures vary with the scope of work of the appraisal review assignment, the requirements of the client, and the complexity of the property appraised. The appraisal reviewer's scope of work should not be confused with the appraiser's scope of work. The appraisal reviewer's scope of work is the problem-solving process of the appraisal reviewer, which involves answering a question about the quality of the work done by the appraiser. The scope of work of an appraisal review can vary widely, from simply checking the math in the appraisal under review to developing the appraisal reviewer's own independent opinion of value.

Traditionally, appraisal review assignments have been described in colloquial terms as either desk reviews or field reviews. Both general types of review can be acceptable for checking the thoroughness and consistency of appraisals. However, it is important to remember that the choice of performing a desk review or a field review is always dictated by the appraisal reviewer's determination of the scope of work of the review assignment.

---
[1] See CUSPAP 8.1.6

A desk review is completed without a field inspection and is often limited to the data presented in the report. The data in the appraisal report may or may not be independently confirmed by the reviewer and additional market data is typically not researched. A field review includes inspection of the exterior and sometimes the interior of the subject property and possibly inspection of the comparable properties to confirm the data provided in the report.

The scope of work of an appraisal review assignment might include the following activities:

- Verifying that the problem statement is complete, accurate, and appropriate for the intended use and user

- Determining if the highest and best use is properly analyzed and supported

- Verifying that mathematical calculations are accurate

- Determining if the appraiser's methodology is appropriate

- Verifying that the data used is appropriate, adequate, and internally consistent

- Determining if the appraisal was completed in accordance with the client's guidelines and appraisal policy requirements, any regulatory requirements, and CUSPAP

- Inspecting the exteriors of comparable properties and the interiors when appropriate

- Performing a limited or full verification of market data and field inspections of comparable properties and areas of market influence

- Performing independent research to gather additional market data

- Verifying results obtained with electronic spreadsheet software or software used in lease-by-lease analysis

Note again that the procedures applied in a given appraisal review assignment are dictated by the scope of work of the appraisal review. This is why disclosure of the scope of work is so critical in an appraisal review assignment. Clients sometimes use a series of appraisers to perform elements of an appraisal review.

Review policies should be flexible enough to allow appraisal reviewers to exercise due diligence in either a desk review or a field review. The scope of work of the review process is usually a function of the complexity of the property and the perceived risk threshold of the client.

Appraisal Review for Litigation Support

Most lawyers are unfamiliar with appraisal reports and therefore need professional assistance in evaluating these documents to prepare a case. An appraiser may review appraisals prepared at the request of the lawyer who engaged the appraiser or at the request of opposing counsel. Related services include the following:

- Advising a lawyer on matters of standards of practice, professional codes of ethics, market data sources, and industry trends
- Helping frame questions for appraisal experts on either side of the case at depositions and during trial testimony
- Case management

When these services are provided without testimony or without the sharing of the appraisal work or conclusions with others, the scope of work may allow a practitioner to serve in the role of a litigation consultant. However, whether the appraiser is acting as a consultant or an expert witness, the Review Standard is applicable if appraisal review services are rendered.

Appraisers are frequently called upon in courts and tribunals such arbitrations and property tax assessment hearings, to testify regarding appraisal methodology or appraisal standards. Principles and processes established by legal precedent create a need for the court to seek testimony in order to qualify (or disqualify) someone offered as an expert witness. Methodology and standards testimony typically involves generally accepted valuation principles and methods and applicable appraisal standards.

APPRAISAL CONSULTING

A real estate appraiser may be called upon to perform an assignment in which the objective is to provide advice, a recommendation, an opinion, or a conclusion about real estate but not develop an opinion of value. Such assignments are broadly categorized as consulting assignments.

Professional appraisers are asked to provide consulting services because they have valuation and market knowledge along with the expertise needed to help clients solve a variety of real estate problems. Given the breadth of potential consulting assignments, appraisers must be particularly careful when providing such services to properly identify the client's problem to be solved and to ascertain whether they have the required competence.

Consulting, as defined in CUSPAP, is the act or process of analysis of real estate data, and recommendations or conclusions on diversified problems in real estate, other than an appraisal or review assignment. It usually entails the analysis, recommendation or opinion to solve a problem, where an opinion of value is a component of the analysis leading to the assignment results.

One example of a common consulting assignment is a feasibility study. The appraiser must develop an opinion of value for a proposed use and test the feasibility of that use by comparing costs and benefits. The objective of this type of consulting assignment is not to develop an opinion of value, but rather to draw a conclusion about feasibility,

> consulting
> The act or process of analysis of real estate data, and recommendations or conclusions on diversified problems in real estate, other than an appraisal or review assignment (CUSPAP, 2010 ed.)

which is assessed by determining whether the financial benefit (value) of an action or project is equal to or greater than the cost, or to analyze alternative actions or projects.

Other Types of Consulting Services

Consulting services may or may not involve developing an opinion of value. Those that do not involve development of an opinion of value are not addressed in the Appraisal or Review Standard of CUSPAP.[2] Some common assignments that are likely to fall under the broader category of consulting services include the following:

- Land use studies
- Market studies
- Marketability studies
- Due diligence for a client's acquisition or sale decision
- Operations audits
- Absorption analyses
- Risk analysis
- Cash flow and investment analysis
- Feasibility analysis
- Reserve fund studies
- Portfolio analyses
- Regulatory and administrative evaluations of appraisal services
- Adaptive reuse analyses, i.e., analysis of an existing property's proposed change of use
- Property inspections
- Capital market analyses
- Studies that provide support for litigation

Some of these services could require the development of an opinion of value – e.g., marketability studies, absorption studies, portfolio analysis, risk analysis, some aspects of litigation support – and if so would be categorized as consulting assignments under the Consulting Standard of CUSPAP. Other services generally do not require the development of an opinion of value.

In both appraisal and consulting assignments, appraisers must always maintain their objectivity and support their findings with facts extracted from competent research.

Competency Issues

The Ethics Standard of CUSPAP states that it is unethical for members to undertake an assignment lacking the necessary competence. Appraisers must disclose any lack of knowledge or experience necessary to complete an assignment before accepting the assignment, and must take all steps necessary or appropriate to complete the assignment competently. As appraisers diversify their professional activities and enter new areas, they may not have sufficient experience to recognize the requirements of certain consulting assignments. A clear understanding of the client's problem to be

---

[2]   Standard 3 of the Uniform Standards of Professional Appraisal Practice differentiates between appraisal review and appraisal consulting assignments. The former must not be labeled as the latter.

solved and the appraiser's ability to complete the assignment in a competent manner is imperative.

Litigation Support and Consulting

The function of litigation support is to provide advisory and support services to a litigation team or to the experts who will testify. Various activities previously discussed can fall into this category, but the principal distinction is that the scope of work is, or may be, that of an advisor to an advocate and is rendered for confidential use, not for direct use by those who are not a part of the litigation team. Thus, the work is generally covered under the attorney work product privilege and is confidential.

For many lawyers and trial teams, the most important function in litigation support is making the members of the team fully aware of the appraisal principles and standards that guide not only the adverse witnesses but their own witnesses. This provides a basis for ensuring that the principles and requirements that the courts apply to appraisal experts are met in their own presentation of the case and that they can recognize the mistakes and weaknesses of the adverse party. It is also important that other witnesses and participants in litigation have the same understandings and that they play clearly defined roles.

Given the scope of many trials, many experts may be needed. For example, an appraiser who competently performs the valuation process may be supported by legal witnesses who are expert in zoning and land use matters, market experts who can testify about market developments and trends, cost experts, managers or operators of similar properties, and others who provide additional bases or support for the appraisal expert. For the testimony of these experts to be relevant, litigation support may involve educating or orienting the experts to appraisal requirements so they can determine how best to explain their work where it relates to the appraisal and appraisers to experts' work and processes. This form of support can aid the court and juries by excluding extraneous testimony and providing focus.

There are many other areas in which appraisal practitioners provide litigation support and counselling. These range from assisting in the preparation of graphics to ensure that trial exhibits are accurate and clear, evaluating trial materials, performing research, responding to trial developments, and performing many other functions. When performed with high ethics and an understanding and application of standards, litigation support should ultimately improve the operation of the judicial system and the fairness of court decisions.

CHAPTER 28

STATISTICS IN APPRAISAL

An understanding of statistics has become important to appraisers as the single-property appraisal mind-set and mass appraisal techniques have merged. The traditional real property appraiser plays an important role in this changing world by bridging the gaps between purely mathematical valuation models, local market conditions, and the physical real estate being analyzed. The use of statistical models and more formal applications of statistical processes provide added support for a value opinion or analysis.

Statistics has been described as the science of data, which "involves collecting, classifying, summarizing, organizing, analyzing, and interpreting numerical information."[1] Based on this definition, traditional appraisal methods have always been steeped in statistics. Although the study of data has always been at the core of the valuation process, the tools necessary for more rigorous analysis and interpretation of numerical data have raised expectations for more "statistical" support for value conclusions. As a result, the profession has evolved to the point at which appraisers are expected to have a more formal understanding of statistics, statistical models, and automated valuation modeling (AVM). With this in mind, an alternative and narrower definition of statistics provides a better description of the focus of this chapter: summary measures that have been computed from relatively little data, gathered by sampling a much larger collection of data called a population.[2]

Statistical applications are generally divided into two types: descriptive statistics and inferential statistics. The category of descriptive statistics deals with the use of summary measures, charts, and tables to describe a sample or population. Inferential statistics involves the use of sample data in support of opinions (i.e., inferences) concerning a population represented by a sample. Statistical inferences can include, among other things, estimates of actual but unknown population central tendency and dispersion, outcome predictions, and the underlying structure of cause-and-effect relationships.

---

[1]   James T. McClave, P. George Benson, and Terry Sincich, *Statistics for Business and Economics*, 9th ed. (Upper Saddle River, N.J.: Prentice-Hall, 2005), 5.

[2]   Heinz Kohler, *Statistics for Business and Economics* (Stamford, Conn.: Thomson, 2002), 4.

While descriptive statistical tools such as tables, charts, and graphs are important and useful, they are not discussed in depth in this chapter. Much has been written about these tools and how they relate to appraisal, and this material is readily accessible in publications such as The Appraisal Journal.[3] Instead, this chapter concentrates on development of a basic understanding of inferential statistics leading up to a discussion of simple and multiple linear regression. Because the field of statistics is a discipline unto itself, appraisers should decide the extent to which statistical methods will be used in their practices and determine the education and training they will need to master the necessary elements of statistics and provide credible appraisal services. With this in mind, this chapter can be viewed as an introductory lesson and first step on the path to statistical competence, starting with precise definitions of fundamental statistical terminology.

SAMPLE AND POPULATION, INFERENCE, AND DESCRIPTION

A population consists of all of the items under consideration such as all of the rental units located in garden-level apartment developments in a given market area. A parameter is a summary measure that describes a characteristic of a population, i.e., a variable. The mean size of all of the units in garden-level apartment developments in a given market area is an example of a parameter where size is the variable and the population mean is the parameter. In contrast, a sample is a subset of a population that has been selected for analysis. A statistic is a summary measure derived from sample data. The mean size of all of the apartment units in a sample selected from garden-level apartment developments in a given market area is an example of a statistic. Statistics are used to estimate parameters. That is, parameter values are inferred through the analysis of statistics.

As stated earlier, descriptive statistics is concerned with data collection, presentation, and quantification. For example, descriptive statistics on a sample might include the sample size, the collection method, and the date. Descriptive statistics might also include numerically quantifying the dispersion and central tendencies of the sample variables by reporting minimum and maximum values, ranges, quartiles, standard deviations, means, medians, or modes. Specific examples of descriptive charts, graphs, and tables include histograms, pie charts, bar charts, line graphs, scatter plots, ordered arrays, relative frequency distributions, and percentage distributions. Descriptive statistical methods are applicable to population data as well as sample data.

Fundamentally, inferential statistics involves estimating a population parameter using sample data or reaching a conclusion concerning one or more populations based on sample data. For example, the Canadian Real Estate Association (CREA) publishes monthly median home price statistics for various markets throughout Canada. Changes in the price level of the underlying population of homes are generally inferred from this sample statistic. The reliability and validity of this inference

---

[3]   See, for example, a series of three articls by Bryan L. Goddard: "Graphics Improve the Analysis of Income Data", The Appraisal Journal (October 2000): 388-394; "The Power of Computer Graphics for Comparative Analysis", *The Appraisal Journal* (April 2000): 134-141; and :The Role of Graphic Analysis in Appraisals:, The Appraisal Journal (October 1999): 429-435.

– i.e., how accurate the inference is – depend on a number of factors including sample size and how well the sample represents the population. A measure of accuracy is usually reported along with an inference. The measure of accuracy states the degree of uncertainty associated with the inference.[4] Uncertainty cannot, however, be quantified when the sample is a non-probability sample.[5] Median home price statistics reported by CREA are derived from non-probability samples, so a degree of uncertainty is not reported and cannot be calculated due to the manner in which the data is collected.

These terms and concepts are important in all types of real estate appraisals. When most appraisers gather comparable sales, they must recognize that only some of the properties in the population of which the sales are a part will have sold in a given time frame. Thus, the sales may or may not represent that population and would not constitute a random or unbiased sample. To report that "the mean sales price of the properties sold in the subject property's market area between 2007 and 2008 was $175,000" would be more accurate than to report that "the average price for properties in the neighbourhood in 2007 was $175,000". The latter statement implies that all properties were sold.

MEASURES OF CENTRAL TENDENCY

Central tendency refers to a typical value that describes a sample or population variable. The three most frequently used measures of central tendency are the median, mean, and mode.

Median

The median is the middle value in an ordered array, i.e., a data set arranged numerically from lowest to highest or highest to lowest. The median is unaffected by extreme values in sample data. As a result, it is often reported when one or more extreme values distorts the ability of the mean to accurately depict central tendency.

If a data set contains an odd number of observations, the median value is the observation at the $(n + 1) \div 2$ position in the ordered array, where n represents sample size. If the data set has an even number of observations, then the median is the value halfway between the two middle observation values. For example, if the data set has 15 observations, the median is the eighth data point in an ordered array of the data. If the data set contains 14 observations, then the median would be the midpoint between the seventh and eighth data points in the ordered array.

Arithmetic Mean

The arithmetic mean is the most commonly reported measure of central tendency. It is often referred to as the sample mean or population mean or simply as the mean.

---

[4] For example, polling data usually includes an inference and its associated margin of error, which describes a confidence interval at some preselected confidence level (generally 90%, 95%, or occasionally 99%).

[5] With a non-probability sample, the probability of any given sample item being chosen from the underlying population is unknown. Examples of non-probability samples include convenience samples, intact groups, and self-selection.

Sample mean is represented by the symbol x. Population mean is symbolized as the Greek letter μ. Sample mean is calculated by summing the values of all observations on a variable and dividing by sample size (n). This is written mathematically as:

$$\bar{x} = \frac{\sum_{i=1}^{n} x_i}{n}$$

In contrast, population mean is calculated by summing the values of all items in a population and dividing by population size (N). Mathematically, this is written as:

$$\bar{x} = \frac{\sum_{i=1}^{N} x_i}{n}$$

Because the arithmetic mean includes all observations on a variable, its calculation is affected by any extreme values, which may distort its depiction of central tendency. When this occurs, the population mean is not the best representation of central tendency.

The mean is very amenable to statistical inference when the population distribution is known or can be reliably approximated or when the sample is adequately large. A t-distribution is the most frequently used measure to assess the degree of uncertainty associated with statistical inferences based on the mean.

Geometric Mean

Central tendency for compound financial returns over time can be measured by the geometric mean. The geometric mean is mathematically calculated as:

$$\bar{R} = [(1+R_1) \times (1+R_2) \times \ldots \times (1+R_N)]^{1/n} - 1$$

where R_i is the rate of return in period i and n represents the number of compounding periods. The geometric mean is an important financial concept. For instance, the internal rate of return is a geometric mean.

Mode

The mode is the most frequently occurring observation in a sample data set. It is not affected by extreme values, but it is more variable from sample to sample. If more than one mode occurs, the data set is multi-modal. For example, a data set with two modes is referred to as bimodal. The mode is undefined for some data distributions (e.g., the uniform distribution), and unlike the mean and median, the mode does not have statistical tools useful for making inferences based on the mode.

Numerical Example

Table 28.1 shows an ordered array (in ascending order) of a 36-item random sample of garden-level apartment rents. The data set illustrates the sample mean, median, and mode. The same data is used later to illustrate measures of dispersion and shape.

Because the sample has an even number of observations, the median is the midpoint between the 18th and 19th ordered observations, which is $825. The most frequently occurring rent is $850, which occurs six times and is the mode. Since the observations in the sample were randomly selected, the measures of central tendency can be used to infer the corresponding population central tendency.[6]

Table 28.1: Garden-Level Apartment Rents

Monthly Rent		
$600	805	850
650	815	850
695	820	860
710	820	860
715	825	890
730	825	890
735	825	920
735	825	920
760	850	930
760	850	970
785	850	995
800	850	Σ_x = $29,370
800		

$$\text{Sample mean} = \bar{x} = \frac{\sum_{i=1}^{n} x_i}{n} = \frac{\$29,370}{36} = \$815.83$$

MEASURES OF DISPERSION

Measures of dispersion indicate how much variation occurs in a given variable. These measures are useful because they can be compared to the characteristics of a known distribution – such as the normal distribution – to determine whether a particular set of parametric inferential statistics can be used.[7] They also facilitate comparison of two data sets to determine which is more variable.

Standard Deviation and Variance

The two fundamental measures of dispersion – standard deviation and variance – take into account how all of the data is distributed. In addition, the standard deviation lends itself to further statistical treatment, allowing inferences to be drawn and statements to be made regarding the degree of uncertainty associated with

---

[6] Often inferences can be improved by use of a stratified random sample. For example, if garden apartment units exist in one-bedroom and two-bedroom configurations in a given market and it is known that one-bedroom units represent 35% of the garden apartment population, then a stratified random sample consisting of 35% one-bedroom garden apartment units and 65% two-bedroom garden apartment units would provide improved inferences on population parameters by ensuring that the unit type variability within the sample is consistent with the underlying population.

[7] For example, if the data is sufficiently close to being normally distributed, then statistical methods based on the normal distribution can be employed to make inferences about the parameters of the underlying population.

NORMAL DISTRIBUTIONS

A normal distribution or normal curve is an important tool in statistical inference. A normal curve is produced when a normal distribution is plotted on a graph to illustrate a distribution of data. Although the original data may not be normally distributed, the results of repeated random samples may approximate a normal distribution. Sales are often treated as though they were normally distributed in competitive, open-market situations.

A normal curve often takes the form of a bell curve. One major characteristic of a bell curve is its symmetry. Both halves of the curve have the same shape and contain the same number of observations. The mean, median, and mode are the same value and fall at the midpoint, or apex, of the curve.

Figure 28.1 is a bell curve that illustrates the 36 house sales. It shows that 68.26% of the observations will fall within the range of the mean, plus or minus one standard deviation; 95.44% will fall within plus or minus two standard deviations; and 99.74% will fall within plus or minus three standard deviations. The figure depicts an analysis of the probable population distribution for the 36 sales, assuming a normal distribution.

Under the bell curve, the ranges for one, two, and three standard deviations are shown. The percentage of the population that will fall within a given distance from the mean or within any specified range can be calculated. For example, the percentage of sales included within a range of $81,989 to $91,989 (i.e., the mean of $86,989 plus or minus $5,000) may be estimated by calculating the Z value for this range with the formula presented below and then consulting a table of areas under the normal curve for the calculated value of Z.

Z = the deviation of X from the mean measured in standard deviations

$$Z = \frac{X - \text{Mean}}{\text{Standard Deviation}}$$

$$Z = \frac{\$91,989 - \$86,989}{\$6,828} = 0.73$$

This formula shows that $81,989 and $91,989 each deviate from the mean of $86,989 by 0.73 standard deviations.

The percentage of sales within this Z range of plus or minus 0.73 standard deviations can be found in published Z-tables. The table indicates that 26.73% of the sales fall between $86,989 and $91,989 or between $86,989 and $81,989; therefore, 53.46% of the sales will fall between $81,989 and $91,989.

an inference. For this reason the standard deviation is a commonly calculated and reported sample statistic. The sample standard deviation is denoted by the letter S, and the population standard deviation is denoted by the Greek letter σ.

Calculations for these two standard deviation measures are:

$$\sigma = \sqrt{\frac{\sum (x_i - \mu)^2}{N}}$$

and

$$S = \sqrt{\frac{\sum (x_i - \bar{x})^2}{n-1}}$$

where N = population size and n = sample size.

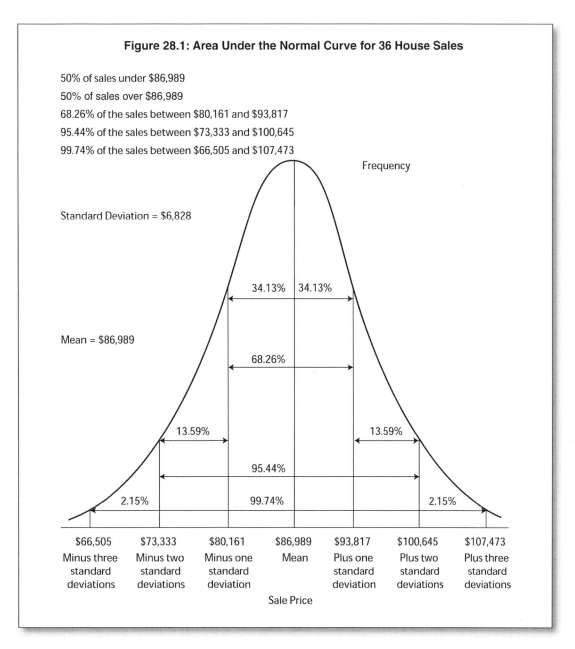

Figure 28.1: Area Under the Normal Curve for 36 House Sales

50% of sales under $86,989

50% of sales over $86,989

68.26% of the sales between $80,161 and $93,817

95.44% of the sales between $73,333 and $100,645

99.74% of the sales between $66,505 and $107,473

Frequency

Standard Deviation = $6,828

34.13% 34.13%

Mean = $86,989

68.26%

13.59%   13.59%

95.44%

2.15%   99.74%   2.15%

$66,505	$73,333	$80,161	$86,989	$93,817	$100,645	$107,473
Minus three standard deviations	Minus two standard deviations	Minus one standard deviation	Mean	Plus one standard deviation	Plus two standard deviations	Plus three standard deviations

Sale Price

Variance is simply the square of the standard deviation. Sample variance equals S^2 and population variance equals σ^2. The sample standard deviation for the sample of 36 apartment unit rents is calculated in Table 28.2.

When data is normally distributed, approximately 67% of the observations are expected to lie within ±1 standard deviation of the mean, 80% within ±1.28 standard deviations of the mean, and 95% within ±2 standard deviations of the mean. For this data set, 25 observations (69%) lie within ±1 standard deviation of the mean, 30 observations (83%) lie within ±1.28 standard deviations of the mean, and 34 observations

Table 28.2: Sample Standard Deviation (S) Calculation

Rent (x_i)	Sample Mean ($\bar{x}$)	($x_i - \bar{x}$)	($x_i - \bar{x}$)^2
600	815.8333	-215.8333	46,584.01
650	815.8333	-165.8333	27,500.68
695	815.8333	-120.8333	14,600.69
710	815.8333	-105.8333	11,200.69
715	815.8333	-100.8333	10,167.35
730	815.8333	-85.8333	7,367.36
735	815.8333	-80.8333	6,534.02
735	815.8333	-80.8333	6,534.02
760	815.8333	-55.8333	3,117.36
760	815.8333	-55.8333	3,117.36
785	815.8333	-30.8333	950.69
800	815.8333	-15.8333	250.69
800	815.8333	-15.8333	250.69
805	815.8333	-10.8333	117.36
815	815.8333	-0.8333	0.69
820	815.8333	4.1667	17.36
820	815.8333	4.1667	17.36
825	815.8333	9.1667	84.03
825	815.8333	9.1667	84.03
825	815.8333	9.1667	84.03
825	815.8333	9.1667	84.03
850	815.8333	34.1667	1,167.36
850	815.8333	34.1667	1,167.36
850	815.8333	34.1667	1,167.36
850	815.8333	34.1667	1,167.36
850	815.8333	34.1667	1,167.36
850	815.8333	34.1667	1,167.36
860	815.8333	44.1667	1,950.70
860	815.8333	44.1667	1,950.70
890	815.8333	74.1667	5,500.70
890	815.8333	74.1667	5,500.70
920	815.8333	104.1667	10,850.70
920	815.8333	104.1667	10,850.70
930	815.8333	114.1667	13,034.04
970	815.8333	154.1667	23,767.37
995	815.8333	179.1667	32,100.71

$$\Sigma(x_i - x)^2 = 251,175.00$$

$$S = \sqrt{\frac{\Sigma(x_i - \bar{x})^2}{n-1}} = \sqrt{\frac{251,175.00}{31-1}} = \$84.71$$

(94%) lie within ±2 standard deviations of the mean. Based on these measures, the data appears to be approximately normal.

Coefficient of Variation

The coefficient of variation (CV) is useful for relative comparisons of dispersion among multiple sets of data because dispersion is standardized to each sample's mean. This is done by stating standard deviation as a percentage of the sample mean as follows:

$$CV = \frac{S}{x} \times 100\%$$

The sample having the greatest coefficient of variation has the most widely dispersed data.

For the apartment rent data set, the coefficient of variation is

$$CV = \frac{\$84.71}{\$815.83} \times 100\% = 10.38\%$$

Range

The range is a simple measure of the spread of the data. It is the difference between the values of the largest observation and the smallest observation. When data is normally distributed, the range will be approximately equal to 6 standard deviations. The range for the apartment rent data is $995 – $600, or $395. This range equates to 4.66 standard deviations, i.e., less dispersion than would be expected for a normally distributed data set.

Interquartile Range

A data set's ordered array can be divided into four subsets of identical size by identifying quartiles. Quartiles are useful for analyzing the shape of the data distribution, which will be illustrated in the next section of this chapter.

Quartile 1 (Q1) ends at the midpoint between the lowest value and the median. Quartile 2 (Q2) ends at the median, and Quartile 3 (Q3) ends at the midpoint between the highest value and the median.

For the apartment rent data (36 observations), the position for Q1 is 9.25 (37 ÷ 4) rounded down to the ninth ordered observation. Position 9 in the ordered array corresponds to $760, which is Q1. Q2 is the median, which is $825. The position for Q3 is 27.75 (111 ÷ 4) rounded up to the 28th ordered observation. Position 28 in the ordered array corresponds to $860.

The interquartile range is Q3 - Q1, or $860 - $760 = $100. When data is normally distributed, the interquartile range should be approximately equal to 1.33 standard deviations. For the apartment rent data, the interquartile range is 1.18 standard deviations ($100 ÷ $84.71).

MEASURES OF SHAPE

Measures of shape are essential for determining how close to normal a data distribution is and the extent to which extreme values are distorting the difference between the median and the mean. The normal distribution, which is the basis for many statistical inferences, is symmetrical, i.e., its median and mean are equal. Figure 28.2 shows a normal distribution with a mean of $815.83 and a standard distribution of $84.71. This plot, generated using Minitab statistical software, illustrates how the apartment rent data set would have been distributed if it were perfectly normal. The mean and median would both have been $815.83, and the distribution would have been symmetrical.

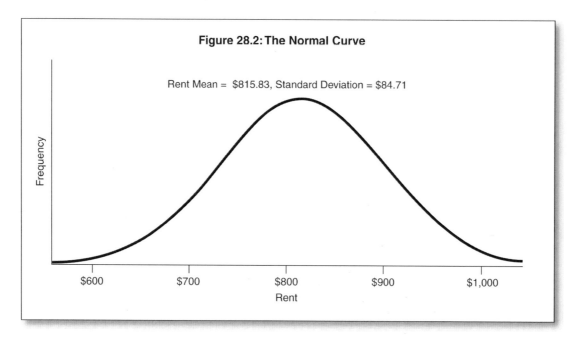

Figure 28.2: The Normal Curve

Rent Mean = $815.83, Standard Deviation = $84.71

A useful graphic illustration of shape is the box and whisker plot, which helps illustrate the extent of *skewness*, or lack of skewness, in the data distribution. (Skewness will be discussed shortly; see Figure 28.3.) A box and whisker plot is based on what is referred to as a *five-number summary*. The summary includes the following:

1. The lowest value
2. Q1
3. The median
4. Q3
5. The highest value

The five-number summary for the chapter's example data is $600, $760, $825, $860, and $995. The corresponding box and whisker plot, along with the sample mean, is shown in Figure 28.4.

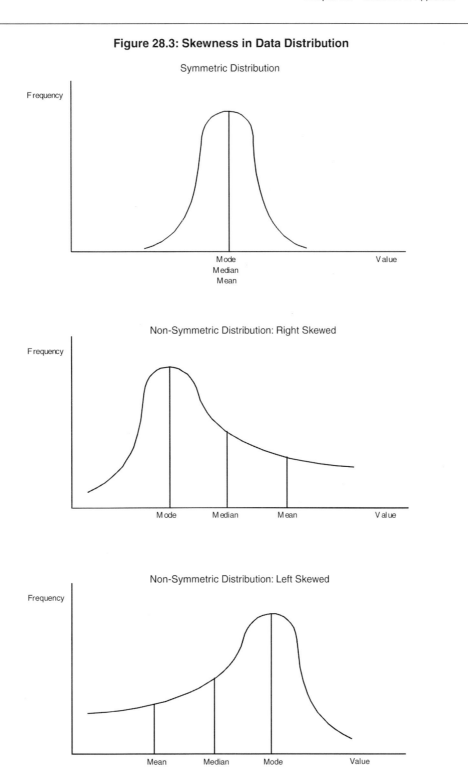

Figure 28.3: Skewness in Data Distribution

The apartment rent data is not perfectly normal. Figure 28.4 shows that the sample data is skewed (i.e., concentrated more densely) to the left, both in terms of the inter-quartile range ($825 – $760 > $860 – $825) and in terms of the tails ($760 – $600 > $995 – $860). Another indication of skewness is the relationship between the median and the mean. When data is left-skewed, the mean will be less than the median. When the data is right-skewed, the mean will be greater than the median. The mean is included in this box and whisker plot to further illustrate the degree of left skewness.

Skewness can also be captured through a graphic depiction of a frequency or percentage distribution. These graphic displays are called histograms. Figure 28.5 illustrates a combination frequency and percentage distribution for the apartment rent data and the related percentage histogram.

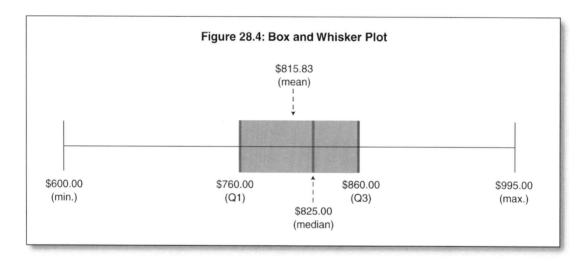

Figure 28.4: Box and Whisker Plot

$815.83
(mean)

$600.00
(min.)

$760.00
(Q1)

$860.00
(Q3)

$995.00
(max.)

$825.00
(median)

Figure 28.5: Frequency and Percentage Distributions with Percentage Histogram

Rent Category	Frequency (Count)	Percentage of Total
Less than $650	1	2.8%
$650 to $699	2	5.6%
$700 to $749	5	13.9%
$750 to $799	3	8.3%
$800 to $849	10	27.8%
$859 to $899	10	27.8%
$900 to $949	3	8.3%
$950 or more	2	5.6%

The percentage histogram is derived from conversion of the numerical price data (monthly rent) to categorical data (rent category) reflecting percentages of the sample items within each class. If the rent data was symmetrical, the distributions to the right and left of center would be mirror images. Instead, the left side extends further from the centre, i.e., left skewness. Numerical data can be either discrete (counts) or continuous (measures). In contrast, categorical data refers to membership or lack of membership in a class, category, or cohort group. Categorical data can either be nominal (e.g., brick, stone, stucco) or ordinal, in which the category names imply scale (e.g., small, medium, large). The categories in this histogram are ordinal because they reflect the progression of rent.

Spreadsheet programs and statistical software packages such as Excel, Minitab, and SPSS provide more quantitative assessments of skewness within their descriptive statistics measures. All rely on the same calculation of skewness:

$$\text{Skewness} = \frac{n}{(n-1)(n-2)} \Sigma \left(\frac{x_i - \bar{x}}{S} \right)^3$$

If a data distribution is symmetrical, the value in the parentheses following the summation sign is zero and the measure of skewness is zero. If the data distribution is left-skewed, the value in the parentheses following the summation sign is negative and the measure of skewness is negative. If it is right-skewed, the value in the parentheses following the summation sign is positive and the measure of skewness is positive. Skewness for the apartment rent data is -0.312, indicating left skewness as depicted in the box and whisker plot and the percentage histogram.

Kurtosis

The statistical term kurtosis refers to the degree of "peakedness" in a data distribution – that is, the height of the probability distribution and thickness of its tails. Curves with kurtosis of 3 are called mesokurtic.[8] The normal distribution has kurtosis equal to 3. More peaked curves (leptokurtic) have values larger than 3 and less peaked curves (platykurtic) have values less than 3. The apartment rent data set is less peaked (kurtosis = 0.42) than a normal distribution.

Normality

The apartment rent data appear to be approximately normal based on a menu of measures, including the proportions of observations lying within the mean plus or minus 1, 1.28, and 2 standard deviations and the number of standard deviations encompassed by the range and the interquartile range. However, as these statistics show, the fit to normality is seldom perfect. The rent data is slightly left-skewed and, as mentioned previously, the range is 4.66 standard deviations, slightly less than the normal expectation of 6 standard deviations.

Quantitative tests for normality and normal probability plots are useful for assessing the degree of departure from normality. Data points that are perfectly normal will line up along a straight-line normal probability plot, whereas data points that depart from normal will depart from a straight line that is representative of a perfectly normal distribution. The normal probability plot shown in Figure 28.6 confirms

---

[8]   Kurtosis values are most often calculated using Excel, Minitab, SPSS, or other statistical software. They are seldom calculated by hand.

the prior assessment that the apartment rent data is not perfectly normal, but does provide a reasonably close fit. The normal probability plot was generated in Minitab, and the output includes other useful information such as the mean, the standard deviation, and the results of a Komolgorov-Smirnov test (KS test) for normality. The p-value[9] from the KS test indicates that the hypothesis that the data was drawn from a normally distributed population cannot be rejected.[10]

To reiterate the importance of the measures of shape, these metrics are helpful in assessing the extent to which a data distribution conforms to the normal distribution and determining if extreme values are distorting the difference between the median and the mean. If the data distribution is too far from normal, then inferential tests based on assumptions of normality (e.g., t-tests and F-tests) may not be applicable to small samples. In addition, if extreme values in the data are distorting the arithmetic mean, then the median is likely to be a better indicator of central tendency.

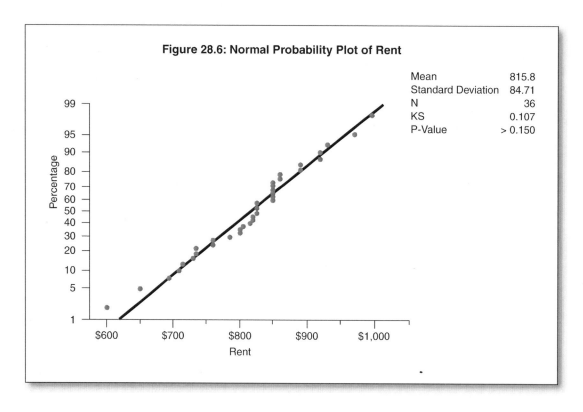

Figure 28.6: Normal Probability Plot of Rent

Mean	815.8
Standard Deviation	84.71
N	36
KS	0.107
P-Value	> 0.150

---

9 The p-value represents the probability of something occurring if the assumption underlying the analysis is true. For example, in this test the analyst asks, "If the population is normal, what is the probability of drawing a sample that departs from normal to the extent this one does?" The p-value of 15% indicates that the analyst could expect a sample derived from a normal population to depart from normal to the extent this one does 15% of the time.

10 Generally speaking, a p-value of 5% or less would provide convincing evidence of a sample drawn from a non-normal population. Minitab provides two additional normality tests (Anderson-Darling and Ryan-Joiner tests), which also fall to reject the normality hypothesis. Normality tests are also available in SPSS.

CENTRAL LIMIT THEOREM AND INFERENCE

Although the most popular and user-friendly inference tests are based on the assumption that a sample has been derived from a normally distributed population (i.e., the so-called "bell curve" with skewness = 0 and kurtosis = 3), normality-based inferences concerning non-normally distributed populations can be made if the sample size is large enough. The adequacy of the sample size depends on the underlying population distribution. Generally speaking, the sampling distribution of a mean[11] drawn from the population – regardless of the shape of the underlying population distribution – will be approximately normal with a sample size of at least 30, according to the central limit theorem. If the underlying population is fairly symmetrical (like the apartment rent data), the sampling distribution of the mean will be approximately normal with a sample size of at least 15. If the underlying population is normally distributed, then the sampling distribution of the mean is also normal, regardless of sample size.[12] The central limit theorem's importance is that it allows inferences to be drawn without knowing the actual distribution of the underlying population.[13]

The apartment rent data sample consists of 36 observations, so it can be used to make inferences about the mean of the underlying population rent because of the size of the sample under the central limit theorem. The rent data has been drawn from a population with an unknown mean and standard deviation.[14] The sample data can be used to infer the underlying population mean because a probability sample (e.g., a simple random sample) was drawn. The sample mean (x) is $815.83 and the sample standard deviation (S) is $84.71.

A confidence interval reflects the degree of uncertainty associated with an inference. It is a range accompanied with a statement of probability or confidence that the range contains the parameter being estimated. Any inference should be accompanied by such a statement. Excel, Minitab, and SPSS will calculate a confidence

---

[11] The *sampling distribution of the mean* refers to the distribution of the sample mean. Creation of a distribution of a sample mean entails taking numerous random samples from a given population, calculating the mean of each random sample, and the examining the distribution of those means.

[12] See David M. Levine, Timothy C. Krehbiel, and Mark L. Berenson, *Business Statistics: A First Course*, 3rd ed. (Upper Saddle River, N.J.: Prentice-Hall, 2003), 237-239.

[13] Inferences on medians (as opposed to inferences on means), derived from a discipline called *nonparametric statistics*, are useful for analyzing small samples when the underlying population distribution is unknown and the sample is so small that the central limit theorem cannot be relied upon to ensure approximate normality of the sampling distribution of the mean. Although nonparametric median tests are beyond the scope of this chapter, note that many software packages provide a number of nonparametric tests that are appropriate for making inferences about central tendency and distribution from a single sample and comparing the central tendencies of two or more small samples. For example, the SPSS and Minitab software packages include several nonparametric single-sample analysis tools as well as independent-sample comparison tests and related-sample comparison tests. Because real property data sets often consist of small-sized samples, it is often useful to be able to apply a level of understanding sufficient for most real estate applications. See Mark L. Berenson, David M. Levine, and Timothy C. Krehbiel, *Basic Statistics: Concepts and Applications*, 9th ed. (Upper Saddle River, N.J.: Prentice-Hall, 2004), Chapter 10, Sections 10.4 and 10.5 (Wilcoxon Rank Sum Test and Wilcoxon Signed Rank Test), Chapter 11, Sections 11.4 and 11.5 (Kruskal-Wallis Rank Test and Friedman Rank Test), and Chapter 12, Sections 12.2, 12.3 and 12.4 (Chi Square Tests).

[14] Population standard deviation is rarely known when making inferences about the true population mean. This is because μ must be known in order to calculate. Logically, if μ is known, then there is no need to infer it. However, in rare cases a population has been studied so many times that many estimates on *S* have been previously published and they can be relied upon as estimators of σ rather than using *S* from a sample.

interval from a data set, given input on the level of confidence sought. The associated confidence intervals on the true population mean price for the apartment rent data are:

90% confidence	$791.98 \leq \mu \leq \$839.68$
95% confidence	$787.17 \leq \mu \leq \$844.49$
99% confidence	$777.37 \leq \mu \leq \$854.29$

With 90% confidence, the degree of uncertainty concerning the value of the true mean is 10%. Uncertainty reduces to 5% and 1% as confidence rises, but the associated "cost of less uncertainty" is a wider confidence interval. The level of uncertainty is referred to as "alpha" (α) in statistics, and the confidence level is $1 - \alpha$. Alpha is the probability of making a "Type I Error"– inferring μ to be within a confidence interval when it is not. "Type II Errors" are referred to as "beta" (β) – inferring μ to be outside of the confidence interval when it is actually within the interval.

Sample Size

Suppose a client requires a narrower confidence interval without increasing α. Notice that the width of the confidence interval is reduced when n is increased due to division by the square root of n. Additionally, the value of t becomes smaller at a given confidence level as sample size increases. As a result, narrower confidence intervals can be achieved by collecting a larger sample.

A requisite sample size can be estimated to accommodate a predetermined amount of sampling error (e). The equation for sample size is:

$$n = \frac{Z^2 \sigma^2}{e^2}$$

Z (the standard normal distribution) is used in this calculation because the value of t cannot be determined until a sample size has been selected. Consequently, this calculation yields an approximate sample size. Furthermore, it is not unusual for some proportion of collected data to be unusable due to missing variables or "nonresponse". It is good practice to attempt to collect a sample that is comfortably larger than indicated by the sample size calculation. As calculated here, sample size is an estimate of the number of usable observations needed to control the size of sampling error at a given level of confidence.

The sampling error from the 36-unit rent sample for the 95% confidence interval on true mean monthly apartment rent is $28.66 [($844.49 – $787.17) ÷ 2]. Suppose, however, that the needs of the client dictate that a sampling error no larger than $15 is acceptable at a 95% confidence level. In order to calculate a revised sample size, Z is derived from the standard normal distribution and is equal to 1.96 at a 95% confidence level. The population standard deviation (σ) is unknown, but can be estimated as $84.71 based on the previous calculation of S.[15] On this basis, the sample size would have to be increased to at least 123 observations, computed as follows:

$$n = \frac{1.96^2 \times 84.71^2}{15^2} = 122.5$$

---

[15] The population standard deviation is usually unknown and must be estimated based on prior research, a pilot sample, or other bases used to support an assumption.

Sample size is always rounded up. Furthermore, since t_{122} is approximately 1.9799, the sample size could be increased to 126 based on the difference between the standard normal Z and t_{122}, as follows:

$$123 \times \frac{1.9799^2}{1.96^2} = 125.5$$

As this example demonstrates, increased inference precision can add to data collection expense. Here an approximate 90% reduction in sampling error from $28.66 to $15 results in a need to increase sample size by 350%.[16]

REGRESSION ANALYSIS

Regression analysis is a statistical technique in which a mathematical equation can be derived to quantify the relationship between a dependent (outcome) variable and one or more independent (input) variables. In appraisal, the dependent variable is usually price or rent. The independent variables are usually broadly derived from the four forces that affect value (social, economic, governmental, and environmental) and the physical characteristics of the land and improvements. Often, data collection protocols control for the four forces that affect value by focusing on property sales or rents that are subject to common social, economic, governmental, and environmental influences. The relevant physical characteristics of comparable property data (sites and improvement information) must be included as independent variables, unless all of the comparable properties and the subject property are identical in some physical aspect, e.g., all are stucco, all have 2-car attached garages, or all are located on interior lots of identical size. In some instances it is also necessary to include a date of sale variable (or variable set) to account for economic change over time. In addition, it is not uncommon to include an environmental variable or variables when investigating the effects of an external environmental factor such as traffic noise or factory odour.

Regression models have been used by property tax assessors for many years, especially in highly developed residential markets, within the broad context of mass appraisal modeling because regression modeling is more resource-efficient and may be more accurate than performing a traditional appraisal for each property in a large assessment district with an active real property market. Regression modeling is often the logical choice for tax assessment when the alternative is to appraise each property individually and resource constraints prohibit doing so as often as would be necessary to ensure equitable taxation.

Regression models (along with expert systems and neural networks, which are discussed briefly later) also form the basis for many automated valuation models (AVMs), of which mass appraisal models are a subset.[17] AVMs became important in the 1990s as residential lenders began to concentrate on shortening loan approval turnaround time to compete more intensely on transaction fees. The use of information technology and automated word processing by appraisers has mitigated the

---

[16] Obviously, mean apartment rent could be known with certainty by analyzing a census of all apartments in a market. In many cases, however, it simply is not possible or is too costly to collect data on each item in a population.

[17] See CUSPAP 12.38 (2010) for Standards guidelines respecting AVMs.

threat of AVMs to residential appraisal practice somewhat by shortening turnaround times and improving efficiency.

Simple Linear Regression

In its simplest form, linear regression captures a relationship between a single dependent variable and a single independent, or predictor, variable. This relationship is usually written as follows:

$$Y_i = \alpha + \beta x_i + \varepsilon$$

which reflects an underlying linear deterministic relationship of the form $Y = \alpha + \beta x$ plus a stochastic (random) component (ε). The slope of the regression line is b and the intercept is a. The impact of variables, other than the single independent variable, that may influence the value of the dependent variable is not included in a simple linear regression model.

In real estate appraisal, Y could be modeled as market rent and x could be apartment living area, for example. The random component reflects sampling error plus the imperfection of real estate markets in terms of the influence of factors such as information advantages, the negotiating strengths of the parties to a sale or lease transaction, and any other influential variables not included in the model. The simple linear regression model yields an estimate of the equation above in the form

$$\hat{Y}_i = a + b x_i + e$$

where a is an estimator of α, b is an estimator of β, and e is an estimator of ε. The outcome variable ($\hat{Y}^i$) is the expected market price (for example, model's estimate of market rent) of property i conditional on the value of x.

The presence of the random error term is an indication that regression models are inferential (stochastic). Regression models provide estimates of the outcome variables that should be accompanied by a statement about the degree of uncertainty associated with the estimate. In addition, they provide estimates of the coefficient on the independent variable, b in this context, which also incorporate a degree of uncertainty.

The apartment rent data set described previously is augmented by adding living area to demonstrate a simple linear regression model. The additional data is presented in Table 28.3.

Note that the range in rent per square foot is $0.35 ($1.20 − $0.85), an indication that living area probably is not the sole factor determining rent. Otherwise, rent per square foot would exhibit minimal variation. A simple linear regression model will uncover the extent to which rent is explained by the living area variable. The model can be run on a number of statistical software packages. The following output was derived using Minitab:

Regression equation:	price = $336.17 + $0.57359 × floor area (sq. ft.)
t-statistic on floor area:	6.55
Model F-statistic:	42.86
R^2:	.558
Adjusted R^2:	.545

This output says that the best-fitting linear relationship between living area and rent is a line with intercept $336.17 and a slope of $0.57359 per square foot of floor area. The model F-statistic is highly significant, meaning the model predicts rent better than merely relying on mean unit rent. The t-statistic on floor area is also highly significant, meaning that living area is an important factor for rent estimation. The coefficient of determination, R^2, can vary from 0 to 1, with 0 indicating no explanatory power whatsoever and 1 indicating perfect explanatory power (a deterministic model). The R^2 of .558 indicates that 55.8% of the variation in rent is accounted for by variation in floor area. Adjusted R^2 is useful for comparing multiple competing models having differing sets of independent variables because the measure accounts for the number of explanatory variables in relation to sample size. The model having the highest adjusted R^2 is usually the preferred model. In this instance, because there is only one independent variable, there is no competing model.

Obtaining an understanding of the intercept and slope is referred to as structural modeling because it uncovers the structure of the relationship between the dependent variable and the independent variable. In a simple linear model it facilitates development of a "best fit" line in two-dimensional space, which can be overlaid on a scatter plot of the data to demonstrate unexplained variation in the dependent variable (see Figure 28.7).

The scatter plot shows that rent generally rises linearly with floor area. The regression line shown on the chart is the best-fitting straight line, which minimizes the squares of the errors between the data and the line's fit to the data. Differences between actual prices and the regression line can be attributed to one of two causes – randomness in pricing (the stochastic element of price) or other unaccounted-for variables that are also important in determining rent. Such elements might include unit characteristics such as bedroom counts, bathroom counts, and tenant amenities such as a pool, spa, and exercise facility. Simple linear regression becomes multiple linear regression when more than one independent variable is included in a model to account for additional elements of comparison.

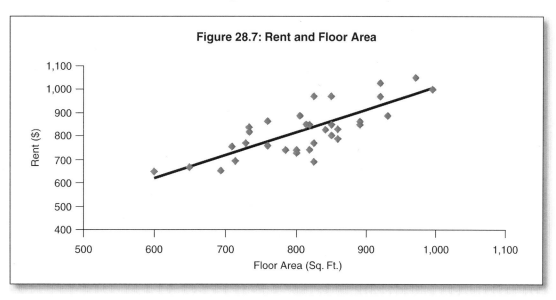

Figure 28.7: Rent and Floor Area

Table 28.3: Living Area and Monthly Rent

	Rent	Living Area (Sq. Ft.)	Rent per Sq. Ft.
	$600	650	$0.92
	650	670	0.97
	695	655	1.06
	710	755	0.94
	715	695	1.03
	730	770	0.95
	735	840	0.88
	735	820	0.90
	760	865	0.88
	760	760	1.00
	785	740	1.06
	800	740	1.08
	800	730	1.10
	805	890	0.90
	815	850	0.96
	820	850	0.96
	820	740	1.11
	825	970	0.85
	825	970	0.85
	825	770	1.07
	825	690	1.20
	850	850	1.00
	850	970	0.88
	850	970	0.88
	850	970	0.88
	850	805	1.06
	850	850	1.00
	860	830	1.04
	860	790	1.09
	890	860	1.03
	890	850	1.05
	920	970	0.95
	920	1,030	0.89
	930	890	1.04
	970	1,050	0.92
	995	1,000	1.00
Median	$825.00	845	$0.985
Mean	$815.83	836	$0.983
S	$84.71	110	$0.087
Minimum	$600.00	650	$0.85
Maximum	$995.00	1,050	$1.20

Regression models can either be predictive or structural, i.e., constructed for the purpose of understanding the structure of the relationship among variables. Predictive models are predominant in most valuation settings. Two forms of predictive models are generally employed. One form is used to estimate the mean outcome, and the other form estimates a single, specific outcome. The primary difference is that the confidence interval for an estimation of the mean outcome is narrower than the confidence interval for estimation of a single, specific outcome. Furthermore, regression models are not usually employed to estimate outcomes using inputs that are outside the ranges of the independent variables.

For example, assume the appraiser wants to predict rent for an 810 square foot apartment using the sample data. The predicted mean rent for units of this size and the predicted rent for a single, specific 810 square foot unit are the same at $800.78. However, the confidence interval widths vary considerably, as follows:

95% confidence interval on mean rent of 810 square foot units: $780.86 to $820.70
95% confidence interval on rent of a single 810 square foot unit: $682.91 to $918.65

SPSS and Minitab are capable of calculating and reporting confidence intervals for the mean and for a single outcome. The confidence intervals for the data are illustrated in Figure 28.8 along with the regression line for unit rent. Note that the prediction confidence intervals are narrowest near the mean unit size and grow wider for single units. For this reason, the confidence intervals must be calculated separately for any given value of the independent variable (or values for the independent variables in multiple linear regression). This is a time-consuming process, which is best accomplished electronically in SPSS or Minitab. Note also that the limits of the known data are shown at the ends of each plotted line. Appraisers must be cautioned that beyond the limits of known data any conclusions drawn by the appraiser will constitute forecasts or predictions and that usable confidence is further reduced or eliminated statistically.

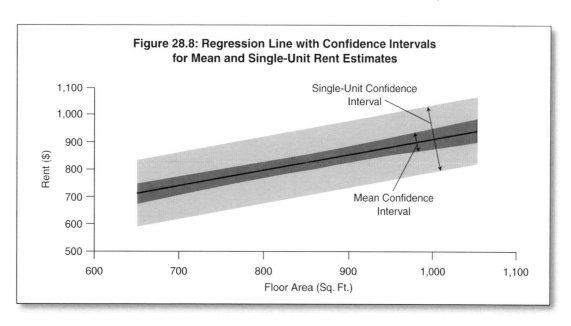

Figure 28.8: Regression Line with Confidence Intervals for Mean and Single-Unit Rent Estimates

Multiple Linear Regression

To demonstrate a multiple linear regression model, suppose that further investigation of the rent data reveals variation in bedroom counts, bath counts, and common amenities.[18] Characteristics such as these can be modeled by use of numerical variables and by the creation of indicator variables (also known as dummy variables) to convert categorical data such as common amenities into numerical variables. To create a common amenity variable indicative of the presence of a pool, spa, and exercise facility, units in apartment complexes that have the feature are coded 1 and units in apartment complexes that do not have a pool, spa, and exercise facility are coded 0. Bedroom and bath counts are entered as discrete numerical data. The revised sample data set is shown in Table 28.4.

A multiple regression model yields the following price equation using Minitab:

Unit rent = $209.06 + $0.4703 × unit sq. ft. + $50.10 × bedrooms + $58.27 × bathrooms
+ $79.77 × pool/spa/exercise

t-statistics:

Living area (sq. ft.)	3.83 (p = .001)
Bedrooms	2.06 (p = .048)
Baths	3.45 (p = .002)
Pool/spa/exercise	5.22 (p = .000)

Model F-statistic = 37.80 (p = .000)
R^2 = .830
Adjusted R^2 = .808

This result indicates that living area, bedroom count, bath count, and amenities consisting of a pool, spa, and exercise facility are all significant in the determination of unit rent (t-statistics are all significant at $\alpha \leq$ .05).[19] The model's F-statistic is also large enough to be highly significant. This model is preferred to the simple linear regression model because adjusted R^2 has gone up from .545 to .808, despite the loss in degrees of freedom resulting from adding more variables while keeping sample size constant. The expanded multiple linear regression model accounts for 83% of the variation in unit rent, which is a vast improvement over the 55.8% coefficient of determination for the simple linear regression model.

To predict mean rent and a specific unit rent for an 810 square foot apartment unit having 2 bedrooms, 1.5 baths, and use of an on-site pool, spa, and exercise facility, the calculation would be:

Unit rent = $209.06 + $.4703 × 810 + $50.10 × 2 + $58.27 × 1.5 + $79.77 × 1 = $857.38

Note that the Minitab estimate is $857.40, which is unaffected by rounding.

The associated 95% confidence intervals derived in Minitab are

95% confidence interval on mean unit rent: $827.55 to $887.24
95% confidence interval on a single unit rent: $776.00 to $938.79

---

[18] Obviously, other elements of comparison may be important such as differences in age and condition, location, access, neighbouring land use, and other characteristics.

[19] The p values stated after the t and F statistics are the probabilities of the model result occurring by chance. When the p value is less than .05, then the variable (or model in the case of the F statistic) is said to be significant at the 5% level (i.e., $\alpha \leq$ .05). Here most of the results are significant at the 1% level.

Table 28.4: Rent, Living Area, Room Counts, and Amenities

Rent	Living Area (Sq. Ft.)	Bedrooms	Baths	Pool/Spa/Exercise
$600	650	1	1	0
650	670	1	1	0
695	655	1	2	1
710	755	1	1	0
715	695	1	2	1
730	770	2	1	0
735	840	2	1	0
735	820	2	1	0
760	865	2	1	0
760	760	1	2	0
785	740	1	1.5	1
800	740	1	2	1
800	730	1	2	1
805	890	2	2	0
815	850	2	2	0
820	850	2	2	0
820	740	1	2	1
825	970	2	2	0
825	970	2	2	0
825	770	1	2	1
825	690	1	2	1
850	850	2	1	1
850	970	2	2	0
850	970	2	2	0
850	970	2	2	0
850	805	2	1	1
850	850	2	2	0
860	830	2	2	0
860	790	2	1	1
890	860	2	2	0
890	850	2	2	1
920	970	2	2	0
920	1,030	2	2	0
930	890	2	2	1
970	1,050	2	2.5	0
995	1,000	2	2.5	0

One benefit of the expanded multiple regression model's higher explanatory power is more predictive precision in comparison to the simple linear regression model, as indicated by the resulting tighter confidence intervals for the predicted mean and for a single unit rent prediction.[20]

---

[20] Another way to develop such a model would be to create indicator variables for discrete numerical variables such as bedroom counts and bath counts. This allows the rent contributions of these features to vary instead of being constrained to a single linear coefficient. Often creation of indicator (dummy) variables to describe discrete numerical variables will improve the model fit. For example, addition of bathroom dummy variables to reflect 1, 1½, 2, and 2½ bath categories to this model increases R^2 to .854 and adjusted R^2 to .824.

DEVELOPING STATISTICAL MODELS

Model specification is the process of developing statistical models. For valuation purposes, model specification includes two key considerations: the functional form of the relationship between the dependent variable and the independent variables and the choice of variables to include in the model.

Functional Form

Functional form issues arise because of the regression model's presumed linear relationship between dependent and independent variables, even though many of these relationships are likely to be curvilinear.[21] For example, many characteristics of real property are thought to be subject to increasing or diminishing marginal utility. Consider bathroom counts. Keeping floor area and bedroom count constant, adding bathrooms could initially result in increasing marginal utility. However, as more bathrooms are added above some optimum level, the contribution to value begins to diminish (imagine a three-bedroom home with six baths and the contribution to value added by the fourth, fifth, and sixth baths. Other independent variables that may have a curvilinear relationship to price or rent include property age, floor area, lot area, garage stall count, bedroom count, and proximity (e.g., distance) measures. Furthermore, the nature of the functional relationship between these variables and price or rent can vary by market area whether defined geographically (i.e., region of the country) or economically (i.e., market norms).

Because the underlying functional form of the relationship between an independent variable set and a price or rent outcome variable is unknown, regression model builders must search for the functional form that best fits the data being analyzed. This involves variable transformations such as logarithms, exponents, polynomials, reciprocals, and square roots. In some cases, a transformation applies to an entire equation. In others, transformations apply only to certain variables.

Two examples of transformations of entire equations include a hypothesized multiplicative model and a hypothesized exponential model. Transformations are done in these cases to convert the underlying relationships from a non-linear to a linear form amenable to regression analysis. These transformations are illustrated in Figure 28.9.

Figure 28.9: Multiplicative and Exponential Model Transformations

Underlying Multiplicative Price (P) Model	**Underlying Exponential Price (P) Model**
$P = \alpha x_1^{\beta_1} x_2^{\beta_2} \varepsilon$	$P = e^{(\alpha + \beta_1 x_1 + \beta_2 x_2 + \varepsilon)}$
Log Transformation to Linear Form	**Log Transformation to Linear Form**
$\ln(P) = \ln\alpha + \beta_1 \ln x_1 + \beta_2 \ln x_2 + \ln\varepsilon$	$\ln(P) = \alpha + \beta_1 x_1 + \beta_2 x_2 + \varepsilon$

---

[21]   Curvilinear relationships are characterized by curved lines instead of straight lines. Examples include logarithmic curves, exponential curves, inverse curves, and polynominal curves.

The transformed multiplicative model is linear in the relationship between the logs of the independent and dependent variables, and the exponents of these variables are transformed into the linear regression coefficient estimates. The estimated coefficients can either be placed into the underlying model to directly estimate price (or value), or the linear model can be used to estimate the log of price, which can then be converted to price. This sort of multiplicative model accommodates a variety of variable relationship shapes, depending on the value of the exponents (the βs). Models of this type are used extensively in mass appraisal for property tax assessment. Transformations of exponential models into the log-linear form and the prior log-log transformation are often useful for controlling heteroscedasticity, which is explained later in this chapter.

It is also possible, and often appropriate, to include other variable transformations. For example, one variable may be curvilinear while others are linear in relation to the dependent variable. The curvilinear variable could be modeled as a quadratic (e.g., floor area) while the others are modeled in linear form. An estimation model of this sort would be similar to the following:

$$P = \alpha + \beta_1 x_1 + \beta_2 x_2 + \beta_3 x_2^{\,2} + \varepsilon$$

In this case x_2 is entered in a quadratic form. If x_2 were to represent floor area, a positive coefficient on x_2 along with a negative coefficient on x_2^2 could indicate price increasing with floor area but at a decreasing rate as the negative x_2^2 variable diminishes the positive contribution of the x_2 variable. The decision to include a quadratic term should be based on whether its inclusion is theoretically supported and it significantly improves the model, which would be shown by a significant t-statistic on the squared variable coefficient, improvement in adjusted R_2, or both.

Indicator variables are another form of variable transformation (e.g., the dummy variable used in the apartment illustration to indicate the presence of a pool/spa/exercise facility in the apartment complex). Indicator variables transform categorical variables into numerical variables so that their effects can be included in a regression model. Dummy variables are the simplest single-category form of indicator variables, coded 1 if the observation is included in the category and 0 if it is not. Sometimes more than one category is required to completely exhaust categorical variable possibilities. For example, suppose a data set spans four years (2005 to 2008), and the year of sale is being entered as a set of indicator variables. Dummy variables would be created for 2005, 2006, and 2007, each coded 1 or 0 depending on the year of sale for each observation, assuming the valuation date is 2008. The year 2008 is accounted for in the model when the variables 2005 = 0, 2006 = 0, and 2007 = 0. As a result no variable is created for 2008. The coefficients on the variables 2005, 2006, and 2007 indicate the adjustments required to account for these earlier transactions. The general rules are the following:

1. Create one less dummy variable than the number of categories.
2. All of the dummy variables from an indicator variable set must be included in the model even though some of them may not be significant. That is, the decision to include or exclude a categorical variable implies that all of

the dummy variables related to the categorical variable set must either be included or excluded.[22]

Variable Inclusion

Decisions to include or exclude variables determine whether or not a model is under-specified or over-specified. Two problems arise relating to variable inclusion. First, if relevant variables are excluded from the model, its ability to account for change in the dependent variable is diminished. Second, misspecification leads to biased estimates of population parameters (i.e., the independent variable coefficients) because correlation among independent variables causes the model to adjust coefficient estimates when the model is under- or over-specified. Coefficients on included variables are altered in the regression model to account for their correlations with relevant excluded variables. Conversely, coefficients on relevant included variables are altered to account for correlations with irrelevant included variables.

The apartment unit rent data illustration demonstrates the underspecification effect. The model was initially under-specified because it included only one independent variable, living area. However, three other variables were found to be significant: bedroom count, bath count, and on-site pool/spa/exercise facility. These additional variables are correlated with living area. A correlation matrix (Table 28.5) quantifies these relationships.

Table 28.5: Rent Data Variable Correlations

	Living Area	Bedrooms	Bath	Pool/Spa/Exercise
Living Area	1			
Bedrooms	.780	1		
Baths	.419	.041	1	
Pool/Spa/Exercise	-.493	-.450	-.008	1

Note: Correlation, symbolized as r, can range from -1 to +1. Perfect negative correlation is -1, whereas perfect positive correlation is +1. When r=0, two variables are uncorrelated (i.e., independent or orthogonal).

All three of the additional variables are significantly correlated with living area, indicating that omission of these variables from the model would distort the coefficient on living area. This, in fact, occurred. The coefficient on living area was $0.574 per square foot in the simple linear regression model but was reduced to $0.47 in the multiple regression model. The $0.574 coefficient value was distorted by omitting variables that should have been included in the model. The multiple regression model provides a better estimate of unit rent and a less-distorted estimate of the effect of living area on rent.

In addition, the newly included variables are correlated with each other, sharing some explanatory power. For example, living area and bedrooms are correlated with

22   See Terry Dielman, *Applied Regression Analysis for Business and Economics*, 3rd ed. (Pacific Grove, Calif.: Duxbury, 2001), 406. "[I]ndicator variables are designed to have a particular meaning as a group. They are either all retained in the equation or all dropped from the equation as a group. Dropping individual indicators changes the meaning of the remaining indicators."

pool/spa/exercise facility. It appears as though these amenities are more prevalent when living area is smaller and bedroom counts are lower. As a result of this correlation, the coefficient on pool/spa/exercise facility would be distorted if living area and bedroom count were inadvertently omitted from the model. The multiple regression model provides a better estimate of unit rent and a less-distorted estimate of the contributory value of additional living area unclouded by the simple regression model's attempt to account for bedrooms, baths, and amenities. Since all four of the variables are significant, all of them should be included in the multiple regression model.

MODEL VALIDATION

Statistics reference books offer several suggestions for regression model validation including the following:

- Collecting new data to assess the model's predictive ability on the new data
- Comparison of results with theory and with previously published empirical studies
- Data splitting

Collection of new data is generally not a practical option in applied valuation settings. Nevertheless, it is possible and recommended to assess the signs of the variables in the regression equation and compare them with theoretical and intuitive expectations. Also, the need to stay current on relevant published studies is obvious and needs little discussion. However, data splitting provides the most practical sample-specific and model-specific means of model validation and is worthy of further examination.

Data splitting, which is also known as cross-validation, requires that the data set be divided into two subsets: a model-building set and a validation set (usually referred to as a holdout sample). The holdout sample should be randomly chosen from the full data set, and it can be a small proportion of the full data set, e.g., 10% to 20%.

Two validation routines are possible and recommended. The first routine is to compare the coefficients and significance levels derived from the model-building set with the coefficients and significance levels derived from a regression model employing all of the data. The results should be consistent; otherwise a small number of influential observations may be affecting the model disproportionately. The second routine is to use the regression model derived from the model building set to predict the dependent variable values for the holdout sample. One measure of how well the model predicts is to compute the correlation between the actual values in the holdout sample and the predicted values. When the model is valid, the correlation should be high.[23]

---

[23]   If the data set is too small to accommodate data splitting into a model-building sample and a holdout sample, then an alternative but time-consuming data-splitting procedure may be employed. The alternative procedure is to remove one observation from the data set, run the regression model with the remaining $n-1$ observations, use the model to predict the value for the omitted observation, and repeat the procedure by sequentially omitting each observation in turn and re-estimating the model and predicting the value for each omitted observation. This procedure will generate n holdout samples of size = 1. The predicted value for each holdout observation should correlate highly with the actual observed values. A subroutine in SAS can automate this procedure. Unfortunately, the procedure cannot be automated in SPSS, Minitab, or Excel.

If the results from these two validation routines are satisfactory, the model is likely to be valid. A final regression model employing all of the data would therefore be appropriate for valuation purposes.[24]

UNDERLYING REGRESSION MODEL ASSUMPTIONS

In addition to the linearity of the relationship of variables, regression modeling has several other important theoretical underpinnings, generally referred to as the assumptions of regression. The additional assumptions are the following:

- Errors are normally distributed
- Variance is homoscedastic
- Errors are independent
- The explanatory variables are not highly interrelated

The normality assumption means that the errors around the regression line are normally distributed for each independent variable value. Regression models are fairly resistant to violations of the normality assumption as long as error distributions are not dramatically different from normal.[25] This assumption is important because it is the basis for the validity of the F-tests and t-tests of model and variable significance, and it provides the mathematical basis for the calculation of confidence intervals. The detrimental effects of non-normality are diminished as sample size increases.

Homoscedasticity refers to variation around the regression line being equal for all values of the independent variable. When this assumption is violated (i.e., when the data is *heteroscedastic*), significant variable coefficients are apt to appear to be insignificant and confidence intervals will be skewed due to systematic variation in error variance. Visual examination of a plot of residuals against the independent variables or the fitted values of the dependent variable is a simple means of checking for violation of the homoscedasticity assumption. The data set is not heteroscedastic when the distribution of residuals is similar across the range of each independent variable or the fitted values of the dependent variable. However, a plot showing systematic narrowing or widening of the range of residual values as the values of an independent variable or fitted values of the dependent variable change is an indication of violation of this assumption. Figure 28.10 plots the residuals (e) against the fitted values of the dependent variable ($\hat{Y}$). Note that the residuals are more tightly packed when the fitted values of the dependent variable are small and less tightly packed when the fitted values are large. The data appear to be heteroscedastic, and error variance is directly related to the value of the dependent variable.

Suggested corrections for violation of this assumption include the following:

- Replacing the values of the dependent variable with the natural logarithm of the dependent variable, i.e., log transformation
- Replacing the values of the dependent variable with the square root of the dependent variable, i.e., square root transformation

---

[24] See John Neter, William Wasserman, and Michael H. Kutner, *Applied Linear Statistical Models: Regression, Analysis of Variance, and Experimental Designs*, 3rd ed. (Homewood, Ill: Irwin, 1990), 465-470, for a more complete discussion of model validation.

[25] Levine, et al., 436.

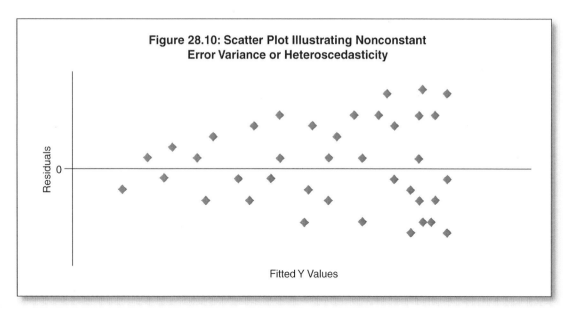

Figure 28.10: Scatter Plot Illustrating Nonconstant Error Variance or Heteroscedasticity

These two transformations replace the dependent variable with less-variable functional forms. However, the replacement variables are undefined for negative numbers.

Violation of the assumption of error independence most often occurs with time-series data. Residuals in sequential time periods may be correlated as a result of occurrences in a prior time period influencing subsequent time periods. This phenomenon is referred to as serial correlation or autocorrelation. Variable coefficient estimates remain unbiased under conditions of autocorrelation; however, the standard errors of the coefficients are biased, which affects the validity of t-statistics produced by a regression model.[26]

High interrelation among independent variables is referred to as multicollinearity. When this occurs, the independent variables share explanatory power, and the coefficients on the correlated independent variables are consequently biased. Multicollinearity is often difficult to correct. When possible, gathering more data (increasing n) may help. Also, data reduction methods such as factor analysis and the use of proxy variables can be employed to gather correlated variables together into a single representative construct. Ridge regression has also historically been suggested as a means of dealing with multicollinearity.[27]

It is important to note that multicollinearity has no effect on a model's predictive ability, assuming the model is well specified. Multicollinearity does seriously affect structural interpretation of a model's coefficients. If multicollinearity results in inclusion of superfluous variables that would otherwise be excluded, then the loss in

---

[26] The Durbin-Watson test is one well-known means of testing for first-order autocorrelation (correlation between a residual and the next residual in a time sequence). An easy-to-read and understandable text dealing solely with regression modeling and devoting an entire chapter to identification of and correlation for violations of underlying regression model assumptions is Terry Dielman, *Applied Regression Analysis*, 3rd ed. (Pacific Grove, Calif.: Duxbury, 2001).

[27] See also Graeme J. Newell, "The Application of Ridge Regression to Real Estate Appraisal", *The Appraisal Journal* (January 1982): 116-119; Alan K. Reichert, James S. Moore, and Chien-Ching Cho, "Stabilizing Statistical Appraisal Models Using Ridge Regression", *The Real Estate Appraiser and Analyst* (Fall 1985): 17-22; Doug Sweetland, "Ridge Regression: A Word of Caution", *The Appraisal Journal* (April 1986): 294-300; and Jonathon Mark, "Multiple Regression Analysis and Mass Assessment: A Review of the Issues", *The Appraisal Journal* (January 1988): 89-109.

degrees of freedom due to their inclusion will lead to a loss of some predictive power. Investigation of the existence of multicollinearity includes analysis of an independent variable correlation matrix and an examination of regression model multicollinearity diagnostics including variance inflation factors (VIFs), which most statistical packages will generate but which are not available in Excel. The general rule of thumb is that no VIF should be greater than 10 and the mean VIF should not be considerably larger than 1.[28] Note that a VIF of 10 equates to multiple correlation of 0.95, which may be excessive in many instances. Some analysts suggest a maximum VIF of 5 as a criterion for multicollinearity, which implies multiple correlation below 0.90.[29] In the multiple regression example using the garden apartment observations, variance inflation factors are 4.7 (living area), 3.4 (bedrooms), 1.7 (baths), and 1.4 (pool/spa/exercise).

DATA SUFFICIENCY

The thought process involved in making a decision regarding how many data observations are necessary for application of a regression model differs from the calculation of sample size for inferences about a mean, which was presented earlier in the chapter. In regard to a regression model, the measure of data sufficiency is based on degrees of freedom, i.e., the relationship between the number of observations (n) and the number of independent variables in the model (k). When the ratio of n to k is too low, the model is "overfitted" and the regression outcome is in danger of being data-specific, not representative of the underlying population.

For example, consider a ratio of n to k of 2:1. It is always possible to connect two points with a straight line. In this case, the coefficient of determination, R^2, would always be equal to 1 in a simple linear regression model. However, the model may not actually explain anything. Since R^2 and the ability to generalize from a sample to a population are affected by the ratio of n to k, many researchers suggest that the minimum ratio be in the range of 10 to 15 observations per independent variable,[30] with a ratio of 4:1 to 6:1 being an absolute minimum.[31] One indication of an overfit model due to a ratio of n to k that is too low is an increase in adjusted R^2 as the least-significant variables are removed from the model.

The multiple regression model example using the apartment rent data includes 36 observations (n) and four independent variables (k). The ratio of n to k is 9:1, which is less than optimal but more than the absolute minimum. If additional variables such as apartment age, location, condition, parking ratio, and the like were to be added to the regression model, then more data would be required to accommodate the expansion of the model.

---

[28] Neter, et al., 409-410.

[29] Joseph F. Hair, Rolph E. Anderson, Ronald L. Tatham, and William C. Black, *Multivariate Data Analysis with Readings*, 3rd ed. (New York: Macmillan, 1992), 48.

[30] Hair, et al., 46.

[31] Hair, et al., caution readers that a ratio of 4:1 is an absolute minimum, whereas Neter, et al., refer to a ratio of 6:1 to 10:1 as a minimum.

STATISTICAL APPLICATIONS IN APPRAISAL PRACTICE

The advent of personal computers, spreadsheet programs, and statistical software allows appraisers to incorporate statistics into their analyses and appraisal reports easily and accurately. In the early years of personal computing, statistical analysis was generally limited to providing descriptive statistics and accompanying charts, tables, and graphs. As graphical user interfaces became more prevalent in operating systems, statistical programs such as SPSS, Minitab, and SAS became more user-friendly, largely because the user no longer had to write programming code.

Also, as computer users became more sophisticated, spreadsheet programs added statistical tools to accommodate the needs of customers. Currently, Microsoft Excel includes a statistical tool pack that will generate statistical output such as correlation matrices, F-tests of variances, t-tests of means, and linear regression models. However, Excel provides very little in the way of diagnostics to accompany its inferential tools. Excel's statistical strength continues to be in its charting capabilities.

Automated Valuation Models

Tax assessment mass appraisal techniques existed long before the advent of auto-mated valuation models (AVMs), and they are now considered to be a subset of the AVM universe. Mass appraisal models were developed by property tax assessors to improve productivity and equity in non-rural locations where manpower was insuf-ficient to carry out the assessed value estimation function. In addition, in the early years of mass appraisal, tax assessors were in a unique position to take advantage of large amounts of data that had been converted into a computer-readable format. Assessors continue to use AVMs as a means of automating assessment and make use of the large amounts of digitally coded data they possess. Internet access to more reliable data from taxing authorities and third-party data sources has enabled most appraisers to access the large data resources required for statistical analyses.

Initial research on AVMs pitted neural networks and expert systems against regression-based models. Neural networks "learn" the relationships among variables to develop and continually update an internal and unknowable price-estimation algo-rithm. Neural networks are essentially "atheoretical" in terms of their algorithms and can only be tested by comparing estimation results to a known standard. Because of their "black box" decision model, they have not developed a large practical follow-ing. Expert systems develop decision models that attempt to mimic expert (e.g., appraiser) behaviour. They essentially automate the human problem-solving process. For example, some AVMs employ an expert systems layer for such tasks as selecting comparable sales or comparable rents.

Regression-based AVMs apply multiple regression models at some level within the valuation product to produce a value-estimation equation, a value estimate, adjustment coefficients for automatically selected comparable sales or rents, or some combination of these outputs. Many AVMs now include other features that enable appraisers, appraisal reviewers, and underwriters to produce and review descriptive statistics by user-defined property characteristics, market area, subdivision, postal code, city, or regional district. These features provide scales of reasonableness against which human appraiser contentions, assumptions, and conclusions can be measured. In addition to this quality control function, AVMs also enhance a lender's ability to pre-qualify borrowers, conduct audits, mitigate loss, assess portfolios of loans, provide home equity loans, and engage in numerous other functions.

A variety of AVM products are offered nationally and new products emerge constantly. As the lending industry works through issues and problems related to data reporting, data transfer, data accuracy, and modeling, AVM standards are continually being refined by the federal government's Canada Mortgage and Housing Corporation and industry organizations such as the Canadian Bankers Association and Credit Union Central of Canada. US organizations with Canadian influence include the Joint Industry Task Force on Automated Valuation Models, the Real Estate Information Providers Association, the Mortgage Bankers Association, and the Mortgage Industry Standards Maintenance Organization.

Although AVMs were initially perceived as a means of replacing human appraisers with machines, they have developed more recently into underwriting devices and tools designed to assist appraisers and appraisal reviewers. Today, practicing real estate appraisers are working to gain an understanding of AVM technology, shifting markets for appraisal services, and determining how to take advantage of new business opportunities resulting from AVMs.

Custom Valuation Models

Custom valuation models represent another opportunity for appraisers to incorporate statistical applications into their practices. Given access to adequate amounts of data, which are more readily available in single-unit residential and rental apartment markets than in most commercial markets, appraisers with adequate statistical modeling skills and appropriate software can apply statistical models to customized, unique valuation questions. Applications vary widely and include the following:

- Property tax assessment and equity studies
- Price or rent trend analysis
- Augmentation of traditional valuation approaches
- Impact studies addressing the effects of nuisances or environmental hazards
- Preparation of value estimates for litigation

Some custom applications are straightforward and easily modeled, and others are complex and difficult to model. Production of a credible work product is of paramount importance. Appraisers should not attempt to build a statistical model that is beyond the limits of their education and experience. As with any appraisal specialty, the ability to address complex statistical problems grows with experience. Experience is best gained by collaboration with a more qualified statistical analyst and continuing education to build skill sets. Perhaps more than most appraisal specialties, the use of statistical applications to solve complex appraisal problems requires knowledge beyond what is currently available in the tightly focused world of appraisal education. With this in mind, a community college or introductory undergraduate course in business statistics coupled with an upper-level course in regression analysis and specialized appraisal courses dealing with statistics are most likely the best first steps toward preparing to engage in the development of custom applications of statistical valuation modeling.

MISUSE OF STATISTICAL METHODS

Statistical methods are powerful tools for summarizing and describing data. They are also useful for making inferences about population parameters and the construction of predictive models. Unfortunately, they are also easily and frequently misused. Abuse usually falls into one or both of two categories:

- Overt attempts to mislead
- Ignorance

Manipulating the scale of charts, providing insufficient categories in frequency distributions and related histograms, and intentionally omitting variables in regression models are examples of attempts to mislead. Unknowingly violating the underlying assumptions of regression, using too low a ratio of n to k, and failing to recognize the limitations on sample representativeness could be the result of simple ignorance.

One rarely discussed problem in appraisal applications of statistical analysis is how well a statistical sample represents the larger population. This problem stems from the fact that real property sales are generally not randomly selected from the population they are purported to represent. In some instances, sales are representative even though they have not been randomly selected, and inferences are appropriate. However, in other instances some underlying cause may have been a temporary or location-specific influence on the decision to offer certain properties for sale, and data affected by that influence may not be representative of the market as a whole. In these situations, inferences derived from sales data may not provide a true picture of the overall market.

It is incumbent upon professional appraisers to present charts, tables, and graphs that accurately reflect the data being presented. In addition, appraisers who employ inferential statistical methods should be competent, i.e., educated in inferential methods and experienced with the software being used. The burden of proof of competence and lack of bias ultimately lies with the appraiser.

Frequently encountered problems of statistical misuse include the following:

- Failure to fully understand the ramifications of violating the assumptions underlying regression models

- Failure to test and assess the validity of a regression model and its underlying assumptions

- Failure to correct regression models when necessary in order to adequately comply with the underlying assumptions

Three particularly problematic areas explained earlier in the chapter are multicollinearity, heteroscedasticity, and autocorrelation. Multicollinearity often results in variable signs that are theoretically or intuitively incorrect and the apparent insignificance of variables that share explanatory power. Heteroscedasticity masks the significance of otherwise significant explanatory variables. Autocorrelation fails to account for historical influence on a time-series variable.

Other frequently encountered problems result from the misspecification of regression models. They include "overfitting" where the ratio of n to k is too low, inclusion of irrelevant variables, and omission of important variables. Note that inclusion of any variable, relevant or not, will result in an increase in the coefficient of determination, R^2. Adjusted R^2 provides a test of whether inclusion of an additional variable adds sufficient explanatory power. When adjusted R^2 does not increase with the addition of another variable, the additional variable is most likely irrelevant.[32]

In conclusion, credible regression modeling includes an assessment of data sufficiency, a residual analysis, an assessment of which variables should be included in a model, and model validation. Regarding data sufficiency, due to the ratio of n to k an analyst often has too few observations to facilitate inclusion of all of the variables known or thought to be important. To ensure credibility, the analyst must assess the need for and availability of additional data or explore means of variable reduction such as factor analysis or proxy variables. In addition, the appraiser's workfile should include an analysis of residuals regarding the assumptions underlying any model employed and an assessment of functional form and support for the variables included.

As a final cautionary statement, be aware that although modern statistical software is easy to use, its use can contribute to production of a less-than-credible work product when the steps required to ensure credible model building are overlooked.

---

[32] The additional variable should probably be included, however, if there is strong theoretical support for its importance to the relationship being studied.

CHAPTER 29

VALUATION OF PARTIAL INTERESTS

As discussed in earlier chapters, an appraisal assignment may call for the valuation of the most complete interest in real property (the fee simple interest) or an interest less than fee, i.e., a partial interest. The most common types of partial interests to be appraised include the following:

- Leased fee interests
- Leasehold interests
- Subleasehold interests
- Mortgage and equity interests
- Life estates
- Estates for years
- Remainder Interest (also known as Remainderman)

Chapter 6 defines common types of real property interests and ownership interests. This chapter outlines the techniques typically used in the valuation of the most commonly encountered partial interests, as well as other special forms of ownership such as condominium and cooperative ownership.

VALUATION OF LEASEHOLD AND LEASED FEE

The valuation of a leased fee interest is usually accomplished using the income approach. Regardless of the capitalization method selected, the value of the leased fee interest represents the owner's interest in the property. The benefits that accrue to an owner of a leased fee interest generally consist of income throughout the lease and the reversion at the end of the lease.

The market value of a leasehold interest depends on how contract rent compares to market rent, as shown in Figure 29.1. A leasehold interest may acquire value if the lease allows for subletting and the term is long enough so that market participants will pay something for the advantageous lease.

When analyzing a leasehold interest, it is essential that the appraiser analyze all of the economic benefits or disadvantages created by the lease. An appraiser should ask the following questions:

- What is the term of the lease?
- What is the likelihood that the tenant will be able to meet all of the rental payments on time?
- Are the various clauses and stipulations in the lease typical of the market, or do they create special advantages or disadvantages for either party?
- Is either the leased fee interest or the leasehold interest transferable, or does the lease prohibit transfers?
- Is the lease written in a manner that will accommodate reasonable change over time, or will it eventually become cumbersome to the parties?

An appraiser cannot simply assume that each of the interests created by the lease has market value. Many leases create no separate value for the tenant. For example, when the tenant cannot or will not pay the rent, the market value of the leased fee interest may be reduced to an amount less than the market value of a comparable property that is unleased or a comparable property leased to a more reliable tenant at below-market terms.

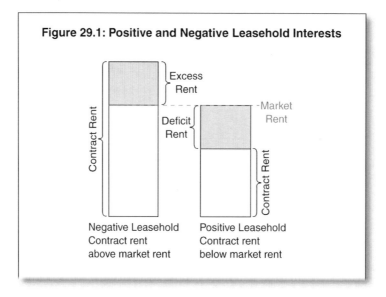

Figure 29.1: Positive and Negative Leasehold Interests

Valuation of Sublease Interests

In sublease situations, the discount rates used in valuing different lease interests will vary because the rates selected must reflect the risks involved. Generally, the leased fee interest entails less risk than the leasehold interest because the owner of the leased fee interest has the first claim on the income and is entitled to a reversion whereas the owner of the leasehold is not. Also, the leased fee interest involves less risk because the rent is fixed and not subject to the volatility of the market. In turn, the lessee assumes less risk than the sublessee because the subleasehold will only have value if it is rented to a subsequent subtenant for an amount that is more than the sublessee pays the original tenant.

VALUATION OF MORTGAGE AND EQUITY INTERESTS

Because the equity side of the real estate market dominates sales activity, appraisers must thoroughly understand the benefits that accrue to equity owners and know how equity yield is calculated. Equity owners look for two kinds of benefits:

1. Income, usually on an annual basis
2. Reversion at the end of the ownership period

Income is the annual cash flow that flows to the equity holder after payment of annual debt service to the mortgage holder. The reversion is the equity proceeds of resale after any outstanding mortgage balance and all selling expenses have been paid. Any refinancing benefits taken during the ownership period are usually viewed as a form of partial early reversion. In investment analysis assignments, the sum of all benefits received over the ownership period is analyzed in comparison to the equity invested to reveal the equity yield rate. In valuation assignments, an equity yield rate is applied to the forecast benefits to produce a present value conclusion. If the market value of the equity interest is sought, the equity yield rate can be derived from the market.

For the investor, the prime measures of investment performance are the equity yield rate and the first-year dividend, usually expressed as the equity capitalization rate (also known as the *equity dividend rate*). An investor may compare the expected equity yield on a real property investment with the yields on alternative investments with commensurate risk (e.g., stocks and bonds) and with a lender's yield on mortgages secured by similar real property. Usually the equity investor will seek a higher yield than the lender because the equity investor has a less secure position. The lender can foreclose on the mortgage and take title to the real property if the mortgage terms are not fulfilled.

To estimate equity yield rates, appraisers must research the market. This research can take many forms and may include one or more of the following analyses:

- Comparison of equity yield rates extracted from recent comparable sales. These equity yield rates are retrospective, however, and the appraiser's focus is more often prospective.3

- Verification of the prospective equity yields considered by market participants, particularly buyers, in recent or anticipated sales.

- Comparison of the equity yield rates achieved by alternative investments of comparable risk such as stocks and bonds.

- Review of published investor surveys, which can provide guidelines for appraisers.

Appropriate equity yield rates vary with property characteristics. To develop an equity yield rate from recent comparable sales, an appraiser analyzes the forecast benefits of equity ownership in relation to the equity capital invested. Note that a distinction must be drawn between historical equity yield rates, which relate to the past, and currently required equity yield rates, which apply to anticipated future benefits.

Since yield is a significant consideration in the lender's decision to invest in a mortgage interest in real estate, the lender's yield must be understood and often calculated. In the absence of points, participation, or accrual features, the lender's yield is equivalent to the interest rate.

The monetary benefits that accrue to the lender are similar to the benefits received by the equity owner, i.e., periodic income from debt service and the reversion from payment of the outstanding principal at maturity or prior. In some depressed markets, lenders may find that the property securing the loan has declined in value to the point that the loan balance exceeds the property's value. In this case, there is no longer any value in the equity interest in the property, and the value of the loan may be calculated based on the actual cash flows to the property rather than the cash flows projected when the loan contract was obtained. To do otherwise would be to estimate the value of the mortgage interest as greater than the value of the property.

The lender's interest in a property is more secure than the equity interest because debt service is paid before any other claims on net operating income and the lender can foreclose if the borrower defaults on the loan. As an interest in real property becomes less senior – e.g., a mortgage interest that corresponds to a junior lien – the rate of return requirement to attract a purchaser rises. The combination of mortgage and equity interests divides a real property interest into tiers of risk:

- The first mortgage interest in the property is a low-risk investment.

- The second mortgage interest would require a higher rate of return to compensate for the increased risk.

- The equity interest would require an even higher rate of return because of its higher risk despite the potentially higher profits.

VALUATION OF LIFE ESTATES

A life estate consists of the ownership rights held during the lifetime of a designated party, known as the *life tenant*. Upon the death of the life tenant, the life estate terminates and the ownership rights that were held by the life tenant pass to the holder of the remainder interest. An assignment involving a life estate might involve the valuation of both the life tenant's interest and the remainder interest.

To value the remainder interest, an appraiser:

- Estimates the expected time of death of the holder of the life estate. Actuarial studies from Statistics Canada provide life expectancy statistics by province and gender.

- Forecasts the future value of the fee simple interest in the property at the time of death, i.e., the reversion.

- Discounts the forecast future value of the fee simple interest in the property at an appropriate rate to derive the current value of the remainder interest. The discount rate selected depends on the age and life expectancy of the person who holds the life estate and must reflect the risk in forecasting the future value of the fee simple interest.

The life estate is generally valued as the residual, i.e., the difference between the value of the fee simple interest and the current value of the remainder interest.

VALUATION OF TRANSFERABLE DEVELOPMENT RIGHTS

Appraisers can value transferable development rights (TDRs) with ordinary direct comparison techniques if there are sufficient transactions to constitute a market. When market sales are lacking, the appraiser may apply the income approach. In such cases, the economic concept of contribution provides a foundation, and the value added to the property due to the acquisition of the TDR is adjusted for the administrative, legal, and other costs incurred. Some, though not all, of the property's net value increase can be attributed to the TDR. No one is likely to undertake such a complicated procedure without the prospect of a reasonable profit.

VALUATION OF AIR RIGHTS

When the air space above a specific land area is developable, the rights to use and control that space can be valued separately from the complete rights of ownership of the surface and air rights. For the air rights to have value there must be economic demand for the legal use of air rights.

In residual analysis, the appraiser researches the market to develop an opinion of the income and operating expenses appropriate for the space occupied by the air rights. Net operating income is capitalized using an appropriate market-extracted yield or capitalization rate, taking into account the difference in risks between ownership of the fee simple interest and air rights. The residual value of the air rights is calculated by deducting the total cost of construction from the value indication derived from the income approach.

VALUATION OF WATER RIGHTS

Some jurisdictions grant individuals and private organizations the rights to water. The water rights granted can have value, separate from the underlying real estate across which the water flows. Water rights separated from the fee simple interest may have a different market value than the water rights as part of the fee simple interest. Identifying the specific type of water rights being appraised – e.g., prescriptive water rights, appropriative water rights, groundwater rights, riparian rights, contractual entitlements – is essential because the comparability and transferability of those rights is affected by the limitations on use and access imposed by different types of ownership interests. The ownership of water rights can be complex and even contentious, and an appraiser may need legal counsel to fully analyze the issues involved in identifying and appraising water rights separately.[1]

In Canada, water rights are generally conveyed with the underlying land, and in this circumstance, they do not have severable value. Where water rights are severable, they are often bought and sold in an identifiable market, making direct comparisons possible. If ground leases for the use of water are available, that information may be applicable in the income approach. The rates charged by local utilities for water are not usually an indicator of the value of the water to a property owner because of the many additional costs (administration, overhead, etc.) built into the consumer price of water.

When valuing water rights attached to land, most commonly with the before-and-after valuation technique, an appraiser must consider the cost of bringing water to a property, which may be borne by the owner of the water rights or by the provider of the water (e.g., the local water district).

VALUATION OF SUBSURFACE RIGHTS

Appraising the right to obtain and market the minerals present underground requires the consideration of a wide variety of physical and business characteristics that affect the value and use of land subject to a subsurface mining easement. Analysis of the estimated mineral reserves, the quality of the resource, the capacity for extraction, market demand and pricing for the commodity, transportation costs, and many other factors may be outside a real property appraiser's field of expertise. Due to the complexity of identifying and analyzing relevant characteristics, assignments to value subsurface rights generally involve the collaboration of business appraisers, real property appraisers, geologists, and other experts.

A contractual royalty rate granting rights to extract a mineral from the land can provide an indication of the income-generating potential of the land. A capitalization or yield rate applied to the royalty rent would not reflect expenses of operation, capital costs, and other expenses related to the mining operation. Deriving appropriate discount rates for the mineral rights alone from sales of entire mines can be difficult because of the presence of other assets and liabilities, such as other mine operations, pension fund liabilities, and employee benefit liabilities. Similarly, direct comparison of sales must factor in any business value or other non-realty components present in comparable mining operations.

VALUATION OF CONDOMINIUMS, COOPERATIVES, AND CORPORATE SHARE UNITS

Real estate that is divided into condominium or cooperative units can be valued using most traditional appraisal methodologies.

To value individual condominium units (residential, office, industrial, or other property types), appraisers generally use the direct comparison approach. Recent

---

[1]   See *www.watergovernance.ca* for details of water rights across Canada

sales of units of comparable size, location, and quality are the best indicators of value. The income approach may also be applicable if some condominium units are rented rather than occupied by the owners. For example, a leased office condominium unit could be valued by the income approach using traditional techniques. The cost approach is usually not applicable in the appraisal of any type of condominium unit because it is difficult to estimate site value and the contributory value of common elements.[2]

To value entire condominium projects, whether they are newly constructed buildings or conversions, appraisers typically use the direct comparison approach to establish individual unit prices and apply discounted cash flow analysis to value the whole project. Using the latter technique, the appraiser estimates the amount and timing of all capital outlays, expected monetary receipts, and returns. These amounts are discounted at a rate consistent with competitive investment yields. The estimates of future sellout prices and the timing of sales are key elements in the valuation.

Although similar data may be used in both applications, the valuation of individual condominium units is distinct from the valuation of an entire condominium project. The aggregate of individual unit values does not reflect the market value of the overall project, as the aggregate sum does not reflect carrying or holding costs, marketing expense, or the timing of cash flows. It is improper to represent the sum of the individual unit values as the market value of the entire project. Likewise, individual units are not valued by appraising the entirety and then allocating the total value to individual units. Each assignment has separate and distinct considerations.

Various forms of cooperative ownership exist. Non-profit cooperatives have been created through government social housing programs. Private cooperatives were commonly used before the existence and widespread acceptability of condominium or strata title ownership, or in situations where moratoriums prohibit stratas. If an active market for units in a private cooperatively-owned property exists, appraisers can value individual units using the direct comparison approach. However, appraisers must remember that prices are influenced by the amount and terms of the mortgage financing placed on the building by the corporation. Often corporate by-laws impose limitations on the property's marketability, which can affect the validity of comparable sales data. Similarly, entrepreneurs have occasionally put certain real estate – usually apartment buildings or recreational acreages – into the name of a corporation that held no other assets, with the number of shares equal to the number of apartments or recreational lots. Shares in the corporation were sold, accompanied by a license or other right that gave exclusive occupancy to a particular apartment or recreational lot. These corporate share arrangements were usually employed as an alternative to strata titling, again to avoid zoning and subdivision controls on such subdivisions. In Canada, these private cooperatives and corporate share arrangements are usually prohibited by regulators, through policies that closed these loopholes.

---

[2]   See Claim Prevention Bulletins CP-09 and CP-16 for further information on condominium appraisal; at *www.aicanada.ca*

CHAPTER 30

VALUATION FOR FINANCIAL REPORTING

The end of the Cold War introduced new open market concepts to formerly closed societies and provided new opportunities for worldwide economic cooperation that previously could not have been attempted. It also provided opportunities for all countries to join in global systems of finance and economics. At the same time that international markets opened up and expanded, the global economy demonstrated that the collapse of an important economic segment could affect all countries. In the late 1990s, currency crises in Mexico, Russia, and Southeast Asia illustrated the increasing interdependence of national economies and how failure in one country affects the world economy. Had these situations not been addressed by the global financial community, including entities such as the International Monetary Fund, there could have been a critical economic problem worldwide.

INTERNATIONAL VALUATION STANDARDS COMMITTEE (IVSC)

The International Valuation Standards Committee (IVSC), formed in 1981 and now representing more than 50 nations, originally bore the name, The International Assets Valuation Standards Committee, or TIAVSC. The committee's original name marked its original focus on the development of international standards for the valuation of fixed assets. Its early work dealt with international accounting standards, the development of appraisal standards for financial reporting, and the harmonization of appraisal standards in all countries.

The United Nations recognized TIAVSC as a non-government member in 1985. The Committee's subsequent name change reflected growing worldwide recognition of the close relationships among the principles applied in all valuation fields, the importance of appraisals of all types of assets and liabilities in financial reporting, and the need to bring all valuation fields under a common umbrella of terms, principles, and standards. The IVSC has published International Valuation Standards (IVS) since 1985. Appendix A provides more information on the goals and content of International Valuation Standards.

As investors expand their activities beyond their national borders, Canadian appraisers are increasingly called upon to prepare appraisal reports on Canadian properties for overseas clients under the International Valuation Standards, established by the International Valuation Standards Committee, and to consult with appraisers in foreign countries on behalf of Canadian clients that need appraisal reports that follow familiar Canadian standards. For some 40 years, Canadian appraisers with international clients having real estate in Canada have needed to prepare appraisal reports that comply with the standards imposed by regulators, lenders, and stakeholders in other countries. The fact that an appraisal may be prepared in one country but used in another and that generally accepted valuation principles (or GAVP, promulgated by IVS and its predecessor) were similar, if not identical, in countries with established appraisal standards spurred the development – and ongoing refinement – of international valuation standards.

VALUATION FOR FINANCIAL REPORTING TODAY

Early on in the development of accounting principles, including those relating to the accumulation of accounting data for preparing earnings statements, balance sheets, and other statements for financial reporting, Canadian accounting policy setters (today the Accounting Standards Board, or AcSB) elected to adopt what was considered a "conservative approach" when financial information was publicly disclosed or reported to third parties. The axiom of "cost or market, whichever is lower" was the vehicle for this approach. Under this system, original accounting entries commonly reflected the cost of assets such as real estate. Similar principles were applied to other tangible assets and, customarily, to liabilities. With market changes, it was common for real estate to appreciate in market value while the books of account (and related financial reports) reflected real estate and many other assets at original cost less depreciation. Because the depreciation reported in that context was customarily based on income tax or other tabular approaches to depreciation, significant differences developed between current prices and the figures shown on balance sheets.

Although in Canada steps have been taken on several occasions to move to a system that would reflect current values in financial reporting, until recently, the concept has generally been resisted, even though it was adopted for international accounting standards more than 30 years ago. In the United Kingdom, most of Europe, and many other countries, accounting procedures have called for appraisals (often termed *valuations* elsewhere) prepared by independent experts to be used for financial reporting purposes, and appraisal standards were developed and promulgated for this purpose. This was a principal reason for the establishment of the IVSC, which also assists in the globalization of appraisal standards for all purposes and the harmonization of accounting standards where they called for valuations in financial reporting.

Starting about 2002, as part of a larger move to international accounting practises and standards, Canadian accounting organizations and regulators began to move away from cost-based asset reporting towards fair value asset reporting. The use of IFRS (International Financial Reporting Systems) will be required for Canadian publicly accountable profit-oriented enterprises for financial periods beginning on or after January 1, 2011. This group includes public companies and other "profit-oriented enterprises that are responsible to large or diverse groups of shareholders".

The International Accounting Standards Board defines *fair value* as "The amount for which an asset could be exchanged between knowledgeable, willing parties in an arms-length transaction". This definition is very close to the traditional definition of *market value* used by real estate appraisers. One of the major differences calls for the real estate appraiser, working with the accountant or business valuer, to determine whether the value of the asset as a stand-alone property has a highest and best use greater than the highest and best use of that asset to the business as a whole. In other words, if the loss of that asset would lower the value of the entire business by more than would be gained by its sale as a stand-alone property, then the value in use equates to the highest and best use for financial reporting under fair value.

> fair value
> The amount for which an asset could be exchanged between knowledgeable, willing parties in an arms-length transaction. (IVS 2, 3.2; GN 3, 3.1 Also the International Accounting Standards Board, or IASB)

Real estate appraisers can play a major role in valuation for financial reporting, working as part of a team with accountants, business valuers, and personal property appraisers. Corporate assets must be valued for inclusion on corporate financial statements. A corporate merger or acquisition also triggers a valuation of the entire business, requiring allocations of value for tangible and intangible assets in order to determine if there is any residual goodwill in the business value. Another source of work for appraisers is cost segregation. Accountants need information on the value and depreciation of building components, both long- and short-lived items. Valuation for financial reporting has long been a staple for valuers internationally, and this work is now available for appraisers in Canada who have the appropriate training and competency.[1]

The relevant set of professional standards that apply in a particular assignment for financial reporting depends on whether law, regulation, or agreement with the client requires compliance with USPAP, IVS or other standards. Members of the Appraisal Institute of Canada must comply with CUSPAP because the Institute requires it, however, these standards were amended in 2010 to provide for conformity with IVS; an appraiser may comply with USPAP and IVS simultaneously. Compliance with IVS, Accounting Standards Board (AcSB), or other standards is determined by the intended use of the appraisal, which drives the scope of work decision.

> In general, compliance with IVS is a requirement for Canadian appraisals when the appraisal reports and conclusions are to be used for the purposes of financial reporting, by publicly accountable enterprises. The Canadian Institute of Chartered Accountants has adopted the following definition for the purposes of applicable accounting standards. "A **publicly accountable enterprise** is an entity, other than a not-for-profit organization, or a government or other entity in the public sector, that:

---

[1]   For more information, see the UBC Real Estate Division *Continuing Professional Development* course "Valuation for Financial Reporting".

     i.   has issued, or is in the process of issuing, debt or equity instruments that are, or will be, outstanding and traded in a public market (a domestic or foreign stock exchange or an over-the-counter market, including local and regional markets); or

    ii.   holds assets in a fiduciary capacity for a broad group of outsiders as one of its primary businesses.

Banks, credit unions, insurance companies, securities brokers/dealers, mutual funds, and investment banks typically meet the second criterion above. Other entities may also hold assets in a fiduciary capacity for a broad group of outsiders because they hold and manage financial resources entrusted to them by clients, customers, or members not involved in the management of the entity. However, if they do so for reasons incidental to a primary business (as, for example, may be the case for travel or real estate agents, cooperative enterprises requiring a nominal membership deposit, or sellers that receive payment in advance of delivery of the goods or services, such as utility companies), that does not make them publicly accountable."

Therefore, IVS standards do not apply to the majority of appraisal assignments completed in Canada (i.e., mortgage, litigation, purchase and sale, insurance), which are prepared for purposes other than financial reporting.

PROFESSIONAL PRACTICE

Current Standards-related material is presented in this appendix, but readers should be aware that Standards are revised regularly. Readers should consult the most recent editions of any publications referenced in this appendix.

A profession is distinguished from a trade or service industry by a combination of the following factors:

- High standards of competence in a specialized field
- A distinct body of knowledge that is continually augmented by the contributions of members and can be imparted to future generations
- A code of ethics and standards of practice and members who are willing to be subject to peer review

Professional appraisal practice is founded on an established body of knowledge. In solving most appraisal problems, however, the conclusions depend largely on the ability, judgment, and integrity of individual appraisers. To form a sound conclusion, relevant data must be available and the appraiser must be committed to finding and analyzing the data. A valid analysis also depends on the skillful application of appraisal techniques. While experience, training, and knowledge are important to the gathering of relevant and important data and to the analysis processes, objectivity and independence require that judgments are drawn from the evidence and not substituted for the supporting evidence necessary to derive market value.

Since appraisal applies the scientific processes of economic analyses (i.e., the valuation process) and the professional purposes of appraisal are to develop conclusions in an impartial, objective manner, without bias or any desire to accommodate their own interests or the interests of their clients, appraisers avoid personal beliefs or biases and search for market evidence to support their appraisal opinion. It is this level of independence and freedom from either personal views or personal financial gain, and strict adherence to scientific principles contained in the valuation process, that separate the profession of appraisal from other fields that also deal with real estate values.

Professional appraisal organizations are typically formed for three purposes:

- To establish criteria for selecting and recognizing individuals with real estate valuation skills who were committed to competent and ethical practice

- To develop a system of education to train new appraisers and sharpen the skills of practicing appraisers

- To formulate a code of professional ethics and standards of professional practice to guide real estate appraisers and serve as a model for other practitioners

The heart of the Appraisal Institute of Canada's commitment to professionalism is contained in the Canadian Uniform Standards of Professional Appraisal Practice (CUSPAP), and its Bylaws and Regulations.

CANADIAN UNIFORM STANDARDS OF PROFESSIONAL APPRAISAL PRACTICE

The heart of the Appraisal Institute of Canada's commitment to professionalism is contained in the Canadian Uniform Standards of Professional Appraisal Practice, which include the Ethics Rule that governs all real property-related activity of its members, and the Appraisal, Review, and Consulting Standards Rules, along with the related Comments and Practice Notes. This Canadian Edition of the Appraisal of Real Estate describes the Appraisal, Review, and Consulting requirements.

Adopted in 2000 and taking effect on January 1, 2001, The Canadian Uniform Standards of Professional Appraisal Practice are familiarly known as CUSPAP, Canadian Uniform Standards, or simply "The Standards". Their foundation was the Code of Ethics that the Institute had developed and enhanced since its formation in 1938, and the Uniform Standards of Professional Appraisal Practice, or USPAP, developed and maintained by the Appraisal Foundation, based in Washington, DC, USA. The 2002 edition of CUSPAP incorporated for the first time materials from the International Valuation Standards Commission, or IVSC, a non-governmental organization that develops valuation standards related to International Financial Reporting Standards (IFRS), both developed under the umbrella of the United Nations Although uniquely Canadian, the Standards continue to incorporate further IVSC standards, as the international standards become more widely accepted.

The Standards meet the sponsor criteria of the Appraisal Foundation in their international membership category, and endorse International Valuation Standards as an authority promoting worldwide acceptance of standards for property valuation.

Members of the AIC and other users of CUSPAP completing reports in accordance with the standards as well as intended users of professional appraisal services will find contained herein the requirements necessary to meet compliancy with the IVS relative to IFRS and Valuation for Financial Reporting (VFR).

With the advent of IFRS and the transition within Canada to International Accounting Standards (IAS) in 2011, the Board of Directors of the AIC has recognized the need for valuation standards that address emerging valuation requirements for IFRS and diversification of the scope of work available to AIC Appraisers. Members of the Appraisal Institute of Canada (AIC) accepting assignments with respect to VFR and IFRS must, in addition to CUSPAP, obtain and be familiar with the current edition (eighth) of the IVS.[1]

The Canadian Uniform Standards of Professional Appraisal Practice were developed and are maintained by the Standards Committee of the Appraisal Institute of Canada as a working model for appraisers, consultants, and regulators. The document recognizes the need to separate the compliance role from the broader objective of servicing client issues while, at the same time, respecting both domestic protocol and international market requirements.

Four Standards have been developed:

- Ethics Standard
- Appraisal Standard
- Review Standard
- Consulting Standard

Each Standard consists of Rules and Comments; Practise Notes, and Definitions can apply to all of the Standards.

- **Rules** provide minimum performance Standards for ethics, appraisal, review, and consulting assignments.

- **Comments** clarify, interpret, explain, and elaborate on the Rules, and form an integral part of the Standards; for the purpose of the Standards, their application is compulsory.

- **Practice Notes** offer advice, examples, and resolution; their application is not compulsory.

- **Definitions** form an integral part of the Standards; for the purpose of the Standards, their application is compulsory.

Foreword to the Standards

The intent of the Standards is to promote and maintain a high level of public trust in professional appraisal practice by establishing requirements for appraisal, review, and consulting assignments. The Standards begin with the Ethics Standard which set out the requirements for integrity, impartiality, objectivity, independent judgement, and ethical conduct.

The Standards apply to all activities of any member involving an analysis, opinion, or conclusion relating to the nature, quality, utility, or value of a specified interest in or aspects of identified real estate.

---

[1]   Copies are available at *www.ivsc.org/order/index.html*

A Member of the Appraisal Institute of Canada must develop and communicate his or her analysis, opinions, and advice in a manner that will be meaningful to the client, that will not be misleading in the marketplace, and that will be in compliance with the Standards.

An appraiser must not render appraisal, review, or consulting services in a careless or negligent manner. This requires an appraiser to use due diligence and due care. The fact that the carelessness or negligence of an appraiser has not caused an error that significantly affects his or her opinions or conclusions and thereby seriously harms an intended user does not excuse such carelessness or negligence.

Authority for interpretation and application of the Standards is found in the terms of reference of appropriate Committees of the Institute.

Rules

The Rules are based upon accepted appraisal teaching that incorporates the minimum compulsory content of principles for appraising, reviewing, or consulting assignments necessary to provide a credible result. It is not anticipated that the fundamental concepts incorporated in the rules will change significantly over time; nonetheless, the Standards Committee as required will amend them.

Comments

Comments are provided to expand upon the interpretation and application of Rules. They are an integral part of the Standards and must be viewed as extensions of the Rules having the same force and effect. It may be anticipated that comments will be added or changed more frequently than Rules to respond to those industry issues that develop over time. Amendments to Comments will be made only if critical to the implementation of the Rules.

Practice Notes

Practice notes supplement the general discipline of applying Standards that an appraiser learns through a combination of education and experience. The practice notes are not binding on the appraiser. They are intended to provide a convenient resource for everyday application, giving examples for application of Rules for appraisal, review, and consulting. As new issues emerge that require practical examples for implementation, Practice Notes will be developed to promote discussion and provide leadership to appraisers in understanding how to comply with Standards.

How to Use the Document

The Standards are set up in three tiers or levels. The three tiers (Rules, Comments, and Practice Notes), apply to three Standards for the common appraisal activities: appraisals, review, and consulting.

Tier one for each Standard is an expression of the Rules for that Standard. In the majority of assignments, reference need only be made to the Rules that are written to be as concise as possible.

Each section and sub-section of the Standards is numbered for standardization of reference.

If further explanation of a Rule is required, links are provided to the Comments or second tier. The numbers in brackets at the end of a section refer to the line number at the beginning of the appropriate Comment.

The third tier of reference is the Practice Notes. When there is a Practice Note linked to a Rule, the sub-section reference will also be shown. Note that a link is referenced not only at the Rule level, but also at the Comments level, when applicable. This minimizes the need to navigate back and forth through the pages of the document in order to retrieve the full text of Comments and Practice Notes linked to a particular Rule. While Comments follow immediately after the Rules for each Standard, Practice Notes form a single section. A Practice Note may be linked to Rules under more than one Standard.

A comprehensive Index provides back-up features for quick access to linked Rules, Comments, and Practice Notes.

Linking to subordinate tiers is even simpler in the AIC website version of the Standards (*www.aicanada.org*). A left mouse click on a section number will take the reader directly to the appropriate referred link.

Jurisdictional Exception

An ethical problem arises for an appraisal when an assignment entails a legal condition that voids the force of a part or parts of CUSPAP, because Standards compliance would be contrary to law or public policy applicable to the assignment.

CUSPAP provides for jurisdictional exceptions, which an appraiser can invoke to disregard a part or parts of the Standards that are determined to be contrary to law or public policy in a given jurisdiction and only that part shall be void and of no force or effect in that jurisdiction.

Examples of a jurisdictional exception would be where an expropriation appraisal assignment dictated different valuation procedures than CUSPAP require, or an assessor who is obliged by provincial law to apply valuation procedures that contradict CUSPAP, e.g., for example, in one province applicable law prevented assessors from applying the income approach in determining assessed values, even where the property being assessed would trade based on its net income.

The use of Jurisdictional Exception is strictly limited to providing a severability clause that preserves the remainder of the Standards when one or more of its parts are determined as contrary to law or public policy of a jurisdiction.

Jurisdiction relates to the legal authority to legislate, apply, or interpret law at the federal, provincial, or local levels of government. It is misleading not to identify the part or parts disregarded and the legal authority justifying this action. In every case, it is ultimately the responsibility of the appraiser under the "Reasonable Appraiser" test, and not the client or other intended users, to determine whether the use of the Jurisdictional Exception is appropriate.

CUSPAP Definitions

Definitions form an integral part of The Standards and for the purpose of these Standards, their application is compulsory. The following definitions are taken from the Standards (CUSPAP), 2010 edition:

AACI: Accredited Appraiser Canadian Institute designation

AIC: Appraisal Institute of Canada

ACCEPTED APPRAISAL STANDARDS: a level of professional practice qualifications that affect current appraisal teachings, experience, and work performance that reasonable appraisers would believe to be justified

ACCRUED DEPRECIATION: the difference between an improvement's cost new and its value as of any given date

AD VALOREM FEE: a fee levied in proportion to the value of the property being appraised

APPRAISAL: a formal opinion of value: prepared as a result of a retainer; intended for reliance by identified parties, and for which the appraiser assumes responsibility

> Comment: An expression of value is not an appraisal if it is not the result of a retainer, if it is not intended to be relied upon, and if it is one for which the appraiser would not be expected to accept responsibility.

APPRAISAL PRACTICE: the work or services performed by appraisers, defined by three terms in these standards: appraisal, review, and consulting

> Comment: These three terms are intentionally generic, and not mutually exclusive. For example, an estimate of value may be required as part of a review or consulting service. The use of other nomenclature by an appraiser (e.g. analysis, counselling, evaluation, study, submission, valuation) does not exempt an appraiser from adherence to these standards.

APPRAISAL REPORT:

Types include:
- Narrative - comprehensive and detailed
- Short Narrative - concise and briefly descriptive
- Form - a standardized format combining check-off boxes and narrative comments

APPRAISAL REVIEW: the act or process of developing and communicating an opinion about all or part of an appraisal

> Comment: The subject of an appraisal review assignment may be all or part of an appraisal report, the work file, or a combination of these.

ASSEMBLAGE: the merging of adjacent properties into one common ownership or use

ASSIGNMENT: an appraisal, consulting, or review service provided as a consequence of an agreement between an appraiser and client

ASSUMPTION: that which is taken to be true

BIAS: a preference or inclination used in the development or communication of an appraisal, review, or consulting assignment that precludes an appraiser's impartiality

CRA: Canadian Residential Appraiser designation

CLIENT: the party or parties who engages an appraiser in a specific assignment

COMPETENCE: having the required or adequate ability or qualities to perform the specific assignment.

CONFIDENTIAL INFORMATION: information, not otherwise publicly available, provided in the trust that the recipient will not disclose it to another

CONSULTING: the act or process of analysis of real estate data, and recommendations or conclusions on diversified problems in real estate, other than an appraisal or review assignment

CONTINGENT FEE: compensation that is dependent on the result

CO-SIGNATURE: personalized evidence indicating authentication of the work performed by the members as joint authors, where each is responsible for content, analyses, and the conclusions in the report; a member cannot co-sign a report with a student or non-member

> Comment: A signature can be represented by a hand written mark, a digitized image controlled by a personalized identification number, or other media, where the member has sole personalized control of affixing the signature.

COUNCIL: the National Governing Council of the Institute

DEPRECIATION: a loss in property value from any cause

EFFECTIVE DATE: the date at which the analyses, opinions, and advice in an appraisal, review, or consulting service apply

EXTERNAL VALUER: appraiser who together with any associates has no material link with the client, an agent acting on behalf of the client, or the subject of the assignment

EXTRAORDINARY ASSUMPTION: an assumption, directly related to a specific assignment, which, if found to be false, could alter the appraiser's opinions or conclusions

EXTRAORDINARY LIMITING CONDITION: a necessary modification or exclusion of a Standard Rule; may diminish the reliability of the report

FEASIBILITY ANALYSIS: a study of the cost-benefit relationship of an economic endeavour

HAZARDOUS SUBSTANCE: any material within, around, or near the property in question that has sufficient form, quantity, and bioavailability to create a negative impact on value

HIGHEST AND BEST USE: the reasonably probable and legal use of property, that is physically possible, appropriately supported, and financially feasible, and that results in the highest value

HYPOTHETICAL CONDITION: that which is contrary to what exists, but is supposed for the purpose of analysis

INSTITUTE: the Appraisal Institute of Canada and its authorized Committees

INTANGIBLE PROPERTY (INTANGIBLE ASSETS): non physical assets, including but not limited to franchises, trademarks, patents, copyrights, goodwill, equities, mineral rights, securities, and contracts, as distinguished from physical assets such as facilities and equipment

INTENDED USE: the use or uses of an appraiser's reported appraisal, consulting, or review assignment opinions and conclusions, as identified by the appraiser based on communication with the client at the time of the assignment

INTENDED USER: the client and any other party as identified, by name or type, as users of the appraisal, consulting, or review report, by the appraiser based on communication with the client at the time of the assignment

INTERNAL VALUER: an appraiser who is in the employ of either the entity that owns the assets or the accounting firm responsible for the preparing the entity's financial records and/or reports. Appraisers in this category should refer to IVS for further clarification

INVESTMENT ANALYSIS: a study that reflects the relationship between acquisition price and anticipated future benefits of a real estate investment

JURISDICTIONAL EXCEPTION: permits the appraiser to disregard a part or parts of these Standards that are determined to be contrary to law or public policy in a given jurisdiction and only that part shall be void and of no force or effect in that jurisdiction

LARGER PARCEL: the subject property when considered together with contiguous or nearby property, the value of which is impacted by common ownership

LEASE: a legal agreement which grants to another the right to use, occupy, or control all or part of a property for a stated period of time at a stated rental

LIMITING CONDITION: a statement in the appraisal identifying conditions that impact the value conclusion

MARKET ANALYSIS: a study of real estate market conditions for a specific type of property

P.APP: Professional Appraiser designation

PERSONAL PROPERTY: identifiable portable and tangible objects which are considered by the general public as being "personal", e.g., furnishings, artwork, antiques, gems and jewellery, collectibles, machinery and equipment; all property, tangible and intangible, that is not classified as real estate

PROFESSIONAL ASSISTANCE: Professional assistance involves support to the member that has a direct and significant bearing on the outcome of his or her report. A member may rely on significant professional, valuation, consulting, or review appraisal assistance of an employee. Insured members of the Institute or other professionals would generally provide such assistance. Inspection of a property is professional assistance as it forms part of the analysis leading to an opinion

PROFESSIONAL PRACTICE PEER GROUP: committees authorized under the by-laws of the Institute to administer Canadian Uniform Standards

REAL ESTATE: land, buildings, and other affixed improvements, as a tangible entity

REAL PROPERTY: the interests, benefits, and rights inherent in the ownership of real estate

> Comment: In some jurisdictions, the terms real estate and real property have the same legal meaning. The separate definitions recognize the traditional distinction between the two concepts in appraisal theory.

REASONABLE APPRAISER: an appraiser that provides appraisal, appraisal review, and consulting services within an acceptable standard of skill and expertise, and based on rational assumptions

RECERTIFICATION OF VALUE: an inspection performed to confirm whether the hypothetical conditions in the appraisal have been met

REPORT: any communication, written or oral, of an appraisal, review, or consulting service that is transmitted to the client upon completion of an assignment

> Comment: Most reports are written and most clients mandate written reports. Oral report requirements are included to cover court testimony and other oral communications of an appraisal, review, or consulting service.

RETAINER: engagement by a client of an appraiser to produce a formal report for an intended use

SCOPE OF WORK: the type and extent of research and analysis in an assignment. Scope of work includes, but is not limited to, the following:

- the degree to which the property is inspected or identified
- the extent of research into physical or economic factors that could affect the property
- the extent of data research
- the type and extent of analysis applied to arrive at opinions or conclusions

SIGNATURE: personalized evidence indicating authentication of the work performed by the member, where the member is responsible for content, analyses, and the conclusions in the report

> Comment: A signature can be represented by a hand written mark, a digitized image controlled by a personalized identification number, or other media, where the member has sole personalized control of affixing the signature

TECHNICAL ASSISTANCE: involves support to the member in the preparation of a report, such as collecting property data and other information, but does not in itself include interpretation or analysis; a member may rely on technical assistance from Student members of the Institute or others, keeping in mind that the responsibility for the finished product rests with the member signing the report

UNIT OF MEASUREMENT: a feature of a property that can be measured, for purposes of comparison, with the same common element or component of another property, e.g., a selling price per "unit" could express a figure on a per square foot basis, per acre basis, or per suite basis

VALUE: the monetary relationship between properties and those who buy, sell, or use those properties

> Comment: Value expresses an economic concept. As such, it is never a fact, but always an opinion of the worth of a property at a given time in accordance with a specific definition of value. In appraisal practice, value must always be qualified, e.g., market value, liquidation value, investment value, rental value.

WORKFILE: documentation necessary to support an appraiser's analyses, opinions, and conclusions

Ethics Standard – Rules

Preamble

Members` of the Institute pledge to conduct themselves in a manner that is not detrimental to the public, the Institute, or the real property appraisal profession. Members' relationships with other members and the Institute shall portray courtesy and good faith and show respect for the Institute and its procedures.

Rules

It is unethical for a member:

1. to knowingly fail to comply with Bylaws, Regulations and Standards, and the Professional Liability Insurance Program, of the Institute
2. to knowingly engage in conduct that will prejudice his/her professional status, the reputation of the Institute, the appraisal profession or any other member
3. to knowingly act in a manner that is misleading
4. to act in a manner that is fraudulent
5. to knowingly complete an assignment that a reasonable appraiser could not support

6. to claim qualifications, including Continuing Professional Development credits, improperly
7. to undertake an assignment lacking the necessary competence
8. to refuse to co-operate with the Institute
9. to not create a workfile for each assignment
10. to disclose results of an assignment to anyone but the client, except with the client's permission
11. to fail to reveal any conflict of interest
12. to accept an appraisal assignment that is contingent on the result

Appraisal Standard – Rules

This Standard deals with the procedures for the development and communication of a formal opinion of value, and incorporates the minimum content necessary to produce a credible report that will not be misleading.

Rules

In the report, the appraiser must:

1. identify the client and other intended users, by name
2. identify the intended use of the appraiser's opinions and conclusions
3. identify the purpose of the assignment, including a relevant definition of value
4. identify the scope of work necessary to complete the assignment
5. identify whether the appraisal is current, retrospective, prospective, or an update
6. provide an analysis of reasonable exposure time linked to a market value opinion
7. identify the effective date of the appraiser's opinions and conclusions
8. identify the date of the report
9. identify the location and characteristics of the property and the interest appraised
10. identify all assumptions and limiting conditions
11. identify any hypothetical conditions (including proposed improvements)
12. identify land use controls
13. state the existing use and the use reflected in the appraisal
14. define and resolve the highest and best use
15. describe and analyze all data relevant to the assignment
16. describe and apply the appraisal procedures relevant to the assignment
17. support the reason for the exclusion of any of the usual valuation procedures
18. detail the reasoning supporting the analyses, opinions, and conclusions of each valuation approach
19. when developing an opinion of the value of a leased fee or a leasehold estate, analyze the effect on value, if any, of the terms and conditions of the lease(s)
20. analyze the effect on value of an assemblage
21. analyze the effect on value of anticipated public or private improvements
22. analyze the effect on value of any personal property
23. analyze any agreement for sale, option, or listing of the property
24. analyze any prior sales of the property

25. review and reconcile the data, analyses, and conclusions of each valuation approach into a final value estimate
26. report the final value estimate
27. include a signed certification of value

Note: An appraiser who signs a certification of value accepts responsibility for the appraisal and the contents of the appraisal report.

An appraisal report completed pursuant to CUSPAP for Financial Reporting purposes pursuant to International Valuation Standard 1 (IVS-1) must meet additional CUSPAP standards. See CUSPAP Appraisal Rules section 6.3.

Review Standard – Rules

In performing an appraisal review assignment, an appraiser acting as a reviewer must develop and report a credible opinion as to the quality of another appraiser's work and must clearly disclose the scope of work performed in the review assignment.

This Standard deals with the procedures for the development and communication of a real property appraisal review, and incorporates the minimum content necessary to produce a credible review report that is not misleading. The Appraisal Review determines compliance with the Appraisal Standard. This Standard does not dictate the form, format, or style of appraisal review reports, which are functions of the needs of users and appraisers. The substantive content of the appraisal review report determines its compliance.

There is a distinction between the terms *technical review* and *administrative review*. A technical review is work performed by an independent third party appraiser in accordance with this Review Standard, of an appraisal report prepared by another appraiser for the purpose of forming an opinion as to whether the analysis, opinions, and conclusions in the report under review are appropriate and reasonable. The review appraiser does not sign or co-sign the appraisal report that is under review. An administrative review is work performed by clients and users of appraisal services as a due diligence function in the context of making a business decision.
This Standard is not applicable to:

- Administrative Review
- Supervisory co-signing
- Professional Practice Peer Review

Rules

In the report, the review appraiser must:

1. identify the client and other intended users, by name
2. identify the intended use of the review appraiser's opinions and conclusions
3. identify the purpose of the appraisal review assignment
4. identify the report under review, the appraiser(s) that completed the report under review, the real estate and real property interest appraised, and the effective date of the opinion in the report under review
5. identify the date of the review

6.   identify the scope of work of the review process that was conducted
7.   identify all assumptions and limiting conditions
8.   provide an opinion as to the completeness of the report under review within the scope of work applicable in the review assignment
9.   provide an opinion as to the apparent adequacy and relevance of the data and the propriety of any adjustments to the data
10. provide an opinion as to the appropriateness and proper application of the appraisal methods and techniques used
11. provide an opinion as to whether the analyses, opinions, and conclusions in the report under review are appropriate and reasonable
12. provide the reasons developed for any disagreement or agreement with the appraisal report being reviewed
13. include all known pertinent information
14. include a signed certification

Note: A review appraiser who signs a certification accepts responsibility for the review and the contents of the review report.

Consulting Standard – Rules

This Standard deals with the procedures for the development and communication of a real property consulting service and incorporates the minimum content necessary to produce a credible result that is not misleading.

Rules

In the report, the consultant must:

1.   identify the client and other intended users, by name
2.   identify the intended use of the opinions and conclusions
3.   identify the purpose of the consultation
4.   identify the real estate/property under consideration, if any
5.   identify the effective date of the consulting service
6.   identify the date of the report
7.   identify the scope of work and the extent of the data collection process
8.   identify all assumptions and limiting conditions
9.   identify any hypothetical conditions (including proposed improvements)
10. collect, verify, reconcile, and report all pertinent data as may be required to complete the consulting service
11. describe and apply the consulting procedures relevant to the assignment
12. detail the reasoning that supports the analyzes, opinions, and conclusions
13. report the consultant's final conclusions/recommendations (if any)
14. include a signed certification

Note: A consultant who signs a certification accepts responsibility for the consultation and the contents of the consultation report.

INTERNATIONAL VALUATION STANDARDS (IVS)

As the established international standard setter for valuation, the International Valuation Standards (IVS) develops and maintains standards for the reporting and disclosure of valuations, especially those that will be relied upon by investors and other third party stakeholders. It also supports the need to develop a framework of guidance on best practice for valuations of the various classes of assets and liabilities and for the consistent delivery of the standards by properly trained professionals around the globe.

The International Valuation Standards Board (IVSB) is the standard-setting body of the International Valuation Standard Council (IVSC). The IVSB members are appointed by the IVSC Trustees having regard to criteria set out in the By Laws of the organization and the IVSB has autonomy in the development and approval of the International Valuation Standards (IVS).

Valuations are widely used and relied upon in the financial and other markets, whether for inclusion in financial statements, for regulatory compliance, or to support secured lending and transactional activity. The objective of the IVSB is to contribute to the efficiency of those markets by providing a framework for the delivery of credible and consistent valuation opinions. The IVSB achieves this objective by developing and maintaining the IVS and promoting the use of those standards.

The IVS are designed to:

- promote consistency and aid the understanding of valuations of all types by identifying or developing globally accepted principles and terminology

- identify and promulgate common principles for the undertaking of valuation assignments and the reporting of valuations

- identify the appropriate valuation objectives and solutions for the major purposes for which valuations are required

- identify specific issues that require consideration when valuing different types of assets or liabilities

- promote the convergence of existing valuation standards that are in use in different sectors and states

The material in these standards meets at least one of the above criteria.

Where a statement is made that a valuation will be or has been undertaken in accordance with these standards, it is implicit that all relevant individual standards are complied with. Where a departure is necessary to comply with any legislative or regulatory requirements, this should be clearly explained.

In developing the IVS, the IVSB:

- follows due process in the development of any new standard that involves consultation with providers and users of valuation services, and public exposure of all new standards and material alterations to existing standards

- liaises with other bodies that have a standard setting function for valuation within a defined geographic area or for a defined sector or group of individuals

- is subject to oversight by the Board of Trustees of the IVSC to ensure that it acts in the public interest.

IVSC is the successor body to the International Valuation Standards Committee, which from the early 1980s until 2007 developed and published the IVS. In 2006 and 2007, the outgoing Committee established a Critical Review Group with a remit of considering how the standards could be improved to meet the requirements of the evolving market for valuation. The report of the Critical Review Group was published and comments invited on its recommendations. The IVSB has accepted the major recommendations of the Critical Review Group in developing this, the ninth edition of the standards. This has resulted in major changes to the scope and presentation of the standards.

The standards apply to assets and liabilities. To assist the legibility of these standards, the words asset or assets are deemed to include liability or liabilities, except where it is expressly stated otherwise, or is clear from the context that liabilities are excluded.

Structure

In the 2011 edition, the standards are organized as follows:

100 Series – General Standards

The General Standards have general application for all valuation purposes, subject only to specified variations or additional requirements in standards that are appropriate to specific applications or to specific types of asset or liability.

    IVS 101 – General Concepts and Principles
    IVS 102 – Valuation Approaches
    IVS 103 – Bases of Value
    IVS 104 – Scope of Work
    IVS 105 – Valuation Reporting

200 Series – Application Standards

The Application Standards describe common different purposes for which valuations are required, relate these to the IVS general standards, and set out any specific valuation requirements for each purpose.

    IVS 201.01 – Fair Value under International Financial Reporting Standards
    IVS 201.02 – Valuations for Depreciation
    IVS 201.03 – Valuations for Lease Accounting
    IVS 201.04 – Valuations for Impairment Testing
    IVS 201.05 – Valuations of Property, Plant and Equipment in the Public Sector
    IVS 202.01 – Valuations of Property Interests for Secured Lending

300 Series – Asset Standards

The Asset Standards describe matters that influence the value of different types of asset, how the principles in the General Standards are applied to their valuation, and any variations or additional requirements to these principles.

IVS 301.01 – Valuations of Businesses and Business Interests
IVS 301.02 – Valuations of Intangible Assets
IVS 302.01 – Valuations of Plant and Equipment
IVS 303.01 – Valuations of Property Interests
IVS 303.02 – Valuations of Historic Property
IVS 303.03 – Valuations of Investment Property under Construction
IVS 303.04 – Valuations of Trade Related Property
IVS 304.01 – Valuations of Financial Instruments
IVS 305.01 – reserved for future standard on valuing non financial liabilities
IVS 306.01 – reserved for future standard on Biological Assets
IVS 307.01 – reserved for future standard on Extractive Industries

As mentioned earlier, IVS are not mandatory standards for appraisers in Canada, unless the intended use of the valuation work involves financial reporting, pursuant to International Financial Reporting Standards (IFRS), which entails a body of knowledge in the accounting profession. Real estate valuations pursuant to IFRS entail fair value concepts, rather than market value, as CUSPAP defines such.

Fair value is the estimated price for the transfer of an asset or liability between identified knowledgeable and willing parties that reflects the respective interests of those parties.

The definition of fair value in International Financial Reporting Standards (IFRS) is different from the above and is generally consistent with market value.

For purposes other than use in financial statements, fair value can be distinguished from market value. Fair value requires the assessment of the price that is fair between two identified parties taking into account the respective advantages or disadvantages that each will gain from the transaction. In contrast, market value requires any advantages that would not be available to market participants generally to be disregarded.

Fair value is a broader concept than market value. Although in many cases the price that is fair between two parties will equate to that obtainable in the market, there will be cases where the assessment of fair value will involve taking into account matters that have to be disregarded in the assessment of market value, such as any element of special value arising because of the combination of the interests.

Examples of the use of fair value include:

- estimating a price that is fair for a shareholding in a non quoted business, where the holdings of two specific parties may mean that the price that is fair between them is different from the price that might be obtainable in the market

- estimating the price that would be fair between a lessor and a lessee for either the permanent transfer of the leased asset or the cancelation of the lease liability.[2]

---

[2]   See IVSC2010 Exposure Draft page 22

FINANCIAL FORMULAS

BASIC FORMULAS

Symbols

I = income	**Subscript:**
R = capitalization rate	O = overall property
V = value	M = mortgage
M = mortgage ratio	E = equity
DCR = debt coverage ratio	L = land
F = capitalization factor (multiplier)	B = building
GIM = gross income multiplier	LF = leased fee
EGIM = effective gross income multiplier	LH = leasehold
NIR = net income ratio	

Basic Income/Cap Rate/Value Formulas

$$I = R \times V$$
$$R = I/V$$
$$V = I/R$$

Basic Value/Income/Factor Formulas

$$V = I \times F$$
$$I = V/F$$
$$F = V/I$$

Adaptations for Mortgage/Equity Components

Band of Investment (using ratios)

$$R_O = M \times R_M + [(1 - M) \times R_E]$$
$$R_E = (R_O - M \times R_M)/(1 - M)$$

Equity Residual

$$V_O = [(I_O - V_M \times R_M)/R_E] + V_M$$
$$R_E = (I_O - V_M \div R_M)/V_E$$

> **Cap Rate/Factor Relationships**
> $$R = 1/F$$
> $$R_O = NIR/GIM$$
> $$R_O = NIR/EGIM$$
> Note: NIR may relate to scheduled gross or effective gross income; care should be taken to ensure consistency.

Mortgage Residual

$$V_O = [(I_o - V_E \times R_E)/R_M] + V_E$$

Debt Coverage Ratio

$$R_O = DCR \times M \times R_M$$
$$DCR = R_O/(M \times R_M)$$
$$M = R_O/(DCR \times R_M)$$

Adaptations for Land/Building Components

Land Residual

$$V_O = [(I_o - V_B \times R_B)/R_L] + V_B$$
$$R_L = (I_o - V_B \times R_B)/V_L$$

Building Residual

$$V_O = [(I_o - V_L \times R_L)/R_B] + V_L$$
$$R_B = (I_o - V_L \times R_L)/V_B$$

DISCOUNTED CASH FLOW ANALYSIS FORMULAS

Symbols

PV = present value

CF = cash flow

Y = yield rate

R = capitalization rate

Δ = change

a = annualizer

$1/S_{n|}$ = sinking fund factor

$1/n$ = 1/projection period

CR = compound rate of change

V = value

Subscript:

n = projection periods

O = overall property

I = income

Discounted Cash Flows/Present Value (DCF/PV)

$$PV = \frac{CF_1}{1 + Y} + \frac{CF_2}{(1 + Y)^2} + \frac{CF_3}{(1 + Y)^3} + \cdots + \frac{CF_n}{(1 + Y)^n}$$

Basic Cap Rate/Yield Rate/Value Change Formulas

$$R = Y - \Delta a$$
$$Y = R + \Delta a$$
$$\Delta a = Y - R$$
$$\Delta = (Y - R)/a$$

Adaptations for Common Income/Value Patterns

Pattern	Premise	Cap Rate (R)	Yield Rate (Y)	Value Change (D)
Perpetuity	$\Delta = O$	$R = Y$	$Y = R$	
Level annuity*	$a = 1/S_{n\rceil}$	$R = Y - \Delta 1/S_{n\rceil}$	$Y = R + \Delta 1/S_{n\rceil}$	$\Delta = (Y - R)/(1/S_{n\rceil})$
Straight-line change	$a = 1/n$	$R = Y - \Delta 1/n$	$Y = R + \Delta 1/n$	$\Delta = (Y - R)/(1/n)$
Exponential change	$\Delta a = CR$	$R_O = Y_O - CR$	$Y_O = R_O + CR$	$\Delta = (1 + CR)^n - 1$

* Inwood premise: $1/S_{n\rceil}$ at Y rate; Hoskold premise: $1/S_{n\rceil}$ at safe rate

Straight-Line Change* in Income	Straight-Line Change* in Value	Compound Rate of Change
$\$\Delta_I = V \times \Delta 1/n \times Y$	$\$\Delta 1/n = \$\Delta_I/Y$	$CR = \sqrt[n]{FV/PV} - 1$
$\Delta_I = (Y \times \Delta 1/n)/(Y - \Delta 1/n)$	$\Delta 1/n = (Y \times \Delta_I)/(Y \times \Delta_I)$	$CR = Y_O - R_O$

* In these formulas, Δ_I is the ratio of one year's change in income to the first year's income.

Six Functions of One

The following formulas may be used to convert the annual constant (R_M) for a monthly payment loan to the corresponding monthly functions.

Function for Monthly Frequency	Formula
Amount of one	$S^n = R_M/(R_M - I)$
Amount of one per month	$S^n = 12/(R_M - I)$
Sinking fund factor	$1/S_{n\rceil} = (R_M - I)/12$
Present value of one	$1/S_{n\rceil} = (R_M - I)/R_M$
Present value of one per month	$a_{n\rceil} = 12/R_M$
Partial payment	$1/a_{n\rceil} = R_M/12$

In these formulas, I = nominal interest rate.

Note: Section 6 of Canada's Interest Act provides that, for loans secured by a mortgage on real property (or hypothetically on immovables) and that are payable on a sinking fund plan (that is, involves payments that combine interest charges and principal repayment), the loan contract must expressly state the rate of interest chargeable on that money, calculated yearly or half-yearly, not in advance; exceptions exist for certain types of loans. Section 10 of the Interest Act limits penalties that apply to early repayment of mortgages. For the purpose of illustrating financial calculations, the examples in this Appendix do not consider statutory provisions such as those set out above that, for some mortgages, can affect interest calculations and the valuation of the unpaid balances.

Present Value of Level Annuities

The Inwood Premise

The Inwood premise applies to income that is an ordinary level annuity. It holds that the present value of a stream of income is based on a single discount rate. Each instalment of income is discounted with a single discount rate, and the total discounted values of the instalments are accumulated to obtain the present value of the income stream. The present value of a series of $1 payments can be found in compound interest tables for a given rate and a given period of time. It is assumed that the income will be sufficient to return all investment capital to the investor and to pay the specified return on the investment.

In most mortgages, the amount of interest declines gradually over the holding period and is calculated as a specified percentage of the unrecaptured capital. Any excess over the required interest payment is considered a return of capital and reduces the amount of capital remaining in the investment. Because the instalments are always the same amount, the principal portion of the payments increases by the same amounts that the interest portion of the payments decreases. It is also valid, but not customary, to see the interest payments as constant, always amounting to the specified return on the original investment, with any excess over the required, fixed-interest payments credited to a hypothetical sinking fund that grows with interest at the same rate to repay the original investment.

An Inwood capitalization rate can be constructed by adding the interest rate to a sinking fund factor $(1/S_{\overline{n}|})$ that is based on the same interest rate and duration as the income stream. The resulting capitalization rate is simply the reciprocal of the ordinary level annuity (present value of one per period) factor found in financial tables. Thus, the Inwood premise is consistent with the use of compound interest tables to calculate the present value of the income stream.

The Inwood premise applies only to a level stream of income. Therefore, the present value of any expected reversion or other benefit not included in the income stream must be added to obtain the total present value of the investment. For example, assume that the NOI of a property is $10,000 per year for five years. What is the value of the property assuming an overall yield rate (Y_O) of 10% under the Inwood premise?

Solution 1

Apply the PV of 1 per period (ordinary level annuity) factor to the NOI:

   3.79079 × $10,000 = $37,908 (rounded)

Solution 2

The general yield capitalization formula can also be used for a level income with a percentage change in value:

   $R_O = Y_O - \Delta_O \, 1/S_{\overline{n}|}$

Because there is no reversion, the property will lose 100% of its value. Δ_O is thus -1.0 and the yield capitalization formula becomes:

   $R_O = Y_O + 1/S_{\overline{n}|}$

With appropriate inputs, this equation represents the Inwood premise. By substituting the data given in the example, R_O can be solved for as follows:

$R_O = 0.10 + 0.163797$
$R_O = 0.263797$

The value of the property may be estimated using the basic valuation formula:

$V_O = NOI / R_O$
$= \$10,000 / 0.263797$
$= \$37,908$ (rounded)

Note that the sinking fund factor $(1/S_{\overline{n}|})$ is based on a 10% discount rate, which implies that a portion of the NOI could be reinvested at 10% to replace the investment. It can be said that Y_O represents the return on capital and $1/S_{\overline{n}|}$ represents the return of capital.

The Inwood premise assumes a constant rate of return on capital each year with the return of capital being reinvested in a sinking fund at the same yield rate as Y_O. The amount accumulated in this sinking fund can be used to replace the asset at the end of its economic life. Using the assumptions applied in the preceding example, the NOI for the first year may be allocated as follows:

NOI	$10,000.00
Return on capital (10% of $37,908)	– $3,790.80
Return of capital	$6,209.20

If the return of capital ($6,209.20) is placed in a sinking fund earning 10%, the fund will accumulate to $37,908 over five years. The sinking fund accumulation factor (future value of one per period), $S_{\overline{n}|}$, is applied to the return of capital:

$6.1051 \times \$6,209.20 = \$37,908$

This is the exact amount required to replace the asset.

The Hoskold Premise

The Hoskold premise differs from the Inwood premise in that it employs two separate interest rates:

- A speculative rate, representing a fair rate of return on capital commensurate with the risks involved

- A safe rate for a sinking fund, designed to return all the invested capital to the investor in a lump sum at the termination of the investment

In contrast to the Inwood premise, the Hoskold premise assumes that the portion of NOI needed to recover or replace capital (the return of capital) is reinvested at a "safe rate" – e.g., the prevailing rate for insured savings accounts or government bonds – which is lower than the "speculative" yield rate (Y_O) used to value the other portion of NOI. Like the Inwood premise, the Hoskold technique was designed to be applied when the asset value of the investment decreases to zero over the holding period. However, Hoskold assumed that funds would have to be set aside at a lower, safe rate to replace the asset at the end of the holding period. Hoskold suggested that this technique might be appropriate for valuing wasting assets such as a mine where the value is reduced to zero as minerals are extracted; thus funds have to be set aside to invest in a new mine once the minerals are totally depleted, i.e., the reversion equals zero.

Using the same NOI, yield, and term set forth in the previous example, assume that a portion of NOI has to be set aside at a 5% safe rate to allow for the recovery of capital at the end of every five-year period. All other assumptions remain the same. This problem may be solved with the same yield capitalization formula applied in the Inwood calculation, but the sinking fund factor $(1/S_{\overline{n}|})$ is based on the safe rate of 5% rather than the yield rate of 10%. Thus, the overall rate is calculated as follows:

$$R_o = Y_o + 1/S_{\overline{n}|}$$
$$= 0.10 + 0.180975$$
$$= 0.280975$$

Because the sinking fund factor $(1/S_{\overline{n}|})$ is calculated at a 5% rate rather than the 10% rate, the capitalization rate is higher and the value is lower. The value is calculated as:

$$V_o = NOI / R_o$$
$$= \$10,000 / 0.280975$$
$$= \$35,590 \text{ (rounded)}$$

The lower value is a result of setting aside the portion of NOI earning 5% to allow for the recovery of capital ($35,590) at the end of five years. The income allocation for the first year can be shown as follows:

NOI	$10,000
Return on capital (10% of $35,590)	− 3,559
Return of capital	$6,441

To find the future value of $6,441 at 5% for five years, apply the sinking fund accumulation factor (future value of one per period), $S_{\overline{n}|}$, to the return of capital:

$$5.525631 \times \$6,441.00 = \$35,590$$

The result is the exact amount required to recover the capital invested.

Present Value of Increasing/Decreasing Annuities

Straight-Line Changes

To obtain the present value of an annuity that has a starting income of d at the end of the first period and increases h dollars per period for n periods:

$$PV = (d + h\,n)a_{\overline{n}|} - \frac{h\,(n - a_{\overline{n}|})}{i}$$

To obtain the present value of an annuity that has a starting income of d at the end of the first period and decreases h dollars per period for n periods, simply make h negative in the formula.

Exponential-Curve (Constant-Ratio) Changes

To obtain the present value of an annuity that starts at $1 at the end of the first period and increases each period thereafter at the rate x for n periods:

$$PV = \frac{1-(1+x)^n / (1+i)^n}{i-x}$$

where i is the periodic discount rate and x is the ratio between the increase in income for any period and the income for the previous period.

To obtain the present value of an annuity that starts at $1 at the end of the first period and decreases each period thereafter at rate x, simply make x negative in the formula.

RATES OF RETURN

Symbols

PV = present value
NPV = net present value
CF = cash flow
i = discount rate (in NPV formula)
n = projection period
IRR = internal rate of return
PI = profitability index
MIRR = modified internal rate of return
FVCFj = future value of a series of cash flows
i = reinvestment rate (in MIRR formula)

Subscript:
0 = at time zero
1 = end of 1st period
2 = end of 2nd period
3 = end of 3rd period
n = end period of series

Net Present Value (NPV)

$$NPV = CF_0 + \frac{CF_1}{1+i} + \frac{CF_2}{(1+i)^2} + \frac{CF_3}{(1+i)^3} + \cdots + \frac{CF_n}{(1+i)^n}$$

Internal Rate of Return (IRR)

Where NPV = 0; IRR = i

Profitability Index (PI)

$PI = PV/CF_0$

Modified Internal Rate of Return (MIRR)

$$MIRR = \sqrt[n]{\frac{FVCFj}{CF_0}} - 1$$

$$MIRR = \sqrt[n]{\frac{CF_1(1+i)^{n-1} + CF_2(1+i)^{n-2} + CF_3(1+i)^{n-3} + \cdots + CF_n}{CF_0}} - 1$$

Note: In these formulas, individual CFs may be positive or negative for PV and NPV solutions; however, CF_0 is treated as a positive value for PI and MIRR solutions.

MORTGAGE INTERESTS

Mortgage investments have a great impact on real property value and equity yield rates. Since yield is a significant consideration in the lender's decision to invest in a mortgage interest in real estate, the lender's yield must be understood and often calculated. In the absence of points and any participation or accrual feature, the lender's yield equals the interest rate.

Mortgage information used to value income-producing properties may include the following:

1. The monthly or periodic payments and annual debt service on a level-payment, fully amortized loan

2. The accompanying partial payment factors and annual constants (RM)

3. The balance outstanding balance (B) on an amortized loan at any time before the end of its term, expressed as a dollar amount or a percentage of the original loan amount

4. The percentage or proportion of the principal amount paid off before full amortization (P)

Mortgage Components

Periodic (Monthly) Payment

The monthly payment factor for a fully amortized, monthly payment loan with equal payments is the direct reduction loan factor, or monthly constant, for the loan, given the interest rate and amortization period. Thus, the monthly payment factor for a 30-year, fully amortized, level monthly payment loan at 15.5% interest per year, compounded monthly is 0.013045. This number can be obtained from a direct reduction loan table or by solving for the monthly payment (PMT) on a financial calculator, given the number of periods (n), the interest rate (i), and the principal loan amount.

If the loan had an initial principal amount of $160,000, the monthly payment required to amortize the principal over 30 years and provide interest at a rate of 15.5% per year, compounded monthly on the outstanding balance each month would be:

$160,000 × 0.013045 = $2,087.20

Annual Debt Service and Loan Constant

Cash flows are typically converted to an annual basis for real property valuation, so it is useful to calculate the amount of annual debt service as well as the monthly payments. For the 30-year, fully amortized, level monthly payment loan of $160,000 at a 15.5% interest per year, compounded monthly, the annual debt service is:

$2,087.20 × 12 = $25,046.40

The annual loan constant is simply the ratio of annual debt service to the loan principal. (The annual loan constant, often called the *mortgage constant,* describes a rate although it is actually the annual debt service per dollar of mortgage loan outstanding, which may be expressed as a dollar amount.) The annual loan constant is expressed as R_M to signify that it is a capitalization rate for the loan or debt portion of the real property investment. For the loan mentioned, the annual loan constant can be calculated as follows:

$$R_M = \frac{\text{annual debt service}}{\text{loan principal}}$$

$$= \frac{\$25,046.40}{\$160,000.00}$$

$$= 0.156540$$

The annual loan constant can also be obtained when the amount of the loan principal is not known. In this case, the monthly payment factor is simply multiplied by 12.

$$R_M = \text{monthly payment factor} \times 12$$
$$= 0.013045 \times 12$$
$$= 0.156540$$

Although these figures are rounded to the nearest cent, in actual practice most loan constants are rounded up to make sure that the loan will be repaid during the stated amortization period.

Outstanding Balance

Properties are frequently sold, or loans may be refinanced, before the loan on the property is fully amortized. Furthermore, loans often mature before the completion of loan amortization. In such cases, there is an outstanding balance or balloon payment due on the note; from the lender's point of view, this is the loan or debt reversion to the lender.

The outstanding balance (B) on any level-payment, amortized loan is the present value of the debt service over the remaining amortization period discounted at the interest rate. Thus, at the end of 10 years, the balance for the 30-year note discussed above would be the present value of 20 years of remaining payments. The balance is calculated by multiplying the monthly payment by the present value of one per period factor (monthly) for 20 years at the interest rate. The balloon payment, or future value, may be calculated as follows:

$$B = \$2,087.20 \times 73.861752$$
$$= \$154,164.25$$

Similarly, the outstanding balance at the end of 18 years would be equal to the monthly payment times the present value of one per period factor (monthly) for 12 years at the interest rate.

$$B = \$2,087.20 \times 65.222881$$
$$= \$136,133.20$$

The outstanding balance on a loan can also be expressed as a percentage of the original principal. This is useful, and sometimes necessary, if dollar amounts are not given or are unavailable. For a 10-year projection with 20 years remaining on the note, the outstanding balance is:

$$B = \frac{\$154,164.25}{\$160,000.00}$$
$$= 0.963527$$

For an 18-year projection with 12 years remaining on the note, the balance is:

$$B = \frac{\$136,133.20}{\$160,000.00}$$
$$= 0.850833$$

A percentage balance can also be calculated as the ratio of the present value of one per period factor for the remaining term of the loan at the specified interest rate divided by the present value of one per period factor for the full term of the loan at the interest rate. This can be expressed as:

$$B = \frac{PV\ 1/P\ \text{remaining term}}{PV\ 1/P\ \text{full term}}$$

In the case of the 30-year loan at an interest rate of 15.5% per annum, compounded monthly, the balance for a 10-year projection with 20 years remaining is calculated as:

$$B = \frac{73.861752}{76.656729}$$
$$= 0.963539$$

For an 18-year projection with 12 years remaining, the balance would be:

$$B = \frac{65.222881}{76.656729}$$
$$= 0.850844$$

These results are similar to those obtained using dollar amounts.

Percentage of Loan Paid Off

It is often necessary to calculate the percentage of the loan paid off before full amortization over the projection period, especially in Ellwood mortgage-equity analysis. The percentage of the loan paid off is expressed as P and is most readily calculated as the complement of B.

$P = 1 - B$

For the 30-year note, P is calculated as follows:

$P_{10} = 1 - 0.963539$
$\quad = 0.036461$

$P_{18} = 1 - 0.850844$
$\quad = 0.149156$

The percentage of the loan paid off prior to full amortization over the projection period (P) can also be calculated directly. There are many different procedures for this operation and they are not all presented here. Financial calculators often provide an amortization or AMORT function.

The simplest, most direct procedure is to calculate P as the ratio of the sinking fund factor for the full term (monthly) divided by the sinking fund factor for the projection period (monthly).

$$P = \frac{1/S_{\overline{n}|}}{1/S_{\overline{n}|P}}$$

For the 30-year monthly payment note at 15.5% per annum, compounded monthly, the calculations are:

$$P_{10} = \frac{0.000129}{0.003524}$$

$\quad = 0.036606$

$$P_{18} = \frac{0.000129}{0.000862}$$

$\quad = 0.149652$

Any differences are due to rounding.

Lender's Yield

To illustrate how the lender's yield on a mortgage loan investment is calculated, consider a mortgage loan with the following characteristics.

Loan amount	$100,000
Interest rate	13.5% per annum, compounded monthly
Term	25 years
Payment	Monthly
Balance in five years	$96,544
Points	3
Other costs	Borrower to pay all other costs

If the mortgage runs full term, the yield can be obtained using a calculator.

$$n = 300$$
$$PMT = \$1,165.65$$
$$PV = \$97,000 \ (\$100,000 \ \text{less 3 points, or} \ \$3,000)^*$$
$$i = 13.97\% \ \text{per annum, compounded monthly}$$

* Each point is equal to 1% of the loan amount: $\$100,000 \times 0.01 = \$1,000$.

The lender's yield is greater than the nominal interest rate because of the points paid by the borrower. In effect, the lender only loaned $97,000 ($100,000 − $3,000) but receives a stream of debt service payments based on $100,000. If the mortgage is paid off in five years, the lender's yield is calculated with these figures.

$$n = 60$$
$$PMT = \$1,165.65$$
$$PV = \$97,000$$
$$FV = \$96,544$$
$$i = 14.36\% \ \text{per annum, compounded monthly}$$

If there were no points in either of these examples, the yield to the lender would be 13.5% per annum, compounded monthly in each case. Points or any other monetary payments that reduce the lender's investment are important considerations in calculating the lender's yield. The lender's yield may be supplemented through the syndication process.

In some depressed markets, lenders may find that the property securing the loan has declined in value to the point that the loan balance exceeds the property's value. In this case, there is no longer any equity interest in the property, and the value of the loan may often be calculated based on the actual cash flows to the property rather than the cash flows projected when the loan contract was obtained. To do otherwise would be to estimate the value of the mortgage interest as greater than the value of the property.

MORTGAGE/EQUITY FORMULAS

Symbols

r = basic capitalization rate	**Subscript:**
Y = yield rate	E = equity
M – mortgage ratio	M = mortgage
C = mortgage coefficient	P = projection
P = ratio paid off—mortgage	O = overall property
$1/S_{\overline{n}\rceil}$ = sinking fund factor	I = income
R = capitalization rate	1 = 1st mortgage
$S_{\overline{n}\rceil}$ = future value of one per period	2 = 2nd mortgage

Δ = change
J = J factor (changing income)
n = projection period
NOI = net operating income
B = mortgage balance
I = nominal interest rate

Basic Capitalization Rate (r)

$r = Y_E - MC$

$r = Y_E - (M_1C_1 + M_2C_2)$

$C = Y_E + P\, 1/S_{n\rceil} - R_M$

$P = (R_M - I)/(R_{Mp} - I)$

$P = 1/S_{n\rceil} \times S_{n\rceil}\, P$

Capitalization Rates (R)

Level income

$R = Y_E - MC - \Delta\, 1/S_{n\rceil}$

$R = r - \Delta\, 1/S_{n\rceil}$

J-factor changing income

$$R_o = \frac{Y_E - MC - \Delta_o 1/S_{n\rceil}}{1 + \Delta_I J}$$

$$R_o = \frac{r - \Delta_o 1/S_{n\rceil}}{1 + \Delta_I J}$$

Required Change in Value (D)

Level income

$$\Delta = \frac{r - R}{1/S_{n\rceil}}$$

$$\Delta = \frac{Y_E - MC - R}{1/S_{n\rceil}}$$

J-factor changing income

$$\Delta_o = \frac{r - R_o(1 + \Delta_I J)}{1/S_{n\rceil}}$$

$$*\Delta_o = \frac{r - R_o}{R_o J + I/S_{n\rceil}}$$

Note: For multiple mortgage situations, insert M and C for each mortgage.
* This formula assumes value and income change at the same ratio.

Equity yield (YE)

Level income

$Y_E = R_E + \Delta_E\, 1/S_{n\rceil}$

J-factor changing income

$$Y_E = R_E + \Delta_E 1/S_{n\rceil} + \frac{[R_o \Delta_I]J}{1 - M}$$

Change in equity

$\Delta_E = (\Delta_o + MP) / (1 - M)$

$\Delta_E = [V_o(1 + \Delta_o) - B - V_E] / V_E$

Assumed mortgage situation

Level income

$$V_0 = \frac{NOI + BC}{Y_E - \Delta_0 1/S_{\overline{n}|}}$$

J-factor changing income

$$V_0 = \frac{NOI(1 + \Delta_i J) + BC}{Y_E - \Delta_0 1/S_{\overline{n}|}}$$

Mortgage/Equity Without Algebra Format

Loan ratio × annual constant	= _____
Equity ratio × equity yield rate	= + _____
Loan ratio × paid off loan ratio × SFF	= − _____
Basic rate (r)	= _____
+ Dep or − App × SFF	= ± _____
Cap rate (R)	= _____

Note: SFF is sinking fund factor at equity yield rate for projection period. Dep/App is the change in value from depreciation or appreciation during the projection period.

MORTGAGE-EQUITY ANALYSIS

L.W. Ellwood was the first to organize, develop, and promulgate the use of mortgage-equity analysis in yield capitalization for real property valuation. He theorized that mortgage money plays a major role in determining real property prices and values. Ellwood saw real property investments as a combination of two components – debt and equity – and held that the return requirements of both components must be satisfied through income, reversion, or a combination of the two. Thus, Ellwood developed an approach for estimating property value that made explicit assumptions as to what a mortgage lender and an equity investor would expect from the property.

In general, mortgage-equity analysis involves estimating the value of a property based on both mortgage and equity return requirements. The value of the equity interest in the property is found by discounting the equity dividends available to the equity investor. The equity yield rate (Y_E) is used as the discount rate. The total value of the property is equal to the present value of the equity position plus the value of the mortgage. This is true whether the value is found using discounted cash flow analysis or yield capitalization formulas that have been developed for mortgage-equity analysis.

Applications

Mortgage-equity analysis can facilitate the valuation process in many ways. It may be used in the following situations:

1. To compose overall rates

2. To analyze and test the capitalization rates obtained with other capitalization techniques

3.   as an investment analysis tool to test the values indicated by the direct comparison and cost approaches

4.   to analyze a capitalization rate graphically

Given a set of assumptions concerning the NOI, mortgage (amount, rate, and term), reversion (rate of appreciation or depreciation), equity yield rate, and projection period, mortgage-equity analysis may be employed to estimate the present value of the equity and to arrive at the total property value. The following example illustrates a general approach to mortgage-equity analysis.

   Given:

Annual NOI (level)	$25,000
Projection period	10 years
Loan amount	$168,000
Loan terms*	
Interest rate	9% per annum, compounded monthly
Amortization term (monthly payments)	25 years
Estimated reversion	$201,600
Equity yield rate	15%

* Contract terms are at current market rates.

Using these assumptions, cash flow to the equity investor can be projected as follows:

Annual Cash Flow from Operations – Years 1–10

Annual net operating income	$25,000
Annual debt service	16,918
Equity dividend	$8,082

Cash Flow from Reversion – Year 10

Estimated resale price	$201,600
Mortgage balance	139,002
Cash flow from reversion	$62,598

Using the present value factor for a 15% effective annual yield rate and a 10-year holding period, the present value of the cash flows to the equity investor may be calculated as follows:

Years	Cash Flow	Present Value Factor	Present Value
1–10	$8,082	5.018769*	$40,562
10	$62,598	0.247185†	15,473
Present value of equity			$56,035

* Ordinary level annuity (present value of one per period) factor
† Reversion (present value of one) factor

The total property value can now be found by adding the present value of the equity to the present value of the loan.[1]

---

[1]   Because the loan is assumed to be at current market rates, the face amount of the loan is equal to the value of the loan to the lender.

Present value of the equity	$56,035
Present value of the loan	168,000
Total value	$224,035

This example illustrates a fairly straightforward application of mortgage-equity analysis. The present value of the equity was easily calculated by discounting the dollar estimates of the cash flows. The assumptions in this example were simplified in several ways. First, the income was assumed to be level. In a more complex situation, income may be expected to change over the holding period. Second, the loan amount was specified in dollars.[2] If the loan amount were assumed to be based on a loan-to-value ratio, the dollar amount of the loan would depend on the property value being calculated. In such a case, the cash flows to the equity investor could not be specified in dollars and discounted as they were in the example. Third, the resale price was specified in dollars.[3] Investors often assume that property values will change by a specified percentage amount over the holding period (see Chapter 23). Thus, the resale price depends on the property value being calculated. Finally, in the preceding example the total property value is greater than the loan amount. If the opposite were true, the value of the loan could not exceed the combined debt and equity interests in the property.

When either the loan amount or the resale price depends on the value of the property, the cash flows cannot be projected in dollar amounts and discounted. An alternative procedure must be used to solve for the present value. One such alternative is to use a yield capitalization formula that has been developed to solve this type of problem.[4] This is what L.W. Ellwood did when he developed the Ellwood equation, which is illustrated in the following section.

Mortgage-Equity Formula

The general mortgage-equity formula is:

$$R_O = \frac{Y_E - M[Y_E + P1/S_{\overline{n}|} - R_M] - \Delta_O 1/S_{\overline{n}|}}{1 + \Delta_I J}$$

where:

R_O = overall capitalization rate
Y_E = equity yield rate
M = loan-to-value ratio
P = percentage of loan paid off
$1/S_{\overline{n}|}$ = sinking fund factor at the equity yield rate

---

[2] This might be the case if the property were being valued subject to an existing loan. Such a situation is illustrated later in this appendix. Alternatively, the dollar amount may have resulted from a separate calculation of the maximum amount that could be borrowed to meet a minimum debt coverage ratio.

[3] This situation might occur if there is a purchase option in a lease that the appraiser believes will be exercised. Alternatively, a dollar estimate may be the result of a separate estimate of the resale price calculated by applying a capitalization rate to the income at the end of the holding period.

[4] A computer can be programmed to handle this type of valuation problem. For a discussion of this procedure, see Jeffrey D. Fisher, "Using Circular Reference in Spreadsheets to Estimate Value", *The Quarterly Byte*, vol. 5, no. 4 (Fourth Quarter 1989).

R_M = mortgage capitalization rate or mortgage constant
Δ_O = change in total property value
Δ_I = total ratio change in income
J = J factor (This symbol is discussed later in this appendix.)

The part of the formula represented as $Y_E - M [Y_E + P\ 1/S_{n\rceil} - R_M]$ can be referred to as the *basic capitalization rate* (r). It satisfies the lender's requirement and adjusts for amortization. It also satisfies the investor's equity yield requirement before any adjustment is made for income and value changes. Therefore, the basic rate starts with an investor's yield requirement and adjusts it to reflect the effect of financing. The resulting basic capitalization rate is a building block from which an overall capitalization rate can be developed with additional assumptions.

If level income and no change in property value are anticipated, the basic rate will be identical to the overall capitalization rate. The last part of the numerator, $\Delta_O\ 1/S_{n\rceil}$, allows the appraiser to adjust the basic rate to reflect an expected change in overall property value. If the value change is positive, referred to as property appreciation, the overall capitalization rate is reduced to reflect this anticipated monetary benefit; if the change is negative, referred to as depreciation, the overall capitalization rate is increased.

Finally, the denominator, $1 + \Delta_I\ J$, accounts for any change in income. The J factor is always positive. Thus, if the change in income is positive, the denominator will be greater than one and the overall rate will be reduced. If the change in income is negative, the overall rate will be increased. For level-income applications, $\Delta = 0$, so the denominator is $1 + 0$, or 1.

Akerson Format

The mortgage-equity procedure developed by Charles B. Akerson substitutes an arithmetic format for the algebraic equation in the Ellwood formula.[5] This format is applicable to level-income situations; when modified with the J or K factor, it can also be applied to changing-income situations.

The Akerson format for level-income situations is:

Loan ratio × annual constant	= _____
Equity ratio × equity yield rate	= + _____
Loan ratio × % paid off in projection period × $1/S_{n\rceil}$	= − _____
Basic rate (r)	= _____
+ dep or − app × $1/S_{n\rceil}$	= ± _____
Overall capitalization rate	= _____

where $1/S_{n\rceil}$ is the sinking fund factor at the equity yield rate for the projection period and dep/app denotes the change in value from property depreciation or appreciation during the projection period.

[5]   The format was first presented by Charles B. Akerson in "Ellwood without Algebra", *The Appraisal Journal* (July 1970).

Level-Income Applications

Mortgage-equity analysis can be used to value real property investments with level income streams or variable income streams converted to level equivalents using overall capitalization rates and residual techniques.

Use of Overall Capitalization Rates

In the simplest application of the mortgage-equity formula and the Akerson format, a level income and a stable or changing overall property value are assumed. The following example illustrates the application of the mortgage-equity formula using an overall capitalization rate applied to a level flow of income.

NOI (level)	$25,000
Projection period	10 years
Loan terms	
Interest rate	9% per annum, compounded monthly
Amortization term (monthly payments)	25 years
Loan-to-value ratio	75%
Property value change	20% gain
Equity yield rate	15%

The overall rate is calculated as follows:

$$R_o = \frac{Y_E - M[Y_E + P1/S_{\overline{n}|} - R_M] - \Delta_o 1/S_{\overline{n}|}}{1 + \Delta_i J}$$

$$R_o = \frac{0.15 - 0.75(0.15 + 0.1726 \times 0.04925 - 0.1007) - (0.20 \times 0.04925)}{1 + 0 \times J}$$

$$R_o = \frac{0.15 - 0.75(0.057801) - 0.009850}{1}$$

$$R_o = \frac{0.15 - 0.043350 - 0.009850}{1}$$

$$R_o = \frac{0.096800}{1}$$

$$R_o = 0.0968 \text{ (rounded)}$$

The capitalized value of the investment is $25,000/0.0968 = $258,264.

Using the same data and assumptions, an identical value can be derived by applying the Akerson format:

0.75 × 0.100704	=	0.075528
0.25 × 0.15	= +	0.037500
-0.75 × 0.172608 × 0.049252	= −	0.006376
Basic rate (r)	=	0.106652
0.20 × -0.049252	= −	0.009850
R_o	=	0.096802
The capitalized value is $25,000/0.0968	=	$258,264

The answer derived in this example is virtually the same as the answer that would be derived using DCF analysis. In fact, it is possible to check the answer found with the Ellwood formula by discounting the implied cash flows. This is true because the dollar amount of the loan and resale price are approximately the same in both examples. That is, the implied amount of the loan is 75% of $224,014, or approximately $168,000, and the implied resale price is 90% of $224,014, or approximately $201,600. It is important to realize, however, that this was not known until the problem was solved. The examples were designed to produce the same answer to demonstrate that both problems are based on the same concepts of discounted cash flow analysis.

Use of Residual Techniques

Land and building residual techniques can be applied with land and building capitalization rates based on mortgage-equity procedures. The general mortgage-equity formula or the Akerson format is applied to derive a basic rate, which is used to develop land and building capitalization rates.

For example, assume that a commercial property is expected to produce level annual income of $15,000 per year over a 10-year term. Mortgage financing is available at a 75% loan-to-value ratio, and monthly payments at 11% interest per annum, compounded monthly are made over an amortization term of 25 years. The land is currently valued at $65,000 and is forecast to have a value of $78,000 at the end of the projection period, indicating a 20% positive change in land value. The building is expected to have no value at the end of the projection period and the equity yield rate is 15%.

The first step in valuing this property is to derive the basic rate (r) using the Ellwood Formula:

$$r = Y_E - M (Y_E + P\ 1/S_{n\rceil} - R_M)$$
$$r = 0.15 - 0.75\ (0.15 + 0.137678 \times 0.049252 - 0.117614)$$
$$= 0.15 - 0.029375$$
$$= 0.120625$$

The Akerson format can also be used to derive the basic rate:

0.75×0.117614	$=\quad 0.088211$
0.25×0.15	$=\quad 0.037500$
$0.75 \times 0.137678 \times 0.049252$	$=-\ \underline{0.005086}$
Basic capitalization rate (r)	$=\quad 0.120625$

Next, the land and building capitalization rates are calculated. To solve for the land capitalization rate, R_L, the calculations are:

$$R_L = r - \Delta_L\ 1/S_{n\rceil}$$
$$= 0.120625 - (0.20 \times 0.049252)$$
$$= 0.120625 - 0.009850$$
$$= 0.110775$$

The building capitalization rate, R_B, is calculated as follows:

$R_B = r - \Delta_B\ 1/S_{n\rceil}$
$= 0.120625 - (-1.0 \times 0.049252)$
$= 0.120625 + 0.049252$
$= 0.169877$

These rates can be used to value the property with the building residual technique:

NOI $15,000
Land income
  $(V_L \times R_L) = \$65,000 \times 0.110775$ $-\ \underline{7,200}$
Residual income attributable to building $7,800
Capitalized value of building
  $(I_B \div R_B) = \$7,800/0.169877$ $45,916
Plus land value $+\ \underline{65,000}$
Indicated property value $110,916

When the rates are used in the land residual technique, a similar property value is indicated:

NOI $15,000
Building income
  $(V_B \times R_B) = \$46,000 \times 0.169877$ $-\ \underline{7,814}$
Residual income attributable to land $7,186
Capitalized value of land
  $(I_L \div R_L) = \$7,186/0.110775$ $64,870
Plus building value $+\ \underline{46,000}$
Indicated total property value $110,870

Changing-Income Applications

The general mortgage-equity formula can be applied to income streams that are forecast to change on a curvilinear or exponential-curve (constant-ratio) basis by using a J factor for curvilinear change or a K factor for constant-ratio change. The J factor, used in the stabilizer $(1 + \Delta_I\ J)$, may be obtained from precomputed tables or calculated with the J-factor formula.[6] The K factor, an income adjuster or stabilizer used to convert a changing income stream into its level equivalent, can be calculated with the K-factor formula.[7]

---

[6] Before the advent of financial calculators, present value and future value problems were solved using precomputed tables of compound interest factors. Although the tables are no longer used in everyday practice, they remain useful for checking results of calculations made with calculators and computers and in teaching the mathematics of finance. See James J. Mason, ed., comp., *American Institute of Real Estate Appraisers Financial Tables*, rev. ed. (Chicago: American Institute of Real Estate Appraisers, with tables computed by Financial Publishing Company, 1982), 461-473.

[7] Charles B. Akerson, *Capitalization Theory and Techniques: Study Guide*, 2nd ed. (Chicago: Appraisal Institute, with tables computed by Financial Publishing Company, 2000), T-47 to T-52.

Use of the J Factor

The J-factor formula for curvilinear income reflects an income stream that changes from time zero in relation to a sinking fund accumulation curve. The formula is:

$$J = 1/S_{\overline{n}|} \times \left[\frac{n}{1 - 1/(1+Y)^n} \right] - \frac{1}{Y}$$

where:

$1/S_{\overline{n}|}$ = sinking fund factor at equity yield rate

n = projection period

Y = equity yield rate

Consider the facts set forth in the level annuity example, but assume a 20% increase in income. Note that the J factor is applied to the income in the year prior to the first year of the holding period.

$$R_o = \frac{0.15 - 0.75(0.15 + 0.172608 \times 0.049252 - 0.100704) - (0.20 \times 0.049252)}{1 + (0.20 \times 0.3259)}$$

$$R_o = \frac{0.15 - 0.043348 - 0.009850}{1 + 0.0652}$$

$$R_o = \frac{0.096802}{1.0652}$$

$$= 0.09088$$

The capitalized value is $25,000/0.09088 = $275,088.

The net operating incomes for the projection period that are implied by the curvilinear J-factor premise are calculated in the following table.

Period	1st Year Adjustment*		$S_{\overline{n}|}$		Periodic Adjustment		Base NOI†		NOI
1	$246.26	×	1/1.000000	=	$246	+	$25,000	=	$25,246
2	$246.26	×	1/0.465116	=	$529	+	$25,000	=	$25,529
3	$246.26	×	1/0.287977	=	$855	+	$25,000	=	$25,855
4	$246.26	×	1/0.200265	=	$1,230	+	$25,000	=	$26,230
5	$246.26	×	1/0.148316	=	$1,660	+	$25,000	=	$26,660
6	$246.26	×	1/0.114237	=	$2,156	+	$25,000	=	$27,156
7	$246.26	×	1/0.090360	=	$2,725	+	$25,000	=	$27,725
8	$246.26	×	1/0.072850	=	$3,380	+	$25,000	=	$28,380
9	$246.26	×	1/0.059574	=	$4,134	+	$25,000	=	$29,134
10	$246.26	×	1/0.049252	=	$5,000	+	$25,000	=	$30,000

* This adjustment was derived by multiplying the NOI ($25,000) by the assumed increase in the NOI (20%); the resulting figure ($5,000) was then multiplied by the sinking fund factor for the anticipated 15% equity yield rate over the 10-year projection period ($1/S_{\overline{n}|}$ = 0.049252).

† The base NOI is the income for the year prior to the beginning of the projection period.

Mathematical proof of the example is provided below.

Valuation of Equity

Period	NOI		Debt Service		Cash to Equity		PVF at 15%		PV
1	$25,246	–	$20,772	=	$4,474	× 0.869565	=	$3,890
2	$25,529	–	$20,772	=	$4,757	× 0.756144	=	$3,597
3	$25,855	–	$20,772	=	$5,083	× 0.657516	=	$3,342
4	$26,230	–	$20,772	=	$5,458	× 0.571753	=	$3,121
5	$26,660	–	$20,772	=	$5,888	× 0.497177	=	$2,927
6	$27,156	–	$20,772	=	$6,384	× 0.432328	=	$2,760
7	$27,725	–	$20,772	=	$6,953	× 0.375937	=	$2,614
8	$28,380	–	$20,772	=	$7,608	× 0.326902	=	$2,487
9	$29,134	–	$20,772	=	$8,362	× 0.284262	=	$2,377
10	$30,000	–	$20,772	=	$9,228	× 0.247185	=	$2,281
					$159,400*	× 0.247185	=	$39,401

Value of equity at 15% = $68,797

Check: $275,088 × 0.25 = $68,772

* The reversion is calculated as follows:	Resale ($275,088 × 1.20) =	$330,106
	Loan balance ($275,088 × 0.75)(1 – 0.1726) =	170,706
	Equity proceeds =	$159,400

Use of the K Factor

The K-factor formula, which is applied to income that changes on an exponential-curve (constant-ratio) basis, is expressed as:

$$K = \frac{1-(1+C)^n / S^n}{(Y-C)a_{\overline{n}|}}$$

where:

K = factor

C = constant-ratio change in income

S^n = future value factor

Y = equity yield rate

$a_{\overline{n}|}$ = present value factor for ordinary level annuity

When the general mortgage-equity formula is used to derive an overall capitalization rate applicable to an income expected to change on a constant-ratio basis, K is substituted for the denominator $(1 + \Delta_I J)$. The following example is based on the same property used for the level-income and J-factor examples, but it assumes that NOI will increase by 2% per year, on a compound basis. This property can be valued using the K factor in the mortgage-equity formula.

$$R_o = \frac{Y_E - M[Y_E + P1/S_{\overline{n}|} - R_M] - \Delta_o 1/S_{\overline{n}|}}{K}$$

$$R_o = \frac{0.15 - 0.75\,(0.15 + 0.172608 \times 0.049252 - 0.100704) - (0.20 \times 0.049252)}{1.070877}$$

$$= 0.090395$$

The capitalized value of the investment is $25,000/0.090395 = $276,564.

Note that the indicated values based on the J-factor and K-factor premises are very close, i.e., $275,088 and $276,564. The indicated value based on a level-income assumption is much lower, i.e., $238,264. This is because all of the yield has to occur on resale, not in increased income.

Table B.1: J-Factor Income Pattern and K-Factor Income Pattern

	J Factor	K Factor
Year 1	$25,246	$25,000
Year 2	$25,529	$25,500
Year 3	$25,855	$26,010
Year 4	$26,230	$26,530
Year 5	$26,660	$27,060
Year 6	$27,156	$27,602
Year 7	$27,725	$28,154
Year 8	$28,380	$28,717
Year 9	$29,134	$29,291
Year 10	$30,000	$29,877

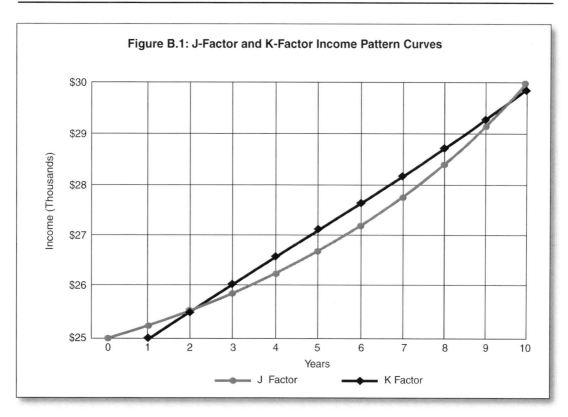

Figure B.1: J-Factor and K-Factor Income Pattern Curves

Based on the income data in Table B.1, J-factor and K-factor income patterns are plotted on the graph in Figure B.1. Both examples assume a 20% increase in overall property value. In the J-factor example, income is projected to increase by 20%. In the K-factor example, income is projected to increase at a constant ratio of 2% per year. Under the J-factor assumption, the value of the property is $275,088 and the R_O is 9.088%. Under the K-factor assumption, the value of the property is $276,569, and the R_O is 9.039%.

Solving for Equity Yield

Given an actual or proposed equity sale price and a forecast of equity benefits, an equity yield rate can be estimated. When level income is forecast, a formula is used. The calculations can be performed by iteration or with the financial functions of a calculator. When income is expected to change on a curvilinear basis or a constant-ratio basis, formulas must be used to solve for the yield. A calculator cannot be used to solve the problem conveniently, and the iteration technique is too time-consuming.

Level-Income Example

Consider a property that is purchased for $250,000. The net operating income is forecast to remain level at $35,000 per year and the buyer believes that property value will decline 15% over a five-year ownership period. The mortgage amount is $200,000 and monthly payments are at 10% per annum, compounded monthly with an amortization term of 20 years. The investment forecast is outlined below:

Purchase		Holding Period	
Sale price	$250,000	NOI	$35,000
Mortgage	– 200,000	Debt service	– 23,161*
Equity	$50,000	Equity dividend	$11,839

Resale After 5 Years	
Sale price	$212,500
Mortgage balance	$179,605†
Equity reversion	$32,895
Original equity	$50,000
Equity change	-$17,105

* $200,000 × 0.115803 mortgage constant
† Unamortized portion of $200,000 mortgage at end of 5-year projection period

$$R_E \text{ (equity capitalization rate)} = \frac{\$11,839}{\$50,000} = 0.236780$$

$$\Delta_E \text{ (equity change)} = \frac{-\$17,105}{\$50,000} = -0.342100$$

The equity yield rate may now be computed through iteration or by using the formula and interpolation. Iteration is performed using the formula:

$$Y_E = R_E + \Delta_E \ 1/S_{n\rceil}$$

Because the sinking fund factor for five years at the Y_E rate cannot be identified without knowing Y_E, a trial-and-error procedure must be used to develop Y_E. Without discounting, the 34.21% equity decline over the five-year holding period would subtract 6.84% each year from the equity capitalization rate of 23.67%. Consequently, Y_E will be less than 23.67% and more than 16.83% (23.67% − 6.84%).

The first computation is performed with a Y_E of 18%. When the correct equity yield rate is applied, the equation will balance.

Estimated Y_E	R_E	+	Δ_E	×	$1/S_{n\rceil}$	=	Indicated Y_E
0.1800	0.2368	+	(-0.3425)	×	0.139778	=	0.1889
0.2000	0.2368	+	(-0.3425)	×	0.134380	=	0.1908
0.1900	0.2368	+	(-0.3425)	×	0.137050	=	0.1899

Therefore, $Y_E = 0.1900$, or 19.0%.

This procedure for computing Y_E is correct because Y_E is defined as the rate that makes the present value of the future equity benefits equal to the original equity. The future benefits in this case are the equity dividend of $11,839 per year for five years and the equity reversion of $32,895 at the end of the five-year period.

If Y_E is 19%, the present value of the two benefits can be computed.

$$\begin{aligned}
\$11,839 \times 3.057635 &= \quad \$36,199 \\
\$32,895 \times 0.419049 &= + \underline{\;13,785} \\
&\quad\;\; \$49,984
\end{aligned}$$

Thus, the equity yield rate has been proven to be 19.0%. Precision to 0.03% represents a level of accuracy in keeping with current practice and the normal requirements of the calculation. This example is based on level income, but the same procedure can be applied to changing income streams by incorporating J and K factors into the formula.

J-Factor Premise Example

Consider the information set forth in the previous example, but assume that income is expected to decline 15% according to the J-factor premise.

$$R_O = \$35,000/\$250,000 = 0.14 \qquad M = \$200,000/\$250,000 = 0.80$$

$$Y_E = R_E + \frac{\Delta_E}{S_{n\rceil}} + \frac{R_O \Delta_I}{1-M} J$$

Try 15%,

$$0.2368 + {-0.3421} \times 0.1483 + \frac{0.14 \times {-0.15}}{0.2} \times 0.4861 = 0.135$$

Try 12%,

$$0.2368 + {-0.3421} \times 0.1574 + \frac{0.14 \times {-0.15}}{0.2} \times 0.5077 = 0.130$$

Try 13%,

$$0.2368 + -0.3421 \times 0.1543 + \frac{0.14 \times -0.15}{0.2} \times 0.5004 = 0.131472$$

Therefore, $Y_E = 13.15\%$ (rounded).

K-Factor Premise Example

Consider the same information, but assume that income is expected to decrease at a compound rate of 3% per year, indicating a constant-ratio change in income.

$$Y_E = R_E + \Delta_E 1 / S_{\overline{n}|} + \frac{R_o(K-1)}{1-M}$$

Try 13%,

$$0.2368 + -0.3421 \times 0.1543 + \frac{0.14 \times (0.9487 - 1)}{0.2} = 0.148$$

Try 15%,

$$0.2368 + -0.3421 \times 0.1483 + \frac{0.14 \times (0.9497 - 1)}{0.2} = 0.151$$

Therefore, $Y_E = 15.1\%$.

Rate Analysis

Rate analysis allows an appraiser to test the reasonableness of the value conclusions derived through the application of overall capitalization rates. Once an overall capitalization rate has been developed with mortgage-equity analysis or another technique, its reliability and consistency with market expectations of equity yield and value change can be tested using Ellwood graphic analysis.

To create a graph for rate analysis, the appraiser chooses equity yield rates that cover a realistic range of rates expected and demanded by investors. It is often wise to include a rate that is at the low end of the range of market acceptance as well as a rate at the high end of the range. For the analysis to be useful to the client, the range of yield rates chosen should be in line with investors' perceptions of the market.

In most real estate investments, there is no assurance that the investment can be liquidated at the convenience of the equity investor or on the terms dictated by the investor. For example, in the early 1990s most liquidity evaporated from the market. Moreover, in negotiating a purchase price, the prospects for profit within a plausible range of possibilities may be greater than the chance of achieving a specific equity yield rate, which cannot be determined until the property is resold. However, the appraiser's value judgments can easily be subjected to realistic tests. The appraiser should ask the following questions:

- What resale prices correspond to various yield levels?

- Can the property suffer some loss in value and still produce an acceptable profit?

- How sensitive is the equity yield rate to possible fluctuations in value?

- What percentage of the investor's return is derived from annual cash flows, and what percentage comes from the reversion? (Reversion is generally considered riskier.)

- What prospective equity yield rates can be inferred from the overall capitalization rates found in the marketplace?

Many of these questions focus on the relationship between the change in property value and the equity yield rate. The unknown variable in rate analysis is the change in property value (Δ_O). The formula for the required change in property value in a level-income application is:

$$\Delta_O = \frac{r - R_O}{1/S_{\overline{n}|}}$$

Level-Income Example

Consider an investment that will generate stable income and has an overall capitalization rate of 10%. The purchase can be financed with a 75% loan at 10% interest per annum, compounded monthly, amortized over 25 years with level monthly payments. If the investment is held for 10 years, what levels of depreciation or appreciation should be expected with equity yield rates of 9%, 12% and 15%?

To solve this problem, the appraiser must first find the basic rate (r) and the sinking fund factor for each equity yield rate. The Ellwood Tables[8] are the source of the following figures:

Y_E	r	$1/S_{\overline{n}|}$
9%	0.096658	0.065820
12%	0.105185	0.056984
15%	0.113584	0.049252

When the difference between r and the overall rate (R_O) is divided by the corresponding sinking fund factor, the result is the expected change in property value. If r is greater than R_O, a value increase is indicated; if r is less than R_O, value loss is indicated. Analysis of the 10% overall capitalization rate is shown below:

$$Y_E = \frac{r - R_O}{1/S_{\overline{n}|}}$$

9%	-0.0508 (5.1% depreciation)
12%	0.0910 (9.1% appreciation)
15%	0.2758 (27.6% appreciation)

The formula produces answers consistent with the notion that a loss is negative and a gain is positive. In some texts, the numerator in this formula is expressed as $R_O - r$.

---

[8] L.W. Ellwood, *Ellwood Tables for Real Estate Appraising and Financing*, 4th ed. (Cambridge, Mass.: Ballinger Publishing Co., 1977).

Use of this formula results in a change of sign, i.e., positive answers indicate deprecia-tion and negative answers indicate appreciation.

J-Factor Premise

A similar analysis can be performed when income is presumed to change commensu-rately with value according to the J-factor premise. In this case, the expected change in overall property value is calculated by dividing $(r - R_O)$ by $(R_O J + 1/S_{n})$.

Graphic Rate Analysis

Various systems have been developed to employ mortgage-equity concepts in graphic rate analysis. The graphic analysis of capitalization rates is a helpful analytical tool

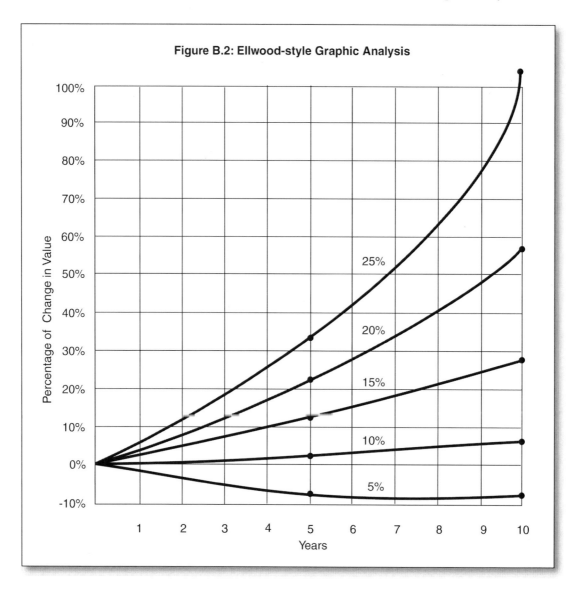

Figure B.2: Ellwood-style Graphic Analysis

used by practicing appraisers and investment analysts. Rate analysis in graphic or tabular form is particularly useful in interpreting market data. Although analyzing a market-oriented overall capitalization rate cannot reveal a property's eventual equity yield rate or resale price, the analysis can reveal combinations of Y_E and Δ_O implicit in the overall rate. Thus, an appraiser can use rate analysis to decide whether a particular combination of Y_E and Δ_O is consistent with market behaviour.

The accompanying figures illustrate two types of graphic analysis. Figure B.2 shows Ellwood-style graphic analysis, with time on the horizontal axis and the percentage change in property value on the vertical axis. Figure B.3 illustrates another type of graphic analysis with the equity yield rate on the horizontal axis and the percentage change in value on the vertical axis. Graphs like these can be constructed manually by plotting three or more key points and connecting the points with a smooth curve; they can also be constructed using a computer.

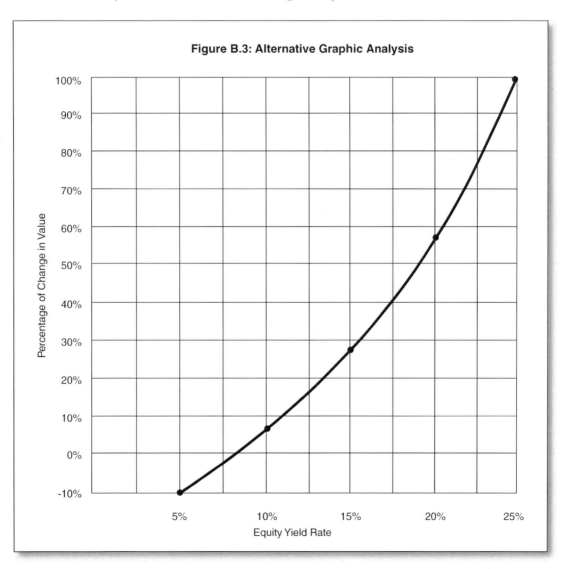

Figure B.3: Alternative Graphic Analysis

The graph in Figure B.2 shows change in value and income under the J-factor premise with respect to time for equity yield rates of 5%, 10%, 15%, 20%, and 25%. It is assumed that $R_O = 0.11$, $I = 0.125$, $R_M = 0.135$, $M = 0.7$, and $\Delta_O = \Delta_I$.

The graph in Figure B.3 shows the change in value and income under the J-factor premise for equity yield rates ranging from 5% to 25% over a 10-year holding period. Again, it is assumed that $R_O = 0.11$, $I = 0.125$, $R_M = 0.135$, $M = 0.7$, and $\Delta_O = \Delta_I$.

After a graph is created, the appraiser must interpret it. Usually the appraiser determines the range of property value changes (Δ_O) anticipated by the market and then forms an opinion as to the reasonableness of the overall capitalization rate. If the value changes are in line with the expectations of market participants and there is nothing unusual about the subject property, the overall rate being tested may be reasonable. If the value changes are not within the range expected by the marketplace, the overall capitalization rate should either be considered unreasonable and in need of further analysis or must be explained and accounted for.

Rate Extraction

Rate extraction is a technique that allows an appraiser to infer the market's expectation of yield and change in property value from a market-oriented overall capitalization rate. The key is to determine what assumptions about the yield rate and the change in property value are consistent with the overall capitalization rates derived from comparable sales. Although a specific yield rate or change in value cannot be identified using this approach, an analyst can determine what change in property value is needed to produce a given yield rate. That is, for each assumed yield rate, there is only one assumption about the change in property value that can be used with that rate to obtain the overall capitalization rate implied by comparable sales.

The following example illustrates this technique. The subject property is an apartment complex. Data on three comparable properties is given.

Factual Data on Three Apartment Complexes

	Sale 1	Sale 2	Sale 3
Number of units	240	48	148
Sale price	$4,678,000	$811,000	$3,467,000
Cash down payment	$1,300,000	$462,145	$1,370,000
Gross income	$594,540	$126,240	$507,120
NOI	$368,600	$71,500	$293,400

Comparative Factors

	Sale 1	Sale 2	Sale 3
Price per unit	$19,492	$16,896	$23,426
Gross income per unit			
Annually	$2,477	$2,638	$3,426
Monthly	$206	$219	$285
Gross income multiplier (GIM)	7.870	6.420	6.830
Overall capitalization rate (R_O)	0.079	0.088	0.085
Loan-to-value ratio (M)	0.722	0.430	0.605

Mortgage constant (R_M)	0.107	0.127	0.136
Percent paid off (P)	-0.125	0.016	0.032
Equity capitalization rate (R_E)	0.006	0.059	0.006
Debt coverage ratio (DCR)	1.021	1.610	1.030

Using the mortgage-equity J-factor formula, pairs of Y_E and Δ_O can be extracted for each comparable sale. The formula for change in income and value is:

$$\Delta_{O-I} = \frac{Y_E - MY_E + (P1/S_{\overline{n}|} - R_M) - R_O}{R_O J + 1/S_{\overline{n}|}}$$

The overall rate for each of the sales can be used in this formula to solve for the combinations of Y_E and Δ_O that would produce that overall capitalization rate. This data is shown in the following table:

Calculated Required Changes for the Three Sales (Five-Year Projection)

%Y_E	% $\Delta_{O=I}$		
	Sale 1	Sale 2	Sale 3
10	19.9	10.7	16.1
12	23.2	16.8	20.8
14	26.7	23.3	25.7
16	30.5	30.3	31.0
18	34.5	37.8	36.6
20	38.8	45.8	42.7
22	43.4	54.3	49.1
24	48.3	63.4	55.9
26	53.7	73.2	63.2
28	59.0	83.4	70.9
30	64.9	94.6	79.2

Note that the rate of change in property value is assumed to equal the rate of change in income. This reflects the appraiser's belief that this assumption is consistent with market perceptions. The relationship between equity yield and change in value and income can now be graphed (see Figure B.4).

Once the graph is completed, the appraiser can draw certain conclusions. If the sales used accurately reflect market perceptions, every pair of equity yield rate and change in property value is a perfect pair. When the figures are inserted into the mortgage-equity formula to derive an overall capitalization rate, the resulting value estimate will be market-oriented.

In this case, any pair of Y_E and Δ_O that does not coincide with the lines on the graph is not market-oriented. The lines have different slopes and cross at some point because each sale has a different loan-to-value ratio (M). Furthermore, because of the differences in the loan-to-value ratios, some variation in the yield rate that equity investors would require for each of the sales would be expected. For example, Sale 1 had the highest loan-to-value ratio and, therefore, probably had the highest required yield rate because of its greater risk. The curves indicate reasonable assumptions about yield rates and changes in value that are consistent with the prices paid for comparable sales and the manner in which they were financed.

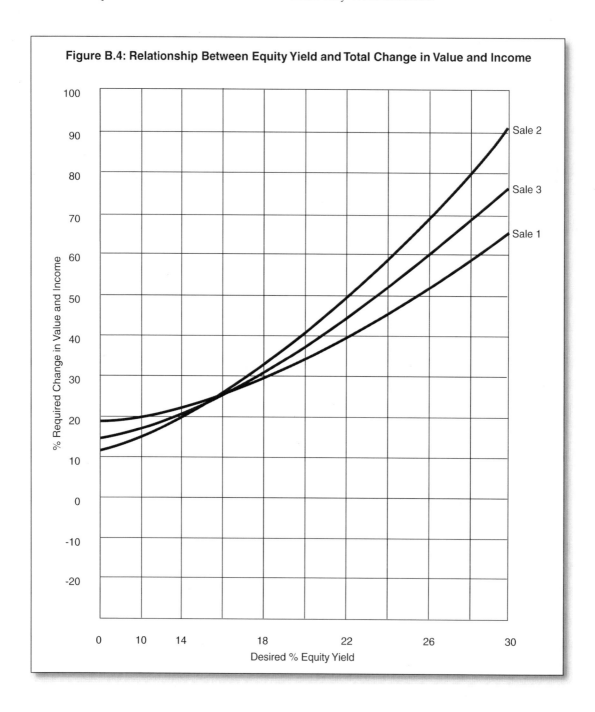

Figure B.4: Relationship Between Equity Yield and Total Change in Value and Income

The graph can also be used to reflect the most likely pair of Y_E and Δ_O for developing an overall capitalization rate. By verifying current investor perceptions of the yield anticipated for the type of property being appraised, the appraiser can determine the necessary property value change. Then, with the mortgage-equity formula, the overall capitalization rate can be calculated. This overall rate will reflect typical investor assumptions for both yield and change in property value.

COMPOUND INTEREST (FUTURE VALUE OF ONE)

This factor reflects the amount to which an investment or deposit will grow in a given number of time periods, including the accumulation of interest at the effective rate per period. It is also known as the amount of one.

$$S^n = (1 + i)^n$$

where: S^n = future value factor

          i = effective rate of interest

         n = number of compounding periods

and $S^n = (e)^{in}$ for continuous compounding

where: S^n = future value factor

         i = nominal rate of interest

        n = number of years

        e = 2.718282

This factor is used to solve problems dealing with compound growth.

When money is invested or deposited at the beginning of a period in an account that bears interest at a fixed rate, it grows according to the interest rate and the number of compounding (conversion) periods that remains in the account. To illustrate how and why this growth occurs, consider an investment of $1.00, a nominal interest rate of 10% with annual compounding, and an investment holding period of five years.

Original investment	$1.00
Interest, first year at 10%	0.10
Accumulation, end of 1 year	$1.10
Interest, second year at 10%	0.11
Accumulation, end of 2 years	$1.21
Interest, third year at 10%	0.121
Accumulation, end of 3 years	$1.331
Interest, fourth year at 10%	0.1331
Accumulation, end of 4 years	$1.4641
Interest, fifth year at 10%	0.14641
Accumulation, end of 5 years	$1.61051

Figure B.5: Compound Interest Table for 10%

10% RATE i / n	1 AMOUNT OF $1 — The amount to which $1 will grow with compound interest	2 AMOUNT OF $1 PER PERIOD — The amount to which $1 per period will grow with compound interest	3 SINKING FUND FACTOR — The amount per period which will grow with compound interest to $1	4 PRESENT WORTH OF $1 — What $1 due in the future is worth today	5 PRESENT WORTH OF $1 PER PERIOD — What $1 payable periodically is worth today	6 PARTIAL PAYMENT — The installment to repay $1 with interest	n
1	1.100 000	1.000 000	1.000 000	.909 091	.909 091	1.100 000	1
2	1.210 000	2.100 000	.476 190	.826 446	1.735 537	.576 190	2
3	1.331 000	3.310 000	.302 115	.751 315	2.486 852	.402 115	3
4	1.464 100	4.641 000	.215 471	.683 013	3.169 865	.315 471	4
5	1.610 510	6.105 100	.163 797	.620 921	3.790 787	.263 797	5
6	1.771 561	7.715 610	.129 607	.564 474	4.355 261	.229 607	6
7	1.948 717	9.487 171	.105 405	.513 158	4.868 419	.205 405	7
8	2.143 589	11.435 888	.087 444	.466 507	5.334 926	.187 444	8
9	2.357 948	13.579 477	.073 641	.424 098	5.759 024	.173 641	9
10	2.593 742	15.937 425	.062 745	.385 543	6.144 567	.162 745	10
11	2.853 117	18.531 167	.053 963	.350 494	6.495 061	.153 963	11
12	3.138 428	21.384 284	.046 763	.318 631	6.813 692	.146 763	12
13	3.452 271	24.522 712	.040 779	.289 664	7.103 356	.140 779	13
14	3.797 498	27.974 983	.035 746	.263 331	7.366 687	.135 746	14
15	4.177 248	31.772 482	.031 474	.239 392	7.606 080	.131 474	15
16	4.594 973	35.949 730	.027 817	.217 629	7.823 709	.127 817	16
17	5.054 470	40.544 703	.024 664	.197 845	8.021 553	.124 664	17
18	5.559 917	45.599 173	.021 930	.179 859	8.201 412	.121 930	18
19	6.115 909	51.159 090	.019 547	.163 508	8.364 920	.119 547	19
20	6.727 500	57.274 999	.017 460	.148 644	8.513 564	.117 460	20
21	7.400 250	64.002 499	.015 624	.135 131	8.648 694	.115 624	21
22	8.140 275	71.402 749	.014 005	.122 846	8.771 540	.114 005	22
23	8.954 302	79.543 024	.012 572	.111 678	8.883 218	.112 572	23
24	9.849 733	88.497 327	.011 300	.101 526	8.984 744	.111 300	24
25	10.834 706	98.347 059	.010 168	.092 296	9.077 040	.110 168	25
26	11.918 177	109.181 765	.009 159	.083 905	9.160 945	.109 159	26
27	13.109 994	121.099 942	.008 258	.076 278	9.237 223	.108 258	27
28	14.420 994	134.209 936	.007 451	.069 343	9.306 567	.107 451	28
29	15.863 093	148.630 930	.006 728	.063 039	9.369 606	.106 728	29
30	17.449 402	164.494 023	.006 079	.057 309	9.426 914	.106 079	30
31	19.194 342	181.943 425	.005 496	.052 099	9.479 013	.105 496	31
32	21.113 777	201.137 767	.004 972	.047 362	9.526 376	.104 972	32
33	23.225 154	222.251 544	.004 499	.043 057	9.569 432	.104 499	33
34	25.547 670	245.476 699	.004 074	.039 143	9.608 575	.104 074	34
35	28.102 437	271.024 368	.003 690	.035 584	9.644 159	.103 690	35
36	30.912 681	299.126 805	.003 343	.032 349	9.676 508	.103 343	36
37	34.003 949	330.039 486	.003 030	.029 408	9.705 917	.103 030	37
38	37.404 343	364.043 434	.002 747	.026 735	9.732 651	.102 747	38
39	41.144 778	401.447 778	.002 491	.024 304	9.756 956	.102 491	39
40	45.259 255	442.592 556	.002 259	.022 095	9.779 051	.102 259	40
41	49.785 181	487.851 811	.002 050	.020 086	9.799 137	.102 050	41
42	54.763 699	537.636 992	.001 860	.018 260	9.817 397	.101 860	42
43	60.240 069	592.400 692	.001 688	.016 600	9.833 998	.101 688	43
44	66.264 076	652.640 761	.001 532	.015 091	9.849 089	.101 532	44
45	72.890 484	718.904 837	.001 391	.013 719	9.862 808	.101 391	45
46	80.179 532	791.795 321	.001 263	.012 472	9.875 280	.101 263	46
47	88.197 485	871.974 853	.001 147	.011 338	9.886 618	.101 147	47
48	97.017 234	960.172 338	.001 041	.010 307	9.896 926	.101 041	48
49	106.718 957	1057.189 572	.000 946	.009 370	9.906 296	.100 946	49
50	117.390 853	1163.908 529	.000 859	.008 519	9.914 814	.100 859	50
51	129.129 938	1281.299 382	.000 780	.007 744	9.922 559	.100 780	51
52	142.042 932	1410.429 320	.000 709	.007 040	9.929 599	.100 709	52
53	156.247 225	1552.472 252	.000 644	.006 400	9.935 999	.100 644	53
54	171.871 948	1708.719 477	.000 585	.005 818	9.941 817	.100 585	54
55	189.059 142	1880.591 425	.000 532	.005 289	9.947 106	.100 532	55
56	207.965 057	2069.650 567	.000 483	.004 809	9.951 915	.100 483	56
57	228.761 562	2277.615 624	.000 439	.004 371	9.956 286	.100 439	57
58	251.637 719	2506.377 186	.000 399	.003 974	9.960 260	.100 399	58
59	276.801 490	2758.014 905	.000 363	.003 613	9.963 873	.100 363	59
60	304.481 640	3034.816 395	.000 330	.003 284	9.967 157	.100 330	60
n	$S^n = (1+i)^n$	$S_{\overline{n}|} = \dfrac{S^n-1}{i}$	$\dfrac{1}{S_{\overline{n}|}} = \dfrac{i}{S^n-1}$	$\dfrac{1}{S^n} = \dfrac{1}{(1+i)^n}$	$a_{\overline{n}|} = \dfrac{1-1/S^n}{i}$	$\dfrac{1}{a_{\overline{n}|}} = \dfrac{i}{1-1/S^n}$	n

$$S = 1+i$$

The use of precomputed tables of loan factors has largely been supplanted by the use of financial calculators and computer applications. The tables remain useful to illustrate the mathematics of finance, particularly the relative rates of change of loan factors over time for different interest rates. Tables for additional interest rates can be found in various publications:

- Compound Interest and Discount Factor Tables for Appraisers – The Six Functions of One Dollar, Appraisal Institute of Canada, Winnipeg, 1991
- Charles B. Akerson, The Appraiser's Workbook, 2nd ed. (Chicago: Appraisal Institute, 1996).
- Charles B. Akerson, Capitalization Theory and Techniques: Study Guide, 2nd ed. (Chicago: Appraisal Institute, with tables computed by Financial Publishing Company, 2000).
- L.W. Ellwood, Ellwood Tables for Real Estate Appraising and Financing, 4th ed. (Cambridge, Mass.: Ballinger Publishing Co., 1977).
- James J. Mason, ed., comp., American Institute of Real Estate Appraisers Financial Tables, rev. ed. (Chicago: American Institute of Real Estate Appraisers, with tables computed by Financial Publishing Company, 1982), 461–473.

One dollar grows to $1.61051 in five years with interest at 10%, so the future value of one factor at 10% annually for five years is 1.610510; $1,000 would grow 1,000 times this amount to $1,610.51 over the same five years at the same 10% annual rate. When interest is not collected or withdrawn as it is earned, it is added to the capital amount and additional interest accumulates in subsequent periods. This process is called *compounding*.

The results of compounding can be calculated with the formula $(1 + i)^n$, where n is the number of compounding periods and i is the interest rate per period.

n		
1	$1.10 \times 1 = 1.10^1$	$= 1.10$
2	$1.10 \times 1.10 = 1.10^2$	$= 1.21$
3	$1.10 \times 1.10 \times 1.10 = 1.10^3$	$= 1.331$
4	$1.10 \times 1.10 \times 1.10 \times 1.10 = 1.10^4$	$= 1.461$
5	$1.10 \times 1.10 \times 1.10 \times 1.10 \times 1.10 = 1.10^5$	$= 1.61051$

Thus, the factors in Figure B.5, the amount of one or the future value of one, reflect the growth of $1.00 accumulating at interest for the number of compounding periods shown at the left and right sides of each page of tables. For example, the 10% annual column reveals a factor of 2.593742 for 10 periods. This means that $1.00 deposited at 10% interest compounded annually for 10 years will grow to $1.00 × 2.593742, or just over $2.59. In other words, $1.10^{10} = 2.593742$. The factors for seven and eight years indicate that $1.00 (or any investment earning 10% per year, compounded annually) will double in value in approximately 7.5 years. Similarly, an investment of $10,000 made 10 years ago, earning no periodic income during the 10-year holding period, must be liquidated in the current market at $10,000 × 2.593742, or $25,937.42, to realize a 10% effective annual return on the original investment.

This factor reflects the growth of the original deposit measured from the beginning deposit period. Thus, at the end of the first period at a rate of 10%, the original $1.00 has grown to $1.10 and the factor is 1.100000, as shown above.

REVERSION FACTORS (PRESENT VALUE OF ONE)

This factor is the present value of $1 (or other currency) to be collected at a given future time discounted at the effective interest rate for the number of periods between now and the date of collection. It is the reciprocal of the corresponding compound interest factor.

$$1/S^n = \frac{1}{(1+i)^n}$$

where: $1/S^n$ = present value factor
             i = effective rate of interest
             n = number of compounding periods

and

$$1/S^n = \frac{1}{(e)^{in}} \text{ for continuous compounding}$$

where: $1/S^n$ = present value factor
    i = nominal rate of interest
    n = number of years
    e = 2.718282

This factor is used to solve problems that involve compound discounting.

As demonstrated in the discussion of future value, $1.00 compounded annually at 10% will grow to $1.610151 in five years. Accordingly, the amount that will grow to $1.00 in five years is $1.00 divided by 1.61051, or $0.62092. In the 10% table, the present value of one factor for five years is 0.620921. In other words, $1.00 to be collected five years from today has a present value of $0.620921 when discounted at 10% per year. And $10,000 to be collected five years from today, discounted at the same 10% annual rate, has a present value of $10,000 × 0.620921, or $6,209.21. The $10,000 sum to be received in five years is a reversion.

ORDINARY LEVEL ANNUITY (PRESENT VALUE OF ONE PER PERIOD)

This factor represents the present value of a series of future instalments or payments of $1 (or other currency) per period for a given number of periods discounted at an effective interest rate. It is commonly referred to as the *Inwood coefficient*.

$$a_{\overline{n}|} = \frac{1-1/S^n}{i}$$

where: $a_{\overline{n}|}$ = level annuity factor
    $1/S^n$ = present value factor
    i = rate of interest yield

This factor is used in solving problems that deal with the compound discounting of cash flows that are level or effectively level.

Finding the present value of a future income stream is a discounting procedure in which future payments are treated as a series of reversions. The present value of a series of future receipts may be quickly ascertained using the precomputed present value of one per period factors for the selected discount rate provided the receipts are all equal in amount, equally spaced over time, and receivable at the end of each period.

If, for example, 10% per year, compounded annually is a fair rate of interest or discount, it would be justifiable to pay $0.909091 (I.e., the annual present value of $1 at 10%) for the right to receive $1.00 one year from today. Assuming that the cost of this right is $0.909091, the $1.00 received at the end of the year could be divided between principal and interest as follows.

Return of principal	$0.90909
Interest on principal for one year @ 10%	0.09091
Total received	$1.00000

If approximately $0.091 is the present value of the right to receive $1.00 of income one year from today at 10% interest, the present value of the right to receive $1.00 two years from today is less. According to the present value formula, the present value of $1.00 to be received two years from today is $0.826446. The present value of $1.00 payable at the end of two years can be confirmed with these calculations.

Return on principal	$0.82645*
Interest for first year at 10% on $0.82645	0.08264
	$0.90909
Interest for second year at 10% on $0.90909	0.09091
Total principal repayment + interest received	$1.00000

* Present value factor, 0.826446 × $1.00 = $0.82645 (rounded).

Similarly, the present value of the right to receive $1.00 at the end of three years is $0.751315, at the end of four years, it is $0.683013 and at the end of the fifth year it is $0.620921. The present value of these rights to receive income at one-year intervals for five years is accumulated as the present value of $1.00 per year. This is known as the *compound interest valuation premise,* also referred to as the *ordinary annuity factor.* Therefore, the sum of the five individual rights to receive $1.00 each year, payable at the end of the year, for five years is $3.790787, i.e., the 10% annual present value of one per period factor for five years.

Sum of Individual Present Values of $1.00
Payable at the End of the Period

Present value of $1.00 due in 1 year	$0.909091*
Present value of $1.00 due in 2 years	0.826446*
Present value of $1.00 due in 3 years	0.751315*
Present value of $1.00 due in 4 years	0.683013*
Present value of $1.00 due in 5 years	0.620921*
Total present value of $1.00 per year for 5 years	$3.790786**

* 10% present value of one factor.
** 10% present value of one per period factor is 3.790787; the difference is due to rounding.

The present value of one per period table for five annual discounting periods (n = 5) gives a factor that represents the total of the present values of a series of periodic amounts of $1.00, payable at the end of each period. The calculation presented above is unnecessary because multiplying $1.00 by the factor for the present value of $1 per year for five years produces the same present value ($1.00 × 3.790787 = $3.790787).

For appraisal purposes, the present value of one per period factor may be multiplied by a periodic income with the characteristics of an ordinary annuity to derive the present value of the right to receive that income stream. The future payments of income provide for recapture of, and interest on, this present value. Present value factors are multipliers and perform the same function as capitalization rates.

The 10% ordinary annuity factor for five years, 3.790787, represents the present value of each $1.00 of annual end-of-year collection based on a nominal annual discount rate of 10%. Tables and formulas for semi-annual, quarterly and monthly payments are also available. The ordinary annuity factor for semi-annual payments in the 10% nominal annual rate table is 7.721735. If the payment continues for five years, each $1.00 of semi-annual payment represents $10.00 received but reflects only $7.72 of the discounted present value of monthly payments for five years. In the table for a 10% nominal rate, the monthly factor is 47.065369, indicating that the present value of an ordinary annuity income stream of 60 monthly payments of $1.00 each discounted at a nominal rate of 10% is 47.065369 × $1.00, or about $47.065.

Based on a 10% nominal rate, semi-annual payments would involve an effective rate of 5%. In the 5% annuity table, the factor for 10 periods is 7.721735; this is the same factor shown in the 10% semi-annual table for a five-year period. Thus, annuity factors for more frequent payment periods can be derived using nominal annual rate tables. Pre-programmed financial calculators can be used to facilitate these calculations.

In computing the present value of an annuity income stream, it may be desirable to assume that periodic payments are made at the beginning rather than the end of each payment period. The present value of an annuity payable in advance is equal to the present value of an ordinary annuity in arrears multiplied by the base, i.e., 1 plus the effective interest rate for the discounting period: 1 + i. Thus, the present value of semi-annual payments in advance over a five-year period discounted at a nominal rate of 10% becomes $1.00 × 7.721735 × 1.05 = $8.107822, or $8.11, compared to $7.72 as computed for payments received at the end of each payment period.

ORDINARY ANNUITIES CHANGING IN CONSTANT AMOUNTS

Present Value of Annual Payments Starting at One and Changing in Constant Amounts

$$PVF = (1+hn)a_{\overline{n}|} - \frac{h(n - a_{\overline{n}|})}{i}$$

where:

PVF = present value factor

h^* = annual increase or decrease after first year

n = number of years

$a_{\overline{n}|}$ = PVF for ordinary level annuity

i = rate of interest yield

* h is positive for an increase and negative for a decrease

This factor is used to solve problems dealing with the compound discounting of cash flows that are best represented by a straight-line pattern of change.

This factor is similar to the ordinary level annuity table, but the annual receipts are converted into constant dollar amounts. For instance, assume that the amount to be received one year from today is $10,000, additional future receipts are expected to increase $1,000 per year for the next nine years and 15% per year is a fair rate of interest. According to the 15% annual present value of one factor, it would be justifiable to pay $67,167 for the right to receive $10,000 one year from today and nine additional payments growing at $1,000 per year for nine additional years. The table for 15% indicates that the factor to be applied to the initial receipt is 6.7167.

Proof:

Year	Income	×	Present Value Factor	=	Present Value
1	$10,000	×	0.869565	=	$8,695.65
2	11,000	×	0.756144	=	8,317.58
3	12,000	×	0.657516	=	7,890.19
4	13,000	×	0.571753	=	7,432.79
5	14,000	×	0.497177	=	6,960.48
6	15,000	×	0.432328	=	6,484.92
7	16,000	×	0.375937	=	6,014.99
8	17,000	×	0.326902	=	5,557.33
9	18,000	×	0.284262	=	5,116.72
10	19,000	×	0.247185	=	4,696.52
Present value					$67,167.17

$$\frac{\text{Present value}}{\text{Initial receipt}} = \text{Factor}$$

$$\frac{\$67,167.17}{\$10,000.00} = 6.7167$$

ORDINARY ANNUITIES CHANGING IN CONSTANT RATIO

Present Value of Annual Payments Starting at One and Changing in Constant Ratio

$$PVF = \frac{1-(1+x)^n / (1+i)^n}{i-x}$$

where:

PVF = present value factor
x^* = constant ratio change in income
n = number of years
i = rate of interest or yield

* x is positive for an increase and negative for a decrease

This factor is used to solve problems dealing with the compound discounting of cash flows that are best represented by an exponential-curve pattern of change.

SINKING FUND FACTORS

Periodic Payment to Grow to One

This factor represents the level periodic investment or deposit required to accumulate to $1 (or other unit of currency) in a given number of periods including interest at the effective rate. It is commonly known as the amortization rate and is the reciprocal of the corresponding sinking fund accumulation factor.

$$1/S_{\overline{n}|} = \frac{i}{S^n - 1}$$

where:
$1/S_{\overline{n}|}$ = sinking fund factor
i = effective rate of interest
n = number of compounding periods
S^n = future value factor

This factor is used to solve problems that involve calculating required sinking fund deposits or providing for the change in capital value in investment situations where the income or payments are level.

When deposits are made at the end of each compounding period, sinking fund factors reflect the fractional portion of $1.00 that must be deposited periodically at a specified interest rate to accumulate to $1.00 by the end of the series of deposits.

If $10,000 is to be accumulated over a 10-year period and annual deposits are compounded at 10% interest, the factor shown on the 10-year line of the annual column in the 10% sinking fund table indicates that each annual deposit must amount to $10,000 × 0.062745, or $627.45.

SINKING FUND ACCUMULATION FACTORS

Future Value of Periodic Payments of One

The future value of periodic payments of one factor represents the total accumulation of principal and interest on a series of deposits or instalments of $1 (or other currency) per period for a given number of periods with interest at the effective rate per period. It is also known as the amount of one per period. It is the reciprocal of the corresponding sinking factor.

$$S_{\overline{n}|} = \frac{S^n - 1}{i}$$

where:
$S_{\overline{n}|}$ = sinking fund accumulation factor
i = effective rate of interest
S^n = future value factor

This factor is used to solve problems that involve the growth of sinking funds or the calculation of capital recovery in investment situations where the income or payments are level.

Sinking fund accumulation factors are similar to the future value of one (amount of one) factors except that deposits are periodic (in a series) and are assumed to be made at the end of the first compounding period and at the end of each period thereafter. Thus, the initial deposit, which is made at the end of the first period, has earned no interest and the factor for this period is 1.000000.

If compounding at 10% per year for 10 years is assumed, a factor of 15.937425 reveals that a series of 10 deposits of $1.00 each made at the end of each year for 10 years will accumulate to $1.00 × 15.937425, or almost $15.94.

DIRECT REDUCTION LOAN FACTORS

Monthly Payment and Annual Constant per One of Loan

Payment: $$1/a_{\overline{n}|} = \frac{i}{1-1/S^n}$$

Annual constant: $$R_M = 12/a_{\overline{n}|}$$

where:

$1/a_{\overline{n}|}$ = direct reduction loan factor

$1/S^n$ = present value factor

i = effective rate of interest

R_M = annual constant

Part paid off: $$P = \frac{R_M - 12i}{R_{Mp} - 12i}$$

where:

R_M = actual annual constant

R_{Mp} = annual constant for projection period

i = effective rate of interest

This factor is used to solve problems dealing with monthly payment, direct reduction loans. Payments and constants for quarterly, semi-annual, and annual payment loans can be obtained by calculating the reciprocals of the present value of one per period factors.

These factors, which are known as *mortgage constants for loan amortization,* reflect the amount of ordinary annuity payment that $1.00 will purchase. They indicate the periodic payment that will extinguish the debt and pay interest on the declining balance of the debt over the life of the payments. The mortgage constant may be expressed in terms of the periodic payments. A mortgage constant related to a monthly payment is the ratio of the monthly payment amount to the original amount of the loan. Whether payments are monthly, semi-annual, or annual, the mortgage constant is usually expressed in terms of the total payments in one year as a percentage of the original loan amount. This is called the annual constant and is represented by the symbol R_M. As the loan is paid off and the outstanding balance is reduced, a new annual mortgage constant can be calculated as the ratio of total annual payments to the unpaid balance of the loan at that time.

A loan of $10,000 to be amortized in 10 annual end-of-year payments at a mortgage interest rate of 10% would require level annual payments of $10,000 × 0.162745, the 10% direct reduction annual factor for 10 years. If monthly payments were made at 10% over 10 years, the amount of each payment would be $132.15, i.e.,

$10,000 × 0.013215. The annual mortgage constant in this case would be 0.15858, or 12 × 0.013215.

Direct reduction factors consist of the interest rate plus the sinking fund factor at the specific point in time. They are reciprocals of the corresponding ordinary level-annuity factors.

INTERRELATIONSHIPS AMONG THE FACTORS

Note that mathematical relationships exist among the formulas for the various factors. These relationships can be useful in understanding the factors and solving appraisal problems. For example, appraisers should know that the factors in the ordinary level annuity and direct reduction loan tables are reciprocals; the factors in the ordinary level annuity table can be used as multipliers instead of using the direct reduction loan factors as divisors.

Reciprocals

The factors in some of the tables are reciprocals of those in other tables. This is indicated by their formulas.

Future Value of One and Reversion Factors

$$S^n \text{ and } \frac{1}{S^n}$$

The reversion factor at 12% for 10 years with annual compounding is 0.321973, which is the reciprocal of the future value of one factor.

0.321973 = 1/3.105848

Sinking Fund Accumulations and Sinking Fund Factors

$$S_{n\rceil} \text{ and } 1/S_{n\rceil}$$

The sinking fund factor at 12% for 10 years with annual compounding is 0.056984, which is the reciprocal of the sinking fund accumulation factor.

0.056984 = 1/17.548735

Ordinary Level Annuity and Direct Reduction Loan Factors

$$a_{n\rceil} \text{ and } 1/a_{n\rceil}$$

The direct reduction loan factor at 12% for 10 years with annual compounding is 0.176984, which is the reciprocal of the ordinary level annuity factor.

0.056984 = 1/17.548735
0.176984 = 1/5.650223

Summations

Ordinary Level Annuity Factors

An ordinary level annuity factor represents the sum of the reversion factors for all periods up to and including the period being considered. For example, the ordinary level annuity factor for five years at 12% with annual compounding is 3.604776, which is the sum of all the reversion factors for Years 1 through 5.

```
0.892857
0.797194
0.711780
0.635518
0.567427
3.604776
```

Direct Reduction Loan Factors

A direct reduction loan factor represents the sum of the interest, yield, or discount rate stated at the top of the table and the sinking fund factor. For example, the direct reduction loan factor at 12% for 10 years with monthly compounding is 0.1721651, which is the sum of 0.12 plus the monthly sinking fund factor of 0.0043471 times 12 $(0.12 + 0.0521651 = 0.1721651)$.

Conversely, the sinking fund factor can be obtained by subtracting the interest rate from the direct reduction loan factor. The sinking fund factor at 12% for 10 years with monthly compounding is $0.1721651 - 0.12 = 0.0521651$. In addition, the interest rate can be obtained by subtracting the sinking fund factor from the direct reduction loan factor. Given a mortgage constant of 0.1721651 with monthly compounding for 10 years, the interest rate is $0.1721651 - 0.0521651 = 0.12000$, or 12%.

STEPS FOR THE HP10BII FINANCIAL CALCULATOR

The financial problems in this book are mostly solved mathematically, using financial formulae and algebra. In some cases, the problems have also been solved using factors from published Financial Tables. However, most practitioners solve complex mathematical problems using a financial calculator. Therefore, this appendix provides steps for how to solve the financial problems throughout the book using the Hewlett-Packard HP10BII financial calculator. Note that every financial calculator has its own programming specifics that guide how a problem must be solved. The HP10BII has the following specifics:

- Interest rates are entered as nominal rates, or annual rates with a stated compounding frequency; many calculators and spreadsheet programs instead use periodic rates (e.g., rate per day, per month, or per quarter).

- Periods per year (P/YR) refers to the frequency of the payments, the scale of N (periods), and the compounding frequency of the nominal interest rate; some calculators and spreadsheet programs have the payment frequency and compounding frequency entered separately.

- The cash flows must be entered as positive or negative numbers, to reflect the direction of cash flows in the transaction; e.g., for a mortgage loan from the borrower's perspective, the present value (PV) is a positive, while the payments (PMT) are a negative cash flow, as is the balloon payment or outstanding balance (entered as FV).

- Payments default to the end of the period, but the calculator can instead be set to handle payments that are made in advance (BEG/END).

CHAPTER 14

Page 14.10: Discounting Annual Income Loss

PV of payments of $91,000 per year for 10 years at a rate of j_1=15% **[end of period payments]**

Press	Display	Comments
15 I/YR	15	
1 ■ P/YR	1	
91000 +/- PMT	-91,000	
10 N	10	
0 FV	0	
PV	456,707.944953	

PV of payments of $91,000 per year for 10 years at a rate of j_1=15% **[beginning of period payments]**

Press	Display	Comments
BEG/END	BEGIN	
15 I/YR	15	
1 ■ P/YR	1	
91000 +/- PMT	-91,000	
10 N	10	
0 FV	0	
PV	525,214.136696	
■ BEG/END		*remove BEGIN function*

Page 14.12: Comparable with Beneficial Financing, fully amortized

Monthly payment for a $170,000 mortgage loan at a rate of j_2 = 7% over a 20-year amortization

Press	Display	Comments
7 ■ NOM%	7	
2 ■ P/YR	2	
EFF%	7.1225	
12 ■ P/YR		
■ NOM%	6.90004739713	
170000 PV		
240 N		
0 FV		
PMT	-1,307.82808098	
1307.83 +/- PMT	-1,307.83	

PV of monthly payments of $1,307.83 over 20 years at a market rate of j_2=9%

Press	Display	Comments
9 ■ NOM%		
2 ■ P/YR		
EFF%	9.2025	
12 ■ P/YR		
■ NOM%	8.83574763	
1307.83 +/- PMT		
240 N		
0 FV		
PV	147,081.134347	

Page 14.12: Comparable with Beneficial Financing, partially amortized

Monthly payment and outstanding at the end of a 5-year term for a $170,000 mortgage loan at a rate of $j_2 = 7\%$ over a 20-year amortization

Press	Display	Comments
7 ■ NOM%		
2 ■ P/YR		
EFF%	7.1225	
12 ■ P/YR		
■ NOM%	6.90004739713	
170000 PV		
240 N		
0 FV		
PMT	-1,307.82808098	
1307.83 +/- PMT	-1,307.83	
60 INPUT ■ AMORT= = =	146,412.278272	

PV of monthly payments of $1,307.83 and an outstanding balance of $146,412.28 over 5 years at a market rate of $j_2=9\%$

Press	Display	Comments
9 ■ NOM%		
2 ■ P/YR		
EFF%	9.2025	
12 ■ P/YR		
■ NOM%	8.83574763	
1307.83 +/- PMT		
146412.28 +/- FV		
60 N		
PV	157,524.102598	

Page 14.13: Calculations for Figure 14.1 (beneficial financing)

Monthly payment and outstanding balance for a $200,000 mortgage loan at an interest rate of $j_2 = 5.5\%$ over a 25-year amortization and a 8-year term

Press	Display	Comments
5.5 ■ NOM%		
2 ■ P/YR		
EFF%	5.575625	
12 ■ P/YR		
■ NOM%	5.43801806193	
200000 PV		
300 N		
0 FV		
PMT	-1,220.78296533	
1220.79 +/- PMT	-1,220.79	
96 INPUT ■ AMORT= = =	162,285.848835	

The present value of the contract payment of $1,220.79 and the outstanding balance owing at the end of the 8-year term of $162,085.85 discounted at a market rate of $j_2 = 7\%$.

Press	Display	Comments
7 ■ NOM%		
2 ■ P/YR		
EFF%	7.1225	
12 ■ P/YR		
■ NOM%	6.90004739713	
1220.79 +/- PMT		
162285.85 +/- FV		
96 N		
PV	183,460.711762	

CHAPTER 15

Page 15.8: Lease calculations

<u>Sale C</u>: PV of annual payments of $5,500 for 7 years at a rate of $j_1 = 9\%$ **[end of period payments]**

Press	Display	Comments
9 I/YR		
1 ■ P/YR		
5500 +/- PMT		
7 N		
0 FV		
PV	27,681.2405929	

<u>Sale C</u>: PV of annual payments of \$5,500 for 7 years at a rate of j_1=9% **[beginning of period payments]**

Press	Display	Comments
BEG/END	BEGIN	
9 I/YR		
1 ■ P/YR		
5500 +/- PMT		
7 N		
0 FV		
PV	30,172.5522463	
■ BEG/END		*remove BEGIN function*

<u>Sale E</u>: PV of annual payments of \$11,700 for 10 years at a rate of j_1=9% **[end of period payments]**

Press	Display	Comments
9 I/YR		
1 ■ P/YR		
11700 +/- PMT		
10 N		
0 FV		
PV	75,086.5951036	

<u>Sale E</u>: PV of annual payments of \$11,700 for 10 years at a rate of j_1=9% **[beginning of period payments]**

Press	Display	Comments
BEG/END	BEGIN	
9 I/YR		
1 ■ P/YR		
11700 +/- PMT		
10 N		
0 FV		
PV	81,844.3886629	
■ BEG/END		*remove BEGIN function*

CHAPTER 16

Page 16.18: Calculations for Table 16.4

PV of cash flows for 5 semi-annual periods at a rate of $j_2 = 23\%$

$PV = -\$635,300(1+i_{sa})^{-1} + \$320,400(1+i_{sa})^{-2} + \$439,640(1+i_{sa})^{-3} + \$438,880(1+i_{sa})^{-4} + \$488,120(1+i_{sa})^{-5}$

Where $i_{sa} = 11.5\%$ (23%/ 2)

$PV = \$572,288$

Press	Display	Comments
Solution 1		
23 I/YR		
2 ■ P/YR		
635300 +/- FV		
1 N		
0 PMT		
PV	569,775.784753	
→M		
320400 FV		
2 N		
PV	-257,716.825193	
M+		
439640 FV		
3 N		
PV	-317,155.755495	
M+		
438880 FV		
4 N		
PV	-283,952.908009	
M+		
488120 FV		
5 N		
PV	-283,238.486913	
M+		
RM	-572,288.190857	
Solution 2		
■ C ALL		
23 I/YR		
2 ■ P/YR		
0 CFj		
635300 +/- CFj		
320400 CFj		
439640 CFj		
438880 CFj		
488120 CFj		
■ NPV	572,288.190856	

Page 16.19: Calculations for Table 16.5

PV of cash flows for 5 semi-annual periods at a rate of $j_2 = 15.5\%$

$PV = -\$635,300(1+i_{sa})^{-1} + \$282,000(1+i_{sa})^{-2} + \$399,320(1+i_{sa})^{-3} + \$396,640(1+i_{sa})^{-4} + \$443,960(1+i_{sa})^{-5}$

Where $i_{sa} = 7.75\%$ (15.5%/ 2)

PV = \$572,422

Press	Display	Comments
Solution 1		
15.5 I/YR		
2 ∎ P/YR		
635300 +/- FV		
1 N		
0 PMT		
PV	589,605.568445	
→M		
282000 FV		
2 N		
PV	-242,892.749285	
M+		
399320 FV		
3 N		
PV	-319,204.662239	
M+		
396640 FV		
4 N		
PV	-294,257.400529	
M+		
443960 FV		
5 N		
PV	-305,673.259881	
M+		
RM	-572,422.503489	
Solution 2		
∎ C ALL		
15.5 I/YR		
2 ∎ P/YR		
0 CFj		
635300 +/- CFj		
282000 CFj		
399320 CFj		
396640 CFj		
443960 CFj		
∎ NPV	572,422.503489	

CHAPTER 19

Page 19.36: Calculating external obsolescence

PV of payments of $7,000 per year for 3 years at a rate of j_1=13%

Press	Display	Comments
Press		
13 I/YR		
1 ■ P/YR		
7000 +/- PMT		
3 N		
0 FV		
PV	16,528.068185	

CHAPTER 22

Page 22.8: Mortgage Constant

Rm calculation for a $1 mortgage loan at a rate of $j_2 = 7\%$ over a 25-year amortization

Press	Display	Comments
7 ■ NOM%		
2 ■ P/YR		
EFF%	7.1225	
12 ■ P/YR		
■ NOM%	6.90004739713	
1 PV		
300 N		
0 FV		
PMT	-7.00415754E-3	*monthly payment*
X 12 =	-8.40498905E-2	R_m *(mortgage constant)*

Page 22.14: Mortgage Annual Debt Service

Mortgage payment calculation is as follows: $375,000 mortgage loan at a rate of $j_2 = 7\%$ over a 25-year amortization

Press	Display	Comments
7 ■ NOM%		
2 ■ P/YR		
EFF%	7.1225	
12 ■ P/YR		
■ NOM%	6.90004739713	
375000 PV		
300 N		
0 FV		
PMT	-2,626.550779	*monthly payment*
X 12 =	-31,518.7089348	*annual debt service*

CHAPTER 23

Page 23.15: Mortgage Level Income with Change in Value

Calculation for sinking fund factor of 0.084321

Find the pmt on a $1 FV over 8 years at a rate of j_1=11%

Press	Display	Comments
11 I/YR		
1 ■ P/YR		
1 FV		
8 N		
0 PV		
PMT	-8.43210542E-2	

Page 23.19: Level-Equivalent Income

Press	Display	Comments
■ C ALL		
12 I/YR		
1 ■ P/YR		
0 CFj		
200000 CFj		
208000 CFj		
216320 CFj		
224973 CFj		
233972 CFj		
■ NPV	774,096.463248	

This is easily converted to a level equivalent by multiplying by the instalment to amortize one factor, 0.277410*.

*Calculation for annuity factor:
Find the payment for $1 PV over 5 years at j_1=12%

Press	Display	Comments
12 I/YR		
1 ■ P/YR		
1 PV		
5 N		
0 FV		
PMT	-2.77409732E-1	

Level-equivalent income = $774,096 x 0.277410 = $214,742

Next, the overall capitalization rate is developed using the level income property model.

$$R_o = Y_o - \Delta\, a$$
$$R_o = 0.12 - 0.15(0.157410^*)$$
$$R_o = 0.096389$$

*Calculation for sinking fund factor of 0.157410

Find the pmt on a \$1 FV over 5 years at a rate of $j_1 = 12\%$

Press	Display	Comments
12 I/YR		
1 ■ P/YR		
1 FV		
5 N		
0 PV		
PMT	-1.57409732E-1	

The value can then be obtained with the model $V = I / R$.

$V_o = \$214{,}742 / 0.096389 = \$2{,}227{,}868$

CHAPTER 24

Page 24.4: Table 24.1, Five-Year DCF Analysis of a Shopping Centre

Press	Display	Comments
■ C ALL		
11 I/YR		
1 ■ P/YR		
0 CFj		
172584 CFj		
147290 CFj		
204326 CFj		
210486 CFj		
216822 + 3084822 = CFj		
■ NPV	2,522,445.02385	

Total leased fee present value indication = \$2,522,445

Page 24.6: Table 24.3: Projected Cash Flow in Each Year

Press	Display	Comments
■ C ALL		
1 ■ P/YR		
817000 +/- CFj		
49823 CFj		
51937 CFj		
49024 CFj		
55810 CFj		
52815 + 948672 = CFj		
■ IRR/YR	9.02128201864	

The yield on this investment is approximately 9%.

Page 24.20: Table 24.10: Forecasting Cash Flows

Present value is the PV of the cash flows plus the PV of the reversion value of $4,487,802

$$PV = \$308,154(1.095)^{-1} + \$357,474(1.095)^{-2} + \$366,460(1.095)^{-3} + \$298,222(1.095)^{-4} + \$388,497(1.095)^{-5} + \$4,487,802(1.095)^{-5}$$

Present value at the cash flows and reversion at j_1=9.5% is $4,163,668.

Press	Display	Comments
■ C ALL		
9.5 I/YR		
1 ■ P/YR		
0 CFj		
308154 CFj		
357474 CFj		
366460 CFj		
298222 CFj		
388497 + 4487802 = CFj		
■ NPV	4,163,667.6709	

BIBLIOGRAPHY

General

Akerson, Charles B. *The Appraiser's Workbook.* 2nd ed. Chicago: Appraisal Institute, 1996.

American Society of Farm Managers and Rural Appraisers and Appraisal Institute. *The Appraisal of Rural Property,* 2nd ed. Denver and Chicago: ASFMRA and Appraisal Institute, 2000.

Appraisal Institute. *The Dictionary of Real Estate Appraisal.* 4th ed. Chicago, 2002.

Benson, Marjorie Lynn, Marie-Ann Bowden, *Understanding Property; a Guide to Canada's Property Law;* Carswell Thomson Canada Ltd, Toronto, 1997

Bonbright, James C. *The Valuation of Property.* Vol. 1. New York: McGraw-Hill, 1937.

Brooks, S. Michael, *Canadian Real Property Theory and Commercial Practise,* Real Property Association of Canada, Toronto, 2006

Davies, Pearl Janet. *Real Estate in American History.* Washington, D.C.: Public Affairs Press, 1958.

Eaton, James D. *Real Estate Valuation in Litigation.* 2nd ed. Chicago: Appraisal Institute, 1995.

Fisher, Clifford E., Jr. *Mathematics for Real Estate Appraisers.* Chicago: Appraisal Institute, 1996.

Fisher, Jeffrey D., and Dennis S. Tosh. *Questions and Answers To Help You Pass the Real Estate Appraisal Exams.* 4th ed. Chicago: Dearborn Real Estate Education, 2004.

Friedman, Edith J., ed. *Encyclopedia of Real Estate Appraising.* Englewood Cliffs, N.J.: Prentice-Hall, Inc., 1978.

Graaskamp, James A. *Graaskamp on Real Estate.* Stephen P. Jarchot, ed. Washington, D.C.: Urban Land Institute, 1991.

Greer, Gaylon E. *The Real Estate Investment Decision.* Lexington, Mass.: D. C. Heath, 1980.

Hines, Mary Alice. *Real Estate Appraisal.* New York: Macmillan Publishing Co., Inc., 1981.

International Association of Assessing Officers. *Property Appraisal and Assessment Administration.* Chicago, 1990.

Kahn, Sanders A., and Frederick E. Case. *Real Estate Appraisal and Investment.* 2nd ed. New York: Ronald Press, 1977.

Kinnard, William N., Jr., and Byrl N. Boyce. *Appraising Real Property.* Lexington, Mass: D. C. Heath, 1984.

Klink, James J. *Real Estate Accounting and Reporting: A Guide for Developers, Investors and Lenders.* New York: John Wiley & Sons, Inc., 1995.

Ontario Real Estate Association. *Real Estate Encyclopedia, Canadian Edition.* , Alliance for Canadian Real Estate Association, Don Mills, Ontario, 2005

Reilly, John W. *The Language of Real Estate.* 5th ed. Chicago: Real Estate Education Co., 2000.

Ring, Alfred A., and James H. Boykin. *The Valuation of Real Estate.* 4th ed. Englewood Cliffs, N.J.: Prentice-Hall, 1993.

Ring, Alfred A., and Jerome Dasso. *Real Estate Principles and Practices.* 11th ed. Englewood Cliffs, N.J.: Prentice-Hall, 1989.

Shenkel, William M. *Modern Real Estate Appraisal.* New York: McGraw-Hill, 1978.

Shlaes, Jared. *Real Estate Counselling in a Plain Brown Wrapper.* Chicago: Counsellors of Real Estate, 1992.

Siedel, George J., and Robert J. Aalberts. *Real Estate Law.* 6th ed. Mason, Ohio: Thomson/West, 2006.

Smith, Halbert C., and Jerry D. Beloit. *Real Estate Appraisal.* 3rd ed. Columbus, Ohio: Century VII Publishing Company, 1995.

Smith, Halbert C., Carl J. Tschappat, and Ronald L. Racster. *Real Estate and Urban Development.* 3rd ed. Homewood, Ill.: Richard D. Irwin, 1981.

Talamo, John. *The Real Estate Dictionary.* 6th ed. Boston: Laventhal & Horwath/Financial Publishing Co., 1998.

Ventrolo, William L., and Martha R. Williams. *Fundamentals of Real Estate Appraisal.* 5th ed. Chicago: Real Estate Education Co., 1990.

Wendt, Paul F. *Real Estate Appraisal Review and Outlook.* Athens, Ga.: University of Georgia Press, 1974.

West, Bill W., and Richard L. Dickinson. *Street Talk in Real Estate.* Alameda/Sacramento, Calif.: Unique Pub., 1987.

Young, Janice F., and Stephanie Coleman. "Common Errors and Issues in Reports". *The Appraisal Journal* (Summer 2007).

UBC Real Estate Division. 2008. *Real Estate Investment Analysis and Advanced Income Appraisal.* Vancouver: UBC Real Estate Division

UBC Real Estate Division. 2009. *Statistical and Computer Applications in Valuation (BUSI 344 Course Workbook).* Vancouver: UBC Real Estate Division

Periodicals

American Council of Life Insurance Investment Bulletins. American Council of Life Insurance, Washington, D.C.

> Annual and quarterly reports on the lending actities and holdings of life insurance companies. *www.acli.com*

American Housing Survey. Bureau of the Census for the Department of Housing and Urban Development, Washington, D.C.

> Biannual updates. Data on U.S. housing markets in 47 selected metropolitan areas, including information on apartments, single-family homes, mobile homes, and owner demographics. *www.census.gov/hhes/www/housing/ahs/ahs.html*

The Appraisal Journal. Appraisal Institute, Chicago.

> Quarterly. Oldest periodical in the appraisal field. Includes technical articles on all phases of real property appraisal and regular feature on legal decisions. *www.appraisalinstitute.org/taj/*

Appraiser News Online. Appraisal Institute, Chicago.

> Twice monthly. News bulletin covering current events and trends in appraisal practice. *www.appraisalinstitute.org/ano/*

Bank of Canada Review. Bank of Canada, Ottawa.

> Quarterly, featuring articles related to the Canadian economy and to central banking, with summary statistical tables. *www.bankofcanada.ca*

Buildings. Stamats Communications, Inc., Cedar Rapids, Iowa.

> Monthly. Journal of building construction and management. *www.buildings.com/*

Canada Year Book, Statistics Canada, Ottawa.

> Annual - the newest facts and analysis related to current events, important issues and trends in Canada for over 140 years.

Canadian Property Valuation. Appraisal Institute of Canada, Ottawa, Ontario.

> Quarterly. General and technical articles on appraisal and expropriation in Canada. Includes information on institute programs, news, etc. *www.aicanada.ca/*

Crittenden Report on Real Estate Financing. Crittenden Publishing, Inc., Novato, Calif.

> Weekly. Real estate finance information. *www.crittendenreport.com*

Emerging Trends in Real Estate. PricewaterhouseCoopers LLP and Urban Land Institute, New York and Washington, D.C.

> Annual. *www.pwcreval.com*

Journal of the American Society of Farm Managers and Rural Appraisers. Denver.

> Annual. Includes appraisal articles. *www.asfmra.org/publications/*

Journal of Property Management. Institute of Real Estate Management, Chicago.

> Bimonthly. Covers a broad range of property investment and management issues. *www.irem.org*

Journal of Property Tax Assessment & Administration. International Association of Assessing Officers, Kansas City, Mo.
> Bimonthly. Includes articles on property taxation and assessment administration. Formerly *Assessment Journal. www.iaao.org*

Journal of Real Estate Literature. American Real Estate Society, Clemson, S.C.
> Semiannual. Contains review articles, case studies, doctoral dissertations, and reviews of technical literature, data sets, computer applications, and software.

Journal of Real Estate Portfolio Management. American Real Estate Society, Clemson, S.C.
> Semiannual. Contains the results of applied research on real estate investment and portfolio management.

Journal of Real Estate Research. American Real Estate Society, Clemson, S.C.
> Quarterly. Publishes the results of applied research on real estate development, finance, investment, management, market analysis, marketing, and valuation. *www.aresnet.org*

Just Compensation: A Monthly Report on Condemnation Cases. Sherman Oaks, Calif.
> Monthly. Reports on condemnation cases. *www.justcompensation.com*

Korpacz Real Estate Investor Survey. Peter Korpacz, Florham Park, N.J.
> Quarterly. Survey of a cross-section of the major participants in real estate equity markets. *www.pwcreval.com/survey/home.asp*

Land Economics. University of Wisconsin, Madison.
> Quarterly. Devoted to the study of economics and social institutes. Includes reports on university research and trends in land utilization. Frequently publishes articles on developments in other countries.
> *www.wisc.edu/wisconsinpress/journals/journals/le.html*

Land Lines. Lincoln Institute of Land Policy, Cambridge, Mass.
> Quarterly. Publishes articles focusing on research and scholarly studies of land policy and land-related taxation. *www.lincolninst.edu*

NCREIF Quarterly Real Estate Performance Report. National Council of Real Estate Investment Fiduciaries, which maintains the NCREIF Classic Property Index (formerly the Russell-NCREIF Property Index).
> Quarterly. Tracks the performance of properties acquired on behalf of tax-exempt institutions, on an unleveraged basis, and held in fiduciary trusts. The index is calculated on the basis of four different rates of return (total return, income return, capital appreciation return, and annual/annualized return). *www.ncreif.com*

PREA Quarterly. Pension Real Estate Association, Glastonbury, Conn.
> Quarterly. Contains articles and information areas such as real estate securities, legislative issues, capital flows and market research, as well as articles exploring issues and trends of importance to institutional real estate investors. *www.prea.org*

Real Estate Economics. American Real Estate and Urban Economics Association, Richmond, Va.
> Quarterly. Focuses on research and scholarly studies of current and emerging real estate issues. Formerly *Journal of the American Real Estate and Urban Economics Association. www.areuea.org/publications/ree/*

Real Estate Issues. The Counsellors of Real Estate, Chicago.

> Quarterly. Focuses on practical applications and applied theory for a cross section of real estate practitioners and related professionals. *www.cre.org/publications/rei.cfm*

Real Estate Law Journal. Thomson/West, St. Paul, Minn.

> Quarterly. Publishes articles on legal issues and reviews current litigation of concern to real estate professionals.

Right of Way. International Right of Way Association, Torrance, Calif.

> Bimonthly. Publishes articles on all phases of right-of-way activity– e.g., condemnation, negotiation, pipelines, electric power transmission lines, highways. Includes association news. *www.irwaonline.org*

Survey of Current Business. U.S. Bureau of Economic Analysis, U.S. Department of Commerce, Washington, D.C.

> Monthly. Includes statistical and price data. Biennial supplement, *Business Statistics. www.bea.gov/scb/index.htm*

Valuation. American Society of Appraisers, Herndon, Va.

> Annual. Articles on real property valuation and the appraisal of personal and intangible property. Includes society news. Previously published as *Technical Valuation. www.appraisers.org/pubs/valuation/*

Valuation. Appraisal Institute, Chicago.

> Quarterly. Provides timely, practical information and ideas to assist real estate appraisers in conducting their businesses effectively. Previously published as *Valuation Insights & Perspectives. www.appraisalinstitute.org/vip/*

Valuation Strategies. Thomson/TTA, Stamford, Conn.

> Published bimonthly. Includes technical articles, case studies, and research on all aspects of real estate valuation. *ria.thomson.com/journals/*

Wharton Real Estate Review. Samuel Zell and Robert Lurie Real Estate Center, University of Pennsylvania, Philadelphia.

> Semi-annual. Provides a forum for scholars, real estate practitioners, and public officials to introduce new ideas, present research and analytical findings, and promote widespread discussion of topical issues. *realestate.wharton.upenn.edu/review.php*

Chapter 1

American Institute of Real Estate Appraisers. *Appraisal Thought: A 50-Year Beginning.* Chicago, 1982.

Andrews, Richard N.L. *Land in America.* Lexington, Mass.: D.C. Heath, 1979.

Appraisal Institute. *Appraising Residential Properties.* 4th ed. Chicago, 2007.

Benjamin, John D. "The Legal Liability of Real Estate Appraisers". *The Appraisal Journal* (April 1995).

Bleich, Donald H. "Factors that Influence University Student Interest in the Appraisal Profession". *The Appraisal Journal* (Spring 2006).

Closser, Bruce M. "The Evolution of Appraiser Ethics and Standards". *The Appraisal Journal* (Spring 2007).

Davies, Pearl Janet. *Real Estate in American History*. Washington, D.C.: Public Affairs Press, 1958.

Derbes, Max J., Jr. "When Are Appraisers Not Liable?" *The Appraisal Journal* (October 1995).

Finch, J. Howard. "The Role of Professional Designations as Quality Signals". *The Appraisal Journal* (April 1999).

Gaglione, Claudia L. "Third-Party Liability: Does Privity Matter". *Valuation Insights & Perspectives* vol. 2, no. 3 (Third Quarter 1997).

Kinnard, William N., Jr., ed. 1984 *Real Estate Valuation Colloquium: A Redefinition of Real Estate Appraisal Precepts and Practices*. Boston: Oelgeschlager, Gunn & Hain and Lincoln Institute of Land Policy, 1986.

Kratovil, Robert, and Raymond J. Werner. *Real Estate Law*. 8th ed. Englewood Cliffs, N.J.: Prentice-Hall, 1983.

Levine, Mark Lee. "The Death of Privity: Recent Decisions". *The Appraisal Journal* (July 1998).

___. *Real Estate Appraisers' Liability*. New York: Clark Boardman Callaghan, 1991.

Love, Terrence L. *The Guide to Appraisal Office Policies and Procedures*. Chicago: Appraisal Institute, 1991.

Martin, Michael M. "The Ethics of Desire". *The Appraisal Journal* (July 1997).

Miller, Norman G., and Sergey Markosyan. "The Academic Roots and Evolution of Real Estate Appraisal". *The Appraisal Journal* (April 2003).

Miller, Norman G., and Margot Weinstein. *Commercial Real Estate Career Education and Resource Guide*. North Palm Beach, Fla.: The Hoyt Institute of Real Estate, 2006.

Nahorney, Daniel J., and Vicki Lankarge. *How to Get Started in the Real Estate Appraisal Business*. New York: McGraw-Hill Companies, 2006.

Noyes, C. Reinold. *The Institution of Property*. London: Longmans, Green and Company, 1936.

Parli, Richard L. "The Education of a Profession". *The Appraisal Journal* (Fall 2007).

Smalley, Steven P. "Appraisal: Science or Art?" *The Appraisal Journal* (April 1995).

Chapter 2

American Institute of Real Estate Appraisers. *Appraisal Thought: A 50-Year Beginning*. Chicago, 1982.

Davies, Pearl Janet. *Real Estate in American History*. Washington, D.C.: Public Affairs Press, 1958.

Dorchester, John D., Jr. "Market Value for Financial Reporting: The Premise", *The Appraisal Journal* (Winter 2004).

Glanville, Brian A., and Alison L. Gerlach. "In All Fairness", *The Appraisal Journal* (Spring 2004).

Heilbroner, Robert L. *The Worldly Philosophers*. Rev. ed. New York: Simon and Schuster, 1964.

Hodges, McCloud B., Jr. "Three Approaches?" *The Appraisal Journal* (October 1993).

Jevons, W. Stanley. *The Theory of Political Economy*. 5th ed. New York: Augustus M. Kelley, 1965.

King, Alfred M. *Fair Value for Financial Reporting: Meeting the New FASB Requirements*. Hoboken, N.J.: John Wiley & Sons, Inc., 2006.

Noyes, C. Reinold. *The Institution of Property*. London: Longmans, Green and Company, 1936.

Roll, Eric. *A History of Economic Thought*. 3rd ed. Englewood Cliffs, N.J.: Prentice-Hall, 1964.

Samuelson, Paul A., and William D. Nordhaus. *Economics*. 13th ed. New York: McGraw-Hill, 1989.

Solot, Sanders K. "The First Appraisal". *The Real Estate Appraiser & Analyst* (April 1987).

Vane, Howard R., and John L. Thompson. *Monetarism– Theory, Evidence, and Policy*. New York: Halsted Press, 1979.

Wilson, Donald C. "How Tactical Utility Influences Price and Value". *The Appraisal Journal* (January 1998).

Yovino-Young, Michael. "Appraising from the Middle Ages to the Millennium". *Valuation Insights & Perspectives* (Third Quarter 1999).

Chapter 3

Hoover, Edgar M. *The Location of Economic Activity*. New York: McGraw-Hill, 1963.

Noyes, C. Reinold. *The Institution of Property*. London: Longmans, Green and Company, 1936.

Mitchell, Phillip S. "The Evolving Appraisal Paradigm". *The Appraisal Journal* (April 1993).

Pearson, Thomas D. "Education for Professionalism: A Common Body of Knowledge for Appraisers, Part I: Background and Historical Trends". *The Appraisal Journal* (October 1988).

___. "Education for Professionalism: A Common Body of Knowledge for Appraisers, Part II: The Body of Knowledge". *The Appraisal Journal* (January 1989).

Chapter 4

American Society of Farm Managers and Rural Appraisers and Appraisal Institute. *The Appraisal of Rural Property*. 2nd ed. Denver and Chicago, 2000.

Dollars and Cents of Shopping Centers/The SCORE: 2008. Washington, D.C.: Urban Land Institute and International Council of Shopping Centers, 2008 (updated biannually).

Garreau, Joel. *Edge City: Life on the New Frontier*. New York: Doubleday, 1991.

Girling, Cynthia L., and Kenneth I. Helphand. *Yard-Street-Park: The Design of Suburban Open Space*. New York: John Wiley & Sons, Inc., 1994.

Jackson, Kenneth T. *Crabgrass Frontier: The Suburbanization of the United States*. New York: Oxford University Press, 1985.

Jacobs, Jane. *The Death and Life of Great American Cities*. New York: Random House, 1961.

Perin, Constance. *Everything in Its Place: Social Order and Land Use in America*. Princeton, N.J.: Princeton University Press, 1977.

Rabianski, Joseph. "Apartment Market Area Delineation". *The Appraisal Journal* (Winter 2006).

Rogers, Jean, Norman D. Flynn, Thomas A. Motta, William D. Endsley, and Soula Porxenos. *Real Property Markets: The "Real" Solution for Economic Development*. Chicago: Appraisal Institute, 2004.

Schwanke, Dean. *Mixed Use Development Handbook*. 2nd ed. Washington, D.C.: Urban Land Institute, 2003.

Chapter 5

Anderson, Joshua. "The ABCs of CMBS". *Valuation Insights & Perspectives*, (Third Quarter 1999).

The Appraisal Journal "Financial Views" column, including:

DeLisle, James. "Real Estate Capital Markets Update, Settling into the Transitional Economic Environment". (April 2001).

___. "Still Bouncing and Being Bounced Along". (April 2003).

___. "Out of the Economic Doldrums?" (October 2003).

___. "The Three Rs of Election Year Economics: Recovery, Rhetoric, and 'Rithmetic". (Spring 2004).

___. "Impact of Hurricane Katrina Ripples Across Economy". (Fall 2005).

___. "Economy Set for Soft Landing". (Fall 2006).

___. "At the Crossroads of Expansion and Recession". (Fall 2007).

Brueggeman, William B., and Jeffrey D. Fisher. *Real Estate Finance and Investments*. 13th ed. Boston: McGraw-Hill/Irwin, 2008.

Clauretie, Terence M., and G. Stacy Sirmans. *Real Estate Finance: Theory and Practice*. 3rd ed. Upper Saddle River, N.J.: Prentice Hall, 1999.

Dannis, Charles G. "Discover the Benefits of the NCREIF Property Index". *The Appraisal Journal* (October 1997).

Downs, Anthony. *Niagara of Capital: How Global Capital Has Transformed Housing and Real Estate Markets*. Washington, D.C.: Urban Land Institute, 2007.

Economic Report of the President. Washington, D.C.: Council of Economic Advisors (updated annually) http://w3.access.gpo.gov/eop/.

Fabozzi, Frank J., ed. *Handbook of Commercial Mortgage-Backed Securities*, 2nd ed. New Hope, Penn.: Frank J. Fabozzi Associates, 1998.

___. *Trends in Commercial Mortgage-Backed Securities*. New Hope, Penn.: Frank J. Fabozzi Associates, 1998.

Jones, Lawrence. D. 1995. "The Evolving Canadian Housing Finance System and the Role of Government". *Housing Finance International*: pp. 27-35.

Kelly, Kevin. *New Rules for the New Economy: 10 Radical Strategies for a Connected World*. New York: Viking, 1998.

Leon, Hortense. "Foreign Investment in U.S. Real Estate Continues to Rise". *National Real Estate Investor* (May 2005).

Oliner, Stephen, and Daniel E. Sichel. "The Resurgence of Growth in the Late 1990s: Is Information Technology the Story?" *Journal of Economic Perspectives* (Fall 2000).

Pratt, Shannon P. *Cost of Capital: Estimation and Applications.* New York: John Wiley & Sons, Inc., 1998.

Roulac, Stephen E. "Global Capital Flows: The New Market Dynamic". *Mortgage Banking* (February 2000), Commercial CREF Conference Special Issue.

Siklos, Pierre L. 2001. *Money Banking and Financial Institutions: Canada in the Global Environment.* Toronto: McGraw-Hill Ryerson.

Smith, Steve. "Predatory Lending, Mortgage Fraud, and Client Pressures". *The Appraisal Journal* (April 2002).

Stocks Bonds Bills and Inflation Yearbook. Chicago: R.G. Ibbotson Associates, (updated annually).

Winger, Alan R. "A Layman's Approach to Risk Analysis". *Real Estate Review* (Winter 1996).

Yun, Lawrence, Keunwon Chung, and Ken Fears. "Foreign Investment in U.S. Real Estate". *Real Estate Insights* (December 2006).

Chapter 6

Kratovil, Robert, and Raymond J. Werner. *Real Estate Law.* 10th ed. Englewood Cliffs, N.J.: Prentice-Hall, 1993.

Sackman, Julius L., and Patrick J. Rohan. *Nichols' Law of Eminent Domain.* 3rd rev. ed. Albany, N.Y.: Matthew Bender, 1973 (looseleaf service).

UBC Real Estate Division. 2010. *Real Property Law.* Vancouver: UBC Real Estate Division.

Webb, Dennis. *Valuing Undivided Interests in Real Property: Partnerships and Cotenancies.* Chicago: Appraisal Institute, 2004.

Wolf, Peter. *Land in America: Its Value, Use, and Control.* New York: Pantheon, 1981.

Chapter 7

Coleman, Stephanie. *Scope of Work.* Chicago: Appraisal Institute, 2006.

___. "Scope of Work and Problem Identification: The Significant Seven". *The Appraisal Journal* (Summer 2006).

Schmutz, George L. *The Appraisal Process.* North Hollywood, Calif.: the author, 1941; New York: Prentice-Hall, Inc., 1949.

Chapter 8

"AI, MISMO Unite to Develop Common Data Standards for Valuation, Mortgage Industries". *Valuation Insights & Perspectives* (Third Quarter 2005).

Britt, Phil. "MISMO and XML: Keeping Up with the Mortgage Industry". *Valuation Insights & Perspectives* (Second Quarter 2004).

___. "The Big Dig for Data". *Valuation* (Fourth Quarter 2007).

Byrne, Therese E. *A Guide to Real Estate Information Sources*, 1980.

Castle, Gilbert H., III, ed. *GIS in Real Estate: Integrating, Analyzing, and Presenting Locational Information.* Chicago: Appraisal Institute, 1998.

Cirincione, John, Daniel Szparaga, and Grant Ian Thrall, "XML-Based Data Standards Being Developed for the Mortgage Industry May Significantly Impact the GIS Community". *Geospatial Solutions* (June 2005).

Epley, Donald R. "Data Management and Continual Verification for Accurate Appraisal Reports". *The Appraisal Journal* (Winter 2006).

Friedman, Thomas. *The World Is Flat: A Brief History of the Twenty-First Century.* New York: Farrar, Straus and Giroux, 2005.

Gordon Jenkins and Ray Lancashire, *The Electronic Commerce Handbook: A Quick Read on How Electronic Commerce Can Keep You Competitive* (Etobicoke, Ontario, Canada: EDI Council of Canada, 1994).

Gilon, Paul, and C.A. Cardenas. "Appraisers and Cyberspace: An Introduction to the Internet". *The Appraisal Journal* (October 1995).

Linné, Mark R. "The Emergence of Real Estate Data Standards: Opportunities for Public and Private Sector Collaboration". *Fair & Equitable* (March 2008).

Minnerly, W. Lee. *Electronic Data Interchange (EDI) and the Appraisal Office.* Chicago: Appraisal Institute, 1996.

Nielson, Donald A. "World Wide Web Data Sources for the Appraiser: U.S. Census Changes for the Year 2000". *Valuation Insights & Perspectives* (First Quarter 2000).

Rayburn, William B., and Dennis S. Tosh. "Artificial Intelligence: The Future of Appraising". *The Appraisal Journal* (October 1995). Ross, John W. "The Appraisal Institute's Continued Forays into Setting Technology Standards [Viewpoint]". *Valuation Insights & Perspectives* (Second Quarter 2004).

Thrall, Grant Ian. *Business Geography and New Real Estate Market Analysis.* New York: Oxford University Press, 2002.

UBC Real Estate Division. 2009. *Statistical and Computer Applications in Valuation (BUSI 344 Course Workbook).* Vancouver: UBC Real Estate Division

U.S. Census Bureau. *Statistical Abstract of the United States: 2007.* Washington, D.C.: U.S. Government Printing Office, 2006. *www.census.gov*

Valuation "Cool Tools" column, including:

Pugh, Wayne. "Collaborate Online to Complete Reports". (First Quarter 2007).

___. "Safeguard your Systems with Online Backup and Ultimate Rebooting". (Second Quarter 2007).

___. "Where Can I Find Free Comparable Commercial Data?" (First Quarter 2005).

Chapter 9

General Surveys

American Institute of Real Estate Appraisers. *Real Estate Market Analysis and Appraisal.* Research Series Report 3. Chicago, 1988.

Appraisal Institute. *Real Estate Market Analysis: Supply and Demand Factors.* Chicago, 1993.

Carn, Neil, Joseph Rabianski, Maury Seldin, and Ron Racster. *Real Estate Market Analysis: Applications and Techniques.* Englewood Cliffs, N.J.: Prentice-Hall, 1988.

Clapp, John M. *Handbook for Real Estate Market Analysis.* Englewood Cliffs, N.J.: Prentice-Hall, 1987.

Epley, Donald R., and Joseph Rabianski. *Principles of Real Estate Decisions.* Englewood Cliffs, N.J.: Prentice-Hall, Inc., 1986.

Fanning, Stephen F. *Market Analysis for Real Estate: Concepts and Applications in Valuation and Highest and Best Use.* Chicago: Appraisal Institute, 2005.

Graaskamp, James A. *A Guide to Feasibility Analysis.* Chicago: Society of Real Estate Appraisers, 1970.

Malizia, Emil E. "Clarifying the Structure and Advancing the Practice of Real Estate Market Analysis". *The Appraisal Journal* (January 1995).

Myers, Dowell, and Phillip S. Mitchell. "Identifying a Well-Founded Market Analysis". *The Appraisal Journal* (October 1993).

Seldin, Maury, and James H. Boykin. *Real Estate Analyses.* Homewood, Ill.: American Society of Real Estate Counsellors and Dow Jones-Irwin, 1990.

Vandell, Kerry D. "Market Analysis: Can We Do Better?" *The Appraisal Journal* (July 1988).

Wincott, D. Richard. "Market Analysis in the Appraisal Process". *The Appraisal Journal* (January 1995).

Economic Base Analysis, Location Theory, and Census Data

Haggett, Peter. *Locational Analysis in Human Geography.* New York: St. Martin's, 1965.

Hoover, Edgar M. *The Location of Economic Activity.* New York: McGraw-Hill, 1963.

Perin, Constance. *Everything in Its Place: Social Order and Land Use in America.* Princeton, N.J.: Princeton University Press, 1977.

Specific Property Types

Gimmy, Arthur E., Joseph S. Rabianski, Stephen Rushmore, James D. Vernor, and Marvin L. Wolverton. "Market Analysis Applied: Snapshots of Four Property Types". *Valuation Insights & Perspectives* (Fall 1996).

Hughes, William T., Jr. "Determinants of Demand for Industrial Property". *The Appraisal Journal* (April 1994).

Kimball, J.R. "Office Space Demand Analysis". *The Appraisal Journal* (October 1987).

Kimball, J.R., and Barbara S. Bloomberg. "The Demographics of Subdivision Analysis". *The Appraisal Journal* (October 1986).

Mills, Arlen, and Anthony Reynolds. "Apartment Property Market Analysis". *The Real Estate Appraiser & Analyst* (December 1991).

Mills, Arlen, Richard Parli, and Anthony Reynolds. *The Valuation of Apartment Properties.* 2nd ed. Chicago, Appraisal Institute, 2008.

Myers, Dowell. "Housing Market Research: A Time for a Change". *Urban Land* (October 1988).

Rabianski, Joseph S., and Roy T. Black. "Why Analysts Often Make Wrong Estimates About the Demand for Industrial Space". *Real Estate Review* (Spring 1997).

Rushmore, Stephen, and Erich Baum. *Hotels and Motels– Valuations and Market Studies.* Chicago: Appraisal Institute, 2001.

Vernor, James D., and Joseph Rabianski. *Shopping Center Appraisal and Analysis.* Chicago: Appraisal Institute, 1992.

Chapter 10

American Society of Farm Managers and Rural Appraisers and Appraisal Institute. *The Appraisal of Rural Property.* 2nd ed. Chicago and Denver, 2000.

Andrews, Richard N.L. *Land in America.* Lexington, Mass.: D.C. Heath, 1979.

Bible, Douglas S., and Chengo Hsieh. "Determinants of Vacant Land Values and Implications for Appraisers". *The Appraisal Journal* (July 1999).

Boykin, James H. *Land Valuation: Adjustment Procedures and Assignments.* Chicago: Appraisal Institute, 2001.

Graham, J. Edward, Jr., and William W. Hall, Jr. "Hurricanes, Housing Market Activity, and Coastal Real Estate Values". *The Appraisal Journal* (October 2001).

Keating, David M. *The Valuation of Wetlands.* 2nd ed. Chicago: Appraisal Institute, 2002.

Layne, David. *Principles of Right of Way.* Torrance, Calif.: International Right of Way Association, 2004.

Major, Christopher, and Kenneth M. Lusht. "Beach Proximity and the Distribution of Property Values in Shore Communities". *The Appraisal Journal* (Fall 2004).

Owens, Robert W. "Appraising Floodplain Properties". *The Appraisal Journal* (April 1991).

Rinehart, James R. "Estimating the Effect of a View on Undeveloped Property Values". *The Appraisal Journal* (January 1999).

Rubenstein, Harvey M. *A Guide to Site Planning and Landscape Construction.* New York: John Wiley & Sons, Inc., 1996.

Uniform Appraisal Standards for Federal Land Acquisitions. Washington, D.C.: Interagency Land Acquisition Conference, 2000.

Witherspoon, Robert E., Jon P. Abbett, and Robert M. Gladstone. *Mixed-Use Developments: New Ways of Land Use.* Washington, D.C.: Urban Land Institute, 1976.

Chapter 11

Brand, Stewart. *How Buildings Learn: What Happens After They're Built.* New York: Viking Penguin, 1994.

Carson Dunlap & Associates Limited. *The Illustrated Home.* Chicago: Dearborn Real Estate Education, 2003.

Ching, Francis D.K., and Cassandra Adams. *Building Construction Illustrated.* 3rd ed. New York: John Wiley & Sons, Inc., 2001.

Duffy, Francis, and Kenneth Powell. *The New Office.* London: Conran Octopus Books, 1997.

Guidry, Krisandra. "Sick Commercial Buildings: What Appraisers Need To Know". *The Appraisal Journal* (January 2002).

Harris, Cyril M. *Dictionary of Architecture and Construction.* New York: McGraw-Hill, 1975.

Harrison, Henry S. *Houses– The Illustrated Guide to Construction, Design & Systems.* 3rd ed. Chicago: Real Estate Education Company, a division of Dearborn Financial, 1998.

Keune, Russell V., ed. *The Historic Preservation Yearbook.* Bethesda, Md.: Adler and Adler, 1984.

Love, Terrence L. "New Light Construction Technologies for Residential and Small Commercial Buildings". *The Appraisal Journal* (January 1997).

McKnight, Douglas. "A Practical Guide to Evaluating the Functional Utility of Warehouses". *The Appraisal Journal* (January 1999).

McMorrough, Julia. *Materials, Structures, and Standards.* Gloucester, Mass.: Rockport Publishers, Inc., 2006.

R.S. Means, Inc. *Means Illustrated Construction Dictionary.* 3rd. ed. Kingston, Mass.: R.S. Means, Inc., 2000.

Myers, John. "Fundamentals of Production that Influence Industrial Facility Designs". *The Appraisal Journal* (April 1994).

PKF Consulting and Urban Land Institute. *Hotel Development.* Washington, D.C.: Urban Land Institute, 1996.

Reynolds, Judith. *Historic Properties: Preservation and the Valuation Process.* 3rd ed. Chicago: Appraisal Institute, 2006.

Roddewig, Richard J., ed. *Valuing Contaminated Properties: An Appraisal Institute Anthology.* Chicago: Appraisal Institute, 2002.

Ruegg, Rosalie T., and Harold E. Marshall. *Building Economics: Theory and Practice.* New York: Van Nostrand Reinhold, 1990.

Sanders, Michael V. "Mold: What Appraisers Should Know". *Valuation Insights & Perspectives* (Third Quarter 2005).

Sharkawy, M. Atef., and Joseph Rabianski. "How Design Elements Create and Enhance Real Estate Value". *Real Estate* Review (Summer 1995).

Simmons, H. Leslie, Harold B. Olin, John L. Schmidt, and Walter H. Lewis. *Construction Principles, Materials and Methods.* 7th ed. New York: John Wiley & Sons, Inc., 2001.

Simons, Robert A. *When Bad Things Happen to Good Property.* Washington, D.C.: Environmental Law Institute, 2005.

Simpson, John A. *Property Inspection: An Appraiser's Guide.* Chicago: Appraisal Institute, 1997.

UBC Real Estate Division. 2009. *Commercial Property Analysis.* Vancouver: UBC Real Estate Division

UBC Real Estate Division. 2009. *Residential Property Analysis.* Vancouver: UBC Real Estate Division.

Wang, Ko, and Marvin L. Wolverton. *Real Estate Valuation Theory.* Boston: Kluwer Academic, 2002.

White, John Robert, ed. *The Office Building: From Concept to Investment Reality.* Chicago: Appraisal Institute, Counsellors of Real Estate, and Society of Industrial and Office Realtors Educational Fund, 1993.

Green Building

Council of Energy Ministers. 2007. *Moving Forward on Energy Efficiency in Canada: A Foundation for Action.* Government of Canada. ISBN 978-0-662-46749-6.

Elkington, John. *Cannibals with Forks: The Triple Bottom Line of 21st Century Business.* Stony Creek, Conn.: New Society Publishers, 1998.

Frej, Anne, ed. *Green Office Buildings: A Practical Guide to Development.* Washington, D.C.: Urban Land Institute, 2005.

Guidry, Krisandra. "How Green is Your Building?: An Appraiser's Guide to Sustainable Design". *The Appraisal Journal* (Winter 2004).

Lucuik, Mark et al. 2005. *A Business Case for Green Buildings in Canada.* Canada Green Building Council.

McDonough, Bill, and Michael Braungart. *Cradle to Cradle: Remaking the Way We Make Things.* New York: North Point Press, 2002.Rocky Mountain Institute. *Green Development: Integrating Ecology and Real Estate.* New York: John Wiley & Sons, Inc. 1998.

UBC Real Estate Division. 2010. *Green Value: Valuing Sustainable Commercial Buildings.* (CPD 125 course workbook).

UBC Real Estate Division. 2008. *Getting to Green – Energy Efficient and Sustainable Housing.* (CPD 126 course workbook).

U.S. Green Building Council. *LEED Green Building Rating System.* Washington, D.C.: USGBC. *www.usgbc.org*

Valuation (Second Quarter 2007), "Appraising in a Green World: Where Value and Sustainability Meet" issue, including the following articles:

Bergsman, Steve. "Sustainable by All Accords".

Nicolay, Claire. "The Greening of Real Estate Appraisal".

Price-Robinson, Kathy. "Green Building: Lenders' and Builders' Perspectives".

Chapter 12

Abson, Gary K. "Highest and Best Use: Theory and Practice". *Canadian Appraiser* (Spring 1989).

American Institute of Real Estate Appraisers. *Readings in Highest and Best Use.* Chicago, 1981.

Beckwith, Paul. " Highest and best use analysis". *Canadian Property Valuation* (Fall 2010).

Fanning, Stephen F. *Market Analysis for Real Estate: Concepts and Applications in Valuation and Highest and Best Use.* Chicago: Appraisal Institute, 2005.

Finch, J. Howard. "Highest and Best Use and the Special-Purpose Property". *The Appraisal Journal* (April 1996).

Galleshaw, Mark. "Evaluating Interim Uses". *The Appraisal Journal* (January 1994).

Graaskamp, James A. *A Guide to Feasibility Analysis.* Chicago: Society of Real Estate Appraisers, 1970.

Greer, Gaylon E. *The Real Estate Investment Decision.* Lexington, Mass.: D.C. Heath, 1979.

Lennhoff, David C., and William A. Elgie. "Highest and Best User". *The Appraisal Journal* (July 1995).

Lennhoff, David C., and Richard L. Parli. "A Higher and Better Definition". *The Appraisal Journal* (Winter 2004).

Love, Terrence L., Sr. "The Appraiser's Role in Zoning Litigation". *The Appraisal Journal* (July 1998).

North, Lincoln W. *The Concept of Highest and Best Use.* Winnipeg, Manitoba: Appraisal Institute of Canada, 1981.

Parli, Richard. "What's Financial Feasibility Got To Do With It?" *The Appraisal Journal* (October 2001).

Rattermann, Mark R. "Highest and Best Use Problems in Market Value Appraisals". *The Appraisal Journal* (Winter 2008).

Seldin, Maury, and James H. Boykin. *Real Estate Analyses.* Homewood, Ill.: American Society of Real Estate Counsellors and Dow Jones-Irwin, 1990.

Young, Janice F. and Stephanie Coleman. "Common Errors and Issues in Reports". *The Appraisal Journal* (Summer, 2007).

Chapter 13

Akerson, Charles B. *The Appraiser's Workbook.* 2nd ed. Chicago: Appraisal Institute, 1996.

Boronico, Jess S., and Donald M. Moliver. "Appraisal Reliability and the Sales Comparison Approach". *The Appraisal Journal* (October 1997).

Crookham, James. "Sales Comparison Approach: Revisited". *The Appraisal Journal* (April 1995).

Rattermann, Mark R. "Consistency Problems in Residential Appraisals". *The Appraisal Journal* (October 1994).

___. "The Market History of the Subject: Analytical Tool or Fourth Approach to Value?" *The Appraisal Journal* (Spring 2005).

___. *Valuation by Comparison: Residential Analysis and Logic.* Chicago: Appraisal Institute, 2007.

Rodgers, Thomas. 1994. "Property-to-Property Comparison". *Appraisal Journal* (January 1994)

Williams, J. Greg. 1995. "Value by Deductive Reasoning". *Appraisal Journal* (July 1995)

Wilson, Donald C. 1997. "The Principle of Rank Substitution". *Appraisal Journal* (January 1997)

Wincott, D. Richard. "A Primer on Comparable Sale Confirmation". *The Appraisal Journal* (July 2002).

Chapter 14

Asabere, Paul K., and Forrest E. Huffman. "Sales Comparison Adjustments for FHA and VA Financing After Deregulation". *The Appraisal Journal* (Spring 2007).

Ramsland, Maxwell O., Jr. "Market-Supported Adjustments Using Multiple Regression Analysis". *The Appraisal Journal* (April 1998).

Slade, Barrett A. "Conditions of Sale Adjustment: The Influence of Buyer and Seller Motivations on Sale Price". *The Appraisal Journal* (Winter 2004).

UBC Real Estate Division. 2008. *Adjustment Support in the Direct Comparison Approach: Hybrid Adjustment Technique.* (CPD 123 course workbook).

Chapter 16

American Society of Farm Managers and Rural Appraisers and Appraisal Institute. *The Appraisal of Rural Property,* 2nd ed. Denver and Chicago, 2000.

Bible, Douglas S., and Chengo Hsieh. "Determinants of Vacant Land Values and Implications for Appraisers". *The Appraisal Journal* (July 1999).

Boykin, James H. "Impropriety of Using Dissimilar-size Comparable Land Sales". *The Appraisal Journal* (July 1996).

___. *Land Valuation: Adjustment Procedures and Assignments.* Chicago: Appraisal Institute, 2001.

Emerson, Don, M. *Subdivision Valuation.* Chicago: Appraisal Institute, 2008.

Ennis, David. "Property Markets and Monopoly Elements". *Canadian Appraiser* (Spring 2002)

Entreken, Henry C., Jr. "Analysis of Land Value Under Differing Land Use Restrictions". *The Appraisal Journal* (October 1994).

Foster, S.G., "Appraisal Process in the Valuation of Water Lots". *Canadian Appraiser*, Volume 27, Boo4 4.

Lovell, Douglas D., and Robert S. Martin. *Subdivision Analysis.* Chicago: Appraisal Institute, 1993.

Miller, Steven E. "Land Value in a Collapsing Market". *The Appraisal Journal* (January 1994).

Chapter 17

Coggin, Dana T. "Let's Not Abandon the Cost Approach". *The Appraisal Journal* (January 1994).

Dannis, Charles G. "Pulling Back the Curtain on Tradition". *The Appraisal Journal* (January 1993).

Iwan, Gregory A. "The Cost Approach: Inflexible or Infeasible?" *The Appraisal Journal* (January 1993).

Marchitelli, Richard. "Rethinking the Cost Approach". *The Appraisal Journal* (July 1992).

Mason, James J. "Under the Microscope: The Cost Approach". *The Appraisal Journal* (January 1993).

Oetzel, Terrell R. "Some Thoughts on the Cost Approach". *The Appraisal Journal* (January 1993).

Ramsett, David E. "The Cost Approach: An Alternative View". *The Appraisal Journal* (April 1998).

Zillioux, Victoria Cassens. "The Cost Approach Dilemma: The Responsibilities Behind the Issue". *Valuation Insights & Perspectives* (Fourth Quarter 2006).

Chapter 18

Ruegg, Rosalie T., and Harold E. Marshall. *Building Economics: Theory and Practice.* New York: Van Nostrand Reinhold, 1990.

Building Cost Manuals

Building Construction Cost Data. Duxbury, Mass.: Robert Snow Means Co. (annual). *www.rsmeans.com*
Lists average unit prices on many building construction items for use in engineering estimates. Components arranged according to uniform system adopted by the American Institute of Architects, Associated General Contractors, and Construction Specifications Institute.

Dodge Building Cost Calculator & Valuation Guide. New York: McGraw-Hill Information Systems Co. (looseleaf service, quarterly supplements). *www.fwdodge.com*
Lists building costs for common types and sizes of buildings. Local cost modifiers and historical local cost index tables included. Formerly *Dow Building Cost Calculator.*

Marshall Valuation Service. Los Angeles: Marshall and Swift Publication Co. (looseleaf service, monthly supplements). *www.marshallswift.com*
Cost data for determining replacement costs of buildings and other improvements in the United States and Canada. Includes current cost multipliers and local modifiers.

Residential Cost Handbook. Los Angeles: Marshall and Swift Publication Co. (looseleaf service, quarterly supplements). *www.marshallswift.com*
Presents square-foot method and segregated-cost method. Local modifiers and cost-trend modifiers included.

Chapter 19

Akerson, Charles B. *The Appraiser's Workbook.* 2nd ed. Chicago: Appraisal Institute, 1996.

Cappello, Steve. "Incurable What?! Incurable Functional Obsolescence". *Assessment Journal* (July/August 1995).

Derbes, Max J., Jr. "Accrued Depreciation Redefined and Reordered". *The Appraisal Journal* (April 1998).

Ellsworth, Richard K. "Estimating Depreciation for Infrequently Transacted Assets". *The Appraisal Journal* (January 2000).

Ramsett, David E. "The Cost Approach: An Alternative View". *The Appraisal Journal* (April 1998).

Williams, Thomas P. "Categorizing External Obsolescence". *The Appraisal Journal* (April 1996).

Wolverton, Marvin L. "Empirical Analysis of the Breakdown Method of Estimating Physical Depreciation". *The Appraisal Journal* (April 1998).

Chapter 20

Akerson, Charles B. *Capitalization Theory and Techniques: Study Guide.* 2nd ed. Chicago: Appraisal Institute, 2000.

American Institute of Real Estate Appraisers. *Readings in the Income Capitalization Approach to Real Property Valuation,* Volume II. Chicago, 1985.

Burton, James H. *Evolution of the Income Approach.* Chicago: American Institute of Real Estate Appraisers, 1982.

Clayton, J. and Hamilton, S.W. "Risk and Return in the Canadian Real Estate Market". *Revue Canadienne des Sciences de l'Administration.* Volume 16. Issue 2. June 1999.

Fisher, Clifford E., Jr. *Rates and Ratios Used in the Income Capitalization Approach.* Chicago: Appraisal Institute, 1995.

UBC Real Estate Division. 2008. *Real Estate Investment Analysis and Advanced Income Appraisal.* Vancouver: UBC Real Estate Division. Chapter 7: Income Method of Valuation.

Chapter 21

American Institute of Real Estate Appraisers. *Forecasting: Market Determinants Affecting Cash Flows and Reversions.* Research Series Report 4. Chicago, 1989.

Sources of Operating Costs and Ratios

Only a few of the many published sources are cited below.

Building Owners and Managers Association International. *Downtown and Suburban Office Building Experience Exchange Report.* Washington, D.C.
Published annually since 1920. Includes analysis of expenses and income quoted in cents per square foot as well as national, regional, and selected city averages.

Dun & Bradstreet, Inc. *Key Business Ratios in 125 Lines.* New York.
Published annually. Contains balance sheet and profit-and-loss ratios.

Institute of Real Estate Management. *Income/Expense Analysis: Apartments, Condominiums &*
Cooperatives. Chicago.
Published annually since 1954. Data arranged by building type, then by national, regional,
metropolitan, and selected city groupings. Operating costs listed per room, per square
foot, etc. Formerly *Apartment Building Experience Exchange.*

___. *Income/Expense Analysis: Suburban Office Buildings.* Chicago.
Published annually since 1976. Data analyzed based on gross area and gross and net
rentable office areas. Includes dollar-per-square-foot calculations; national, regional,
and metropolitan comparisons; and detailed analyses for selected cities.

Urban Land Institute and International Council of Shopping Centers. *Dollars and Cents of*
Shopping Centers/The Score: 2008. Washington, D.C.
First issued in 1961. Updated biannually. Includes income and expense data for neighbour-
hood, community, and regional centers as well as statistics for specific tenant types.

Chapter 22

Mason, James J., ed. and comp. *AIREA Financial Tables.* Chicago: American Institute of Real
Estate Appraisers, 1981.

Chapter 24

Greer, Gaylon E. *Investment Analysis for Real Estate Decisions.* 4th ed. Chicago: Dearborn
Financial Publishing, 1997.

Chapter 25

Emerson, Ralph, III. "Proper Reconciliation in Narrative Reports Favours Substance Over
Form". *The Appraisal Journal* (January 1998).

Lambert, D.W., "The Three Approaches to Value - Market, Market and Market". *Canadian*
Appraiser, Volume 20 Book 1 (revisited 1988, Volume 32, Book 2)

Roberts, Joe R., and Eric Roberts. "The Myth About Appraisals". *The Appraisal Journal* (April
1991).

Spence, Mark T., and James A. Thorson. "The Effect of Expertise on the Quality of Appraisal
Services". *Journal of Real Estate Research*, Volume 15, no. 1/2 (1998).

Chapter 26

Appraisal Institute of Canada. *Canadian Uniform Standards of Professional Appraisal Practice*
(CUSPAP).

Blankenship, Alan. *The Appraisal Writing Handbook.* Chicago: Appraisal Institute, 1998.

Coleman, Stephanie. *Scope of Work.* Chicago: Appraisal Institute, 2006.

Craft, J.L. "Logic and Rhetoric in Appraisal Reporting". *The Appraisal Journal* (April 1995).

Eaton, J.D. "FRCP: The Other Appraisal Report Standard". *Valuation Insights & Perspectives* (Second Quarter 1999).

Horevitz, Ann Marie. "Appraisal Writing, Aristotle, and the Art of Persuasion". *The Appraisal Journal* (July 1997).

Klaasen, Romain L. "It's Only Words But Writers Beware!" *Canadian Appraiser*, Volume 36, Book 2, 1992

Rattermann, Mark R. *Using the Individual Condominium Unit Appraisal Report Forms: Fannie Mae Form 1073 and Exterior-Only Form 1075*. Chicago: Appraisal Institute, 2006.

___. *Using Residential Appraisal Report Forms: URAR 2005 (Form 1004) and Exterior Inspection (Form 2055)*. Chicago: Appraisal Institute, 2005.

___. *Using the Small Residential Income Property Appraisal Report (Fannie Mae Form 1025/Freddie Mac Form 72)*. Chicago: Appraisal Institute, 2006.

Rex, Charles W., III, and Susan Motycka Rex. "Market Analysis in Appraisal Reports: Vitalizing Key Data Sections". *Valuation Insights & Perspectives* (Fall 1996).

Tardiff, Frank D. "Using an Engagement Letter to Minimize Discrepancies Between Appraised Value and Transaction Price". *The Appraisal Journal* (January 1994).

Wilson, L. Deane. "Are Appraisal Reports Logical Fallacies?" *The Appraisal Journal* (April 1996).

Chapter 27

Appraisal Institute of Canada. *Canadian Uniform Standards of Professional Appraisal Practice.* Review and Consulting Standards,

Grover, Michael M. *Expert Witness – The Forensic Appraiser..* September, 1991. Winnipeg: Appraisal Institute of Canada.

Sevelka, Tony. . "Appraisal Review: An Emerging Discipline" Part I and Part II". *Canadian Appraiser*. Spring 1997.

Chapter 28

Berenson, Mark L., David M. Levine, and Timothy C. Krehbiel. *Basic Business Statistics: Concepts and Applications*. 9th ed. Upper Saddle River, N.J.: Prentice-Hall, 2004.

Canning, George. 2002. "What Makes AVMs Work?" Vancouver: UBC Real Estate Division.

City of Calgary Assessment Department. "Regression Modeling in Calgary – A Practical Approach". *Assessment Journal*. Vol. 5, Num. 4, August 1998. International Association of Assessing Officers.

Dielman, Terry. *Applied Regression Analysis*. 3rd ed. Pacific Grove, Calif.: Duxbury, 2001.

Goddard, Bryan L. "Graphics Improve the Analysis of Income Data". *The Appraisal Journal* (October 2000).

___. "The Power of Computer Graphics for Comparative Analysis". *The Appraisal Journal* (April 2000).

___. "The Role of Graphic Analysis in Appraisals". *The Appraisal Journal* (October 1999).

Guy, Rebecca F., and Louis G. Pol. *Statistics for Real Estate Professionals.* New York: Quorum Books, 1989.

Hair, Joseph F., Rolph E. Anderson, Ronald L. Tatham, and William C. Black. *Multivariate Data Analysis with Readings.* 3rd ed. New York: Macmillan, 1992.

Kohler, Heinz. *Statistics for Business and Economics.* Stamford, Conn.: Thomson, 2002.

Levine, David M., Timothy C. Krehbiel, and Mark L. Berenson. *Business Statistics: A First Course.* 3rd ed. Upper Saddle River, N.J.: Prentice-Hall, 2003.

Mark, Jonathon. "Multiple Regression Analysis: A Review of the Issues". *The Appraisal Journal* (January 1988).

McClave, James T., P. George Benson, and Terry Sincich. *Statistics for Business and Economics.* 9th ed. Upper Saddle River, N.J.: Prentice-Hall, 2005.

Neter, John, William Wasserman, and Michael H. Kutner. *Applied Linear Statistical Models: Regression, Analysis of Variance, and Experimental Designs.* 3rd ed. Homewood, Ill.: Irwin, 1990.

Newell, Graeme J. "The Application of Ridge Regression to Real Estate Appraisal". *The Appraisal Journal* (January 1982).

Reichert, Alan K., James S. Moore, and Chien-Ching Cho. "Stabilizing Statistical Appraisal Models Using Ridge Regression". *The Real Estate Appraiser and Analyst* (Fall 1985).

Sweetland, Doug. "Ridge Regression: A Word of Caution". *The Appraisal Journal* (April 1986)

Triola, Mario F., William M. Goodman, Richard Law, *"Elementary Statistics, Canadian Edition*; Pearson Education Canada, 2nd Edition, 2001, 848 pages

UBC Real Estate Division. 2009. *Statistical and Computer Applications in Valuation.* Vancouver, BC: UBC Real Estate Division.

UBC Real Estate Division. 2009. *Advanced Computed Assisted Mass Appraisal.* Vancouver, BC: UBC Real Estate Division.

Chapter 29

Annis, Kristyn, *"Aboriginal Rights and Wind Development in Canada,* Right-of-Way Magazine, International Right of Way Association, Gardena California, July August 2009.

Appraising Easements: Guidelines for Valuation of Land Conservation and Historic Preservation Easements. 3rd ed. Washington, D.C.: Land Trust Alliance and National Trust for Historic Preservation, 1999.

Conroy, Kathleen. *Valuing the Timeshare Property.* Chicago: American Institute of Real Estate Appraisers, 1981.

Dombal, Robert W. *Appraising Condominiums: Suggested Data Analysis Techniques*. Chicago: American Institute of Real Estate Appraisers, 1981.

___. *Residential Condominiums: A Guide to Analysis and Appraisal*. Chicago: American Institute of Real Estate Appraisers, 1976.

Herzog, Steven J. "The Appraisal of Water Rights: Their Nature and Transferability". *The Appraisal Journal* (Winter 2008).

MacCrate, James R., and James B. McEvoy. "Family Limited Partnerships, Corporations, and Valuation Issues". *The Appraisal Journal* (July 2000).

Rattermann, Mark R. *Using the Individual Condominium Unit Appraisal Report: Forms 1073 and 1075*. Chicago: Appraisal Institute, 2006.

Reynolds, Judith. *Historic Properties: Preservation and the Valuation Process*. 3rd ed. Chicago: Appraisal Institute, 2006.

Rothermich, David. "Partitioning Real Property". *The Appraisal Journal* (July 2002).

UBC Real Estate Division. 2010. *BUSI 442 Course Workbook*. Vancouver: UBC Real Estate Division.

UBC Real Estate Division. 2006. *BUSI 452 Course Workbook*. Vancouver: UBC Real Estate Division.

Webb, Dennis A. *Valuing Undivided Interests in Real Property: Partnerships and Cotenancies*. Chicago: Appraisal Institute, 2004.

Chapter 30

Bower, Ray; *Primer on International Valuation Standards*, a 5-part series, 2008 Book 4 to 2009-Book 4, Canadian Property Valuation, Appraisal Institute of Canada, Ottawa, 2008/2009.

Crosson, Stephen T., and Simon D. Neame. "Mark-to-Market in the United Kingdom". *The Appraisal Journal* (Winter 2004).

Dorchester, John D., Jr. "Market Value for Financial Reporting: The Premise". *The Appraisal Journal* (Winter 2004).

Financial Accounting Standards Board. Statement of Financial Accounting Standards No. 157: Fair Value Measurements. (September 2006).

Fishman, Jay E., Shannon P. Pratt, and William J. Morrison. *Standards of Value: Theory and Applications*. Hoboken, N.J.: John Wiley & Sons, Inc., 2007.

Gerlach, Alison. "Valuation for Financial Reporting: Are We There Yet?" Valuation Insights & Perspectives (Fourth Quarter 2006).

Glanville, Brian, and Alison Gerlach. "VFR Is Important for Your Business Sense". *Valuation Insights & Perspectives* (First Quarter 2004).

International Valuation Standards Committee. *International Valuation Standards*. 8th ed. London, 2008.

King, Alfred M. *Fair Value for Financial Reporting: Meeting the New FASB Requirements*. Hoboken, N.J.: John Wiley & Sons, Inc., 2006.

KPMG. 2008. *The Impact of IFRS on the Real Estate Industry: Financial Services. www.kpmg.com*

McCarthy, Ann Marie, and John McCarthy. "Accounting for Change: GASB, FASB and Mark to Market". *Valuation Insights & Perspectives* (Fourth Quarter 2002).

PriceWaterhouseCoopers. 2008. *Putting IFRS in Motion. The Impact of International Financial Reporting Standards (IFRS) on the Canadian Real Estate Sector. www.pwc.com*

UBC Real Estate Division. 2008. *Valuation for Financial Reporting – Real Property Appraisal and IFRS.* (CPD 114 course workbook). Vancouver: UBC Real Estate Division.

INDEX

balloon payments, 23.9
band-of-investment techniques, 20.20,22.6
    and land and building components, 22.9
    and mortgage and equity components,
      22.8
bankers' acceptances, 5.11
banks. *See also* trust companies; credit unions
barns, 11.44
baseboards, 11.8
base lines, 10.3-4
basements, 11.7-8, 11.20,-21
    finishes, 11.24
bathrooms
    adequacy of, 11.36-37
    fixtures, 11.26-27
bays, in commercial buildings, 11.38
beams, structural, 11.8-10, 11.15, 11.19-21
below-the-line expense, 21.3, 21.12
benchmark building, 18.5
blocks. *See* lot and block system
BOMA. *See* Building Owners and Managers
  Association International
bonds, 5.11-.12, 5.14
book depreciation, 17.16, 21.26
    in operating statements, 21.26
book value, 1.15
boundaries
    legal descriptions of, 10.2-3
    of market areas, 4.4-6
bounds, 10.2-3
bracketing, 14.7, 15.6
breakdown method, of estimating depreciation,
  19.1, 19.15-36
building activity, 8.8
building, and architecture, 11.33-35
building capitalization rate, 20.5, 22.9, 22.11,
  22.13-14
building codes, and highest and best use
  analysis, 12.5-7
building components. *See* building description
building costs, 18.1
    and comparative-unit method, 18.3-9
    cost-estimating methods, 18.3-14
    and entrepreneurial profit, 18.3-4, 18.7
    and quantity survey method, 18.11-14
    sources of, 8.9, 18.1-3
    and unit-in-place method, 18.9-11
    See also cost index trending; cost-
      estimating manuals; direct costs;
      indirect costs
building description, 11.3-4
    air-conditioning, 11.8
    and building codes, 11.5-6
    chimneys, stacks, and vents, 11.8
    electrical systems, 11.8

elements of, 11.4-8
equipment and mechanical systems,
  11.3-4, 11.7-8
exterior, 11.4, 11.7-8
exterior doors, 11.8
exterior walls, 11.8
facade, 11.8
flooring, 11.8
footings, 11.8
format, 11.7-8
framing, 11.8
heating systems, 11.8
insulation, 11.8
interior, 11.4, 11.7-11.8
interior doors, 11.8
interior supports, 11.8
interior walls and partitions, 11.8
miscellaneous equipment, 11.8
painting and finishing, 11.8
plumbing systems, 11.8
protection against decay and insect
  damage, 11.8
quality and condition surveys, 11.3-4
roof and drain systems, 11.8
size, 11.6-11.7
special features, 11.8
stairs, ramps, and elevators, 11.8
storage areas, 11.8
substructure, 11.8
superstructure, 11.8
use classification, 11.5
ventilation, 11.6, 11.8
windows, storm windows, and screens,
  11.8
Building Owners and Managers Association
  International (BOMA), 8.15-16, 11.6-7, 21.25
building residual technique, 22.9, 22.13
building style and function, 11.31-46
bundle of rights, 6.1-2
business cycles, 4.6-9
business enterprise value. *See* business value
business value, 2.14-16
    See also fair value; use value
buyers and sellers, 1.9
buyer's market, 9.8

call systems, 11.32
Canadian Uniform Standards of Professional
  Appraisal Practice (CUSPAP), 1.10-11
    and appraisal review, 27.3-4
    and appraiser liability, 1.16
capital
    additions to, 21.26
    as agent of production, 3.2

public records, as source of specific data, 8.17
public utilities, 4.16-18, 6.7-8, 10.17-18
purchase-money mortgages, 5.5

qualifications of appraiser, 26.17-18
qualitative analysis, 13.11-13, 14.1-2, 14.6-7, 15.9-11
    See also ranking analysis; relative comparison analysis
quality and condition survey, 11.46-49
quantitative adjustments, 13.11, 14.1-6, 15.7
quantitative analysis, 13.11-13
    See also graphic analysis; paired data analysis
quantity of evidence, as reconciliation criterion, 25.5
quantity survey method, 17.2, 18.3, 18.11-14

ramps, in public buildings, 11.21
random samples, 28.4-5
range
    statistical, 28.10
    of value, 7.15-16, 25.7
ranking analysis, 13.13, 14.6-7, 14.23
rate extraction, and yield capitalization, 24.1-12
rates. *See* discount rates; income rates; interest rates; rates of return; yield rates
rates of return, 20.16-18
    return of capital, 20.17-18
    return on capital, 20.17-18
raw land, 10.1-2
real estate
    definition of, 1.6-8
    cycles, 4.6-9
    See also real estate markets
real estate financial officers, 1.9
real estate investment trusts (REITs), 5.13-14
real estate markets, 4.1-32
    characteristics of, 4.1-6
    definition of, 4.1
real estate operating companies (REOCs), 5.4
real estate salespeople, 1.9
real estate taxes. *See* ad valorem taxes; property taxes
real property
    definition of, 1.6-8
    and economic forces, 1.4
    and environmental forces, 1.2
    equity interests in, 5.29-31
    and government forces, 1.2-4
    identification of, 1.6-8
    mortgage interests in, 120
    ownership, public and private, 6.11-12
    and social forces, 1.5-6
real property consulting, 27.5-6
real property rights
    in appraisal reports, 26.10
    and income approach, 20.3
    in direct comparison approach, 13.6, 13.12-13
    See also fee simple estate; leased fee interests; leasehold interests; partial interests
recapture rate, 23.14-15
recession, 3.10, 4.6
reconciliation of value indications, 25.1-7
    accuracy of, 25.5
    in appraisal reports, 7.15-16, 26.16
    appropriateness of, 25.4-5
    criteria for, 25.4-6
    definition of, 7.15
    and final value opinion, 25.6-7
    quantity of evidence in, 25.5-6
    questions asked, 25.2
    in direct comparison approach, 13.16-17
reconstructed operating statement, 20.15, 20.21, 21.13-29
recovery of demand, 4.8-9
rectangular survey system, 10.2-4
refuse and refuse collection. *See* rubbish removal
regional shopping centers, 4.22-24
    See also super-regional shopping centers
regression analysis, 14.4-5, 14.19-23, 28.17-33
    model assumptions, 28.28-30
    model specification, 28.24-27
    model validation, 28.27-28
    multiple regression, 14.4-5, 28.22-23
    simple linear regression, 14.4, 28.18-21
    See also statistics
regression, principle of, 3.10
reinvestment concepts, 24.10-12
REITs. *See* real estate investment trusts (REITs)
relative comparison analysis, 13.13, 14.6-7, 15.5-6, 15.10-11
remainderman, 6.7, 29.4-5
remaining economic life, 11.49, 19.2, 19.6-7
remaining useful life, 19.3, 19.6-7
REMIC. *See* real estate mortgage investment conduit (REMIC)
renewal options in leases, 21.9
rent
    analysis of, 21.2-4
    types of, 20.9-12
rent concessions, 21.7
repairs. *See* maintenance and repairs
replacement allowance, 20.16
    as variable expense, 21.22-24